THE
WORD STUDY
NEW TESTAMENT

Containing the numbering system to
the WORD STUDY CONCORDANCE
and the *Key Number Index*
to Standard Reference Works

edited by
RALPH D. WINTER
and
ROBERTA H. WINTER

based on the
Authorized Version of the Holy Bible

Tyndale House Publishers, Inc.
Wheaton, Illinois, U.S.A.

Introduction, numbering system and
Key Number Index to Standard
Reference Works, copyright ©1978
by Ralph D. Winter. All rights
reserved.

The Large Print Edition of the
Authorized Version was used by
permission of the American Bible
Society.

Published cooperatively by: Tyndale
House Publishers, Inc., Wheaton,
Illinois; William Carey Library, Pasa-
dena, California.

Library of Congress Catalog Card
Number 78-68102   ISBN 0-8423-8390-5

CONTENTS

INTRODUCTION to the Word Study New Testament

The most fundamental fact about the New Testament is that its secrets are available only to those who are willing to obey what they find. "Believe that you may know" (John 10:25-28) is a basic teaching of the New Testament itself.

A second, balancing truth, is that although the Bible was inspired by God in its original language, we do not regard any *translation* of the Bible as perfect. All scholars and translators are human and fallible. A serious Bible student will often consult more than one translation to find what he wants to know. But unless he has studied Greek, the original language of the New Testament, he is forced to rely on the translators' choices of English words. Theological seminaries have long recognized this fact and assiduously require all students who plan to become ministers to study the biblical languages. While even that does not solve all problems, the person who reads no Greek at all often feels a bit left out. He may not be able to spend three years in seminary studies, nor have time to learn Greek and Hebrew on his own. Even those pastors acquainted with Hebrew and Greek are often too busy to make practical use of their knowledge. Eventually they may almost forget Greek and Hebrew completely.

For all such people the *Word Study New Testament* (and its companion volume, the *Word Study Concordance*) will be a great help. Here under every noun, verb, adjective, and adverb the reader will find the key number assigned to that word by Strong in *Strong's Exhaustive Concordance of the Bible*. The Bible student can turn directly to that number in the *Word Study Concordance* and see the Greek word and, in English, all the various biblical references where that Greek word was used.

Those who know Greek, or those who would like to consult what well-known scholars have said about a specific Greek word, will find in the "Key Number Index to Standard Reference Works" appended to this volume a cross-reference to Moulton and Geden's *Concordance to the Greek New Testament,* to Arndt and Gingrich's *Greek-English Lexicon of the New Testament,* and to Kittel's *A Theological Dictionary of the New Testament.*

Thus by availing himself of the numbering system in *The Word Study New Testament* and its companion volume, *The Word Study Concordance,* the Bible student will save a huge amount of time and will be much more likely and able to go on to make use of these widely acclaimed reference materials.

We wish to express our gratitude to the many who have helped in the preparation of this volume. They include our parents, our four daughters, our Sunday school class, and the students at Bethany Missionary Fellowship in Minneapolis, Minnesota. We especially wish to thank Clara Wong, who through many hours of arduous work checked and typed the numbers under each entry herein.

That the study of the Bible may be enriched and made exciting through the use of this volume is the author's earnest prayer.

RALPH D. WINTER
ROBERTA H. WINTER

How to Use the Word Study New Testament

13 Ye are the salt of the earth: but if the
salt have lost his savor, wherewith shall it
be salted? it is thenceforth good for nothing,
but to be cast out, and to be trodden under
foot of men.

1. The key number under each noun, verb, adjective, or adverb identifies the Greek word for which that English word is a translation. This number is that assigned by James Strong in his "Concise Dictionary of the Words in the Greek Testament" found in the appendix to his *Exhaustive Concordance of the Bible.*

2. That number will allow you in seconds to look up the Greek word in *The Word Study Concordance,* and there find out all the other occurrences of that Greek word in the New Testament. You may also locate that same key number in the "Key Number Index to Standard Reference Works" at the back of *The Word Study New Testament,* which will lead you to where that Greek word is discussed in Moulton and Geden's *Concordance of the Greek New Testament,* Arndt and Gingrich's *Greek-English Lexicon of the New Testament* and the multi-volume *A Theological Dictionary of the New Testament* by Kittel.

3. Dots following a number (see figure above) merely indicate that the sense of the Greek word includes more than the single English word under which that number occurs.

Guide to Key Number Index to Standard Reference Works

WSC	F	A&G/M&G	K
1	4	1/46	1:1
2 *	5	1/1	1:3
3 *	1	1/1	1:4
4	1	1/1	
5	3	1/1	1:5
6 *	4	1/1	1:6

1) The first column in the Index is the *key number* assigned by James Strong in his "Concise Dictionary of the Words in the Greek New Testament" appended to his *Exhaustive Concordance of the Bible.* These numbers have been used throughout the companion volume to this book, *The Word Study Concordance,* and have also been included in the 1978 edition of Moulton and Geden's *Concordance of the Greek New Testament,* and in the index volume (Volume 10) of Kittel's *A Theological Dictionary of the New Testament.*

2) The second column gives the number of occurrences (or the frequency) of that Greek word in the New Testament.

3) The third column refers to the pages where the word is discussed in Arndt and Gingrich and (after the slash) in Moulton and Geden.

4) The fourth column gives the volume and page number where Kittel treats the word (e.g., 1:6 = Volume 1, page 6).

The third and fourth columns will be of great help to students of Greek. Thus, those who do not have a copy of the *Word Study Concordance* will still find the *Word Study New Testament* very useful by itself. We strongly recommend, however, that the *Word Study New Testament* and the *Word Study Concordance* be used together as they were designed, since a reading of the biblical *contexts* is the most important basis of understanding the meaning of the Greek word.

THE GOSPEL ACCORDING TO
ST. MATTHEW

The Genealogy of Jesus Christ

1 The book of the generation of Jesus Christ, the son of David, the son of Abraham.

2 Abraham begat Isaac; and Isaac begat Jacob; and Jacob begat Judah and his brethren;

3 And Judah begat Pharez and Zerah of Tamar; and Pharez begat Hezron; and Hezron begat Ram;

4 And Ram begat Ammin'adab; and Ammin'adab begat Nahshon; and Nahshon begat Salmon;

5 And Salmon begat Boaz of Rachab; and Boaz begat Obed of Ruth; and Obed begat Jesse;

6 And Jesse begat David the king. And David the king begat Solomon of her that had been the wife of Uri'ah;

7 And Solomon begat Rehobo'am; and Rehobo'am begat Abi'jah; and Abi'jah begat Asa;

8 And Asa begat Jehosh'aphat; and Jehosh'aphat begat Jeho'ram; and Jeho'ram begat Uzzi'ah;

9 And Uzzi'ah begat Jotham; and Jotham begat Ahaz; and Ahaz begat Hezeki'ah;

10 And Hezeki'ah begat Manas'seh; and Manas'seh begat Amon; and Amon begat Josi'ah;

11 And Josi'ah begat Jeconi'ah and his brethren, about the time they were carried away to Babylon.

12 And after they were brought to Babylon, Jeconi′ah[2423] begat[1080] She-al′ti-el[4528];[3350] and She-al′ti-el[4528] begat[1080] Zerub′babel[1080];

13 And Zerub′babel[2216] begat Abi′ud[2216]; and Abi′-ud begat Eli′akim[1080]; and Eli′akim[1662][10] begat Azor[1662][10];

14 And Azor[1080] begat[107] Zadok[1080]; and Zadok[4524] begat[4524] Achim[107][1080]; and Achim[885] begat[885] Eli′ud[1080];

15 And Eli′ud[1664] begat Ele-a′zar[1664]; and Ele-a′zar begat Matthan[1664][1080]; and Matthan[1648] begat Jacob[1648];[1080]

16 And Jacob[3157] begat Joseph[3157] the husband[1080][2384] of Mary[2384][1080], of whom was[2501] born[1080] Jesus[435], who[2424] is called Christ.[3137]

17 So all the generations[5547] from Abraham[1074] to David are fourteen[11] generations; and from David[1138] until the[1180] carrying[1074] away into Babylon[1138] are fourteen generations;[3350] and from the carrying[897] away into Babylon[1180] unto[1074] Christ are fourteen[3350] generations.[897][5547][1180][1074]

The Birth of Jesus Christ

18 Now the birth[1083] of Jesus[2424] Christ[5547] was on this wise: When as his[3423] mother[1063] Mary[3384] was[3137][3423] espoused to Joseph, before they[2501] came together, she was found with child[4905] of the Holy Ghost.

19 Then[2147] Joseph her[1722] husband, being[40] a[4151] just man,[2501] and not[435] willing to[5607] make her a public[1342] example, was minded[2309] to[3856] put her away[3856] privily.[1014][630][630][2977]

20 But while[1760] he[1760] thought on these things, behold, the angel of the Lord appeared unto him[2400] in a dream[32], saying, Joseph[2962], thou[5316] son of David, fear[3677] not to[2501] take unto[5207] thee Mary[1138] thy[5399] wife: for[3880] that which is conceived in her[3137] is of the Holy Ghost.[1135][1063][1080][846]

21 And she[40][4151] shall bring forth a son, and thou[5088][5207]

shalt call his name JESUS: for he shall save his people from their sins.

22 Now all this was done, that it might be fulfilled which was spoken of the Lord by the prophet, saying,

23 Behold, a virgin shall be with child, and shall bring forth a son, and they shall call his name Imman'u-el, which being interpreted is, God with us.

24 Then Joseph being raised from sleep did as the angel of the Lord had bidden him, and took unto him his wife:

25 And knew her not till she had brought forth her firstborn son: and he called his name JESUS.

The Visit of the Wise Men

2 Now when Jesus was born in Bethlehem of Judea in the days of Herod the king, behold, there came wise men from the east to Jerusalem,

2 Saying, Where is he that is born King of the Jews? for we have seen his star in the east, and are come to worship him.

3 When Herod the king had heard these things, he was troubled, and all Jerusalem with him.

4 And when he had gathered all the chief priests and scribes of the people together, he demanded of them where Christ should be born.

5 And they said unto him, In Bethlehem of Judea: for thus it is written by the prophet,

6 And thou Bethlehem, in the land of

Judah, art not the least among the princes of Judah: for out of thee shall come a Governor, that shall rule my people Israel.

7 Then Herod, when he had privily called the wise men, inquired of them diligently what time the star appeared.

8 And he sent them to Bethlehem, and said, Go and search diligently for the young child; and when ye have found him, bring me word again, that I may come and worship him also.

9 When they had heard the king, they departed; and, lo, the star, which they saw in the east, went before them, till it came and stood over where the young child was.

10 When they saw the star, they rejoiced with exceeding great joy.

11 And when they were come into the house, they saw the young child with Mary his mother, and fell down, and worshipped him: and when they had opened their treasures, they presented unto him gifts; gold, and frankincense, and myrrh.

12 And being warned of God in a dream that they should not return to Herod, they departed into their own country another way.

The Slaying of the Infants

13 And when they were departed, behold, the angel of the Lord appeareth to Joseph in a dream, saying, Arise, and take the young child and his mother, and flee into Egypt, and be thou there until I bring thee word: for Herod will seek the young child to destroy him.

14 When he arose, he took the young child and his mother by night, and departed into Egypt:

15 And was there until the death of Herod: that it might be fulfilled which was spoken of the Lord by the prophet, saying, Out of Egypt have I called my son.

16 Then Herod, when he saw that he was mocked of the wise men, was exceeding wroth, and sent forth, and slew all the children that were in Bethlehem, and in all the coasts thereof, from two years old and under, according to the time which he had diligently inquired of the wise men.

17 Then was fulfilled that which was spoken by Jeremiah the prophet, saying,

18 In Ramah was there a voice heard, lamentation, and weeping, and great mourning, Rachel weeping for her children, and would not be comforted, because they are not.

19 But when Herod was dead, behold, an angel of the Lord appeareth in a dream to Joseph in Egypt,

20 Saying, Arise, and take the young child and his mother, and go into the land of Israel: for they are dead which sought the young child's life.

21 And he arose, and took the young child and his mother, and came into the land of Israel.

22 But when he heard that Archela'us did reign in Judea in the room of his father Herod, he was afraid to go thither: notwith-

standing, being warned of God in a dream, he
turned aside into the parts of Galilee:

23 And he came and dwelt in a city called
Nazareth: that it might be fulfilled which was
spoken by the prophets, He shall be called a
Nazarene.

The Preaching of John the Baptist

3 In those days came John the Baptist,
preaching in the wilderness of Judea,

2 And saying, Repent ye: for the kingdom
of heaven is at hand.

3 For this is he that was spoken of by the
prophet Isaiah, saying, The voice of one crying
in the wilderness, Prepare ye the way of the
Lord, make his paths straight.

4 And the same John had his raiment of
camel's hair, and a leathern girdle about his
loins; and his meat was locusts and wild
honey.

5 Then went out to him Jerusalem, and all
Judea, and all the region round about Jordan,

6 And were baptized of him in Jordan, confessing their sins.

7 But when he saw many of the Pharisees
and Sadducees come to his baptism, he said
unto them, O generation of vipers, who
hath warned you to flee from the wrath to
come?

8 Bring forth therefore fruits meet for
repentance:

9 And think not to say within yourselves,
We have Abraham to our father: for I say

unto you, that God is able of these stones to raise up children unto Abraham.

10 And now also the axe is laid unto the root of the trees: therefore every tree which bringeth not forth good fruit is hewn down, and cast into the fire.

11 I indeed baptize you with water unto repentance: but he that cometh after me is mightier than I, whose shoes I am not worthy to bear: he shall baptize you with the Holy Ghost, and with fire:

12 Whose fan is in his hand, and he will thoroughly purge his floor, and gather his wheat into the garner; but he will burn up the chaff with unquenchable fire.

The Baptism of Jesus

13 Then cometh Jesus from Galilee to Jordan unto John, to be baptized of him.

14 But John forbade him, saying, I have need to be baptized of thee, and comest thou to me?

15 And Jesus answering said unto him, Suffer it to be so now: for thus it becometh us to fulfil all righteousness. Then he suffered him.

16 And Jesus, when he was baptized, went up straightway out of the water: and, lo, the heavens were opened unto him, and he saw the Spirit of God descending like a dove, and lighting upon him:

17 And lo a voice from heaven, saying, This is my beloved Son, in whom I am well pleased.

The Temptation of Jesus

4 Then was Jesus led up of the Spirit into the wilderness to be tempted of the devil.

2 And when he had fasted forty days and forty nights, he was afterward ahungered.

3 And when the tempter came to him, he said, If thou be the Son of God, command that these stones be made bread.

4 But he answered and said, It is written, Man shall not live by bread alone, but by every word that proceedeth out of the mouth of God.

5 Then the devil taketh him up into the holy city, and setteth him on a pinnacle of the temple,

6 And saith unto him, If thou be the Son of God, cast thyself down: for it is written, He shall give his angels charge concerning thee: and in their hands they shall bear thee up, lest at any time thou dash thy foot against a stone.

7 Jesus said unto him, It is written again, Thou shalt not tempt the Lord thy God.

8 Again, the devil taketh him up into an exceeding high mountain, and showeth him all the kingdoms of the world, and the glory of them;

9 And saith unto him, All these things will I give thee, if thou wilt fall down and worship me.

10 Then saith Jesus unto him, Get thee hence, Satan: for it is written, Thou shalt worship the Lord thy God, and him only shalt thou serve.

11 Then the devil leaveth him, and, behold, angels came and ministered unto him.

Jesus Begins His Ministry

12 Now when Jesus had heard that John was cast into prison, he departed into Galilee;

13 And leaving Nazareth, he came and dwelt in Caper′na-um, which is upon the sea-coast, in the borders of Zeb′ulun and Naph′-tali:

14 That it might be fulfilled which was spoken by Isaiah the prophet, saying,

15 The land of Zeb′ulun, and the land of Naph′tali, by the way of the sea, beyond Jordan, Galilee of the Gentiles;

16 The people which sat in darkness saw great light; and to them which sat in the region and shadow of death light is sprung up.

17 From that time Jesus began to preach, and to say, Repent: for the kingdom of heaven is at hand.

Jesus Calls Four Fishermen

18 And Jesus, walking by the sea of Galilee, saw two brethren, Simon called Peter, and Andrew his brother, casting a net into the sea: for they were fishers.

19 And he saith unto them, Follow me, and I will make you fishers of men.

20 And they straightway left their nets, and followed him.

21 And going on from thence, he saw other two brethren, James the son of Zeb′edee, and John his brother, in a ship with Zeb′edee

their father, mending their nets; and he called
them.

22 And they immediately left the ship and
their father, and followed him.

Jesus Ministers to a Great Multitude

23 And Jesus went about all Galilee,
teaching in their synagogues, and preaching
the gospel of the kingdom, and healing all
manner of sickness and all manner of disease
among the people.

24 And his fame went throughout all Syria:
and they brought unto him all sick people
that were taken with divers diseases and
torments, and those which were possessed with
devils, and those which were lunatic, and those
that had the palsy; and he healed them.

25 And there followed him great multitudes
of people from Galilee, and from Decap′olis,
and from Jerusalem, and from Judea, and from
beyond Jordan.

The Beginning of the Sermon on the Mount

5 And seeing the multitudes, he went up
into a mountain: and when he was set,
his disciples came unto him:

2 And he opened his mouth, and taught
them, saying,

The Beatitudes

3 Blessed are the poor in spirit: for theirs
is the kingdom of heaven.

4 Blessed are they that mourn: for they
shall be comforted.

5 Blessed are the meek: for they shall inherit the earth.

6 Blessed are they which do hunger and thirst after righteousness: for they shall be filled.

7 Blessed are the merciful: for they shall obtain mercy.

8 Blessed are the pure in heart: for they shall see God.

9 Blessed are the peacemakers: for they shall be called the children of God.

10 Blessed are they which are persecuted for righteousness' sake: for theirs is the kingdom of heaven.

11 Blessed are ye, when men shall revile you, and persecute you, and shall say all manner of evil against you falsely, for my sake.

12 Rejoice, and be exceeding glad: for great is your reward in heaven: for so persecuted they the prophets which were before you.

The Salt of the Earth

13 Ye are the salt of the earth: but if the salt have lost his savor, wherewith shall it be salted? it is thenceforth good for nothing, but to be cast out, and to be trodden under foot of men.

The Light of the World

14 Ye are the light of the world. A city that is set on a hill cannot be hid.

15 Neither do men light a candle, and put

it under a bushel, but on a candlestick; and it giveth light unto all that are in the house.

16 Let your light so shine before men, that they may see your good works, and glorify your Father which is in heaven.

Jesus' Attitude toward the Law

17 Think not that I am come to destroy the law, or the prophets: I am not come to destroy, but to fulfil.

18 For verily I say unto you, Till heaven and earth pass, one jot or one tittle shall in no wise pass from the law, till all be fulfilled.

19 Whosoever therefore shall break one of these least commandments, and shall teach men so, he shall be called the least in the kingdom of heaven: but whosoever shall do and teach them, the same shall be called great in the kingdom of heaven.

20 For I say unto you, That except your righteousness shall exceed the righteousness of the scribes and Pharisees, ye shall in no case enter into the kingdom of heaven.

Jesus' Attitude toward Anger

21 Ye have heard that it was said by them of old time, Thou shalt not kill; and whosoever shall kill shall be in danger of the judgment:

22 But I say unto you, That whosoever is angry with his brother without a cause shall be in danger of the judgment: and whosoever shall say to his brother, Raca, shall be in danger of the council: but whosoever shall

say,[2036] Thou fool,[3474] shall be in danger of[1777] hell[1067] fire.[4442]

23 Therefore if thou bring[4374] thy gift[1435] to the altar, and there rememberest[2379] that[2546] thy brother[80] hath aught[3415] against thee;[3100]

24 Leave[863] there thy gift[1435] before[1715] the altar,[2379] and go thy[5217] way;[5217] first[1259] be reconciled to thy brother,[80] and then[2064] come and[4374] offer thy gift.[1435]

25 Agree[2132][2468] with thine adversary[476] quickly,[5035] while thou art in the way[3598] with him; lest at any time the adversary[476] deliver[3860] thee to the judge,[2923] and the judge[2923] deliver[3860] thee to the officer,[5257] and thou be cast[906] into prison.[5438]

26 Verily[281] I say unto thee, Thou shalt by no means come out thence,[1831] till thou hast[1564] paid[591] the uttermost[2078] farthing.[2835]

Jesus' Attitude toward Adultery

27 Ye have heard[191] that it was said[4483] by them[744] of old time, Thou shalt[3431] not commit[3431] adultery:

28 But I say unto you, That whosoever looketh[991] on a woman[1135] to lust[1937] after her hath committed[3431] adultery with her already[2235] in his heart.[2588]

29 And if thy right[1188] eye[3788] offend[4624] thee, pluck[1807] it out,[1807] and cast[906] it from thee: for it is profit-able[4851] for thee that one of thy members[3196] should[3650] perish,[622] and not that thy whole[3650] body[4983] should be cast[906] into hell.[1067]

30 And if thy right[1188] hand[5495] offend[4624] thee, cut[1581] it off,[1581] and cast[906] it from thee: for it is profitable for thee that one of thy members[3196] should[4851] perish,[622] and not that thy whole[3650] body[4983] should[906] be cast into hell.[1067]

Jesus' Attitude toward Divorce

31 It hath been said, Whosoever shall put away his wife, let him give her a writing of divorcement:

32 But I say unto you, That whosoever shall put away his wife, saving for the cause of fornication, causeth her to commit adultery: and whosoever shall marry her that is divorced committeth adultery.

Jesus' Attitude toward Oaths

33 Again, ye have heard that it hath been said by them of old time, Thou shalt not forswear thyself, but shalt perform unto the Lord thine oaths:

34 But I say unto you, Swear not at all; neither by heaven; for it is God's throne:

35 Nor by the earth; for it is his footstool: neither by Jerusalem; for it is the city of the great King.

36 Neither shalt thou swear by thy head, because thou canst not make one hair white or black.

37 But let your communication be, Yea, yea; Nay, nay: for whatsoever is more than these cometh of evil.

Love for Enemies

38 Ye have heard that it hath been said, An eye for an eye, and a tooth for a tooth:

39 But I say unto you, That ye resist not evil: but whosoever shall smite thee on thy right cheek, turn to him the other also.

40 And if any man will sue thee at the law,

and take away thy coat, let him have thy cloak also.

41 And whosoever shall compel thee to go a mile, go with him twain.

42 Give to him that asketh thee, and from him that would borrow of thee turn not thou away.

43 Ye have heard that it hath been said, Thou shalt love thy neighbor, and hate thine enemy.

44 But I say unto you, Love your enemies, bless them that curse you, do good to them that hate you, and pray for them which despitefully use you, and persecute you;

45 That ye may be the children of your Father which is in heaven: for he maketh his sun to rise on the evil and on the good, and sendeth rain on the just and on the unjust.

46 For if ye love them which love you, what reward have ye? do not even the publicans the same?

47 And if ye salute your brethren only, what do ye more than others? do not even the publicans so?

48 Be ye therefore perfect, even as your Father which is in heaven is perfect.

Jesus' Teaching on Almsgiving

6 Take heed that ye do not your alms before men, to be seen of them: otherwise ye have no reward of your Father which is in heaven.

2 Therefore when thou doest thine alms, do not sound a trumpet before thee, as the

hypocrites do in the synagogues and in the streets, that they may have glory of men. Verily I say unto you, They have their reward.

3 But when thou doest alms, let not thy left hand know what thy right hand doeth: 4 That thine alms may be in secret; and thy Father which seeth in secret himself shall reward thee openly.

Jesus' Teaching on Prayer

5 And when thou prayest, thou shalt not be as the hypocrites are: for they love to pray standing in the synagogues and in the corners of the streets, that they may be seen of men. Verily I say unto you, They have their reward.

6 But thou, when thou prayest, enter into thy closet, and when thou hast shut thy door, pray to thy Father which is in secret; and thy Father which seeth in secret shall reward thee openly.

7 But when ye pray, use not vain repetitions, as the heathen do: for they think that they shall be heard for their much speaking. 8 Be not ye therefore like unto them: for your Father knoweth what things ye have need of, before ye ask him.

9 After this manner therefore pray ye: Our Father which art in heaven, Hallowed be thy name.

10 Thy kingdom come. Thy will be done in earth, as it is in heaven.

11 Give us this day our daily bread.

12 And forgive us our debts, as we forgive
our debtors.

13 And lead us not into temptation, but
deliver us from evil: For thine is the kingdom,
and the power, and the glory, for ever. Amen.

14 For if ye forgive men their trespasses,
your heavenly Father will also forgive you:

15 But if ye forgive not men their trespasses, neither will your Father forgive your
trespasses.

Jesus' Teaching on Fasting

16 Moreover when ye fast, be not, as the
hypocrites, of a sad countenance: for they
disfigure their faces, that they may appear
unto men to fast. Verily I say unto you,
They have their reward.

17 But thou, when thou fastest, anoint thine
head, and wash thy face;

18 That thou appear not unto men to fast,
but unto thy Father which is in secret: and
thy Father which seeth in secret shall reward
thee openly.

Treasure in Heaven

19 Lay not up for yourselves treasures upon
earth, where moth and rust doth corrupt, and
where thieves break through and steal:

20 But lay up for yourselves treasures in
heaven, where neither moth nor rust doth
corrupt, and where thieves do not break
through nor steal:

21 For where your treasure is, there will
your heart be also.

The Light of the Body

22 The light of the body is the eye: if therefore thine eye be single, thy whole body shall be full of light.

23 But if thine eye be evil, thy whole body shall be full of darkness. If therefore the light that is in thee be darkness, how great is that darkness!

God and Mammon

24 No man can serve two masters: for either he will hate the one, and love the other; or else he will hold to the one, and despise the other. Ye cannot serve God and mammon.

Care and Anxiety

25 Therefore I say unto you, Take no thought for your life, what ye shall eat, or what ye shall drink; nor yet for your body, what ye shall put on. Is not the life more than meat, and the body than raiment?

26 Behold the fowls of the air: for they sow not, neither do they reap, nor gather into barns; yet your heavenly Father feedeth them. Are ye not much better than they?

27 Which of you by taking thought can add one cubit unto his stature?

28 And why take ye thought for raiment? Consider the lilies of the field, how they grow; they toil not, neither do they spin:

29 And yet I say unto you, That even Solomon in all his glory was not arrayed like one of these.

30 Wherefore, if God so clothe the grass of the field, which today is, and tomorrow is cast into the oven, shall he not much more clothe you, O ye of little faith?

31 Therefore take no thought, saying, What shall we eat? or, What shall we drink? or, Wherewithal shall we be clothed?

32 (For after all these things do the Gentiles seek:) for your heavenly Father knoweth that ye have need of all these things.

33 But seek ye first the kingdom of God, and his righteousness; and all these things shall be added unto you.

34 Take therefore no thought for the morrow: for the morrow shall take thought for the things of itself. Sufficient unto the day is the evil thereof.

Judging Others

7 Judge not, that ye be not judged.
2 For with what judgment ye judge, ye shall be judged: and with what measure ye mete, it shall be measured to you again.
3 And why beholdest thou the mote that is in thy brother's eye, but considerest not the beam that is in thine own eye?
4 Or how wilt thou say to thy brother, Let me pull out the mote out of thine eye; and, behold, a beam is in thine own eye?
5 Thou hypocrite, first cast out the beam out of thine own eye; and then shalt thou see clearly to cast out the mote out of thy brother's eye.

6 Give not that which is holy unto the dogs, neither cast ye your pearls before swine, lest they trample them under their feet, and and turn again and rend you.

Ask, Seek, Knock

7 Ask, and it shall be given you; seek, and ye shall find; knock, and it shall be opened unto you:

8 For every one that asketh receiveth; and he that seeketh findeth; and to him that knocketh it shall be opened.

9 Or what man is there of you, whom if his son ask bread, will he give him a stone?

10 Or if he ask a fish, will he give him a serpent?

11 If ye then, being evil, know how to give good gifts unto your children, how much more shall your Father which is in heaven give good things to them that ask him?

12 Therefore all things whatsoever ye would that men should do to you, do ye even so to them: for this is the law and the prophets.

The Narrow Gate

13 Enter ye in at the strait gate: for wide is the gate, and broad is the way, that leadeth to destruction, and many there be which go in thereat:

14 Because strait is the gate, and narrow is the way, which leadeth unto life, and few there be that find it.

A Tree Is Known by Its Fruit

15 Beware of false prophets, which come to you in sheep's clothing, but inwardly they are ravening wolves.

16 Ye shall know them by their fruits. Do men gather grapes of thorns, or figs of thistles?

17 Even so every good tree bringeth forth good fruit; but a corrupt tree bringeth forth evil fruit.

18 A good tree cannot bring forth evil fruit, neither can a corrupt tree bring forth good fruit.

19 Every tree that bringeth not forth good fruit is hewn down, and cast into the fire.

20 Wherefore by their fruits ye shall know them.

I Never Knew You

21 Not every one that saith unto me, Lord, Lord, shall enter into the kingdom of heaven; but he that doeth the will of my Father which is in heaven.

22 Many will say to me in that day, Lord, Lord, have we not prophesied in thy name? and in thy name have cast out devils? and in thy name done many wonderful works?

23 And then will I profess unto them, I never knew you: depart from me, ye that work iniquity.

The Two Foundations

24 Therefore whosoever heareth these sayings of mine, and doeth them, I will liken him unto a wise man, which built his house upon a rock:

25 And the rain descended, and the floods came, and the winds blew, and beat upon that house; and it fell not: for it was founded upon a rock.

26 And every one that heareth these sayings of mine, and doeth them not, shall be likened unto a foolish man, which built his house upon the sand:

27 And the rain descended, and the floods came, and the winds blew, and beat upon that house; and it fell: and great was the fall of it.

28 And it came to pass, when Jesus had ended these sayings, the people were astonished at his doctrine:

29 For he taught them as one having authority, and not as the scribes.

Jesus Cleanses a Leper

8 When he was come down from the mountain, great multitudes followed him.

2 And, behold, there came a leper and worshipped him, saying, Lord, if thou wilt, thou canst make me clean.

3 And Jesus put forth his hand, and touched him, saying, I will; be thou clean. And immediately his leprosy was cleansed.

4 And Jesus saith unto him, See thou tell no man; but go thy way, show thyself to the priest, and offer the gift that Moses commanded, for a testimony unto them.

A Centurion's Servant Healed

5 And when Jesus was entered into Caper'-na-um, there came unto him a centurion, beseeching him,

6 And saying, Lord, my servant lieth at home sick of the palsy, grievously tormented.

7 And Jesus saith unto him, I will come and heal him.

8 The centurion answered and said, Lord, I am not worthy that thou shouldest come under my roof: but speak the word only, and my servant shall be healed.

9 For I am a man under authority, having soldiers under me: and I say to this man, Go, and he goeth; and to another, Come, and he cometh; and to my servant, Do this, and he doeth it.

10 When Jesus heard it, he marveled, and said to them that followed, Verily I say unto you, I have not found so great faith, no, not in Israel.

11 And I say unto you, That many shall come from the east and west, and shall sit down with Abraham, and Isaac, and Jacob, in the kingdom of heaven:

12 But the children of the kingdom shall be cast out into outer darkness: there shall be weeping and gnashing of teeth.

13 And Jesus said unto the centurion, Go thy way; and as thou hast believed, so be it done unto thee. And his servant was healed in the selfsame hour.

Jesus Heals Peter's Mother-in-Law

14 And when Jesus was come into Peter's house, he saw his wife's mother laid, and sick of a fever.

15 And he touched her hand, and the

fever left her: and she arose, and ministered unto them.

16 When the even was come, they brought unto him many that were possessed with devils: and he cast out the spirits with his word, and healed all that were sick:

17 That it might be fulfilled which was spoken by Isaiah the prophet, saying, Himself took our infirmities, and bare our sicknesses.

The Would-be Followers of Jesus

18 Now when Jesus saw great multitudes about him, he gave commandment to depart unto the other side.

19 And a certain scribe came, and said unto him, Master, I will follow thee whithersoever thou goest.

20 And Jesus saith unto him, The foxes have holes, and the birds of the air have nests; but the Son of man hath not where to lay his head.

21 And another of his disciples said unto him, Lord, suffer me first to go and bury my father.

22 But Jesus said unto him, Follow me; and let the dead bury their dead.

Jesus Calms a Storm

23 And when he was entered into a ship, his disciples followed him.

24 And, behold, there arose a great tempest in the sea, insomuch that the ship was covered with the waves: but he was asleep.

25 And his disciples came to him, and awoke him, saying, Lord, save us: we perish.

26 And he saith unto them, Why are ye fearful, O ye of little faith? Then he arose, and rebuked the winds and the sea; and there was a great calm.

27 But the men marveled, saying, What manner of man is this, that even the winds and the sea obey him!

The Gergesene Demoniacs

28 And when he was come to the other side into the country of the Ger'gesenes, there met him two possessed with devils, coming out of the tombs, exceeding fierce, so that no man might pass by that way.

29 And, behold, they cried out, saying, What have we to do with thee, Jesus, thou Son of God? art thou come hither to torment us before the time?

30 And there was a good way off from them a herd of many swine feeding.

31 So the devils besought him, saying, If thou cast us out, suffer us to go away into the herd of swine.

32 And he said unto them, Go. And when they were come out, they went into the herd of swine: and, behold, the whole herd of swine ran violently down a steep place into the sea, and perished in the waters.

33 And they that kept them fled, and went their ways into the city, and told every thing, and what was befallen to the possessed of the devils.

34 And, behold, the whole city came out to meet Jesus: and when they saw him, they besought him that he would depart out of their coasts.

Jesus Heals a Palsied Man

9 And he entered into a ship, and passed over, and came into his own city.

2 And, behold, they brought to him a man sick of the palsy, lying on a bed: and Jesus seeing their faith said unto the sick of the palsy; Son, be of good cheer; thy sins be forgiven thee.

3 And, behold, certain of the scribes said within themselves, This man blasphemeth.

4 And Jesus knowing their thoughts said, Wherefore think ye evil in your hearts?

5 For whether is easier, to say, Thy sins be forgiven thee; or to say, Arise, and walk?

6 But that ye may know that the Son of man hath power on earth to forgive sins, (then saith he to the sick of the palsy,) Arise, take up thy bed, and go unto thine house.

7 And he arose, and departed to his house.

8 But when the multitudes saw it, they marveled, and glorified God, which had given such power unto men.

The Call of Matthew

9 And as Jesus passed forth from thence, he saw a man, named Matthew, sitting at the receipt of custom: and he saith unto him, Follow me. And he arose, and followed him.

10 And it came to pass, as Jesus sat at meat in the house, behold, many publicans and sinners came and sat down with him and his disciples.

11 And when the Pharisees saw it, they said unto his disciples, Why eateth your master with publicans and sinners?

12 But when Jesus heard that, he said unto them, They that be whole need not a physician, but they that are sick.

13 But go ye and learn what that meaneth, I will have mercy, and not sacrifice: for I am not come to call the righteous, but sinners to repentance.

The Question about Fasting

14 Then came to him the disciples of John, saying, Why do we and the Pharisees fast oft, but thy disciples fast not?

15 And Jesus said unto them, Can the children of the bridechamber mourn, as long as the bridegroom is with them? but the days will come, when the bridegroom shall be taken from them, and then shall they fast.

16 No man putteth a piece of new cloth unto an old garment; for that which is put in to fill it up taketh from the garment, and the rent is made worse.

17 Neither do men put new wine into old bottles: else the bottles break, and the wine runneth out, and the bottles perish: but they put new wine into new bottles, and both are preserved.

The Ruler's Daughter and the Woman
Who Touched Jesus' Garment

18 While he spake these things unto them, behold, there came a certain ruler, and worshipped him, saying, My daughter is even now dead: but come and lay thy hand upon her, and she shall live.

19 And Jesus arose, and followed him, and so did his disciples.

20 And, behold, a woman, which was diseased with an issue of blood twelve years, came behind him, and touched the hem of his garment:

21 For she said within herself, If I may but touch his garment, I shall be whole.

22 But Jesus turned him about, and when he saw her, he said, Daughter, be of good comfort; thy faith hath made thee whole. And the woman was made whole from that hour.

23 And when Jesus came into the ruler's house, and saw the minstrels and the people making a noise,

24 He said unto them, Give place: for the the maid is not dead, but sleepeth. And they laughed him to scorn.

25 But when the people were put forth, he went in, and took her by the hand, and the maid arose.

26 And the fame hereof went abroad into all that land.

Two Blind Men Receive Sight

27 And when Jesus departed thence, two blind men followed him, crying, and

saying, Thou Son of David, have mercy on us.

28 And when he was come into the house, the blind men came to him: and Jesus saith unto them, Believe ye that I am able to do this? They said unto him, Yea, Lord.

29 Then touched he their eyes, saying, According to your faith be it unto you.

30 And their eyes were opened; and Jesus straitly charged them, saying, See that no man know it.

31 But they, when they were departed, spread abroad his fame in all that country.

A Dumb Man Speaks

32 As they went out, behold, they brought to him a dumb man possessed with a devil.

33 And when the devil was cast out, the dumb spake: and the multitudes marveled, saying, It was never so seen in Israel.

34 But the Pharisees said, He casteth out devils through the prince of the devils.

The Harvest Is Plenteous

35 And Jesus went about all the cities and villages, teaching in their synagogues, and preaching the gospel of the kingdom, and healing every sickness and every disease among the people.

36 But when he saw the multitudes, he was moved with compassion on them, because they fainted, and were scattered abroad, as sheep having no shepherd.

37 Then saith he unto his disciples, The harvest truly is plenteous, but the laborers are few;

38 Pray ye therefore the Lord of the harvest, that he will send forth laborers into his harvest.

Jesus Chooses the Twelve

10 And when he had called unto him his twelve disciples, he gave them power against unclean spirits, to cast them out, and to heal all manner of sickness and all manner of disease.

2 Now the names of the twelve apostles are these; The first, Simon, who is called Peter, and Andrew his brother; James the son of Zeb'edee, and John his brother;

3 Philip, and Bartholomew; Thomas, and Matthew the publican; James the son of Al'pheus, and Lebbe'us, whose surname was Thad'deus;

4 Simon the Canaanite, and Judas Iscar'i-ot, who also betrayed him.

The Mission of the Twelve

5 These twelve Jesus sent forth, and commanded them, saying, Go not into the way of the Gentiles, and into any city of the Samaritans enter ye not:

6 But go rather to the lost sheep of the house of Israel.

7 And as ye go, preach, saying, The kingdom of heaven is at hand.

8 Heal the sick, cleanse the lepers, raise

the dead, cast out devils: freely ye have received, freely give.

9 Provide neither gold, nor silver, nor brass in your purses;

10 Nor scrip for your journey, neither two coats, neither shoes, nor yet staves: for the workman is worthy of his meat.

11 And into whatsoever city or town ye shall enter, inquire who in it is worthy; and there abide till ye go thence.

12 And when ye come into a house, salute it.

13 And if the house be worthy, let your peace come upon it: but if it be not worthy, let your peace return to you.

14 And whosoever shall not receive you, nor hear your words, when ye depart out of that house or city, shake off the dust of your feet.

15 Verily I say unto you, It shall be more tolerable for the land of Sodom and Gomor'-rah in the day of judgment, than for that city.

Coming Persecutions

16 Behold, I send you forth as sheep in the midst of wolves: be ye therefore wise as serpents, and harmless as doves.

17 But beware of men: for they will deliver you up to the councils, and they will scourge you in their synagogues;

18 And ye shall be brought before governors and kings for my sake, for a testimony against them and the Gentiles.

19 But when they deliver you up, take no

thought how or what ye shall speak: for it shall be given you in that same hour what ye shall speak.

20 For it is not ye that speak, but the Spirit of your Father which speaketh in you.

21 And the brother shall deliver up the brother to death, and the father the child: and the children shall rise up against their parents, and cause them to be put to death.

22 And ye shall be hated of all men for my name's sake: but he that endureth to the end shall be saved.

23 But when they persecute you in this city, flee ye into another: for verily I say unto you, Ye shall not have gone over the cities of Israel, till the Son of man be come.

24 The disciple is not above his master, nor the servant above his lord.

25 It is enough for the disciple that he be as his master, and the servant as his lord. If they have called the master of the house Beel'zebub, how much more shall they call them of his household?

Whom to Fear

26 Fear them not therefore: for there is nothing covered, that shall not be revealed; and hid, that shall not be known.

27 What I tell you in darkness, that speak ye in light: and what ye hear in the ear, that preach ye upon the housetops.

28 And fear not them which kill the body, but are not able to kill the soul: but rather

fear him which is able to destroy both soul and body in hell.

29 Are not two sparrows sold for a farthing? and one of them shall not fall on the ground without your Father.

30 But the very hairs of your head are all numbered.

31 Fear ye not therefore, ye are of more value than many sparrows.

32 Whosoever therefore shall confess me before men, him will I confess also before my Father which is in heaven.

33 But whosoever shall deny me before men, him will I also deny before my Father which is in heaven.

Not Peace, but a Sword

34 Think not that I am come to send peace on earth: I came not to send peace, but a sword.

35 For I am come to set a man at variance against his father, and the daughter against her mother, and the daughter-in-law against her mother-in-law.

36 And a man's foes shall be they of his own household.

37 He that loveth father or mother more than me is not worthy of me: and he that loveth son or daughter more than me is not worthy of me.

38 And he that taketh not his cross, and followeth after me, is not worthy of me.

39 He that findeth his life shall lose it: and he that loseth his life for my sake shall find it.

Rewards

40 He that receiveth you receiveth me; and he that receiveth me receiveth him that sent me.

41 He that receiveth a prophet in the name of a prophet shall receive a prophet's reward; and he that receiveth a righteous man in the name of a righteous man shall receive a righteous man's reward.

42 And whosoever shall give to drink unto one of these little ones a cup of cold water only in the name of a disciple, verily I say unto you, he shall in no wise lose his reward.

The Messengers from John the Baptist

11 And it came to pass, when Jesus had made an end of commanding his twelve disciples, he departed thence to teach and to preach in their cities.

2 Now when John had heard in the prison the works of Christ, he sent two of his disciples,

3 And said unto him, Art thou he that should come, or do we look for another?

4 Jesus answered and said unto them, Go and show John again those things which ye do hear and see:

5 The blind receive their sight, and the lame walk, the lepers are cleansed, and the deaf hear, the dead are raised up, and the poor have the gospel preached to them.

6 And blessed is he, whosoever shall not be offended in me.

7 And as they departed, Jesus began to say

unto the multitudes concerning John,[2491] What[5101] went[1831] ye out[1831] into[3793] the wilderness to[2491] see?[2300] A reed[2563] shaken[4531] with the wind?[417]

8 But what[5101] went[1831] ye out[1831] for[1492] to see? A man clothed[444] in[294] soft[3120] raiment?[2440] behold,[2400] they that[5409] wear soft clothing[3120] are in kings'[935] houses.[3624]

9 But what[5101] went[1831] ye out[1831] for[1492] to see? A prophet?[4396] yea,[3483] I say unto you, and more than[4053] a prophet.[4396]

10 For this is he, of whom it is[1125] written, Behold, I send[649] my messenger[32] before[1715] thy face,[4383] which[2400] shall prepare[2680] thy way[3598] before thee.

11 Verily[281] I say unto you, Among them that[1084] are born of women there hath not risen a greater[3187] than John[1135] the Baptist:[1453] notwithstanding,[1453] he that is least[2491] in the kingdom[932] of heaven is greater[3772] than[3398] he.

12 And[3187] from the days[2250] of John the Baptist until now the kingdom[932] of heaven[2491] suffereth[910] violence,[737] and the violent[3772] take it[726] by force.[971]

13 For all the prophets[973] and the law[3551] prophe-[726]sied until John.[4396]

14 And if ye[2491] will receive it,[2309][1209] this is Eli'jah,[2243] which was[3195] for to come.[2064]

15 He that hath ears[2064] to hear, let him hear.

16 But whereunto[3775] shall I[191] liken[191] this genera-[191]tion? It is[5101] like unto[3666] children[3666] sitting in[1074] the markets,[3664] and calling[3808] unto their fellows,[2521][58][4377]

17 And saying, We have[832] piped[2083] unto you, and ye have not danced;[3738] we have[3738] mourned[2354] unto you, and ye have not lamented.

18 For John came[2875] neither eating[2875] nor drink-ing,[2491][2064] and they say,[2068] He hath a devil.[4095]

19 The Son[5207] of man[444] came[2064] eating[2068] and[1140] drink-[4095]

ing, and they say, Behold a man gluttonous, and a winebibber, a friend of publicans and sinners. But wisdom is justified of her children.

Woes to Unrepentant Cities

20 Then began he to upbraid the cities wherein most of his mighty works were done, because they repented not:

21 Woe unto thee, Chora'zin! woe unto thee, Bethsai'da! for if the mighty works, which were done in you, had been done in Tyre and Sidon, they would have repented long ago in sackcloth and ashes.

22 But I say unto you, It shall be more tolerable for Tyre and Sidon at the day of judgment, than for you.

23 And thou, Caper'na-um, which art exalted unto heaven, shalt be brought down to hell: for if the mighty works, which have been done in thee, had been done in Sodom, it would have remained until this day.

24 But I say unto you, That it shall be more tolerable for the land of Sodom in the day of judgment, than for thee.

Come unto Me and Rest

25 At that time Jesus answered and said, I thank thee, O Father, Lord of heaven and earth, because thou hast hid these things from the wise and prudent, and hast revealed them unto babes.

26 Even so, Father; for so it seemed good in thy sight.

27 All things are delivered unto me of my Father: and no man knoweth the Son, but the Father; neither knoweth any man the Father, save the Son, and he to whomsoever the Son will reveal him.

28 Come unto me, all ye that labor and are heavy laden, and I will give you rest.

29 Take my yoke upon you, and learn of me; for I am meek and lowly in heart: and ye shall find rest unto your souls.

30 For my yoke is easy, and my burden is light.

The Disciples Pluck Grain on the Sabbath

12 At that time Jesus went on the sabbath day through the corn; and his disciples were ahungered, and began to pluck the ears of corn, and to eat.

2 But when the Pharisees saw it, they said unto him, Behold, thy disciples do that which is not lawful to do upon the sabbath day.

3 But he said unto them, Have ye not read what David did, when he was ahungered, and they that were with him;

4 How he entered into the house of God, and did eat the showbread, which was not lawful for him to eat, neither for them which were with him, but only for the priests?

5 Or have ye not read in the law, how that on the sabbath days the priests in the temple profane the sabbath, and are blameless?

6 But I say unto you, That in this place is one greater than the temple.

7 But if ye had known what this meaneth,

I will have mercy, and not sacrifice, ye would not have condemned the guiltless.

8 For the Son of man is Lord even of the sabbath day.

The Man with a Withered Hand

9 And when he was departed thence, he went into their synagogue:

10 And, behold, there was a man which had his hand withered. And they asked him, saying, Is it lawful to heal on the sabbath days? that they might accuse him.

11 And he said unto them, What man shall there be among you, that shall have one sheep, and if it fall into a pit on the sabbath day, will he not lay hold on it, and lift it out?

12 How much then is a man better than a sheep? Wherefore it is lawful to do well on the sabbath days.

13 Then saith he to the man, Stretch forth thine hand. And he stretched it forth; and it was restored whole, like as the other.

14 Then the Pharisees went out, and held a council against him, how they might destroy him.

The Chosen Servant

15 But when Jesus knew it, he withdrew himself from thence: and great multitudes followed him, and he healed them all;

16 And charged them that they should not make him known:

17 That it might be fulfilled which was spoken by Isaiah the prophet, saying,

18 Behold my servant, whom I have chosen; my beloved, in whom my soul is well pleased: I will put my Spirit upon him, and he shall show judgment to the Gentiles.

19 He shall not strive, nor cry; neither shall any man hear his voice in the streets.

20 A bruised reed shall he not break, and smoking flax shall he not quench, till he send forth judgment unto victory.

21 And in his name shall the Gentiles trust.

A Divided House Cannot Stand

22 Then was brought unto him one possessed with a devil, blind, and dumb: and he healed him, insomuch that the blind and dumb both spake and saw.

23 And all the people were amazed, and said, Is not this the Son of David?

24 But when the Pharisees heard it, they said, This fellow doth not cast out devils, but by Beel'zebub the prince of the devils.

25 And Jesus knew their thoughts, and said unto them, Every kingdom divided against itself is brought to desolation; and every city or house divided against itself shall not stand:

26 And if Satan cast out Satan, he is divided against himself; how shall then his kingdom stand?

27 And if I by Beel'zebub cast out devils, by whom do your children cast them out? therefore they shall be your judges.

28 But if I cast out devils by the Spirit of

God, then the kingdom of God is come unto you.

29 Or else, how can one enter into a strong man's house, and spoil his goods, except he first bind the strong man? and then he will spoil his house.

30 He that is not with me is against me; and he that gathereth not with me scattereth abroad.

31 Wherefore I say unto you, All manner of sin and blasphemy shall be forgiven unto men: but the blasphemy against the Holy Ghost shall not be forgiven unto men.

32 And whosoever speaketh a word against the Son of man, it shall be forgiven him: but whosoever speaketh against the Holy Ghost, it shall not be forgiven him, neither in this world, neither in the world to come.

33 Either make the tree good, and his fruit good; or else make the tree corrupt, and his fruit corrupt: for the tree is known by his fruit.

34 O generation of vipers, how can ye, being evil, speak good things? for out of the abundance of the heart the mouth speaketh.

35 A good man out of the good treasure of the heart bringeth forth good things: and an evil man out of the evil treasure bringeth forth evil things.

36 But I say unto you, That every idle word that men shall speak, they shall give account thereof in the day of judgment.

37 For by thy words thou shalt be justified, and by thy words thou shalt be condemned.

An Evil Generation Seeks a Sign

38 Then certain of the scribes and of the Pharisees answered, saying, Master, we would see a sign from thee.

39 But he answered and said unto them, An evil and adulterous generation seeketh after a sign; and there shall no sign be given to it, but the sign of the prophet Jonah:

40 For as Jonah was three days and three nights in the whale's belly; so shall the Son of man be three days and three nights in the heart of the earth.

41 The men of Nin'eveh shall rise in judgment with this generation, and shall condemn it: because they repented at the preaching of Jonah; and, behold, a greater than Jonah is here.

42 The queen of the south shall rise up in the judgment with this generation, and shall condemn it: for she came from the uttermost parts of the earth to hear the wisdom of Solomon; and, behold, a greater than Solomon is here.

The Return of the Unclean Spirit

43 When the unclean spirit is gone out of a man, he walketh through dry places, seeking rest, and findeth none.

44 Then he saith, I will return into my house from whence I came out; and when he is come, he findeth it empty, swept, and garnished.

45 Then goeth he, and taketh with himself seven other spirits more wicked than himself,

and they enter in and dwell there: and the last state of that man is worse than the first. Even so shall it be also unto this wicked generation.

Jesus' Mother and Brethren

46 While he yet talked to the people, behold, his mother and his brethren stood without, desiring to speak with him.

47 Then one said unto him, Behold, thy mother and thy brethren stand without, desiring to speak with thee.

48 But he answered and said unto him that told him, Who is my mother? and who are my brethren?

49 And he stretched forth his hand toward his disciples, and said, Behold my mother and my brethren!

50 For whosoever shall do the will of my Father which is in heaven, the same is my brother, and sister, and mother.

The Parable of the Sower

13 The same day went Jesus out of the house, and sat by the sea side.

2 And great multitudes were gathered together unto him, so that he went into a ship, and sat; and the whole multitude stood on the shore.

3 And he spake many things unto them in parables, saying, Behold, a sower went forth to sow;

4 And when he sowed, some seeds fell by the wayside, and the fowls came and devoured them up:

5 Some fell upon stony places, where they had not much earth: and forthwith they sprung up, because they had no deepness of earth:

6 And when the sun was up, they were scorched; and because they had no root, they withered away.

7 And some fell among thorns; and the thorns sprung up, and choked them:

8 But other fell into good ground, and brought forth fruit, some a hundredfold, some sixtyfold, some thirtyfold.

9 Who hath ears to hear, let him hear.

The Purpose of the Parables

10 And the disciples came, and said unto him, Why speakest thou unto them in parables?

11 He answered and said unto them, Because it is given unto you to know the mysteries of the kingdom of heaven, but to them it is not given.

12 For whosoever hath, to him shall be given, and he shall have more abundance: but whosoever hath not, from him shall be taken away even that he hath.

13 Therefore speak I to them in parables: because they seeing see not; and hearing they hear not, neither do they understand.

14 And in them is fulfilled the prophecy of Isaiah, which saith, By hearing ye shall hear, and shall not understand; and seeing ye shall see, and shall not perceive:

15 For this people's heart is waxed gross, and their ears are dull of hearing, and their

eyes they have closed; lest at any time they should see with their eyes, and hear with their ears, and should understand with their heart, and should be converted, and I should heal them.

16 But blessed are your eyes, for they see: and your ears, for they hear.

17 For verily I say unto you, That many prophets and righteous men have desired to see those things which ye see, and have not seen them; and to hear those things which ye hear, and have not heard them.

Jesus Explains the Parable of the Sower

18 Hear ye therefore the parable of the sower.

19 When any one heareth the word of the kingdom, and understandeth it not, then cometh the wicked one, and catcheth away that which was sown in his heart. This is he which received seed by the wayside.

20 But he that received the seed into stony places, the same is he that heareth the word, and anon with joy receiveth it;

21 Yet hath he not root in himself, but dureth for a while: for when tribulation or persecution ariseth because of the word, by and by he is offended.

22 He also that received seed among the thorns is he that heareth the word; and the care of this world, and the deceitfulness of riches, choke the word, and he becometh unfruitful.

23 But he that received seed into the good

ground is he that heareth the word, and un-
1093   191   3056   4920
derstandeth it; which also beareth fruit, and
1211   2592
bringeth forth, some a hundredfold, some sixty,
4160   1540   1835
some thirty.
5144

The Parable of the Wheat and the Tares

24 Another parable put he forth unto them,
243   3850   3908   3908
saying, The kingdom of heaven is likened unto
932   3772 3666
a man which sowed good seed in his field:
444   4687   2570 4690   68
25 But while men slept, his enemy came and
444   2518   2190   2064
sowed tares among the wheat, and went his
4687 2215 3319,303   4621   565
way.
565
26 But when the blade was sprung up, and
5528 985
brought forth fruit, then appeared the tares
4160   2590   5316   2215
also.

27 So the servants of the householder came
1401   3617
and said unto him, Sir, didst not thou sow
2036   2962 4687   4687
good seed in thy field? from whence then
2570 4690   68   4159
hath it tares?
2215

28 He said unto them, An enemy hath done
5346   2190   4160
this. The servants said unto him, Wilt thou
5346   2036
then that we go and gather them up?
1401   2309
565   4816
29 But he said, Nay; lest while ye gather
5346   4816   4816
up the tares, ye root up also the wheat with
2215   1610   4621   260
them.

30 Let both grow together until the har-
863   297   4885   3360   2326
vest: and in the time of harvest I will say to
2326   2540   2326 2046
the reapers, Gather ye together first the tares,
2327   4816   2215
and bind them in bundles to burn them: but
1210   1197   2618
gather the wheat into my barn.
4863   4621   596

The Parable of the Mustard Seed

31 Another parable put he forth unto them,
243   3850   3908   3908
saying, The kingdom of heaven is like to a
932   3772   3664

grain of mustard seed, which a man took, and sowed in his field:

32 Which indeed is the least of all seeds: but when it is grown, it is the greatest among herbs, and becometh a tree, so that the birds of the air come and lodge in the branches thereof.

The Parable of the Leaven

33 Another parable spake he unto them; The kingdom of heaven is like unto leaven, which a woman took, and hid in three measures of meal, till the whole was leavened.

Jesus' Use of Parables

34 All these things spake Jesus unto the multitude in parables; and without a parable spake he not unto them:

35 That it might be fulfilled which was spoken by the prophet, saying, I will open my mouth in parables; I will utter things which have been kept secret from the foundation of the world.

Jesus Explains the Parable of the Wheat and the Tares

36 Then Jesus sent the multitude away, and went into the house: and his disciples came unto him, saying, Declare unto us the parable of the tares of the field.

37 He answered and said unto them, He that soweth the good seed is the Son of man;

38 The field is the world; the good seed are the children of the kingdom; but the tares are the children of the wicked one;

39 The enemy that sowed them is the devil; the harvest is the end of the world; and the reapers are the angels.

40 As therefore the tares are gathered and burned in the fire; so shall it be in the end of this world.

41 The Son of man shall send forth his angels, and they shall gather out of his kingdom all things that offend, and them which do iniquity;

42 And shall cast them into a furnace of fire: there shall be wailing and gnashing of teeth.

43 Then shall the righteous shine forth as the sun in the kingdom of their Father. Who hath ears to hear, let him hear.

The Hidden Treasure

44 Again, the kingdom of heaven is like unto treasure hid in a field; the which when a man hath found, he hideth, and for joy thereof goeth and selleth all that he hath, and buyeth that field.

The Pearl of Great Price

45 Again the kingdom of heaven is like unto a merchantman, seeking goodly pearls:

46 Who, when he had found one pearl of great price, went and sold all that he had, and bought it.

The Net

47 Again, the kingdom of heaven is like unto a net, that was cast into the sea, and gathered of every kind:

48 Which, when it was full, they drew to shore, and sat down, and gathered the good into vessels, but cast the bad away.

49 So shall it be at the end of the world: the angels shall come forth, and sever the wicked from among the just,

50 And shall cast them into the furnace of fire: there shall be wailing and gnashing of teeth.

Treasures New and Old

51 Jesus saith unto them, Have ye understood all these things? They say unto him, Yea, Lord.

52 Then said he unto them, Therefore every scribe which is instructed unto the kingdom of heaven, is like unto a man that is a householder, which bringeth forth out of his treasure things new and old.

Jesus Rejected at Nazareth

53 And it came to pass, that when Jesus had finished these parables, he departed thence.

54 And when he was come into his own country, he taught them in their synagogue, insomuch that they were astonished, and said, Whence hath this man this wisdom, and these mighty works?

55 Is not this the carpenter's son? is not

his mother called Mary[3137]? and his brethren, James[3384], and Joses[2499-2500], and Simon[4613], and Judas[80]? 56 And his sisters[2385], are they not all[2455] with us? Whence[79] then hath this man all these things[4159]? 57 And they were offended in him. But Jesus[2424] said[2036] unto them, A prophet[4624] is not without[820] honor[2424] save in his own country[4396], and in his own house[3968]. 58 And[3614] he did not many mighty works[1411] there because of their[4160] unbelief[4183].[570]

The Death of John the Baptist

14 At that time[2540] Herod the tetrarch[5076] heard[191] of the fame[2264] of Jesus,

2 And said[189] unto his servants[2424], This is John the Baptist[2036]; he is[910] risen[1453] from the dead[3498]; and therefore mighty works[1411] do[1754] show[1754] forth themselves in him.[1754]

3 For Herod had[2264] laid[2902] hold on John[2491], and bound him[2902], and put[1210] him in prison[5087] for Hero[5438]-di-as'[2266] sake, his brother Philip's[5376] wife.

4 For John[80] said unto him[5376], It is[1135] not lawful[1832] for thee[2491] to have her[1832].

5 And when he would[2309] have put him to death[2309], he feared[615] the multitude[5399], because they[615] counted him[3793] as a prophet.

6 But when Herod's[4396] birthday[2264] was[1077] kept[71], the daughter[2364] of Hero'di-as[2266] danced[3738] before[3319] them, and pleased Herod[700].[2264]

7 Whereupon[3606] he promised[3670] with an oath[3727] to[1325] give her[3670] whatsoever she would ask.[154]

8 And she, being[4264] before instructed of her mother[3384], said[5346], Give[1325] me here[5602] John[2491] Baptist's[910] head[2776] in a charger[4094].

9 And the king was sorry: nevertheless for the oath's sake, and them which sat with him at meat, he commanded it to be given her.

10 And he sent, and beheaded John in the prison.

11 And his head was brought in a charger, and given to the damsel: and she brought it to her mother.

12 And his disciples came, and took up the body, and buried it, and went and told Jesus.

The Feeding of the Five Thousand

13 When Jesus heard of it, he departed thence by ship into a desert place apart: and when the people had heard thereof, they followed him on foot out of the cities.

14 And Jesus went forth, and saw a great multitude, and was moved with compassion toward them, and he healed their sick.

15 And when it was evening, his disciples came to him, saying, This is a desert place, and the time is now past; send the multitude away, that they may go into the villages, and buy themselves victuals.

16 But Jesus said unto them, They need not depart; give ye them to eat.

17 And they say unto him, We have here but five loaves, and two fishes.

18 He said, Bring them hither to me.

19 And he commanded the multitude to sit down on the grass, and took the five loaves, and the two fishes, and looking up to heaven, he blessed, and brake, and gave the loaves to

his disciples, and the disciples to the multitude.

20 And they did all eat, and were filled: and they took up of the fragments that remained twelve baskets full.

21 And they that had eaten were about five thousand men, beside women and children.

Jesus Walks on the Sea

22 And straightway Jesus constrained his disciples to get into a ship, and to go before him unto the other side, while he sent the multitudes away.

23 And when he had sent the multitudes away, he went up into a mountain apart to pray: and when the evening was come, he was there alone.

24 But the ship was now in the midst of the sea, tossed with waves: for the wind was contrary.

25 And in the fourth watch of the night Jesus went unto them, walking on the sea.

26 And when the disciples saw him walking on the sea, they were troubled, saying, It is a spirit; and they cried out for fear.

27 But straightway Jesus spake unto them, saying, Be of good cheer; it is I; be not afraid.

28 And Peter answered him and said, Lord, if it be thou, bid me come unto thee on the water.

29 And he said, Come. And when Peter was come down out of the ship, he walked on the water, to go to Jesus.

30 But when he saw the wind boisterous, he was afraid; and beginning to sink, he cried, saying, Lord, save me.

31 And immediately Jesus stretched forth his hand, and caught him, and said unto him, O thou of little faith, wherefore didst thou doubt?

32 And when they were come into the ship, the wind ceased.

33 Then they that were in the ship came and worshipped him, saying, Of a truth thou art the Son of God.

Jesus Heals the Sick in Gennesaret

34 And when they were gone over, they came into the land of Gennesaret.

35 And when the men of that place had knowledge of him, they sent out into all that country round about, and brought unto him all that were diseased;

36 And besought him that they might only touch the hem of his garment: and as many as touched were made perfectly whole.

The Things That Defile

15 Then came to Jesus scribes and Pharisees, which were of Jerusalem, saying,

2 Why do thy disciples transgress the tradition of the elders? for they wash not their hands when they eat bread.

3 But he answered and said unto them, Why do ye also transgress the commandment of God by your tradition?

4 For God commanded, saying, Honor thy

father and mother: and, He that curseth father or mother, let him die the death.

5 But ye say, Whosoever shall say to his father or his mother, It is a gift, by whatsoever thou mightest be profited by me;

6 And honor not his father or his mother, he shall be free. Thus have ye made the commandment of God of none effect by your tradition.

7 Ye hypocrites, well did Isaiah prophesy of you, saying,

8 This people draweth nigh unto me with their mouth, and honoreth me with their lips; but their heart is far from me.

9 But in vain they do worship me, teaching for doctrines the commandments of men.

10 And he called the multitude, and said unto them, Hear, and understand:

11 Not that which goeth into the mouth defileth a man; but that which cometh out of the mouth, this defileth a man.

12 Then came his disciples, and said unto him, Knowest thou that the Pharisees were offended, after they heard this saying?

13 But he answered and said, Every plant, which my heavenly Father hath not planted, shall be rooted up.

14 Let them alone: they be blind leaders of the blind. And if the blind lead the blind, both shall fall into the ditch.

15 Then answered Peter and said unto him, Declare unto us this parable.

16 And Jesus said, Are ye also yet without understanding?

17 Do not ye yet understand, that whatsoever entereth in at the mouth goeth into the belly, and is cast out into the draught?

18 But those things which proceed out of the mouth come forth from the heart; and they defile the man.

19 For out of the heart proceed evil thoughts, murders, adulteries, fornications, thefts, false witness, blasphemies:

20 These are the things which defile a man: but to eat with unwashen hands defileth not a man.

The Canaanite Woman's Faith

21 Then Jesus went thence, and departed into the coasts of Tyre and Sidon.

22 And, behold, a woman of Canaan came out of the same coasts, and cried unto him, saying, Have mercy on me, O Lord, thou Son of David; my daughter is grievously vexed with a devil.

23 But he answered her not a word. And his disciples came and besought him, saying, Send her away; for she crieth after us.

24 But he answered and said, I am not sent but unto the lost sheep of the house of Israel.

25 Then came she and worshipped him, saying, Lord, help me.

26 But he answered and said, It is not meet to take the children's bread, and to cast it to dogs.

27 And she said, Truth, Lord: yet the dogs eat of the crumbs which fall from their masters' table.

28 Then Jesus answered and said unto her,
O woman, great is thy faith: be it unto thee
even as thou wilt. And her daughter was made
whole from that very hour.

Jesus Heals Many People

29 And Jesus departed from thence, and
came nigh unto the sea of Galilee; and went
up into a mountain, and sat down there.
30 And great multitudes came unto him,
having with them those that were lame, blind,
dumb, maimed, and many others, and cast
them down at Jesus' feet; and he healed them:
31 Insomuch that the multitude wondered,
when they saw the dumb to speak, the
maimed to be whole, the lame to walk, and
the blind to see: and they glorified the God
of Israel.

The Feeding of the Four Thousand

32 Then Jesus called his disciples unto him,
and said, I have compassion on the multitude,
because they continue with me now three days,
and have nothing to eat: and I will not send
them away fasting, lest they faint in the way.
33 And his disciples say unto him, Whence
should we have so much bread in the wilderness, as to fill so great a multitude?
34 And Jesus saith unto them, How many
loaves have ye? And they said, Seven, and a
few little fishes.
35 And he commanded the multitude to sit
down on the ground.
36 And he took the seven loaves and the

fishes, and gave thanks, and brake them, and gave to his disciples, and the disciples to the multitude.

37 And they did all eat, and were filled: and they took up of the broken meat that was left seven baskets full.

38 And they that did eat were four thousand men, beside women and children.

39 And he sent away the multitude, and took ship, and came into the coasts of Mag'-dala.

The Demand for a Sign

16 The Pharisees also with the Sadducees came, and tempting desired him that he would show them a sign from heaven.

2 He answered and said unto them, When it is evening, ye say, It will be fair weather: for the sky is red.

3 And in the morning, It will be foul weather today: for the sky is red and lowering. O ye hypocrites, ye can discern the face of the sky; but can ye not discern the signs of the times?

4 A wicked and adulterous generation seeketh after a sign; and there shall no sign be given unto it, but the sign of the prophet Jonah. And he left them, and departed.

The Leaven of the Pharisees and Sadducees

5 And when his disciples were come to the other side, they had forgotten to take bread.

6 Then Jesus said unto them, Take heed

and beware of the leaven[2219] of the Pharisees[5330] and of the[4337] Sadducees.[4523]

7 And they reasoned[1260] among themselves, saying, It is because we have taken[1438] no bread.[2983]

8 Which when Jesus perceived,[2983] he said[2036] unto them,[740] O ye[1097] of[2424] little faith,[1097] why reason[2036] ye among yourselves,[3640] because ye[5101] have[1260] brought no bread?[1438][740][2983]

9 Do ye not[3768] yet understand,[3539] neither remember[3421] the five[4002] loaves[740] of the five[4000] thousand, and how many[4214] baskets[2894] ye took[2983] up?

10 Neither the seven loaves[2033][740] of the four thousand, and how[4214] many[4711] baskets ye took[5070][2983] up?

11 How is it that ye do not[3539] understand that I spake[2036] it not to you concerning[3539] bread, that ye should beware of the leaven[2219] of the[740] Pharisees[4337] and of the[5330] Sadducees?[4523]

12 Then understood[4920] they how that he bade[2036] them not beware[4337] of the leaven[2219] of bread,[740] but of the doctrine[1322] of the Pharisees[5330] and of the Sadducees.[4523]

Peter's Confession

13 When Jesus came[2064] into[2424] the coasts[2064] of[3313] Caesare'a Phil'ippi,[2542] he[5376] asked his disciples,[2065] saying,[3101] Whom[2542] do men[444] say that I,[5101] the Son of[5207] man, am?[444]

14 And they said,[2036] Some say that thou art John[2491] the Baptist;[910] some, Eli'jah;[243][2243] and others,[2087] Jeremiah,[2408] or one of the prophets.[4396]

15 He saith unto them, But[4396] whom say ye[5101] that I am?

16 And Simon[4613] Peter[4074] answered[611] and said,[2036]

Thou art the Christ,[5547] the Son[5207] of the living[2198] God.[2316]

17 And Jesus[2424] answered[611] and said[2036] unto him, Blessed[3107] art thou, Simon[4613] Bar–jona:[920] for flesh[4561] and blood[129] hath not revealed[601] it unto thee, but my Father[3962] which is[129] in[601] heaven.

18 And I say also[3772] unto thee, That thou art Peter,[4074] and upon this rock[4073] I will build[3618] my church;[1577] and the gates[4439] of hell[86] shall not[2729] prevail[2729] against it.[157.7]

19 And I will give[1325] unto thee the keys[2807] of the kingdom[932] of heaven: and whatsoever[3772] thou shalt bind[1210] on earth[3772] shall be bound[1210] in heaven; and[1093] whatsoever[1093] thou shalt loose[1210] on earth[3772] shall be loosed[3089] in heaven.[1093]

20 Then[3089] charged[3772] he his disciples that they should tell no[1291] man that he[3101] was Jesus[2424] the Christ.[5547][2036]

Jesus Foretells His Death

21 From that time forth began[756] Jesus[2424] to show[1166] unto his disciples, how that he must[846] go[1163] unto Jerusalem,[2414] and suffer[3958] many things[4183] of the[565] elders and chief[749] priests and scribes,[1122] and be killed,[4245][615] and be raised[1453] again the third[5154] day.[2250]

22 Then Peter[4074] took him,[5154] and began[2250] to rebuke him, saying,[4355] Be it[4355] far from[756] thee, Lord:[2008] this shall not[2436] be unto thee.[2962]

23 But he turned,[4762] and said[2036] unto Peter,[4074] Get[5217] thee behind[3694] me, Satan:[4567] thou art an offense[4625] unto me: for thou savorest[5426] not the things[4625] that be of God,[2316] but those that[5426] be of men.[444]

24 Then said[2036] Jesus[2424] unto his disciples,[3101] If any[1536] man will[2309] come[2064] after[3694] me, let him[3101] deny[533] himself,[533] and take[2309] up[2064] his cross,[3694][4716] and follow[533] me.[190][1438][142]

25 For whosoever will save his life shall lose it: and whosoever will lose his life for my sake shall find it.

26 For what is a man profited, if he shall gain the whole world, and lose his own soul? or what shall a man give in exchange for his soul?

27 For the Son of man shall come in the glory of his Father with his angels; and then he shall reward every man according to his works.

28 Verily I say unto you, There be some standing here, which shall not taste of death, till they see the Son of man coming in his kingdom.

The Transfiguration

17 And after six days Jesus taketh Peter, James, and John his brother, and bringeth them up into a high mountain apart,

2 And was transfigured before them: and his face did shine as the sun, and his raiment was white as the light.

3 And, behold, there appeared unto them Moses and Eli'jah talking with him.

4 Then answered Peter, and said unto Jesus, Lord, it is good for us to be here: if thou wilt, let us make here three tabernacles; one for thee, and one for Moses, and one for Eli'jah.

5 While he yet spake, behold, a bright cloud overshadowed them: and behold a voice out of the cloud, which said, This is my beloved Son, in whom I am well pleased; hear ye him.

6 And when the disciples heard it, they fell on their face, and were sore afraid.

7 And Jesus came and touched them, and said, Arise, and be not afraid.

8 And when they had lifted up their eyes, they saw no man, save Jesus only.

9 And as they came down from the mountain, Jesus charged them, saying, Tell the vision to no man, until the Son of man be risen again from the dead.

10 And his disciples asked him, saying, Why then say the scribes that Eli'jah must first come?

11 And Jesus answered and said unto them, Eli'jah truly shall first come, and restore all things.

12 But I say unto you, That Eli'jah is come already, and they knew him not, but have done unto him whatsoever they listed. Likewise shall also the Son of man suffer of them.

13 Then the disciples understood that he spake unto them of John the Baptist.

Jesus Heals a Boy with an Unclean Spirit

14 And when they were come to the multitude, there came to him a certain man, kneeling down to him, and saying,

15 Lord, have mercy on my son; for he is lunatic, and sore vexed: for ofttimes he falleth into the fire, and oft into the water.

16 And I brought him to thy disciples, and they could not cure him.

17 Then Jesus answered and said, O faithless and perverse generation, how long shall I

be with you? how long shall I suffer[430] you?[430]
bring him hither to me.
[5342] 18 And Jesus[5602] rebuked the devil; and he
departed[2424] out[2008] of him: and the child[846,1140] was cured
[1831] from that very hour. [3816] [2323]

19 Then came[5610] the disciples to Jesus apart,[2398]
and said,[2036] Why[1302] could[1410] not[3101] we cast[1544] him[2424] out?[1544]

20 And Jesus[2424] said[2036] unto them, Because of
your unbelief: for verily I say unto you, If ye
have faith[570] as a grain[281] of mustard[4102] seed,[2848] ye shall[2046]
say unto this mountain,[3735] Remove[4615] hence[1782] to[1563] yonder place; and it shall[3327] remove: and nothing
shall be impossible[101] unto you.

21 Howbeit[1085] this kind[1607] goeth not[1607] out[1607] but[1508] by
prayer[4335] and fasting.[3521]

Jesus Again Foretells His Death

22 And while they abode[390] in Galilee,[1056] Jesus[2424]
said[2036] unto them,[390] The Son[5207] of man[444] shall[3195] be[3860]
betrayed into the hands of men:[444]

23 And they shall kill[5495] him, and the third[5154]
day[2250] he shall[1453] be raised[615] again. And they were[5154]
exceeding[4970] sorry.[3076] [3076]

Payment of the Tribute Money

24 And when they were[2064] come to Caper'-[2584]
na-um, they that received[2983] tribute[1323] money came
to Peter, and said,[2036] Doth[5055] not your master pay[1320]
tribute?[4074] [1323]

25 He saith, Yes. And when he was come[1525]
into the house,[3483] Jesus[2424] prevented him, saying,[4399]
What thinkest[1380] thou, Simon?[4613] of whom do the[5101][2983]
kings[935] of the earth[1093] take[2983] custom[5056] or tribute?[2778] of
their own children,[5207] or of strangers?[245]

26 Peter saith unto him, Of strangers. Jesus saith unto him, Then are the children free.

27 Notwithstanding, lest we should offend them, go thou to the sea, and cast a hook, and take up the fish that first cometh up; and when thou hast opened his mouth, thou shalt find a piece of money: that take, and give unto them for me and thee.

Who Is the Greatest?

18 At the same time came the disciples unto Jesus, saying, Who is the greatest in the kingdom of heaven?

2 And Jesus called a little child unto him, and set him in the midst of them,

3 And said, Verily I say unto you, Except ye be converted, and become as little children, ye shall not enter into the kingdom of heaven.

4 Whosoever therefore shall humble himself as this little child, the same is greatest in the kingdom of heaven.

5 And whoso shall receive one such little child in my name receiveth me.

Temptations to Sin

6 But whoso shall offend one of these little ones which believe in me, it were better for him that a millstone were hanged about his neck, and that he were drowned in the depth of the sea.

7 Woe unto the world because of offenses! for it must needs be that offenses come; but woe to that man by whom the offense cometh!

8 Wherefore if thy hand or thy foot offend

thee, cut them off, and cast them from thee: it is better for thee to enter into life halt or maimed, rather than having two hands or two feet to be cast into everlasting fire.

9 And if thine eye offend thee, pluck it out, and cast it from thee: it is better for thee to enter into life with one eye, rather than having two eyes to be cast into hell fire.

The Parable of the Lost Sheep

10 Take heed that ye despise not one of these little ones; for I say unto you, That in heaven their angels do always behold the face of my Father which is in heaven.

11 For the Son of man is come to save that which was lost.

12 How think ye? if a man have a hundred sheep, and one of them be gone astray, doth he not leave the ninety and nine, and goeth into the mountains, and seeketh that which is gone astray?

13 And if so be that he find it, verily I say unto you, he rejoiceth more of that sheep, than of the ninety and nine which went not astray.

14 Even so it is not the will of your Father which is in heaven, that one of these little ones should perish.

A Brother Who Sins

15 Moreover if thy brother shall trespass against thee, go and tell him his fault between thee and him alone: if he shall hear thee, thou hast gained thy brother.

16 But if he will not hear thee, then take

with thee one or two more, that in the mouth of two or three witnesses every word may be established.

17 And if he shall neglect to hear them, tell it unto the church: but if he neglect to hear the church, let him be unto thee as a heathen man and a publican.

18 Verily I say unto you, Whatsoever ye shall bind on earth shall be bound in heaven; and whatsoever ye shall loose on earth shall be loosed in heaven.

19 Again I say unto you, That if two of you shall agree on earth as touching any thing that they shall ask, it shall be done for them of my Father which is in heaven.

20 For where two or three are gathered together in my name, there am I in the midst of them.

The Parable of the Unforgiving Servant

21 Then came Peter to him, and said, Lord, how oft shall my brother sin against me, and I forgive him? till seven times?

22 Jesus saith unto him, I say not unto thee, Until seven times: but, Until seventy times seven.

23 Therefore is the kingdom of heaven likened unto a certain king, which would take account of his servants.

24 And when he had begun to reckon, one was brought unto him, which owed him ten thousand talents.

25 But forasmuch as he had not to pay, his lord commanded him to be sold, and his wife,

and children, and all that he had, and payment to be made.

26 The servant therefore fell down, and worshipped him, saying, Lord, have patience with me, and I will pay thee all.

27 Then the lord of that servant was moved with compassion, and loosed him, and forgave him the debt.

28 But the same servant went out, and found one of his fellow servants, which owed him a hundred pence: and he laid hands on him, and took him by the throat, saying, Pay me that thou owest.

29 And his fellow servant fell down at his feet, and besought him, saying, Have patience with me, and I will pay thee all.

30 And he would not: but went and cast him into prison, till he should pay the debt.

31 So when his fellow servants saw what was done, they were very sorry, and came and told unto their lord all that was done.

32 Then his lord, after that he had called him, said unto him, O thou wicked servant, I forgave thee all that debt, because thou desiredst me:

33 Shouldest not thou also have had compassion on thy fellow servant, even as I had pity on thee?

34 And his lord was wroth, and delivered him to the tormentors, till he should pay all that was due unto him.

35 So likewise shall my heavenly Father do also unto you, if ye from your hearts forgive not every one his brother their trespasses.

Jesus' Teaching on Divorce

19 And it came to pass, that when Jesus had finished these sayings, he departed from Galilee, and came into the coasts of Judea beyond Jordan;

2 And great multitudes followed him; and he healed them there.

3 The Pharisees also came unto him, tempting him, and saying unto him, Is it lawful for a man to put away his wife for every cause?

4 And he answered and said unto them, Have ye not read, that he which made them at the beginning made them male and female,

5 And said, For this cause shall a man leave father and mother, and shall cleave to his wife: and they twain shall be one flesh?

6 Wherefore they are no more twain, but one flesh. What therefore God hath joined together, let not man put asunder.

7 They say unto him, Why did Moses then command to give a writing of divorcement, and to put her away?

8 He saith unto them, Moses because of the hardness of your hearts suffered you to put away your wives: but from the beginning it was not so.

9 And I say unto you, Whosoever shall put away his wife, except it be for fornication, and shall marry another, committeth adultery: and whoso marrieth her which is put away doth commit adultery.

10 His disciples say unto him, If the case of the man be so with his wife, it is not good to marry.

11 But he said unto them, All men cannot receive this saying, save they to whom it is given.

12 For there are some eunuchs, which were so born from their mother's womb: and there are some eunuchs, which were made eunuchs of men: and there be eunuchs, which have made themselves eunuchs for the kingdom of heaven's sake. He that is able to receive it, let him receive it.

Jesus Blesses Little Children

13 Then were there brought unto him little children, that he should put his hands on them, and pray: and the disciples rebuked them.

14 But Jesus said, Suffer little children, and forbid them not, to come unto me; for of such is the kingdom of heaven.

15 And he laid his hands on them, and departed thence.

The Rich Young Ruler

16 And, behold, one came and said unto him, Good Master, what good thing shall I do, that I may have eternal life?

17 And he said unto him, Why callest thou me good? there is none good but one, that is, God: but if thou wilt enter into life, keep the commandments.

18 He saith unto him, Which? Jesus said, Thou shalt do no murder, Thou shalt not commit adultery, Thou shalt not steal, Thou shalt not bear false witness,

19 Honor thy father and thy mother: and, Thou shalt love thy neighbor as thyself.

20 The young man saith unto him, All these things have I kept from my youth up: what lack I yet?

21 Jesus said unto him, If thou wilt be perfect, go and sell that thou hast, and give to the poor, and thou shalt have treasure in heaven: and come and follow me.

22 But when the young man heard that saying, he went away sorrowful: for he had great possessions.

23 Then said Jesus unto his disciples, Verily I say unto you, That a rich man shall hardly enter into the kingdom of heaven.

24 And again I say unto you, It is easier for a camel to go through the eye of a needle, than for a rich man to enter into the kingdom of God.

25 When his disciples heard it, they were exceedingly amazed, saying, Who then can be saved?

26 But Jesus beheld them, and said unto them, With men this is impossible; but with God all things are possible.

27 Then answered Peter and said unto him, Behold, we have forsaken all, and followed thee; what shall we have therefore?

28 And Jesus said unto them, Verily I say unto you, That ye which have followed me, in the regeneration when the Son of man shall sit in the throne of his glory, ye also shall sit upon twelve thrones, judging the twelve tribes of Israel.

29 And every one that hath forsaken houses, or brethren, or sisters, or father, or mother, or wife, or children, or lands, for my name's sake, shall receive a hundredfold, and shall inherit everlasting life.

30 But many that are first shall be last; and the last shall be first.

Laborers in the Vineyard

20 For the kingdom of heaven is like unto a man that is a householder, which went out early in the morning to hire laborers into his vineyard.

2 And when he had agreed with the laborers for a penny a day, he sent them into his vineyard.

3 And he went out about the third hour, and saw others standing idle in the market place,

4 And said unto them; Go ye also into the vineyard, and whatsoever is right I will give you. And they went their way.

5 Again he went out about the sixth and ninth hour, and did likewise.

6 And about the eleventh hour he went out, and found others standing idle, and saith unto them, Why stand ye here all the day idle?

7 They say unto him, Because no man hath hired us. He saith unto them, Go ye also into the vineyard; and whatsoever is right, that shall ye receive.

8 So when even was come, the lord of the vineyard saith unto his steward, Call the laborers, and give them their hire, beginning from the last unto the first.

9 And when they came that were hired about the eleventh hour, they received every man a penny.

10 But when the first came, they supposed that they should have received more; and they likewise received every man a penny.

11 And when they had received it, they murmured against the goodman of the house,

12 Saying, These last have wrought but one hour, and thou hast made them equal unto us, which have borne the burden and heat of the day.

13 But he answered one of them, and said, Friend, I do thee no wrong: didst not thou agree with me for a penny?

14 Take that thine is, and go thy way: I will give unto this last, even as unto thee.

15 Is it not lawful for me to do what I will with mine own? Is thine eye evil, because I am good?

16 So the last shall be first, and the first last: for many be called, but few chosen.

Jesus Foretells His Death a Third Time

17 And Jesus going up to Jerusalem took the twelve disciples apart in the way, and said unto them,

18 Behold, we go up to Jerusalem; and the Son of man shall be betrayed unto the chief priests and unto the scribes, and they shall condemn him to death,

19 And shall deliver him to the Gentiles to mock, and to scourge, and to crucify him: and the third day he shall rise again.

The Request of James and John

20 Then came to him the mother of Zeb'-edee's children with her sons, worshipping him, and desiring a certain thing of him.

21 And he said unto her, What wilt thou? She saith unto him, Grant that these my two sons may sit, the one on thy right hand, and the other on the left, in thy kingdom.

22 But Jesus answered and said, Ye know not what ye ask. Are ye able to drink of the cup that I shall drink of, and to be baptized with the baptism that I am baptized with? They say unto him, We are able.

23 And he saith unto them, Ye shall drink indeed of my cup, and be baptized with the baptism that I am baptized with: but to sit on my right hand, and on my left, is not mine to give, but it shall be given to them for whom it is prepared of my Father.

24 And when the ten heard it, they were moved with indignation against the two brethren.

25 But Jesus called them unto him, and said, Ye know that the princes of the Gentiles exercise dominion over them, and they that are great exercise authority upon them.

26 But it shall not be so among you: but whosoever will be great among you, let him be your minister;

27 And whosoever will be chief among you, let him be your servant:

28 Even as the Son of man came not to be ministered unto, but to minister, and to give his life a ransom for many.

Two Blind Men Receive Sight

29 And as they departed from Jericho, a great multitude followed him.

30 And, behold, two blind men sitting by the wayside, when they heard that Jesus passed by, cried out, saying, Have mercy on us, O Lord, thou Son of David.

31 And the multitude rebuked them, because they should hold their peace: but they cried the more, saying, Have mercy on us, O Lord, thou Son of David.

32 And Jesus stood still, and called them, and said, What will ye that I shall do unto you?

33 They say unto him, Lord, that our eyes may be opened.

34 So Jesus had compassion on them, and touched their eyes: and immediately their eyes received sight, and they followed him.

The Triumphal Entry into Jerusalem

21 And when they drew nigh unto Jerusalem, and were come to Bethphage, unto the mount of Olives, then sent Jesus two disciples,

2 Saying unto them, Go into the village over against you, and straightway ye shall find an ass tied, and a colt with her: loose them, and bring them unto me.

3 And if any man say aught unto you, ye shall say, The Lord hath need of them; and straightway he will send them.

4 All this was done, that it might be fulfilled which was spoken by the prophet, saying,

5 Tell ye the daughter of Zion, Behold, thy King cometh unto thee, meek, and sitting upon an ass, and a colt the foal of an ass.

6 And the disciples went, and did as Jesus commanded them,

7 And brought the ass, and the colt, and put on them their clothes, and they set him thereon.

8 And a very great multitude spread their garments in the way; others cut down branches from the trees, and strewed them in the way.

9 And the multitudes that went before, and that followed, cried, saying, Hosanna to the Son of David: Blessed is he that cometh in the name of the Lord; Hosanna in the highest.

10 And when he was come into Jerusalem, all the city was moved, saying, Who is this?

11 And the multitude said, This is Jesus the prophet of Nazareth of Galilee.

The Cleansing of the Temple

12 And Jesus went into the temple of God, and cast out all them that sold and bought in the temple, and overthrew the tables of the money changers, and the seats of them that sold doves,

13 And said unto them, It is written, My house shall be called the house of prayer; but ye have made it a den of thieves.

14 And the blind and the lame came to him in the temple; and he healed them.

15 And when the chief priests and scribes saw the wonderful things that he did, and the

children crying in the temple, and saying, Hosanna to the Son of David; they were sore displeased,

16 And said unto him, Hearest thou what these say? And Jesus saith unto them, Yea; have ye never read, Out of the mouth of babes and sucklings thou hast perfected praise?

17 And he left them, and went out of the city into Bethany; and he lodged there.

The Cursing of the Fig Tree

18 Now in the morning, as he returned into the city, he hungered.

19 And when he saw a fig tree in the way, he came to it, and found nothing thereon, but leaves only, and said unto it, Let no fruit grow on thee henceforward for ever. And presently the fig tree withered away.

20 And when the disciples saw it, they marveled, saying, How soon is the fig tree withered away!

21 Jesus answered and said unto them, Verily I say unto you, If ye have faith, and doubt not, ye shall not only do this which is done to the fig tree, but also if ye shall say unto this mountain, Be thou removed, and be thou cast into the sea; it shall be done.

22 And all things, whatsoever ye shall ask in prayer, believing, ye shall receive.

Jesus' Authority Questioned

23 And when he was come into the temple, the chief priests and the elders of the people came unto him as he was teaching, and said,

By what authority doest thou these things? and who gave thee this authority?

24 And Jesus answered and said unto them, I also will ask you one thing, which if ye tell me, I in like wise will tell you by what authority I do these things.

25 The baptism of John, whence was it? from heaven, or of men? And they reasoned with themselves, saying, If we shall say, From heaven; he will say unto us, Why did ye not then believe him?

26 But if we shall say, Of men; we fear the people; for all hold John as a prophet.

27 And they answered Jesus, and said, We cannot tell. And he said unto them, Neither tell I you by what authority I do these things.

The Parable of the Two Sons

28 But what think ye? A certain man had two sons; and he came to the first, and said, Son, go work today in my vineyard.

29 He answered and said, I will not; but afterward he repented, and went.

30 And he came to the second, and said likewise. And he answered and said, I go, sir; and went not.

31 Whether of them twain did the will of his father? They say unto him, The first. Jesus saith unto them, Verily I say unto you, That the publicans and the harlots go into the kingdom of God before you.

32 For John came unto you in the way of righteousness, and ye believed him not; but the publicans and the harlots believed him:

and ye, when ye had seen it, repented not afterward, that ye might believe him.

The Parable of the Wicked Husbandmen

33 Hear another parable: There was a certain householder, which planted a vineyard, and hedged it round about, and digged a winepress in it, and built a tower, and let it out to husbandmen, and went into a far country:

34 And when the time of the fruit drew near, he sent his servants to the husbandmen, that they might receive the fruits of it.

35 And the husbandmen took his servants, and beat one, and killed another, and stoned another.

36 Again, he sent other servants more than the first: and they did unto them likewise.

37 But last of all he sent unto them his son, saying, They will reverence my son.

38 But when the husbandmen saw the son, they said among themselves, This is the heir; come, let us kill him, and let us seize on his inheritance.

39 And they caught him, and cast him out of the vineyard, and slew him.

40 When the lord therefore of the vineyard cometh, what will he do unto those husbandmen?

41 They say unto him, He will miserably destroy those wicked men, and will let out his vineyard unto other husbandmen, which shall render him the fruits in their seasons.

42 Jesus saith unto them, Did ye never read

in the Scriptures, The stone which the builders rejected, the same is become the head of the corner: this is the Lord's doing, and it is marvelous in our eyes?

43 Therefore say I unto you, The kingdom of God shall be taken from you, and given to a nation bringing forth the fruits thereof.

44 And whosoever shall fall on this stone shall be broken: but on whomsoever it shall fall, it will grind him to powder.

45 And when the chief priests and Pharisees had heard his parables, they perceived that he spake of them.

46 But when they sought to lay hands on him, they feared the multitude, because they took him for a prophet.

The Parable of the Marriage Feast

22 And Jesus answered and spake unto them again by parables, and said,

2 The kingdom of heaven is like unto a certain king, which made a marriage for his son,

3 And sent forth his servants to call them that were bidden to the wedding: and they would not come.

4 Again, he sent forth other servants, saying, Tell them which are bidden, Behold, I have prepared my dinner: my oxen and my fatlings are killed, and all things are ready: come unto the marriage.

5 But they made light of it, and went their ways, one to his farm, another to his merchandise:

6 And the remnant took his servants, and entreated them spitefully, and slew them.

7 But when the king heard thereof, he was wroth: and he sent forth his armies, and destroyed those murderers, and burned up their city.

8 Then saith he to his servants, The wedding is ready, but they which were bidden were not worthy.

9 Go ye therefore into the highways, and as many as ye shall find, bid to the marriage.

10 So those servants went out into the highways, and gathered together all as many as they found, both bad and good: and the wedding was furnished with guests.

11 And when the king came in to see the guests, he saw there a man which had not on a wedding garment:

12 And he saith unto him, Friend, how camest thou in hither not having a wedding garment? And he was speechless.

13 Then said the king to the servants, Bind him hand and foot, and take him away, and cast him into outer darkness; there shall be weeping and gnashing of teeth.

14 For many are called, but few are chosen.

Paying Taxes to Caesar

15 Then went the Pharisees, and took counsel how they might entangle him in his talk.

16 And they sent out unto him their disciples with the Hero'di-ans, saying, Master, we know that thou art true, and teachest the way of God in truth, neither carest thou for any

man: for thou regardest not the person of
men.

17 Tell us therefore, What thinkest thou?
Is it lawful to give tribute unto Caesar, or
not?

18 But Jesus perceived their wickedness, and
said, Why tempt ye me, ye hypocrites?
19 Show me the tribute money. And they
brought unto him a penny.
20 And he saith unto them, Whose is this
image and superscription?
21 They say unto him, Caesar's. Then saith
he unto them, Render therefore unto Caesar
the things which are Caesar's; and unto God
the things that are God's.
22 When they had heard these words, they
marveled, and left him, and went their way.

The Question about the Resurrection

23 The same day came to him the Sadducees, which say that there is no resurrection,
and asked him,
24 Saying, Master, Moses said, If a man
die, having no children, his brother shall
marry his wife, and raise up seed unto his
brother.
25 Now there were with us seven brethren:
and the first, when he had married a wife,
deceased, and, having no issue, left his wife
unto his brother:
26 Likewise the second also, and the third,
unto the seventh.
27 And last of all the woman died also.
28 Therefore in the resurrection, whose wife

shall she be of the seven? for they all had her.

29 Jesus answered and said unto them, Ye do err, not knowing the Scriptures, nor the power of God.

30 For in the resurrection they neither marry, nor are given in marriage, but are as the angels of God in heaven.

31 But as touching the resurrection of the dead, have ye not read that which was spoken unto you by God, saying,

32 I am the God of Abraham, and the God of Isaac, and the God of Jacob? God is not the God of the dead, but of the living.

33 And when the multitude heard this, they were astonished at his doctrine.

The Great Commandment

34 But when the Pharisees had heard that he had put the Sadducees to silence, they were gathered together.

35 Then one of them, which was a lawyer, asked him a question, tempting him, and saying,

36 Master, which is the great commandment in the law?

37 Jesus said unto him, Thou shalt love the Lord thy God with all thy heart, and with all thy soul, and with all thy mind.

38 This is the first and great commandment.

39 And the second is like unto it, Thou shalt love thy neighbor as thyself.

40 On these two commandments hang all the law and the prophets.

The Question about David's Son

41 While the Pharisees were gathered to-gether, Jesus asked them,

42 Saying, What think ye of Christ? whose son is he? They say unto him, The son of David.

43 He saith unto them, How then doth David in spirit call him Lord, saying,

44 The LORD said unto my Lord, Sit thou on my right hand, till I make thine enemies thy footstool?

45 If David then call him Lord, how is he his son?

46 And no man was able to answer him a word, neither durst any man from that day forth ask him any more questions.

Jesus Denounces the Scribes and Pharisees

23 Then spake Jesus to the multitude, and to his disciples,

2 Saying, The scribes and the Pharisees sit in Moses' seat:

3 All therefore whatsoever they bid you observe, that observe and do; but do not ye after their works: for they say, and do not.

4 For they bind heavy burdens and grievous to be born, and lay them on men's shoulders; but they themselves will not move them with one of their fingers.

5 But all their works they do for to be seen of men: they make broad their phylacteries, and enlarge the borders of their garments,

6 And love the uppermost rooms at feasts, and the chief seats in the synagogues,

7 And greetings in the markets, and to be called of men[783], Rabbi[58], Rabbi[2564].

8 But be[444] not ye called[2564] Rabbi[4461]: for one is your Master[2564], even Christ[4461]; and[2519] all ye are brethren[5547].

9 And[80] call[2564] no man your father upon the earth[1093]: for one[2564] is your Father[3962], which is in heaven[3962].

10 Neither[3772] be[2564] ye called[2564] masters[2519]: for one is your Master[2519], even Christ[5547].

11 But he that is greatest[3187] among you shall be your servant[1249].

12 And whosoever shall exalt[5312] himself shall be abased[5013]; and he that shall humble[5013] himself shall be exalted[5312].[1438][1438]

13 But woe[3759] unto you, scribes[1122] and Pharisees[5330], hypocrites[5273]! for ye shut up[2808] the kingdom[932] of heaven[3772] against[1715] men[444]: for ye neither go in[1525] yourselves, neither suffer[863] ye them that are entering[1525] to go in[1525].

14 Woe[3759] unto you, scribes[1122] and Pharisees[5330], hypocrites[5273]! for ye devour[2719] widows'[5503] houses[3614], and for a pretense[4392] make long[3117] prayer[4336]: therefore[4336] ye shall receive[2983] the greater[4053] damnation[2917].

15 Woe[3759] unto you, scribes[1122] and Pharisees[5330], hypocrites[5273]! for ye compass[4013] sea[2281] and land[3584] to make[4160] one proselyte[4339]; and when[1362] he is made[5207], ye make[4160] him twofold more the child of[1096] hell[1067] than yourselves.

16 Woe[3759] unto you, ye blind[5185] guides[3595], which say, Whosoever shall swear[3660] by the temple[3485], it is nothing; but whosoever shall swear[3660] by the gold[5557] of the temple[3485], he is a debtor[3784]!

17 Ye fools[3474] and blind[5185]: for whether[5101] is

greater, the gold, or the temple that sanctifieth the gold?

18 And, Whosoever shall swear by the
altar, it is nothing; but whosoever sweareth
by the gift that is upon it, he is guilty.

19 Ye fools and blind: for whether is
greater, the gift, or the altar that sanctifieth
the gift?

20 Whoso therefore shall swear by the
altar, sweareth by it, and by all things thereon.

21 And whoso shall swear by the temple,
sweareth by it, and by him that dwelleth
therein.

22 And he that shall swear by heaven,
sweareth by the throne of God, and by him
that sitteth thereon.

23 Woe unto you, scribes and Pharisees,
hypocrites! for ye pay tithe of mint and anise
and cummin, and have omitted the weightier
matters of the law, judgment, mercy, and
faith: these ought ye to have done, and not
to leave the other undone.

24 Ye blind guides, which strain at a gnat,
and swallow a camel.

25 Woe unto you, scribes and Pharisees,
hypocrites! for ye make clean the outside of
the cup and of the platter, but within they
are full of extortion and excess.

26 Thou blind Pharisee, cleanse first that
which is within the cup and platter, that the
outside of them may be clean also.

27 Woe unto you, scribes and Pharisees,
hypocrites! for ye are like unto whited sepulchres, which indeed appear beautiful outward,

but are within full of dead men's bones, and of all uncleanness.

28 Even so ye also outwardly appear righteous unto men, but within ye are full of hypocrisy and iniquity.

29 Woe unto you, scribes and Pharisees, hypocrites! because ye build the tombs of the prophets, and garnish the sepulchres of the righteous,

30 And say, If we had been in the days of our fathers, we would not have been partakers with them in the blood of the prophets.

31 Wherefore ye be witnesses unto yourselves, that ye are the children of them which killed the prophets.

32 Fill ye up then the measure of your fathers.

33 Ye serpents, ye generation of vipers, how can ye escape the damnation of hell?

34 Wherefore, behold, I send unto you prophets, and wise men, and scribes: and some of them ye shall kill and crucify; and some of them shall ye scourge in your synagogues, and persecute them from city to city:

35 That upon you may come all the righteous blood shed upon the earth, from the blood of righteous Abel unto the blood of Zechari'ah son of Berechi'ah, whom ye slew between the temple and the altar.

36 Verily I say unto you, All these things shall come upon this generation.

Jesus Laments over Jerusalem

37 O Jerusalem, Jerusalem, thou that killest the prophets, and stonest them which are sent

unto thee, how often would I have gathered thy children together, even as a hen gathereth her chickens under her wings, and ye would not!

38 Behold, your house is left unto you desolate.

39 For I say unto you, Ye shall not see me henceforth, till ye shall say, Blessed is he that cometh in the name of the Lord.

The Destruction of the Temple and Signs before the End

24 And Jesus went out, and departed from the temple: and his disciples came to him for to show him the buildings of the temple.

2 And Jesus said unto them, See ye not all these things? verily I say unto you, There shall not be left here one stone upon another, that shall not be thrown down.

3 And as he sat upon the mount of Olives, the disciples came unto him privately, saying, Tell us, when shall these things be? and what shall be the sign of thy coming, and of the end of the world?

4 And Jesus answered and said unto them, Take heed that no man deceive you.

5 For many shall come in my name, saying, I am Christ; and shall deceive many.

6 And ye shall hear of wars and rumors of wars: see that ye be not troubled: for all these things must come to pass, but the end is not yet.

7 For nation shall rise against nation, and

kingdom against kingdom: and there shall be famines, and pestilences, and earthquakes, in divers places.

8 All these are the beginning of sorrows.

9 Then shall they deliver you up to be afflicted, and shall kill you: and ye shall be hated of all nations for my name's sake.

10 And then shall many be offended, and shall betray one another, and shall hate one another.

11 And many false prophets shall rise, and shall deceive many.

12 And because iniquity shall abound, the love of many shall wax cold.

13 But he that shall endure unto the end, the same shall be saved.

14 And this gospel of the kingdom shall be preached in all the world for a witness unto all nations; and then shall the end come.

15 When ye therefore shall see the abomination of desolation, spoken of by Daniel the prophet, stand in the holy place, (whoso readeth, let him understand,)

16 Then let them which be in Judea flee into the mountains:

17 Let him which is on the housetop not come down to take any thing out of his house:

18 Neither let him which is in the field return back to take his clothes.

19 And woe unto them that are with child, and to them that give suck in those days!

20 But pray ye that your flight be not in the winter, neither on the sabbath day:

21 For then shall be great tribulation, such as was not since the beginning of the world to this time, no, nor ever shall be.

22 And except those days should be shortened, there should no flesh be saved: but for the elect's sake those days shall be shortened.

23 Then if any man shall say unto you, Lo, here is Christ, or there; believe it not.

24 For there shall arise false Christs, and false prophets, and shall show great signs and wonders; insomuch that, if it were possible, they shall deceive the very elect.

25 Behold, I have told you before.

26 Wherefore if they shall say unto you, Behold, he is in the desert; go not forth: behold, he is in the secret chambers; believe it not.

27 For as the lightning cometh out of the east, and shineth even unto the west; so shall also the coming of the Son of man be.

28 For wheresoever the carcass is, there will the eagles be gathered together.

The Coming of the Son of Man

29 Immediately after the tribulation of those days shall the sun be darkened, and the moon shall not give her light, and the stars shall fall from heaven, and the powers of the heavens shall be shaken:

30 And then shall appear the sign of the Son of man in heaven: and then shall all the tribes of the earth mourn, and they shall see the Son of man coming in the clouds of heaven with power and great glory.

31 And he shall send his angels with a great sound of a trumpet, and they shall gather together his elect from the four winds, from one end of heaven to the other.

32 Now learn a parable of the fig tree; When his branch is yet tender, and putteth forth leaves, ye know that summer is nigh:

33 So likewise ye, when ye shall see all these things, know that it is near, even at the doors.

34 Verily I say unto you, This generation shall not pass, till all these things be fulfilled.

35 Heaven and earth shall pass away, but my words shall not pass away.

No Man Knoweth the Day and Hour

36 But of that day and hour knoweth no man, no, not the angels of heaven, but my Father only.

37 But as the days of Noah were, so shall also the coming of the Son of man be.

38 For as in the days that were before the flood they were eating and drinking, marrying and giving in marriage, until the day that Noah entered into the ark,

39 And knew not until the flood came, and took them all away; so shall also the coming of the Son of man be.

40 Then shall two be in the field; the one shall be taken, and the other left.

41 Two women shall be grinding at the mill; the one shall be taken, and the other left.

42 Watch therefore; for ye know not what hour your Lord doth come.

43 But know this, that if the goodman of the house had known in what watch the thief would come, he would have watched, and would not have suffered his house to be broken up.

44 Therefore be ye also ready: for in such an hour as ye think not the Son of man cometh.

The Unfaithful Servant

45 Who then is a faithful and wise servant, whom his lord hath made ruler over his household, to give them meat in due season?

46 Blessed is that servant, whom his lord when he cometh shall find so doing.

47 Verily I say unto you, That he shall make him ruler over all his goods.

48 But and if that evil servant shall say in his heart, My lord delayeth his coming;

49 And shall begin to smite his fellow servants, and to eat and drink with the drunken;

50 The lord of that servant shall come in a day when he looketh not for him, and in an hour that he is not aware of,

51 And shall cut him asunder, and appoint him his portion with the hypocrites: there shall be weeping and gnashing of teeth.

The Parable of the Ten Virgins

25 Then shall the kingdom of heaven be likened unto ten virgins, which took their lamps, and went forth to meet the bridegroom.

2 And five of them were wise, and five were foolish.

3 They that were foolish took their lamps, and took no oil with them:

4 But the wise took oil in their vessels with their lamps.

5 While the bridegroom tarried, they all slumbered and slept.

6 And at midnight there was a cry made, Behold, the bridegroom cometh; go ye out to meet him.

7 Then all those virgins arose, and trimmed their lamps.

8 And the foolish said unto the wise, Give us of your oil; for our lamps are gone out.

9 But the wise answered saying, Not so; lest there be not enough for us and you: but go ye rather to them that sell, and buy for yourselves.

10 And while they went to buy, the bridegroom came; and they that were ready went in with him to the marriage: and the door was shut.

11 Afterward came also the other virgins, saying, Lord, Lord, open to us.

12 But he answered and said, Verily I say unto you, I know you not.

13 Watch therefore; for ye know neither the day nor the hour wherein the Son of man cometh.

The Parable of the Talents

14 For the kingdom of heaven is as a man traveling into a far country, who called his

own servants, and delivered unto them his goods.

15 And unto one he gave five talents, to another two, and to another one; to every man according to his several ability; and straightway took his journey.

16 Then he that had received the five talents went and traded with the same, and made them other five talents.

17 And likewise he that had received two, he also gained other two.

18 But he that had received one went and digged in the earth, and hid his lord's money.

19 After a long time the lord of those servants cometh, and reckoneth with them.

20 And so he that had received five talents came and brought other five talents, saying, Lord, thou deliveredst unto me five talents: behold, I have gained beside them five talents more.

21 His lord said unto him, Well done, thou good and faithful servant: thou hast been faithful over a few things, I will make thee ruler over many things: enter thou into the joy of thy lord.

22 He also that had received two talents came and said, Lord, thou deliveredst unto me two talents: behold, I have gained two other talents beside them.

23 His lord said unto him, Well done, good and faithful servant; thou hast been faithful over a few things, I will make thee ruler over many things: enter thou into the joy of thy lord.

24 Then he which had received the one talent came and said, Lord, I knew thee that thou art a hard man, reaping where thou hast not sown, and gathering where thou hast not strewed:

25 And I was afraid, and went and hid thy talent in the earth: lo, there thou hast that is thine.

26 His lord answered and said unto him, Thou wicked and slothful servant, thou knewest that I reap where I sowed not, and gather where I have not strewed:

27 Thou oughtest therefore to have put my money to the exchangers, and then at my coming I should have received mine own with usury.

28 Take therefore the talent from him, and give it unto him which hath ten talents.

29 For unto every one that hath shall be given, and he shall have abundance: but from him that hath not shall be taken away even that which he hath.

30 And cast ye the unprofitable servant into outer darkness: there shall be weeping and gnashing of teeth.

The Judgment of the Nations

31 When the Son of man shall come in his glory, and all the holy angels with him, then shall he sit upon the throne of his glory:

32 And before him shall be gathered all nations: and he shall separate them one from another, as a shepherd divideth his sheep from the goats:

33 And he shall set the sheep on his right hand, but the goats on the left.

34 Then shall the King say unto them on his right hand, Come, ye blessed of my Father, inherit the kingdom prepared for you from the foundation of the world:

35 For I was ahungered, and ye gave me meat: I was thirsty, and ye gave me drink: I was a stranger, and ye took me in:

36 Naked, and ye clothed me: I was sick, and ye visited me: I was in prison, and ye came unto me.

37 Then shall the righteous answer him, saying, Lord, when saw we thee ahungered, and fed thee? or thirsty, and gave thee drink?

38 When saw we thee a stranger, and took thee in? or naked, and clothed thee?

39 Or when saw we thee sick, or in prison, and came unto thee?

40 And the King shall answer and say unto them, Verily I say unto you, Inasmuch as ye have done it unto one of the least of these my brethren, ye have done it unto me.

41 Then shall he say also unto them on the left hand, Depart from me, ye cursed, into everlasting fire, prepared for the devil and his angels:

42 For I was ahungered, and ye gave me no meat: I was thirsty, and ye gave me no drink:

43 I was a stranger, and ye took me not in: naked, and ye clothed me not: sick, and in prison, and ye visited me not.

44 Then shall they also answer him, saying,

Lord, when saw we thee ahungered, or athirst, or a stranger, or naked, or sick, or in prison, and did not minister unto thee?

45 Then shall he answer them, saying, Verily I say unto you, Inasmuch as ye did it not to one of the least of these, ye did it not to me.

46 And these shall go away into everlasting punishment: but the righteous into life eternal.

The Leaders Plot against Jesus

26 And it came to pass, when Jesus had finished all these sayings, he said unto his disciples,

2 Ye know that after two days is the feast of the passover, and the Son of man is betrayed to be crucified.

3 Then assembled together the chief priests, and the scribes, and the elders of the people, unto the palace of the high priest, who was called Cai'aphas,

4 And consulted that they might take Jesus by subtilty, and kill him.

5 But they said, Not on the feast day, lest there be an uproar among the people.

Jesus Anointed at Bethany

6 Now when Jesus was in Bethany, in the house of Simon the leper,

7 There came unto him a woman having an alabaster box of very precious ointment, and poured it on his head, as he sat at meat.

8 But when his disciples saw it, they had

indignation, saying, To what purpose is this waste?

9 For this ointment might have been sold for much, and given to the poor.

10 When Jesus understood it, he said unto them, Why trouble ye the woman? for she hath wrought a good work upon me.

11 For ye have the poor always with you, but me ye have not always.

12 For in that she hath poured this ointment on my body, she did it for my burial.

13 Verily I say unto you, Wheresoever this gospel shall be preached in the whole world, there shall also this, that this woman hath done, be told for a memorial of her.

Judas Agrees to Betray Jesus

14 Then one of the twelve, called Judas Iscar′i-ot, went unto the chief priests,

15 And said unto them, What will ye give me, and I will deliver him unto you? And they covenanted with him for thirty pieces of silver.

16 And from that time he sought opportunity to betray him.

Jesus Eats the Passover with His Disciples

17 Now the first day of the feast of unleavened bread the disciples came to Jesus, saying unto him, Where wilt thou that we prepare for thee to eat the passover?

18 And he said, Go into the city to such a man, and say unto him, The Master saith, My time is at hand; I will keep the passover at thy house with my disciples.

19 And the disciples did as Jesus had
appointed them; and they made ready the
passover.

20 Now when the even was come, he sat
down with the twelve.

21 And as they did eat, he said, Verily
I say unto you, that one of you shall betray
me.

22 And they were exceeding sorrowful, and
began every one of them to say unto him,
Lord, is it I?

23 And he answered and said, He that dippeth his hand with me in the dish, the same
shall betray me.

24 The Son of man goeth as it is written
of him: but woe unto that man by whom the
Son of man is betrayed! it had been good for
that man if he had not been born.

25 Then Judas, which betrayed him, answered and said, Master, is it I? He said unto
him, Thou hast said.

26 And as they were eating, Jesus took
bread, and blessed it, and brake it, and gave
it to the disciples, and said, Take, eat; this
is my body.

27 And he took the cup, and gave thanks,
and gave it to them, saying, Drink ye all of it;

28 For this is my blood of the new testament, which is shed for many for the remission of sins.

29 But I say unto you, I will not drink
henceforth of this fruit of the vine, until that
day when I drink it new with you in my
Father's kingdom.

Peter's Denial Foretold

30 And when they had sung a hymn, they went out into the mount of Olives.

31 Then saith Jesus unto them, All ye shall be offended because of me this night: for it is written, I will smite the shepherd, and the sheep of the flock shall be scattered abroad.

32 But after I am risen again, I will go before you into Galilee.

33 Peter answered and said unto him, Though all men shall be offended because of thee, yet will I never be offended.

34 Jesus said unto him, Verily I say unto thee, That this night, before the cock crow, thou shalt deny me thrice.

35 Peter said unto him, Though I should die with thee, yet will I not deny thee. Likewise also said all the disciples.

Jesus Prays in Gethsemane

36 Then cometh Jesus with them unto a place called Gethsem'ane, and saith unto the disciples, Sit ye here, while I go and pray yonder.

37 And he took with him Peter and the two sons of Zeb'edee, and began to be sorrowful and very heavy.

38 Then saith he unto them, My soul is exceeding sorrowful, even unto death: tarry ye here, and watch with me.

39 And he went a little further, and fell on his face, and prayed, saying, O my Father, if it be possible, let this cup pass from me: nevertheless, not as I will, but as thou wilt.

40 And he cometh unto the disciples, and findeth them asleep, and saith unto Peter, What, could ye not watch with me one hour?

41 Watch and pray, that ye enter not into temptation: the spirit indeed is willing, but the flesh is weak.

42 He went away again the second time, and prayed, saying, O my Father, if this cup may not pass away from me, except I drink it, thy will be done.

43 And he came and found them asleep again: for their eyes were heavy.

44 And he left them, and went away again, and prayed the third time, saying the same words.

45 Then cometh he to his disciples, and saith unto them, Sleep on now, and take your rest: behold, the hour is at hand, and the Son of man is betrayed into the hands of sinners.

46 Rise, let us be going: behold, he is at hand that doth betray me.

The Betrayal and Arrest of Jesus

47 And while he yet spake, lo, Judas, one of the twelve, came, and with him a great multitude with swords and staves, from the chief priests and elders of the people.

48 Now he that betrayed him gave them a sign, saying, Whomsoever I shall kiss, that same is he; hold him fast.

49 And forthwith he came to Jesus, and said, Hail, Master; and kissed him.

50 And Jesus said unto him, Friend, where-

fore art thou come? Then came they, and laid hands on Jesus, and took him.

51 And, behold, one of them which were with Jesus stretched out his hand, and drew his sword, and struck a servant of the high priest, and smote off his ear.

52 Then said Jesus unto him, Put up again thy sword into his place: for all they that take the sword shall perish with the sword.

53 Thinkest thou that I cannot now pray to my Father, and he shall presently give me more than twelve legions of angels?

54 But how then shall the Scriptures be fulfilled, that thus it must be?

55 In that same hour said Jesus to the multitudes, Are ye come out as against a thief with swords and staves for to take me? I sat daily with you teaching in the temple, and ye laid no hold on me.

56 But all this was done, that the Scriptures of the prophets might be fulfilled. Then all the disciples forsook him, and fled.

Jesus before the Council

57 And they that had laid hold on Jesus led him away to Cai'aphas the high priest, where the scribes and the elders were assembled.

58 But Peter followed him afar off unto the high priest's palace, and went in, and sat with the servants, to see the end.

59 Now the chief priests, and elders, and all the council, sought false witness against Jesus, to put him to death;

60 But found none: yea, though many false witnesses came, yet found they none. At the last came two false witnesses,

61 And said, This fellow said, I am able to destroy the temple of God, and to build it in three days.

62 And the high priest arose, and said unto him, Answerest thou nothing? what is it which these witness against thee?

63 But Jesus held his peace. And the high priest answered and said unto him, I adjure thee by the living God, that thou tell us whether thou be the Christ, the Son of God.

64 Jesus saith unto him, Thou hast said: nevertheless I say unto you, Hereafter shall ye see the Son of man sitting on the right hand of power, and coming in the clouds of heaven.

65 Then the high priest rent his clothes, saying, He hath spoken blasphemy; what further need have we of witnesses? behold, now ye have heard his blasphemy.

66 What think ye? They answered and said, He is guilty of death.

67 Then did they spit in his face, and buffeted him; and others smote him with the palms of their hands,

68 Saying, Prophesy unto us, thou Christ, Who is he that smote thee?

Peter Denies Jesus

69 Now Peter sat without in the palace: and a damsel came unto him, saying, Thou also wast with Jesus of Galilee.

70 But he denied before them all, saying, I know not what thou sayest.

71 And when he was gone out into the porch, another maid saw him, and said unto them that were there, This fellow was also with Jesus of Nazareth.

72 And again he denied with an oath, I do not know the man.

73 And after a while came unto him they that stood by, and said to Peter, Surely thou also art one of them; for thy speech betrayeth thee.

74 Then began he to curse and to swear, saying, I know not the man. And immediately the cock crew.

75 And Peter remembered the word of Jesus, which said unto him, Before the cock crow, thou shalt deny me thrice. And he went out, and wept bitterly.

Jesus Brought before Pilate

27 When the morning was come, all the chief priests and elders of the people took counsel against Jesus to put him to death:

2 And when they had bound him, they led him away, and delivered him to Pontius Pilate the governor.

The Death of Judas

3 Then Judas, which had betrayed him, when he saw that he was condemned, repented himself, and brought again the thirty pieces of silver to the chief priests and elders,

4 Saying, I have sinned in that I have betrayed the innocent blood. And they said, What is that to us? see thou to that.

5 And he cast down the pieces of silver in the temple, and departed, and went and hanged himself.

6 And the chief priests took the silver pieces, and said, It is not lawful for to put them into the treasury, because it is the price of blood.

7 And they took counsel, and bought with them the potter's field, to bury strangers in.

8 Wherefore that field was called, The field of blood, unto this day.

9 Then was fulfilled that which was spoken by Jeremiah the prophet, saying, And they took the thirty pieces of silver, the price of him that was valued, whom they of the children of Israel did value;

10 And gave them for the potter's field, as the Lord appointed me.

Pilate Questions Jesus

11 And Jesus stood before the governor: and the governor asked him, saying, Art thou the King of the Jews? And Jesus said unto him, Thou sayest.

12 And when he was accused of the chief priests and elders, he answered nothing.

13 Then said Pilate unto him, Hearest thou not how many things they witness against thee?

14 And he answered him to never a word; insomuch that the governor marveled greatly.

Jesus Sentenced to Die

15 Now at that feast the governor was wont to release unto the people a prisoner, whom they would.

16 And they had then a notable prisoner, called Barab′bas.

17 Therefore when they were gathered together, Pilate said unto them, Whom will ye that I release unto you? Barab′bas, or Jesus which is called Christ?

18 For he knew that for envy they had delivered him.

19 When he was set down on the judgment seat, his wife sent unto him, saying, Have thou nothing to do with that just man: for I have suffered many things this day in a dream because of him.

20 But the chief priests and elders persuaded the multitude that they should ask Barab′bas, and destroy Jesus.

21 The governor answered and said unto them, Whether of the twain will ye that I release unto you? They said, Barab′bas.

22 Pilate saith unto them, What shall I do then with Jesus which is called Christ? They all say unto him, Let him be crucified.

23 And the governor said, Why, what evil hath he done? But they cried out the more, saying, Let him be crucified.

24 When Pilate saw that he could prevail nothing, but that rather a tumult was made, he took water, and washed his hands before the multitude, saying, I am innocent of the blood of this just person: see ye to it.

25 Then answered all the people, and said, His blood be on us, and on our children.

26 Then released he Barab'bas unto them: and when he had scourged Jesus, he delivered him to be crucified.

27 Then the soldiers of the governor took Jesus into the common hall, and gathered unto him the whole band of soldiers.

28 And they stripped him, and put on him a scarlet robe.

29 And when they had platted a crown of thorns, they put it upon his head, and a reed in his right hand: and they bowed the knee before him, and mocked him, saying, Hail, King of the Jews!

30 And they spit upon him, and took the reed, and smote him on the head.

31 And after that they had mocked him, they took the robe off from him, and put his own raiment on him, and led him away to crucify him.

The Crucifixion

32 And as they came out, they found a man of Cyre'ne, Simon by name: him they compelled to bear his cross.

33 And when they were come unto a place called Gol'gotha, that is to say, a place of a skull,

34 They gave him vinegar to drink mingled with gall: and when he had tasted thereof, he would not drink.

35 And they crucified him, and parted his garments, casting lots: that it might be fulfilled

which was spoken by the prophet, They parted my garments among them, and upon my vesture did they cast lots.

36 And sitting down they watched him there;

37 And set up over his head his accusation written, THIS IS JESUS THE KING OF THE JEWS.

38 Then were there two thieves crucified with him; one on the right hand, and another on the left.

39 And they that passed by reviled him, wagging their heads,

40 And saying, Thou that destroyest the temple, and buildest it in three days, save thyself. If thou be the Son of God, come down from the cross.

41 Likewise also the chief priests mocking him, with the scribes and elders, said,

42 He saved others; himself he cannot save. If he be the King of Israel, let him now come down from the cross, and we will believe him.

43 He trusted in God; let him deliver him now, if he will have him: for he said, I am the Son of God.

44 The thieves also, which were crucified with him, cast the same in his teeth.

45 Now from the sixth hour there was darkness over all the land unto the ninth hour.

46 And about the ninth hour Jesus cried with a loud voice, saying, Eli, Eli, lama sabach'thani? that is to say, My God, my God, why hast thou forsaken me?

47 Some of them that stood there, when they heard that, said, This man calleth for Eli′jah.

48 And straightway one of them ran, and took a sponge, and filled it with vinegar, and put it on a reed, and gave him to drink.

49 The rest said, Let be, let us see whether Eli′jah will come to save him.

50 Jesus, when he had cried again with a loud voice, yielded up the ghost.

51 And, behold, the veil of the temple was rent in twain from the top to the bottom; and the earth did quake, and the rocks rent;

52 And the graves were opened; and many bodies of the saints which slept arose,

53 And came out of the graves after his resurrection, and went into the holy city, and appeared unto many.

54 Now when the centurion, and they that were with him, watching Jesus, saw the earthquake, and those things that were done, they feared greatly, saying, Truly this was the Son of God.

55 And many women were there beholding afar off, which followed Jesus from Galilee, ministering unto him:

56 Among which was Mary Mag′dalene, and Mary the mother of James and Joses, and the mother of Zeb′edee's children.

The Burial of Jesus

57 When the even was come, there came a rich man of Arimathe′a, named Joseph, who also himself was Jesus' disciple:

58 He went to Pilate, and begged the body

of Jesus. Then Pilate commanded the body to be delivered.

59 And when Joseph had taken the body, he wrapped it in a clean linen cloth,

60 And laid it in his own new tomb, which he had hewn out in the rock: and he rolled a great stone to the door of the sepulchre, and departed.

61 And there was Mary Mag'dalene, and the other Mary, sitting over against the sepulchre.

The Guard at the Tomb

62 Now the next day, that followed the day of the preparation, the chief priests and Pharisees came together unto Pilate,

63 Saying, Sir, we remember that that deceiver said, while he was yet alive, After three days I will rise again.

64 Command therefore that the sepulchre be made sure until the third day, lest his disciples come by night, and steal him away, and say unto the people, He is risen from the dead: so the last error shall be worse than the first.

65 Pilate said unto them, Ye have a watch: go your way, make it as sure as ye can.

66 So they went, and made the sepulchre sure, sealing the stone, and setting a watch.

The Resurrection

28 In the end of the sabbath, as it began to dawn toward the first day of the week, came Mary Mag'dalene and the other Mary to see the sepulchre.

2 And, behold, there was a great earthquake: for the angel of the Lord descended from heaven, and came and rolled back the stone from the door, and sat upon it.

3 His countenance was like lightning, and his raiment white as snow:

4 And for fear of him the keepers did shake, and became as dead men.

5 And the angel answered and said unto the women, Fear not ye: for I know that ye seek Jesus, which was crucified.

6 He is not here: for he is risen, as he said. Come, see the place where the Lord lay.

7 And go quickly, and tell his disciples that he is risen from the dead; and, behold, he goeth before you into Galilee; there shall ye see him: lo, I have told you.

8 And they departed quickly from the sepulchre with fear and great joy; and did run to bring his disciples word.

9 And as they went to tell his disciples, behold, Jesus met them, saying, All hail. And they came and held him by the feet, and worshipped him.

10 Then said Jesus unto them, Be not afraid: go tell my brethren that they go into Galilee, and there shall they see me.

The Report of the Guard

11 Now when they were going, behold, some of the watch came into the city, and showed unto the chief priests all the things that were done.

12 And when they were assembled with the

elders, and had taken counsel, they gave large money unto the soldiers,

13 Saying, Say ye, His disciples came by night, and stole him away while we slept.

14 And if this come to the governor's ears, we will persuade him, and secure you.

15 So they took the money, and did as they were taught: and this saying is commonly reported among the Jews until this day.

Jesus Commissions the Eleven

16 Then the eleven disciples went away into Galilee, into a mountain where Jesus had appointed them.

17 And when they saw him, they worshipped him: but some doubted.

18 And Jesus came and spake unto them, saying, All power is given unto me in heaven and in earth.

19 Go ye therefore, and teach all nations, baptizing them in the name of the Father, and of the Son, and of the Holy Ghost:

20 Teaching them to observe all things whatsoever I have commanded you: and, lo, I am with you alway, even unto the end of the world. Amen.

THE GOSPEL ACCORDING TO
ST. MARK

The Preaching of John the Baptist

1 The beginning of the gospel of Jesus Christ, the Son of God.

2 As it is written in the prophets, Behold, I send my messenger before thy face, which shall prepare thy way before thee.

3 The voice of one crying in the wilderness, Prepare ye the way of the Lord, make his paths straight.

4 John did baptize in the wilderness, and preach the baptism of repentance for the remission of sins.

5 And there went out unto him all the land of Judea, and they of Jerusalem, and were all baptized of him in the river of Jordan, confessing their sins.

6 And John was clothed with camel's hair, and with a girdle of a skin about his loins; and he did eat locusts and wild honey;

7 And preached, saying, There cometh one mightier than I after me, the latchet of whose shoes I am not worthy to stoop down and unloose.

8 I indeed have baptized you with water: but he shall baptize you with the Holy Ghost.

The Baptism of Jesus

9 And it came to pass in those days, that Jesus came from Nazareth of Galilee, and was baptized of John in Jordan.

10 And straightway coming up out of the

water, he saw the heavens opened, and the Spirit like a dove descending upon him:

11 And there came a voice from heaven, saying, Thou art my beloved Son, in whom I am well pleased.

The Temptation of Jesus

12 And immediately the Spirit driveth him into the wilderness.

13 And he was there in the wilderness forty days tempted of Satan; and was with the wild beasts; and the angels ministered unto him.

Jesus Begins His Ministry

14 Now after that John was put in prison, Jesus came into Galilee, preaching the gospel of the kingdom of God,

15 And saying, The time is fulfilled, and the kingdom of God is at hand: repent ye, and believe the gospel.

Jesus Calls Four Fishermen

16 Now as he walked by the sea of Galilee, he saw Simon and Andrew his brother casting a net into the sea: for they were fishers.

17 And Jesus said unto them, Come ye after me, and I will make you to become fishers of men.

18 And straightway they forsook their nets, and followed him.

19 And when he had gone a little further thence, he saw James the son of Zeb'edee, and John his brother, who also were in the ship mending their nets.

20 And straightway he called them: and they left their father Zeb'edee in the ship with the hired servants, and went after him.

A Man with an Unclean Spirit

21 And they went into Caper'na-um; and straightway on the sabbath day he entered into the synagogue, and taught.

22 And they were astonished at his doctrine: for he taught them as one that had authority, and not as the scribes.

23 And there was in their synagogue a man with an unclean spirit; and he cried out,

24 Saying, Let us alone; what have we to do with thee, thou Jesus of Nazareth? art thou come to destroy us? I know thee who thou art, the Holy One of God.

25 And Jesus rebuked him, saying, Hold thy peace, and come out of him.

26 And when the unclean spirit had torn him, and cried with a loud voice, he came out of him.

27 And they were all amazed, insomuch that they questioned among themselves, saying, What thing is this? what new doctrine is this? for with authority commandeth he even the unclean spirits, and they do obey him.

28 And immediately his fame spread abroad throughout all the region round about Galilee.

Jesus Heals Simon's Mother-in-Law

29 And forthwith, when they were come out of the synagogue, they entered into the house of Simon and Andrew, with James and John.

30 But Simon's wife's mother lay sick of a
fever; and anon they tell him of her.

31 And he came and took her by the hand,
and lifted her up; and immediately the fever
left her, and she ministered unto them.

Jesus Heals Many at Evening

32 And at even, when the sun did set, they
brought unto him all that were diseased, and
them that were possessed with devils.

33 And all the city was gathered together
at the door.

34 And he healed many that were sick of
divers diseases, and cast out many devils; and
suffered not the devils to speak, because they
knew him.

Jesus Departs on a Preaching Tour

35 And in the morning, rising up a great
while before day, he went out, and departed
into a solitary place, and there prayed.

36 And Simon and they that were with him
followed after him.

37 And when they had found him, they said
unto him, All men seek for thee.

38 And he said unto them, Let us go into
the next towns, that I may preach there also:
for therefore came I forth.

39 And he preached in their synagogues
throughout all Galilee, and cast out devils.

Jesus Cleanses a Leper

40 And there came a leper to him, beseeching him, and kneeling down to him, and

saying unto him, If thou wilt, thou canst make me clean.

41 And Jesus, moved with compassion, put forth his hand, and touched him, and saith unto him, I will; be thou clean.

42 And as soon as he had spoken, immediately the leprosy departed from him, and he was cleansed.

43 And he straitly charged him, and forthwith sent him away;

44 And saith unto him, See thou say nothing to any man: but go thy way, show thyself to the priest, and offer for thy cleansing those things which Moses commanded, for a testimony unto them.

45 But he went out, and began to publish it much, and to blaze abroad the matter, insomuch that Jesus could no more openly enter into the city, but was without in desert places: and they came to him from every quarter.

Jesus Heals a Palsied Man

2 And again he entered into Caper'na-um after some days; and it was noised that he was in the house.

2 And straightway many were gathered together, insomuch that there was no room to receive them, no, not so much as about the door: and he preached the word unto them.

3 And they come unto him, bringing one sick of the palsy, which was borne of four.

4 And when they could not come nigh unto him for the press, they uncovered the roof where he was: and when they had broken it

up, they let down the bed wherein the sick of the palsy lay.

5 When Jesus saw their faith, he said unto the sick of the palsy, Son, thy sins be forgiven thee.

6 But there were certain of the scribes sitting there, and reasoning in their hearts,

7 Why doth this man thus speak blasphemies? who can forgive sins but God only?

8 And immediately, when Jesus perceived in his spirit that they so reasoned within themselves, he said unto them, Why reason ye these things in your hearts?

9 Whether is it easier to say to the sick of the palsy, Thy sins be forgiven thee; or to say, Arise, and take up thy bed, and walk?

10 But that ye may know that the Son of man hath power on earth to forgive sins, (he saith to the sick of the palsy,)

11 I say unto thee, Arise, and take up thy bed, and go thy way into thine house.

12 And immediately he arose, took up the bed, and went forth before them all; insomuch that they were all amazed, and glorified God, saying, We never saw it on this fashion.

The Call of Levi

13 And he went forth again by the sea side; and all the multitude resorted unto him, and he taught them.

14 And as he passed by, he saw Levi the son of Alpheus sitting at the receipt of custom, and said unto him, Follow me. And he arose and followed him.

15 And it came to pass, that, as Jesus sat at meat in his house, many publicans and sinners sat also together with Jesus and his disciples; for there were many, and they followed him.

16 And when the scribes and Pharisees saw him eat with publicans and sinners, they said unto his disciples, How is it that he eateth and drinketh with publicans and sinners?

17 When Jesus heard it, he saith unto them, They that are whole have no need of the physician, but they that are sick: I came not to call the righteous, but sinners to repentance.

The Question about Fasting

18 And the disciples of John and of the Pharisees used to fast: and they come and say unto him, Why do the disciples of John and of the Pharisees fast, but thy disciples fast not?

19 And Jesus said unto them, Can the children of the bridechamber fast, while the bridegroom is with them? as long as they have the bridegroom with them, they cannot fast.

20 But the days will come, when the bridegroom shall be taken away from them, and then shall they fast in those days.

21 No man also seweth a piece of new cloth on an old garment; else the new piece that filled it up taketh away from the old, and the rent is made worse.

22 And no man putteth new wine into old bottles; else the new wine doth burst the

bottles, and the wine[3631] is[1632] spilled, and the bottles[779] will[779] be marred: but new wine[3631] must be[992] put[622] into[2537] new[779] bottles.[3501]

The Disciples Pluck Grain on the Sabbath

23 And it came[1096] to pass, that he went through the corn[4702] fields on the sabbath[4521] day;[3899] and his disciples[3101] began,[756] as they went,[3598] to pluck[5089] the ears of corn.[4719]

24 And the Pharisees said unto him,[5330] Behold,[2396] why do they on the sabbath[4521] day that which is[5101] not[4160] lawful?[1832]

25 And he said unto them, Have ye never[3763] read what[5101] David[1138] did,[4160] when he had need,[314] and was[5532] ahungered, he, and they[3983] that were with him?

26 How he went into[1525] the house of[3624] God[2316] in the days of Abi'athar[8] the high[749] priest, and did[5315] eat the showbread,[4286][740] which is not lawful to eat[1832][5315] but[1508] for the priests,[2409] and gave[1325] also to them which[5607] were with him?

27 And he said unto them, The sabbath[4521] was[1096] made for man,[444] and not man[444] for the sab-[4521] bath:

28 Therefore the Son[5207] of man[444] is Lord[2962] also of the sabbath.[4521]

The Man with a Withered Hand

3 And he entered[1525] again into[1525] the synagogue;[4864] and there was a man[444] there[1563] which had a withered hand.[3583]

2 And they watched him,[3906] whether he would heal[2323] him on the sabbath[4521] day; that they might[2723] accuse him.

3 And he saith unto the man which had the withered hand, Stand forth.

4 And he saith unto them, Is it lawful to do good on the sabbath days, or to do evil? to save life, or to kill? But they held their peace.

5 And when he had looked round about on them with anger, being grieved for the hardness of their hearts, he saith unto the man, Stretch forth thine hand. And he stretched it out: and his hand was restored whole as the other.

6 And the Pharisees went forth, and straightway took counsel with the Hero'di-ans against him, how they might destroy him.

A Multitude at the Seaside

7 But Jesus withdrew himself with his disciples to the sea: and a great multitude from Galilee followed him, and from Judea,

8 And from Jerusalem, and from Idume'a, and from beyond Jordan; and they about Tyre and Sidon, a great multitude, when they had heard what great things he did, came unto him.

9 And he spake to his disciples, that a small ship should wait on him because of the multitude, lest they should throng him.

10 For he had healed many; insomuch that they pressed upon him for to touch him, as many as had plagues.

11 And unclean spirits, when they saw him, fell down before him, and cried, saying, Thou art the Son of God.

12 And he straitly charged them that they
should not make him known.

Jesus Chooses the Twelve

13 And he goeth up into a mountain, and
calleth unto him whom he would: and they
came unto him.

14 And he ordained twelve, that they should
be with him, and that he might send them
forth to preach,

15 And to have power to heal sicknesses,
and to cast out devils:

16 And Simon he surnamed Peter;

17 And James the son of Zeb'edee, and
John the brother of James; and he surnamed
them Bo-aner'ges, which is, The sons of
thunder:

18 And Andrew, and Philip, and Bartholomew, and Matthew, and Thomas, and James
the son of Al'pheus, and Thad'de-us, and
Simon the Canaanite,

19 And Judas Iscar'i-ot, which also betrayed
him.

A Divided House Cannot Stand

And they went into a house.

20 And the multitude cometh together
again, so that they could not so much as eat
bread.

21 And when his friends heard of it, they
went out to lay hold on him: for they said,
He is beside himself.

22 And the scribes which came down from
Jerusalem said, He hath Beel'zebub, and by

the prince of the devils casteth he out devils.

23 And he called them unto him, and said unto them in parables, How can Satan cast out Satan?

24 And if a kingdom be divided against itself, that kingdom cannot stand.

25 And if a house be divided against itself, that house cannot stand.

26 And if Satan rise up against himself, and be divided, he cannot stand, but hath an end.

27 No man can enter into a strong man's house, and spoil his goods, except he will first bind the strong man; and then he will spoil his house.

28 Verily I say unto you, All sins shall be forgiven unto the sons of men, and blasphemies wherewith soever they shall blaspheme:

29 But he that shall blaspheme against the Holy Ghost hath never forgiveness, but is in danger of eternal damnation:

30 Because they said, He hath an unclean spirit.

Jesus' Mother and Brethren

31 There came then his brethren and his mother, and, standing without, sent unto him, calling him.

32 And the multitude sat about him, and they said unto him, Behold, thy mother and thy brethren without seek for thee.

33 And he answered them, saying, Who is my mother, or my brethren?

34 And he looked round about on them

which sat about him, and said, Behold my
mother and my brethren!

35 For whosoever shall do the will of God,
the same is my brother, and my sister, and
mother.

The Parable of the Sower

4 And he began again to teach by the sea
side: and there was gathered unto him a
great multitude, so that he entered into a
ship, and sat in the sea; and the whole multitude was by the sea on the land.

2 And he taught them many things by
parables, and said unto them in his doctrine,

3 Hearken; Behold, there went out a sower
to sow:

4 And it came to pass, as he sowed, some
fell by the wayside, and the fowls of the air
came and devoured it up.

5 And some fell on stony ground, where
it had not much earth; and immediately it
sprang up, because it had no depth of earth:

6 But when the sun was up, it was scorched;
and because it had no root, it withered away.

7 And some fell among thorns, and the
thorns grew up, and choked it, and it yielded
no fruit.

8 And other fell on good ground, and did
yield fruit that sprang up and increased, and
brought forth, some thirty, and some sixty,
and some a hundred.

9 And he said unto them, He that hath
ears to hear, let him hear.

10 And when he was alone, they that were

about him with the twelve asked of him the parable.

11 And he said unto them, Unto you it is given to know the mystery of the kingdom of God: but unto them that are without, all these things are done in parables:

12 That seeing they may see, and not perceive; and hearing they may hear, and not understand; lest at any time they should be converted, and their sins should be forgiven them.

13 And he said unto them, Know ye not this parable? and how then will ye know all parables?

14 The sower soweth the word.

15 And these are they by the wayside, where the word is sown; but when they have heard, Satan cometh immediately, and taketh away the word that was sown in their hearts.

16 And these are they likewise which are sown on stony ground; who, when they have heard the word, immediately receive it with gladness;

17 And have no root in themselves, and so endure but for a time: afterward, when affliction or persecution ariseth for the word's sake, immediately they are offended.

18 And these are they which are sown among thorns; such as hear the word,

19 And the cares of this world, and the deceitfulness of riches, and the lusts of other things entering in, choke the word, and it becometh unfruitful.

20 And these are they which are sown on

good ground; such as hear the word, and receive it, and bring forth fruit, some thirty-fold, some sixty, and some a hundred.

A Candle under a Bushel

21 And he said unto them, Is a candle brought to be put under a bushel, or under a bed? and not to be set on a candlestick?

22 For there is nothing hid, which shall not be manifested; neither was any thing kept secret, but that it should come abroad.

23 If any man have ears to hear, let him hear.

24 And he said unto them, Take heed what ye hear. With what measure ye mete, it shall be measured to you; and unto you that hear shall more be given.

25 For he that hath, to him shall be given; and he that hath not, from him shall be taken even that which he hath.

The Parable of the Growing Seed

26 And he said, So is the kingdom of God, as if a man should cast seed into the ground;

27 And should sleep, and rise night and day, and the seed should spring and grow up, he knoweth not how.

28 For the earth bringeth forth fruit of herself; first the blade, then the ear, after that the full corn in the ear.

29 But when the fruit is brought forth, immediately he putteth in the sickle, because the harvest is come.

The Parable of the Mustard Seed

30 And he said, Whereunto shall we liken the kingdom of God? or with what comparison shall we compare it?

31 It is like a grain of mustard seed, which, when it is sown in the earth, is less than all the seeds that be in the earth:

32 But when it is sown, it groweth up, and becometh greater than all herbs, and shooteth out great branches; so that the fowls of the air may lodge under the shadow of it.

Jesus' Use of Parables

33 And with many such parables spake he the word unto them, as they were able to hear it.

34 But without a parable spake he not unto them: and when they were alone, he expounded all things to his disciples.

Jesus Calms a Storm

35 And the same day, when the even was come, he saith unto them, Let us pass over unto the other side.

36 And when they had sent away the multitude, they took him even as he was in the ship. And there were also with him other little ships.

37 And there arose a great storm of wind, and the waves beat into the ship, so that it was now full.

38 And he was in the hinder part of the ship, asleep on a pillow: and they awake him, and say unto him, Master, carest thou not that we perish?

39 And he arose, and rebuked the wind, and said unto the sea, Peace, be still. And the wind ceased, and there was a great calm.

40 And he said unto them, Why are ye so fearful? how is it that ye have no faith?

41 And they feared exceedingly, and said one to another, What manner of man is this, that even the wind and the sea obey him?

The Gadarene Demoniac Healed

5 And they came over unto the other side of the sea, into the country of the Gad'-arenes.

2 And when he was come out of the ship, immediately there met him out of the tombs a man with an unclean spirit,

3 Who had his dwelling among the tombs; and no man could bind him, no, not with chains:

4 Because that he had been often bound with fetters and chains, and the chains had been plucked asunder by him, and the fetters broken in pieces: neither could any man tame him.

5 And always, night and day, he was in the mountains, and in the tombs, crying, and cutting himself with stones.

6 But when he saw Jesus afar off, he ran and worshipped him,

7 And cried with a loud voice, and said, What have I to do with thee, Jesus, thou Son of the most high God? I adjure thee by God, that thou torment me not.

8 For he said unto him, Come out of the man, thou unclean spirit.

9 And he asked him, What is thy name? And he answered, saying, My name is Legion: for we are many.

10 And he besought him much that he would not send them away out of the country.

11 Now there was there nigh unto the mountains a great herd of swine feeding.

12 And all the devils besought him, saying, Send us into the swine, that we may enter into them.

13 And forthwith Jesus gave them leave. And the unclean spirits went out, and entered into the swine; and the herd ran violently down a steep place into the sea, (they were about two thousand,) and were choked in the sea.

14 And they that fed the swine fled, and told it in the city, and in the country. And they went out to see what it was that was done.

15 And they come to Jesus, and see him that was possessed with the devil, and had the legion, sitting, and clothed, and in his right mind; and they were afraid.

16 And they that saw it told them how it befell to him that was possessed with the devil, and also concerning the swine.

17 And they began to pray him to depart out of their coasts.

18 And when he was come into the ship, he that had been possessed with the devil prayed him that he might be with him.

19 Howbeit Jesus suffered him not, but saith unto him, Go home to thy friends, and

tell them how great things the Lord hath done
for thee, and hath had compassion on thee.

20 And he departed, and began to publish
in Decap′olis how great things Jesus had done
for him: and all men did marvel.

Jairus' Daughter and the Woman Who
Touched Jesus' Garment

21 And when Jesus was passed over again
by ship unto the other side, much people
gathered unto him; and he was nigh unto the
sea.

22 And, behold, there cometh one of the
rulers of the synagogue, Jai′rus by name; and
when he saw him, he fell at his feet,

23 And besought him greatly, saying, My
little daughter lieth at the point of death: I
pray thee, come and lay thy hands on her,
that she may be healed; and she shall live.

24 And Jesus went with him. And much
people followed him, and thronged him.

25 And a certain woman, which had an
issue of blood twelve years,

26 And had suffered many things of many
physicians, and had spent all that she had,
and was nothing bettered, but rather grew
worse,

27 When she had heard of Jesus, came in
the press behind, and touched his garment.

28 For she said, If I may touch but his
clothes, I shall be whole.

29 And straightway the fountain of her blood
was dried up; and she felt in her body that
she was healed of that plague.

30 And Jesus, immediately knowing in himself that virtue had gone out of him, turned him about in the press, and said, Who touched my clothes?

31 And his disciples said unto him, Thou seest the multitude thronging thee, and sayest thou, Who touched me?

32 And he looked round about to see her that had done this thing.

33 But the woman fearing and trembling, knowing what was done in her, came and fell down before him, and told him all the truth.

34 And he said unto her, Daughter, thy faith hath made thee whole; go in peace, and be whole of thy plague.

35 While he yet spake, there came from the ruler of the synagogue's house certain which said, Thy daughter is dead; why troublest thou the Master any further?

36 As soon as Jesus heard the word that was spoken, he saith unto the ruler of the synagogue, Be not afraid, only believe.

37 And he suffered no man to follow him, save Peter, and James, and John the brother of James.

38 And he cometh to the house of the ruler of the synagogue, and seeth the tumult, and them that wept and wailed greatly.

39 And when he was come in, he saith unto them, Why make ye this ado, and weep? the damsel is not dead, but sleepeth.

40 And they laughed him to scorn. But when he had put them all out, he taketh the father and the mother of the damsel, and them

that were with him, and entereth in where the damsel was lying.

41 And he took the damsel by the hand, and said unto her, Tal′itha cu′mi; which is, being interpreted, Damsel, (I say unto thee,) arise.

42 And straightway the damsel arose, and walked; for she was of the age of twelve years. And they were astonished with a great astonishment.

43 And he charged them straitly that no man should know it; and commanded that something should be given her to eat.

Jesus Rejected at Nazareth

6 And he went out from thence, and came into his own country; and his disciples follow him.

2 And when the sabbath day was come, he began to teach in the synagogue: and many hearing him were astonished, saying, From whence hath this man these things? and what wisdom is this which is given unto him, that even such mighty works are wrought by his hands?

3 Is not this the carpenter, the son of Mary, the brother of James, and Joses, and of Judas, and Simon? and are not his sisters here with us? And they were offended at him.

4 But Jesus said unto them, A prophet is not without honor, but in his own country, and among his own kin, and in his own house.

5 And he could there do no mighty work,

save that he laid his hands upon a few sick folk, and healed them.

6 And he marveled because of their unbelief. And he went round about the villages, teaching.

The Mission of the Twelve

7 And he called unto him the twelve, and began to send them forth by two and two; and gave them power over unclean spirits;

8 And commanded them that they should take nothing for their journey, save a staff only; no scrip, no bread, no money in their purse:

9 But be shod with sandals; and not put on two coats.

10 And he said unto them, In what place soever ye enter into a house, there abide till ye depart from that place.

11 And whosoever shall not receive you, nor hear you, when ye depart thence, shake off the dust under your feet for a testimony against them. Verily I say unto you, It shall be more tolerable for Sodom and Gomor'rah in the day of judgment, than for that city.

12 And they went out, and preached that men should repent.

13 And they cast out many devils, and anointed with oil many that were sick, and healed them.

The Death of John the Baptist

14 And king Herod heard of him; (for his name was spread abroad;) and he said, That

John the Baptist was risen from the dead, and
therefore mighty works do show forth themselves in him.

15 Others said, That it is Eli'jah. And others
said, That it is a prophet, or as one of the
prophets.

16 But when Herod heard thereof, he said,
It is John, whom I beheaded: he is risen from
the dead.

17 For Herod himself had sent forth and
laid hold upon John, and bound him in prison
for Hero'di-as' sake, his brother Philip's wife;
for he had married her.

18 For John had said unto Herod, It is not
lawful for thee to have thy brother's wife.

19 Therefore Hero'di-as had a quarrel
against him, and would have killed him; but
she could not:

20 For Herod feared John, knowing that he
was a just man and a holy, and observed him;
and when he heard him, he did many things,
and heard him gladly.

21 And when a convenient day was come,
that Herod on his birthday made a supper to
his lords, high captains, and chief estates of
Galilee;

22 And when the daughter of the said
Hero'di-as came in, and danced, and pleased
Herod and them that sat with him, the king
said unto the damsel, Ask of me whatsoever
thou wilt, and I will give it thee.

23 And he sware unto her, Whatsoever thou
shalt ask of me, I will give it thee, unto the
half of my kingdom.

24 And she went forth, and said unto her mother, What shall I ask? And she said, The head of John the Baptist.

25 And she came in straightway with haste unto the king, and asked, saying, I will that thou give me by and by in a charger the head of John the Baptist.

26 And the king was exceeding sorry; yet for his oath's sake, and for their sakes which sat with him, he would not reject her.

27 And immediately the king sent an executioner, and commanded his head to be brought: and he went and beheaded him in the prison,

28 And brought his head in a charger, and gave it to the damsel; and the damsel gave it to her mother.

29 And when his disciples heard of it, they came and took up his corpse, and laid it in a tomb.

The Feeding of the Five Thousand

30 And the apostles gathered themselves together unto Jesus, and told him all things, both what they had done, and what they had taught.

31 And he said unto them, Come ye yourselves apart into a desert place, and rest a while: for there were many coming and going, and they had no leisure so much as to eat.

32 And they departed into a desert place by ship privately.

33 And the people saw them departing, and many knew him, and ran afoot thither out of

all cities, and outwent them, and came together unto him.

34 And Jesus, when he came out, saw much people, and was moved with compassion toward them, because they were as sheep not having a shepherd: and he began to teach them many things.

35 And when the day was now far spent, his disciples came unto him, and said, This is a desert place, and now the time is far passed:

36 Send them away, that they may go into the country round about, and into the villages, and buy themselves bread: for they have nothing to eat.

37 He answered and said unto them, Give ye them to eat. And they say unto him, Shall we go and buy two hundred pennyworth of bread, and give them to eat?

38 He saith unto them, How many loaves have ye? go and see. And when they knew, they say, Five, and two fishes.

39 And he commanded them to make all sit down by companies upon the green grass.

40 And they sat down in ranks, by hundreds, and by fifties.

41 And when he had taken the five loaves and the two fishes, he looked up to heaven, and blessed, and brake the loaves, and gave them to his disciples to set before them; and the two fishes divided he among them all.

42 And they did all eat, and were filled.

43 And they took up twelve baskets full of the fragments, and of the fishes.

44 And they that did eat of the loaves were about five thousand men.

Jesus Walks on the Sea

45 And straightway he constrained his disciples to get into the ship, and to go to the other side before unto Bethsai′da, while he sent away the people.

46 And when he had sent them away, he departed into a mountain to pray.

47 And when even was come, the ship was in the midst of the sea, and he alone on the land.

48 And he saw them toiling in rowing; for the wind was contrary unto them: and about the fourth watch of the night he cometh unto them, walking upon the sea, and would have passed by them.

49 But when they saw him walking upon the sea, they supposed it had been a spirit, and cried out:

50 For they all saw him, and were troubled. And immediately he talked with them, and saith unto them, Be of good cheer: it is I; be not afraid.

51 And he went up unto them into the ship; and the wind ceased: and they were sore amazed in themselves beyond measure, and wondered.

52 For they considered not the miracle of the loaves; for their heart was hardened.

Jesus Heals the Sick in Gennesaret

53 And when they had passed over, they came into the land of Gennes′aret, and drew to the shore.

54 And when they were come out of the ship, straightway they knew him,

55 And ran through that whole region round about, and began to carry about in beds those that were sick, where they heard he was.

56 And whithersoever he entered, into villages, or cities, or country, they laid the sick in the streets, and besought him that they might touch if it were but the border of his garment: and as many as touched him were made whole.

The Things That Defile

7 Then came together unto him the Pharisees, and certain of the scribes, which came from Jerusalem.

2 And when they saw some of his disciples eat bread with defiled, that is to say, with unwashen hands, they found fault.

3 For the Pharisees, and all the Jews, except they wash their hands oft, eat not, holding the tradition of the elders.

4 And when they come from the market, except they wash, they eat not. And many other things there be, which they have received to hold, as the washing of cups, and pots, brazen vessels, and of tables.

5 Then the Pharisees and scribes asked him, Why walk not thy disciples according to the tradition of the elders, but eat bread with unwashen hands?

6 He answered and said unto them, Well hath Isaiah prophesied of you hypocrites, as

it is written, This people honoreth me with their lips, but their heart is far from me.

7 Howbeit in vain do they worship me, teaching for doctrines the commandments of men.

8 For laying aside the commandment of God, ye hold the tradition of men, as the washing of pots and cups: and many other such like things ye do.

9 And he said unto them, Full well ye reject the commandment of God, that ye may keep your own tradition.

10 For Moses said, Honor thy father and thy mother; and, Whoso curseth father or mother, let him die the death:

11 But ye say, If a man shall say to his father or mother, It is Corban, that is to say, a gift, by whatsoever thou mightest be profited by me; he shall be free.

12 And ye suffer him no more to do aught for his father or his mother;

13 Making the word of God of none effect through your tradition, which ye have delivered: and many such like things do ye.

14 And when he had called all the people unto him, he said unto them, Hearken unto me every one of you, and understand:

15 There is nothing from without a man, that entering into him can defile him: but the things which come out of him, those are they that defile the man.

16 If any man have ears to hear, let him hear.

17 And when he was entered into the house

from the people, his disciples asked him concerning the parable.

18 And he saith unto them, Are ye so without understanding also? Do ye not perceive,
that whatsoever thing from without entereth
into the man, it cannot defile him;

19 Because it entereth not into his heart,
but into the belly, and goeth out into the
draught, purging all meats?

20 And he said, That which cometh out of
the man, that defileth the man.

21 For from within, out of the heart of men,
proceed evil thoughts, adulteries, fornications,
murders,

22 Thefts, covetousness, wickedness, deceit,
lasciviousness, an evil eye, blasphemy, pride,
foolishness:

23 All these evil things come from within,
and defile the man.

The Syrophoenician Woman's Faith

24 And from thence he arose, and went into
the borders of Tyre and Sidon, and entered
into a house, and would have no man know
it: but he could not be hid.

25 For a certain woman, whose young
daughter had an unclean spirit, heard of him,
and came and fell at his feet:

26 The woman was a Greek, a Syrophoeni'-
cian by nation; and she besought him that he
would cast forth the devil out of her daughter.

27 But Jesus said unto her, Let the children
first be filled: for it is not meet to take the

children's bread, and to cast it unto the
dogs.

28 And she answered and said unto him,
Yes, Lord: yet the dogs under the table eat
of the children's crumbs.

29 And he said unto her, For this saying go
thy way; the devil is gone out of thy daughter.

30 And when she was come to her house,
she found the devil gone out, and her daughter
laid upon the bed.

Jesus Heals a Deaf and Dumb Man

31 And again, departing from the coasts of
Tyre and Sidon, he came unto the sea of
Galilee, through the midst of the coasts of
Decap'olis.

32 And they bring unto him one that was
deaf, and had an impediment in his speech;
and they beseech him to put his hand upon
him.

33 And he took him aside from the multitude, and put his fingers into his ears, and he
spit, and touched his tongue;

34 And looking up to heaven, he sighed,
and saith unto him, Eph'phatha, that is, Be
opened.

35 And straightway his ears were opened,
and the string of his tongue was loosed, and
he spake plain.

36 And he charged them that they should
tell no man: but the more he charged them,
so much the more a great deal they published
it;

37 And were beyond measure astonished,

saying, He hath done all things well: he maketh both the deaf to hear, and the dumb to speak.

The Feeding of the Four Thousand

8 In those days the multitude being very great, and having nothing to eat, Jesus called his disciples unto him, and saith unto them,

2 I have compassion on the multitude, because they have now been with me three days, and have nothing to eat:

3 And if I send them away fasting to their own houses, they will faint by the way: for divers of them came from far.

4 And his disciples answered him, From whence can a man satisfy these men with bread here in the wilderness?

5 And he asked them, How many loaves have ye? And they said, Seven.

6 And he commanded the people to sit down on the ground: and he took the seven loaves, and gave thanks, and brake, and gave to his disciples to set before them; and they did set them before the people.

7 And they had a few small fishes: and he blessed, and commanded to set them also before them.

8 So they did eat, and were filled: and they took up of the broken meat that was left seven baskets.

9 And they that had eaten were about four thousand: and he sent them away.

10 And straightway he entered into a ship

with his disciples, and came into the parts of Dalmanu'tha.

The Demand for a Sign

11 And the Pharisees came forth, and began to question with him, seeking of him a sign from heaven, tempting him.

12 And he sighed deeply in his spirit, and saith, Why doth this generation seek after a sign? verily I say unto you, There shall no sign be given unto this generation.

13 And he left them, and entering into the ship again departed to the other side.

The Leaven of the Pharisees

14 Now the disciples had forgotten to take bread, neither had they in the ship with them more than one loaf.

15 And he charged them, saying, Take heed, beware of the leaven of the Pharisees, and of the leaven of Herod.

16 And they reasoned among themselves, saying, It is because we have no bread.

17 And when Jesus knew it, he saith unto them, Why reason ye, because ye have no bread? perceive ye not yet, neither understand? have ye your heart yet hardened?

18 Having eyes, see ye not? and having ears, hear ye not? and do ye not remember?

19 When I brake the five loaves among five thousand, how many baskets full of fragments took ye up? They say unto him, Twelve.

20 And when the seven among four thou-

sand, how many baskets full of fragments took ye up? And they said, Seven.

21 And he said unto them, How is it that ye do not understand?

A Blind Man Healed at Bethsaida

22 And he cometh to Bethsai'da; and they bring a blind man unto him, and besought him to touch him.

23 And he took the blind man by the hand, and led him out of the town; and when he had spit on his eyes, and put his hands upon him, he asked him if he saw aught.

24 And he looked up, and said, I see men as trees, walking.

25 After that he put his hands again upon his eyes, and made him look up; and he was restored, and saw every man clearly.

26 And he sent him away to his house, saying, Neither go into the town, nor tell it to any in the town.

Peter's Confession

27 And Jesus went out, and his disciples, into the towns of Caesare'a Phil'ippi: and by the way he asked his disciples, saying unto them, Whom do men say that I am?

28 And they answered, John the Baptist: but some say, Eli'jah; and others, One of the prophets.

29 And he saith unto them, But whom say ye that I am? And Peter answereth and saith unto him, Thou art the Christ.

30 And he charged them that they should tell no man of him.

Jesus Foretells His Death

31 And he began to teach them, that the Son of man must suffer many things, and be rejected of the elders, and of the chief priests, and scribes, and be killed, and after three days rise again.

32 And he spake that saying openly. And Peter took him, and began to rebuke him.

33 But when he had turned about and looked on his disciples, he rebuked Peter, saying, Get thee behind me, Satan: for thou savorest not the things that be of God, but the things that be of men.

34 And when he had called the people unto him with his disciples also, he said unto them, Whosoever will come after me, let him deny himself, and take up his cross, and follow me.

35 For whosoever will save his life shall lose it; but whosoever shall lose his life for my sake and the gospel's, the same shall save it.

36 For what shall it profit a man, if he shall gain the whole world, and lose his own soul?

37 Or what shall a man give in exchange for his soul?

38 Whosoever therefore shall be ashamed of me and of my words, in this adulterous and sinful generation, of him also shall the Son of man be ashamed, when he cometh in the glory of his Father with the holy angels.

9 And he said unto them, Verily I say unto
you, That there be some of them that
stand here, which shall not taste of death, till
they have seen the kingdom of God come with
power.

The Transfiguration

2 And after six days Jesus taketh with him
Peter, and James, and John, and leadeth them
up into a high mountain apart by themselves:
and he was transfigured before them.

3 And his raiment became shining, exceeding white as snow; so as no fuller on earth
can white them.

4 And there appeared unto them Eli'jah
with Moses: and they were talking with
Jesus.

5 And Peter answered and said to Jesus,
Master, it is good for us to be here: and let
us make three tabernacles; one for thee, and
one for Moses, and one for Eli'jah.

6 For he wist not what to say; for they
were sore afraid.

7 And there was a cloud that overshadowed
them: and a voice came out of the cloud, saying, This is my beloved Son: hear him.

8 And suddenly, when they had looked
round about, they saw no man any more, save
Jesus only with themselves.

9 And as they came down from the mountain, he charged them that they should tell no
man what things they had seen, till the Son
of man were risen from the dead.

10 And they kept that saying with them-

selves, questioning one with another what the
rising from the dead should mean.

11 And they asked him, saying, Why say
the scribes that Eli′jah must first come?

12 And he answered and told them, Eli′jah
verily cometh first, and restoreth all things;
and how it is written of the Son of man, that
he must suffer many things, and be set at
nought.

13 But I say unto you, That Eli′jah is indeed
come, and they have done unto him whatsoever they listed, as it is written of him.

Jesus Heals a Boy with an Unclean Spirit

14 And when he came to his disciples, he
saw a great multitude about them, and the
scribes questioning with them.

15 And straightway all the people, when they
beheld him, were greatly amazed, and running
to him saluted him.

16 And he asked the scribes, What question
ye with them?

17 And one of the multitude answered and
said, Master, I have brought unto thee my
son, which hath a dumb spirit;

18 And wheresoever he taketh him, he
teareth him; and he foameth, and gnasheth
with his teeth, and pineth away: and I spake
to thy disciples that they should cast him out;
and they could not.

19 He answereth him, and saith, O faithless
generation, how long shall I be with you?
how long shall I suffer you? bring him unto
me.

20 And they brought him unto him: and
when he saw him, ⁵³⁴² straightway the spirit tare
him; and he fell on the ground, and wallowed
foaming.

21 And he asked his father, How long is it
ago since this came unto him? And he said,
Of a child.

22 And ofttimes it hath cast him into the
fire, and into the waters, to destroy him: but
if thou canst do any thing, have compassion
on us, and help us.

23 Jesus said unto him, If thou canst believe, all things are possible to him that
believeth.

24 And straightway the father of the child
cried out, and said with tears, Lord, I believe;
help thou mine unbelief.

25 When Jesus saw that the people came
running together, he rebuked the foul spirit,
saying unto him, Thou dumb and deaf spirit,
I charge thee, come out of him, and enter no
more into him.

26 And the spirit cried, and rent him sore,
and came out of him: and he was as
one dead; insomuch that many said, He is
dead.

27 But Jesus took him by the hand, and
lifted him up; and he arose.

28 And when he was come into the house,
his disciples asked him privately, Why could
not we cast him out?

29 And he said unto them, This kind can
come forth by nothing, but by prayer and
fasting.

Jesus Again Foretells His Death

30 And they departed thence, and passed through Galilee; and he would not that any man should know it.

31 For he taught his disciples, and said unto them, The Son of man is delivered into the hands of men, and they shall kill him; and after that he is killed, he shall rise the third day.

32 But they understood not that saying, and were afraid to ask him.

Who Is the Greatest?

33 And he came to Caper'na-um: and being in the house he asked them, What was it that ye disputed among yourselves by the way?

34 But they held their peace: for by the way they had disputed among themselves, who should be the greatest.

35 And he sat down, and called the twelve, and saith unto them, If any man desire to be first, the same shall be last of all, and servant of all.

36 And he took a child, and set him in the midst of them: and when he had taken him in his arms, he said unto them,

37 Whosoever shall receive one of such children in my name, receiveth me; and whosoever shall receive me, receiveth not me, but him that sent me.

He That Is Not against Us Is for Us

38 And John answered him, saying, Master, we saw one casting out devils in thy name,

and he followeth not us; and we forbade him,
because he followeth not us.

39 But Jesus said, Forbid him not: for there
is no man which shall do a miracle in my
name, that can lightly speak evil of me.

40 For he that is not against us is on our part.

41 For whosoever shall give you a cup of
water to drink in my name, because ye belong
to Christ, verily I say unto you, he shall not
lose his reward.

Temptations to Sin

42 And whosoever shall offend one of these
little ones that believe in me, it is better for
him that a millstone were hanged about his
neck, and he were cast into the sea.

43 And if thy hand offend thee, cut it off:
it is better for thee to enter into life maimed,
than having two hands to go into hell, into
the fire that never shall be quenched:

44 Where their worm dieth not, and the
fire is not quenched.

45 And if thy foot offend thee, cut it off:
it is better for thee to enter halt into life,
than having two feet to be cast into hell, into
the fire that never shall be quenched:

46 Where their worm dieth not, and the
fire is not quenched.

47 And if thine eye offend thee, pluck it
out: it is better for thee to enter into the
kingdom of God with one eye, than having
two eyes to be cast into hell fire:

48 Where their worm dieth not, and the
fire is not quenched.

49 For every one shall be salted with fire, and every sacrifice shall be salted with salt.

50 Salt is good: but if the salt have lost his saltness, wherewith will ye season it? Have salt in yourselves, and have peace one with another.

Jesus' Teaching on Divorce

10 And he arose from thence, and cometh into the coasts of Judea by the farther side of Jordan: and the people resort unto him again; and, as he was wont, he taught them again.

2 And the Pharisees came to him, and asked him, Is it lawful for a man to put away his wife? tempting him.

3 And he answered and said unto them, What did Moses command you?

4 And they said, Moses suffered to write a bill of divorcement, and to put her away.

5 And Jesus answered and said unto them, For the hardness of your heart he wrote you this precept.

6 But from the beginning of the creation God made them male and female.

7 For this cause shall a man leave his father and mother, and cleave to his wife;

8 And they twain shall be one flesh: so then they are no more twain, but one flesh.

9 What therefore God hath joined together, let not man put asunder.

10 And in the house his disciples asked him again of the same matter.

11 And he saith unto them, Whosoever shall

put away his wife, and marry another, committeth adultery against her.

12 And if a woman shall put away her husband, and be married to another, she committeth adultery.

Jesus Blesses Little Children

13 And they brought young children to him, that he should touch them; and his disciples rebuked those that brought them.

14 But when Jesus saw it, he was much displeased, and said unto them, Suffer the little children to come unto me, and forbid them not; for of such is the kingdom of God.

15 Verily I say unto you, Whosoever shall not receive the kingdom of God as a little child, he shall not enter therein.

16 And he took them up in his arms, put his hands upon them, and blessed them.

The Rich Young Ruler

17 And when he was gone forth into the way, there came one running, and kneeled to him, and asked him, Good Master, what shall I do that I may inherit eternal life?

18 And Jesus said unto him, Why callest thou me good? there is none good but one, that is, God.

19 Thou knowest the commandments, Do not commit adultery, Do not kill, Do not steal, Do not bear false witness, Defraud not, Honor thy father and mother.

20 And he answered and said unto him,

Master, all these have I observed from my
youth.

21 Then Jesus beholding him loved him,
and said unto him, One thing thou lackest:
go thy way, sell whatsoever thou hast, and
give to the poor, and thou shalt have treasure in heaven: and come, take up the cross,
and follow me.

22 And he was sad at that saying, and went
away grieved: for he had great possessions.

23 And Jesus looked round about, and saith
unto his disciples, How hardly shall they that
have riches enter into the kingdom of God!

24 And the disciples were astonished at his
words. But Jesus answereth again, and saith
unto them, Children, how hard is it for them
that trust in riches to enter into the kingdom
of God!

25 It is easier for a camel to go through the
eye of a needle, than for a rich man to enter
into the kingdom of God.

26 And they were astonished out of measure, saying among themselves, Who then can
be saved?

27 And Jesus looking upon them saith, With
men it is impossible, but not with God: for
with God all things are possible.

28 Then Peter began to say unto him, Lo,
we have left all, and have followed thee.

29 And Jesus answered and said, Verily I
say unto you, There is no man that hath left
house, or brethren, or sisters, or father, or
mother, or wife, or children, or lands, for my
sake, and the gospel's,

30 But he shall receive a hundredfold now in this time, houses, and brethren, and sisters, and mothers, and children, and lands, with persecutions; and in the world to come eternal life.

31 But many that are first shall be last; and the last first.

Jesus Foretells His Death a Third Time

32 And they were in the way going up to Jerusalem; and Jesus went before them: and they were amazed; and as they followed, they were afraid. And he took again the twelve, and began to tell them what things should happen unto him,

33 Saying, Behold, we go up to Jerusalem; and the Son of man shall be delivered unto the chief priests, and unto the scribes; and they shall condemn him to death, and shall deliver him to the Gentiles:

34 And they shall mock him, and shall scourge him, and shall spit upon him, and shall kill him; and the third day he shall rise again.

The Request of James and John

35 And James and John, the sons of Zeb'-edee, come unto him, saying, Master, we would that thou shouldest do for us whatso-ever we shall desire.

36 And he said unto them, What would ye that I should do for you?

37 They said unto him, Grant unto us that we may sit, one on thy right hand, and the other on thy left hand, in thy glory.

38 But Jesus said unto them, Ye know not what ye ask: can ye drink of the cup that I drink of? and be baptized with the baptism that I am baptized with?

39 And they said unto him, We can. And Jesus said unto them, Ye shall indeed drink of the cup that I drink of; and with the baptism that I am baptized withal shall ye be baptized:

40 But to sit on my right hand and on my left hand is not mine to give; but it shall be given to them for whom it is prepared.

41 And when the ten heard it, they began to be much displeased with James and John.

42 But Jesus called them to him, and saith unto them, Ye know that they which are accounted to rule over the Gentiles exercise lordship over them; and their great ones exercise authority upon them.

43 But so shall it not be among you: but whosoever will be great among you, shall be your minister:

44 And whosoever of you will be the chiefest, shall be servant of all.

45 For even the Son of man came not to be ministered unto, but to minister, and to give his life a ransom for many.

Blind Bartimeus Receives Sight

46 And they came to Jericho: and as he went out of Jericho with his disciples and a great number of people, blind Bartime′us, the son of Time′us, sat by the highway side begging.

47 And when he heard that it was Jesus of Nazareth, he began to cry out, and say, Jesus, thou Son of David, have mercy on me.

48 And many charged him that he should hold his peace: but he cried the more a great deal, Thou Son of David, have mercy on me.

49 And Jesus stood still, and commanded him to be called. And they call the blind man, saying unto him, Be of good comfort, rise; he calleth thee.

50 And he, casting away his garment, rose, and came to Jesus.

51 And Jesus answered and said unto him, What wilt thou that I should do unto thee? The blind man said unto him, Lord, that I might receive my sight.

52 And Jesus said unto him, Go thy way; thy faith hath made thee whole. And immediately he received his sight, and followed Jesus in the way.

The Triumphal Entry into Jerusalem

11 And when they came nigh to Jerusalem, unto Bethphage and Bethany, at the mount of Olives, he sendeth forth two of his disciples,

2 And saith unto them, Go your way into the village over against you: and as soon as ye be entered into it, ye shall find a colt tied, whereon never man sat; loose him, and bring him.

3 And if any man say unto you, Why do ye this? say ye that the Lord hath need of him; and straightway he will send him hither.

4 And they went their way, and found the colt tied by the door without in a place where two ways met; and they loose him.

5 And certain of them that stood there said unto them, What do ye, loosing the colt?

6 And they said unto them even as Jesus had commanded: and they let them go.

7 And they brought the colt to Jesus, and cast their garments on him; and he sat upon him.

8 And many spread their garments in the way; and others cut down branches off the trees, and strewed them in the way.

9 And they that went before, and they that followed, cried, saying, Hosanna; Blessed is he that cometh in the name of the Lord:

10 Blessed be the kingdom of our father David, that cometh in the name of the Lord: Hosanna in the highest.

11 And Jesus entered into Jerusalem, and into the temple: and when he had looked round about upon all things, and now the eventide was come, he went out unto Bethany with the twelve.

The Cursing of the Fig Tree

12 And on the morrow, when they were come from Bethany, he was hungry:

13 And seeing a fig tree afar off having leaves, he came, if haply he might find any thing thereon: and when he came to it, he found nothing but leaves; for the time of figs was not yet.

14 And Jesus answered and said unto it,

No man eat fruit of thee hereafter for ever. And his disciples heard it.

The Cleansing of the Temple

15 And they come to Jerusalem: and Jesus went into the temple, and began to cast out them that sold and bought in the temple, and overthrew the tables of the money changers, and the seats of them that sold doves;

16 And would not suffer that any man should carry any vessel through the temple.

17 And he taught, saying unto them, Is it not written, My house shall be called of all nations the house of prayer? but ye have made it a den of thieves.

18 And the scribes and chief priests heard it, and sought how they might destroy him: for they feared him, because all the people was astonished at his doctrine.

19 And when even was come, he went out of the city.

The Lesson from the Withered Fig Tree

20 And in the morning, as they passed by, they saw the fig tree dried up from the roots.

21 And Peter calling to remembrance saith unto him, Master, behold, the fig tree which thou cursedst is withered away.

22 And Jesus answering saith unto them, Have faith in God.

23 For verily I say unto you, That whosoever shall say unto this mountain, Be thou removed, and be thou cast into the sea; and shall not doubt in his heart, but shall be-

lieve that those things which he saith shall come to pass;[1096] he shall have whatsoever he saith.[2036]

24 Therefore I say unto you, What things soever ye desire,[3745] [154] when ye pray,[4336] believe[3745] that ye receive[4336] them,[4100] and ye shall have them.[2983]

25 And when ye stand[2476] praying,[4336] forgive,[863] if ye have aught[5100] against any;[5100] that your Father also which is in heaven[3772] may forgive[863] you your[3962] trespasses.[3900]

26 But[235] if ye do not forgive,[863] neither will your Father[3962] which is[863] in heaven[3772] forgive[863] your trespasses.[3900]

Jesus' Authority Questioned

27 And they come again to Jerusalem: and as he was walking[4043] in[2064] the temple,[2411] there[2414] come to him the chief priests,[749] and the scribes,[1122] and the elders,[4245]

28 And say unto him, By what authority doest thou[4160] these things? and who[4169] gave[1325] thee this authority[1849] to do these things?[5101]

29 And Jesus[2424] answered[4160] and said unto them, I will also ask[1905] of you one question,[2036] and answer me,[1905] and I will tell[2046] you by what authority[4169] I do[4160] these things.[1849]

30 The baptism of John,[908] was it from heaven,[3772] or of men?[444] answer me.[2491]

31 And they reasoned with themselves,[3049] saying, If we shall say,[2036] From heaven;[3772] he will say, Why then did ye not believe[4100] him?[2046]

32 But if we shall say,[2036] Of men;[444] they feared[5399] the people:[2992] for all men counted[537] John,[2491] that he was a prophet[4396] indeed.[3689]

33 And they answered and said unto Jesus, We cannot tell. And Jesus answering saith unto them, Neither do I tell you by what authority I do these things.

The Parable of the Wicked Husbandmen

12 And he began to speak unto them by parables. A certain man planted a vineyard, and set a hedge about it, and digged a place for the winevat, and built a tower, and let it out to husbandmen, and went into a far country.

2 And at the season he sent to the husbandmen a servant, that he might receive from the husbandmen of the fruit of the vineyard.

3 And they caught him, and beat him, and sent him away empty.

4 And again he sent unto them another servant; and at him they cast stones, and wounded him in the head, and sent him away shamefully handled.

5 And again he sent another; and him they killed, and many others; beating some, and killing some.

6 Having yet therefore one son, his well-beloved, he sent him also last unto them, saying, They will reverence my son.

7 But those husbandmen said among themselves, This is the heir; come, let us kill him, and the inheritance shall be ours.

8 And they took him, and killed him, and cast him out of the vineyard.

9 What shall therefore the lord of the vine-

yard do? he will come and destroy the husbandmen, and will give the vineyard unto others.

10 And have ye not read this Scripture; The stone which the builders rejected is become the head of the corner:

11 This was the Lord's doing, and it is marvelous in our eyes?

12 And they sought to lay hold on him, but feared the people; for they knew that he had spoken the parable against them: and they left him, and went their way.

Paying Taxes to Caesar

13 And they send unto him certain of the Pharisees and of the Hero'dians, to catch him in his words.

14 And when they were come, they say unto him, Master, we know that thou art true, and carest for no man; for thou regardest not the person of men, but teachest the way of God in truth: Is it lawful to give tribute to Caesar, or not?

15 Shall we give, or shall we not give? But he, knowing their hypocrisy, said unto them, Why tempt ye me? bring me a penny, that I may see it.

16 And they brought it. And he saith unto them, Whose is this image and superscription? And they said unto him, Caesar's.

17 And Jesus answering said unto them, Render to Caesar the things that are Caesar's, and to God the things that are God's. And they marveled at him.

The Question about the Resurrection

18 Then come unto him the Sadducees, which say there is no resurrection; and they asked him, saying,

19 Master, Moses wrote unto us, If a man's brother die, and leave his wife behind him, and leave no children, that his brother should take his wife, and raise up seed unto his brother.

20 Now there were seven brethren: and the first took a wife, and dying left no seed.

21 And the second took her, and died, neither left he any seed: and the third likewise.

22 And the seven had her, and left no seed: last of all the woman died also.

23 In the resurrection therefore, when they shall rise, whose wife shall she be of them? for the seven had her to wife.

24 And Jesus answering said unto them, Do ye not therefore err, because ye know not the Scriptures, neither the power of God?

25 For when they shall rise from the dead, they neither marry, nor are given in marriage; but are as the angels which are in heaven.

26 And as touching the dead, that they rise; have ye not read in the book of Moses, how in the bush God spake unto him, saying, I am the God of Abraham, and the God of Isaac, and the God of Jacob?

27 He is not the God of the dead, but the God of the living: ye therefore do greatly err.

The Great Commandment

28 And one of the scribes came, and having heard them reasoning together, and perceiving that he had answered them well, asked him, Which is the first commandment of all?

29 And Jesus answered him, The first of all the commandments is, Hear, O Israel; The Lord our God is one Lord:

30 And thou shalt love the Lord thy God with all thy heart, and with all thy soul, and with all thy mind, and with all thy strength: this is the first commandment.

31 And the second is like, namely this, Thou shalt love thy neighbor as thyself. There is none other commandment greater than these.

32 And the scribe said unto him, Well, Master, thou hast said the truth: for there is one God; and there is none other but he:

33 And to love him with all the heart, and with all the understanding, and with all the soul, and with all the strength, and to love his neighbor as himself, is more than all whole burnt offerings and sacrifices.

34 And when Jesus saw that he answered discreetly, he said unto him, Thou art not far from the kingdom of God. And no man after that durst ask him any question.

The Question about David's Son

35 And Jesus answered and said, while he taught in the temple, How say the scribes that Christ is the son of David?

36 For David himself said by the Holy

Ghost, The LORD said to my Lord, Sit thou on my right hand, till I make thine enemies thy footstool.

37 David therefore himself calleth him Lord; and whence is he then his son? And the common people heard him gladly.

Jesus Denounces the Scribes

38 And he said unto them in his doctrine, Beware of the scribes, which love to go in long clothing, and love salutations in the market places,

39 And the chief seats in the synagogues, and the uppermost rooms at feasts:

40 Which devour widows' houses, and for a pretense make long prayers: these shall receive greater damnation.

The Widow's Offering

41 And Jesus sat over against the treasury, and beheld how the people cast money into the treasury: and many that were rich cast in much.

42 And there came a certain poor widow, and she threw in two mites, which make a farthing.

43 And he called unto him his disciples, and saith unto them, Verily I say unto you, That this poor widow hath cast more in, than all they which have cast into the treasury:

44 For all they did cast in of their abundance; but she of her want did cast in all that she had, even all her living.

The Destruction of the Temple and Signs before the End

13 And as he went out of the temple, one of his disciples saith unto him, Master, see what manner of stones and what buildings are here!

2 And Jesus answering said unto him, Seest thou these great buildings? there shall not be left one stone upon another, that shall not be thrown down.

3 And as he sat upon the mount of Olives, over against the temple, Peter and James and John and Andrew asked him privately,

4 Tell us, when shall these things be? and what shall be the sign when all these things shall be fulfilled?

5 And Jesus answering them began to say, Take heed lest any man deceive you:

6 For many shall come in my name, saying, I am Christ; and shall deceive many.

7 And when ye shall hear of wars and rumors of wars, be ye not troubled: for such things must needs be; but the end shall not be yet.

8 For nation shall rise against nation, and kingdom against kingdom: and there shall be earthquakes in divers places, and there shall be famines and troubles: these are the beginnings of sorrows.

9 But take heed to yourselves: for they shall deliver you up to councils; and in the synagogues ye shall be beaten: and ye shall be brought before rulers and kings for my sake, for a testimony against them.

10 And the gospel must first be published among all nations.

11 But when they shall lead you, and deliver you up, take no thought beforehand what ye shall speak, neither do ye premeditate: but whatsoever shall be given you in that hour, that speak ye: for it is not ye that speak, but the Holy Ghost.

12 Now the brother shall betray the brother to death, and the father the son; and children shall rise up against their parents, and shall cause them to be put to death.

13 And ye shall be hated of all men for my name's sake: but he that shall endure unto the end, the same shall be saved.

14 But when ye shall see the abomination of desolation, spoken of by Daniel the prophet, standing where it ought not, (let him that readeth understand,) then let them that be in Judea flee to the mountains:

15 And let him that is on the housetop not go down into the house, neither enter therein, to take any thing out of his house:

16 And let him that is in the field not turn back again for to take up his garment.

17 But woe to them that are with child, and to them that give suck in those days!

18 And pray ye that your flight be not in the winter.

19 For in those days shall be affliction, such as was not from the beginning of the creation which God created unto this time, neither shall be.

20 And except that the Lord had shortened

those days, no flesh should be saved: but for the elect's sake, whom he hath chosen, he hath shortened the days.

21 And then if any man shall say to you, Lo, here is Christ; or, lo, he is there; believe him not:

22 For false Christs and false prophets shall rise, and shall show signs and wonders, to seduce, if it were possible, even the elect.

23 But take ye heed: behold, I have foretold you all things.

The Coming of the Son of Man

24 But in those days, after that tribulation, the sun shall be darkened, and the moon shall not give her light,

25 And the stars of heaven shall fall, and the powers that are in heaven shall be shaken.

26 And then shall they see the Son of man coming in the clouds with great power and glory.

27 And then shall he send his angels, and shall gather together his elect from the four winds, from the uttermost part of the earth to the uttermost part of heaven.

28 Now learn a parable of the fig tree: When her branch is yet tender, and putteth forth leaves, ye know that summer is near:

29 So ye in like manner, when ye shall see these things come to pass, know that it is nigh, even at the doors.

30 Verily I say unto you, that this generation shall not pass, till all these things be done.

31 Heaven and earth shall pass away: but my words shall not pass away.

32 But of that day and that hour knoweth no man, no, not the angels which are in heaven, neither the Son, but the Father.

33 Take ye heed, watch and pray: for ye know not when the time is.

34 For the Son of man is as a man taking a far journey, who left his house, and gave authority to his servants, and to every man his work, and commanded the porter to watch.

35 Watch ye therefore: for ye know not when the master of the house cometh, at even, or at midnight, or at the cockcrowing, or in the morning:

36 Lest coming suddenly he find you sleeping.

37 And what I say unto you I say unto all, Watch.

The Leaders Plot against Jesus

14 After two days was the feast of the passover, and of unleavened bread: and the chief priests and the scribes sought how they might take him by craft, and put him to death.

2 But they said, Not on the feast day, lest there be an uproar of the people.

Jesus Anointed at Bethany

3 And being in Bethany, in the house of Simon the leper, as he sat at meat, there came a woman having an alabaster box of

ointment of spikenard very precious; and she brake the box, and poured it on his head.

4 And there were some that had indignation within themselves, and said, Why was this waste of the ointment made?

5 For it might have been sold for more than three hundred pence, and have been given to the poor. And they murmured against her.

6 And Jesus said, Let her alone; why trouble ye her? she hath wrought a good work on me.

7 For ye have the poor with you always, and whensoever ye will ye may do them good: but me ye have not always.

8 She hath done what she could: she is come aforehand to anoint my body to the burying.

9 Verily I say unto you, Wheresoever this gospel shall be preached throughout the whole world, this also that she hath done shall be spoken of for a memorial of her.

Judas Agrees to Betray Jesus

10 And Judas Iscar'i-ot, one of the twelve, went unto the chief priests, to betray him unto them.

11 And when they heard it, they were glad, and promised to give him money. And he sought how he might conveniently betray him.

Jesus Eats the Passover with His Disciples

12 And the first day of unleavened bread, when they killed the passover, his disciples

said unto him, Where wilt thou that we go and prepare that thou mayest eat the passover?

13 And he sendeth forth two of his disciples, and saith unto them, Go ye into the city, and there shall meet you a man bearing a pitcher of water: follow him.

14 And wheresoever he shall go in, say ye to the goodman of the house, The Master saith, Where is the guest chamber, where I shall eat the passover with my disciples?

15 And he will show you a large upper room furnished and prepared: there make ready for us.

16 And his disciples went forth, and came into the city, and found as he had said unto them: and they made ready the passover.

17 And in the evening he cometh with the twelve.

18 And as they sat and did eat, Jesus said, Verily I say unto you, One of you which eateth with me shall betray me.

19 And they began to be sorrowful, and to say unto him one by one, Is it I? and another said, Is it I?

20 And he answered and said unto them, It is one of the twelve, that dippeth with me in the dish.

21 The Son of man indeed goeth, as it is written of him: but woe to that man by whom the Son of man is betrayed! good were it for that man if he had never been born.

22 And as they did eat, Jesus took bread, and blessed, and brake it, and gave to them, and said, Take, eat; this is my body.

23 And he took the cup, and when he had given thanks, he gave it to them: and they all drank of it.

24 And he said unto them, This is my blood of the new testament, which is shed for many.

25 Verily I say unto you, I will drink no more of the fruit of the vine, until that day that I drink it new in the kingdom of God.

Peter's Denial Foretold

26 And when they had sung a hymn, they went out into the mount of Olives.

27 And Jesus saith unto them, All ye shall be offended because of me this night: for it is written, I will smite the shepherd, and the sheep shall be scattered.

28 But after that I am risen, I will go before you into Galilee.

29 But Peter said unto him, Although all shall be offended, yet will not I.

30 And Jesus saith unto him, Verily I say unto thee, That this day, even in this night, before the cock crow twice, thou shalt deny me thrice.

31 But he spake the more vehemently, If I should die with thee, I will not deny thee in any wise. Likewise also said they all.

Jesus Prays in Gethsemane

32 And they came to a place which was named Gethsemane: and he saith to his disciples, Sit ye here, while I shall pray.

33 And he taketh with him Peter and

James and John, and began to be sore amazed,
and to be very heavy;

34 And saith unto them, My soul is exceeding sorrowful unto death: tarry ye here,
and watch.

35 And he went forward a little, and fell
on the ground, and prayed that, if it were
possible, the hour might pass from him.

36 And he said, Abba, Father, all things
are possible unto thee; take away this cup
from me: nevertheless, not what I will, but
what thou wilt.

37 And he cometh, and findeth them sleeping, and saith unto Peter, Simon, sleepest
thou? couldest not thou watch one hour?

38 Watch ye and pray, lest ye enter into
temptation. The spirit truly is ready, but the
flesh is weak.

39 And again he went away, and prayed,
and spake the same words.

40 And when he returned, he found them
asleep again, (for their eyes were heavy,)
neither wist they what to answer him.

41 And he cometh the third time, and
saith unto them, Sleep on now, and take your
rest: it is enough, the hour is come; behold,
the Son of man is betrayed into the hands of
sinners.

42 Rise up, let us go; lo, he that betrayeth
me is at hand.

The Betrayal and Arrest of Jesus

43 And immediately, while he yet spake,
cometh Judas, one of the twelve, and with

him a great multitude with swords and staves, from the chief priests and the scribes and the elders.

44 And he that betrayed him had given them a token, saying, Whomsoever I shall kiss, that same is he; take him, and lead him away safely.

45 And as soon as he was come, he goeth straightway to him, and saith, Master, Master; and kissed him.

46 And they laid their hands on him, and took him.

47 And one of them that stood by drew a sword, and smote a servant of the high priest, and cut off his ear.

48 And Jesus answered and said unto them, Are ye come out, as against a thief, with swords and with staves to take me?

49 I was daily with you in the temple teaching, and ye took me not: but the Scriptures must be fulfilled.

50 And they all forsook him, and fled.

The Young Man Who Fled

51 And there followed him a certain young man, having a linen cloth cast about his naked body; and the young men laid hold on him:

52 And he left the linen cloth, and fled from them naked.

Jesus before the Council

53 And they led Jesus away to the high priest: and with him were assembled all the chief priests and the elders and the scribes.

54 And Peter followed him afar off, even into the palace of the high priest: and he sat with the servants, and warmed himself at the fire.

55 And the chief priests and all the council sought for witness against Jesus to put him to death; and found none.

56 For many bare false witness against him, but their witness agreed not together.

57 And there arose certain, and bare false witness against him, saying,

58 We heard him say, I will destroy this temple that is made with hands, and within three days I will build another made without hands.

59 But neither so did their witness agree together.

60 And the high priest stood up in the midst, and asked Jesus, saying, Answerest thou nothing? what is it which these witness against thee?

61 But he held his peace, and answered nothing. Again the high priest asked him, and said unto him, Art thou the Christ, the Son of the Blessed?

62 And Jesus said, I am: and ye shall see the Son of man sitting on the right hand of power, and coming in the clouds of heaven.

63 Then the high priest rent his clothes, and saith, What need we any further witnesses?

64 Ye have heard the blasphemy: what

think ye? And they all condemned him to be
guilty of death.

65 And some began to spit on him, and to
cover his face, and to buffet him, and to say
unto him, Prophesy: and the servants did
strike him with the palms of their hands.

Peter Denies Jesus

66 And as Peter was beneath in the palace,
there cometh one of the maids of the high
priest:

67 And when she saw Peter warming himself, she looked upon him, and said, And thou
also wast with Jesus of Nazareth.

68 But he denied, saying, I know not,
neither understand I what thou sayest. And
he went out into the porch; and the cock
crew.

69 And a maid saw him again, and began
to say to them that stood by, This is one of
them.

70 And he denied it again. And a little
after, they that stood by said again to Peter,
Surely thou art one of them: for thou
art a Galilean, and thy speech agreeth thereto.

71 But he began to curse and to swear,
saying, I know not this man of whom ye
speak.

72 And the second time the cock crew.
And Peter called to mind the word that
Jesus said unto him, Before the cock crow
twice, thou shalt deny me thrice. And when
he thought thereon, he wept.

Jesus before Pilate

15 And straightway in the morning the chief priests held a consultation with the elders and scribes and the whole council, and bound Jesus, and carried him away, and delivered him to Pilate.

2 And Pilate asked him, Art thou the King of the Jews? And he answering said unto him, Thou sayest it.

3 And the chief priests accused him of many things; but he answered nothing.

4 And Pilate asked him again, saying, Answerest thou nothing? behold how many things they witness against thee.

5 But Jesus yet answered nothing; so that Pilate marveled.

Jesus Sentenced to Die

6 Now at that feast he released unto them one prisoner, whomsoever they desired.

7 And there was one named Barab'bas, which lay bound with them that had made insurrection with him, who had committed murder in the insurrection.

8 And the multitude crying aloud began to desire him to do as he had ever done unto them.

9 But Pilate answered them, saying, Will ye that I release unto you the King of the Jews?

10 For he knew that the chief priests had delivered him for envy.

11 But the chief priests moved the people, that he should rather release Barab'bas unto them.

12 And Pilate[4091] answered and said again unto them, What will ye[5101][2309] then that I shall do[2036] unto him whom ye call[5101] the King of the Jews[4160]?

13 And they cried[935] out[2896] again, Crucify[2453] him.[4717]

14 Then Pilate[4091] said unto them, Why, what[1063] evil[2556] hath he done[4160]? And they cried[5101] out the[2896] more exceedingly,[4044-4056] Crucify[4717] him.

15 And so Pilate,[4091] willing[1014] to content the[4160] people, released[3793][630] Barab'bas[912] unto them, and de-[(4160)] livered Jesus, when[2424] he had[5417] scourged him, to[5417][3860] be crucified.[4717]

16 And the soldiers led[4757] him[520] away into the[520][2080] hall, called Preto'ri-um;[833][3603] and they call[4232] together[4779] the whole band.[3650][4686]

17 And they clothed[3650][4686] him with purple,[4209] and platted a crown[4120] of thorns,[4735][174] and put it about[4060][4060] his head,

18 And began[756] to salute[782] him, Hail, King[5463][935] of the Jews![2453]

19 And they smote[5180] him on the head[2776] with a reed, and did spit upon[2563][1716] him, and bowing[5087] their knees[1119] worshipped[4352] him.

20 And when they had mocked[1702] him, they took off[1562] the purple[4209] from him,[1562] and put his[1746][2398] own clothes on[2440][1746] him, and led him out[1806] to[1806] crucify him.[4717]

The Crucifixion

21 And they compel one[29] Simon[5100] a Cyre'nian,[4613][2956] who passed by,[3855] coming out of the country,[2064] the[2956] father of Alexander[3962][223] and Rufus,[4504] to bear his[142] cross.[4716]

22 And they bring[5342] him unto the place[5117]

Gol′gotha, which is, being interpreted, The place of a skull.

23 And they gave him to drink wine mingled with myrrh: but he received it not.

24 And when they had crucified him, they parted his garments, casting lots upon them, what every man should take.

25 And it was the third hour, and they crucified him.

26 And the superscription of his accusation was written over, THE KING OF THE JEWS.

27 And with him they crucify two thieves; the one on his right hand, and the other on his left.

28 And the Scripture was fulfilled, which saith, And he was numbered with the transgressors.

29 And they that passed by railed on him, wagging their heads, and saying, Ah, thou that destroyest the temple, and buildest it in three days,

30 Save thyself, and come down from the cross.

31 Likewise also the chief priests mocking said among themselves with the scribes, He saved others; himself he cannot save.

32 Let Christ the King of Israel descend now from the cross, that we may see and believe. And they that were crucified with him reviled him.

33 And when the sixth hour was come, there was darkness over the whole land until the ninth hour.

34 And at the ninth hour Jesus cried with

a loud voice, saying, E′lo-i, E′lo-i, lama sabach′thani? which is, being interpreted, My God, my God, why hast thou forsaken me?

35 And some of them that stood by, when they heard it, said, Behold, he calleth Eli′jah.

36 And one ran and filled a sponge full of vinegar, and put it on a reed, and gave him to drink, saying, Let alone; let us see whether Eli′jah will come to take him down.

37 And Jesus cried with a loud voice, and gave up the ghost.

38 And the veil of the temple was rent in twain from the top to the bottom.

39 And when the centurion, which stood over against him, saw that he so cried out, and gave up the ghost, he said, Truly this man was the Son of God.

40 There were also women looking on afar off: among whom was Mary Mag′dalene, and Mary the mother of James the less and of Joses, and Salo′me;

41 Who also, when he was in Galilee, followed him, and ministered unto him; and many other women which came up with him unto Jerusalem.

The Burial of Jesus

42 And now when the even was come, because it was the preparation, that is, the day before the sabbath,

43 Joseph of Arimathe′a, an honorable counselor, which also waited for the kingdom of God, came, and went in boldly unto Pilate, and craved the body of Jesus.

44 And Pilate marveled if he were already dead: and calling unto him the centurion, he asked him whether he had been any while dead.

45 And when he knew it of the centurion, he gave the body to Joseph.

46 And he bought fine linen, and took him down, and wrapped him in the linen, and laid him in a sepulchre which was hewn out of a rock, and rolled a stone unto the door of the sepulchre.

47 And Mary Mag'dalene and Mary the mother of Joses beheld where he was laid.

The Resurrection

16 And when the sabbath was past, Mary Mag'dalene, and Mary the mother of James, and Salo'me, had bought sweet spices, that they might come and anoint him.

2 And very early in the morning, the first day of the week, they came unto the sepulchre at the rising of the sun.

3 And they said among themselves, Who shall roll us away the stone from the door of the sepulchre?

4 And when they looked, they saw that the stone was rolled away: for it was very great.

5 And entering into the sepulchre, they saw a young man sitting on the right side, clothed in a long white garment; and they were affrighted.

6 And he saith unto them, Be not affrighted: ye seek Jesus of Nazareth, which was cruci-

fied: he is risen; he is not here: behold the
place where they laid him.

7 But go your way, tell his disciples and
Peter that he goeth before you into Galilee:
there shall ye see him, as he said unto you.

8 And they went out quickly, and fled from
the sepulchre; for they trembled and were
amazed: neither said they any thing to any
man; for they were afraid.

Jesus Appears to Mary Magdalene

9 Now when Jesus was risen early the
first day of the week, he appeared first to
Mary Mag'dalene, out of whom he had cast
seven devils.

10 And she went and told them that had
been with him, as they mourned and wept.

11 And they, when they had heard that he
was alive, and had been seen of her, believed
not.

Jesus Appears to Two Disciples

12 After that he appeared in another form
unto two of them, as they walked, and went
into the country.

13 And they went and told it unto the
residue: neither believed they them.

Jesus Commissions the Eleven

14 Afterward he appeared unto the eleven
as they sat at meat, and upbraided them with
their unbelief and hardness of heart, because
they believed not them which had seen him
after he was risen.

15 And he said unto them, Go ye into all the world, and preach the gospel to every creature.

16 He that believeth and is baptized shall be saved; but he that believeth not shall be damned.

17 And these signs shall follow them that believe; In my name shall they cast out devils; they shall speak with new tongues;

18 They shall take up serpents; and if they drink any deadly thing, it shall not hurt them; they shall lay hands on the sick, and they shall recover.

The Ascension

19 So then, after the Lord had spoken unto them, he was received up into heaven, and sat on the right hand of God.

20 And they went forth, and preached every where, the Lord working with them, and confirming the word with signs following. Amen.

THE GOSPEL ACCORDING TO
ST. LUKE

Dedication to Theophilus

1 Forasmuch as many have taken in hand to set forth in order a declaration of those things which are most surely believed among us,

2 Even as they delivered them unto us, which from the beginning were eyewitnesses, and ministers of the word;

3 It seemed good to me also, having had perfect understanding of all things from the very first, to write unto thee in order, most excellent The-oph'ilus,

4 That thou mightest know the certainty of those things, wherein thou hast been instructed.

The Birth of John the Baptist Foretold

5 There was in the days of Herod, the king of Judea, a certain priest named Zechari'ah, of the course of Abi'jah: and his wife was of the daughters of Aaron, and her name was Elisabeth.

6 And they were both righteous before God, walking in all the commandments and ordinances of the Lord blameless.

7 And they had no child, because that Elisabeth was barren; and they both were now well stricken in years.

8 And it came to pass, that, while he executed the priest's office before God in the order of his course,

9 According to the custom of the priest's office, his lot was to burn incense when he went into the temple of the Lord.

10 And the whole multitude of the people were praying without at the time of incense.

11 And there appeared unto him an angel of the Lord standing on the right side of the altar of incense.

12 And when Zechari′ah saw him, he was troubled, and fear fell upon him.

13 But the angel said unto him, Fear not, Zechari′ah: for thy prayer is heard; and thy wife Elisabeth shall bear thee a son, and thou shalt call his name John.

14 And thou shalt have joy and gladness; and many shall rejoice at his birth.

15 For he shall be great in the sight of the Lord, and shall drink neither wine nor strong drink; and he shall be filled with the Holy Ghost, even from his mother's womb.

16 And many of the children of Israel shall he turn to the Lord their God.

17 And he shall go before him in the spirit and power of Eli′jah, to turn the hearts of the fathers to the children, and the disobedient to the wisdom of the just; to make ready a people prepared for the Lord.

18 And Zechari′ah said unto the angel, Whereby shall I know this? for I am an old man, and my wife well stricken in years.

19 And the angel answering said unto him, I am Gabriel, that stand in the presence of God; and am sent to speak unto thee, and to show thee these glad tidings.

20 And, behold, thou shalt be dumb, and not able to speak, until the day that these things shall be performed, because thou believest not my words, which shall be fulfilled in their season.

21 And the people waited for Zechari'ah, and marveled that he tarried so long in the temple.

22 And when he came out, he could not speak unto them: and they perceived that he had seen a vision in the temple; for he beckoned unto them, and remained speechless.

23 And it came to pass, that, as soon as the days of his ministration were accomplished, he departed to his own house.

24 And after those days his wife Elisabeth conceived, and hid herself five months, saying,

25 Thus hath the Lord dealt with me in the days wherein he looked on me, to take away my reproach among men.

Jesus' Birth Foretold

26 And in the sixth month the angel Gabriel was sent from God unto a city of Galilee, named Nazareth,

27 To a virgin espoused to a man whose name was Joseph, of the house of David; and the virgin's name was Mary.

28 And the angel came in unto her, and said, Hail, thou that art highly favored, the Lord is with thee: blessed art thou among women.

29 And when she saw him, she was troubled

at his saying, and cast in her mind what
manner of salutation this should be.

30 And the angel said unto her, Fear not,
Mary: for thou hast found favor with God.

31 And, behold, thou shalt conceive in thy
womb, and bring forth a son, and shalt call
his name JESUS.

32 He shall be great, and shall be called the
Son of the Highest; and the Lord God shall
give unto him the throne of his father David:

33 And he shall reign over the house of
Jacob for ever; and of his kingdom there shall
be no end.

34 Then said Mary unto the angel, How
shall this be, seeing I know not a man?

35 And the angel answered and said unto
her, The Holy Ghost shall come upon thee,
and the power of the Highest shall overshadow
thee: therefore also that holy thing which shall
be born of thee shall be called the Son of God.

36 And, behold, thy cousin Elisabeth, she
hath also conceived a son in her old age; and
this is the sixth month with her, who was
called barren.

37 For with God nothing shall be impossible.

38 And Mary said, Behold the handmaid
of the Lord; be it unto me according to thy
word. And the angel departed from her.

Mary Visits Elisabeth

39 And Mary arose in those days, and went
into the hill country with haste, into a city of
Judah;

40 And entered into the house of Zechari'ah, and saluted Elisabeth.

41 And it came to pass, that, when Elisabeth heard the salutation of Mary, the babe leaped in her womb; and Elisabeth was filled with the Holy Ghost:

42 And she spake out with a loud voice, and said, Blessed art thou among women, and blessed is the fruit of thy womb.

43 And whence is this to me, that the mother of my Lord should come to me?

44 For, lo, as soon as the voice of thy salutation sounded in mine ears, the babe leaped in my womb for joy.

45 And blessed is she that believed: for there shall be a performance of those things which were told her from the Lord.

46 And Mary said, My soul doth magnify the Lord,

47 And my spirit hath rejoiced in God my Saviour.

48 For he hath regarded the low estate of his handmaiden: for, behold, from henceforth all generations shall call me blessed.

49 For he that is mighty hath done to me great things; and holy is his name.

50 And his mercy is on them that fear him from generation to generation.

51 He hath showed strength with his arm; he hath scattered the proud in the imagination of their hearts.

52 He hath put down the mighty from their seats, and exalted them of low degree.

53 He hath filled the hungry with good

things; and the rich he hath sent empty away.

54 He hath holpen his servant Israel, in remembrance of his mercy;

55 As he spake to our fathers, to Abraham, and to his seed for ever.

56 And Mary abode with her about three months, and returned to her own house.

The Birth of John the Baptist

57 Now Elisabeth's full time came that she should be delivered; and she brought forth a son.

58 And her neighbors and her cousins heard how the Lord had showed great mercy upon her; and they rejoiced with her.

59 And it came to pass, that on the eighth day they came to circumcise the child; and they called him Zechari′ah, after the name of his father.

60 And his mother answered and said, Not so; but he shall be called John.

61 And they said unto her, There is none of thy kindred that is called by this name.

62 And they made signs to his father, how he would have him called.

63 And he asked for a writing table, and wrote, saying, His name is John. And they marveled all.

64 And his mouth was opened immediately, and his tongue loosed, and he spake, and praised God.

65 And fear came on all that dwelt round about them: and all these sayings were noised

abroad[1255] throughout all[3650] the hill[3714] country of Judea[2448,2449].

66 And all they that heard[191] them laid[5087] them up[5087] in their hearts[2588], saying, What[5101] manner[686] of child[3813] shall this be? And the hand[5495] of the Lord[2962] was with him.

Zechariah's Prophecy

67 And his father[3962] Zechari′ah[2197] was filled[4130] with the Holy[40] Ghost[4151], and prophesied[4395], saying,

68 Blessed[2128] be the Lord[2962] God[2316] of Israel[2474]; for he hath visited[1980] and redeemed[3085] his people[2992],

69 And hath raised up[1453] a horn[2768] of salvation[4991] for us in the house[3624] of his servant[3816] David[1138];

70 As[2531] he spake[2980] by the mouth[4750] of his holy[40] prophets[4396], which have been since the world began[165]:

71 That we should be saved[4991] from our enemies[4991], and from the hand[5495] of all that hate[3404] us[2190];

72 To perform[4160] the mercy[1656] promised to our fathers[3962], and to remember[3415] his holy[40] covenant[1242];

73 The oath[3727] which he sware[3660] to our father[3962] Abraham[11],

[11] 74 That he would grant[1325] unto us, that we, being delivered[4506] out of the hand[5495] of our enemies[2190], might serve[3000] him without fear[870],

75 In holiness[3742] and righteousness[1343] before him[1799], all the days[2250] of our life[2222].

76 And thou, child[3813], shalt be called[2564] the prophet[4396] of the Highest[5310]: for thou shalt go[4313] before[4396] the face[4383] of the Lord[2962] to prepare[2090] his ways[3598];

77 To give knowledge of salvation unto his people by the remission of their sins,

78 Through the tender mercy of our God; whereby the dayspring from on high hath visited us,

79 To give light to them that sit in darkness and in the shadow of death, to guide our feet into the way of peace.

80 And the child grew, and waxed strong in spirit, and was in the deserts till the day of his showing unto Israel.

The Birth of Jesus

2 And it came to pass in those days, that there went out a decree from Caesar Augustus, that all the world should be taxed.

2 (And this taxing was first made when Cyre′ni-us was governor of Syria.)

3 And all went to be taxed, every one into his own city.

4 And Joseph also went up from Galilee, out of the city of Nazareth, into Judea, unto the city of David, which is called Bethlehem, (because he was of the house and lineage of David,)

5 To be taxed with Mary his espoused wife, being great with child.

6 And so it was, that, while they were there, the days were accomplished that she should be delivered.

7 And she brought forth her firstborn son, and wrapped him in swaddling clothes, and laid him in a manger; because there was no room for them in the inn.

The Shepherds and the Angels

8 And there were in the same country shepherds abiding in the field, keeping watch over their flock by night.

9 And, lo, the angel of the Lord came upon them, and the glory of the Lord shone round about them; and they were sore afraid.

10 And the angel said unto them, Fear not: for, behold, I bring you good tidings of great joy, which shall be to all people.

11 For unto you is born this day in the city of David a Saviour, which is Christ the Lord.

12 And this shall be a sign unto you; Ye shall find the babe wrapped in swaddling clothes, lying in a manger.

13 And suddenly there was with the angel a multitude of the heavenly host praising God, and saying,

14 Glory to God in the highest, and on earth peace, good will toward men.

15 And it came to pass, as the angels were gone away from them into heaven, the shepherds said one to another, Let us now go even unto Bethlehem, and see this thing which is come to pass, which the Lord hath made known unto us.

16 And they came with haste, and found Mary and Joseph, and the babe lying in a manger.

17 And when they had seen it, they made known abroad the saying which was told them concerning this child.

18 And all they that heard it wondered at

those things which were told them by the shepherds.

19 But Mary kept all these things, and pondered them in her heart.

20 And the shepherds returned, glorifying and praising God for all the things that they had heard and seen, as it was told unto them.

The Presentation of Jesus in the Temple

21 And when eight days were accomplished for the circumcising of the child, his name was called JESUS, which was so named of the angel before he was conceived in the womb.

22 And when the days of her purification according to the law of Moses were accomplished, they brought him to Jerusalem, to present him to the Lord;

23 (As it is written in the law of the Lord, Every male that openeth the womb shall be called holy to the Lord;)

24 And to offer a sacrifice according to that which is said in the law of the Lord, A pair of turtledoves, or two young pigeons.

25 And, behold, there was a man in Jerusalem, whose name was Simeon; and the same man was just and devout, waiting for the consolation of Israel: and the Holy Ghost was upon him.

26 And it was revealed unto him by the Holy Ghost, that he should not see death, before he had seen the Lord's Christ.

27 And he came by the Spirit into the temple: and when the parents brought in the

child Jesus, to do for him after the custom
of the law,

28 Then took he him up in his arms, and
blessed God, and said,

29 Lord, now lettest thou thy servant depart in peace, according to thy word:

30 For mine eyes have seen thy salvation,

31 Which thou hast prepared before the
face of all people;

32 A light to lighten the Gentiles, and the
glory of thy people Israel.

33 And Joseph and his mother marveled at
those things which were spoken of him.

34 And Simeon blessed them, and said
unto Mary his mother, Behold, this child is
set for the fall and rising again of many in
Israel; and for a sign which shall be spoken
against;

35 (Yea, a sword shall pierce through thy
own soul also;) that the thoughts of many
hearts may be revealed.

36 And there was one Anna, a prophetess,
the daughter of Phan'u-el, of the tribe of
Asher: she was of a great age, and had lived
with a husband seven years from her virginity;

37 And she was a widow of about fourscore
and four years, which departed not from the
temple, but served God with fastings and
prayers night and day.

38 And she coming in that instant gave
thanks likewise unto the Lord, and spake of
him to all them that looked for redemption in
Jerusalem.

The Return to Nazareth

39 And when they had performed all things according to the law of the Lord, they returned into Galilee, to their own city Nazareth.

40 And the child grew, and waxed strong in spirit, filled with wisdom; and the grace of God was upon him.

The Boy Jesus in the Temple

41 Now his parents went to Jerusalem every year at the feast of the passover.

42 And when he was twelve years old, they went up to Jerusalem after the custom of the feast.

43 And when they had fulfilled the days, as they returned, the child Jesus tarried behind in Jerusalem; and Joseph and his mother knew not of it.

44 But they, supposing him to have been in the company, went a day's journey; and they sought him among their kinsfolk and acquaintance.

45 And when they found him not, they turned back again to Jerusalem, seeking him.

46 And it came to pass, that after three days they found him in the temple, sitting in the midst of the doctors, both hearing them, and asking them questions.

47 And all that heard him were astonished at his understanding and answers.

48 And when they saw him, they were amazed: and his mother said unto him, Son, why hast thou thus dealt with us? behold, thy father and I have sought thee sorrowing.

49 And he said unto them, How is it that ye sought me? wist ye not that I must be about my Father's business?

50 And they understood not the saying which he spake unto them.

51 And he went down with them, and came to Nazareth, and was subject unto them: but his mother kept all these sayings in her heart.

52 And Jesus increased in wisdom and stature, and in favor with God and man.

The Preaching of John the Baptist

3 Now in the fifteenth year of the reign of Tibe′ri-us Caesar, Pontius Pilate being governor of Judea, and Herod being tetrarch of Galilee, and his brother Philip tetrarch of Iturae′a and of the region of Trachoni′tis, and Lysa′ni-as the tetrarch of Abile′ne,

2 Annas and Cai′aphas being the high priests, the word of God came unto John the son of Zechari′ah in the wilderness.

3 And he came into all the country about Jordan, preaching the baptism of repentance for the remission of sins;

4 As it is written in the book of the words of Isaiah the prophet, saying, The voice of one crying in the wilderness, Prepare ye the way of the Lord, make his paths straight.

5 Every valley shall be filled, and every mountain and hill shall be brought low; and the crooked shall be made straight, and the rough ways shall be made smooth;

6 And all flesh shall see the salvation of God.

7 Then said he to the multitude that came forth to be baptized of him, O generation of vipers, who hath warned you to flee from the wrath to come?

8 Bring forth therefore fruits worthy of repentance, and begin not to say within your-selves, We have Abraham to our father: for I say unto you, That God is able of these stones to raise up children unto Abraham.

9 And now also the axe is laid unto the root of the trees: every tree therefore which bringeth not forth good fruit is hewn down, and cast into the fire.

10 And the people asked him, saying, What shall we do then?

11 He answereth and saith unto them, He that hath two coats, let him impart to him that hath none; and he that hath meat, let him do likewise.

12 Then came also publicans to be bap-tized, and said unto him, Master, what shall we do?

13 And he said unto them, Exact no more than that which is appointed you.

14 And the soldiers likewise demanded of him, saying, And what shall we do? And he said unto them, Do violence to no man, neither accuse any falsely; and be content with your wages.

15 And as the people were in expectation, and all men mused in their hearts of John, whether he were the Christ, or not;

16 John answered, saying unto them all, I indeed baptize you with water; but one

mightier than I cometh, the latchet of whose shoes I am not worthy to unloose: he shall baptize you with the Holy Ghost and with fire:

17 Whose fan is in his hand, and he will thoroughly purge his floor, and will gather the wheat into his garner; but the chaff he will burn with fire unquenchable.

18 And many other things in his exhortation preached he unto the people.

19 But Herod the tetrarch, being reproved by him for Hero'di-as his brother Philip's wife, and for all the evils which Herod had done,

20 Added yet this above all, that he shut up John in prison.

The Baptism of Jesus

21 Now when all the people were baptized, it came to pass, that Jesus also being baptized, and praying, the heaven was opened,

22 And the Holy Ghost descended in a bodily shape like a dove upon him, and a voice came from heaven, which said, Thou art my beloved Son; in thee I am well pleased.

The Genealogy of Jesus

23 And Jesus himself began to be about thirty years of age, being (as was supposed) the son of Joseph, which was the son of Heli,

24 Which was the son of Matthat, which was the son of Levi, which was the son of

Melchi[3197], which was the son of Janna[2388], which was the son of Joseph[2501],

25 Which was the son of Mattathi′as[3161], which was the son of Amos[301], which was the son of Nahum[3486], which was the son of Esli[2069], which was the son of Nag′gai[3477],

26 Which was the son of Ma′ath[3092], which was the son of Mattathi′as[3161], which was the son of Sem′e-i[4584], which was the son of Joseph[2501], which was the son of Judah[2455],

27 Which was the son of Joanna[2490], which was the son of Rhesa[4488], which was the son of Zerub′-babel[2216], which was the son of She-al′ti-el[4528], which was the son of Neri[3518],

28 Which was the son of Melchi[3197], which was the son of Addi[78], which was the son of Cosam[2973], which was the son of Elmo′dam[1678], which was the son of Er[2262],

29 Which was the son of Jose[2499], which was the son of Eli-e′zer[2500], which was the son of Jorim[1663], which was the son of Matthat[3158], which was the son of Levi[3018],

30 Which was the son of Simeon[4826], which was the son of Judah[2455], which was the son of Joseph[2501], which was the son of Jonan[2494], which was the son of Eli′akim[1662],

31 Which was the son of Me′le-a[3190], which was the son of Menan[3104], which was the son of Mat′tatha[3160], which was the son of Nathan[3481], which was the son of David[1138],

32 Which was the son of Jesse[2421], which was the son of Obed[5601], which was the son of Boaz[1003], which was the son of Salmon[4533], which was the son of Nahshon[3476],

33 Which was the son of Ammin´adab, which was the son of Ram,[284] which was the son of Hezron,[689] which was[2074] the son of Pharez,[5329] which was the son of Judah,

34 Which was the son[2455] of Jacob, which was the son[2384] of Isaac, which was the[2464] son of Abraham, which was the son of Terah,[11] which was[2291] the son of Nahor,

35 Which was[3493] the son of Serug,[4562] which was the son of Re´u,[4466] which was the son of Peleg,[5317] which was the son of Eber,[1443] which was the son of Salah,

36 Which was[4527] the son of Ca-i´nan, which was the son of Arphax´ad,[2536] which was the son of Shem,[742] which was the son of Noah,[3575] which was the son of Lamech,[4590]

37 Which was the son[2984] of Methu´selah, which was the son of Enoch,[3103] which was the son of Jared,[1802] which was the son of Mahal´aleel,[3121] which was[2391] the son of Ca-i´nan,

38 Which was the son[2536] of Enos, which was the son of Seth,[1800] which was the son of Adam,[76] which was the son[4589] of God.[2316]

The Temptation of Jesus

4 And Jesus being full of the Holy Ghost[40] returned[2424] from Jordan,[4134] and was led by the Spirit[5290] into the wilderness,[2446][71]

2 Being forty[4151] days[2250] tempted[2048] of the devil.[1228] And in those[3985] days[5062] he did[3985] eat nothing: and when they were[2250] ended,[5315] he afterward hungered.[5305]

3 And the devil[4931] said[4931] unto him,[5305] If thou be[3983] the Son[1228] of God,[2036] command this stone that it[2036][3037] be made[5207] bread.[2316][1096][740]

4 And Jesus answered him, saying, It is written, That man shall not live by bread alone, but by every word of God.

5 And the devil, taking him up into a high mountain, showed unto him all the kingdoms of the world in a moment of time.

6 And the devil said unto him, All this power will I give thee, and the glory of them: for that is delivered unto me; and to whomsoever I will, I give it.

7 If thou therefore wilt worship me, all shall be thine.

8 And Jesus answered and said unto him, Get thee behind me, Satan: for it is written, Thou shalt worship the Lord thy God, and him only shalt thou serve.

9 And he brought him to Jerusalem, and set him on a pinnacle of the temple, and said unto him, If thou be the Son of God, cast thyself down from hence:

10 For it is written, He shall give his angels charge over thee, to keep thee:

11 And in their hands they shall bear thee up, lest at any time thou dash thy foot against a stone.

12 And Jesus answering said unto him, It is said, Thou shalt not tempt the Lord thy God.

13 And when the devil had ended all the temptation, he departed from him for a season.

Jesus Begins His Ministry

14 And Jesus returned in the power of the Spirit into Galilee: and there went out a

fame of him through all the region round about.

15 And he taught in their synagogues, being glorified of all.

Jesus Rejected at Nazareth

16 And he came to Nazareth, where he had been brought up: and, as his custom was, he went into the synagogue on the sabbath day, and stood up for to read.

17 And there was delivered unto him the book of the prophet Isaiah. And when he had opened the book, he found the place where it was written,

18 The Spirit of the Lord is upon me, because he hath anointed me to preach the gospel to the poor; he hath sent me to heal the brokenhearted, to preach deliverance to the captives, and recovering of sight to the blind, to set at liberty them that are bruised,

19 To preach the acceptable year of the Lord.

20 And he closed the book, and he gave it again to the minister, and sat down. And the eyes of all them that were in the synagogue were fastened on him.

21 And he began to say unto them, This day is this Scripture fulfilled in your ears.

22 And all bare him witness, and wondered at the gracious words which proceeded out of his mouth. And they said, Is not this Joseph's son?

23 And he said unto them, Ye will surely say unto me this proverb, Physician, heal

thyself: whatsoever we have heard done in Caper'na-um, do also here in thy country.

24 And he said, Verily I say unto you, No prophet is accepted in his own country.

25 But I tell you of a truth, many widows were in Israel in the days of Eli'jah, when the heaven was shut up three years and six months, when great famine was throughout all the land;

26 But unto none of them was Eli'jah sent, save unto Zar'ephath, a city of Sidon, unto a woman that was a widow.

27 And many lepers were in Israel in the time of Eli'sha the prophet; and none of them was cleansed, saving Na'aman the Syrian.

28 And all they in the synagogue, when they heard these things, were filled with wrath,

29 And rose up, and thrust him out of the city, and led him unto the brow of the hill whereon their city was built, that they might cast him down headlong.

30 But he, passing through the midst of them, went his way,

31 And came down to Caper'na-um, a city of Galilee, and taught them on the sabbath days.

32 And they were astonished at his doctrine: for his word was with power.

A Man with an Unclean Spirit

33 And in the synagogue there was a man, which had a spirit of an unclean devil, and cried out with a loud voice,

34 Saying, Let us alone; what have we to do with thee, thou Jesus of Nazareth? art thou come to destroy us? I know thee who thou art; the Holy One of God.

35 And Jesus rebuked him, saying, Hold thy peace, and come out of him. And when the devil had thrown him in the midst, he came out of him, and hurt him not.

36 And they were all amazed, and spake among themselves, saying, What a word is this! for with authority and power he commandeth the unclean spirits, and they come out.

37 And the fame of him went out into every place of the country round about.

Jesus Heals Simon's Mother-in-Law

38 And he arose out of the synagogue, and entered into Simon's house. And Simon's wife's mother was taken with a great fever; and they besought him for her.

39 And he stood over her, and rebuked the fever; and it left her: and immediately she arose and ministered unto them.

Jesus Heals Many at Evening

40 Now when the sun was setting, all they that had any sick with divers diseases brought them unto him; and he laid his hands on every one of them, and healed them.

41 And devils also came out of many, crying out, and saying, Thou art Christ the Son of God. And he rebuking them suffered them not to speak: for they knew that he was Christ.

Jesus Departs on a Preaching Tour

42 And when it was day, he departed and went into a desert place: and the people sought him, and came unto him, and stayed him, that he should not depart from them.

43 And he said unto them, I must preach the kingdom of God to other cities also: for therefore am I sent.

44 And he preached in the synagogues of Galilee.

The Great Catch of Fish

5 And it came to pass, that, as the people pressed upon him to hear the word of God, he stood by the lake of Gennes'aret,

2 And saw two ships standing by the lake: but the fishermen were gone out of them, and were washing their nets.

3 And he entered into one of the ships, which was Simon's, and prayed him that he would thrust out a little from the land. And he sat down, and taught the people out of the ship.

4 Now when he had left speaking, he said unto Simon, Launch out into the deep, and let down your nets for a draught.

5 And Simon answering said unto him, Master, we have toiled all the night, and have taken nothing: nevertheless at thy word I will let down the net.

6 And when they had this done, they inclosed a great multitude of fishes: and their net brake.

7 And they beckoned unto their partners,

which were in the other ship, that they should come and help them. And they came, and filled both the ships, so that they began to sink.

8 When Simon Peter saw it, he fell down at Jesus' knees, saying, Depart from me; for I am a sinful man, O Lord.

9 For he was astonished, and all that were with him, at the draught of the fishes which they had taken:

10 And so was also James, and John, the sons of Zebedee, which were partners with Simon. And Jesus said unto Simon, Fear not; from henceforth thou shalt catch men.

11 And when they had brought their ships to land, they forsook all, and followed him.

Jesus Cleanses a Leper

12 And it came to pass, when he was in a certain city, behold a man full of leprosy: who seeing Jesus fell on his face, and besought him, saying, Lord, if thou wilt, thou canst make me clean.

13 And he put forth his hand, and touched him, saying, I will: be thou clean. And immediately the leprosy departed from him.

14 And he charged him to tell no man: But go, and show thyself to the priest, and offer for thy cleansing, according as Moses commanded, for a testimony unto them.

15 But so much the more went there a fame abroad of him: and great multitudes came together to hear, and to be healed by him of their infirmities.

16 And he withdrew himself into the wilderness, and prayed.

Jesus Heals a Palsied Man

17 And it came to pass on a certain day, as he was teaching, that there were Pharisees and doctors of the law sitting by, which were come out of every town of Galilee, and Judea, and Jerusalem: and the power of the Lord was present to heal them.

18 And, behold, men brought in a bed a man which was taken with a palsy: and they sought means to bring him in, and to lay him before him.

19 And when they could not find by what way they might bring him in because of the multitude, they went upon the housetop, and let him down through the tiling with his couch into the midst before Jesus.

20 And when he saw their faith, he said unto him, Man, thy sins are forgiven thee.

21 And the scribes and the Pharisees began to reason, saying, Who is this which speaketh blasphemies? Who can forgive sins, but God alone?

22 But when Jesus perceived their thoughts, he answering said unto them, What reason ye in your hearts?

23 Whether is easier, to say, Thy sins be forgiven thee; or to say, Rise up and walk?

24 But that ye may know that the Son of man hath power upon earth to forgive sins, (he said unto the sick of the palsy,) I say

unto thee, Arise, and take up thy couch, and go into thine house.

25 And immediately he rose up before them, and took up that whereon he lay, and departed to his own house, glorifying God.

26 And they were all amazed, and they glorified God, and were filled with fear, saying, We have seen strange things today.

The Call of Levi

27 And after these things he went forth, and saw a publican, named Levi, sitting at the receipt of custom: and he said unto him, Follow me.

28 And he left all, rose up, and followed him.

29 And Levi made him a great feast in his own house: and there was a great company of publicans and of others that sat down with them.

30 But their scribes and Pharisees murmured against his disciples, saying, Why do ye eat and drink with publicans and sinners?

31 And Jesus answering said unto them, They that are whole need not a physician; but they that are sick.

32 I came not to call the righteous, but sinners to repentance.

The Question about Fasting

33 And they said unto him, Why do the disciples of John fast often, and make prayers, and likewise the disciples of the Pharisees; but thine eat and drink?

34 And he said unto them, Can ye make

the children of the bridechamber fast, while the bridegroom is with them?

35 But the days will come, when the bridegroom shall be taken away from them, and then shall they fast in those days.

36 And he spake also a parable unto them; No man putteth a piece of a new garment upon an old; if otherwise, then both the new maketh a rent, and the piece that was taken out of the new agreeth not with the old.

37 And no man putteth new wine into old bottles; else the new wine will burst the bottles, and be spilled, and the bottles shall perish.

38 But new wine must be put into new bottles; and both are preserved.

39 No man also having drunk old wine straightway desireth new; for he saith, The old is better.

The Disciples Pluck Grain on the Sabbath

6 And it came to pass on the second sabbath after the first, that he went through the corn fields; and his disciples plucked the ears of corn, and did eat, rubbing them in their hands.

2 And certain of the Pharisees said unto them, Why do ye that which is not lawful to do on the sabbath days?

3 And Jesus answering them said, Have ye not read so much as this, what David did, when himself was ahungered, and they which were with him;

4 How he went into the house of God, and

did take and eat the showbread, and gave also to them that were with him; which it is not lawful to eat but for the priests alone?

5 And he said unto them, That the Son of man is Lord also of the sabbath.

The Man with a Withered Hand

6 And it came to pass also on another sabbath, that he entered into the synagogue and taught: and there was a man whose right hand was withered.

7 And the scribes and Pharisees watched him, whether he would heal on the sabbath day; that they might find an accusation against him.

8 But he knew their thoughts, and said to the man which had the withered hand, Rise up, and stand forth in the midst. And he arose and stood forth.

9 Then said Jesus unto them, I will ask you one thing; Is it lawful on the sabbath days to do good, or to do evil? to save life, or to destroy it?

10 And looking round about upon them all, he said unto the man, Stretch forth thy hand. And he did so: and his hand was restored whole as the other.

11 And they were filled with madness; and communed one with another what they might do to Jesus.

Jesus Chooses the Twelve

12 And it came to pass in those days, that he went out into a mountain to pray, and continued all night in prayer to God.

13 And when it was day, he called unto him his disciples: and of them he chose twelve, whom also he named apostles;

14 Simon, (whom he also named Peter,) and Andrew his brother, James and John, Philip and Bartholomew,

15 Matthew and Thomas, James the son of Al'pheus, and Simon called Zelo'tes,

16 And Judas the brother of James, and Judas Iscar'i-ot, which also was the traitor.

Jesus Ministers to a Great Multitude

17 And he came down with them, and stood in the plain, and the company of his disciples, and a great multitude of people out of all Judea and Jerusalem, and from the sea-coast of Tyre and Sidon, which came to hear him, and to be healed of their diseases;

18 And they that were vexed with unclean spirits: and they were healed.

19 And the whole multitude sought to touch him: for there went virtue out of him, and healed them all.

Blessings and Woes

20 And he lifted up his eyes on his disciples, and said, Blessed be ye poor: for yours is the kingdom of God.

21 Blessed are ye that hunger now: for ye shall be filled. Blessed are ye that weep now: for ye shall laugh.

22 Blessed are ye, when men shall hate you, and when they shall separate you from their company, and shall reproach you, and

cast out your name as evil, for the Son of man's sake.

23 Rejoice ye in that day, and leap for joy: for, behold, your reward is great in heaven: for in the like manner did their fathers unto the prophets.

24 But woe unto you that are rich! for ye have received your consolation.

25 Woe unto you that are full! for ye shall hunger. Woe unto you that laugh now! for ye shall mourn and weep.

26 Woe unto you, when all men shall speak well of you! for so did their fathers to the false prophets.

Love for Enemies

27 But I say unto you which hear, Love your enemies, do good to them which hate you,

28 Bless them that curse you, and pray for them which despitefully use you.

29 And unto him that smiteth thee on the one cheek offer also the other; and him that taketh away thy cloak forbid not to take thy coat also.

30 Give to every man that asketh of thee; and of him that taketh away thy goods ask them not again.

31 And as ye would that men should do to you, do ye also to them likewise.

32 For if ye love them which love you, what thank have ye? for sinners also love those that love them.

33 And if ye do good to them which do

good to you, what thank have ye? for sinners also do even the same.

34 And if ye lend to them of whom ye hope to receive, what thank have ye? for sinners also lend to sinners, to receive as much again.

35 But love ye your enemies, and do good, and lend, hoping for nothing again; and your reward shall be great, and ye shall be the children of the Highest: for he is kind unto the unthankful and to the evil.

36 Be ye therefore merciful, as your Father also is merciful.

Judging Others

37 Judge not, and ye shall not be judged: condemn not, and ye shall not be condemned: forgive, and ye shall be forgiven:

38 Give, and it shall be given unto you; good measure, pressed down, and shaken together, and running over, shall men give into your bosom. For with the same measure that ye mete withal it shall be measured to you again.

39 And he spake a parable unto them; Can the blind lead the blind? shall they not both fall into the ditch?

40 The disciple is not above his master: but every one that is perfect shall be as his master.

41 And why beholdest thou the mote that is in thy brother's eye, but perceivest not the beam that is in thine own eye?

42 Either how canst thou say to thy brother, Brother, let me pull out the mote that is in

thine eye, when thou thyself beholdest not the beam that is in thine own eye? Thou hypocrite, cast out first the beam out of thine own eye, and then shalt thou see clearly to pull out the mote that is in thy brother's eye.

A Tree Is Known by Its Fruit

43 For a good tree bringeth not forth corrupt fruit; neither doth a corrupt tree bring forth good fruit.

44 For every tree is known by his own fruit. For of thorns men do not gather figs, nor of a bramble bush gather they grapes.

45 A good man out of the good treasure of his heart bringeth forth that which is good; and an evil man out of the evil treasure of his heart bringeth forth that which is evil: for of the abundance of the heart his mouth speaketh.

The House Built on a Rock

46 And why call ye me, Lord, Lord, and do not the things which I say?

47 Whosoever cometh to me, and heareth my sayings, and doeth them, I will show you to whom he is like:

48 He is like a man which built a house, and digged deep, and laid the foundation on a rock: and when the flood arose, the stream beat vehemently upon that house, and could not shake it; for it was founded upon a rock.

49 But he that heareth, and doeth not, is like a man that without a foundation built a house upon the earth; against which the

stream did beat vehemently, and immediately it fell; and the ruin of that house was great.

A Centurion's Servant Healed

7 Now when he had ended all his sayings in the audience of the people, he entered into Caper′na-um.

2 And a certain centurion's servant, who was dear unto him, was sick, and ready to die.

3 And when he heard of Jesus, he sent unto him the elders of the Jews, beseeching him that he would come and heal his servant.

4 And when they came to Jesus, they besought him instantly, saying, That he was worthy for whom he should do this:

5 For he loveth our nation, and he hath built us a synagogue.

6 Then Jesus went with them. And when he was now not far from the house, the centurion sent friends to him, saying unto him, Lord, trouble not thyself; for I am not worthy that thou shouldest enter under my roof:

7 Wherefore neither thought I myself worthy to come unto thee: but say in a word, and my servant shall be healed.

8 For I also am a man set under authority, having under me soldiers, and I say unto one, Go, and he goeth; and to another, Come, and he cometh; and to my servant, Do this, and he doeth it.

9 When Jesus heard these things, he marveled at him, and turned him about, and said unto the people that followed him, I say unto

you, I have not found so great faith, no, not in Israel.

10 And they that were sent, returning to the house, found the servant whole that had been sick.

Jesus Raises the Widow's Son at Nain

11 And it came to pass the day after, that he went into a city called Nain; and many of his disciples went with him, and much people.

12 Now when he came nigh to the gate of the city, behold, there was a dead man carried out, the only son of his mother, and she was a widow: and much people of the city was with her.

13 And when the Lord saw her, he had compassion on her, and said unto her, Weep not.

14 And he came and touched the bier: and they that bare him stood still. And he said, Young man, I say unto thee, Arise.

15 And he that was dead sat up, and began to speak. And he delivered him to his mother.

16 And there came a fear on all: and they glorified God, saying, That a great prophet is risen up among us; and, That God hath visited his people.

17 And this rumor of him went forth throughout all Judea, and throughout all the region round about.

The Messengers from John the Baptist

18 And the disciples of John showed him of all these things.

19 And John calling unto him two of his disciples sent them to Jesus, saying, Art thou he that should come? or look we for another?

20 When the men were come unto him, they said, John Baptist hath sent us unto thee, saying, Art thou he that should come? or look we for another?

21 And in that same hour he cured many of their infirmities and plagues, and of evil spirits; and unto many that were blind he gave sight.

22 Then Jesus answering said unto them, Go your way, and tell John what things ye have seen and heard; how that the blind see, the lame walk, the lepers are cleansed, the deaf hear, the dead are raised, to the poor the gospel is preached.

23 And blessed is he, whosoever shall not be offended in me.

24 And when the messengers of John were departed, he began to speak unto the people concerning John, What went ye out into the wilderness for to see? A reed shaken with the wind?

25 But what went ye out for to see? A man clothed in soft raiment? Behold, they which are gorgeously appareled, and live delicately, are in kings' courts.

26 But what went ye out for to see? A prophet? Yea, I say unto you, and much more than a prophet.

27 This is he, of whom it is written, Behold, I send my messenger before thy face, which shall prepare thy way before thee.

28 For I say unto you, Among those that [1084] are born of women there is not a greater [3187] prophet than John [1135] the Baptist: but he that [3187] is least [4396] in the [2491] kingdom [910] of God [2316] is greater [3187] than [3398] he. [932]

29 And all the people that heard him, and the publicans, justified [2992] God, [191] being [2316] baptized [907] with the [5057] baptism [1344] of John. [908]

30 But the [908] Pharisees [2491] and lawyers rejected [3544] [114] the counsel [5330] of God against themselves, being [907] not baptized [1012] of him. [2316]

31 And [907] the Lord said, [2962] Whereunto [2036] then [5101] shall I liken the men [3666] [3666] of this [444] generation? and [1074] to what are they like? [5101]

32 They are like [3664] unto children sitting in the market place, and calling [3664] one to [3813] another, and [2521] saying, We [58] have piped [4377] unto [240] you, [4377] [240] and ye have not danced; [832] we have mourned to you, and ye [3738] have not wept. [3738] [2354]

33 For John [2799] the Baptist came [2799] neither eating bread nor [2491] drinking [910] wine; [2064] and ye say, [2068] He hath a devil. [740] [4095] [3631]

34 The [1140] Son of man is come eating and drinking; [5207] and ye say, [444] Behold [2064] a gluttonous [2068] man, [4095] and a winebibber, [2400] a friend of publicans [5314] and sinners! [444] [3630] [5384] [5057]

35 But [268] wisdom is justified of all her chil- [4678] [1344] dren. [5043]

Jesus at the Home of Simon the Pharisee

36 And one of the Pharisees desired him [5100] that he would eat with him. [5330] And he went [5315] into the Pharisee's house, and sat down to [5330] [3614] [1525] [347] meat.

37 And, behold, a woman in the city, which was a sinner, when she knew that Jesus sat at meat in the Pharisee's house, brought an alabaster box of ointment,

38 And stood at his feet behind him weeping, and began to wash his feet with tears, and did wipe them with the hairs of her head, and kissed his feet, and anointed them with the ointment.

39 Now when the Pharisee which had bidden him saw it, he spake within himself, saying, This man, if he were a prophet, would have known who and what manner of woman this is that toucheth him; for she is a sinner.

40 And Jesus answering said unto him, Simon, I have somewhat to say unto thee. And he saith, Master, say on.

41 There was a certain creditor which had two debtors: the one owed five hundred pence, and the other fifty.

42 And when they had nothing to pay, he frankly forgave them both. Tell me therefore, which of them will love him most?

43 Simon answered and said, I suppose that he, to whom he forgave most. And he said unto him, Thou hast rightly judged.

44 And he turned to the woman, and said unto Simon, Seest thou this woman? I entered into thine house, thou gavest me no water for my feet: but she hath washed my feet with tears, and wiped them with the hairs of her head.

45 Thou gavest me no kiss: but this wom-

an, since the time I came in, hath not ceased to kiss my feet.

46 My head with oil thou didst not anoint: but this woman hath anointed my feet with ointment.

47 Wherefore I say unto thee, Her sins, which are many, are forgiven; for she loved much: but to whom little is forgiven, the same loveth little.

48 And he said unto her, Thy sins are forgiven.

49 And they that sat at meat with him began to say within themselves, Who is this that forgiveth sins also?

50 And he said to the woman, Thy faith hath saved thee; go in peace.

Some Women Accompany Jesus

8 And it came to pass afterward, that he went throughout every city and village, preaching and showing the glad tidings of the kingdom of God: and the twelve were with him,

2 And certain women, which had been healed of evil spirits and infirmities, Mary called Magdalene, out of whom went seven devils,

3 And Joanna the wife of Chuza Herod's steward, and Susanna, and many others, which ministered unto him of their substance.

The Parable of the Sower

4 And when much people were gathered together, and were come to him out of every city, he spake by a parable:

5 A sower went out to sow his seed: and
as he sowed, some fell by the wayside; and it
was trodden down, and the fowls of the air
devoured it.

6 And some fell upon a rock; and as soon
as it was sprung up, it withered away, because
it lacked moisture.

7 And some fell among thorns; and the
thorns sprang up with it, and choked it.

8 And other fell on good ground, and
sprang up, and bare fruit a hundredfold. And
when he had said these things, he cried, He
that hath ears to hear, let him hear.

9 And his disciples asked him, saying, What
might this parable be?

10 And he said, Unto you it is given to
know the mysteries of the kingdom of God:
but to others in parables; that seeing they
might not see, and hearing they might not
understand.

11 Now the parable is this: The seed is the
word of God.

12 Those by the wayside are they that hear;
then cometh the devil, and taketh away the
word out of their hearts, lest they should
believe and be saved.

13 They on the rock are they, which, when
they hear, receive the word with joy; and
these have no root, which for a while believe,
and in time of temptation fall away.

14 And that which fell among thorns are they,
which, when they have heard, go forth, and
are choked with cares and riches and pleasures
of this life, and bring no fruit to perfection.

15 But that on the good ground are they, which in an honest and good heart, having heard the word, keep it, and bring forth fruit with patience.

A Light under a Vessel

16 No man, when he hath lighted a candle, covereth it with a vessel, or putteth it under a bed; but setteth it on a candlestick, that they which enter in may see the light. 17 For nothing is secret, that shall not be made manifest; neither any thing hid, that shall not be known and come abroad. 18 Take heed therefore how ye hear: for whosoever hath, to him shall be given; and whosoever hath not, from him shall be taken even that which he seemeth to have.

Jesus' Mother and Brethren

19 Then came to him his mother and his brethren, and could not come at him for the press. 20 And it was told him by certain which said, Thy mother and thy brethren stand without, desiring to see thee. 21 And he answered and said unto them, My mother and my brethren are these which hear the word of God, and do it.

Jesus Calms a Storm

22 Now it came to pass on a certain day, that he went into a ship with his disciples: and he said unto them, Let us go over unto the other side of the lake. And they launched forth.

23 But as they sailed, he fell asleep: and there came down a storm of wind on the lake; and they were filled with water, and were in jeopardy.

24 And they came to him, and awoke him, saying, Master, Master, we perish. Then he arose, and rebuked the wind and the raging of the water: and they ceased, and there was a calm.

25 And he said unto them, Where is your faith? And they being afraid wondered, saying one to another, What manner of man is this! for he commandeth even the winds and water, and they obey him.

The Gadarene Demoniac Healed

26 And they arrived at the country of the Gad'arenes, which is over against Galilee.

27 And when he went forth to land, there met him out of the city a certain man, which had devils long time, and ware no clothes, neither abode in any house, but in the tombs.

28 When he saw Jesus, he cried out, and fell down before him, and with a loud voice said, What have I to do with thee, Jesus, thou Son of God most high? I beseech thee, torment me not.

29 (For he had commanded the unclean spirit to come out of the man. For oftentimes it had caught him: and he was kept bound with chains and in fetters; and he brake the bands, and was driven of the devil into the wilderness.)

30 And Jesus asked him, saying, What is

thy name? And he said, Legion: because many devils were entered into him.

31 And they besought him that he would not command them to go out into the deep.

32 And there was there a herd of many swine feeding on the mountain: and they besought him that he would suffer them to enter into them. And he suffered them.

33 Then went the devils out of the man, and entered into the swine: and the herd ran violently down a steep place into the lake, and were choked.

34 When they that fed them saw what was done, they fled, and went and told it in the city and in the country.

35 Then they went out to see what was done; and came to Jesus, and found the man, out of whom the devils were departed, sitting at the feet of Jesus, clothed, and in his right mind: and they were afraid.

36 They also which saw it told them by what means he that was possessed of the devils was healed.

37 Then the whole multitude of the country of the Gad'arenes round about besought him to depart from them; for they were taken with great fear: and he went up into the ship, and returned back again.

38 Now the man, out of whom the devils were departed, besought him that he might be with him: but Jesus sent him away, saying,

39 Return to thine own house, and show how great things God hath done unto thee. And he went his way, and published through-

out the whole city how great things Jesus had done unto him.

Jairus' Daughter and the Woman Who Touched Jesus' Garment

40 And it came to pass, that, when Jesus was returned, the people gladly received him: for they were all waiting for him.

41 And, behold, there came a man named Jai'rus, and he was a ruler of the synagogue: and he fell down at Jesus' feet, and besought him that he would come into his house:

42 For he had one only daughter, about twelve years of age, and she lay a dying. But as he went the people thronged him.

43 And a woman having an issue of blood twelve years, which had spent all her living upon physicians, neither could be healed of any,

44 Came behind him, and touched the border of his garment: and immediately her issue of blood stanched.

45 And Jesus said, Who touched me? When all denied, Peter and they that were with him said, Master, the multitude throng thee and press thee, and sayest thou, Who touched me?

46 And Jesus said, Somebody hath touched me: for I perceive that virtue is gone out of me.

47 And when the woman saw that she was not hid, she came trembling, and falling down before him, she declared unto him before all the people for what cause she had touched him, and how she was healed immediately.

48 And he said unto her, Daughter, be of good comfort: thy faith hath made thee whole; go in peace.

49 While he yet spake, there cometh one from the ruler of the synagogue's house, saying to him, Thy daughter is dead; trouble not the Master.

50 But when Jesus heard it, he answered him, saying, Fear not: believe only, and she shall be made whole.

51 And when he came into the house, he suffered no man to go in, save Peter, and James, and John, and the father and the mother of the maiden.

52 And all wept, and bewailed her: but he said, Weep not; she is not dead, but sleepeth.

53 And they laughed him to scorn, knowing that she was dead.

54 And he put them all out, and took her by the hand, and called, saying, Maid, arise.

55 And her spirit came again, and she arose straightway: and he commanded to give her meat.

56 And her parents were astonished: but he charged them that they should tell no man what was done.

The Mission of the Twelve

9 Then he called his twelve disciples together, and gave them power and authority over all devils, and to cure diseases.

2 And he sent them to preach the kingdom of God, and to heal the sick.

3 And he said unto them, Take nothing for

your journey, neither staves, nor scrip, neither bread, neither money; neither have two coats apiece.

4 And whatsoever house ye enter into, there abide, and thence depart.

5 And whosoever will not receive you, when ye go out of that city, shake off the very dust from your feet for a testimony against them.

6 And they departed, and went through the towns, preaching the gospel, and healing everywhere.

The Death of John the Baptist

7 Now Herod the tetrarch heard of all that was done by him: and he was perplexed, because that it was said of some, that John was risen from the dead;

8 And of some, that Eli′jah had appeared; and of others, that one of the old prophets was risen again.

9 And Herod said, John have I beheaded; but who is this, of whom I hear such things? And he desired to see him.

The Feeding of the Five Thousand

10 And the apostles, when they were returned, told him all that they had done. And he took them, and went aside privately into a desert place belonging to the city called Bethsai′da.

11 And the people, when they knew it, followed him: and he received them, and spake unto them of the kingdom of God, and healed them that had need of healing.

12 And when the day began to wear away, then came the twelve, and said unto him, Send the multitude away, that they may go into the towns and country round about, and lodge, and get victuals: for we are here in a desert place.

13 But he said unto them, Give ye them to eat. And they said, We have no more but five loaves and two fishes; except we should go and buy meat for all this people.

14 For they were about five thousand men. And he said to his disciples, Make them sit down by fifties in a company.

15 And they did so, and made them all sit down.

16 Then he took the five loaves and the two fishes, and looking up to heaven, he blessed them, and brake, and gave to the disciples to set before the multitude.

17 And they did eat, and were all filled: and there was taken up of fragments that remained to them twelve baskets.

Peter's Declaration

18 And it came to pass, as he was alone praying, his disciples were with him; and he asked them, saying, Whom say the people that I am?

19 They answering said, John the Baptist; but some say, Eli′jah; and others say, that one of the old prophets is risen again.

20 He said unto them, But whom say ye that I am? Peter answering said, The Christ of God.

Jesus Foretells His Death

21 And he straitly charged them, and commanded them to tell no man that thing;

22 Saying, The Son of man must suffer many things, and be rejected of the elders and chief priests and scribes, and be slain, and be raised the third day.

23 And he said to them all, If any man will come after me, let him deny himself, and take up his cross daily, and follow me.

24 For whosoever will save his life shall lose it: but whosoever will lose his life for my sake, the same shall save it.

25 For what is a man advantaged, if he gain the whole world, and lose himself, or be cast away?

26 For whosoever shall be ashamed of me and of my words, of him shall the Son of man be ashamed, when he shall come in his own glory, and in his Father's, and of the holy angels.

27 But I tell you of a truth, there be some standing here, which shall not taste of death, till they see the kingdom of God.

The Transfiguration

28 And it came to pass about an eight days after these sayings, he took Peter and John and James, and went up into a mountain to pray.

29 And as he prayed, the fashion of his countenance was altered, and his raiment was white and glistering.

30 And, behold, there talked with him two men, which were Moses and Eli'jah:

31 Who appeared in glory, and spake of his decease which he should accomplish at Jerusalem.

32 But Peter and they that were with him were heavy with sleep: and when they were awake, they saw his glory, and the two men that stood with him.

33 And it came to pass, as they departed from him, Peter said unto Jesus, Master, it is good for us to be here: and let us make three tabernacles; one for thee, and one for Moses, and one for Eli′jah: not knowing what he said.

34 While he thus spake, there came a cloud, and overshadowed them: and they feared as they entered into the cloud.

35 And there came a voice out of the cloud, saying, This is my beloved Son: hear him.

36 And when the voice was past, Jesus was found alone. And they kept it close, and told no man in those days any of those things which they had seen.

Jesus Heals a Boy with an Unclean Spirit

37 And it came to pass, that on the next day, when they were come down from the hill, much people met him.

38 And, behold, a man of the company cried out, saying, Master, I beseech thee, look upon my son; for he is mine only child.

39 And, lo, a spirit taketh him, and he suddenly crieth out; and it teareth him that he foameth again, and bruising him, hardly departeth from him.

40 And I besought thy disciples to cast him out; and they could not.

41 And Jesus answering said, O faithless and perverse generation, how long shall I be with you, and suffer you? Bring thy son hither.

42 And as he was yet a coming, the devil threw him down, and tare him. And Jesus rebuked the unclean spirit, and healed the child, and delivered him again to his father.

43 And they were all amazed at the mighty power of God.

Jesus Again Foretells His Death

But while they wondered every one at all things which Jesus did, he said unto his disciples,

44 Let these sayings sink down into your ears: for the Son of man shall be delivered into the hands of men.

45 But they understood not this saying, and it was hid from them, that they perceived it not: and they feared to ask him of that saying.

Who Is the Greatest?

46 Then there arose a reasoning among them, which of them should be greatest.

47 And Jesus, perceiving the thought of their heart, took a child, and set him by him,

48 And said unto them, Whosoever shall receive this child in my name receiveth me; and whosoever shall receive me, receiveth him that sent me: for he that is least among you all, the same shall be great.

He That Is Not against Us Is for Us

49 And John answered and said, Master, we saw one casting out devils in thy name; and we forbade him, because he followeth not with us.

50 And Jesus said unto him, Forbid him not: for he that is not against us is for us.

Jesus Rebukes James and John

51 And it came to pass, when the time was come that he should be received up, he stead-fastly set his face to go to Jerusalem,

52 And sent messengers before his face: and they went, and entered into a village of the Samaritans, to make ready for him.

53 And they did not receive him, because his face was as though he would go to Jeru-salem.

54 And when his disciples James and John saw this, they said, Lord, wilt thou that we command fire to come down from heaven, and consume them, even as Eli′jah did?

55 But he turned, and rebuked them, and said, Ye know not what manner of spirit ye are of.

56 For the Son of man is not come to destroy men's lives, but to save them. And they went to another village.

The Would-be Followers of Jesus

57 And it came to pass, that, as they went in the way, a certain man said unto him, Lord, I will follow thee whithersoever thou goest.

58 And Jesus said unto him, Foxes have holes, and birds of the air have nests; but the Son of man hath not where to lay his head.

59 And he said unto another, Follow me. But he said, Lord, suffer me first to go and bury my father.

60 Jesus said unto him, Let the dead bury their dead: but go thou and preach the kingdom of God.

61 And another also said, Lord, I will follow thee; but let me first go bid them farewell, which are at home at my house.

62 And Jesus said unto him, No man, having put his hand to the plow, and looking back, is fit for the kingdom of God.

The Mission of the Seventy

10 After these things the Lord appointed other seventy also, and sent them two and two before his face into every city and place, whither he himself would come.

2 Therefore said he unto them, The harvest truly is great, but the laborers are few: pray ye therefore the Lord of the harvest, that he would send forth laborers into his harvest.

3 Go your ways: behold, I send you forth as lambs among wolves.

4 Carry neither purse, nor scrip, nor shoes: and salute no man by the way.

5 And into whatsoever house ye enter, first say, Peace be to this house.

6 And if the son of peace be there, your peace shall rest upon it: if not, it shall turn to you again.

7 And in the same house remain, eating and drinking such things as they give: for the laborer is worthy of his hire. Go not from house to house.

8 And into whatsoever city ye enter, and they receive you, eat such things as are set before you:

9 And heal the sick that are therein, and say unto them, The kingdom of God is come nigh unto you.

10 But into whatsoever city ye enter, and they receive you not, go your ways out into the streets of the same, and say,

11 Even the very dust of your city, which cleaveth on us, we do wipe off against you: notwithstanding, be ye sure of this, that the kingdom of God is come nigh unto you.

12 But I say unto you, that it shall be more tolerable in that day for Sodom, than for that city.

Woes to Unrepentant Cities

13 Woe unto thee, Chora′zin! woe unto thee, Bethsai′da! for if the mighty works had been done in Tyre and Sidon, which have been done in you, they had a great while ago repented, sitting in sackcloth and ashes.

14 But it shall be more tolerable for Tyre and Sidon at the judgment, than for you.

15 And thou, Caper′na-um, which art ex-alted to heaven, shalt be thrust down to hell.

16 He that heareth you heareth me; and he that despiseth you despiseth me; and he

that despiseth me despiseth him that sent me.

The Return of the Seventy

17 And the seventy returned again with joy, saying, Lord, even the devils are subject unto us through thy name.

18 And he said unto them, I beheld Satan as lightning fall from heaven.

19 Behold, I give unto you power to tread on serpents and scorpions, and over all the power of the enemy; and nothing shall by any means hurt you.

20 Notwithstanding, in this rejoice not, that the spirits are subject unto you; but rather rejoice, because your names are written in heaven.

Jesus Rejoices

21 In that hour Jesus rejoiced in spirit, and said, I thank thee, O Father, Lord of heaven and earth, that thou hast hid these things from the wise and prudent, and hast revealed them unto babes: even so, Father; for so it seemed good in thy sight.

22 All things are delivered to me of my Father: and no man knoweth who the Son is, but the Father; and who the Father is, but the Son, and he to whom the Son will reveal him.

23 And he turned him unto his disciples, and said privately, Blessed are the eyes which see the things that ye see:

24 For I tell you, that many prophets and kings have desired to see those things which ye see, and have not seen them; and to hear

those things which ye hear, and have not
heard them.

The Good Samaritan

25 And, behold, a certain lawyer stood up,
and tempted him, saying, Master, what shall
I do to inherit eternal life?
26 He said unto him, What is written in
the law? how readest thou?
27 And he answering said, Thou shalt love
the Lord thy God with all thy heart, and
with all thy soul, and with all thy strength,
and with all thy mind; and thy neighbor as
thyself.
28 And he said unto him, Thou hast
answered right: this do, and thou shalt
live.
29 But he, willing to justify himself, said
unto Jesus, And who is my neighbor?
30 And Jesus answering said, A certain
man went down from Jerusalem to Jericho,
and fell among thieves, which stripped him of
his raiment, and wounded him, and departed,
leaving him half dead.
31 And by chance there came down a certain priest that way; and when he saw him, he
passed by on the other side.
32 And likewise a Levite, when he was at
the place, came and looked on him, and
passed by on the other side.
33 But a certain Samaritan, as he journeyed,
came where he was; and when he saw him,
he had compassion on him,
34 And went to him, and bound up his

wounds, pouring in oil and wine, and set him on his own beast, and brought him to an inn, and took care of him.

35 And on the morrow when he departed, he took out two pence, and gave them to the host, and said unto him, Take care of him: and whatsoever thou spendest more, when I come again, I will repay thee.

36 Which now of these three, thinkest thou, was neighbor unto him that fell among the thieves?

37 And he said, He that showed mercy on him. Then said Jesus unto him, Go, and do thou likewise.

Jesus Visits Martha and Mary

38 Now it came to pass, as they went, that he entered into a certain village: and a certain woman named Martha received him into her house.

39 And she had a sister called Mary, which also sat at Jesus' feet, and heard his word.

40 But Martha was cumbered about much serving, and came to him, and said, Lord, dost thou not care that my sister hath left me to serve alone? bid her therefore that she help me.

41 And Jesus answered and said unto her, Martha, Martha, thou art careful and troubled about many things:

42 But one thing is needful; and Mary hath chosen that good part, which shall not be taken away from her.

Jesus' Teaching on Prayer

11 And it came to pass, that, as he was praying in a certain place, when he ceased, one of his disciples said unto him, Lord, teach us to pray, as John also taught his disciples.

2 And he said unto them, When ye pray, say, Our Father which art in heaven, Hallowed be thy name. Thy kingdom come. Thy will be done, as in heaven, so in earth.

3 Give us day by day our daily bread.

4 And forgive us our sins; for we also forgive every one that is indebted to us. And lead us not into temptation; but deliver us from evil.

5 And he said unto them, Which of you shall have a friend, and shall go unto him at midnight, and say unto him, Friend, lend me three loaves;

6 For a friend of mine in his journey is come to me, and I have nothing to set before him?

7 And he from within shall answer and say, Trouble me not: the door is now shut, and my children are with me in bed; I cannot rise and give thee.

8 I say unto you, Though he will not rise and give him, because he is his friend, yet because of his importunity he will rise and give him as many as he needeth.

9 And I say unto you, Ask, and it shall be given you; seek, and ye shall find; knock, and it shall be opened unto you.

10 For every one that asketh receiveth; and he that seeketh findeth; and to him that knocketh it shall be opened.

11 If a son shall ask bread of any of you that is a father, will he give him a stone? or if he ask a fish, will he for a fish give him a serpent?

12 Or if he shall ask an egg, will he offer him a scorpion?

13 If ye then, being evil, know how to give good gifts unto your children; how much more shall your heavenly Father give the Holy Spirit to them that ask him?

A Divided House Cannot Stand

14 And he was casting out a devil, and it was dumb. And it came to pass, when the devil was gone out, the dumb spake; and the people wondered.

15 But some of them said, He casteth out devils through Beel'zebub the chief of the devils.

16 And others, tempting him, sought of him a sign from heaven.

17 But he, knowing their thoughts, said unto them, Every kingdom divided against itself is brought to desolation; and a house divided against a house falleth.

18 If Satan also be divided against himself, how shall his kingdom stand? because ye say that I cast out devils through Beel'zebub.

19 And if I by Beel'zebub cast out devils, by whom do your sons cast them out? therefore shall they be your judges.

20 But if I with the finger of God cast out devils, no doubt the kingdom of God is come upon you.

21 When a strong man armed keepeth his palace, his goods are in peace:

22 But when a stronger than he shall come upon him, and overcome him, he taketh from him all his armor wherein he trusted, and divideth his spoils.

23 He that is not with me is against me; and he that gathereth not with me scattereth.

The Return of the Unclean Spirit

24 When the unclean spirit is gone out of a man, he walketh through dry places, seeking rest; and finding none, he saith, I will return unto my house whence I came out.

25 And when he cometh, he findeth it swept and garnished.

26 Then goeth he, and taketh to him seven other spirits more wicked than himself; and they enter in, and dwell there: and the last state of that man is worse than the first.

True Blessedness

27 And it came to pass, as he spake these things, a certain woman of the company lifted up her voice, and said unto him, Blessed is the womb that bare thee, and the paps which thou hast sucked.

28 But he said, Yea, rather, blessed are they that hear the word of God, and keep it.

An Evil Generation Seeks a Sign

29 And when the people were gathered thick together, he began to say, This is an

evil generation: they seek a sign; and there shall no sign be given it, but the sign of Jonah the prophet.

30 For as Jonah was a sign unto the Nin'-evites, so shall also the Son of man be to this generation.

31 The queen of the south shall rise up in the judgment with the men of this genera-tion, and condemn them: for she came from the utmost parts of the earth to hear the wisdom of Solomon; and, behold, a greater than Solomon is here.

32 The men of Nin'eveh shall rise up in the judgment with this generation, and shall con-demn it: for they repented at the preaching of Jonah; and, behold, a greater than Jonah is here.

The Light of the Body

33 No man, when he hath lighted a candle, putteth it in a secret place, neither under a bushel, but on a candlestick, that they which come in may see the light.

34 The light of the body is the eye: therefore when thine eye is single, thy whole body also is full of light; but when thine eye is evil, thy body also is full of dark-ness.

35 Take heed therefore, that the light which is in thee be not darkness.

36 If thy whole body therefore be full of light, having no part dark, the whole shall be full of light, as when the bright shining of a candle doth give thee light.

Jesus Denounces the Pharisees and Lawyers

37 And as he spake, a certain Pharisee besought him to dine with him: and he went in, and sat down to meat.

38 And when the Pharisee saw it, he marveled that he had not first washed before dinner.

39 And the Lord said unto him, Now do ye Pharisees make clean the outside of the cup and the platter; but your inward part is full of ravening and wickedness.

40 Ye fools, did not he, that made that which is without, make that which is within also?

41 But rather give alms of such things as ye have; and, behold, all things are clean unto you.

42 But woe unto you, Pharisees! for ye tithe mint and rue and all manner of herbs, and pass over judgment and the love of God: these ought ye to have done, and not to leave the other undone.

43 Woe unto you, Pharisees! for ye love the uppermost seats in the synagogues, and greetings in the markets.

44 Woe unto you, scribes and Pharisees, hypocrites! for ye are as graves which appear not, and the men that walk over them are not aware of them.

45 Then answered one of the lawyers, and said unto him, Master, thus saying thou reproachest us also.

46 And he said, Woe unto you also, ye lawyers! for ye lade men with burdens

grievous to be borne, and ye yourselves touch [1419] [4379] not the burdens with one of your fingers, [1147]

47 Woe unto you! for ye build the sepul-[3759] [3618] [3419] chres of the prophets, and your fathers killed [4396] [3962] [615] them.

48 Truly ye bear witness that ye allow the [686] [3140] [4909] deeds of your fathers: for they indeed killed [2041] [3962] [615] them, and ye build their sepulchres. [3618] [3419]

49 Therefore also said the wisdom of God, [2036] [4678] [2316] I will send them prophets and apostles, and [649] [4396] [652] some of them they shall slay and persecute: [615] [1559]

50 That the blood of all the prophets, [129] [4396] which was shed from the foundation of the [1632] [2602] world, may be required of this generation; [2889] [1567]

51 From the blood of Abel unto the blood [129] [6] [1074] of Zechari′ah, which perished between the altar [2197] [622] [3342] [2379] and the temple: verily I say unto you, It shall [3624] [3483] be required of this generation. [1567]

52 Woe unto you, lawyers! for ye have [3759] [1074] [3544] [142] taken away the key of knowledge: ye entered [2807] [1108] [1525] not in yourselves, and them that were entering [1525] [1525] in ye hindered. [2967]

53 And as he said these things unto them, the scribes and the Pharisees began to urge [1122] [5330] [756] [1758] him vehemently, and to provoke him to speak [1171] [653] [653] of many things:

54 Laying wait for him, and seeking to [4118] [4119] [1748] [2212] [2340] catch something out of his mouth, that they [4750] might accuse him. [5100] [2723]

A Warning against Hypocrisy

12 In the mean time, when there were [1996] [1996] gathered together an innumerable mul-[3461] titude of people, insomuch that they trode one [3793] [2662] [240]

upon another, he began to say unto his disciples first of all, Beware ye of the leaven of the Pharisees, which is hypocrisy.

2 For there is nothing covered, that shall not be revealed; neither hid, that shall not be known.

3 Therefore, whatsoever ye have spoken in darkness shall be heard in the light; and that which ye have spoken in the ear in closets shall be proclaimed upon the housetops.

Whom to Fear

4 And I say unto you my friends, Be not afraid of them that kill the body, and after that have no more that they can do.

5 But I will forewarn you whom ye shall fear: Fear him, which after he hath killed hath power to cast into hell; yea, I say unto you, Fear him.

6 Are not five sparrows sold for two farthings, and not one of them is forgotten before God?

7 But even the very hairs of your head are all numbered. Fear not therefore: ye are of more value than many sparrows.

Confessing Christ before Men

8 Also I say unto you, Whosoever shall confess me before men, him shall the Son of man also confess before the angels of God:

9 But he that denieth me before men shall be denied before the angels of God.

10 And whosoever shall speak a word against the Son of man, it shall be forgiven

him: but unto him that blasphemeth against the Holy Ghost it shall not be forgiven.

11 And when they bring you unto the synagogues, and unto magistrates, and powers, take ye no thought how or what thing ye shall answer, or what ye shall say:

12 For the Holy Ghost shall teach you in the same hour what ye ought to say.

The Parable of the Rich Fool

13 And one of the company said unto him, Master, speak to my brother, that he divide the inheritance with me.

14 And he said unto him, Man, who made me a judge or a divider over you?

15 And he said unto them, Take heed, and beware of covetousness: for a man's life consisteth not in the abundance of the things which he possesseth.

16 And he spake a parable unto them, saying, The ground of a certain rich man brought forth plentifully:

17 And he thought within himself, saying, What shall I do, because I have no room where to bestow my fruits?

18 And he said, This will I do: I will pull down my barns, and build greater; and there will I bestow all my fruits and my goods.

19 And I will say to my soul, Soul, thou hast much goods laid up for many years; take thine ease, eat, drink, and be merry.

20 But God said unto him, Thou fool, this night thy soul shall be required of thee: then

whose[5101] shall those things be, which thou hast[2090] provided?

21 So is he that layeth up treasure[2343] for himself, and is[4147] not rich[4147] toward God.[2316]

Care and Anxiety

22 And he said unto his disciples, Therefore I say unto you,[2036] Take no thought[3101] for your life,[5590] what[5101] ye shall eat;[3309] neither[3309] for the body,[4983] what[5101] ye shall put on.[1746]

23 The life[5590] is more than[4118-4119] meat,[5160] and the body[4983] is more than raiment.

24 Consider the ravens:[1742] for they neither sow[2657] nor reap;[2876] which[2325] neither have storehouse[5009] nor barn;[596] and God[2316] feedeth[5142] them: how much more[4214] are[3123] ye better[1308] than the fowls?[4071]

25 And which[1308] of you with[5101] taking thought[3309] can add[4369] to his stature[2244] one cubit?[4083]

26 If ye then be not able[1410] to do that thing which is least,[1646] why[3777] take[5101] ye thought[3309] for the rest?[3062]

27 Consider the lilies[2657] how they grow:[2918] they toil not,[2872] they spin[3514] not; and yet I[837] say unto you, that Solomon[4672] in all his glory[1391] was[2749] not[4016] arrayed[4016] like one of these.

28 If then God[2316] so clothe[294] the grass,[5528] which is today[4594] in the field,[68] and tomorrow[839] is cast[906] into the oven;[2823] how much more[4214] will he clothe[3123] you, O ye of little faith?[3640]

29 And seek[2212] not ye what[5101] ye shall eat,[5315] or what ye shall drink,[4095] neither be[3349] ye of doubtful mind.[3349]

30 For all these things[3956] do[1934] the nations[1484] of the world[2889] seek after:[1934] and your Father[3962] knoweth[1492] that ye have need[5535] of these things.

31 But rather seek ye the kingdom of God; and all these things shall be added unto you.

Treasure in Heaven

32 Fear not, little flock; for it is your Father's good pleasure to give you the kingdom.

33 Sell that ye have, and give alms; provide yourselves bags which wax not old, a treasure in the heavens that faileth not, where no thief approacheth, neither moth corrupteth.

34 For where your treasure is, there will your heart be also.

Watchful Servants

35 Let your loins be girded about, and your lights burning;

36 And ye yourselves like unto men that wait for their lord, when he will return from the wedding; that, when he cometh and knocketh, they may open unto him immediately.

37 Blessed are those servants, whom the lord when he cometh shall find watching: verily I say unto you, that he shall gird himself, and make them to sit down to meat, and will come forth and serve them.

38 And if he shall come in the second watch, or come in the third watch, and find them so, blessed are those servants.

39 And this know, that if the goodman of the house had known what hour the thief would come, he would have watched, and not have suffered his house to be broken through.

40 Be ye therefore ready also: for the Son
of man cometh at an hour when ye think
not.

The Unfaithful Servant

41 Then Peter said unto him, Lord, speakest thou this parable unto us, or even to all?

42 And the Lord said, Who then is that
faithful and wise steward, whom his lord shall
make ruler over his household, to give them
their portion of meat in due season?

43 Blessed is that servant, whom his lord
when he cometh shall find so doing.

44 Of a truth I say unto you, that he will
make him ruler over all that he hath.

45 But and if that servant say in his heart,
My lord delayeth his coming; and shall begin
to beat the menservants and maidens, and to
eat and drink, and to be drunken;

46 The lord of that servant will come in a
day when he looketh not for him, and at an
hour when he is not aware, and will cut him
in sunder, and will appoint him his portion
with the unbelievers.

47 And that servant, which knew his lord's
will, and prepared not himself, neither did
according to his will, shall be beaten with
many stripes.

48 But he that knew not, and did commit
things worthy of stripes, shall be beaten with
few stripes. For unto whomsoever much is
given, of him shall be much required; and
to whom men have committed much, of him
they will ask the more.

Jesus the Cause of Division

49 I am come to send fire on the earth; and what will I, if it be already kindled?

50 But I have a baptism to be baptized with; and how am I straitened till it be accomplished!

51 Suppose ye that I am come to give peace on earth? I tell you, Nay; but rather division:

52 For from henceforth there shall be five in one house divided, three against two, and two against three.

53 The father shall be divided against the son, and the son against the father; the mother against the daughter, and the daughter against the mother; the mother-in-law against her daughter-in-law, and the daughter-in-law against her mother-in-law.

Discerning the Times

54 And he said also to the people, When ye see a cloud rise out of the west, straightway ye say, There cometh a shower; and so it is.

55 And when ye see the south wind blow, ye say, There will be heat; and it cometh to pass.

56 Ye hypocrites, ye can discern the face of the sky and of the earth; but how is it that ye do not discern this time?

Agree with Your Adversary

57 Yea, and why even of yourselves judge ye not what is right?

58 When thou goest with thine adversary to the magistrate, as thou art in the way, give diligence that thou mayest be delivered from him; lest he hale thee to the judge, and the judge deliver thee to the officer, and the officer cast thee into prison.

59 I tell thee, thou shalt not depart thence, till thou hast paid the very last mite.

Repent or Perish

13 There were present at that season some that told him of the Galileans, whose blood Pilate had mingled with their sacrifices.

2 And Jesus answering said unto them, Suppose ye that these Galileans were sinners above all the Galileans, because they suffered such things?

3 I tell you, Nay: but, except ye repent, ye shall all likewise perish.

4 Or those eighteen, upon whom the tower in Silo′am fell, and slew them, think ye that they were sinners above all men that dwelt in Jerusalem?

5 I tell you, Nay: but, except ye repent, ye shall all likewise perish.

The Parable of the Barren Fig Tree

6 He spake also this parable; A certain man had a fig tree planted in his vineyard; and he came and sought fruit thereon, and found none.

7 Then said he unto the dresser of his vineyard, Behold, these three years I come

seeking fruit on this fig tree, and find none:
cut it down; why cumbereth it the ground?
8 And he answering said unto him, Lord,
let it alone this year also, till I shall dig about
it, and dung it:

9 And if it bear fruit, well: and if not,
then after that thou shalt cut it down.

A Crippled Woman Healed on the Sabbath

10 And he was teaching in one of the
synagogues on the sabbath.

11 And, behold, there was a woman which
had a spirit of infirmity eighteen years, and
was bowed together, and could in no wise lift
up herself.

12 And when Jesus saw her, he called her
to him, and said unto her, Woman, thou art
loosed from thine infirmity.

13 And he laid his hands on her: and immediately she was made straight, and glorified
God.

14 And the ruler of the synagogue answered
with indignation, because that Jesus had
healed on the sabbath day, and said unto the
people, There are six days in which men
ought to work: in them therefore come and be
healed, and not on the sabbath day.

15 The Lord then answered him, and said,
Thou hypocrite, doth not each one of you on
the sabbath loose his ox or his ass from the
stall, and lead him away to watering?

16 And ought not this woman, being a
daughter of Abraham, whom Satan hath

bound, lo, these eighteen years, be loosed from
this bond on the sabbath day?

17 And when he had said these things, all
his adversaries were ashamed: and all the
people rejoiced for all the glorious things that
were done by him.

The Parable of the Mustard Seed

18 Then said he, Unto what is the kingdom
of God like? and whereunto shall I resemble
it?

19 It is like a grain of mustard seed, which
a man took, and cast into his garden; and it
grew, and waxed a great tree; and the fowls
of the air lodged in the branches of it.

The Parable of the Leaven

20 And again he said, Whereunto shall I
liken the kingdom of God?

21 It is like leaven, which a woman took
and hid in three measures of meal, till the
whole was leavened.

The Narrow Gate

22 And he went through the cities and
villages, teaching, and journeying toward Jerusalem.

23 Then said one unto him, Lord, are there
few that be saved? And he said unto them,

24 Strive to enter in at the strait gate: for
many, I say unto you, will seek to enter in,
and shall not be able.

25 When once the master of the house is
risen up, and hath shut to the door, and ye

begin to stand without, and to knock at the door, saying, Lord, Lord, open unto us; and he shall answer and say unto you, I know you not whence ye are:

26 Then shall ye begin to say, We have eaten and drunk in thy presence, and thou hast taught in our streets.

27 But he shall say, I tell you, I know you not whence ye are; depart from me, all ye workers of iniquity.

28 There shall be weeping and gnashing of teeth, when ye shall see Abraham, and Isaac, and Jacob, and all the prophets, in the kingdom of God, and you yourselves thrust out.

29 And they shall come from the east, and from the west, and from the north, and from the south, and shall sit down in the kingdom of God.

30 And, behold, there are last which shall be first; and there are first which shall be last.

Jesus Laments over Jerusalem

31 The same day there came certain of the Pharisees, saying unto him, Get thee out, and depart hence; for Herod will kill thee.

32 And he said unto them, Go ye, and tell that fox, Behold, I cast out devils, and I do cures today and tomorrow, and the third day I shall be perfected.

33 Nevertheless I must walk today, and tomorrow, and the day following: for it cannot be that a prophet perish out of Jerusalem.

34 O Jerusalem, Jerusalem, which killest

the prophets, and stonest them that are sent unto thee; how often would I have gathered thy children together, as a hen doth gather her brood under her wings, and ye would not!

35 Behold, your house is left unto you desolate: and verily I say unto you, Ye shall not see me, until the time come when ye shall say, Blessed is he that cometh in the name of the Lord.

Jesus Heals the Man Who Had Dropsy

14 And it came to pass, as he went into the house of one of the chief Pharisees to eat bread on the sabbath day, that they watched him.

2 And, behold, there was a certain man before him which had the dropsy.

3 And Jesus answering spake unto the lawyers and Pharisees, saying, Is it lawful to heal on the sabbath day?

4 And they held their peace. And he took him, and healed him, and let him go;

5 And answered them, saying, Which of you shall have an ass or an ox fallen into a pit, and will not straightway pull him out on the sabbath day?

6 And they could not answer him again to these things.

A Lesson to Guests and a Host

7 And he put forth a parable to those which were bidden, when he marked how they chose out the chief rooms; saying unto them,

8 When thou art bidden of any man to a

wedding, sit not down in the highest room; lest a more honorable man than thou be bidden of him;

9 And he that bade thee and him come and say to thee, Give this man place; and thou begin with shame to take the lowest room.

10 But when thou art bidden, go and sit down in the lowest room; that when he that bade thee cometh, he may say unto thee, Friend, go up higher: then shalt thou have worship in the presence of them that sit at meat with thee.

11 For whosoever exalteth himself shall be abased; and he that humbleth himself shall be exalted.

12 Then said he also to him that bade him, When thou makest a dinner or a supper, call not thy friends, nor thy brethren, neither thy kinsmen, nor thy rich neighbors; lest they also bid thee again, and a recompense be made thee.

13 But when thou makest a feast, call the poor, the maimed, the lame, the blind:

14 And thou shalt be blessed; for they cannot recompense thee: for thou shalt be recompensed at the resurrection of the just.

The Parable of the Great Supper

15 And when one of them that sat at meat with him heard these things, he said unto him, Blessed is he that shall eat bread in the kingdom of God.

16 Then said he unto him, A certain man made a great supper, and bade many:

17 And sent his servant at supper time to say to them that were bidden, Come; for all things are now ready.

18 And they all with one consent began to make excuse. The first said unto him, I have bought a piece of ground, and I must needs go and see it: I pray thee have me excused.

19 And another said, I have bought five yoke of oxen, and I go to prove them: I pray thee have me excused.

20 And another said, I have married a wife, and therefore I cannot come.

21 So that servant came, and showed his lord these things. Then the master of the house being angry said to his servant, Go out quickly into the streets and lanes of the city, and bring in hither the poor, and the maimed, and the halt, and the blind.

22 And the servant said, Lord, it is done as thou hast commanded, and yet there is room.

23 And the lord said unto the servant, Go out into the highways and hedges, and compel them to come in, that my house may be filled.

24 For I say unto you, That none of those men which were bidden shall taste of my supper.

The Cost of Discipleship

25 And there went great multitudes with him: and he turned, and said unto them,

26 If any man come to me, and hate not his father, and mother, and wife, and children, and brethren, and sisters, yea, and his own life also, he cannot be my disciple.

27 And whosoever doth not bear his cross, and come after me, cannot be my disciple.

28 For which of you, intending to build a tower, sitteth not down first, and counteth the cost, whether he have sufficient to finish it?

29 Lest haply, after he hath laid the foundation, and is not able to finish it, all that behold it begin to mock him,

30 Saying, This man began to build, and was not able to finish.

31 Or what king, going to make war against another king, sitteth not down first, and consulteth whether he be able with ten thousand to meet him that cometh against him with twenty thousand?

32 Or else, while the other is yet a great way off, he sendeth an ambassage, and desireth conditions of peace.

33 So likewise, whosoever he be of you that forsaketh not all that he hath, he cannot be my disciple.

Tasteless Salt

34 Salt is good: but if the salt have lost his savor, wherewith shall it be seasoned?

35 It is neither fit for the land, nor yet for the dunghill; but men cast it out. He that hath ears to hear, let him hear.

The Parable of the Lost Sheep

15 Then drew near unto him all the publicans and sinners for to hear him.

2 And the Pharisees and scribes murmured,

saying, This man receiveth sinners, and eateth with them.

3 And he spake this parable unto them, saying,

4 What man of you, having a hundred sheep, if he lose one of them, doth not leave the ninety and nine in the wilderness, and go after that which is lost, until he find it?

5 And when he hath found it, he layeth it on his shoulders, rejoicing.

6 And when he cometh home, he calleth together his friends and neighbors, saying unto them, Rejoice with me; for I have found my sheep which was lost.

7 I say unto you, that likewise joy shall be in heaven over one sinner that repenteth, more than over ninety and nine just persons, which need no repentance.

The Parable of the Lost Coin

8 Either what woman having ten pieces of silver, if she lose one piece, doth not light a candle, and sweep the house, and seek diligently till she find it?

9 And when she hath found it, she calleth her friends and her neighbors together, saying, Rejoice with me; for I have found the piece which I had lost.

10 Likewise, I say unto you, there is joy in the presence of the angels of God over one sinner that repenteth.

The Parable of the Lost Son

11 And he said, A certain man had two sons:

12 And the younger of them said to his father, Father, give me the portion of goods that falleth to me. And he divided unto them his living.

13 And not many days after the younger son gathered all together, and took his journey into a far country, and there wasted his substance with riotous living.

14 And when he had spent all, there arose a mighty famine in that land; and he began to be in want.

15 And he went and joined himself to a citizen of that country; and he sent him into his fields to feed swine.

16 And he would fain have filled his belly with the husks that the swine did eat: and no man gave unto him.

17 And when he came to himself, he said, How many hired servants of my father's have bread enough and to spare, and I perish with hunger!

18 I will arise and go to my father, and will say unto him, Father, I have sinned against heaven, and before thee,

19 And am no more worthy to be called thy son: make me as one of thy hired servants.

20 And he arose, and came to his father. But when he was yet a great way off, his father saw him, and had compassion, and ran, and fell on his neck, and kissed him.

21 And the son said unto him, Father, I have sinned against heaven, and in thy sight, and am no more worthy to be called thy son.

22 But the father said to his servants,

Bring forth the best robe, and put it on him; and put a ring on his hand, and shoes on his feet:

23 And bring hither the fatted calf, and kill it; and let us eat, and be merry:

24 For this my son was dead, and is alive again; he was lost, and is found. And they began to be merry.

25 Now his elder son was in the field: and as he came and drew nigh to the house, he heard music and dancing.

26 And he called one of the servants, and asked what these things meant.

27 And he said unto him, Thy brother is come; and thy father hath killed the fatted calf, because he hath received him safe and sound.

28 And he was angry, and would not go in: therefore came his father out, and entreated him.

29 And he answering said to his father, Lo, these many years do I serve thee, neither transgressed I at any time thy commandment; and yet thou never gavest me a kid, that I might make merry with my friends:

30 But as soon as this thy son was come, which hath devoured thy living with harlots, thou hast killed for him the fatted calf.

31 And he said unto him, Son, thou art ever with me, and all that I have is thine.

32 It was meet that we should make merry, and be glad: for this thy brother was dead, and is alive again; and was lost, and is found.

The Parable of the Dishonest Steward

16 And he said also unto his disciples, There was a certain rich man, which had a steward; and the same was accused unto him that he had wasted his goods.

2 And he called him, and said unto him, How is it that I hear this of thee? give an account of thy stewardship; for thou mayest be no longer steward.

3 Then the steward said within himself, What shall I do? for my lord taketh away from me the stewardship: I cannot dig; to beg I am ashamed.

4 I am resolved what to do, that, when I am put out of the stewardship, they may receive me into their houses.

5 So he called every one of his lord's debtors unto him, and said unto the first, How much owest thou unto my lord?

6 And he said, A hundred measures of oil. And he said unto him, Take thy bill, and sit down quickly, and write fifty.

7 Then said he to another, And how much owest thou? And he said, A hundred measures of wheat. And he said unto him, Take thy bill, and write fourscore.

8 And the lord commended the unjust steward, because he had done wisely: for the children of this world are in their generation wiser than the children of light.

9 And I say unto you, Make to yourselves friends of the mammon of unrighteousness; that, when ye fail, they may receive you into everlasting habitations.

10 He that is faithful in that which is least is faithful also in much: and he that is unjust in the least is unjust also in much.

11 If therefore ye have not been faithful in the unrighteous mammon, who will commit to your trust the true riches?

12 And if ye have not been faithful in that which is another man's, who shall give you that which is your own?

13 No servant can serve two masters: for either he will hate the one, and love the other; or else he will hold to the one, and despise the other. Ye cannot serve God and mammon.

14 And the Pharisees also, who were covetous, heard all these things: and they derided him.

15 And he said unto them, Ye are they which justify yourselves before men; but God knoweth your hearts: for that which is highly esteemed among men is abomination in the sight of God.

The Law and the Kingdom of God

16 The law and the prophets were until John: since that time the kingdom of God is preached, and every man presseth into it.

17 And it is easier for heaven and earth to pass, than one tittle of the law to fail.

Jesus' Teaching on Divorce

18 Whosoever putteth away his wife, and marrieth another, committeth adultery: and

whosoever marrieth her that is put away from her husband committeth adultery.

The Rich Man and Lazarus

19 There was a certain rich man, which was clothed in purple and fine linen, and fared sumptuously every day:

20 And there was a certain beggar named Lazarus, which was laid at his gate, full of sores,

21 And desiring to be fed with the crumbs which fell from the rich man's table: moreover the dogs came and licked his sores.

22 And it came to pass, that the beggar died, and was carried by the angels into Abraham's bosom: the rich man also died, and was buried;

23 And in hell he lifted up his eyes, being in torments, and seeth Abraham afar off, and Lazarus in his bosom.

24 And he cried and said, Father Abraham, have mercy on me, and send Lazarus, that he may dip the tip of his finger in water, and cool my tongue; for I am tormented in this flame.

25 But Abraham said, Son, remember that thou in thy lifetime receivedst thy good things, and likewise Lazarus evil things: but now he is comforted, and thou art tormented.

26 And beside all this, between us and you there is a great gulf fixed: so that they which would pass from hence to you cannot; neither can they pass to us, that would come from thence.

27 Then he said, I pray thee therefore,
father, that thou wouldest send him to my
father's house:

28 For I have five brethren; that he may
testify unto them, lest they also come into
this place of torment.

29 Abraham saith unto him, They have
Moses and the prophets; let them hear them.

30 And he said, Nay, father Abraham: but
if one went unto them from the dead, they
will repent.

31 And he said unto him, If they hear not
Moses and the prophets, neither will they be
persuaded, though one rose from the dead.

Causing to Sin

17 Then said he unto the disciples, It is
impossible but that offenses will come:
but woe unto him, through whom they come!

2 It were better for him that a millstone
were hanged about his neck, and he cast into
the sea, than that he should offend one of
these little ones.

3 Take heed to yourselves: If thy brother
trespass against thee, rebuke him; and if he
repent, forgive him.

4 And if he trespass against thee seven
times in a day, and seven times in a day turn
again to thee, saying, I repent; thou shalt
forgive him.

Increase Our Faith

5 And the apostles said unto the Lord,
Increase our faith.

6 And the Lord said, If ye had faith as a grain of mustard seed, ye might say unto this sycamine tree, Be thou plucked up by the root, and be thou planted in the sea; and it should obey you.

The Servant's Duty

7 But which of you, having a servant plowing or feeding cattle, will say unto him by and by, when he is come from the field, Go and sit down to meat?

8 And will not rather say unto him, Make ready wherewith I may sup, and gird thyself, and serve me, till I have eaten and drunken; and afterward thou shalt eat and drink?

9 Doth he thank that servant because he did the things that were commanded him? I trow not.

10 So likewise ye, when ye shall have done all those things which are commanded you, say, We are unprofitable servants: we have done that which was our duty to do.

Jesus Cleanses Ten Lepers

11 And it came to pass, as he went to Jerusalem, that he passed through the midst of Samaria and Galilee.

12 And as he entered into a certain village, there met him ten men that were lepers, which stood afar off:

13 And they lifted up their voices, and said, Jesus, Master, have mercy on us.

14 And when he saw them, he said unto them, Go show yourselves unto the priests.

And it came to pass, that, as they went, they were cleansed.

15 And one of them, when he saw that he was healed, turned back, and with a loud voice glorified God,

16 And fell down on his face at his feet, giving him thanks: and he was a Samaritan.

17 And Jesus answering said, Were there not ten cleansed? but where are the nine?

18 There are not found that returned to give glory to God, save this stranger.

19 And he said unto him, Arise, go thy way: thy faith hath made thee whole.

The Coming of the Kingdom

20 And when he was demanded of the Pharisees, when the kingdom of God should come, he answered them and said, The kingdom of God cometh not with observation:

21 Neither shall they say, Lo here! or, lo there! for, behold, the kingdom of God is within you.

22 And he said unto the disciples, The days will come, when ye shall desire to see one of the days of the Son of man, and ye shall not see it.

23 And they shall say to you, See here; or, see there: go not after them, nor follow them.

24 For as the lightning, that lighteneth out of the one part under heaven, shineth unto the other part under heaven; so shall also the Son of man be in his day.

25 But first must he suffer many things, and be rejected of this generation.

26 And as it was in the days of Noah, so shall it be also in the days of the Son of man.

27 They did eat, they drank, they married wives, they were given in marriage, until the day that Noah entered into the ark, and the flood came, and destroyed them all.

28 Likewise also as it was in the days of Lot; they did eat, they drank, they bought, they sold, they planted, they builded;

29 But the same day that Lot went out of Sodom it rained fire and brimstone from heaven, and destroyed them all.

30 Even thus shall it be in the day when the Son of man is revealed.

31 In that day, he which shall be upon the housetop, and his stuff in the house, let him not come down to take it away: and he that is in the field, let him likewise not return back.

32 Remember Lot's wife.

33 Whosoever shall seek to save his life shall lose it; and whosoever shall lose his life shall preserve it.

34 I tell you, in that night there shall be two men in one bed; the one shall be taken, and the other shall be left.

35 Two women shall be grinding together; the one shall be taken, and the other left.

36 Two men shall be in the field; the one shall be taken, and the other left.

37 And they answered and said unto him, Where, Lord? And he said unto them, Wheresoever the body is, thither will the eagles be gathered together.

The Parable of the Widow and the Judge

18 And he spake a parable unto them to this end, that men ought always to pray, and not to faint;

2 Saying, There was in a city a judge, which feared not God, neither regarded man:

3 And there was a widow in that city; and she came unto him, saying, Avenge me of mine adversary.

4 And he would not for a while: but afterward he said within himself, Though I fear not God, nor regard man;

5 Yet because this widow troubleth me, I will avenge her, lest by her continual coming she weary me.

6 And the Lord said, Hear what the unjust judge saith.

7 And shall not God avenge his own elect, which cry day and night unto him, though he bear long with them?

8 I tell you that he will avenge them speedily. Nevertheless, when the Son of man cometh, shall he find faith on the earth?

The Parable of the Pharisee and the Publican

9 And he spake this parable unto certain which trusted in themselves that they were righteous, and despised others:

10 Two men went up into the temple to pray; the one a Pharisee, and the other a publican.

11 The Pharisee stood and prayed thus with himself, God, I thank thee, that I am

not as other men are, extortioners, unjust, adulterers, or even as this publican.

12 I fast twice in the week, I give tithes of all that I possess.

13 And the publican, standing afar off, would not lift up so much as his eyes unto heaven, but smote upon his breast, saying, God be merciful to me a sinner.

14 I tell you, this man went down to his house justified rather than the other: for every one that exalteth himself shall be abased; and he that humbleth himself shall be exalted.

Jesus Blesses Little Children

15 And they brought unto him also infants, that he would touch them: but when his disciples saw it, they rebuked them.

16 But Jesus called them unto him, and said, Suffer little children to come unto me, and forbid them not: for of such is the kingdom of God.

17 Verily I say unto you, Whosoever shall not receive the kingdom of God as a little child shall in no wise enter therein.

The Rich Young Ruler

18 And a certain ruler asked him, saying, Good Master, what shall I do to inherit eternal life?

19 And Jesus said unto him, Why callest thou me good? none is good, save one, that is, God.

20 Thou knowest the commandments, Do not commit adultery, Do not kill, Do not

steal, Do not bear false witness, Honor thy father and thy mother.

21 And he said, All these have I kept from my youth up.

22 Now when Jesus heard these things, he said unto him, Yet lackest thou one thing: sell all that thou hast, and distribute unto the poor, and thou shalt have treasure in heaven: and come, follow me.

23 And when he heard this, he was very sorrowful: for he was very rich.

24 And when Jesus saw that he was very sorrowful, he said, How hardly shall they that have riches enter into the kingdom of God!

25 For it is easier for a camel to go through a needle's eye, than for a rich man to enter into the kingdom of God.

26 And they that heard it said, Who then can be saved?

27 And he said, The things which are impossible with men are possible with God.

28 Then Peter said, Lo, we have left all, and followed thee.

29 And he said unto them, Verily I say unto you, There is no man that hath left house, or parents, or brethren, or wife, or children, for the kingdom of God's sake,

30 Who shall not receive manifold more in this present time, and in the world to come life everlasting.

Jesus Foretells His Death a Third Time

31 Then he took unto him the twelve, and said unto them, Behold, we go up to Jeru-

salem, and all things that are written by the prophets concerning the 1125 Son of man shall be 4396 5207 444 accomplished. 5055

32 For he shall be delivered unto the 3860 Gentiles, and shall be mocked, and spitefully 1484 1702 5195 entreated, and spitted on:

33 And they shall scourge him, and put 1716 him to death; and the third day he shall rise 3146 3146 615 again. 615 5154 2250 450

34 And they understood none of these things: and this saying was hid from them, 4920 neither knew they the things which were 4487 2928 spoken. 1097

A Blind Beggar Healed near Jericho

35 And it came to pass, that as he was 1096 come nigh unto Jericho, a certain blind man 1448 2410 5100 5185 sat by the wayside begging: 2521 3598 4319

36 And hearing the multitude pass by, he 191 3793 1279 asked what it meant. 4441 5101 1498

37 And they told him, that Jesus of Naza- 518 2424 3480 reth passeth by. 3928

38 And he cried, saying, Jesus, thou Son of 994 2424 5207 David, have mercy on me. 1138 1653

39 And they which went before rebuked 4254 2008 him, that he should hold his peace: but he cried so much the more, Thou Son of David, 2896 4183 3123 4623 5207 1138 have mercy on me. 1653

40 And Jesus stood, and commanded him 2424 2476 2753 to be brought unto him: and when he was 71 1448 1448 come near, he asked him,

41 Saying, What wilt thou that I shall do 5101 2309 4160 unto thee? And he said, Lord, that I may 2036 2962 308 receive my sight. 308

42 And Jesus said unto him, Receive thy
sight: thy faith hath saved thee.

43 And immediately he received his sight,
and followed him, glorifying God: and all the
people, when they saw it, gave praise unto
God.

Jesus and Zaccheus

19 And Jesus entered and passed through
Jericho.

2 And, behold, there was a man named
Zacche′us, which was the chief among the
publicans, and he was rich.

3 And he sought to see Jesus who he was;
and could not for the press, because he was
little of stature.

4 And he ran before, and climbed up into
a sycamore tree to see him; for he was to
pass that way.

5 And when Jesus came to the place, he
looked up, and saw him, and said unto him,
Zacche′us, make haste, and come down; for
today I must abide at thy house.

6 And he made haste, and came down, and
received him joyfully.

7 And when they saw it, they all murmured,
saying, That he was gone to be guest with a
man that is a sinner.

8 And Zacche′us stood, and said unto the
Lord; Behold, Lord, the half of my goods I
give to the poor; and if I have taken any
thing from any man by false accusation, I
restore him fourfold.

9 And Jesus said unto him, This day is

salvation come to this house, forasmuch as he also is a son of Abraham.

10 For the Son of man is come to seek and to save that which was lost.

The Parable of the Ten Pounds

11 And as they heard these things, he added and spake a parable, because he was nigh to Jerusalem, and because they thought that the kingdom of God should immediately appear.

12 He said therefore, A certain nobleman went into a far country to receive for himself a kingdom, and to return.

13 And he called his ten servants, and delivered them ten pounds, and said unto them, Occupy till I come.

14 But his citizens hated him, and sent a message after him, saying, We will not have this man to reign over us.

15 And it came to pass, that when he was returned, having received the kingdom, then he commanded these servants to be called unto him, to whom he had given the money, that he might know how much every man had gained by trading.

16 Then came the first, saying, Lord, thy pound hath gained ten pounds.

17 And he said unto him, Well, thou good servant: because thou hast been faithful in a very little, have thou authority over ten cities.

18 And the second came, saying, Lord, thy pound hath gained five pounds.

19 And he said likewise to him, Be thou also over five cities.

20 And another came, saying, Lord, behold, here is thy pound, which I have kept laid up in a napkin:

21 For I feared thee, because thou art an austere man: thou takest up that thou layedst not down, and reapest that thou didst not sow.

22 And he saith unto him, Out of thine own mouth will I judge thee, thou wicked servant. Thou knewest that I was an austere man, taking up that I laid not down, and reaping that I did not sow:

23 Wherefore then gavest not thou my money into the bank, that at my coming I might have required mine own with usury?

24 And he said unto them that stood by, Take from him the pound, and give it to him that hath ten pounds.

25 (And they said unto him, Lord, he hath ten pounds.)

26 For I say unto you, That unto every one which hath shall be given; and from him that hath not, even that he hath shall be taken away from him.

27 But those mine enemies, which would not that I should reign over them, bring hither, and slay them before me.

The Triumphal Entry into Jerusalem

28 And when he had thus spoken, he went before, ascending up to Jerusalem.

29 And it came to pass, when he was come

nigh to Bethphage and Bethany, at the mount called the mount of Olives, he sent two of his disciples,

30 Saying, Go ye into the village over against you; in the which at your entering ye shall find a colt tied, whereon yet never man sat: loose him, and bring him hither.

31 And if any man ask you, Why do ye loose him? thus shall ye say unto him, Because the Lord hath need of him.

32 And they that were sent went their way, and found even as he had said unto them.

33 And as they were loosing the colt, the owners thereof said unto them, Why loose ye the colt?

34 And they said, The Lord hath need of him.

35 And they brought him to Jesus: and they cast their garments upon the colt, and they set Jesus thereon.

36 And as he went, they spread their clothes in the way.

37 And when he was come nigh, even now at the descent of the mount of Olives, the whole multitude of the disciples began to rejoice and praise God with a loud voice for all the mighty works that they had seen;

38 Saying, Blessed be the King that cometh in the name of the Lord: peace in heaven, and glory in the highest.

39 And some of the Pharisees from among the multitude said unto him, Master, rebuke thy disciples.

40 And he answered and said unto them, I tell you that, if these should hold their peace, the stones would immediately cry out.

41 And when he was come near, he beheld the city, and wept over it,

42 Saying, If thou hadst known, even thou, at least in this thy day, the things which belong unto thy peace! but now they are hid from thine eyes.

43 For the days shall come upon thee, that thine enemies shall cast a trench about thee, and compass thee round, and keep thee in on every side,

44 And shall lay thee even with the ground, and thy children within thee; and they shall not leave in thee one stone upon another; because thou knewest not the time of thy visitation.

The Cleansing of the Temple

45 And he went into the temple, and began to cast out them that sold therein, and them that bought;

46 Saying unto them, It is written, My house is the house of prayer; but ye have made it a den of thieves.

47 And he taught daily in the temple. But the chief priests and the scribes and the chief of the people sought to destroy him,

48 And could not find what they might do: for all the people were very attentive to hear him.

Jesus' Authority Questioned

20 And it came to pass, that on one of those days, as he taught the people in the temple, and preached the gospel, the chief priests and the scribes came upon him with the elders,

2 And spake unto him, saying, Tell us, by what authority doest thou these things? or who is he that gave thee this authority?

3 And he answered and said unto them, I will also ask you one thing; and answer me:

4 The baptism of John, was it from heaven, or of men?

5 And they reasoned with themselves, saying, If we shall say, From heaven; he will say, Why then believed ye him not?

6 But and if we say, Of men; all the people will stone us: for they be persuaded that John was a prophet.

7 And they answered, that they could not tell whence it was.

8 And Jesus said unto them, Neither tell I you by what authority I do these things.

The Parable of the Wicked Husbandmen

9 Then began he to speak to the people this parable; A certain man planted a vineyard, and let it forth to husbandmen, and went into a far country for a long time.

10 And at the season he sent a servant to the husbandmen, that they should give him of the fruit of the vineyard: but the husbandmen beat him, and sent him away empty.

11 And again he sent another servant: and

they beat him also, and entreated him shamefully, and sent him away empty.

12 And again he sent a third: and they wounded him also, and cast him out.

13 Then said the lord of the vineyard, What shall I do? I will send my beloved son: it may be they will reverence him when they see him.

14 But when the husbandmen saw him, they reasoned among themselves, saying, This is the heir: come, let us kill him, that the inheritance may be ours.

15 So they cast him out of the vineyard, and killed him. What therefore shall the lord of the vineyard do unto them?

16 He shall come and destroy these husbandmen, and shall give the vineyard to others. And when they heard it, they said, God forbid.

17 And he beheld them, and said, What is this then that is written, The stone which the builders rejected, the same is become the head of the corner?

18 Whosoever shall fall upon that stone shall be broken; but on whomsoever it shall fall, it will grind him to powder.

Paying Taxes to Caesar

19 And the chief priests and the scribes the same hour sought to lay hands on him; and they feared the people: for they perceived that he had spoken this parable against them.

20 And they watched him, and sent forth

spies, which should feign themselves just men, that they might take hold of his words, that so they might deliver him unto the power and authority of the governor.

21 And they asked him, saying, Master, we know that thou sayest and teachest rightly, neither acceptest thou the person of any, but teachest the way of God truly:

22 Is it lawful for us to give tribute unto Caesar, or no?

23 But he perceived their craftiness, and said unto them, Why tempt ye me?

24 Show me a penny. Whose image and superscription hath it? They answered and said, Caesar's.

25 And he said unto them, Render therefore unto Caesar the things which be Caesar's, and unto God the things which be God's.

26 And they could not take hold of his words before the people: and they marveled at his answer, and held their peace.

The Question about the Resurrection

27 Then came to him certain of the Sadducees, which deny that there is any resurrection; and they asked him,

28 Saying, Master, Moses wrote unto us, If any man's brother die, having a wife, and he die without children, that his brother should take his wife, and raise up seed unto his brother.

29 There were therefore seven brethren: and the first took a wife, and died without children.

30 And the second[1208] took[2983] her to wife,[1135] and he died[599] childless.[815]

31 And the third[5154] took[2983] her; and in like manner the seven[5615] also: and they left[2641] no children,[2033] and died.[5043][599]

32 Last[5305] of all the woman[1135] died[599] also.

33 Therefore in the resurrection[386] whose[5101] wife[1135] of them is she? for seven[2033] had her to wife.[1135]

34 And[1096] Jesus answering said[2036] unto them, The children[2424] of this world[165] marry,[1060] and are given[5207] in marriage:[1548]

35 But they which[1548] shall be accounted[2661] worthy to obtain[5177] that world,[165] and the resurrection[386] from the dead,[3498] neither[3777] marry,[1060] nor[3777] are given[1548] in marriage:[1548]

36 Neither[3777] can they[1410] die[599] any more:[2089] for they are equal[2465] unto the angels;[2465] and are the children[5207] of God,[2316] being[5607] the children[5207] of the resurrection.[386]

37 Now that the dead[3498] are raised,[1453] even Moses[3475] showed[3377] at the bush,[942] when he calleth the Lord[2962] the God[2316] of Abraham,[11] and the God[2316] of Isaac,[2464] and the God[2316] of Jacob.[2384]

38 For he is not a God[2316] of the dead,[3498] but of the living:[2198] for all live[2198] unto him.

39 Then certain[5100] of the scribes[1122] answering said,[2036] Master,[1320] thou hast well[2573] said.[2036]

40 And after that they durst[5111] not ask[1905] him any question[2089] at all.

The Question about David's Son

41 And he said[2036] unto them, How say they that Christ[5547] is David's[1138] son?[5207]

42 And David[1138] himself saith in the book[976] of

Psalms, The LORD said unto my Lord, Sit thou on my right hand,

43 Till I make thine enemies thy footstool.

44 David therefore calleth him Lord, how is he then his son?

Jesus Denounces the Scribes

45 Then in the audience of all the people he said unto his disciples,

46 Beware of the scribes, which desire to walk in long robes, and love greetings in the markets, and the highest seats in the synagogues, and the chief rooms at feasts;

47 Which devour widows' houses, and for a show make long prayers: the same shall receive greater damnation.

The Widow's Offering

21 And he looked up, and saw the rich men casting their gifts into the treasury.

2 And he saw also a certain poor widow casting in thither two mites.

3 And he said, Of a truth I say unto you, that this poor widow hath cast in more than they all:

4 For all these have of their abundance cast in unto the offerings of God: but she of her penury hath cast in all the living that she had.

The Destruction of the Temple and Signs before the End

5 And as some spake of the temple, how it was adorned with goodly stones and gifts, he said,

6 As for these things which ye behold, the days will come, in the which there shall not be left one stone upon another, that shall not be thrown down.

7 And they asked him, saying, Master, but when shall these things be? and what sign will there be when these things shall come to pass?

8 And he said, Take heed that ye be not deceived: for many shall come in my name, saying, I am Christ; and the time draweth near: go ye not therefore after them.

9 But when ye shall hear of wars and commotions, be not terrified: for these things must first come to pass; but the end is not by and by.

10 Then said he unto them, Nation shall rise against nation, and kingdom against kingdom:

11 And great earthquakes shall be in divers places, and famines, and pestilences; and fearful sights and great signs shall there be from heaven.

12 But before all these, they shall lay their hands on you, and persecute you, delivering you up to the synagogues, and into prisons, being brought before kings and rulers for my name's sake.

13 And it shall turn to you for a testimony.

14 Settle it therefore in your hearts, not to meditate before what ye shall answer:

15 For I will give you a mouth and wisdom, which all your adversaries shall not be able to gainsay nor resist.

16 And ye shall be betrayed both by parents, and brethren, and kinsfolk, and friends; and some of you shall they cause to be put to death.

17 And ye shall be hated of all men for my name's sake.

18 But there shall not a hair of your head perish.

19 In your patience possess ye your souls.

20 And when ye shall see Jerusalem compassed with armies, then know that the desolation thereof is nigh.

21 Then let them which are in Judea flee to the mountains; and let them which are in the midst of it depart out; and let not them that are in the countries enter thereinto.

22 For these be the days of vengeance, that all things which are written may be fulfilled.

23 But woe unto them that are with child, and to them that give suck, in those days! for there shall be great distress in the land, and wrath upon this people.

24 And they shall fall by the edge of the sword, and shall be led away captive into all nations: and Jerusalem shall be trodden down of the Gentiles, until the times of the Gentiles be fulfilled.

The Coming of the Son of Man

25 And there shall be signs in the sun, and in the moon, and in the stars; and upon the earth distress of nations, with perplexity; the sea and the waves roaring;

26 Men's hearts failing them for fear, and

for looking after those things which are coming on the earth: for the powers of heaven shall be shaken.

27 And then shall they see the Son of man coming in a cloud with power and great glory.

28 And when these things begin to come to pass, then look up, and lift up your heads; for your redemption draweth nigh.

29 And he spake to them a parable; Behold the fig tree, and all the trees;

30 When they now shoot forth, ye see and know of your own selves that summer is now nigh at hand.

31 So likewise ye, when ye see these things come to pass, know ye that the kingdom of God is nigh at hand.

32 Verily I say unto you, This generation shall not pass away, till all be fulfilled.

33 Heaven and earth shall pass away: but my words shall not pass away.

34 And take heed to yourselves, lest at any time your hearts be overcharged with surfeiting, and drunkenness, and cares of this life, and so that day come upon you unawares.

35 For as a snare shall it come on all them that dwell on the face of the whole earth.

36 Watch ye therefore, and pray always, that ye may be accounted worthy to escape all these things that shall come to pass, and to stand before the Son of man.

37 And in the daytime he was teaching in the temple; and at night he went out, and abode in the mount that is called the mount of Olives.

38 And all the people came early in the morning to him in the temple, for to hear him.

The Plot against Jesus

22 Now the feast of unleavened bread drew nigh, which is called the passover.

2 And the chief priests and scribes sought how they might kill him; for they feared the people.

3 Then entered Satan into Judas surnamed Iscar′i-ot, being of the number of the twelve.

4 And he went his way, and communed with the chief priests and captains, how he might betray him unto them.

5 And they were glad, and covenanted to give him money.

6 And he promised, and sought opportunity to betray him unto them in the absence of the multitude.

Jesus Eats the Passover with His Disciples

7 Then came the day of unleavened bread, when the passover must be killed.

8 And he sent Peter and John, saying, Go and prepare us the passover, that we may eat.

9 And they said unto him, Where wilt thou that we prepare?

10 And he said unto them, Behold, when ye are entered into the city, there shall a man meet you, bearing a pitcher of water; follow him into the house where he entereth in.

11 And ye shall say unto the goodman of

the house, The Master saith unto thee, Where is the guest chamber, where I shall eat the passover with my disciples?

12 And he shall show you a large upper room furnished: there make ready.

13 And they went, and found as he had said unto them: and they made ready the passover.

14 And when the hour was come, he sat down, and the twelve apostles with him.

15 And he said unto them, With desire I have desired to eat this passover with you before I suffer:

16 For I say unto you, I will not any more eat thereof, until it be fulfilled in the kingdom of God.

17 And he took the cup, and gave thanks, and said, Take this, and divide it among yourselves:

18 For I say unto you, I will not drink of the fruit of the vine, until the kingdom of God shall come.

19 And he took bread, and gave thanks, and brake it, and gave unto them, saying, This is my body which is given for you: this do in remembrance of me.

20 Likewise also the cup after supper, saying, This cup is the new testament in my blood, which is shed for you.

21 But, behold, the hand of him that betrayeth me is with me on the table.

22 And truly the Son of man goeth, as it was determined: but woe unto that man by whom he is betrayed!

23 And they began to inquire among themselves, which of them it was that should do this thing.

The Dispute about Greatness

24 And there was also a strife among them, which of them should be accounted the greatest.

25 And he said unto them, The kings of the Gentiles exercise lordship over them; and they that exercise authority upon them are called benefactors.

26 But ye shall not be so: but he that is greatest among you, let him be as the younger; and he that is chief, as he that doth serve.

27 For whether is greater, he that sitteth at meat, or he that serveth? is not he that sitteth at meat? but I am among you as he that serveth.

28 Ye are they which have continued with me in my temptations.

29 And I appoint unto you a kingdom, as my Father hath appointed unto me;

30 That ye may eat and drink at my table in my kingdom, and sit on thrones judging the twelve tribes of Israel.

Peter's Denial Foretold

31 And the Lord said, Simon, Simon, behold, Satan hath desired to have you, that he may sift you as wheat:

32 But I have prayed for thee, that thy faith fail not: and when thou art converted, strengthen thy brethren.

33 And he said unto him, Lord, I am ready
to go with thee, both into prison, and to
death.

34 And he said, I tell thee, Peter, the cock
shall not crow this day, before that thou shalt
thrice deny that thou knowest me.

Purse, Scrip, and Sword

35 And he said unto them, When I sent
you without purse, and scrip, and shoes,
lacked ye any thing? And they said, Nothing.

36 Then said he unto them, But now, he
that hath a purse, let him take it, and likewise
his scrip: and he that hath no sword, let him
sell his garment, and buy one.

37 For I say unto you, that this that is
written must yet be accomplished in me, And
he was reckoned among the transgressors: for
the things concerning me have an end.

38 And they said, Lord, behold, here are
two swords. And he said unto them, It is
enough.

Jesus Prays in the Garden

39 And he came out, and went, as he was
wont, to the mount of Olives; and his disciples also followed him.

40 And when he was at the place, he said
unto them, Pray that ye enter not into temptation.

41 And he was withdrawn from them about
a stone's cast, and kneeled down, and prayed,

42 Saying, Father, if thou be willing, re-

move this cup from me: nevertheless, not my will, but thine, be done.

43 And there appeared an angel unto him from heaven, strengthening him.

44 And being in an agony he prayed more earnestly: and his sweat was as it were great drops of blood falling down to the ground.

45 And when he rose up from prayer, and was come to his disciples, he found them sleeping for sorrow,

46 And said unto them, Why sleep ye? rise and pray, lest ye enter into temptation.

The Betrayal and Arrest of Jesus

47 And while he yet spake, behold a multitude, and he that was called Judas, one of the twelve, went before them, and drew near unto Jesus to kiss him.

48 But Jesus said unto him, Judas, betrayest thou the Son of man with a kiss?

49 When they which were about him saw what would follow, they said unto him, Lord, shall we smite with the sword?

50 And one of them smote the servant of the high priest, and cut off his right ear.

51 And Jesus answered and said, Suffer ye thus far. And he touched his ear, and healed him.

52 Then Jesus said unto the chief priests, and captains of the temple, and the elders, which were come to him, Be ye come out, as against a thief, with swords and staves?

53 When I was daily with you in the temple, ye stretched forth no hands against me:

but this is your hour,[5610] and the power[1849] of darkness.[4655]

Peter Denies Jesus

54 Then took[4815] they him, and led[4815] him,[71] and brought[1521] him into[1521] the high priest's[749] house.[3624] And Peter[4074] followed[190] afar off.[3113]

55 And when they had kindled[681] a fire in the midst[3319] of the hall,[833] and were[4776] set down[4442] together, Peter[4074] sat down[2521] among them.[3319]

56 But a certain maid[5100] beheld[3814] him[1492] as he sat[2521] by the fire,[2521] and earnestly[5457] looked[1492] upon[816] him, and said,[816] This[2036] man was also with him.

57 And he denied[720] him, saying, Woman,[1135] I know him not.

58 And[1492] after a little[1024] while another[2087] saw[1492] him, and said,[1492] Thou[5346] art also of them. And Peter[4074] said, Man,[2036] I am not.[444]

59 And about the space of one hour[5610] after another[243] confidently[5100] affirmed,[1340] saying,[1339] Of a truth this fellow also was with him; for he is[225] a Galilean.[1057]

60 And Peter[4074] said, Man,[2036] I[444] know[1492] not what thou sayest. And immediately,[3916] while he yet[2089] spake,[2980] the cock[220] crew.[5455]

61 And the Lord[2962] turned,[4762] and looked[1689] upon Peter. And Peter[4074] remembered[5279] the word[3056] of the Lord,[2962] how he had said unto him, Before the cock[220] crow,[5455] thou shalt[533] deny me thrice.[5151]

62 And Peter[4074] went out,[1831][1854] and wept[2799] bitterly.[4090]

Jesus Mocked and Beaten

63 And the men that held[4912] Jesus[2424] mocked[1702] him, and smote[1194] him.

64 And when they had blindfolded him, they struck him on the face, and asked him, saying, Prophesy, who is it that smote thee?

65 And many other things blasphemously spake they against him.

Jesus before the Council

66 And as soon as it was day, the elders of the people and the chief priests and the scribes came together, and led him into their council, saying,

67 Art thou the Christ? tell us. And he said unto them, If I tell you, ye will not believe:

68 And if I also ask you, ye will not answer me, nor let me go.

69 Hereafter shall the Son of man sit on the right hand of the power of God.

70 Then said they all, Art thou then the Son of God? And he said unto them, Ye say that I am.

71 And they said, What need we any further witness? for we ourselves have heard of his own mouth.

Jesus before Pilate

23 And the whole multitude of them arose, and led him unto Pilate.

2 And they began to accuse him, saying, We found this fellow perverting the nation, and forbidding to give tribute to Caesar, saying that he himself is Christ a king.

3 And Pilate asked him, saying, Art thou the King of the Jews? And he answered him and said, Thou sayest it.

4 Then said Pilate to the chief priests and to the people, I find no fault in this man.

5 And they were the more fierce, saying, He stirreth up the people, teaching throughout all Jewry, beginning from Galilee to this place.

Jesus before Herod

6 When Pilate heard of Galilee, he asked whether the man were a Galilean.

7 And as soon as he knew that he belonged unto Herod's jurisdiction, he sent him to Herod, who himself also was at Jerusalem at that time.

8 And when Herod saw Jesus, he was exceeding glad: for he was desirous to see him of a long season, because he had heard many things of him; and he hoped to have seen some miracle done by him.

9 Then he questioned with him in many words; but he answered him nothing.

10 And the chief priests and scribes stood and vehemently accused him.

11 And Herod with his men of war set him at nought, and mocked him, and arrayed him in a gorgeous robe, and sent him again to Pilate.

12 And the same day Pilate and Herod were made friends together; for before they were at enmity between themselves.

Jesus Sentenced to Die

13 And Pilate, when he had called together the chief priests and the rulers and the people,

14 Said unto them, Ye have brought this

man unto me, as one that perverteth the
people; and, behold, I, having examined him
before you, have found no fault in this man
touching those things whereof ye accuse him:

15 No, nor yet Herod: for I sent you to
him; and, lo, nothing worthy of death is done
unto him.

16 I will therefore chastise him, and release
him.

17 (For of necessity he must release one
unto them at the feast.)

18 And they cried out all at once, saying,
Away with this man, and release unto us
Barab'bas:

19 (Who for a certain sedition made in the
city, and for murder, was cast into prison.)

20 Pilate therefore, willing to release Jesus,
spake again to them.

21 But they cried, saying, Crucify him,
crucify him.

22 And he said unto them the third time,
Why, what evil hath he done? I have found
no cause of death in him: I will therefore
chastise him, and let him go.

23 And they were instant with loud voices,
requiring that he might be crucified: and the
voices of them and of the chief priests prevailed.

24 And Pilate gave sentence that it should
be as they required.

25 And he released unto them him that for
sedition and murder was cast into prison,
whom they had desired; but he delivered
Jesus to their will.

The Crucifixion

26 And as they led him away, they laid hold upon one Simon, a Cyre'nian, coming out of the country, and on him they laid the cross, that he might bear it after Jesus.

27 And there followed him a great company of people, and of women, which also bewailed and lamented him.

28 But Jesus turning unto them said, Daughters of Jerusalem, weep not for me, but weep for yourselves, and for your children.

29 For, behold, the days are coming, in the which they shall say, Blessed are the barren, and the wombs that never bare, and the paps which never gave suck.

30 Then shall they begin to say to the mountains, Fall on us; and to the hills, Cover us.

31 For if they do these things in a green tree, what shall be done in the dry?

32 And there were also two others, malefactors, led with him to be put to death.

33 And when they were come to the place, which is called Calvary, there they crucified him, and the malefactors, one on the right hand, and the other on the left.

34 Then said Jesus, Father, forgive them; for they know not what they do. And they parted his raiment, and cast lots.

35 And the people stood beholding. And the rulers also with them derided him, saying, He saved others; let him save himself, if he be Christ, the chosen of God.

36 And the soldiers also mocked him, coming to him, and offering him vinegar,

37 And saying, If thou be the King of the Jews, save thyself.

38 And a superscription also was written over him in letters of Greek, and Latin, and Hebrew, THIS IS THE KING OF THE JEWS.

39 And one of the malefactors which were hanged railed on him, saying, If thou be Christ, save thyself and us.

40 But the other answering rebuked him, saying, Dost not thou fear God, seeing thou art in the same condemnation?

41 And we indeed justly; for we receive the due reward of our deeds: but this man hath done nothing amiss.

42 And he said unto Jesus, Lord, remember me when thou comest into thy kingdom.

43 And Jesus said unto him, Verily I say unto thee, Today shalt thou be with me in paradise.

44 And it was about the sixth hour, and there was a darkness over all the earth until the ninth hour.

45 And the sun was darkened, and the veil of the temple was rent in the midst.

46 And when Jesus had cried with a loud voice, he said, Father, into thy hands I commend my spirit: and having said thus, he gave up the ghost.

47 Now when the centurion saw what was done, he glorified God, saying, Certainly this was a righteous man.

48 And all the people that came together to

that sight, beholding the things which were done, smote their breasts, and returned.

49 And all his acquaintance, and the women that followed him from Galilee, stood afar off, beholding these things.

The Burial of Jesus

50 And, behold, there was a man named Joseph, a counselor; and he was a good man, and a just:

51 (The same had not consented to the counsel and deed of them:) he was of Arimathe'a, a city of the Jews; who also himself waited for the kingdom of God.

52 This man went unto Pilate, and begged the body of Jesus.

53 And he took it down, and wrapped it in linen, and laid it in a sepulchre that was hewn in stone, wherein never man before was laid.

54 And that day was the preparation, and the sabbath drew on.

55 And the women also, which came with him from Galilee, followed after, and beheld the sepulchre, and how his body was laid.

56 And they returned, and prepared spices and ointments; and rested the sabbath day according to the commandment.

The Resurrection

24 Now upon the first day of the week, very early in the morning, they came unto the sepulchre, bringing the spices which they had prepared, and certain others with them.

2 And they found the stone rolled away from the sepulchre.

3 And they entered in, and found not the body of the Lord Jesus.

4 And it came to pass, as they were much perplexed thereabout, behold, two men stood by them in shining garments:

5 And as they were afraid, and bowed down their faces to the earth, they said unto them, Why seek ye the living among the dead?

6 He is not here, but is risen: remember how he spake unto you when he was yet in Galilee,

7 Saying, The Son of man must be delivered into the hands of sinful men, and be crucified, and the third day rise again.

8 And they remembered his words,

9 And returned from the sepulchre, and told all these things unto the eleven, and to all the rest.

10 It was Mary Mag'dalene, and Joanna, and Mary the mother of James, and other women that were with them, which told these things unto the apostles.

11 And their words seemed to them as idle tales, and they believed them not.

12 Then arose Peter, and ran unto the sepulchre; and stooping down, he beheld the linen clothes laid by themselves, and departed, wondering in himself at that which was come to pass.

The Walk to Emmaus

13 And, behold, two of them went that same day to a village called Emma'us, which

was from Jerusalem about threescore furlongs.

14 And they talked together of all these things which had happened.

15 And it came to pass, that, while they communed together and reasoned, Jesus himself drew near, and went with them.

16 But their eyes were holden that they should not know him.

17 And he said unto them, What manner of communications are these that ye have one to another, as ye walk, and are sad?

18 And the one of them, whose name was Cle′opas, answering said unto him, Art thou only a stranger in Jerusalem, and hast not known the things which are come to pass there in these days?

19 And he said unto them, What things? And they said unto him, Concerning Jesus of Nazareth, which was a prophet mighty in deed and word before God and all the people:

20 And how the chief priests and our rulers delivered him to be condemned to death, and have crucified him.

21 But we trusted that it had been he which should have redeemed Israel: and beside all this, today is the third day since these things were done.

22 Yea, and certain women also of our company made us astonished, which were early at the sepulchre;

23 And when they found not his body, they came, saying, that they had also seen a vision of angels, which said that he was alive.

24 And certain of them which were with

us went to the sepulchre, and found it even so as the women had said: but him they saw not.

25 Then he said unto them, O fools, and slow of heart to believe all that the prophets have spoken:

26 Ought not Christ to have suffered these things, and to enter into his glory?

27 And beginning at Moses and all the prophets, he expounded unto them in all the Scriptures the things concerning himself.

28 And they drew nigh unto the village, whither they went: and he made as though he would have gone further.

29 But they constrained him, saying, Abide with us; for it is toward evening, and the day is far spent. And he went in to tarry with them.

30 And it came to pass, as he sat at meat with them, he took bread, and blessed it, and brake, and gave to them.

31 And their eyes were opened, and they knew him; and he vanished out of their sight.

32 And they said one to another, Did not our heart burn within us, while he talked with us by the way, and while he opened to us the Scriptures?

33 And they rose up the same hour, and returned to Jerusalem, and found the eleven gathered together, and them that were with them,

34 Saying, The Lord is risen indeed, and hath appeared to Simon.

35 And they told what things were done in

the way, and how he was known of them in
breaking of bread.

Jesus Appears to His Disciples

36 And as they thus spake, Jesus himself
stood in the midst of them, and saith unto
them, Peace be unto you.

37 But they were terrified and affrighted,
and supposed that they had seen a spirit.

38 And he said unto them, Why are ye
troubled? and why do thoughts arise in your
hearts?

39 Behold my hands and my feet, that it is
I myself: handle me, and see; for a spirit
hath not flesh and bones, as ye see me have.

40 And when he had thus spoken, he
showed them his hands and his feet.

41 And while they yet believed not for
joy, and wondered, he said unto them, Have
ye here any meat?

42 And they gave him a piece of a broiled
fish, and of a honeycomb.

43 And he took it, and did eat before them.

44 And he said unto them, These are the
words which I spake unto you, while I was
yet with you, that all things must be fulfilled,
which were written in the law of Moses, and
in the prophets, and in the psalms, concerning
me.

45 Then opened he their understanding,
that they might understand the Scriptures,

46 And said unto them, Thus it is written,
and thus it behooved Christ to suffer, and to
rise from the dead the third day:

47 And that repentance and remission of sins should be preached in his name among all nations, beginning at Jerusalem.

48 And ye are witnesses of these things.

49 And, behold, I send the promise of my Father upon you: but tarry ye in the city of Jerusalem, until ye be endued with power from on high.

The Ascension

50 And he led them out as far as to Bethany, and he lifted up his hands, and blessed them.

51 And it came to pass, while he blessed them, he was parted from them, and carried up into heaven.

52 And they worshipped him, and returned to Jerusalem with great joy:

53 And were continually in the temple, praising and blessing God. Amen.

THE GOSPEL ACCORDING TO
ST. JOHN

The Word Made Flesh

1 In the beginning was the Word, and the Word was with God, and the Word was God.

2 The same was in the beginning with God.

3 All things were made by him; and without him was not any thing made that was made.

4 In him was life; and the life was the light of men.

5 And the light shineth in darkness; and the darkness comprehended it not.

6 There was a man sent from God, whose name was John.

7 The same came for a witness, to bear witness of the Light, that all men through him might believe.

8 He was not that Light, but was sent to bear witness of that Light.

9 That was the true Light, which lighteth every man that cometh into the world.

10 He was in the world, and the world was made by him, and the world knew him not.

11 He came unto his own, and his own received him not.

12 But as many as received him, to them gave he power to become the sons of God, even to them that believe on his name:

13 Which were born, not of blood, nor of

the will of the flesh, nor of the will of man, but of God.

14 And the Word was made flesh, and dwelt among us, (and we beheld his glory, the glory as of the only begotten of the Father,) full of grace and truth.

15 John bare witness of him, and cried, saying, This was he of whom I spake, He that cometh after me is preferred before me; for he was before me.

16 And of his fulness have all we received, and grace for grace.

17 For the law was given by Moses, but grace and truth came by Jesus Christ.

18 No man hath seen God at any time; the only begotten Son, which is in the bosom of the Father, he hath declared him.

The Testimony of John the Baptist

19 And this is the record of John, when the Jews sent priests and Levites from Jerusalem to ask him, Who art thou?

20 And he confessed, and denied not; but confessed, I am not the Christ.

21 And they asked him, What then? Art thou Eli′jah? And he saith, I am not. Art thou that Prophet? And he answered, No.

22 Then said they unto him, Who art thou? that we may give an answer to them that sent us. What sayest thou of thyself?

23 He said, I am the voice of one crying in the wilderness, Make straight the way of the Lord, as said the prophet Isaiah.

24 And they which were sent were of the Pharisees.

25 And they asked him, and said unto him, Why baptizest thou then, if thou be not that Christ, nor Eli'jah, neither that Prophet?

26 John answered them, saying, I baptize with water: but there standeth one among you, whom ye know not;

27 He it is, who coming after me is preferred before me, whose shoe-latchet I am not worthy to unloose.

28 These things were done in Bethab'ara beyond Jordan, where John was baptizing.

Behold the Lamb of God

29 The next day John seeth Jesus coming unto him, and saith, Behold the Lamb of God, which taketh away the sin of the world!

30 This is he of whom I said, After me cometh a man which is preferred before me; for he was before me.

31 And I knew him not: but that he should be made manifest to Israel, therefore am I come baptizing with water.

32 And John bare record, saying, I saw the Spirit descending from heaven like a dove, and it abode upon him.

33 And I knew him not: but he that sent me to baptize with water, the same said unto me, Upon whom thou shalt see the Spirit descending, and remaining on him, the same is he which baptizeth with the Holy Ghost.

34 And I saw, and bare record that this is the Son of God.

The First Disciples

35 Again the next day after, John stood, and
two of his disciples;

36 And looking upon Jesus as he walked,
he saith, Behold the Lamb of God!

37 And the two disciples heard him speak,
and they followed Jesus.

38 Then Jesus turned, and saw them following, and saith unto them, What seek ye?
They said unto him, Rabbi, (which is to say,
being interpreted, Master,) where dwellest
thou?

39 He saith unto them, Come and see. They
came and saw where he dwelt, and abode
with him that day: for it was about the tenth
hour.

40 One of the two which heard John speak,
and followed him, was Andrew, Simon Peter's
brother.

41 He first findeth his own brother Simon,
and saith unto him, We have found the
Messiah, which is, being interpreted, the
Christ.

42 And he brought him to Jesus. And when
Jesus beheld him, he said, Thou art Simon the
son of Jona: thou shalt be called Cephas,
which is by interpretation, A stone.

The Call of Philip and Nathanael

43 The day following Jesus would go forth
into Galilee, and findeth Philip, and saith
unto him, Follow me.

44 Now Philip was of Bethsai'da, the city of
Andrew and Peter.

45 Philip findeth Nathan'a-el, and saith unto him, We have found him, of whom Moses in the law, and the prophets, did write, Jesus of Nazareth, the son of Joseph.

46 And Nathan'a-el said unto him, Can there any good thing come out of Nazareth? Philip saith unto him, Come and see.

47 Jesus saw Nathan'a-el coming to him, and saith of him, Behold an Israelite indeed, in whom is no guile!

48 Nathan'a-el saith unto him, Whence knowest thou me? Jesus answered and said unto him, Before that Philip called thee, when thou wast under the fig tree, I saw thee.

49 Nathan'a-el answered and saith unto him, Rabbi, thou art the Son of God; thou art the King of Israel.

50 Jesus answered and said unto him, Because I said unto thee, I saw thee under the fig tree, believest thou? thou shalt see greater things than these.

51 And he saith unto him, Verily, verily, I say unto you, Hereafter ye shall see heaven open, and the angels of God ascending and descending upon the Son of man.

The Wedding at Cana

2 And the third day there was a marriage in Cana of Galilee; and the mother of Jesus was there:

2 And both Jesus was called, and his disciples, to the marriage.

3 And when they wanted wine, the mother of Jesus saith unto him, They have no wine.

4 Jesus saith unto her, Woman, what have I
to do with thee? mine hour is not yet come.

5 His mother saith unto the servants, Whatsoever he saith unto you, do it.

6 And there were set there six waterpots of
stone, after the manner of the purifying of the
Jews, containing two or three firkins apiece.

7 Jesus saith unto them, Fill the waterpots
with water. And they filled them up to the
brim.

8 And he saith unto them, Draw out now,
and bear unto the governor of the feast. And
they bare it.

9 When the ruler of the feast had tasted
the water that was made wine, and knew not
whence it was, (but the servants which drew
the water knew,) the governor of the feast
called the bridegroom,

10 And saith unto him, Every man at the
beginning doth set forth good wine; and when
men have well drunk, then that which is
worse: but thou hast kept the good wine until
now.

11 This beginning of miracles did Jesus in
Cana of Galilee, and manifested forth his
glory; and his disciples believed on him.

12 After this he went down to Caper'-
na-um, he, and his mother, and his brethren,
and his disciples; and they continued there not
many days.

The Cleansing of the Temple

13 And the Jews' passover was at hand, and
Jesus went up to Jerusalem,

14 And found in the temple those that sold oxen and sheep and doves, and the changers of money sitting:

15 And when he had made a scourge of small cords, he drove them all out of the temple, and the sheep, and the oxen; and poured out the changers' money, and overthrew the tables;

16 And said unto them that sold doves, Take these things hence; make not my Father's house a house of merchandise.

17 And his disciples remembered that it was written, The zeal of thine house hath eaten me up.

18 Then answered the Jews and said unto him, What sign showest thou unto us, seeing that thou doest these things?

19 Jesus answered and said unto them, Destroy this temple, and in three days I will raise it up.

20 Then said the Jews, Forty and six years was this temple in building, and wilt thou rear it up in three days?

21 But he spake of the temple of his body.

22 When therefore he was risen from the dead, his disciples remembered that he had said this unto them; and they believed the Scripture, and the word which Jesus had said.

Jesus Knows All Men

23 Now when he was in Jerusalem at the passover, in the feast day, many believed in his name, when they saw the miracles which he did.

24 But Jesus did not commit himself unto them, because he knew all men,

25 And needed not that any should testify of man; for he knew what was in man.

Jesus and Nicodemus

3 There was a man of the Pharisees, named Nicode′mus, a ruler of the Jews:

2 The same came to Jesus by night, and said unto him, Rabbi, we know that thou art a teacher come from God: for no man can do these miracles that thou doest, except God be with him.

3 Jesus answered and said unto him, Verily, verily, I say unto thee, Except a man be born again, he cannot see the kingdom of God.

4 Nicode′mus saith unto him, How can a man be born when he is old? can he enter the second time into his mother's womb, and be born?

5 Jesus answered, Verily, verily, I say unto thee, Except a man be born of water and of the Spirit, he cannot enter into the kingdom of God.

6 That which is born of the flesh is flesh; and that which is born of the Spirit is spirit.

7 Marvel not that I said unto thee, Ye must be born again.

8 The wind bloweth where it listeth, and thou hearest the sound thereof, but canst not tell whence it cometh, and whither it goeth: so is every one that is born of the Spirit.

9 Nicode′mus answered and said unto him, How can these things be?

10 Jesus answered and said unto him, Art
thou a master of Israel, and knowest not these
things ?

11 Verily, verily, I say unto thee, We speak
that we do know, and testify that we have
seen; and ye receive not our witness.

12 If I have told you earthly things, and ye
believe not, how shall ye believe, if I tell you
of heavenly things ?

13 And no man hath ascended up to
heaven, but he that came down from heaven,
even the Son of man which is in heaven.

14 And as Moses lifted up the serpent in
the wilderness, even so must the Son of man
be lifted up:

15 That whosoever believeth in him should
not perish, but have eternal life.

God So Loved the World

16 For God so loved the world, that he
gave his only begotten Son, that whosoever
believeth in him should not perish, but have
everlasting life.

17 For God sent not his Son into the world
to condemn the world; but that the world
through him might be saved.

18 He that believeth on him is not condemned: but he that believeth not is condemned already, because he hath not believed
in the name of the only begotten Son of God.

19 And this is the condemnation, that light
is come into the world, and men loved darkness rather than light, because their deeds
were evil.

20 For every one that doeth evil hateth the light, neither cometh to the light, lest his deeds should be reproved.

21 But he that doeth truth cometh to the light, that his deeds may be made manifest, that they are wrought in God.

He Must Increase, but I Must Decrease

22 After these things came Jesus and his disciples into the land of Judea; and there he tarried with them, and baptized.

23 And John also was baptizing in Ae'non near to Salim, because there was much water there: and they came, and were baptized.

24 For John was not yet cast into prison.

25 Then there arose a question between some of John's disciples and the Jews about purifying.

26 And they came unto John, and said unto him, Rabbi, he that was with thee beyond Jordan, to whom thou barest witness, behold, the same baptizeth, and all men come to him.

27 John answered and said, A man can receive nothing, except it be given him from heaven.

28 Ye yourselves bear me witness, that I said, I am not the Christ, but that I am sent before him.

29 He that hath the bride is the bridegroom: but the friend of the bridegroom, which standeth and heareth him, rejoiceth greatly because of the bridegroom's voice: this my joy therefore is fulfilled.

30 He must increase, but I must decrease.

The Testimony from Heaven

31 He that cometh from above is above all: he that is of the earth is earthly, and speaketh of the earth: he that cometh from heaven is above all.

32 And what he hath seen and heard, that he testifieth; and no man receiveth his testimony.

33 He that hath received his testimony hath set to his seal that God is true.

34 For he whom God hath sent speaketh the words of God: for God giveth not the Spirit by measure unto him.

35 The Father loveth the Son, and hath given all things into his hand.

36 He that believeth on the Son hath everlasting life: and he that believeth not the Son shall not see life; but the wrath of God abideth on him.

Jesus and the Woman of Samaria

4 When therefore the Lord knew how the Pharisees had heard that Jesus made and baptized more disciples than John,

2 (Though Jesus himself baptized not, but his disciples,)

3 He left Judea, and departed again into Galilee.

4 And he must needs go through Samaria.

5 Then cometh he to a city of Samaria, which is called Sychar, near to the parcel of ground that Jacob gave to his son Joseph.

6 Now Jacob's well was there. Jesus therefore, being wearied with his journey, sat thus on the well: and it was about the sixth hour.

7 There cometh a woman of Samaria to draw water: Jesus saith unto her, Give me to drink.

8 (For his disciples were gone away unto the city to buy meat.)

9 Then saith the woman of Samaria unto him, How is it that thou, being a Jew, askest drink of me, which am a woman of Samaria? for the Jews have no dealings with the Samaritans.

10 Jesus answered and said unto her, If thou knewest the gift of God, and who it is that saith to thee, Give me to drink; thou wouldest have asked of him, and he would have given thee living water.

11 The woman saith unto him, Sir, thou hast nothing to draw with, and the well is deep: from whence then hast thou that living water?

12 Art thou greater than our father Jacob, which gave us the well, and drank thereof himself, and his children, and his cattle?

13 Jesus answered and said unto her, Whosoever drinketh of this water shall thirst again:

14 But whosoever drinketh of the water that I shall give him shall never thirst; but the water that I shall give him shall be in him a well of water springing up into everlasting life.

15 The woman saith unto him, Sir, give me this water, that I thirst not, neither come hither to draw.

16 Jesus saith unto her, Go, call thy husband, and come hither.

17 The woman answered and said, I have

no husband. Jesus said unto her, Thou hast well said, I have no husband:

18 For thou hast had five husbands; and he whom thou now hast is not thy husband: in that saidst thou truly.

19 The woman saith unto him, Sir, I perceive that thou art a prophet.

20 Our fathers worshipped in this mountain; and ye say, that in Jerusalem is the place where men ought to worship.

21 Jesus saith unto her, Woman, believe me, the hour cometh, when ye shall neither in this mountain, nor yet at Jerusalem, worship the Father.

22 Ye worship ye know not what: we know what we worship; for salvation is of the Jews.

23 But the hour cometh, and now is, when the true worshippers shall worship the Father in spirit and in truth: for the Father seeketh such to worship him.

24 God is a Spirit: and they that worship him must worship him in spirit and in truth.

25 The woman saith unto him, I know that Messiah cometh, which is called Christ: when he is come, he will tell us all things.

26 Jesus saith unto her, I that speak unto thee am he.

27 And upon this came his disciples, and marveled that he talked with the woman: yet no man said, What seekest thou? or, Why talkest thou with her?

28 The woman then left her waterpot, and went her way into the city, and saith to the men,

29 Come, see a man, which told me all things that ever I did: is not this the Christ?

30 Then they went out of the city, and came unto him.

31 In the mean while his disciples prayed him, saying, Master, eat.

32 But he said unto them, I have meat to eat that ye know not of.

33 Therefore said the disciples one to another, Hath any man brought him aught to eat?

34 Jesus saith unto them, My meat is to do the will of him that sent me, and to finish his work.

35 Say not ye, There are yet four months, and then cometh harvest? behold, I say unto you, Lift up your eyes, and look on the fields; for they are white already to harvest.

36 And he that reapeth receiveth wages, and gathereth fruit unto life eternal: that both he that soweth and he that reapeth may rejoice together.

37 And herein is that saying true, One soweth, and another reapeth.

38 I sent you to reap that whereupon ye bestowed no labor: other men labored, and ye are entered into their labors.

39 And many of the Samaritans of that city believed on him for the saying of the woman, which testified, He told me all that ever I did.

40 So when the Samaritans were come unto him, they besought him that he would tarry with them: and he abode there two days.

41 And many more believed because of his
own word;

42 And said unto the woman, Now we believe, not because of thy saying: for we have
heard him ourselves, and know that this is
indeed the Christ, the Saviour of the world.

Jesus Heals a Nobleman's Son

43 Now after two days he departed thence,
and went into Galilee.

44 For Jesus himself testified, that a prophet
hath no honor in his own country.

45 Then when he was come into Galilee,
the Galileans received him, having seen all the
things that he did at Jerusalem at the feast:
for they also went unto the feast.

46 So Jesus came again into Cana of
Galilee, where he made the water wine. And
there was a certain nobleman, whose son was
sick at Caper′na-um.

47 When he heard that Jesus was come out
of Judea into Galilee, he went unto him, and
besought him that he would come down,
and heal his son: for he was at the point of
death.

48 Then said Jesus unto him, Except ye see
signs and wonders, ye will not believe.

49 The nobleman saith unto him, Sir,
come down ere my child die.

50 Jesus saith unto him, Go thy way; thy
son liveth. And the man believed the word
that Jesus had spoken unto him, and he went
his way.

51 And as he was now going down, his

servants met him, and told him, saying, Thy son liveth.

52 Then inquired he of them the hour when he began to amend. And they said unto him, Yesterday at the seventh hour the fever left him.

53 So the father knew that it was at the same hour, in the which Jesus said unto him, Thy son liveth: and himself believed, and his whole house.

54 This is again the second miracle that Jesus did, when he was come out of Judea into Galilee.

The Healing at the Pool

5 After this there was a feast of the Jews; and Jesus went up to Jerusalem.

2 Now there is at Jerusalem by the sheep market a pool, which is called in the Hebrew tongue Bethes'da, having five porches.

3 In these lay a great multitude of impotent folk, of blind, halt, withered, waiting for the moving of the water.

4 For an angel went down at a certain season into the pool, and troubled the water: whosoever then first after the troubling of the water stepped in was made whole of whatsoever disease he had.

5 And a certain man was there, which had an infirmity thirty and eight years.

6 When Jesus saw him lie, and knew that he had been now a long time in that case, he saith unto him, Wilt thou be made whole?

7 The impotent man answered him, Sir,

I have no man, when the water is troubled, to put me into the pool; but while I am coming, another steppeth down before me.

8 Jesus saith unto him, Rise, take up thy bed, and walk.

9 And immediately the man was made whole, and took up his bed, and walked: and on the same day was the sabbath.

10 The Jews therefore said unto him that was cured, It is the sabbath day: it is not lawful for thee to carry thy bed.

11 He answered them, He that made me whole, the same said unto me, Take up thy bed, and walk.

12 Then asked they him, What man is that which said unto thee, Take up thy bed, and walk?

13 And he that was healed wist not who it was: for Jesus had conveyed himself away, a multitude being in that place.

14 Afterward Jesus findeth him in the temple, and said unto him, Behold, thou art made whole: sin no more, lest a worse thing come unto thee.

15 The man departed, and told the Jews that it was Jesus, which had made him whole.

16 And therefore did the Jews persecute Jesus, and sought to slay him, because he had done these things on the sabbath day.

17 But Jesus answered them, My Father worketh hitherto, and I work.

18 Therefore the Jews sought the more to kill him, because he not only had broken the

sabbath, but said also that God was his
Father, making himself equal with God.

The Authority of the Son

19 Then answered Jesus and said unto
them, Verily, verily, I say unto you, The Son
can do nothing of himself, but what he seeth
the Father do: for what things soever he
doeth, these also doeth the Son likewise.
20 For the Father loveth the Son, and
showeth him all things that himself doeth:
and he will show him greater works than
these, that ye may marvel.
21 For as the Father raiseth up the dead,
and quickeneth them; even so the Son quickeneth whom he will.
22 For the Father judgeth no man, but
hath committed all judgment unto the Son:
23 That all men should honor the Son, even
as they honor the Father. He that honoreth
not the Son honoreth not the Father which
hath sent him.
24 Verily, verily, I say unto you, He that
heareth my word, and believeth on him that
sent me, hath everlasting life, and shall not
come into condemnation; but is passed from
death unto life.
25 Verily, verily, I say unto you, The hour
is coming, and now is, when the dead shall
hear the voice of the Son of God: and they
that hear shall live.
26 For as the Father hath life in himself;
so hath he given to the Son to have life in
himself;

27 And hath given him authority to execute judgment also, because he is the Son of man.

28 Marvel not at this: for the hour is coming, in the which all that are in the graves shall hear his voice,

29 And shall come forth; they that have done good, unto the resurrection of life; and they that have done evil, unto the resurrection of damnation.

Witnesses to Jesus

30 I can of mine own self do nothing: as I hear, I judge: and my judgment is just; because I seek not mine own will, but the will of the Father which hath sent me.

31 If I bear witness of myself, my witness is not true.

32 There is another that beareth witness of me; and I know that the witness which he witnesseth of me is true.

33 Ye sent unto John, and he bare witness unto the truth.

34 But I receive not testimony from man: but these things I say, that ye might be saved.

35 He was a burning and a shining light: and ye were willing for a season to rejoice in his light.

36 But I have greater witness than that of John: for the works which the Father hath given me to finish, the same works that I do, bear witness of me, that the Father hath sent me.

37 And the Father himself, which hath sent me, hath borne witness of me. Ye have

neither heard his voice at any time, nor seen his shape.

38 And ye have not his word abiding in you: for whom he hath sent, him ye believe not.

39 Search the Scriptures; for in them ye think ye have eternal life: and they are they which testify of me.

40 And ye will not come to me, that ye might have life.

41 I receive not honor from men.

42 But I know you, that ye have not the love of God in you.

43 I am come in my Father's name, and ye receive me not: if another shall come in his own name, him ye will receive.

44 How can ye believe, which receive honor one of another, and seek not the honor that cometh from God only?

45 Do not think that I will accuse you to the Father: there is one that accuseth you, even Moses, in whom ye trust.

46 For had ye believed Moses, ye would have believed me: for he wrote of me.

47 But if ye believe not his writings, how shall ye believe my words?

The Feeding of the Five Thousand

6 After these things Jesus went over the Sea of Galilee, which is the sea of Ti-be'ri-as.

2 And a great multitude followed him, because they saw his miracles which he did on them that were diseased.

3 And Jesus went up into a mountain, and there he sat with his disciples.

4 And the passover, a feast of the Jews, was nigh.

5 When Jesus then lifted up his eyes, and saw a great company come unto him, he saith unto Philip, Whence shall we buy bread, that these may eat?

6 And this he said to prove him: for he himself knew what he would do.

7 Philip answered him, Two hundred pennyworth of bread is not sufficient for them, that every one of them may take a little.

8 One of his disciples, Andrew, Simon Peter's brother, saith unto him,

9 There is a lad here, which hath five barley loaves, and two small fishes: but what are they among so many?

10 And Jesus said, Make the men sit down. Now there was much grass in the place. So the men sat down, in number about five thousand.

11 And Jesus took the loaves; and when he had given thanks, he distributed to the disciples, and the disciples to them that were set down; and likewise of the fishes as much as they would.

12 When they were filled, he said unto his disciples, Gather up the fragments that remain, that nothing be lost.

13 Therefore they gathered them together, and filled twelve baskets with the fragments of the five barley loaves, which remained over and above unto them that had eaten.

14 Then those men, when they had seen the miracle that Jesus did, said, This is of a truth that Prophet that should come into the world.

15 When Jesus therefore perceived that they would come and take him by force, to make him a king, he departed again into a mountain himself alone.

Jesus Walks on the Sea

16 And when even was now come, his disciples went down unto the sea,

17 And entered into a ship, and went over the sea toward Caper'na-um. And it was now dark, and Jesus was not come to them.

18 And the sea arose by reason of a great wind that blew.

19 So when they had rowed about five and twenty or thirty furlongs, they see Jesus walking on the sea, and drawing nigh unto the ship: and they were afraid.

20 But he saith unto them, It is I; be not afraid.

21 Then they willingly received him into the ship: and immediately the ship was at the land whither they went.

The People Seek Jesus

22 The day following, when the people, which stood on the other side of the sea, saw that there was none other boat there, save that one whereinto his disciples were entered, and that Jesus went not with his disciples into the boat, but that his disciples were gone away alone;

23 (Howbeit there came other boats from
Tibe′ri-as nigh unto the place where they did
eat bread, after that the Lord had given
thanks:)

24 When the people therefore saw that
Jesus was not there, neither his disciples, they
also took shipping, and came to Caper′na-um,
seeking for Jesus.

Jesus the Bread of Life

25 And when they had found him on the
other side of the sea, they said unto him,
Rabbi, when camest thou hither?

26 Jesus answered them and said, Verily,
verily, I say unto you, Ye seek me, not because ye saw the miracles, but because ye did
eat of the loaves, and were filled.

27 Labor not for the meat which perisheth,
but for that meat which endureth unto everlasting life, which the Son of man shall give
unto you: for him hath God the Father
sealed.

28 Then said they unto him, What shall
we do, that we might work the works of
God?

29 Jesus answered and said unto them, This
is the work of God, that ye believe on him
whom he hath sent.

30 They said therefore unto him, What sign
showest thou then, that we may see, and believe thee? what dost thou work?

31 Our fathers did eat manna in the
desert; as it is written, He gave them bread
from heaven to eat.

32 Then Jesus said unto them, Verily, verily, I say unto you, Moses gave you not that bread from heaven; but my Father giveth you the true bread from heaven.

33 For the bread of God is he which cometh down from heaven, and giveth life unto the world.

34 Then said they unto him, Lord, evermore give us this bread.

35 And Jesus said unto them, I am the bread of life: he that cometh to me shall never hunger; and he that believeth on me shall never thirst.

36 But I said unto you, That ye also have seen me, and believe not.

37 All that the Father giveth me shall come to me; and him that cometh to me I will in no wise cast out.

38 For I came down from heaven, not to do mine own will, but the will of him that sent me.

39 And this is the Father's will which hath sent me, that of all which he hath given me I should lose nothing, but should raise it up again at the last day.

40 And this is the will of him that sent me, that every one which seeth the Son, and believeth on him, may have everlasting life: and I will raise him up at the last day.

41 The Jews then murmured at him, because he said, I am the bread which came down from heaven.

42 And they said, Is not this Jesus, the son of Joseph, whose father and mother we know?

how is it then that he saith, I came down from heaven?

43 Jesus therefore answered and said unto them, Murmur not among yourselves.

44 No man can come to me, except the Father which hath sent me draw him: and I will raise him up at the last day.

45 It is written in the prophets, And they shall be all taught of God. Every man therefore that hath heard, and hath learned of the Father, cometh unto me.

46 Not that any man hath seen the Father, save he which is of God, he hath seen the Father.

47 Verily, verily, I say unto you, He that believeth on me hath everlasting life.

48 I am that bread of life.

49 Your fathers did eat manna in the wilderness, and are dead.

50 This is the bread which cometh down from heaven, that a man may eat thereof, and not die.

51 I am the living bread which came down from heaven: if any man eat of this bread, he shall live for ever: and the bread that I will give is my flesh, which I will give for the life of the world.

52 The Jews therefore strove among themselves, saying, How can this man give us his flesh to eat?

53 Then Jesus said unto them, Verily, verily, I say unto you, Except ye eat the flesh of the Son of man, and drink his blood, ye have no life in you.

54 Whoso eateth my flesh, and drinketh my blood, hath eternal life; and I will raise him up at the last day.

55 For my flesh is meat indeed, and my blood is drink indeed.

56 He that eateth my flesh, and drinketh my blood, dwelleth in me, and I in him.

57 As the living Father hath sent me, and I live by the Father; so he that eateth me, even he shall live by me.

58 This is that bread which came down from heaven: not as your fathers did eat manna, and are dead: he that eateth of this bread shall live for ever.

59 These things said he in the synagogue, as he taught in Caper'na-um.

The Words of Eternal Life

60 Many therefore of his disciples, when they had heard this, said, This is a hard saying; who can hear it?

61 When Jesus knew in himself that his disciples murmured at it, he said unto them, Doth this offend you?

62 What and if ye shall see the Son of man ascend up where he was before?

63 It is the Spirit that quickeneth; the flesh profiteth nothing: the words that I speak unto you, they are spirit, and they are life.

64 But there are some of you that believe not. For Jesus knew from the beginning who they were that believed not, and who should betray him.

65 And he said, Therefore said I unto you,

that no man can come unto me, except it
were given unto him of my Father.

66 From that time many of his disciples
went back, and walked no more with him.

67 Then said Jesus unto the twelve, Will
ye also go away?

68 Then Simon Peter answered him, Lord,
to whom shall we go? thou hast the words of
eternal life.

69 And we believe and are sure that thou
art that Christ, the Son of the living
God.

70 Jesus answered them, Have not I chosen
you twelve, and one of you is a devil?

71 He spake of Judas Iscar'i-ot the son of
Simon: for he it was that should betray him,
being one of the twelve.

The Unbelief of Jesus' Brethren

7 After these things Jesus walked in Galilee:
for he would not walk in Jewry, because
the Jews sought to kill him.

2 Now the Jews' feast of tabernacles was at
hand.

3 His brethren therefore said unto him,
Depart hence, and go into Judea, that thy
disciples also may see the works that thou
doest.

4 For there is no man that doeth any thing
in secret, and he himself seeketh to be known
openly. If thou do these things, show thyself
to the world.

5 For neither did his brethren believe in
him.

6 Then Jesus said unto them, My time is not yet come: but your time is always ready.

7 The world cannot hate you; but me it hateth, because I testify of it, that the works thereof are evil.

8 Go ye up unto this feast: I go not up yet unto this feast; for my time is not yet full come.

9 When he had said these words unto them, he abode still in Galilee.

Jesus at the Feast of Tabernacles

10 But when his brethren were gone up, then went he also up unto the feast, not openly, but as it were in secret.

11 Then the Jews sought him at the feast, and said, Where is he?

12 And there was much murmuring among the people concerning him: for some said, He is a good man: others said, Nay; but he deceiveth the people.

13 Howbeit no man spake openly of him for fear of the Jews.

14 Now about the midst of the feast Jesus went up into the temple, and taught.

15 And the Jews marveled, saying, How knoweth this man letters, having never learned?

16 Jesus answered them, and said, My doctrine is not mine, but his that sent me.

17 If any man will do his will, he shall know of the doctrine, whether it be of God, or whether I speak of myself.

18 He that speaketh of himself seeketh his

own glory: but he that seeketh his glory that sent him, the same is true, and no unrighteousness is in him.

19 Did not Moses give you the law, and yet none of you keepeth the law? Why go ye about to kill me?

20 The people answered and said, Thou hast a devil: who goeth about to kill thee?

21 Jesus answered and said unto them, I have done one work, and ye all marvel.

22 Moses therefore gave unto you circumcision; (not because it is of Moses, but of the fathers;) and ye on the sabbath day circumcise a man.

23 If a man on the sabbath day receive circumcision, that the law of Moses should not be broken; are ye angry at me, because I have made a man every whit whole on the sabbath day?

24 Judge not according to the appearance, but judge righteous judgment.

Is This the Christ?

25 Then said some of them of Jerusalem, Is not this he, whom they seek to kill?

26 But, lo, he speaketh boldly, and they say nothing unto him. Do the rulers know indeed that this is the very Christ?

27 Howbeit we know this man whence he is: but when Christ cometh, no man knoweth whence he is.

28 Then cried Jesus in the temple as he taught, saying, Ye both know me, and ye know whence I am: and I am not come of

myself, but he that sent me is true, whom ye know not.

29 But I know him; for I am from him, and he hath sent me.

30 Then they sought to take him: but no man laid hands on him, because his hour was not yet come.

31 And many of the people believed on him, and said, When Christ cometh, will he do more miracles than these which this man hath done?

Officers Sent to Arrest Jesus

32 The Pharisees heard that the people murmured such things concerning him; and the Pharisees and the chief priests sent officers to take him.

33 Then said Jesus unto them, Yet a little while am I with you, and then I go unto him that sent me.

34 Ye shall seek me, and shall not find me: and where I am, thither ye cannot come.

35 Then said the Jews among themselves, Whither will he go, that we shall not find him? will he go unto the dispersed among the Gentiles, and teach the Gentiles?

36 What manner of saying is this that he said, Ye shall seek me, and shall not find me: and where I am, thither ye cannot come?

Rivers of Living Water

37 In the last day, that great day of the feast, Jesus stood and cried, saying, If any man thirst, let him come unto me, and drink.

38 He that believeth on me, as the Scripture hath said, out of his belly shall flow rivers of living water.

39 (But this spake he of the Spirit, which they that believe on him should receive: for the Holy Ghost was not yet given; because that Jesus was not yet glorified.)

Division among the People

40 Many of the people therefore, when they heard this saying, said, Of a truth this is the Prophet.

41 Others said, This is the Christ. But some said, Shall Christ come out of Galilee?

42 Hath not the Scripture said, That Christ cometh of the seed of David, and out of the town of Bethlehem, where David was?

43 So there was a division among the people because of him.

44 And some of them would have taken him; but no man laid hands on him.

The Unbelief of Those in Authority

45 Then came the officers to the chief priests and Pharisees; and they said unto them, Why have ye not brought him?

46 The officers answered, Never man spake like this man.

47 Then answered them the Pharisees, Are ye also deceived?

48 Have any of the rulers or of the Pharisees believed on him?

49 But this people who knoweth not the law are cursed.

50 Nicode'mus saith unto them, (he that came to Jesus by night, being one of them,)

51 Doth our law judge any man, before it hear him, and know what he doeth?

52 They answered and said unto him, Art thou also of Galilee? Search, and look: for out of Galilee ariseth no prophet.

The Woman Caught in Adultery

53 And every man went unto his own
8 house.

1 Jesus went unto the mount of Olives.

2 And early in the morning he came again into the temple, and all the people came unto him; and he sat down, and taught them.

3 And the scribes and Pharisees brought unto him a woman taken in adultery; and when they had set her in the midst,

4 They say unto him, Master, this woman was taken in adultery, in the very act.

5 Now Moses in the law commanded us, that such should be stoned: but what sayest thou?

6 This they said, tempting him, that they might have to accuse him. But Jesus stooped down, and with his finger wrote on the ground, as though he heard them not.

7 So when they continued asking him, he lifted up himself, and said unto them, He that is without sin among you, let him first cast a stone at her.

8 And again he stooped down, and wrote on the ground.

9 And they which heard it, being convicted

by their own conscience, went out one by one, beginning at the eldest, even unto the last: and Jesus was left alone, and the woman standing in the midst.

10 When Jesus had lifted up himself, and saw none but the woman, he said unto her, Woman, where are those thine accusers? hath no man condemned thee?

11 She said, No man, Lord. And Jesus said unto her, Neither do I condemn thee: go, and sin no more.

Jesus the Light of the World

12 Then spake Jesus again unto them, saying, I am the light of the world: he that followeth me shall not walk in darkness, but shall have the light of life.

13 The Pharisees therefore said unto him, Thou bearest record of thyself; thy record is not true.

14 Jesus answered and said unto them, Though I bear record of myself, yet my record is true: for I know whence I came, and whither I go; but ye cannot tell whence I come, and whither I go.

15 Ye judge after the flesh; I judge no man.

16 And yet if I judge, my judgment is true: for I am not alone, but I and the Father that sent me.

17 It is also written in your law, that the testimony of two men is true.

18 I am one that bear witness of myself, and the Father that sent me beareth witness of me.

19 Then said they unto him, Where is thy
Father? Jesus answered, Ye neither know me,
nor my Father: if ye had known me, ye
should have known my Father also.

20 These words spake Jesus in the treasury,
as he taught in the temple: and no man laid
hands on him; for his hour was not yet come.

Whither I Go Ye Cannot Come

21 Then said Jesus again unto them, I go
my way, and ye shall seek me, and shall
die in your sins: whither I go, ye cannot
come.

22 Then said the Jews, Will he kill himself? because he saith, Whither I go, ye cannot come.

23 And he said unto them, Ye are from
beneath; I am from above: ye are of this
world; I am not of this world.

24 I said therefore unto you, that ye shall
die in your sins: for if ye believe not that I
am he, ye shall die in your sins.

25 Then said they unto him, Who art thou?
And Jesus saith unto them, Even the same
that I said unto you from the beginning.

26 I have many things to say and to judge
of you: but he that sent me is true; and I
speak to the world those things which I have
heard of him.

27 They understood not that he spake to
them of the Father.

28 Then said Jesus unto them, When ye
have lifted up the Son of man, then shall ye
know that I am he, and that I do nothing of

myself; but as my Father hath taught me, I speak these things.

29 And he that sent me is with me: the Father hath not left me alone; for I do always those things that please him.

30 As he spake these words, many believed on him.

The Truth Shall Make You Free

31 Then said Jesus to those Jews which believed on him, If ye continue in my word, then are ye my disciples indeed;

32 And ye shall know the truth, and the truth shall make you free.

33 They answered him, We be Abraham's seed, and were never in bondage to any man: how sayest thou, Ye shall be made free?

34 Jesus answered them, Verily, verily, I say unto you, Whosoever committeth sin is the servant of sin.

35 And the servant abideth not in the house for ever: but the Son abideth ever.

36 If the Son therefore shall make you free, ye shall be free indeed.

37 I know that ye are Abraham's seed; but ye seek to kill me, because my word hath no place in you.

38 I speak that which I have seen with my Father: and ye do that which ye have seen with your father.

Your Father the Devil

39 They answered and said unto him, Abraham is our father. Jesus saith unto them,

If ye were Abraham's children, ye would do
the works of Abraham.

40 But now ye seek to kill me, a man that
hath told you the truth, which I have heard
of God: this did not Abraham.

41 Ye do the deeds of your father. Then
said they to him, We be not born of fornication; we have one Father, even God.

42 Jesus said unto them, If God were your
Father, ye would love me: for I proceeded
forth and came from God; neither came I of
myself, but he sent me.

43 Why do ye not understand my speech?
even because ye cannot hear my word.

44 Ye are of your father the devil, and the
lusts of your father ye will do: he was a
murderer from the beginning, and abode not
in the truth, because there is no truth in him.
When he speaketh a lie, he speaketh of his
own: for he is a liar, and the father of
it.

45 And because I tell you the truth, ye believe me not.

46 Which of you convinceth me of sin?
And if I say the truth, why do ye not believe
me?

47 He that is of God heareth God's words:
ye therefore hear them not, because ye are
not of God.

Before Abraham Was, I Am

48 Then answered the Jews, and said unto
him, Say we not well that thou art a Samaritan, and hast a devil?

49 Jesus answered, I have not a devil; but I honor my Father, and ye do dishonor me.

50 And I seek not mine own glory: there is one that seeketh and judgeth.

51 Verily, verily, I say unto you, If a man keep my saying, he shall never see death.

52 Then said the Jews unto him, Now we know that thou hast a devil. Abraham is dead, and the prophets; and thou sayest, If a man keep my saying, he shall never taste of death.

53 Art thou greater than our father Abraham, which is dead? and the prophets are dead: whom makest thou thyself?

54 Jesus answered, If I honor myself, my honor is nothing: it is my Father that honoreth me; of whom ye say, that he is your God:

55 Yet ye have not known him; but I know him: and if I should say, I know him not, I shall be a liar like unto you: but I know him, and keep his saying.

56 Your father Abraham rejoiced to see my day: and he saw it, and was glad.

57 Then said the Jews unto him, Thou art not yet fifty years old, and hast thou seen Abraham?

58 Jesus said unto them, Verily, verily, I say unto you, Before Abraham was, I am.

59 Then took they up stones to cast at him: but Jesus hid himself, and went out of the temple, going through the midst of them, and so passed by.

Jesus Heals the Man Born Blind

9 And as Jesus passed by, he saw a man which was blind from his birth.

2 And his disciples asked him, saying, Master, who did sin, this man, or his parents, that he was born blind?

3 Jesus answered, Neither hath this man sinned, nor his parents: but that the works of God should be made manifest in him.

4 I must work the works of him that sent me, while it is day: the night cometh, when no man can work.

5 As long as I am in the world, I am the light of the world.

6 When he had thus spoken, he spat on the ground, and made clay of the spittle, and he anointed the eyes of the blind man with the clay,

7 And said unto him, Go, wash in the pool of Silo'am, (which is by interpretation, Sent.) He went his way therefore, and washed, and came seeing.

8 The neighbors therefore, and they which before had seen him that he was blind, said, Is not this he that sat and begged?

9 Some said, This is he: others said, He is like him: but he said, I am he.

10 Therefore said they unto him, How were thine eyes opened?

11 He answered and said, A man that is called Jesus made clay, and anointed mine eyes, and said unto me, Go to the pool of Silo'am, and wash: and I went and washed, and I received sight.

12 Then said they unto him, Where is he?
He said, I know not.

The Pharisees Investigate the Healing

13 They brought to the Pharisees him that
aforetime was blind.

14 And it was the sabbath day when Jesus
made the clay, and opened his eyes.

15 Then again the Pharisees also asked him
how he had received his sight. He said unto
them, He put clay upon mine eyes, and I
washed, and do see.

16 Therefore said some of the Pharisees,
This man is not of God, because he keepeth
not the sabbath day. Others said, How can a
man that is a sinner do such miracles? And
there was a division among them.

17 They say unto the blind man again,
What sayest thou of him, that he hath opened
thine eyes? He said, He is a prophet.

18 But the Jews did not believe concerning
him, that he had been blind, and received his
sight, until they called the parents of him
that had received his sight.

19 And they asked them, saying, Is this
your son, who ye say was born blind? how
then doth he now see?

20 His parents answered them and said, We
know that this is our son, and that he was
born blind:

21 But by what means he now seeth, we
know not; or who hath opened his eyes, we
know not: he is of age; ask him: he shall
speak for himself.

22 These words spake his parents, because
they feared the Jews: for the Jews had agreed
already, that if any man did confess that he
was Christ, he should be put out of the
synagogue.

23 Therefore said his parents, He is of
age; ask him.

24 Then again called they the man that
was blind, and said unto him, Give God the
praise: we know that this man is a sinner.

25 He answered and said, Whether he be a
sinner or no, I know not: one thing I know,
that, whereas I was blind, now I see.

26 Then said they to him again, What did
he to thee? how opened he thine eyes?

27 He answered them, I have told you
already, and ye did not hear: wherefore
would ye hear it again? will ye also be his
disciples?

28 Then they reviled him, and said, Thou
art his disciple; but we are Moses' disciples.

29 We know that God spake unto Moses:
as for this fellow, we know not from whence
he is.

30 The man answered and said unto them,
Why herein is a marvelous thing, that ye
know not from whence he is, and yet he hath
opened mine eyes.

31 Now we know that God heareth not
sinners: but if any man be a worshipper of
God, and doeth his will, him he heareth.

32 Since the world began was it not heard
that any man opened the eyes of one that was
born blind.

33 If this man were not of God, he could do nothing.

34 They answered and said unto him, Thou wast altogether born in sins, and dost thou teach us? And they cast him out.

Spiritual Blindness

35 Jesus heard that they had cast him out; and when he had found him, he said unto him, Dost thou believe on the Son of God?

36 He answered and said, Who is he, Lord, that I might believe on him?

37 And Jesus said unto him, Thou hast both seen him, and it is he that talketh with thee.

38 And he said, Lord, I believe. And he worshipped him.

39 And Jesus said, For judgment I am come into this world, that they which see not might see; and that they which see might be made blind.

40 And some of the Pharisees which were with him heard these words, and said unto him, Are we blind also?

41 Jesus said unto them, If ye were blind, ye should have no sin: but now ye say, We see; therefore your sin remaineth.

The Parable of the Sheepfold

10 Verily, verily, I say unto you, He that entereth not by the door into the sheepfold, but climbeth up some other way, the same is a thief and a robber.

2 But he that entereth in by the door is the shepherd of the sheep.

3 To him the porter[2377] openeth;[455] and the sheep[4263] hear[191] his voice:[5456] and he calleth[2564] his own[2398] sheep[4263] by name,[3686] and leadeth[1806] them out.[1806]

4 And when he putteth forth[1544] his own[2398] sheep,[4263] he goeth[4198] before[1715] them, and the sheep[4263] follow[190] him: for they know[1492] his voice.[5456]

5 And a stranger[245] will they[5456] not follow,[190] but will flee[5343] from him; for[190] they know[1492] not the voice[5456] of strangers.[245]

6 This parable[3942] spake[2036] Jesus[2424] unto them; but they understood[1097] not what[5101] things they were which he spake[2980] unto them.

Jesus the Good Shepherd

7 Then said[2036] Jesus[2424] unto them again, Verily, verily,[281] I say unto you, I am the door[2374] of the sheep.[4263][281]

8 All that ever[3745] came[2064] before me are thieves[2812] and robbers:[3027] but the sheep[4263] did not[191] hear[191] them.

9 I am the door:[2374] by me if any man enter[5100] in,[1525] he shall be saved,[4982] and shall go in[1525] and out,[1525] and find[2147] pasture.[3542][1831][1831]

10 The thief[2812] cometh not, but for to steal,[2813] and to kill,[2380] and to[2064] destroy:[622] I am[1508] come[2064] that they might have life,[2222] and that they might have it more[4053] abundantly.

11 I am the good[2570] shepherd:[4166] the good[2570] shepherd giveth[5087] his life[5590] for the sheep.[4263]

12 But he that is a hireling,[3411] and not the[5607] shepherd,[4166] whose own[2398] the sheep[4263] are not, seeth[2334] the wolf[3074] coming,[2064] and leaveth[863] the sheep,[4263] and fleeth;[5343] and the wolf[3074] catcheth[726] them, and scattereth[4650] the sheep.[4263]

13 The hireling fleeth, because he is a hireling, and careth not for the sheep.

14 I am the good shepherd, and know my sheep, and am known of mine.

15 As the Father knoweth me, even so know I the Father: and I lay down my life for the sheep.

16 And other sheep I have, which are not of this fold: them also I must bring, and they shall hear my voice; and there shall be one fold, and one shepherd.

17 Therefore doth my Father love me, because I lay down my life, that I might take it again.

18 No man taketh it from me, but I lay it down of myself. I have power to lay it down, and I have power to take it again. This commandment have I received of my Father.

19 There was a division therefore again among the Jews for these sayings.

20 And many of them said, He hath a devil, and is mad; why hear ye him?

21 Others said, These are not the words of him that hath a devil. Can a devil open the eyes of the blind?

Jesus Rejected by the Jews

22 And it was at Jerusalem the feast of the dedication, and it was winter.

23 And Jesus walked in the temple in Solomon's porch.

24 Then came the Jews round about him, and said unto him, How long dost thou make us to doubt? If thou be the Christ, tell us plainly.

25 Jesus answered them, I told you, and ye believed not: the works that I do in my Father's name, they bear witness of me.

26 But ye believe not, because ye are not of my sheep, as I said unto you.

27 My sheep hear my voice, and I know them, and they follow me:

28 And I give unto them eternal life; and they shall never perish, neither shall any man pluck them out of my hand.

29 My Father, which gave them me, is greater than all; and no man is able to pluck them out of my Father's hand.

30 I and my Father are one.

31 Then the Jews took up stones again to stone him.

32 Jesus answered them, Many good works have I showed you from my Father; for which of those works do ye stone me?

33 The Jews answered him, saying, For a good work we stone thee not; but for blasphemy; and because that thou, being a man, makest thyself God.

34 Jesus answered them, Is it not written in your law, I said, Ye are gods?

35 If he called them gods, unto whom the word of God came, and the Scripture cannot be broken;

36 Say ye of him, whom the Father hath sanctified, and sent into the world, Thou blasphemest; because I said, I am the Son of God?

37 If I do not the works of my Father, believe me not.

38 But if I do, though ye believe not me, believe the works; that ye may know, and believe, that the Father is in me, and I in him.

39 Therefore they sought again to take him; but he escaped out of their hand,

40 And went away again beyond Jordan into the place where John at first baptized; and there he abode.

41 And many resorted unto him and said, John did no miracle: but all things that John spake of this man were true.

42 And many believed on him there.

The Death of Lazarus

11 Now a certain man was sick, named Lazarus, of Bethany, the town of Mary and her sister Martha.

2 (It was that Mary which anointed the Lord with ointment, and wiped his feet with her hair, whose brother Lazarus was sick.)

3 Therefore his sisters sent unto him, saying, Lord, behold, he whom thou lovest is sick.

4 When Jesus heard that, he said, This sickness is not unto death, but for the glory of God, that the Son of God might be glorified thereby.

5 Now Jesus loved Martha, and her sister, and Lazarus.

6 When he had heard therefore that he was sick, he abode two days still in the same place where he was.

7 Then after that saith he to his disciples, Let us go into Judea again.

8 His disciples say unto him, Master, the Jews of late sought to stone thee; and goest thou thither again?

9 Jesus answered, Are there not twelve hours in the day? If any man walk in the day, he stumbleth not, because he seeth the light of this world.

10 But if a man walk in the night, he stumbleth, because there is no light in him.

11 These things said he: and after that he saith unto them, Our friend Lazarus sleepeth; but I go, that I may awake him out of sleep.

12 Then said his disciples, Lord, if he sleep, he shall do well.

13 Howbeit Jesus spake of his death: but they thought that he had spoken of taking of rest in sleep.

14 Then said Jesus unto them plainly, Lazarus is dead.

15 And I am glad for your sakes that I was not there, to the intent ye may believe; nevertheless let us go unto him.

16 Then said Thomas, which is called Did'ymus, unto his fellow disciples, Let us also go, that we may die with him.

Jesus the Resurrection and the Life

17 Then when Jesus came, he found that he had lain in the grave four days already.

18 Now Bethany was nigh unto Jerusalem, about fifteen furlongs off:

19 And many of the Jews came to Martha and Mary, to comfort them concerning their brother.

20 Then Martha, as soon as she heard that Jesus was coming, went and met him: but Mary sat still in the house.

21 Then said Martha unto Jesus, Lord, if thou hadst been here, my brother had not died.

22 But I know, that even now, whatsoever thou wilt ask of God, God will give it thee.

23 Jesus saith unto her, Thy brother shall rise again.

24 Martha saith unto him, I know that he shall rise again in the resurrection at the last day.

25 Jesus said unto her, I am the resurrection, and the life: he that believeth in me, though he were dead, yet shall he live:

26 And whosoever liveth and believeth in me shall never die. Believest thou this?

27 She saith unto him, Yea, Lord: I believe that thou art the Christ, the Son of God, which should come into the world.

Jesus Weeps

28 And when she had so said, she went her way, and called Mary her sister secretly, saying, The Master is come, and calleth for thee.

29 As soon as she heard that, she arose quickly, and came unto him.

30 Now Jesus was not yet come into the town, but was in that place where Martha met him.

31 The Jews then which were with her in the house, and comforted her, when they saw

Mary, that she rose up hastily and went out, followed her, saying, She goeth unto the grave to weep there.

32 Then when Mary was come where Jesus was, and saw him, she fell down at his feet, saying unto him, Lord, if thou hadst been here, my brother had not died.

33 When Jesus therefore saw her weeping, and the Jews also weeping which came with her, he groaned in the spirit, and was troubled,

34 And said, Where have ye laid him? They say unto him, Lord, come and see.

35 Jesus wept.

36 Then said the Jews, Behold how he loved him!

37 And some of them said, Could not this man, which opened the eyes of the blind, have caused that even this man should not have died?

Lazarus Brought to Life

38 Jesus therefore again groaning in himself cometh to the grave. It was a cave, and a stone lay upon it.

39 Jesus said, Take ye away the stone. Martha, the sister of him that was dead, saith unto him, Lord, by this time he stinketh: for he hath been dead four days.

40 Jesus saith unto her, Said I not unto thee, that, if thou wouldest believe, thou shouldest see the glory of God?

41 Then they took away the stone from the place where the dead was laid. And Jesus

lifted up his eyes, and said, Father, I thank thee that thou hast heard me.

42 And I knew that thou hearest me always: but because of the people which stand by I said it, that they may believe that thou hast sent me.

43 And when he thus had spoken, he cried with a loud voice, Lazarus, come forth.

44 And he that was dead came forth, bound hand and foot with graveclothes; and his face was bound about with a napkin. Jesus saith unto them, Loose him, and let him go.

The Plot against Jesus

45 Then many of the Jews which came to Mary, and had seen the things which Jesus did, believed on him.

46 But some of them went their ways to the Pharisees, and told them what things Jesus had done.

47 Then gathered the chief priests and the Pharisees a council, and said, What do we? for this man doeth many miracles.

48 If we let him thus alone, all men will believe on him; and the Romans shall come and take away both our place and nation.

49 And one of them, named Ca'iaphas, being the high priest that same year, said unto them, Ye know nothing at all,

50 Nor consider that it is expedient for us, that one man should die for the people, and that the whole nation perish not.

51 And this spake he not of himself: but

being high priest that year, he prophesied that Jesus should die for that nation;

52 And not for that nation only, but that also he should gather together in one the children of God that were scattered abroad.

53 Then from that day forth they took counsel together for to put him to death.

54 Jesus therefore walked no more openly among the Jews; but went thence unto a country near to the wilderness, into a city called E′phra-im, and there continued with his disciples.

55 And the Jews' passover was nigh at hand: and many went out of the country up to Jerusalem before the passover, to purify themselves.

56 Then sought they for Jesus, and spake among themselves, as they stood in the temple, What think ye, that he will not come to the feast?

57 Now both the chief priests and the Pharisees had given a commandment, that, if any man knew where he were, he should show it, that they might take him.

Jesus Anointed at Bethany

12 Then Jesus six days before the passover came to Bethany, where Lazarus was which had been dead, whom he raised from the dead.

2 There they made him a supper; and Martha served: but Lazarus was one of them that sat at the table with him.

3 Then took Mary a pound of ointment of

spikenard, very costly, and anointed the feet of Jesus, and wiped his feet with her hair: and the house was filled with the odor of the ointment.

4 Then saith one of his disciples, Judas Iscar′i-ot, Simon's son, which should betray him,

5 Why was not this ointment sold for three hundred pence, and given to the poor?

6 This he said, not that he cared for the poor; but because he was a thief, and had the bag, and bare what was put therein.

7 Then said Jesus, Let her alone: against the day of my burying hath she kept this.

8 For the poor always ye have with you; but me ye have not always.

The Plot against Lazarus

9 Much people of the Jews therefore knew that he was there: and they came not for Jesus' sake only, but that they might see Lazarus also, whom he had raised from the dead.

10 But the chief priests consulted that they might put Lazarus also to death;

11 Because that by reason of him many of the Jews went away, and believed on Jesus.

The Triumphal Entry into Jerusalem

12 On the next day much people that were come to the feast, when they heard that Jesus was coming to Jerusalem,

13 Took branches of palm trees, and went forth to meet him, and cried, Hosanna:

Blessed is the King of Israel that cometh in
the name of the Lord.

14 And Jesus, when he had found a young
ass, sat thereon; as it is written,

15 Fear not, daughter of Zion: behold, thy
King cometh, sitting on an ass's colt.

16 These things understood not his disciples at the first: but when Jesus was glorified, then remembered they that these things
were written of him, and that they had done
these things unto him.

17 The people therefore that was with him
when he called Lazarus out of his grave, and
raised him from the dead, bare record.

18 For this cause the people also met him,
for that they heard that he had done this
miracle.

19 The Pharisees therefore said among
themselves, Perceive ye how ye prevail nothing? behold, the world is gone after him.

Some Greeks Seek Jesus

20 And there were certain Greeks among
them that came up to worship at the feast:

21 The same came therefore to Philip,
which was of Bethsai′da of Galilee, and desired him, saying, Sir, we would see Jesus.

22 Philip cometh and telleth Andrew: and
again Andrew and Philip tell Jesus.

23 And Jesus answered them, saying, The
hour is come, that the Son of man should be
glorified.

24 Verily, verily, I say unto you, Except a
corn of wheat fall into the ground and die, it

abideth alone: but if it die, it bringeth forth much fruit.

25 He that loveth his life shall lose it; and he that hateth his life in this world shall keep it unto life eternal.

26 If any man serve me, let him follow me; and where I am, there shall also my servant be: if any man serve me, him will my Father honor.

The Son of Man Must Be Lifted Up

27 Now is my soul troubled; and what shall I say? Father, save me from this hour: but for this cause came I unto this hour.

28 Father, glorify thy name. Then came there a voice from heaven, saying, I have both glorified it, and will glorify it again.

29 The people therefore that stood by, and heard it, said that it thundered: others said, An angel spake to him.

30 Jesus answered and said, This voice came not because of me, but for your sakes.

31 Now is the judgment of this world: now shall the prince of this world be cast out.

32 And I, if I be lifted up from the earth, will draw all men unto me.

33 This he said, signifying what death he should die.

34 The people answered him, We have heard out of the law that Christ abideth for ever: and how sayest thou, The Son of man must be lifted up? who is this Son of man?

35 Then Jesus said unto them, Yet a little while is the light with you. Walk while ye

have the light, lest darkness come upon you: for he that walketh in darkness knoweth not whither he goeth.

36 While ye have light, believe in the light, that ye may be the children of light.

The Unbelief of the Jews

These things spake Jesus, and departed, and did hide himself from them.

37 But though he had done so many miracles before them, yet they believed not on him:

38 That the saying of Isaiah the prophet might be fulfilled, which he spake, Lord, who hath believed our report? and to whom hath the arm of the Lord been revealed?

39 Therefore they could not believe, because that Isaiah said again,

40 He hath blinded their eyes, and hardened their heart; that they should not see with their eyes, nor understand with their heart, and be converted, and I should heal them.

41 These things said Isaiah, when he saw his glory, and spake of him.

42 Nevertheless among the chief rulers also many believed on him; but because of the Pharisees they did not confess him, lest they should be put out of the synagogue:

43 For they loved the praise of men more than the praise of God.

The Judgment of Jesus' Word

44 Jesus cried and said, He that believeth on me, believeth not on me, but on him that sent me.

45 And he that seeth me seeth him that sent me.

46 I am come a light into the world, that whosoever believeth on me should not abide in darkness.

47 And if any man hear my words, and believe not, I judge him not: for I came not to judge the world, but to save the world.

48 He that rejecteth me, and receiveth not my words, hath one that judgeth him: the word that I have spoken, the same shall judge him in the last day.

49 For I have not spoken of myself; but the Father which sent me, he gave me a commandment, what I should say, and what I should speak.

50 And I know that his commandment is life everlasting: whatsoever I speak therefore, even as the Father said unto me, so I speak.

Jesus Washes His Disciples' Feet

13 Now before the feast of the passover, when Jesus knew that his hour was come that he should depart out of this world unto the Father, having loved his own which were in the world, he loved them unto the end.

2 And supper being ended, the devil having now put into the heart of Judas Iscar'i-ot, Simon's son, to betray him;

3 Jesus knowing that the Father had given all things into his hands, and that he was come from God, and went to God;

4 He riseth from supper, and laid aside his garments; and took a towel, and girded himself.

5 After that he poureth water into a basin, and began to wash the disciples' feet, and to wipe them with the towel wherewith he was girded.

6 Then cometh he to Simon Peter: and Peter saith unto him, Lord, dost thou wash my feet?

7 Jesus answered and said unto him, What I do thou knowest not now; but thou shalt know hereafter.

8 Peter saith unto him, Thou shalt never wash my feet. Jesus answered him, If I wash thee not, thou hast no part with me.

9 Simon Peter saith unto him, Lord, not my feet only, but also my hands and my head.

10 Jesus saith to him, He that is washed needeth not save to wash his feet, but is clean every whit: and ye are clean, but not all.

11 For he knew who should betray him; therefore said he, Ye are not all clean.

12 So after he had washed their feet, and had taken his garments, and was set down again, he said unto them, Know ye what I have done to you?

13 Ye call me Master and Lord: and ye say well; for so I am.

14 If I then, your Lord and Master, have washed your feet; ye also ought to wash one another's feet.

15 For I have given you an example, that ye should do as I have done to you.

16 Verily, verily, I say unto you, The servant is not greater than his lord; neither he that is sent greater than he that sent him.

17 If ye know these things, happy are ye if ye do them.

18 I speak not of you all: I know whom I have chosen: but that the Scripture may be fulfilled, He that eateth bread with me hath lifted up his heel against me.

19 Now I tell you before it come, that, when it is come to pass, ye may believe that I am he.

20 Verily, verily, I say unto you, He that receiveth whomsoever I send receiveth me; and he that receiveth me receiveth him that sent me.

Jesus Foretells His Betrayal

21 When Jesus had thus said, he was troubled in spirit, and testified, and said, Verily, verily, I say unto you, that one of you shall betray me.

22 Then the disciples looked one on another, doubting of whom he spake.

23 Now there was leaning on Jesus' bosom one of his disciples, whom Jesus loved.

24 Simon Peter therefore beckoned to him, that he should ask who it should be of whom he spake.

25 He then lying on Jesus' breast saith unto him, Lord, who is it?

26 Jesus answered, He it is, to whom I shall give a sop, when I have dipped it. And when he had dipped the sop, he gave it to Judas Iscar'i-ot, the son of Simon.

27 And after the sop Satan entered into him. Then said Jesus unto him, That thou doest, do quickly.

28 Now no man at the table knew for what
intent he spake this unto him.

29 For some of them thought, because Judas
had the bag, that Jesus had said unto him,
Buy those things that we have need of against
the feast; or, that he should give something
to the poor.

30 He then, having received the sop, went
immediately out; and it was night.

The New Commandment

31 Therefore, when he was gone out, Jesus
said, Now is the Son of man glorified, and
God is glorified in him.

32 If God be glorified in him, God shall
also glorify him in himself, and shall straightway glorify him.

33 Little children, yet a little while I am
with you. Ye shall seek me; and as I said
unto the Jews, Whither I go, ye cannot come;
so now I say to you.

34 A new commandment I give unto you,
That ye love one another; as I have loved
you, that ye also love one another.

35 By this shall all men know that ye
are my disciples, if ye have love one to another.

Peter's Denial Foretold

36 Simon Peter said unto him, Lord,
whither goest thou? Jesus answered him,
Whither I go, thou canst not follow me now;
but thou shalt follow me afterward.

37 Peter said unto him, Lord, why cannot

I follow thee now? I will lay down my life
for thy sake.

38 Jesus answered him, Wilt thou lay down
thy life for my sake? Verily, verily, I say unto
thee, The cock shall not crow, till thou hast
denied me thrice.

Jesus the Way to the Father

14 Let not your heart be troubled: ye believe in God, believe also in me.

2 In my Father's house are many mansions: if it were not so, I would have told
you. I go to prepare a place for you.

3 And if I go and prepare a place for you,
I will come again, and receive you unto myself; that where I am, there ye may be also.

4 And whither I go ye know, and the way
ye know.

5 Thomas saith unto him, Lord, we know
not whither thou goest; and how can we
know the way?

6 Jesus saith unto him, I am the way, the
truth, and the life: no man cometh unto the
Father, but by me.

7 If ye had known me, ye should have
known my Father also: and from henceforth
ye know him, and have seen him.

8 Philip saith unto him, Lord, show us the
Father, and it sufficeth us.

9 Jesus saith unto him, Have I been so
long time with you, and yet hast thou not
known me, Philip? he that hath seen me hath
seen the Father; and how sayest thou then,
Show us the Father?

10 Believest thou not that I am in the Father, and the Father in me? the words that I speak unto you I speak not of myself: but the Father that dwelleth in me, he doeth the works.

11 Believe me that I am in the Father, and the Father in me: or else believe me for the very works' sake.

12 Verily, verily, I say unto you, He that believeth on me, the works that I do shall he do also; and greater works than these shall he do; because I go unto my Father.

13 And whatsoever ye shall ask in my name, that will I do, that the Father may be glorified in the Son.

14 If ye shall ask any thing in my name, I will do it.

The Promise of the Holy Spirit

15 If ye love me, keep my commandments.

16 And I will pray the Father, and he shall give you another Comforter, that he may abide with you for ever;

17 Even the Spirit of truth; whom the world cannot receive, because it seeth him not, neither knoweth him: but ye know him; for he dwelleth with you, and shall be in you.

18 I will not leave you comfortless: I will come to you.

19 Yet a little while, and the world seeth me no more; but ye see me: because I live, ye shall live also.

20 At that day ye shall know that I am in my Father, and ye in me, and I in you.

21 He that hath my commandments, and keepeth them, he it is that loveth me: and he that loveth me shall be loved of my Father, and I will love him, and will manifest myself to him.

22 Judas saith unto him, not Iscar′i-ot, Lord, how is it that thou wilt manifest thyself unto us, and not unto the world?

23 Jesus answered and said unto him, If a man love me, he will keep my words: and my Father will love him, and we will come unto him, and make our abode with him.

24 He that loveth me not keepeth not my sayings: and the word which ye hear is not mine, but the Father's which sent me.

25 These things have I spoken unto you, being yet present with you.

26 But the Comforter, which is the Holy Ghost, whom the Father will send in my name, he shall teach you all things, and bring all things to your remembrance, whatsoever I have said unto you.

27 Peace I leave with you, my peace I give unto you: not as the world giveth, give I unto you. Let not your heart be troubled, neither let it be afraid.

28 Ye have heard how I said unto you, I go away, and come again unto you. If ye loved me, ye would rejoice, because I said, I go unto the Father: for my Father is greater than I.

29 And now I have told you before it come to pass, that, when it is come to pass, ye might believe.

30 Hereafter I will not talk much with you: for the prince of this world cometh, and hath nothing in me.

31 But that the world may know that I love the Father; and as the Father gave me commandment, even so I do. Arise, let us go hence.

Jesus the True Vine

15 I am the true vine, and my Father is the husbandman.

2 Every branch in me that beareth not fruit he taketh away: and every branch that beareth fruit, he purgeth it, that it may bring forth more fruit.

3 Now ye are clean through the word which I have spoken unto you.

4 Abide in me, and I in you. As the branch cannot bear fruit of itself, except it abide in the vine; no more can ye, except ye abide in me.

5 I am the vine, ye are the branches. He that abideth in me, and I in him, the same bringeth forth much fruit; for without me ye can do nothing.

6 If a man abide not in me, he is cast forth as a branch, and is withered; and men gather them, and cast them into the fire, and they are burned.

7 If ye abide in me, and my words abide in you, ye shall ask what ye will, and it shall be done unto you.

8 Herein is my Father glorified, that ye bear much fruit; so shall ye be my disciples.

9 As the Father hath loved me, so have I loved you: continue ye in my love.

10 If ye keep my commandments, ye shall abide in my love; even as I have kept my Father's commandments, and abide in his love.

11 These things have I spoken unto you, that my joy might remain in you, and that your joy might be full.

12 This is my commandment, That ye love one another, as I have loved you.

13 Greater love hath no man than this, that a man lay down his life for his friends.

14 Ye are my friends, if ye do whatsoever I command you.

15 Henceforth I call you not servants; for the servant knoweth not what his lord doeth: but I have called you friends; for all things that I have heard of my Father I have made known unto you.

16 Ye have not chosen me, but I have chosen you, and ordained you, that ye should go and bring forth fruit, and that your fruit should remain; that whatsoever ye shall ask of the Father in my name, he may give it you.

17 These things I command you, that ye love one another.

The World's Hatred

18 If the world hate you, ye know that it hated me before it hated you.

19 If ye were of the world, the world would love his own; but because ye are not of the world, but I have chosen you out of the world, therefore the world hateth you.

20 Remember the word that I said unto you, The servant is not greater than his lord. If they have persecuted me, they will also persecute you; if they have kept my saying, they will keep yours also.

21 But all these things will they do unto you for my name's sake, because they know not him that sent me.

22 If I had not come and spoken unto them, they had not had sin; but now they have no cloak for their sin.

23 He that hateth me hateth my Father also.

24 If I had not done among them the works which none other man did, they had not had sin: but now have they both seen and hated both me and my Father.

25 But this cometh to pass, that the word might be fulfilled that is written in their law, They hated me without a cause.

26 But when the Comforter is come, whom I will send unto you from the Father, even the Spirit of truth, which proceedeth from the Father, he shall testify of me:

27 And ye also shall bear witness, because ye have been with me from the beginning.

16 These things have I spoken unto you, that ye should not be offended.

2 They shall put you out of the synagogues: yea, the time cometh, that whosoever killeth you will think that he doeth God service.

3 And these things will they do unto you, because they have not known the Father, nor me.

4 But these things have I told you, that when the time shall come, ye may remember that I told you of them.

The Work of the Holy Spirit

And these things I said not unto you at the beginning, because I was with you.

5 But now I go my way to him that sent me; and none of you asketh me, Whither goest thou?

6 But because I have said these things unto you, sorrow hath filled your heart.

7 Nevertheless I tell you the truth; It is expedient for you that I go away: for if I go not away, the Comforter will not come unto you; but if I depart, I will send him unto you.

8 And when he is come, he will reprove the world of sin, and of righteousness, and of judgment:

9 Of sin, because they believe not on me;

10 Of righteousness, because I go to my Father, and ye see me no more;

11 Of judgment, because the prince of this world is judged.

12 I have yet many things to say unto you, but ye cannot bear them now.

13 Howbeit when he, the Spirit of truth, is come, he will guide you into all truth: for he shall not speak of himself; but whatsoever he shall hear, that shall he speak: and he will show you things to come.

14 He shall glorify me: for he shall receive of mine, and shall show it unto you.

15 All things that the Father hath are mine: therefore said I, that he shall take of mine, and shall show it unto you.

Sorrow to Turn into Joy

16 A little while, and ye shall not see me: and again, a little while, and ye shall see me, because I go to the Father.

17 Then said some of his disciples among themselves, What is this that he saith unto us, A little while, and ye shall not see me: and again, a little while, and ye shall see me: and, Because I go to the Father?

18 They said therefore, What is this that he saith, A little while? we cannot tell what he saith.

19 Now Jesus knew that they were desirous to ask him, and said unto them, Do ye inquire among yourselves of that I said, A little while, and ye shall not see me: and again, a little while, and ye shall see me?

20 Verily, verily, I say unto you, That ye shall weep and lament, but the world shall rejoice; and ye shall be sorrowful, but your sorrow shall be turned into joy.

21 A woman when she is in travail hath sorrow, because her hour is come: but as soon as she is delivered of the child, she remembereth no more the anguish, for joy that a man is born into the world.

22 And ye now therefore have sorrow: but I will see you again, and your heart shall rejoice, and your joy no man taketh from you.

23 And in that day ye shall ask me nothing.

Verily, verily, I say unto you, Whatsoever ye shall ask the Father in my name, he will give it you.

24 Hitherto have ye asked nothing in my name: ask, and ye shall receive, that your joy may be full.

I Have Overcome the World

25 These things have I spoken unto you in proverbs: but the time cometh, when I shall no more speak unto you in proverbs, but I shall show you plainly of the Father.

26 At that day ye shall ask in my name: and I say not unto you, that I will pray the Father for you:

27 For the Father himself loveth you, because ye have loved me, and have believed that I came out from God.

28 I came forth from the Father, and am come into the world: again, I leave the world, and go to the Father.

29 His disciples said unto him, Lo, now speakest thou plainly, and speakest no proverb.

30 Now are we sure that thou knowest all things, and needest not that any man should ask thee: by this we believe that thou camest forth from God.

31 Jesus answered them, Do ye now believe?

32 Behold, the hour cometh, yea, is now come, that ye shall be scattered, every man to his own, and shall leave me alone: and yet I am not alone, because the Father is with me.

33 These things I have spoken unto you,

that in me ye might have peace. In the world
1515   2889
ye shall have tribulation: but be of good
2347   2293
cheer; I have overcome the world.
3528   2889

Jesus' Prayer for His Disciples

17 These words spake Jesus, and lifted up
2980   2424   1869
his eyes to heaven, and said, Father, the
3788   37.72   2036   3962
hour is come; glorify thy Son, that thy Son
5610 2064   1392   5207   5207
also may glorify thee:
1392

2 As thou hast given him power over all
2531   1325   1849
flesh, that he should give eternal life to as
4561   1325   166   2222
many as thou hast given him.
1325

3 And this is life eternal, that they might
2222   166   1097
know thee the only true God, and Jesus
3441   228   2316   2424
Christ, whom thou hast sent.
5547   649

4 I have glorified thee on the earth: I have
1392   1093   5048
finished the work which thou gavest me to do.
2041   1325   4160

5 And now, O Father, glorify thou me with
3568   3962   1392
thine own self with the glory which I had
1391
with thee before the world was.
2889

6 I have manifested thy name unto the men
5319   3686   444
which thou gavest me out of the world: thine
1325   2889
they were, and thou gavest them me; and they
1325
have kept thy word.
5083   3056

7 Now they have known that all things
3568   1097
whatsoever thou hast given me are of thee.
3745   1325

8 For I have given unto them the words
1325   4487
which thou gavest me; and they have received
1325   2983
them, and have known surely that I came out
1097   230   1831
from thee, and they have believed that thou
4100
didst send me.
649

9 I pray for them: I pray not for the
world, but for them which thou hast given
2889   1325
me; for they are thine.

10 And all mine are thine, and thine are mine; and I am glorified in them.

11 And now I am no more in the world, but these are in the world, and I come to thee. Holy Father, keep through thine own name those whom thou hast given me, that they may be one, as we are.

12 While I was with them in the world, I kept them in thy name: those that thou gavest me I have kept, and none of them is lost, but the son of perdition; that the Scripture might be fulfilled.

13 And now come I to thee; and these things I speak in the world, that they might have my joy fulfilled in themselves.

14 I have given them thy word; and the world hath hated them, because they are not of the world, even as I am not of the world.

15 I pray not that thou shouldest take them out of the world, but that thou shouldest keep them from the evil.

16 They are not of the world, even as I am not of the world.

17 Sanctify them through thy truth: thy word is truth.

18 As thou hast sent me into the world, even so have I also sent them into the world.

19 And for their sakes I sanctify myself, that they also might be sanctified through the truth.

20 Neither pray I for these alone, but for them also which shall believe on me through their word;

21 That they all may be one; as thou, Father, art in me, and I in thee, that they also may be one in us: that the world may believe that thou hast sent me.

22 And the glory which thou gavest me I have given them; that they may be one, even as we are one:

23 I in them, and thou in me, that they may be made perfect in one; and that the world may know that thou hast sent me, and hast loved them, as thou hast loved me.

24 Father, I will that they also, whom thou hast given me, be with me where I am; that they may behold my glory, which thou hast given me: for thou lovedst me before the foundation of the world.

25 O righteous Father, the world hath not known thee: but I have known thee, and these have known that thou hast sent me.

26 And I have declared unto them thy name, and will declare it; that the love wherewith thou hast loved me may be in them, and I in them.

The Betrayal and Arrest of Jesus

18 When Jesus had spoken these words, he went forth with his disciples over the brook Cedron, where was a garden, into the which he entered, and his disciples.

2 And Judas also, which betrayed him, knew the place: for Jesus ofttimes resorted thither with his disciples.

3 Judas then, having received a band of men and officers from the chief priests and

Pharisees, cometh thither with lanterns and torches and weapons.

4 Jesus therefore, knowing all things that should come upon him, went forth, and said unto them, Whom seek ye?

5 They answered him, Jesus of Nazareth. Jesus saith unto them, I am he. And Judas also, which betrayed him, stood with them.

6 As soon then as he had said unto them, I am he, they went backward, and fell to the ground.

7 Then asked he them again, Whom seek ye? And they said, Jesus of Nazareth.

8 Jesus answered, I have told you that I am he: if therefore ye seek me, let these go their way:

9 That the saying might be fulfilled, which he spake, Of them which thou gavest me have I lost none.

10 Then Simon Peter having a sword drew it, and smote the high priest's servant, and cut off his right ear. The servant's name was Malchus.

11 Then said Jesus unto Peter, Put up thy sword into the sheath: the cup which my Father hath given me, shall I not drink it?

Jesus Brought before the High Priest

12 Then the band and the captain and officers of the Jews took Jesus, and bound him,

13 And led him away to Annas first; for he was father-in-law to Cai'aphas, which was the high priest that same year.

14 Now Cai'aphas was he, which gave
counsel to the Jews, that it was expedient that
one man should die for the people.

Peter in the High Priest's Court

15 And Simon Peter followed Jesus, and so
did another disciple: that disciple was known
unto the high priest, and went in with Jesus
into the palace of the high priest.
16 But Peter stood at the door without.
Then went out that other disciple, which was
known unto the high priest, and spake
unto her that kept the door, and brought in
Peter.
17 Then saith the damsel that kept the door
unto Peter, Art not thou also one of this
man's disciples? He saith, I am not.
18 And the servants and officers stood there,
who had made a fire of coals, for it was cold;
and they warmed themselves: and Peter stood
with them, and warmed himself.

The High Priest Questions Jesus

19 The high priest then asked Jesus of his
disciples, and of his doctrine.
20 Jesus answered him, I spake openly to
the world; I ever taught in the synagogue,
and in the temple, whither the Jews always
resort; and in secret have I said nothing.
21 Why askest thou me? ask them which
heard me, what I have said unto them: behold, they know what I said.
22 And when he had thus spoken, one of
the officers which stood by struck Jesus with

the palm of his hand, saying, Answerest thou
the high priest so?
2036
749

23 Jesus answered him, If I have spoken
2424
evil, bear witness of the evil: but if well, why
2560 3140   2556   2573   5101
smitest thou me?
1194
24 Now Annas had sent him bound unto
452   649   1210
Cai'aphas the high priest.
2533   749

Peter Denies Jesus

25 And Simon Peter stood and warmed
4613   4074   2476   2328
himself. They said therefore unto him, Art
2036
not thou also one of his disciples? He denied
3101   720
it, and said, I am not.
2036
26 One of the servants of the high priest,
1401   749
being his kinsman whose ear Peter cut off,
5607   4773   5621   4074   609
saith, Did not I see thee in the garden with
1492   2779
him?

27 Peter then denied again; and immedi-
4074   720   2112
ately the cock crew.
220   5455

Jesus before Pilate

28 Then led they Jesus from Cai'aphas unto
71   2424   2533
the hall of judgment: and it was early; and
4232   4405
they themselves went not into the judgment
846   1525   1525   4232
hall, lest they should be defiled; but that they
3392
might eat the passover.
5315   3957
29 Pilate then went out unto them, and
4091
said, What accusation bring ye against this
2036   5101   2724   5342
man?
444
30 They answered and said unto him, If he
2036   1508
were not a malefactor, we would not have
1508   2555   3860
delivered him up unto thee.

31 Then said Pilate unto them, Take ye
2036   4091   2983
him, and judge him according to your law.
2919   3551

The Jews therefore said unto him, It is not
lawful for us to put any man to death:

32 That the saying of Jesus might be fulfilled, which he spake, signifying what death
he should die.

33 Then Pilate entered into the judgment
hall again, and called Jesus, and said unto
him, Art thou the King of the Jews?

34 Jesus answered him, Sayest thou this thing
of thyself, or did others tell it thee of me?

35 Pilate answered, Am I a Jew? Thine
own nation and the chief priests have delivered
thee unto me: what hast thou done?

36 Jesus answered, My kingdom is not of
this world: if my kingdom were of this world,
then would my servants fight, that I should
not be delivered to the Jews: but now is my
kingdom not from hence.

37 Pilate therefore said unto him, Art thou
a king then? Jesus answered, Thou sayest that
I am a king. To this end was I born, and for
this cause came I into the world, that I
should bear witness unto the truth. Every one
that is of the truth heareth my voice.

38 Pilate saith unto him, What is truth?

Jesus Sentenced to Die

And when he had said this, he went out
again unto the Jews, and saith unto them, I
find in him no fault at all.

39 But ye have a custom, that I should release unto you one at the passover: will ye
therefore that I release unto you the King of
the Jews?

40 Then cried they all again, saying, Not this man, but Barab'bas. Now Barab'bas was a robber.

19 Then Pilate therefore took Jesus, and scourged him.

2 And the soldiers platted a crown of thorns, and put it on his head, and they put on him a purple robe,

3 And said, Hail, King of the Jews! and they smote him with their hands.

4 Pilate therefore went forth again, and saith unto them, Behold, I bring him forth to you, that ye may know that I find no fault in him.

5 Then came Jesus forth, wearing the crown of thorns, and the purple robe. And Pilate saith unto them, Behold the man!

6 When the chief priests therefore and officers saw him, they cried out, saying, Crucify him, crucify him. Pilate saith unto them, Take ye him, and crucify him: for I find no fault in him.

7 The Jews answered him, We have a law, and by our law he ought to die, because he made himself the Son of God.

8 When Pilate therefore heard that saying, he was the more afraid;

9 And went again into the judgment hall, and saith unto Jesus, Whence art thou? But Jesus gave him no answer.

10 Then saith Pilate unto him, Speakest thou not unto me? knowest thou not that I have power to crucify thee, and have power to release thee?

11 Jesus answered, Thou couldest have no power at all against me, except it were given thee from above: therefore he that delivered me unto thee hath the greater sin.

12 And from thenceforth Pilate sought to release him: but the Jews cried out, saying, If thou let this man go, thou art not Caesar's friend: whosoever maketh himself a king speaketh against Caesar.

13 When Pilate therefore heard that saying, he brought Jesus forth, and sat down in the judgment seat in a place that is called the Pavement, but in the Hebrew, Gab'batha.

14 And it was the preparation of the passover, and about the sixth hour: and he saith unto the Jews, Behold your King!

15 But they cried out, Away with him, away with him, crucify him. Pilate saith unto them, Shall I crucify your King? The chief priests answered, We have no king but Caesar.

16 Then delivered he him therefore unto them to be crucified. And they took Jesus, and led him away.

The Crucifixion

17 And he bearing his cross went forth into a place called the place of a skull, which is called in the Hebrew Gol'gotha:

18 Where they crucified him, and two others with him, on either side one, and Jesus in the midst.

19 And Pilate wrote a title, and put it on the cross. And the writing was, JESUS OF NAZARETH THE KING OF THE JEWS.

20 This title then read many of the Jews;
for the place where Jesus was crucified was
nigh to the city: and it was written in Hebrew, and Greek, and Latin.

21 Then said the chief priests of the Jews
to Pilate, Write not, The King of the Jews;
but that he said, I am King of the Jews.

22 Pilate answered, What I have written I
have written.

23 Then the soldiers, when they had crucified Jesus, took his garments, and made four
parts, to every soldier a part; and also his
coat: now the coat was without seam, woven
from the top throughout.

24 They said therefore among themselves,
Let us not rend it, but cast lots for it, whose
it shall be: that the Scripture might be fulfilled, which saith, They parted my raiment
among them, and for my vesture they did
cast lots. These things therefore the soldiers
did.

25 Now there stood by the cross of Jesus
his mother, and his mother's sister, Mary the
wife of Cle'ophas, and Mary Mag'dalene.

26 When Jesus therefore saw his mother,
and the disciple standing by, whom he loved,
he saith unto his mother, Woman, behold thy
son!

27 Then saith he to the disciple, Behold thy
mother! And from that hour that disciple took
her unto his own home.

28 After this, Jesus knowing that all things
were now accomplished, that the Scripture
might be fulfilled, saith, I thirst.

29 Now there was set a vessel full of vinegar: and they filled a sponge with vinegar, and put it upon hyssop, and put it to his mouth.
30 When Jesus therefore had received the vinegar, he said, It is finished: and he bowed his head, and gave up the ghost.

Jesus' Side Pierced

31 The Jews therefore, because it was the preparation, that the bodies should not remain upon the cross on the sabbath day, (for that sabbath day was a high day,) besought Pilate that their legs might be broken, and that they might be taken away.
32 Then came the soldiers, and brake the legs of the first, and of the other which was crucified with him.
33 But when they came to Jesus, and saw that he was dead already, they brake not his legs:
34 But one of the soldiers with a spear pierced his side, and forthwith came there out blood and water.
35 And he that saw it bare record, and his record is true; and he knoweth that he saith true, that ye might believe.
36 For these things were done, that the Scripture should be fulfilled, A bone of him shall not be broken.
37 And again another Scripture saith, They shall look on him whom they pierced.

The Burial of Jesus

38 And after this Joseph of Arimathe'a, being a disciple of Jesus, but secretly for fear

of the Jews, besought Pilate that he might take away the body of Jesus: and Pilate gave him leave. He came therefore, and took the body of Jesus.

39 And there came also Nicode'mus, which at the first came to Jesus by night, and brought a mixture of myrrh and aloes, about a hundred pound weight.

40 Then took they the body of Jesus, and wound it in linen clothes with the spices, as the manner of the Jews is to bury.

41 Now in the place where he was crucified there was a garden; and in the garden a new sepulchre, wherein was never man yet laid.

42 There laid they Jesus therefore because of the Jews' preparation day; for the sepulchre was nigh at hand.

The Resurrection

20 The first day of the week cometh Mary Mag'dalene early, when it was yet dark, unto the sepulchre, and seeth the stone taken away from the sepulchre.

2 Then she runneth, and cometh to Simon Peter, and to the other disciple, whom Jesus loved, and saith unto them, They have taken away the Lord out of the sepulchre, and we know not where they have laid him.

3 Peter therefore went forth, and that other disciple, and came to the sepulchre.

4 So they ran both together: and the other disciple did outrun Peter, and came first to the sepulchre.

5 And he stooping down, and looking in, saw the linen clothes lying; yet went he not in.

6 Then cometh Simon Peter following him, and went into the sepulchre, and seeth the linen clothes lie,

7 And the napkin, that was about his head, not lying with the linen clothes, but wrapped together in a place by itself.

8 Then went in also that other disciple, which came first to the sepulchre, and he saw, and believed.

9 For as yet they knew not the Scripture, that he must rise again from the dead.

10 Then the disciples went away again unto their own home.

Jesus Appears to Mary Magdalene

11 But Mary stood without at the sepulchre weeping: and as she wept, she stooped down, and looked into the sepulchre,

12 And seeth two angels in white sitting, the one at the head, and the other at the feet, where the body of Jesus had lain.

13 And they say unto her, Woman, why weepest thou? She saith unto them, Because they have taken away my Lord, and I know not where they have laid him.

14 And when she had thus said, she turned herself back, and saw Jesus standing, and knew not that it was Jesus.

15 Jesus saith unto her, Woman, why weepest thou? whom seekest thou? She, supposing him to be the gardener, saith unto him, Sir,

if thou have borne him hence, tell me where
thou hast laid him, and I will take him away.

16 Jesus saith unto her, Mary. She turned
herself, and saith unto him, Rabbo′ni; which
is to say, Master.

17 Jesus saith unto her, Touch me not;
for I am not yet ascended to my Father: but
go to my brethren, and say unto them, I
ascend unto my Father, and your Father; and
to my God, and your God.

18 Mary Mag′dalene came and told the
disciples that she had seen the Lord, and that
he had spoken these things unto her.

Jesus Appears to His Disciples

19 Then the same day at evening, being the
first day of the week, when the doors were
shut where the disciples were assembled for
fear of the Jews, came Jesus and stood in the
midst, and saith unto them, Peace be unto
you.

20 And when he had so said, he showed
unto them his hands and his side. Then were
the disciples glad, when they saw the
Lord.

21 Then said Jesus to them again, Peace be
unto you: as my Father hath sent me, even
so send I you.

22 And when he had said this, he breathed
on them, and saith unto them, Receive ye the
Holy Ghost:

23 Whosesoever sins ye remit, they are re-
mitted unto them; and whosesoever sins ye retain, they are retained.

The Unbelief of Thomas

24 But Thomas, one of the twelve, called Did'ymus, was not with them when Jesus came.

25 The other disciples therefore said unto him, We have seen the Lord. But he said unto them, Except I shall see in his hands the print of the nails, and put my finger into the print of the nails, and thrust my hand into his side, I will not believe.

26 And after eight days again his disciples were within, and Thomas with them: then came Jesus, the doors being shut, and stood in the midst, and said, Peace be unto you.

27 Then saith he to Thomas, Reach hither thy finger, and behold my hands; and reach hither thy hand, and thrust it into my side; and be not faithless, but believing.

28 And Thomas answered and said unto him, My Lord and my God.

29 Jesus saith unto him, Thomas, because thou hast seen me, thou hast believed: blessed are they that have not seen, and yet have believed.

The Purpose of the Book

30 And many other signs truly did Jesus in the presence of his disciples, which are not written in this book:

31 But these are written, that ye might believe that Jesus is the Christ, the Son of God; and that believing ye might have life through his name.

Jesus Appears to Seven Disciples

21 After these things Jesus showed himself again to the disciples at the sea of Tibe′ri-as; and on this wise showed he himself.

2 There were together Simon Peter, and Thomas called Did′ymus, and Nathan′a-el of Cana in Galilee, and the sons of Zeb′edee, and two other of his disciples.

3 Simon Peter saith unto them, I go a fishing. They say unto him, We also go with thee. They went forth, and entered into a ship immediately; and that night they caught nothing.

4 But when the morning was now come, Jesus stood on the shore; but the disciples knew not that it was Jesus.

5 Then Jesus saith unto them, Children, have ye any meat? They answered him, No.

6 And he said unto them, Cast the net on the right side of the ship, and ye shall find. They cast therefore, and now they were not able to draw it for the multitude of fishes.

7 Therefore that disciple whom Jesus loved saith unto Peter, It is the Lord. Now when Simon Peter heard that it was the Lord, he girt his fisher's coat unto him, (for he was naked,) and did cast himself into the sea.

8 And the other disciples came in a little ship, (for they were not far from land, but as it were two hundred cubits,) dragging the net with fishes.

9 As soon then as they were come to land,

they saw a fire of coals there, and fish laid thereon, and bread.

10 Jesus saith unto them, Bring of the fish which ye have now caught.

11 Simon Peter went up, and drew the net to land full of great fishes, a hundred and fifty and three: and for all there were so many, yet was not the net broken.

12 Jesus saith unto them, Come and dine. And none of the disciples durst ask him, Who art thou? knowing that it was the Lord.

13 Jesus then cometh, and taketh bread, and giveth them, and fish likewise.

14 This is now the third time that Jesus showed himself to his disciples, after that he was risen from the dead.

Feed My Sheep

15 So when they had dined, Jesus saith to Simon Peter, Simon, son of Jona, lovest thou me more than these? He saith unto him, Yea, Lord; thou knowest that I love thee. He saith unto him, Feed my lambs.

16 He saith to him again the second time, Simon, son of Jona, lovest thou me? He saith unto him, Yea, Lord; thou knowest that I love thee. He saith unto him, Feed my sheep.

17 He saith unto him the third time, Simon, son of Jona, lovest thou me? Peter was grieved because he said unto him the third time, Lovest thou me? And he said unto him, Lord, thou knowest all things; thou knowest that I love thee. Jesus saith unto him, Feed my sheep.

18 Verily, verily, I say unto thee, When thou wast young, thou girdedst thyself, and walkedst whither thou wouldest: but when thou shalt be old, thou shalt stretch forth thy hands, and another shall gird thee, and carry thee whither thou wouldest not.

19 This spake he, signifying by what death he should glorify God. And when he had spoken this, he saith unto him, Follow me.

The Beloved Disciple

20 Then Peter, turning about, seeth the disciple whom Jesus loved following; which also leaned on his breast at supper, and said, Lord, which is he that betrayeth thee?

21 Peter seeing him saith to Jesus, Lord, and what shall this man do?

22 Jesus saith unto him, If I will that he tarry till I come, what is that to thee? follow thou me.

23 Then went this saying abroad among the brethren, that that disciple should not die: yet Jesus said not unto him, He shall not die; but, If I will that he tarry till I come, what is that to thee?

24 This is the disciple which testifieth of these things, and wrote these things: and we know that his testimony is true.

25 And there are also many other things which Jesus did, the which, if they should be written every one, I suppose that even the world itself could not contain the books that should be written. Amen.

THE ACTS OF THE APOSTLES

The Promise of the Holy Spirit

1 The former treatise have I made, O The-oph'ilus, of all that Jesus began both to do and teach,

2 Until the day in which he was taken up, after that he through the Holy Ghost had given commandments unto the apostles whom he had chosen:

3 To whom also he showed himself alive after his passion by many infallible proofs, being seen of them forty days, and speaking of the things pertaining to the kingdom of God:

4 And, being assembled together with them, commanded them that they should not depart from Jerusalem, but wait for the promise of the Father, which, saith he, ye have heard of me.

5 For John truly baptized with water; but ye shall be baptized with the Holy Ghost not many days hence.

The Ascension

6 When they therefore were come together, they asked of him, saying, Lord, wilt thou at this time restore again the kingdom to Israel?

7 And he said unto them, It is not for you to know the times or the seasons, which the Father hath put in his own power.

8 But ye shall receive power, after that the

Holy Ghost is come upon you: and ye shall be witnesses unto me both in Jerusalem, and in all Judea, and in Samaria, and unto the uttermost part of the earth.

9 And when he had spoken these things, while they beheld, he was taken up; and a cloud received him out of their sight.

10 And while they looked steadfastly toward heaven as he went up, behold, two men stood by them in white apparel;

11 Which also said, Ye men of Galilee, why stand ye gazing up into heaven? this same Jesus, which is taken up from you into heaven, shall so come in like manner as ye have seen him go into heaven.

Judas' Successor Chosen

12 Then returned they unto Jerusalem from the mount called Ol'ivet, which is from Jerusalem a sabbath day's journey.

13 And when they were come in, they went up into an upper room, where abode both Peter, and James, and John, and Andrew, Philip, and Thomas, Bartholomew, and Matthew, James the son of Al'pheus, and Simon Zelo'tes, and Judas the brother of James.

14 These all continued with one accord in prayer and supplication, with the women, and Mary the mother of Jesus, and with his brethren.

15 And in those days Peter stood up in the midst of the disciples, and said, (the number of names together were about a hundred and twenty,)

16 Men and brethren, this Scripture must needs have been fulfilled, which the Holy Ghost by the mouth of David spake before concerning Judas, which was guide to them that took Jesus.

17 For he was numbered with us, and had obtained part of this ministry.

18 Now this man purchased a field with the reward of iniquity; and falling headlong, he burst asunder in the midst, and all his bowels gushed out.

19 And it was known unto all the dwellers at Jerusalem; insomuch as that field is called, in their proper tongue, Acel'dama, that is to say, The field of blood.

20 For it is written in the book of Psalms, Let his habitation be desolate, and let no man dwell therein: and, His bishopric let another take.

21 Wherefore of these men which have companied with us all the time that the Lord Jesus went in and out among us,

22 Beginning from the baptism of John, unto that same day that he was taken up from us, must one be ordained to be a witness with us of his resurrection.

23 And they appointed two, Joseph called Barsabas, who was surnamed Justus, and Matthi'as.

24 And they prayed, and said, Thou, Lord, which knowest the hearts of all men, show whether of these two thou hast chosen,

25 That he may take part of this ministry and apostleship, from which Judas by trans-

gression fell, that he might go to his own place.

26 And they gave forth their lots; and the lot fell upon Matthi′as; and he was numbered with the eleven apostles.

The Coming of the Holy Spirit

2 And when the day of Pentecost was fully come, they were all with one accord in one place.

2 And suddenly there came a sound from heaven as of a rushing mighty wind, and it filled all the house where they were sitting.

3 And there appeared unto them cloven tongues like as of fire, and it sat upon each of them.

4 And they were all filled with the Holy Ghost, and began to speak with other tongues, as the Spirit gave them utterance.

5 And there were dwelling at Jerusalem Jews, devout men, out of every nation under heaven.

6 Now when this was noised abroad, the multitude came together, and were confounded, because that every man heard them speak in his own language.

7 And they were all amazed and marveled, saying one to another, Behold, are not all these which speak Galileans?

8 And how hear we every man in our own tongue, wherein we were born?

9 Par′thi-ans, and Medes, and E′lamites, and the dwellers in Mesopota′mi-a, and in Judea, and Cappado′cia, in Pontus, and Asia,

10 Phryg′i-a, and Pamphyl′i-a, in Egypt, and

in the parts of Libya about Cyre'ne, and
strangers of Rome, Jews and proselytes,

11 Cretes and Arabians, we do hear them speak
in our tongues the wonderful works of God.

12 And they were all amazed, and were in
doubt, saying one to another, What meaneth
this?

13 Others mocking said, These men are full
of new wine.

Peter's Address at Pentecost

14 But Peter, standing up with the eleven,
lifted up his voice, and said unto them, Ye
men of Judea, and all ye that dwell at Jerusalem, be this known unto you, and hearken
to my words:

15 For these are not drunken, as ye suppose, seeing it is but the third hour of the
day.

16 But this is that which was spoken by the
prophet Joel;

17 And it shall come to pass in the last
days, saith God, I will pour out of my Spirit
upon all flesh: and your sons and your
daughters shall prophesy, and your young men
shall see visions, and your old men shall
dream dreams:

18 And on my servants and on my hand-
maidens I will pour out in those days of my
Spirit; and they shall prophesy:

19 And I will show wonders in heaven
above, and signs in the earth beneath; blood,
and fire, and vapor of smoke:

20 The sun shall be turned into darkness,

and the moon into blood, before that great and notable day of the Lord come:

21 And it shall come to pass, that whosoever shall call on the name of the Lord shall be saved.

22 Ye men of Israel, hear these words; Jesus of Nazareth, a man approved of God among you by miracles and wonders and signs, which God did by him in the midst of you, as ye yourselves also know:

23 Him, being delivered by the determinate counsel and foreknowledge of God, ye have taken, and by wicked hands have crucified and slain:

24 Whom God hath raised up, having loosed the pains of death: because it was not possible that he should be holden of it.

25 For David speaketh concerning him, I foresaw the Lord always before my face; for he is on my right hand, that I should not be moved:

26 Therefore did my heart rejoice, and my tongue was glad; moreover also my flesh shall rest in hope:

27 Because thou wilt not leave my soul in hell, neither wilt thou suffer thine Holy One to see corruption.

28 Thou hast made known to me the ways of life; thou shalt make me full of joy with thy countenance.

29 Men and brethren, let me freely speak unto you of the patriarch David, that he is both dead and buried, and his sepulchre is with us unto this day.

30 Therefore being a prophet, and knowing that God had sworn with an oath to him, that of the fruit of his loins, according to the flesh, he would raise up Christ to sit on his throne;

31 He, seeing this before, spake of the resurrection of Christ, that his soul was not left in hell, neither his flesh did see corruption.

32 This Jesus hath God raised up, whereof we all are witnesses.

33 Therefore being by the right hand of God exalted, and having received of the Father the promise of the Holy Ghost, he hath shed forth this, which ye now see and hear.

34 For David is not ascended into the heavens: but he saith himself, The LORD said unto my Lord, Sit thou on my right hand,

35 Until I make thy foes thy footstool.

36 Therefore let all the house of Israel know assuredly, that God hath made that same Jesus, whom ye have crucified, both Lord and Christ.

37 Now when they heard this, they were pricked in their heart, and said unto Peter and to the rest of the apostles, Men and brethren, what shall we do?

38 Then Peter said unto them, Repent, and be baptized every one of you in the name of Jesus Christ for the remission of sins, and ye shall receive the gift of the Holy Ghost.

39 For the promise is unto you, and to your children, and to all that are afar off, even as many as the Lord our God shall call.

40 And with many other words did he testify and exhort, saying, Save yourselves from this untoward generation.

41 Then they that gladly received his word were baptized: and the same day there were added unto them about three thousand souls.

42 And they continued steadfastly in the apostles' doctrine and fellowship, and in breaking of bread, and in prayers.

Life among the Believers

43 And fear came upon every soul: and many wonders and signs were done by the apostles.

44 And all that believed were together, and had all things common;

45 And sold their possessions and goods, and parted them to all men, as every man had need.

46 And they, continuing daily with one accord in the temple, and breaking bread from house to house, did eat their meat with gladness and singleness of heart,

47 Praising God, and having favor with all the people. And the Lord added to the church daily such as should be saved.

A Lame Man Healed at the Gate
of the Temple

3 Now Peter and John went up together into the temple at the hour of prayer, being the ninth hour.

2 And a certain man lame from his mother's

womb was carried, whom they laid daily at the gate of the temple which is called Beautiful, to ask alms of them that entered into the temple;

3 Who, seeing Peter and John about to go into the temple, asked an alms.

4 And Peter, fastening his eyes upon him with John, said, Look on us.

5 And he gave heed unto them, expecting to receive something of them.

6 Then Peter said, Silver and gold have I none; but such as I have give I thee: In the name of Jesus Christ of Nazareth rise up and walk.

7 And he took him by the right hand, and lifted him up: and immediately his feet and ankle bones received strength.

8 And he leaping up stood, and walked, and entered with them into the temple, walking, and leaping, and praising God.

9 And all the people saw him walking and praising God:

10 And they knew that it was he which sat for alms at the Beautiful gate of the temple: and they were filled with wonder and amazement at that which had happened unto him.

Peter's Address in Solomon's Porch

11 And as the lame man which was healed held Peter and John, all the people ran together unto them in the porch that is called Solomon's, greatly wondering.

12 And when Peter saw it, he answered unto the people, Ye men of Israel, why marvel

ye at this? or why look ye so earnestly on us, as though by our own power or holiness we had made this man to walk?

13 The God of Abraham, and of Isaac, and of Jacob, the God of our fathers, hath glorified his Son Jesus; whom ye delivered up, and denied him in the presence of Pilate, when he was determined to let him go.

14 But ye denied the Holy One and the Just, and desired a murderer to be granted unto you;

15 And killed the Prince of life, whom God hath raised from the dead; whereof we are witnesses.

16 And his name, through faith in his name, hath made this man strong, whom ye see and know: yea, the faith which is by him hath given him this perfect soundness in the presence of you all.

17 And now, brethren, I wot that through ignorance ye did it, as did also your rulers.

18 But those things, which God before had showed by the mouth of all his prophets, that Christ should suffer, he hath so fulfilled.

19 Repent ye therefore, and be converted, that your sins may be blotted out, when the times of refreshing shall come from the presence of the Lord;

20 And he shall send Jesus Christ, which before was preached unto you:

21 Whom the heaven must receive until the times of restitution of all things, which God hath spoken by the mouth of all his holy prophets since the world began.

22 For Moses truly said unto the fathers, A Prophet shall the Lord your God raise up unto you of your brethren, like unto me; him shall ye hear in all things whatsoever he shall say unto you.

23 And it shall come to pass, that every soul, which will not hear that Prophet, shall be destroyed from among the people.

24 Yea, and all the prophets from Samuel and those that follow after, as many as have spoken, have likewise foretold of these days.

25 Ye are the children of the prophets, and of the covenant which God made with our fathers, saying unto Abraham, And in thy seed shall all the kindreds of the earth be blessed.

26 Unto you first God, having raised up his Son Jesus, sent him to bless you, in turning away every one of you from his iniquities.

Peter and John before the Council

4 And as they spake unto the people, the priests, and the captain of the temple, and the Sadducees, came upon them,

2 Being grieved that they taught the people, and preached through Jesus the resurrection from the dead.

3 And they laid hands on them, and put them in hold unto the next day: for it was now eventide.

4 Howbeit many of them which heard the word believed; and the number of the men was about five thousand.

5 And it came to pass on the morrow, that their rulers, and elders, and scribes,

6 And Annas the high priest, and Cai′a-phas, and John, and Alexander, and as many as were of the kindred of the high priest, were gathered together at Jerusalem.

7 And when they had set them in the midst, they asked, By what power, or by what name, have ye done this?

8 Then Peter, filled with the Holy Ghost, said unto them, Ye rulers of the people, and elders of Israel,

9 If we this day be examined of the good deed done to the impotent man, by what means he is made whole;

10 Be it known unto you all, and to all the people of Israel, that by the name of Jesus Christ of Nazareth, whom ye crucified, whom God raised from the dead, even by him doth this man stand here before you whole.

11 This is the stone which was set at nought of you builders, which is become the head of the corner.

12 Neither is there salvation in any other: for there is none other name under heaven given among men, whereby we must be saved.

13 Now when they saw the boldness of Peter and John, and perceived that they were unlearned and ignorant men, they marveled; and they took knowledge of them, that they had been with Jesus.

14 And beholding the man which was healed standing with them, they could say nothing against it.

15 But when they had commanded them to

go aside out of the council, they conferred
among themselves,

16 Saying, What shall we do to these men?
for that indeed a notable miracle hath been
done by them is manifest to all them
that dwell in Jerusalem; and we cannot
deny it.

17 But that it spread no further among the
people, let us straitly threaten them, that they
speak henceforth to no man in this name.

18 And they called them, and commanded
them not to speak at all nor teach in the
name of Jesus.

19 But Peter and John answered and said
unto them, Whether it be right in the sight of
God to hearken unto you more than unto
God, judge ye.

20 For we cannot but speak the things
which we have seen and heard.

21 So when they had further threatened
them, they let them go, finding nothing how
they might punish them, because of the
people: for all men glorified God for that
which was done.

22 For the man was above forty years
old, on whom this miracle of healing was
showed.

The Believers Pray for Boldness

23 And being let go, they went to their own
company, and reported all that the chief
priests and elders had said unto them.

24 And when they heard that, they lifted
up their voice to God with one accord, and

said, Lord, thou art God, which hast made heaven, and earth, and the sea, and all that in them is;

25 Who by the mouth of thy servant David hast said, Why did the heathen rage, and the people imagine vain things?

26 The kings of the earth stood up, and the rulers were gathered together against the Lord, and against his Christ.

27 For of a truth against thy holy child Jesus, whom thou hast anointed, both Herod, and Pontius Pilate, with the Gentiles, and the people of Israel, were gathered together,

28 For to do whatsoever thy hand and thy counsel determined before to be done.

29 And now, Lord, behold their threatenings: and grant unto thy servants, that with all boldness they may speak thy word,

30 By stretching forth thine hand to heal; and that signs and wonders may be done by the name of thy holy child Jesus.

31 And when they had prayed, the place was shaken where they were assembled together; and they were all filled with the Holy Ghost, and they spake the word of God with boldness.

All Things in Common

32 And the multitude of them that believed were of one heart and of one soul: neither said any of them that aught of the things which he possessed was his own; but they had all things common.

33 And with great power gave the apostles

witness of the resurrection of the Lord Jesus: and great grace was upon them all.

34 Neither was there any among them that lacked: for as many as were possessors of lands or houses sold them, and brought the prices of the things that were sold,

35 And laid them down at the apostles' feet: and distribution was made unto every man according as he had need.

36 And Joses, who by the apostles was surnamed Barnabas, (which is, being interpreted, The son of consolation,) a Levite, and of the country of Cyprus,

37 Having land, sold it, and brought the money, and laid it at the apostles' feet.

Ananias and Sapphira

5 But a certain man named Anani′as, with Sapphi′ra his wife, sold a possession,

2 And kept back part of the price, his wife also being privy to it, and brought a certain part, and laid it at the apostles' feet.

3 But Peter said, Anani′as, why hath Satan filled thine heart to lie to the Holy Ghost, and to keep back part of the price of the land?

4 While it remained, was it not thine own? and after it was sold, was it not in thine own power? why hast thou conceived this thing in thine heart? thou hast not lied unto men, but unto God.

5 And Anani′as hearing these words fell down, and gave up the ghost: and great fear came on all them that heard these things.

6 And the young men arose, wound him up, and carried him out, and buried him.

7 And it was about the space of three hours after, when his wife, not knowing what was done, came in.

8 And Peter answered unto her, Tell me whether ye sold the land for so much? And she said, Yea, for so much.

9 Then Peter said unto her, How is it that ye have agreed together to tempt the Spirit of the Lord? behold, the feet of them which have buried thy husband are at the door, and shall carry thee out.

10 Then fell she down straightway at his feet, and yielded up the ghost: and the young men came in, and found her dead, and, carrying her forth, buried her by her husband.

11 And great fear came upon all the church, and upon as many as heard these things.

Many Signs and Wonders Are Performed

12 And by the hands of the apostles were many signs and wonders wrought among the people; (and they were all with one accord in Solomon's porch.

13 And of the rest durst no man join himself to them: but the people magnified them.

14 And believers were the more added to the Lord, multitudes both of men and women;)

15 Insomuch that they brought forth the sick into the streets, and laid them on beds and couches, that at the least the shadow of Peter passing by might overshadow some of them.

16 There came also a multitude out of the
cities round about unto Jerusalem, bringing
sick folks, and them which were vexed with
unclean spirits: and they were healed every
one.

The Apostles Are Persecuted

17 Then the high priest rose up, and all
they that were with him, (which is the sect of
the Sadducees,) and were filled with indignation,

18 And laid their hands on the apostles, and
put them in the common prison.

19 But the angel of the Lord by night
opened the prison doors, and brought them
forth, and said,

20 Go, stand and speak in the temple to
the people all the words of this life.

21 And when they heard that, they entered
into the temple early in the morning, and
taught. But the high priest came, and they
that were with him, and called the council together, and all the senate of the children of
Israel, and sent to the prison to have them
brought.

22 But when the officers came, and found
them not in the prison, they returned, and
told,

23 Saying, The prison truly found we shut
with all safety, and the keepers standing
without before the doors: but when we had
opened, we found no man within.

24 Now when the high priest and the captain of the temple and the chief priests heard

these things, they doubted of them whereunto this would grow.

25 Then came one and told them, saying, Behold, the men whom ye put in prison are standing in the temple, and teaching the people.

26 Then went the captain with the officers, and brought them without violence: for they feared the people, lest they should have been stoned.

27 And when they had brought them, they set them before the council: and the high priest asked them,

28 Saying, Did not we straitly command you that ye should not teach in this name? and, behold, ye have filled Jerusalem with your doctrine, and intend to bring this man's blood upon us.

29 Then Peter and the other apostles answered and said, We ought to obey God rather than men.

30 The God of our fathers raised up Jesus, whom ye slew and hanged on a tree.

31 Him hath God exalted with his right hand to be a Prince and a Saviour, for to give repentance to Israel, and forgiveness of sins.

32 And we are his witnesses of these things; and so is also the Holy Ghost, whom God hath given to them that obey him.

33 When they heard that, they were cut to the heart, and took counsel to slay them.

34 Then stood there up one in the council, a Pharisee, named Gama'li-el, a doctor of the

law, had in reputation among all the people,
and commanded to put the apostles forth a
little space;

35 And said unto them, Ye men of Israel,
take heed to yourselves what ye intend to do
as touching these men.

36 For before these days rose up Theu'das,
boasting himself to be somebody; to whom a
number of men, about four hundred, joined
themselves: who was slain; and all, as many
as obeyed him, were scattered, and brought to
nought.

37 After this man rose up Judas of Galilee
in the days of the taxing, and drew away
much people after him: he also perished; and
all, even as many as obeyed him, were dispersed.

38 And now I say unto you, Refrain from
these men, and let them alone: for if this
counsel or this work be of men, it will come
to nought:

39 But if it be of God, ye cannot overthrow it; lest haply ye be found even to fight
against God.

40 And to him they agreed: and when they
had called the apostles, and beaten them, they
commanded that they should not speak in the
name of Jesus, and let them go.

41 And they departed from the presence of
the council, rejoicing that they were counted
worthy to suffer shame for his name.

42 And daily in the temple, and in every
house, they ceased not to teach and preach
Jesus Christ.

The Appointment of the Seven

6 And in those days, when the number of the disciples was multiplied, there arose a murmuring of the Grecians against the Hebrews, because their widows were neglected in the daily ministration.

2 Then the twelve called the multitude of the disciples unto them, and said, It is not reason that we should leave the word of God, and serve tables.

3 Wherefore, brethren, look ye out among you seven men of honest report, full of the Holy Ghost and wisdom, whom we may appoint over this business.

4 But we will give ourselves continually to prayer, and to the ministry of the word.

5 And the saying pleased the whole multitude: and they chose Stephen, a man full of faith and of the Holy Ghost, and Philip, and Proch'orus, and Nica'nor, and Timon, and Par'menas, and Nicolas a proselyte of An'ti-och;

6 Whom they set before the apostles: and when they had prayed, they laid their hands on them.

7 And the word of God increased; and the number of the disciples multiplied in Jeru-salem greatly; and a great company of the priests were obedient to the faith.

The Arrest of Stephen

8 And Stephen, full of faith and power, did great wonders and miracles among the people.

9 Then there arose certain of the synagogue,

which is called the synagogue of the Liber-
tines, and Cyre′nians, and Alexandrians, and
of them of Cili′cia and of Asia, disputing with
Stephen.

10 And they were not able to resist the wisdom and the spirit by which he spake.

11 Then they suborned men, which said,
We have heard him speak blasphemous words
against Moses, and against God.

12 And they stirred up the people, and the
elders, and the scribes, and came upon him,
and caught him, and brought him to the
council,

13 And set up false witnesses, which said,
This man ceaseth not to speak blasphemous
words against this holy place, and the law:

14 For we have heard him say, that this
Jesus of Nazareth shall destroy this place, and
shall change the customs which Moses delivered us.

15 And all that sat in the council, looking
steadfastly on him, saw his face as it had been
the face of an angel.

Stephen's Defense

7 Then said the high priest, Are these
things so?

2 And he said, Men, brethren, and fathers,
hearken; The God of glory appeared unto our
father Abraham, when he was in Mesopota′-
mi-a, before he dwelt in Haran,

3 And said unto him, Get thee out of thy
country, and from thy kindred, and come into
the land which I shall show thee.

4 Then came he out of the land of the Chalde´ans, and dwelt in Haran: and from thence, when his father was dead, he removed him into this land, wherein ye now dwell.

5 And he gave him none inheritance in it, no, not so much as to set his foot on: yet he promised that he would give it to him for a possession, and to his seed after him, when as yet he had no child.

6 And God spake on this wise, That his seed should sojourn in a strange land; and that they should bring them into bondage, and entreat them evil four hundred years.

7 And the nation to whom they shall be in bondage will I judge, said God: and after that shall they come forth, and serve me in this place.

8 And he gave him the covenant of circumcision: and so Abraham begat Isaac, and circumcised him the eighth day; and Isaac begat Jacob; and Jacob begat the twelve patriarchs.

9 And the patriarchs, moved with envy, sold Joseph into Egypt: but God was with him,

10 And delivered him out of all his afflictions, and gave him favor and wisdom in the sight of Pharaoh king of Egypt; and he made him governor over Egypt and all his house.

11 Now there came a dearth over all the land of Egypt and Canaan, and great affliction: and our fathers found no sustenance.

12 But when Jacob heard that there was corn in Egypt, he sent out our fathers first.

13 And at the second time Joseph[2501] was made known[1208] to his brethren; and Joseph's[2501] kindred[319] was made known[80] unto Pharaoh.

14 Then[1085] sent[1096] Joseph,[2501] and called[5318] his father[5328] Jacob[649] to him,[2501] and all his[649] kindred,[3333] threescore[3962] and fifteen[2384] souls.[4772] [1440,4002]

15 So Jacob[5590] went[2384] down[2597] into Egypt, and died, he, and our fathers,[125]

16 And[5053] were carried[3962] over into Shechem,[4966] and laid[3346] in the sepulchre that Abraham bought for a[5087] sum of money[3418] of the sons[11] of Hamor,[5608] the father[5092] of[694] Shechem.[5207] [1697]

17 But when[4966] the time of the promise drew[2531] nigh, which[5550] God had[1860] sworn to Abraham,[1448] the people grew[2316] and[3660] multiplied[11] in Egypt,[2992] [837]

18 Till[4129] another king arose, which[125] knew not[891] Joseph.[2087] [935] [450] [1492]

19 The[2501] same dealt subtilely[2686] with our kin-[1085] dred, and evil[2559] entreated our fathers,[3962] so that they cast[1570] out their young[1025] children, to the end they might not live.[2225]

20 In which time Moses was born, and was exceeding fair,[2540] and[3475] nourished[1080] up in his father's[3962] house[791] three months:[397]

21 And[3624] when[3376] he was cast out, Pharaoh's daughter took him up,[1620] and nourished him[5328] for her own[2364] son.[337] [337] [397] [5207]

22 And Moses was learned in all the wis-[5207] dom of the[3475] Egyptians,[3811] and was mighty[4678] in words[124] and in deeds.[1415]

23 And when[3056] he was full[2041] forty years old, it came into his[5550] heart to[4137] visit[5063] his brethren the children of Israel.[305] [2588] [1980] [80]

24 And seeing[5207] one[2474] of them suffer wrong,[1492] [5100] [91]

he defended him, and avenged him that was oppressed, and smote the Egyptian:

25 For he supposed his brethren would have understood how that God by his hand would deliver them; but they understood not.

26 And the next day he showed himself unto them as they strove, and would have set them at one again, saying, Sirs, ye are brethren; why do ye wrong one to another?

27 But he that did his neighbor wrong thrust him away, saying, Who made thee a ruler and a judge over us?

28 Wilt thou kill me, as thou didst the Egyptian yesterday?

29 Then fled Moses at this saying, and was a stranger in the land of Mid'i-an, where he begat two sons.

30 And when forty years were expired, there appeared to him in the wilderness of mount Si'nai an angel of the Lord in a flame of fire in a bush.

31 When Moses saw it, he wondered at the sight: and as he drew near to behold it, the voice of the Lord came unto him,

32 Saying, I am the God of thy fathers, the God of Abraham and the God of Isaac, and the God of Jacob. Then Moses trembled, and durst not behold.

33 Then said the Lord to him, Put off thy shoes from thy feet: for the place where thou standest is holy ground.

34 I have seen, I have seen the affliction of my people which is in Egypt, and I have heard their groaning, and am come down to

deliver them. And now come, I will send thee
into Egypt.

35 This Moses whom they refused, saying,
Who made thee a ruler and a judge? the same
did God send to be a ruler and a deliverer by
the hand of the angel which appeared to him
in the bush.

36 He brought them out, after that he had
showed wonders and signs in the land of
Egypt, and in the Red sea, and in the wilderness forty years.

37 This is that Moses, which said unto the
children of Israel, A Prophet shall the Lord
your God raise up unto you of your brethren,
like unto me; him shall ye hear.

38 This is he, that was in the church in the
wilderness with the angel which spake to him
in the mount Si'nai, and with our fathers:
who received the lively oracles to give unto
us:

39 To whom our fathers would not obey,
but thrust him from them, and in their hearts
turned back again into Egypt,

40 Saying unto Aaron, Make us gods to go
before us: for as for this Moses, which
brought us out of the land of Egypt, we wot
not what is become of him.

41 And they made a calf in those days, and
offered sacrifice unto the idol, and rejoiced in
the works of their own hands.

42 Then God turned, and gave them up to
worship the host of heaven; as it is written in
the book of the prophets, O ye house of
Israel, have ye offered to me slain beasts and

sacrifices by the space of forty years in the wilderness?

43 Yea, ye took up the tabernacle of Moloch, and the star of your god Remphan, figures which ye made to worship them: and I will carry you away beyond Babylon.

44 Our fathers had the tabernacle of witness in the wilderness, as he had appointed, speaking unto Moses, that he should make it according to the fashion that he had seen.

45 Which also our fathers that came after brought in with Joshua into the possession of the Gentiles, whom God drave out before the face of our fathers, unto the days of David;

46 Who found favor before God, and desired to find a tabernacle for the God of Jacob.

47 But Solomon built him a house.

48 Howbeit the Most High dwelleth not in temples made with hands; as saith the prophet,

49 Heaven is my throne, and earth is my footstool: what house will ye build me? saith the Lord: or what is the place of my rest?

50 Hath not my hand made all these things?

51 Ye stiffnecked and uncircumcised in heart and ears, ye do always resist the Holy Ghost: as your fathers did, so do ye.

52 Which of the prophets have not your

fathers persecuted? and they have slain them which showed before of the coming of the Just One; of whom ye have been now the betrayers and murderers:

53 Who have received the law by the disposition of angels, and have not kept it.

The Stoning of Stephen

54 When they heard these things, they were cut to the heart, and they gnashed on him with their teeth.

55 But he, being full of the Holy Ghost, looked up steadfastly into heaven, and saw the glory of God, and Jesus standing on the right hand of God,

56 And said, Behold, I see the heavens opened, and the Son of man standing on the right hand of God.

57 Then they cried out with a loud voice, and stopped their ears, and ran upon him with one accord,

58 And cast him out of the city, and stoned him: and the witnesses laid down their clothes at a young man's feet, whose name was Saul.

59 And they stoned Stephen, calling upon God, and saying, Lord Jesus, receive my spirit.

60 And he kneeled down, and cried with a loud voice, Lord, lay not this sin to their charge. And when he had said this, he fell asleep.

8 And Saul was consenting unto his death.

Saul Persecutes the Church

And at that time there was a great persecution against the church which was at Jerusalem; and they were all scattered abroad
throughout the regions of Judea and Samaria,
except the apostles.

2 And devout men carried Stephen to his
burial, and made great lamentation over him.

3 As for Saul, he made havoc of the church,
entering into every house, and haling men and
women committed them to prison.

The Gospel Is Preached in Samaria

4 Therefore they that were scattered abroad
went every where preaching the word.

5 Then Philip went down to the city of
Samaria, and preached Christ unto them.

6 And the people with one accord gave
heed unto those things which Philip spake,
hearing and seeing the miracles which he
did.

7 For unclean spirits, crying with loud
voice, came out of many that were possessed
with them: and many taken with palsies, and
that were lame, were healed.

8 And there was great joy in that city.

9 But there was a certain man, called
Simon, which beforetime in the same city
used sorcery, and bewitched the people of
Samaria, giving out that himself was some
great one:

10 To whom they all gave heed, from the
least to the greatest, saying, This man is the
great power of God.

11 And to him they had regard, because
that of long time he had bewitched them with
4337   2425   5550   1839
sorceries.
3095

12 But when they believed Philip preaching
the things concerning the kingdom of God,
      4100   5376   2097
                        932   2316
and the name of Jesus Christ, they were
      3686   2424   5547   907
baptized, both men and women.
          435

13 Then Simon himself believed also: and
      4613   1135   4100
when he was baptized, he continued with
907   907   4342
Philip, and wondered, beholding the miracles
5376   1839   2334   1411
and signs which were done.
  4592   1096

14 Now when the apostles which were at
                    652
Jerusalem heard that Samaria had received the
2414   191   4540   1209
word of God, they sent unto them Peter and
3056   2316   649   4074
John:
2491

15 Who, when they were come down,
          2597   2597
prayed for them, that they might receive the
4336   3704   2983
Holy Ghost:
40

16 (For as yet he was fallen upon none of
     3768   1968
them: only they were baptized in the name of
    3440   5225   907   3686
the Lord Jesus.)
   2962   2424

17 Then laid they their hands on them, and
     2007   5495   2007
they received the Holy Ghost.
   2983   40

18 And when Simon saw that through lay-
      2300   4613   2300   1936
ing on of the apostles' hands the Holy Ghost
            652   5495   40
was given, he offered them money,
1325   4374   5536

19 Saying, Give me also this power, that
      1325   1849
on whomsoever I lay hands, he may receive
2007   2007   5495   2983
the Holy Ghost.
   40

20 But Peter said unto him, Thy money
     4074   2036   694
perish with thee, because thou hast thought
1498   3543
that the gift of God may be purchased with
       1431   2316   2932
money.
5536

21 Thou hast neither part nor lot in this
                3310   2819

matter: for thy heart is not right in the sight of God.

22 Repent therefore of this thy wickedness, and pray God, if perhaps the thought of thine heart may be forgiven thee.

23 For I perceive that thou art in the gall of bitterness, and in the bond of iniquity.

24 Then answered Simon, and said, Pray ye to the Lord for me, that none of these things which ye have spoken come upon me.

25 And they, when they had testified and preached the word of the Lord, returned to Jerusalem, and preached the gospel in many villages of the Samaritans.

Philip and the Ethiopian Eunuch

26 And the angel of the Lord spake unto Philip, saying, Arise, and go toward the south, unto the way that goeth down from Jerusalem unto Gaza, which is desert.

27 And he arose and went: and, behold, a man of Ethiopia, a eunuch of great authority under Candace queen of the Ethiopians, who had the charge of all her treasure, and had come to Jerusalem for to worship,

28 Was returning, and sitting in his chariot read Isaiah the prophet.

29 Then the Spirit said unto Philip, Go near, and join thyself to this chariot.

30 And Philip ran thither to him, and heard him read the prophet Isaiah, and said, Understandest thou what thou readest?

31 And he said, How can I, except some

man should guide me? And he desired Philip that he would come up and sit with him.

32 The place of the Scripture which he read was this, He was led as a sheep to the slaughter; and like a lamb dumb before his shearer, so opened he not his mouth:

33 In his humiliation his judgment was taken away: and who shall declare his generation? for his life is taken from the earth.

34 And the eunuch answered Philip, and said, I pray thee, of whom speaketh the prophet this? of himself, or of some other man?

35 Then Philip opened his mouth, and began at the same Scripture, and preached unto him Jesus.

36 And as they went on their way, they came unto a certain water: and the eunuch said, See, here is water; what doth hinder me to be baptized?

37 And Philip said, If thou believest with all thine heart, thou mayest. And he answered and said, I believe that Jesus Christ is the Son of God.

38 And he commanded the chariot to stand still: and they went down both into the water, both Philip and the eunuch; and he baptized him.

39 And when they were come up out of the water, the Spirit of the Lord caught away Philip, that the eunuch saw him no more: and he went on his way rejoicing.

40 But Philip was found at Azo′tus: and passing through he preached in all the cities, till he came to Caesare′a.

ACTS 9

The Conversion of Saul

9 And Saul, yet breathing out threatenings and slaughter against the disciples of the Lord, went unto the high priest,

2 And desired of him letters to Damascus to the synagogues, that if he found any of this way, whether they were men or women, he might bring them bound unto Jerusalem.

3 And as he journeyed, he came near Damascus: and suddenly there shined round about him a light from heaven:

4 And he fell to the earth, and heard a voice saying unto him, Saul, Saul, why persecutest thou me?

5 And he said, Who art thou, Lord? And the Lord said, I am Jesus whom thou persecutest: it is hard for thee to kick against the pricks.

6 And he trembling and astonished said, Lord, what wilt thou have me to do? And the Lord said unto him, Arise, and go into the city, and it shall be told thee what thou must do.

7 And the men which journeyed with him stood speechless, hearing a voice, but seeing no man.

8 And Saul arose from the earth; and when his eyes were opened, he saw no man: but they led him by the hand, and brought him into Damascus.

9 And he was three days without sight, and neither did eat nor drink.

10 And there was a certain disciple at

Damascus, named Anani'as; and to him said
the Lord in a vision, Anani'as. And he said,
Behold, I am here, Lord.

11 And the Lord said unto him, Arise, and
go into the street which is called Straight, and
inquire in the house of Judas for one called
Saul, of Tarsus: for, behold, he prayeth,

12 And hath seen in a vision a man named
Anani'as coming in, and putting his hand on
him, that he might receive his sight.

13 Then Anani'as answered, Lord, I have
heard by many of this man, how much evil
he hath done to thy saints at Jerusalem:

14 And here he hath authority from the
chief priests to bind all that call on thy
name.

15 But the Lord said unto him, Go thy
way: for he is a chosen vessel unto me, to
bear my name before the Gentiles, and kings,
and the children of Israel:

16 For I will show him how great things he
must suffer for my name's sake.

17 And Anani'as went his way, and entered
into the house; and putting his hands on him
said, Brother Saul, the Lord, even Jesus,
that appeared unto thee in the way as thou
camest, hath sent me, that thou mightest receive thy sight, and be filled with the Holy
Ghost.

18 And immediately there fell from his eyes
as it had been scales: and he received sight
forthwith, and arose, and was baptized.

19 And when he had received meat, he was
strengthened.

Saul Preaches at Damascus

Then was Saul certain days with the disciples which were at Damascus.

20 And straightway he preached Christ in the synagogues, that he is the Son of God.

21 But all that heard him were amazed, and said; Is not this he that destroyed them which called on this name in Jerusalem, and came hither for that intent, that he might bring them bound unto the chief priests?

22 But Saul increased the more in strength, and confounded the Jews which dwelt at Damascus, proving that this is very Christ.

Saul Escapes from the Jews

23 And after that many days were fulfilled, the Jews took counsel to kill him:

24 But their laying wait was known of Saul. And they watched the gates day and night to kill him.

25 Then the disciples took him by night, and let him down by the wall in a basket.

Saul at Jerusalem

26 And when Saul was come to Jerusalem, he assayed to join himself to the disciples: but they were all afraid of him, and believed not that he was a disciple.

27 But Barnabas took him, and brought him to the apostles, and declared unto them how he had seen the Lord in the way, and that he had spoken to him, and how he had preached boldly at Damascus in the name of Jesus.

28 And he was with them coming in and going out at Jerusalem.

29 And he spake boldly in the name of the Lord Jesus, and disputed against the Gre'-cians: but they went about to slay him.

30 Which when the brethren knew, they brought him down to Caesare'a, and sent him forth to Tarsus.

31 Then had the churches rest throughout all Judea and Galilee and Samaria, and were edified; and walking in the fear of the Lord, and in the comfort of the Holy Ghost, were multiplied.

Aeneas Healed

32 And it came to pass, as Peter passed throughout all quarters, he came down also to the saints which dwelt at Lydda.

33 And there he found a certain man named Aene'as, which had kept his bed eight years, and was sick of the palsy.

34 And Peter said unto him, Aene'as, Jesus Christ maketh thee whole: arise, and make thy bed. And he arose immediately.

35 And all that dwelt at Lydda and Sharon saw him, and turned to the Lord.

Dorcas Restored to Life

36 Now there was at Joppa a certain disciple named Tab'itha, which by interpretation is called Dorcas: this woman was full of good works and almsdeeds which she did.

37 And it came to pass in those days, that she was sick, and died: whom when

they had[3068] washed, they laid[5087] her in an upper[5253] chamber.

38 And forasmuch as Lydda[3069] was[5607] nigh[1451] to Joppa[2445], and the disciples[3101] had heard that Peter[4074] was there[191], they sent unto him two[649] men[435], desiring[3870] him that he would not delay[3635] to[1330] come to them.

39 Then Peter[4074] arose[450] and went[450] with them. When he was come[3854], they brought[3854] him[4905] into the upper[5253] chamber: and all the widows[321] stood by him weeping[5503], and showing the coats[3936] and garments[2440] which[3745] Dorcas[1393] made[4160], while[5607] she was[5607] with[2799] them.[1925][5509]

40 But Peter[4074] put[1544] them all forth, and kneeled[1119,5087] down, and prayed[1544]; and turning[1994] him to the body said[4336], Tab'itha[4983], arise[450]. And she opened[455] her eyes[3788]: and when she saw[1492] Peter[4074], she sat up.[339][2036][5000][1492]

41 And he gave[1325] her his hand, and lifted[1325] her up[450]; and when he had called[5455] the saints[40] and widows[5503], he presented[3936] her alive.[450][5455][5455][2198]

42 And it was known[1110] throughout all Joppa[2445]; and many[4183] believed[4100] in the Lord.[1096][3650]

43 And it came[1096] to pass[2962], that he tarried[3306] many days[2250] in Joppa[2445] with one[5100] Simon[4613] a tanner.[2425][1038]

Peter and Cornelius

10 There was a certain[5100] man[435] in Caesare'a[2542] called Cornelius[2883], a centurion[1543] of the band called the Italian[2483] band[4686],[3686][2564]

2 A devout[2152] man, and one that feared[5399] God[2316] with all his house[3624], which gave[4160] much[4183] alms[1654] to the people[2992], and prayed[1189] to God[2316] always[1275].

3 He saw[1492] in a vision[3705] evidently[5320], about the

ninth hour of the day, an angel of God coming in to him, and saying unto him, Cornelius.

4 And when he looked on him, he was afraid, and said, What is it, Lord? And he said unto him, Thy prayers and thine alms are come up for a memorial before God.

5 And now send men to Joppa, and call for one Simon, whose surname is Peter:

6 He lodgeth with one Simon a tanner, whose house is by the sea side: he shall tell thee what thou oughtest to do.

7 And when the angel which spake unto Cornelius was departed, he called two of his household servants, and a devout soldier of them that waited on him continually;

8 And when he had declared all these things unto them, he sent them to Joppa.

9 On the morrow, as they went on their journey, and drew nigh unto the city, Peter went up upon the housetop to pray about the sixth hour:

10 And he became very hungry, and would have eaten: but while they made ready, he fell into a trance,

11 And saw heaven opened, and a certain vessel descending unto him, as it had been a great sheet knit at the four corners, and let down to the earth:

12 Wherein were all manner of fourfooted beasts of the earth, and wild beasts, and creeping things, and fowls of the air.

13 And there came a voice to him, Rise, Peter; kill, and eat.

14 But Peter said, Not so, Lord; for I have

never eaten any thing that is common or
unclean.

15 And the voice spake unto him again the
second time, What God hath cleansed, that
call not thou common.

16 This was done thrice: and the vessel
was received up again into heaven.

17 Now while Peter doubted in himself
what this vision which he had seen should
mean, behold, the men which were sent from
Cornelius had made inquiry for Simon's
house, and stood before the gate,

18 And called, and asked whether Simon,
which was surnamed Peter, were lodged there.

19 While Peter thought on the vision, the
Spirit said unto him, Behold, three men seek
thee.

20 Arise therefore, and get thee down, and
go with them, doubting nothing: for I have
sent them.

21 Then Peter went down to the men which
were sent unto him from Cornelius; and said,
Behold, I am he whom ye seek: what is the
cause wherefore ye are come?

22 And they said, Cornelius the centurion,
a just man, and one that feareth God, and of
good report among all the nation of the Jews,
was warned from God by a holy angel to send
for thee into his house, and to hear words of
thee.

23 Then called he them in, and lodged
them. And on the morrow Peter went away
with them, and certain brethren from Joppa
accompanied him.

24 And the morrow after they entered into Caesare'a. And Cornelius waited for them, and had called together his kinsmen and near friends.

25 And as Peter was coming in, Cornelius met him, and fell down at his feet, and worshipped him.

26 But Peter took him up, saying, Stand up; I myself also am a man.

27 And as he talked with him, he went in, and found many that were come together.

28 And he said unto them, Ye know how that it is an unlawful thing for a man that is a Jew to keep company, or come unto one of another nation; but God hath showed me that I should not call any man common or unclean.

29 Therefore came I unto you without gainsaying, as soon as I was sent for: I ask therefore for what intent ye have sent for me?

30 And Cornelius said, Four days ago I was fasting until this hour; and at the ninth hour I prayed in my house, and, behold, a man stood before me in bright clothing,

31 And said, Cornelius, thy prayer is heard, and thine alms are had in remembrance in the sight of God.

32 Send therefore to Joppa, and call hither Simon, whose surname is Peter; he is lodged in the house of one Simon a tanner by the sea side: who, when he cometh, shall speak unto thee.

33 Immediately therefore I sent to thee; and thou hast well done that thou art come.

Now therefore are we all here present before God, to hear all things that are commanded thee of God.

Peter's Address in Cornelius' House

34 Then Peter opened his mouth, and said, Of a truth I perceive that God is no respecter of persons:

35 But in every nation he that feareth him, and worketh righteousness, is accepted with him.

36 The word which God sent unto the children of Israel, preaching peace by Jesus Christ: (he is Lord of all:)

37 That word, I say, ye know, which was published throughout all Judea, and began from Galilee, after the baptism which John preached;

38 How God anointed Jesus of Nazareth with the Holy Ghost and with power: who went about doing good, and healing all that were oppressed of the devil; for God was with him.

39 And we are witnesses of all things which he did both in the land of the Jews, and in Jerusalem; whom they slew and hanged on a tree:

40 Him God raised up the third day, and showed him openly;

41 Not to all the people, but unto witnesses chosen before of God, even to us, who did eat and drink with him after he rose from the dead.

42 And he commanded us to preach unto

the people, and to testify that it is he which was ordained of God to be the Judge of quick and dead.

43 To him give all the prophets witness, that through his name whosoever believeth in him shall receive remission of sins.

The Gentiles Receive the Holy Ghost

44 While Peter yet spake these words, the Holy Ghost fell on all them which heard the word.

45 And they of the circumcision which believed were astonished, as many as came with Peter, because that on the Gentiles also was poured out the gift of the Holy Ghost.

46 For they heard them speak with tongues, and magnify God. Then answered Peter,

47 Can any man forbid water, that these should not be baptized, which have received the Holy Ghost as well as we?

48 And he commanded them to be baptized in the name of the Lord. Then prayed they him to tarry certain days.

Peter's Report to the Church at Jerusalem

11 And the apostles and brethren that were in Judea heard that the Gentiles had also received the word of God.

2 And when Peter was come up to Jerusalem, they that were of the circumcision contended with him,

3 Saying, Thou wentest in to men uncircumcised, and didst eat with them.

4 But Peter rehearsed the matter from the

beginning, and expounded it by order unto
them, saying,

5 I was in the city of Joppa praying: and in
a trance I saw a vision, a certain vessel
descend, as it had been a great sheet, let down
from heaven by four corners; and it came even
to me:

6 Upon the which when I had fastened
mine eyes, I considered, and saw fourfooted
beasts of the earth, and wild beasts, and
creeping things, and fowls of the air.

7 And I heard a voice saying unto me,
Arise, Peter; slay and eat.

8 But I said, Not so, Lord: for nothing
common or unclean hath at any time entered
into my mouth.

9 But the voice answered me again from
heaven, What God hath cleansed, that call not
thou common.

10 And this was done three times: and all
were drawn up again into heaven.

11 And, behold, immediately there were
three men already come unto the house where
I was, sent from Caesare'a unto me.

12 And the Spirit bade me go with them,
nothing doubting. Moreover these six brethren
accompanied me, and we entered into the
man's house:

13 And he showed us how he had seen an
angel in his house, which stood and said unto
him, Send men to Joppa, and call for Simon,
whose surname is Peter;

14 Who shall tell thee words, whereby thou
and all thy house shall be saved.

15 And as I began to speak, the Holy Ghost fell on them, as on us at the beginning.

16 Then remembered I the word of the Lord, how that he said, John indeed baptized with water; but ye shall be baptized with the Holy Ghost.

17 Forasmuch then as God gave them the like gift as he did unto us, who believed on the Lord Jesus Christ, what was I, that I could withstand God?

18 When they heard these things, they held their peace, and glorified God, saying, Then hath God also to the Gentiles granted repentance unto life.

The Church at Antioch

19 Now they which were scattered abroad upon the persecution that arose about Stephen traveled as far as Phoeni'cia, and Cyprus, and An'ti-och, preaching the word to none but unto the Jews only.

20 And some of them were men of Cyprus and Cyre'ne, which, when they were come to An'ti-och, spake unto the Gre'cians, preaching the Lord Jesus.

21 And the hand of the Lord was with them: and a great number believed, and turned unto the Lord.

22 Then tidings of these things came unto the ears of the church which was in Jerusalem: and they sent forth Barnabas, that he should go as far as An'ti-och.

23 Who, when he came, and had seen the grace of God, was glad, and exhorted them

all, that with purpose of heart they would cleave unto the Lord.

24 For he was a good man, and full of the Holy Ghost and of faith: and much people was added unto the Lord.

25 Then departed Barnabas to Tarsus, for to seek Saul:

26 And when he had found him, he brought him unto An'ti-och. And it came to pass, that a whole year they assembled themselves with the church, and taught much people. And the disciples were called Christians first in An'ti-och.

27 And in these days came prophets from Jerusalem unto An'ti-och.

28 And there stood up one of them named Ag'abus, and signified by the Spirit that there should be great dearth throughout all the world: which came to pass in the days of Claudius Caesar.

29 Then the disciples, every man according to his ability, determined to send relief unto the brethren which dwelt in Judea:

30 Which also they did, and sent it to the elders by the hands of Barnabas and Saul.

James Killed and Peter Imprisoned

12 Now about that time Herod the king stretched forth his hands to vex certain of the church.

2 And he killed James the brother of John with the sword.

3 And because he saw it pleased the Jews,

he proceeded further to take Peter also. (Then were the days of unleavened bread.)

4 And when he had apprehended him, he put him in prison, and delivered him to four quaternions of soldiers to keep him; intending after Easter to bring him forth to the people.

5 Peter therefore was kept in prison: but prayer was made without ceasing of the church unto God for him.

Peter Delivered from Prison

6 And when Herod would have brought him forth, the same night Peter was sleeping between two soldiers, bound with two chains: and the keepers before the door kept the prison.

7 And, behold, the angel of the Lord came upon him, and a light shined in the prison: and he smote Peter on the side, and raised him up, saying, Arise up quickly. And his chains fell off from his hands.

8 And the angel said unto him, Gird thyself, and bind on thy sandals. And so he did. And he saith unto him, Cast thy garment about thee, and follow me.

9 And he went out, and followed him; and wist not that it was true which was done by the angel; but thought he saw a vision.

10 When they were past the first and the second ward, they came unto the iron gate that leadeth unto the city; which opened to them of his own accord: and they went out, and passed on through one street; and forthwith the angel departed from him.

11 And when Peter was come to himself, he said, Now I know of a surety, that the Lord hath sent his angel, and hath delivered me out of the hand of Herod, and from all the expectation of the people of the Jews.

12 And when he had considered the thing, he came to the house of Mary the mother of John, whose surname was Mark; where many were gathered together praying.

13 And as Peter knocked at the door of the gate, a damsel came to hearken, named Rhoda.

14 And when she knew Peter's voice, she opened not the gate for gladness, but ran in, and told how Peter stood before the gate.

15 And they said unto her, Thou art mad. But she constantly affirmed that it was even so. Then said they, It is his angel.

16 But Peter continued knocking: and when they had opened the door, and saw him, they were astonished.

17 But he, beckoning unto them with the hand to hold their peace, declared unto them how the Lord had brought him out of the prison. And he said, Go show these things unto James, and to the brethren. And he departed, and went into another place.

18 Now as soon as it was day, there was no small stir among the soldiers, what was become of Peter.

19 And when Herod had sought for him, and found him not, he examined the keepers, and commanded that they should be put to

death. And he went down from Judea to
2718   575   2448,2449
Caesare'a, and there abode.
2542   1304

The Death of Herod

20 And Herod was highly displeased with
2264   2371
them of Tyre and Sidon: but they came with
5183   4606   3918   3661
one accord to him, and, having made Blastus
                              3982   986
the king's chamberlain their friend, desired
935   3982   154
peace; because their country was nourished by
1515   5561   5142   575
the king's country.
937   5561

21 And upon a set day Herod, arrayed in
937   5002 2250 2264 1746
royal apparel, sat upon his throne, and made
937   2066 2523   968   2523   1215
an oration unto them.

22 And the people gave a shout, saying, It
1218   2019
is the voice of a god, and not of a man.
5456   2316   444

23 And immediately the angel of the Lord
3916   32   2962
smote him, because he gave not God the
3960   473   1325   2316
glory: and he was eaten of worms, and gave
1391   1096 4662   1096   1634
up the ghost.

24 But the word of God grew and mul-
3056   2316 837   4129
tiplied.

25 And Barnabas and Saul returned from
921   4569   5290
Jerusalem, when they had fulfilled their
2419   4137   4137
ministry, and took with them John, whose sur-
1248   4838   2491   1941
name was Mark.
3138

Barnabus and Saul Begin Their First
Missionary Journey

13 Now there were in the church that was
1577   5607
at An'ti-och certain prophets and teachers;
490   5100   4396   1320
as Barnabas, and Simeon that was called
490   4826 2564
Niger, and Lucius of Cyre'ne, and Man'a-en,
3526   3066   2956   3127
which had been brought up with Herod the
4939   2264
tetrarch, and Saul.
5076   4569

2 As they ministered to the Lord, and fasted, the Holy Ghost said, Separate me Barnabas and Saul for the work whereunto I have called them.

3 And when they had fasted and prayed, and laid their hands on them, they sent them away.

The Apostles Preach in Cyprus

4 So they, being sent forth by the Holy Ghost, departed unto Seleu′cia; and from thence they sailed to Cyprus.

5 And when they were at Sal′amis, they preached the word of God in the synagogues of the Jews: and they had also John to their minister.

6 And when they had gone through the isle unto Paphos, they found a certain sorcerer, a false prophet, a Jew, whose name was Bar-jesus:

7 Which was with the deputy of the country, Sergius Paulus, a prudent man; who called for Barnabas and Saul, and desired to hear the word of God.

8 But El′ymas the sorcerer (for so is his name by interpretation) withstood them, seeking to turn away the deputy from the faith.

9 Then Saul, (who also is called Paul,) filled with the Holy Ghost, set his eyes on him,

10 And said, O full of all subtilty and all mischief, thou · child of the devil, thou enemy

of all righteousness, wilt thou not cease to pervert the right ways of the Lord?

11 And now, behold, the hand of the Lord is upon thee, and thou shalt be blind, not seeing the sun for a season. And immediately there fell on him a mist and a darkness; and he went about seeking some to lead him by the hand.

12 Then the deputy, when he saw what was done, believed, being astonished at the doctrine of the Lord.

Paul and Barnabas at Antioch of Pisidia

13 Now when Paul and his company loosed from Paphos, they came to Perga in Pamphyl'i-a: and John departing from them returned to Jerusalem.

14 But when they departed from Perga, they came to An'ti-och in Pisid'i-a, and went into the synagogue on the sabbath day, and sat down.

15 And after the reading of the law and the prophets, the rulers of the synagogue sent unto them, saying, Ye men and brethren, if ye have any word of exhortation for the people, say on.

16 Then Paul stood up, and beckoning with his hand said, Men of Israel, and ye that fear God, give audience.

17 The God of this people of Israel chose our fathers, and exalted the people when they dwelt as strangers in the land of Egypt, and with a high arm brought he them out of it.

18 And about the time of forty years suffered he their manners in the wilderness.

19 And when he had destroyed seven nations in the land of Canaan, he divided their land to them by lot.

20 And after that he gave unto them judges about the space of four hundred and fifty years, until Samuel the prophet.

21 And afterward they desired a king: and God gave unto them Saul the son of Kish, a man of the tribe of Benjamin, by the space of forty years.

22 And when he had removed him, he raised up unto them David to be their king; to whom also he gave testimony, and said, I have found David the son of Jesse, a man after mine own heart, which shall fulfil all my will.

23 Of this man's seed hath God, according to his promise, raised unto Israel a Saviour, Jesus:

24 When John had first preached before his coming the baptism of repentance to all the people of Israel.

25 And as John fulfilled his course, he said, Whom think ye that I am? I am not he. But, behold, there cometh one after me, whose shoes of his feet I am not worthy to loose.

26 Men and brethren, children of the stock of Abraham, and whosoever among you feareth God, to you is the word of this salvation sent.

27 For they that dwell at Jerusalem, and their rulers, because they knew him not, nor yet the voices of the prophets which are read

every sabbath day, they have fulfilled them in condemning him.

28 And though they found no cause of death in him, yet desired they Pilate that he should be slain.

29 And when they had fulfilled all that was written of him, they took him down from the tree, and laid him in a sepulchre.

30 But God raised him from the dead:

31 And he was seen many days of them which came up with him from Galilee to Jerusalem, who are his witnesses unto the people.

32 And we declare unto you glad tidings, how that the promise which was made unto the fathers,

33 God hath fulfilled the same unto us their children, in that he hath raised up Jesus again; as it is also written in the second psalm, Thou art my Son, this day have I begotten thee.

34 And as concerning that he raised him up from the dead, now no more to return to corruption, he said on this wise, I will give you the sure mercies of David.

35 Wherefore he saith also in another psalm, Thou shalt not suffer thine Holy One to see corruption.

36 For David, after he had served his own generation by the will of God, fell on sleep, and was laid unto his fathers, and saw corruption:

37 But he, whom God raised again, saw no corruption.

38 Be it known unto you therefore, men and brethren, that through this man is preached unto you the forgiveness of sins:

39 And by him all that believe are justified from all things, from which ye could not be justified by the law of Moses.

40 Beware therefore, lest that come upon you, which is spoken of in the prophets;

41 Behold, ye despisers, and wonder, and perish: for I work a work in your days, a work which ye shall in no wise believe, though a man declare it unto you.

42 And when the Jews were gone out of the synagogue, the Gentiles besought that these words might be preached to them the next sabbath.

43 Now when the congregation was broken up, many of the Jews and religious proselytes followed Paul and Barnabas; who, speaking to them, persuaded them to continue in the grace of God.

44 And the next sabbath day came almost the whole city together to hear the word of God.

45 But when the Jews saw the multitudes, they were filled with envy, and spake against those things which were spoken by Paul, contradicting and blaspheming.

46 Then Paul and Barnabas waxed bold, and said, It was necessary that the word of God should first have been spoken to you: but seeing ye put it from you, and judge yourselves unworthy of everlasting life, lo, we turn to the Gentiles.

47 For so hath the Lord commanded us, saying, I have set thee to be a light of the Gentiles, that thou shouldest be for salvation unto the ends of the earth.

48 And when the Gentiles heard this, they were glad, and glorified the word of the Lord: and as many as were ordained to eternal life believed.

49 And the word of the Lord was published throughout all the region.

50 But the Jews stirred up the devout and honorable women, and the chief men of the city, and raised persecution against Paul and Barnabas, and expelled them out of their coasts.

51 But they shook off the dust of their feet against them, and came unto Ico'ni-um.

52 And the disciples were filled with joy, and with the Holy Ghost.

Paul and Barnabas at Iconium

14 And it came to pass in Ico'ni-um, that they went both together into the synagogue of the Jews, and so spake, that a great multitude both of the Jews and also of the Greeks believed.

2 But the unbelieving Jews stirred up the Gentiles, and made their minds evil affected against the brethren.

3 Long time therefore abode they speaking boldly in the Lord, which gave testimony unto the word of his grace, and granted signs and wonders to be done by their hands.

4 But the multitude of the city was di-

vided: and part held with the Jews, and part with the apostles.

5 And when there was an assault made both of the Gentiles, and also of the Jews with their rulers, to use them despitefully, and to stone them,

6 They were ware of it, and fled unto Lystra and Derbe, cities of Lyca-o'nia, and unto the region that lieth round about:

7 And there they preached the gospel.

Paul Stoned at Lystra

8 And there sat a certain man at Lystra, impotent in his feet, being a cripple from his mother's womb, who never had walked:

9 The same heard Paul speak: who steadfastly beholding him, and perceiving that he had faith to be healed,

10 Said with a loud voice, Stand upright on thy feet. And he leaped and walked.

11 And when the people saw what Paul had done, they lifted up their voices, saying in the speech of Lyca-o'nia, The gods are come down to us in the likeness of men.

12 And they called Barnabas, Jupiter; and Paul, Mercu'ri-us, because he was the chief speaker.

13 Then the priest of Jupiter, which was before their city, brought oxen and garlands unto the gates, and would have done sacrifice with the people.

14 Which when the apostles, Barnabas and Paul, heard of, they rent their clothes, and ran in among the people, crying out,

15 And saying, Sirs, why do ye these
things? We also are men of like passions with
you, and preach unto you that ye should turn
from these vanities unto the living God, which
made heaven, and earth, and the sea, and all
things that are therein:

16 Who in times past suffered all nations to
walk in their own ways.

17 Nevertheless he left not himself without
witness, in that he did good, and gave us rain
from heaven, and fruitful seasons, filling our
hearts with food and gladness.

18 And with these sayings scarce restrained
they the people, that they had not done sacrifice unto them.

19 And there came thither certain Jews
from An'ti-och and Ico'ni-um, who persuaded
the people, and, having stoned Paul, drew him
out of the city, supposing he had been
dead.

20 Howbeit, as the disciples stood round
about him, he rose up, and came into the
city: and the next day he departed with
Barnabas to Derbe.

21 And when they had preached the gospel
to that city, and had taught many, they returned again to Lystra, and to Ico'ni-um, and
An'ti-och,

22 Confirming the souls of the disciples, and
exhorting them to continue in the faith, and
that we must through much tribulation enter
into the kingdom of God.

23 And when they had ordained them elders
in every church, and had prayed with fasting,

they commended them to the Lord, on whom they believed.

The Return to Antioch in Syria

24 And after they had passed throughout Pisid'i-a, they came to Pamphyl'i-a.

25 And when they had preached the word in Perga, they went down into Attali'a:

26 And thence sailed to An'ti-och, from whence they had been recommended to the grace of God for the work which they fulfilled.

27 And when they were come, and had gathered the church together, they rehearsed all that God had done with them, and how he had opened the door of faith unto the Gentiles.

28 And there they abode long time with the disciples.

The Council at Jerusalem

15 And certain men which came down from Judea taught the brethren, and said, Except ye be circumcised after the manner of Moses, ye cannot be saved.

2 When therefore Paul and Barnabas had no small dissension and disputation with them, they determined that Paul and Barnabas, and certain other of them, should go up to Jerusalem unto the apostles and elders about this question.

3 And being brought on their way by the church, they passed through Phoeni'cia and Samaria, declaring the conversion of the Gen-

tiles: and they caused great joy unto all the
4160   3173 5479
brethren.
80

4 And when they were come to Jerusalem,
3854   3854   2419
they were received of the church, and of the
588   1577
apostles and elders, and they declared all
652   4245   312   3745
things that God had done with them.
3745 2316   4160

5 But there rose up certain of the sect of
1817   5100   575   139
the Pharisees which believed, saying, That it
5330   4100
was needful to circumcise them, and to com-
1163   4059   3853
mand them to keep the law of Moses.
5083   3551   3475

6 And the apostles and elders came to-
652   4245   4863
gether for to consider of this matter.
1492   3056

7 And when there had been much disputing,
1096   1096   4183   4803
Peter rose up, and said unto them, Men and
4074 450   2036   435
brethren, ye know how that a good while ago
80   1987   2250   575
God made choice among us, that the Gentiles
2316 1586   1484
by my mouth should hear the word of the
4750   191   3056
gospel, and believe.
2098   4100

8 And God, which knoweth the hearts, bare
2316 2589
them witness, giving them the Holy Ghost,
3140   1325   40
even as he did unto us;
2531

9 And put no difference between us and
1252   1252 3342
them, purifying their hearts by faith.
2511   2588   4102

10 Now therefore why tempt ye God, to
3568   5101 3985   2316 2007
put a yoke upon the neck of the disciples,
2218 2007   5137   3101
which neither our fathers nor we were able
3777   3962   2480
to bear?
941

11 But we believe that through the grace of
4100   5485
the Lord Jesus Christ we shall be saved,
2962 2424 5547   4982
even as they.
5158 2548

12 Then all the multitude kept silence, and
4128   4601
gave audience to Barnabas and Paul, declaring
191   921   3972   1834
what miracles and wonders God had wrought
3745 4592   5059   2316   4160
among the Gentiles by them.
1484

13 And after they had held their peace, James answered, saying, Men and brethren, hearken unto me:

14 Simeon hath declared how God at the first did visit the Gentiles, to take out of them a people for his name.

15 And to this agree the words of the prophets; as it is written,

16 After this I will return, and will build again the tabernacle of David, which is fallen down; and I will build again the ruins thereof, and I will set it up:

17 That the residue of men might seek after the Lord, and all the Gentiles, upon whom my name is called, saith the Lord, who doeth all these things.

18 Known unto God are all his works from the beginning of the world.

19 Wherefore my sentence is, that we trouble not them, which from among the Gentiles are turned to God:

20 But that we write unto them, that they abstain from pollutions of idols, and from fornication, and from things strangled, and from blood.

21 For Moses of old time hath in every city them that preach him, being read in the synagogues every sabbath day.

22 Then pleased it the apostles and elders, with the whole church, to send chosen men of their own company to An'ti-och with Paul and Barnabas; namely, Judas surnamed Barsabas, and Silas, chief men among the brethren:

23 And they wrote letters by them after this manner; The apostles and elders and brethren send greeting unto the brethren which are of the Gentiles in An'ti-och and Syria and Cili'cia:

24 Forasmuch as we have heard, that certain which went out from us have troubled you with words, subverting your souls, saying, Ye must be circumcised, and keep the law; to whom we gave no such commandment:

25 It seemed good unto us, being assembled with one accord, to send chosen men unto you with our beloved Barnabas and Paul,

26 Men that have hazarded their lives for the name of our Lord Jesus Christ.

27 We have sent therefore Judas and Silas, who shall also tell you the same things by mouth.

28 For it seemed good to the Holy Ghost, and to us, to lay upon you no greater burden than these necessary things;

29 That ye abstain from meats offered to idols, and from blood, and from things strangled, and from fornication: from which if ye keep yourselves, ye shall do well. Fare ye well.

30 So when they were dismissed, they came to An'ti-och: and when they had gathered the multitude together, they delivered the epistle:

31 Which when they had read, they rejoiced for the consolation.

32 And Judas and Silas, being prophets also themselves, exhorted the brethren with many words, and confirmed them.

33 And after they had tarried there a space, they were let go in peace from the brethren unto the apostles.

34 Notwithstanding it pleased Silas to abide there still.

35 Paul also and Barnabas continued in An'ti-och, teaching and preaching the word of the Lord, with many others also.

Paul Separates from Barnabas and Begins the Second Missionary Journey

36 And some days after, Paul said unto Barnabas, Let us go again and visit our brethren in every city where we have preached the word of the Lord, and see how they do.

37 And Barnabas determined to take with them John, whose surname was Mark.

38 But Paul thought not good to take him with them, who departed from them from Pamphyl'i-a, and went not with them to the work.

39 And the contention was so sharp between them, that they departed asunder one from the other: and so Barnabas took Mark, and sailed unto Cyprus;

40 And Paul chose Silas, and departed, being recommended by the brethren unto the grace of God.

41 And he went through Syria and Cili'cia, confirming the churches.

Timothy Accompanies Paul and Silas

16 Then came he to Derbe and Lystra: and, behold, a certain disciple was there, named Timothy, the son of a certain woman,

which was a Jewess, and believed; but his father was a Greek:

2 Which was well reported of by the brethren that were at Lystra and Ico'ni-um.

3 Him would Paul have to go forth with him; and took and circumcised him because of the Jews which were in those quarters: for they knew all that his father was a Greek.

4 And as they went through the cities, they delivered them the decrees for to keep, that were ordained of the apostles and elders which were at Jerusalem.

5 And so were the churches established in the faith, and increased in number daily.

Paul's Vision of the Man of Macedonia

6 Now when they had gone throughout Phryg'i-a and the region of Galatia, and were forbidden of the Holy Ghost to preach the word in Asia,

7 After they were come to My'si-a, they assayed to go into Bithyn'i-a: but the Spirit suffered them not.

8 And they passing by My'si-a came down to Tro'as.

9 And a vision appeared to Paul in the night; There stood a man of Macedonia, and prayed him, saying, Come over into Macedonia, and help us.

10 And after he had seen the vision, immediately we endeavored to go into Macedonia, assuredly gathering that the Lord had called us for to preach the gospel unto them.

ACTS 16

The Imprisonment at Philippi

11 Therefore loosing from Tro′as, we came with a straight course to Samothracia, and the next day to Ne-ap′olis;

12 And from thence to Phil′ippi, which is the chief city of that part of Macedonia, and a colony: and we were in that city abiding certain days.

13 And on the sabbath we went out of the city by a river side, where prayer was wont to be made; and we sat down, and spake unto the women which resorted thither.

14 And a certain woman named Lydia, a seller of purple, of the city of Thy-ati′ra, which worshipped God, heard us: whose heart the Lord opened, that she attended unto the things which were spoken of Paul.

15 And when she was baptized, and her household, she besought us, saying, If ye have judged me to be faithful to the Lord, come into my house, and abide there. And she constrained us.

16 And it came to pass, as we went to prayer, a certain damsel possessed with a spirit of divination met us, which brought her masters much gain by soothsaying:

17 The same followed Paul and us, and cried, saying, These men are the servants of the most high God, which show unto us the way of salvation.

18 And this did she many days. But Paul, being grieved, turned and said to the spirit, I command thee in the name of Jesus Christ to come out of her. And he came out the same hour.

19 And when her masters saw that the hope of their gains was gone, they caught Paul and Silas, and drew them into the market place unto the rulers,

20 And brought them to the magistrates, saying, These men, being Jews, do exceedingly trouble our city,

21 And teach customs, which are not lawful for us to receive, neither to observe, being Romans.

22 And the multitude rose up together against them; and the magistrates rent off their clothes, and commanded to beat them.

23 And when they had laid many stripes upon them, they cast them into prison, charging the jailer to keep them safely:

24 Who, having received such a charge, thrust them into the inner prison, and made their feet fast in the stocks.

25 And at midnight Paul and Silas prayed, and sang praises unto God: and the prisoners heard them.

26 And suddenly there was a great earthquake, so that the foundations of the prison were shaken: and immediately all the doors were opened, and every one's bands were loosed.

27 And the keeper of the prison awaking out of his sleep, and seeing the prison doors open, he drew out his sword, and would have killed himself, supposing that the prisoners had been fled.

28 But Paul cried with a loud voice, saying, Do thyself no harm: for we are all here.

29 Then he called for a light, and sprang in, and came trembling, and fell down before Paul and Silas,

30 And brought them out, and said, Sirs, what must I do to be saved?

31 And they said, Believe on the Lord Jesus Christ, and thou shalt be saved, and thy house.

32 And they spake unto him the word of the Lord, and to all that were in his house.

33 And he took them the same hour of the night, and washed their stripes; and was baptized, he and all his, straightway.

34 And when he had brought them into his house, he set meat before them, and rejoiced, believing in God with all his house.

35 And when it was day, the magistrates sent the sergeants, saying, Let those men go.

36 And the keeper of the prison told this saying to Paul, The magistrates have sent to let you go: now therefore depart, and go in peace.

37 But Paul said unto them, They have beaten us openly uncondemned, being Romans, and have cast us into prison; and now do they thrust us out privily? nay verily; but let them come themselves and fetch us out.

38 And the sergeants told these words unto the magistrates: and they feared, when they heard that they were Romans.

39 And they came and besought them, and brought them out, and desired them to depart out of the city.

40 And they went out of the prison, and

entered into the house of Lydia: and when
they had seen the brethren, they comforted
them, and departed.

The Uproar in Thessalonica

17 Now when they had passed through
Amphip'olis and Apollo'ni-a, they came
to Thessaloni'ca, where was a synagogue of the
Jews:

2 And Paul, as his manner was, went in
unto them, and three sabbath days reasoned
with them out of the Scriptures,

3 Opening and alleging, that Christ must
needs have suffered, and risen again from the
dead; and that this Jesus, whom I preach
unto you, is Christ.

4 And some of them believed, and con-
sorted with Paul and Silas; and of the devout
Greeks a great multitude, and of the chief
women not a few.

5 But the Jews which believed not, moved
with envy, took unto them certain lewd fellows
of the baser sort, and gathered a company, and
set all the city on an uproar, and assaulted the
house of Jason, and sought to bring them out
to the people.

6 And when they found them not, they
drew Jason and certain brethren unto the
rulers of the city, crying, These that have
turned the world upside down are come hither
also;

7 Whom Jason hath received: and these all
do contrary to the decrees of Caesar, saying
that there is another king, one Jesus.

8 And they troubled the people and the rulers of the city, when they heard these things.

9 And when they had taken security of Jason, and of the others, they let them go.

The Apostles at Beroea

10 And the brethren immediately sent away Paul and Silas by night unto Beroe′a: who coming thither went into the synagogue of the Jews.

11 These were more noble than those in Thessaloni′ca, in that they received the word with all readiness of mind, and searched the Scriptures daily, whether those things were so.

12 Therefore many of them believed; also of honorable women which were Greeks, and of men, not a few.

13 But when the Jews of Thessaloni′ca had knowledge that the word of God was preached of Paul at Beroe′a, they came thither also, and stirred up the people.

14 And then immediately the brethren sent away Paul to go as it were to the sea: but Silas and Timothy abode there still.

15 And they that conducted Paul brought him unto Athens: and receiving a commandment unto Silas and Timothy for to come to him with all speed, they departed.

Paul at Athens

16 Now while Paul waited for them at Athens, his spirit was stirred in him, when he saw the city wholly given to idolatry.

17 Therefore disputed he in the synagogue with the Jews, and with the devout persons, and in the market daily with them that met with him.

18 Then certain philosophers of the Epi-cure'ans, and of the Sto'ics, encountered him. And some said, What will this babbler say? other some, He seemeth to be a setter forth of strange gods: because he preached unto them Jesus, and the resurrection.

19 And they took him, and brought him unto Areop'agus saying, May we know what this new doctrine, whereof thou speakest, is?

20 For thou bringest certain strange things to our ears: we would know therefore what these things mean.

21 (For all the Athenians, and strangers which were there, spent their time in nothing else, but either to tell or to hear some new thing.)

22 Then Paul stood in the midst of Mars' hill, and said, Ye men of Athens, I perceive that in all things ye are too superstitious.

23 For as I passed by, and beheld your devotions, I found an altar with this inscrip-tion, To the Unknown God. Whom there-fore ye ignorantly worship, him declare I unto you.

24 God that made the world and all things therein, seeing that he is Lord of heaven and earth, dwelleth not in temples made with hands;

25 Neither is worshipped with men's hands,

as though he needed any thing, seeing he giveth to all life, and breath, and all things;

26 And hath made of one blood all nations of men for to dwell on all the face of the earth, and hath determined the times before appointed, and the bounds of their habitation;

27 That they should seek the Lord, if haply they might feel after him, and find him, though he be not far from every one of us:

28 For in him we live, and move, and have our being; as certain also of your own poets have said, For we are also his offspring.

29 Forasmuch then as we are the offspring of God, we ought not to think that the Godhead is like unto gold, or silver, or stone, graven by art and man's device.

30 And the times of this ignorance God winked at; but now commandeth all men every where to repent:

31 Because he hath appointed a day, in the which he will judge the world in righteousness by that man whom he hath ordained; whereof he hath given assurance unto all men, in that he hath raised him from the dead.

32 And when they heard of the resurrection of the dead, some mocked: and others said, We will hear thee again of this matter.

33 So Paul departed from among them.

34 Howbeit certain men clave unto him, and believed: among the which was Di-onys'ius the Areop'agite, and a woman named Dam'-aris, and others with them.

Paul at Corinth

18 After these things Paul departed from Athens, and came to Corinth;

2 And found a certain Jew named Aquila, born in Pontus, lately come from Italy, with his wife Priscilla, (because that Claudius had commanded all Jews to depart from Rome,) and came unto them.

3 And because he was of the same craft, he abode with them, and wrought: (for by their occupation they were tentmakers.)

4 And he reasoned in the synagogue every sabbath, and persuaded the Jews and the Greeks.

5 And when Silas and Timothy were come from Macedonia, Paul was pressed in the spirit, and testified to the Jews that Jesus was Christ.

6 And when they opposed themselves, and blasphemed, he shook his raiment, and said unto them, Your blood be upon your own heads; I am clean: from henceforth I will go unto the Gentiles.

7 And he departed thence, and entered into a certain man's house, named Justus, one that worshipped God, whose house joined hard to the synagogue.

8 And Crispus, the chief ruler of the synagogue, believed on the Lord with all his house; and many of the Corinthians hearing believed, and were baptized.

9 Then spake the Lord to Paul in the night by a vision, Be not afraid, but speak, and hold not thy peace:

10 For I am with thee, and no man shall set on thee to hurt thee: for I have much people in this city.

11 And he continued there a year and six months, teaching the word of God among them.

12 And when Gal′li-o was the deputy of Achai′a, the Jews made insurrection with one accord against Paul, and brought him to the judgment seat,

13 Saying, This fellow persuadeth men to worship God contrary to the law.

14 And when Paul was now about to open his mouth, Gal′li-o said unto the Jews, If it were a matter of wrong or wicked lewdness, O ye Jews, reason would that I should bear with you:

15 But if it be a question of words and names, and of your law, look ye to it; for I will be no judge of such matters.

16 And he drave them from the judgment seat.

17 Then all the Greeks took Sos′thenes, the chief ruler of the synagogue, and beat him before the judgment seat. And Gal′li-o cared for none of those things.

18 And Paul after this tarried there yet a good while, and then took his leave of the brethren, and sailed thence into Syria, and with him Priscilla and Aquila; having shorn his head in Cen′chre-ae: for he had a vow.

19 And he came to Ephesus, and left them there: but he himself entered into the synagogue, and reasoned with the Jews.

20 When they desired him to tarry longer time with them, he consented not;

21 But bade them farewell, saying, I must by all means keep this feast that cometh in Jerusalem: but I will return again unto you, if God will. And he sailed from Eph-esus.

Paul Returns to Antioch and Begins the Third Missionary Journey

22 And when he had landed at Caesare'a, and gone up, and saluted the church, he went down to An'ti-och.

23 And after he had spent some time there, he departed, and went over all the country of Galatia and Phryg'i-a in order, strengthening all the disciples.

Apollos Preaches at Ephesus

24 And a certain Jew named Apol'los, born at Alexandria, an eloquent man, and mighty in the Scriptures, came to Ephesus.

25 This man was instructed in the way of the Lord; and being fervent in the spirit, he spake and taught diligently the things of the Lord, knowing only the baptism of John.

26 And he began to speak boldly in the synagogue: whom when Aquila and Priscilla had heard, they took him unto them, and ex-pounded unto him the way of God more perfectly.

27 And when he was disposed to pass into Achai'a, the brethren wrote, exhorting the disciples to receive him: who, when he was

come, helped them much which had believed
4820 4183 4100
through grace:
5485

28 For he mightily convinced the Jews, and
2159 1246 2453
that publicly, showing by the Scriptures that
1218 1925 1124
Jesus was Christ.
2424 5547

Paul at Ephesus

19 And it came to pass, that, while Apol'los
1096 625
was at Corinth, Paul having passed
2882 3972 1330
through the upper coasts came to Ephesus;
510 3313 2064 2181
and finding certain disciples,
2147 5100 3101

2 He said unto them, Have ye received the
2036 2983 2983
Holy Ghost since ye believed? And they said
40 4100 4100 2036
unto him, We have not so much as heard
191 191
whether there be any Holy Ghost.
40

3 And he said unto them, Unto what then
2036 5101
were ye baptized? And they said, Unto John's
907 907 2036 2491
baptism.
908

4 Then said Paul, John verily baptized with
2036 3972 2491 907
the baptism of repentance, saying unto the
908 3341
people, that they should believe on him which
2992 4100 2064
should come after him, that is, on Christ
5123 5547
Jesus.
2424

5 When they heard this, they were baptized
191 191 907
in the name of the Lord Jesus.

6 And when Paul had laid his hands upon
3686 2962 2424
them, the Holy Ghost came on them; and
2007 3972 2007 5495 2007
they spake with tongues, and prophesied.
40 2064
2980 1100 4395

7 And all the men were about twelve.

8 And he went into the synagogue, and
435 1177
spake boldly for the space of three months,
1525 4864 1525
3955 1909 3376
disputing and persuading the things concerning
1256 3982
the kingdom of God.

9 But when divers were hardened, and be-
932 2316
5100 4645 544

lieved not, but spake evil of that way before the multitude, he departed from them, and separated the disciples, disputing daily in the school of one Tyrannus.

10 And this continued by the space of two years; so that all they which dwelt in Asia heard the word of the Lord Jesus, both Jews and Greeks.

11 And God wrought special miracles by the hands of Paul:

12 So that from his body were brought unto the sick handkerchiefs or aprons, and the diseases departed from them, and the evil spirits went out of them.

13 Then certain of the vagabond Jews, exorcists, took upon them to call over them which had evil spirits the name of the Lord Jesus, saying, We adjure you by Jesus whom Paul preacheth.

14 And there were seven sons of one Sceva, a Jew, and chief of the priests, which did so.

15 And the evil spirit answered and said, Jesus I know, and Paul I know; but who are ye?

16 And the man in whom the evil spirit was leaped on them, and overcame them, and prevailed against them, so that they fled out of that house naked and wounded.

17 And this was known to all the Jews and Greeks also dwelling at Ephesus; and fear fell on them all, and the name of the Lord Jesus was magnified.

18 And many that believed came, and confessed, and showed their deeds.

19 Many of them also which used curious arts brought their books together, and burned them before all men: and they counted the price of them, and found it fifty thousand pieces of silver.

20 So mightily grew the word of God and prevailed.

21 After these things were ended, Paul purposed in the spirit, when he had passed through Macedonia and Achai´a, to go to Jerusalem, saying, After I have been there, I must also see Rome.

22 So he sent into Macedonia two of them that ministered unto him, Timothy and Eras´-tus; but he himself stayed in Asia for a season.

The Riot at Ephesus

23 And the same time there arose no small stir about that way.

24 For a certain man named Deme´tri-us, a silversmith, which made silver shrines for Diana, brought no small gain unto the crafts-men;

25 Whom he called together with the work-men of like occupation, and said, Sirs, ye know that by this craft we have our wealth.

26 Moreover ye see and hear, that not alone at Ephesus, but almost throughout all Asia, this Paul hath persuaded and turned away much people, saying that they be no gods, which are made with hands:

27 So that not only this our craft is in danger to be set at nought; but also that the

temple of the great goddess Diana should be despised, and her magnificence should be destroyed, whom all Asia and the world worshippeth.

28 And when they heard these sayings, they were full of wrath, and cried out, saying, Great is Diana of the Ephesians.

29 And the whole city was filled with confusion: and having caught Gaius and Aristar'-chus, men of Macedonia, Paul's companions in travel, they rushed with one accord into the theatre.

30 And when Paul would have entered in unto the people, the disciples suffered him not.

31 And certain of the chief of Asia, which were his friends, sent unto him, desiring him that he would not adventure himself into the theatre.

32 Some therefore cried one thing, and some another: for the assembly was confused; and the more part knew not wherefore they were come together.

33 And they drew Alexander out of the multitude, the Jews putting him forward. And Alexander beckoned with the hand, and would have made his defense unto the people.

34 But when they knew that he was a Jew, all with one voice about the space of two hours cried out, Great is Diana of the Ephesians.

35 And when the townclerk had appeased the people, he said, Ye men of Ephesus, what man is there that knoweth not how that the

city of the Ephesians is a worshipper of the great goddess Diana, and of the image which fell down from Jupiter?

36 Seeing then that these things cannot be spoken against, ye ought to be quiet, and to do nothing rashly.

37 For ye have brought hither these men, which are neither robbers of churches, nor yet blasphemers of your goddess.

38 Wherefore if Demetrius, and the craftsmen which are with him, have a matter against any man, the law is open, and there are deputies: let them implead one another.

39 But if ye inquire any thing concerning other matters, it shall be determined in a lawful assembly.

40 For we are in danger to be called in question for this day's uproar, there being no cause whereby we may give an account of this concourse.

41 And when he had thus spoken, he dismissed the assembly.

Paul's Journey to Macedonia and Greece

20 And after the uproar was ceased, Paul called unto him the disciples, and embraced them, and departed for to go into Macedonia.

2 And when he had gone over those parts, and had given them much exhortation, he came into Greece,

3 And there abode three months. And when the Jews laid wait for him, as he was about

to sail into Syria, he purposed to return through Macedonia.

4 And there accompanied him into Asia So'pater of Beroe'a; and of the Thessalo'ni-ans, Aristar'chus and Secun'dus; and Gai'us of Derbe, and Timothy; and of Asia, Tych'icus and Troph'imus.

5 These going before tarried for us at Tro'as.

6 And we sailed away from Phil'ippi after the days of unleavened bread, and came unto them to Tro'as in five days; where we abode seven days.

Paul's Farewell Visit at Troas

7 And upon the first day of the week, when the disciples came together to break bread, Paul preached unto them, ready to depart on the morrow; and continued his speech until midnight.

8 And there were many lights in the upper chamber, where they were gathered together.

9 And there sat in a window a certain young man named Eu'tychus, being fallen into a deep sleep: and as Paul was long preaching, he sunk down with sleep, and fell down from the third loft, and was taken up dead.

10 And Paul went down, and fell on him, and embracing him said, Trouble not yourselves; for his life is in him.

11 When he therefore was come up again, and had broken bread, and eaten, and talked a long while, even till break of day, so he departed.

12 And they brought the young man alive, and were not a little comforted.

The Voyage from Troas to Miletus

13 And we went before to ship, and sailed unto Assos, there intending to take in Paul: for so had he appointed, minding himself to go afoot.

14 And when he met with us at Assos, we took him in, and came to Mityle′ne.

15 And we sailed thence, and came the next day over against Chi′os; and the next day we arrived at Samos, and tarried at Trogyl′li-um; and the next day we came to Mile′tus.

16 For Paul had determined to sail by Ephesus, because he would not spend the time in Asia: for he hasted, if it were possible for him, to be at Jerusalem the day of Pentecost.

Paul's Address to the Ephesian Elders

17 And from Mile′tus he sent to Ephesus, and called the elders of the church.

18 And when they were come to him, he said unto them,

Ye know, from the first day that I came into Asia, after what manner I have been with you at all seasons,

19 Serving the Lord with all humility of mind, and with many tears, and temptations, which befell me by the lying in wait of the Jews:

20 And how I kept back nothing that was profitable unto you, but have showed you, and

have taught you publicly, and from house to
house,

21 Testifying both to the Jews, and also to
the Greeks, repentance toward God, and faith
toward our Lord Jesus Christ.

22 And now, behold, I go bound in the
spirit unto Jerusalem, not knowing the things
that shall befall me there:

23 Save that the Holy Ghost witnesseth in
every city, saying that bonds and afflictions
abide me.

24 But none of these things move me,
neither count I my life dear unto myself, so
that I might finish my course with joy, and
the ministry, which I have received of the
Lord Jesus, to testify the gospel of the grace
of God.

25 And now, behold, I know that ye all,
among whom I have gone preaching
the kingdom of God, shall see my face no
more.

26 Wherefore I take you to record this day,
that I am pure from the blood of all men.

27 For I have not shunned to declare unto
you all the counsel of God.

28 Take heed therefore unto yourselves, and
to all the flock, over the which the Holy
Ghost hath made you overseers, to feed the
church of God, which he hath purchased with
his own blood.

29 For I know this, that after my departing
shall grievous wolves enter in among you, not
sparing the flock.

30 Also of your own selves shall men arise,

speaking perverse things, to draw away disciples after them.

31 Therefore watch, and remember, that by
the space of three years I ceased not to warn
every one night and day with tears.

32 And now, brethren, I commend you to
God, and to the word of his grace, which is
able to build you up, and to give you an inheritance among all them which are sanctified.

33 I have coveted no man's silver, or gold,
or apparel.

34 Yea, ye yourselves know, that these
hands have ministered unto my necessities,
and to them that were with me.

35 I have showed you all things, how that
so laboring ye ought to support the weak, and
to remember the words of the Lord Jesus,
how he said, It is more blessed to give than
to receive.

36 And when he had thus spoken, he
kneeled down, and prayed with them all.

37 And they all wept sore, and fell on
Paul's neck, and kissed him,

38 Sorrowing most of all for the words
which he spake, that they should see his face
no more. And they accompanied him unto
the ship.

Paul's Journey to Jerusalem

21 And it came to pass, that after we were
gotten from them, and had launched, we
came with a straight course unto Co′os, and
the day following unto Rhodes, and from
thence unto Pat′ara:

2 And finding a ship sailing over unto Phoeni'cia, we went aboard, and set forth.

3 Now when we had discovered Cyprus, we left it on the left hand, and sailed into Syria, and landed at Tyre: for there the ship was to unlade her burden.

4 And finding disciples, we tarried there seven days: who said to Paul through the Spirit, that he should not go up to Jerusalem.

5 And when we had accomplished those days, we departed and went our way; and they all brought us on our way, with wives and children, till we were out of the city: and we kneeled down on the shore, and prayed.

6 And when we had taken our leave one of another, we took ship; and they returned home again.

7 And when we had finished our course from Tyre, we came to Ptolema'is, and saluted the brethren, and abode with them one day.

8 And the next day we that were of Paul's company departed, and came unto Caesare'a; and we entered into the house of Philip the evangelist, which was one of the seven; and abode with him.

9 And the same man had four daughters, virgins, which did prophesy.

10 And as we tarried there many days, there came down from Judea a certain prophet, named Ag'abus.

11 And when he was come unto us, he took Paul's girdle, and bound his own hands and feet, and said, Thus saith the Holy Ghost, So shall the Jews at Jerusalem bind the man that

owneth this girdle, and shall deliver him into the hands of the Gentiles.

12 And when we heard these things, both we, and they of that place, besought him not to go up to Jerusalem.

13 Then Paul answered, What mean ye to weep and to break mine heart? for I am ready not to be bound only, but also to die at Jerusalem for the name of the Lord Jesus.

14 And when he would not be persuaded, we ceased, saying, The will of the Lord be done.

15 And after those days we took up our carriages, and went up to Jerusalem.

16 There went with us also certain of the disciples of Caesare′a, and brought with them one Mnason of Cyprus, an old disciple, with whom we should lodge.

Paul Arrested in the Temple

17 And when we were come to Jerusalem, the brethren received us gladly.

18 And the day following Paul went in with us unto James; and all the elders were present.

19 And when he had saluted them, he declared particularly what things God had wrought among the Gentiles by his ministry.

20 And when they heard it, they glorified the Lord, and said unto him, Thou seest, brother, how many thousands of Jews there are which believe; and they are all zealous of the law:

21 And they are informed of thee, that thou

teachest all the Jews which are among the
Gentiles to forsake Moses, saying that they
ought not to circumcise their children, neither
to walk after the customs.

22 What is it therefore? the multitude must
needs come together: for they will hear that
thou art come.

23 Do therefore this that we say to thee:
We have four men which have a vow on
them;

24 Them take, and purify thyself with them,
and be at charges with them, that they may
shave their heads: and all may know that those
things, whereof they were informed concerning
thee, are nothing; but that thou thyself also
walkest orderly, and keepest the law.

25 As touching the Gentiles which believe,
we have written and concluded that they observe no such thing, save only that they keep
themselves from things offered to idols, and
from blood, and from strangled, and from
fornication.

26 Then Paul took the men, and the next
day purifying himself with them entered into
the temple, to signify the accomplishment of
the days of purification, until that an offering
should be offered for every one of them.

27 And when the seven days were almost
ended, the Jews which were of Asia, when
they saw him in the temple, stirred up all the
people, and laid hands on him,

28 Crying out, Men of Israel, help: This is
the man, that teacheth all men every where
against the people, and the law, and this

place: and further brought Greeks also into the temple, and hath polluted this holy place.

29 (For they had seen before with him in the city Troph'imus an Ephesian, whom they supposed that Paul had brought into the temple.)

30 And all the city was moved, and the people ran together: and they took Paul, and drew him out of the temple: and forthwith the doors were shut.

31 And as they went about to kill him, tidings came unto the chief captain of the band, that all Jerusalem was in an uproar:

32 Who immediately took soldiers and centurions, and ran down unto them: and when they saw the chief captain and the soldiers, they left beating of Paul.

33 Then the chief captain came near, and took him, and commanded him to be bound with two chains; and demanded who he was, and what he had done.

34 And some cried one thing, some another, among the multitude: and when he could not know the certainty for the tumult, he commanded him to be carried into the castle.

35 And when he came upon the stairs, so it was, that he was borne of the soldiers for the violence of the people.

36 For the multitude of the people followed after, crying, Away with him.

Paul's Defense before the People

37 And as Paul was to be led into the castle, he said unto the chief captain, May I

speak unto thee? Who said, Canst thou speak
Greek?

38 Art not thou that Egyptian, which before
these days madest an uproar, and leddest out
into the wilderness four thousand men that
were murderers?

39 But Paul said, I am a man which am a
Jew of Tarsus, a city in Cili′cia, a citizen of
no mean city: and, I beseech thee, suffer me
to speak unto the people.

40 And when he had given him license,
Paul stood on the stairs, and beckoned with
the hand unto the people. And when there
was made a great silence, he spake unto them
in the Hebrew tongue, saying,

22 Men, brethren, and fathers, hear ye
my defense which I make now unto
you.

2 (And when they heard that he spake in
the Hebrew tongue to them, they kept the
more silence: and he saith,)

3 I am verily a man which am a Jew, born
in Tarsus, a city in Cili′cia, yet brought up
in this city at the feet of Gama′li-el, and
taught according to the perfect manner of the
law of the fathers, and was zealous toward
God, as ye all are this day.

4 And I persecuted this way unto the
death, binding and delivering into prisons
both men and women.

5 As also the high priest doth bear me
witness, and all the estate of the elders: from
whom also I received letters unto the brethren, and went to Damascus, to bring them

which were there bound unto Jerusalem, for to be punished.

Paul Tells of His Conversion

6 And it came to pass, that, as I made my journey, and was come nigh unto Damascus about noon, suddenly there shone from heaven a great light round about me.

7 And I fell unto the ground, and heard a voice saying unto me, Saul, Saul, why persecutest thou me?

8 And I answered, Who art thou, Lord? And he said unto me, I am Jesus of Nazareth, whom thou persecutest.

9 And they that were with me saw indeed the light, and were afraid; but they heard not the voice of him that spake to me.

10 And I said, What shall I do, Lord? And the Lord said unto me, Arise, and go into Damascus; and there it shall be told thee of all things which are appointed for thee to do.

11 And when I could not see for the glory of that light, being led by the hand of them that were with me, I came into Damascus.

12 And one Anani'as, a devout man according to the law, having a good report of all the Jews which dwelt there,

13 Came unto me, and stood, and said unto me, Brother Saul, receive thy sight. And the same hour I looked up upon him.

14 And he said, The God of our fathers hath chosen thee, that thou shouldest know

his will, and see that Just One, and shouldest hear the voice of his mouth.

15 For thou shalt be his witness unto all men of what thou hast seen and heard.

16 And now why tarriest thou? arise, and be baptized, and wash away thy sins, calling on the name of the Lord.

Paul's Call to the Gentiles

17 And it came to pass, that, when I was come again to Jerusalem, even while I prayed in the temple, I was in a trance;

18 And saw him saying unto me, Make haste, and get thee quickly out of Jerusalem: for they will not receive thy testimony concerning me.

19 And I said, Lord, they know that I imprisoned and beat in every synagogue them that believed on thee:

20 And when the blood of thy martyr Stephen was shed, I also was standing by, and consenting unto his death, and kept the raiment of them that slew him.

21 And he said unto me, Depart: for I will send thee far hence unto the Gentiles.

Paul in the Custody of the Chief Captain

22 And they gave him audience unto this word, and then lifted up their voices, and said, Away with such a fellow from the earth: for it is not fit that he should live.

23 And as they cried out, and cast off their clothes, and threw dust into the air,

24 The chief captain commanded him to be

brought into the castle, and bade that he should be examined by scourging; that he might know wherefore they cried so against him.

25 And as they bound him with thongs, Paul said unto the centurion that stood by, Is it lawful for you to scourge a man that is a Roman, and uncondemned?

26 When the centurion heard that, he went and told the chief captain, saying, Take heed what thou doest; for this man is a Roman.

27 Then the chief captain came, and said unto him, Tell me, art thou a Roman? He said, Yea.

28 And the chief captain answered, With a great sum obtained I this freedom. And Paul said, But I was free-born.

29 Then straightway they departed from him which should have examined him: and the chief captain also was afraid, after he knew that he was a Roman, and because he had bound him.

Paul before the Council

30 On the morrow, because he would have known the certainty wherefore he was accused of the Jews, he loosed him from his bands, and commanded the chief priests and all their council to appear, and brought Paul down, and set him before them.

23 And Paul, earnestly beholding the council, said, Men and brethren, I have lived in all good conscience before God until this day.

2 And the high priest Anani′as commanded them that stood by him to smite him on the mouth.

3 Then said Paul unto him, God shall smite thee, thou whited wall: for sittest thou to judge me after the law, and commandest me to be smitten contrary to the law?

4 And they that stood by said, Revilest thou God's high priest?

5 Then said Paul, I wist not, brethren, that he was the high priest: for it is written, Thou shalt not speak evil of the ruler of thy people.

6 But when Paul perceived that the one part were Sadducees, and the other Pharisees, he cried out in the council, Men and brethren, I am a Pharisee, the son of a Pharisee: of the hope and resurrection of the dead I am called in question.

7 And when he had so said, there arose a dissension between the Pharisees and the Sadducees: and the multitude was divided.

8 For the Sadducees say that there is no resurrection, neither angel, nor spirit: but the Pharisees confess both.

9 And there arose a great cry: and the scribes that were of the Pharisees' part arose, and strove, saying, We find no evil in this man: but if a spirit or an angel hath spoken to him, let us not fight against God.

10 And when there arose a great dissension, the chief captain, fearing lest Paul should have been pulled in pieces of them, commanded the soldiers to go down, and to take him by

force from among them, and to bring him into the castle.

11 And the night following the Lord stood by him, and said, Be of good cheer, Paul: for as thou hast testified of me in Jerusalem, so must thou bear witness also at Rome.

The Plot against Paul's Life

12 And when it was day, certain of the Jews banded together, and bound themselves under a curse, saying that they would neither eat nor drink till they had killed Paul.
13 And they were more than forty which had made this conspiracy.
14 And they came to the chief priests and elders, and said, We have bound ourselves under a great curse, that we will eat nothing until we have slain Paul.
15 Now therefore ye with the council signify to the chief captain that he bring him down unto you tomorrow, as though ye would inquire something more perfectly concerning him: and we, or ever he come near, are ready to kill him.
16 And when Paul's sister's son heard of their lying in wait, he went and entered into the castle, and told Paul.
17 Then Paul called one of the centurions unto him, and said, Bring this young man unto the chief captain: for he hath a certain thing to tell him.
18 So he took him, and brought him to the chief captain, and said, Paul the prisoner called me unto him, and prayed me to bring this

young man unto thee, who hath something to
3494 5100 2980
say unto thee.

19 Then the chief captain took him by the
5506 1949 1949
hand, and went with him aside privately, and
5495 402 402 2398
asked him, What is that thou hast to tell me?
4441 5101 518

20 And he said, The Jews have agreed to
2036 2453 4934
desire thee that thou wouldest bring down
2065 3704 2609
Paul tomorrow into the council, as though
3972 839 4892 3195
they would inquire somewhat of him more
3195 4441 5100 197
perfectly.

21 But do not thou yield unto them: for
3982 3982
there lie in wait for him of them more than
1748 4118-4119
forty men, which have bound themselves with
5062 435 332 332
an oath, that they will neither eat nor drink
5315 4095
till they have killed him: and now are they
337
ready, looking for a promise from thee.
2092 4327 1860 575 3568

22 So the chief captain then let the young
5506 630 3494
man depart, and charged him, See thou tell
630 3853 1583
no man that thou hast showed these things
1718
to me.

Paul Sent to Felix the Governor

23 And he called unto him two centurions,
4341 1417 (5100), 1543
saying, Make ready two hundred soldiers to
2090 1250 4757 3704
go to Caesare'a, and horsemen threescore and
4198 2542 2460 1440
ten, and spearmen two hundred, at the third
1187 1250 575 5154
hour of the night;
5610 3571

24 And provide them beasts, that they may
3936 2934
set Paul on, and bring him safe unto Felix the
1913 3972 1913 1295 1295 5344
governor.
2232

25 And he wrote a letter after this manner:
1125 1125 1992 5179

26 Claudius Lys'i-as unto the most ex-
2804 3079 2903
cellent governor Felix sendeth greeting.

27 This man was taken of the Jews, and
2232 5344 5463
435 4815 2453

should have been killed of them: then came I with an army, and rescued him, having understood that he was a Roman.

28 And when I would have known the cause wherefore they accused him, I brought him forth into their council:

29 Whom I perceived to be accused of questions of their law, but to have nothing laid to his charge worthy of death or of bonds.

30 And when it was told me how that the Jews laid wait for the man, I sent straightway to thee, and gave commandment to his accusers also to say before thee what they had against him. Farewell.

31 Then the soldiers, as it was commanded them, took Paul, and brought him by night to Antip′atris.

32 On the morrow they left the horsemen to go with him, and returned to the castle:

33 Who, when they came to Caesare′a, and delivered the epistle to the governor, presented Paul also before him.

34 And when the governor had read the letter, he asked of what province he was. And when he understood that he was of Cili′cia;

35 I will hear thee, said he, when thine accusers are also come. And he commanded him to be kept in Herod′s judgment hall.

Paul's Defense before Felix

24 And after five days Anani′as the high priest descended with the elders, and with a certain orator named Tertul′lus, who informed the governor against Paul.

2 And when he was called forth, Tertul´lus began to accuse him, saying, Seeing that by thee we enjoy great quietness, and that very worthy deeds are done unto this nation by thy providence,

3 We accept it always, and in all places, most noble Felix, with all thankfulness.

4 Notwithstanding, that I be not further tedious unto thee, I pray thee that thou wouldest hear us of thy clemency a few words.

5 For we have found this man a pestilent fellow, and a mover of sedition among all the Jews throughout the world, and a ringleader of the sect of the Nazarenes:

6 Who also hath gone about to profane the temple: whom we took, and would have judged according to our law.

7 But the chief captain Lys´i-as came upon us, and with great violence took him away out of our hands,

8 Commanding his accusers to come unto thee: by examining of whom thyself mayest take knowledge of all these things, whereof we accuse him.

9 And the Jews also assented, saying that these things were so.

10 Then Paul, after that the governor had beckoned unto him to speak, answered, Forasmuch as I know that thou hast been of many years a judge unto this nation, I do the more cheerfully answer for myself:

11 Because that thou mayest understand, that there are yet but twelve days since I went up to Jerusalem for to worship.

12 And they neither found me in the temple disputing with any man, neither raising up the people, neither in the synagogues, nor in the city:

13 Neither can they prove the things whereof they now accuse me.

14 But this I confess unto thee, that after the way which they call heresy, so worship I the God of my fathers, believing all things which are written in the law and in the prophets:

15 And have hope toward God, which they themselves also allow, that there shall be a resurrection of the dead, both of the just and unjust.

16 And herein do I exercise myself, to have always a conscience void of offense toward God, and toward men.

17 Now after many years I came to bring alms to my nation, and offerings.

18 Whereupon certain Jews from Asia found me purified in the temple, neither with multitude, nor with tumult.

19 Who ought to have been here before thee, and object, if they had aught against me.

20 Or else let these same here say, if they have found any evildoing in me, while I stood before the council,

21 Except it be for this one voice, that I cried standing among them, Touching the resurrection of the dead I am called in question by you this day.

22 And when Felix heard these things, having more perfect knowledge of that way,

he deferred them, and said, When Lys'i-as the chief captain shall come down, I will know the uttermost of your matter.

23 And he commanded a centurion to keep Paul, and to let him have liberty, and that he should forbid none of his acquaintance to minister or come unto him.

24 And after certain days, when Felix came with his wife Drusil'la, which was a Jewess, he sent for Paul, and heard him concerning the faith in Christ.

25 And as he reasoned of righteousness, temperance, and judgment to come, Felix trembled, and answered, Go thy way for this time; when I have a convenient season, I will call for thee.

26 He hoped also that money should have been given him of Paul, that he might loose him: wherefore he sent for him the oftener, and communed with him.

27 But after two years Por'ci-us Festus came into Felix' room: and Felix, willing to show the Jews a pleasure, left Paul bound.

Paul Appeals to Caesar

25 Now when Festus was come into the province, after three days he ascended from Caesare'a to Jerusalem.

2 Then the high priest and the chief of the Jews informed him against Paul, and besought him,

3 And desired favor against him, that he would send for him to Jerusalem, laying wait in the way to kill him.

4 But Festus answered, that Paul should be kept at Caesare′a, and that he himself would depart shortly thither.

5 Let them therefore, said he, which among you are able, go down with me, and accuse this man, if there be any wickedness in him.

6 And when he had tarried among them more than ten days, he went down unto Caesare′a; and the next day sitting on the judgment seat commanded Paul to be brought.

7 And when he was come, the Jews which came down from Jerusalem stood round about, and laid many and grievous complaints against Paul, which they could not prove.

8 While he answered for himself, Neither against the law of the Jews, neither against the temple, nor yet against Caesar, have I offended any thing at all.

9 But Festus, willing to do the Jews a pleasure, answered Paul, and said, Wilt thou go up to Jerusalem, and there be judged of these things before me?

10 Then said Paul, I stand at Caesar's judgment seat, where I ought to be judged: to the Jews have I done no wrong, as thou very well knowest.

11 For if I be an offender, or have committed any thing worthy of death, I refuse not to die: but if there be none of these things whereof these accuse me, no man may deliver me unto them. I appeal unto Caesar.

12 Then Festus, when he had conferred with the council, answered, Hast thou appealed unto Caesar? unto Caesar shalt thou go.

Paul Brought before Agrippa and Bernice

13 And after certain days king Agrip′pa and Bernice came unto Caesare′a to salute Festus.

14 And when they had been there many days, Festus declared Paul's cause unto the king, saying, There is a certain man left in bonds by Felix:

15 About whom, when I was at Jerusalem, the chief priests and the elders of the Jews informed me, desiring to have judgment against him.

16 To whom I answered, It is not the manner of the Romans to deliver any man to die, before that he which is accused have the accusers face to face, and have license to answer for himself concerning the crime laid against him.

17 Therefore, when they were come hither, without any delay on the morrow I sat on the judgment seat, and commanded the man to be brought forth.

18 Against whom when the accusers stood up, they brought none accusation of such things as I supposed:

19 But had certain questions against him of their own superstition, and of one Jesus, which was dead, whom Paul affirmed to be alive.

20 And because I doubted of such manner of questions, I asked him whether he would go to Jerusalem, and there be judged of these matters.

21 But when Paul had appealed to be reserved unto the hearing of Augustus, I com-

manded him to be kept till I might send him to Caesar.

22 Then Agrip'pa said unto Festus, I would also hear the man myself. Tomorrow, said he, thou shalt hear him.

23 And on the morrow, when Agrip'pa was come, and Bernice, with great pomp, and was entered into the place of hearing, with the chief captains, and principal men of the city, at Festus' commandment Paul was brought forth.

24 And Festus said, King Agrip'pa, and all men which are here present with us, ye see this man, about whom all the multitude of the Jews have dealt with me, both at Jerusalem, and also here, crying that he ought not to live any longer.

25 But when I found that he had committed nothing worthy of death, and that he himself hath appealed to Augustus, I have determined to send him.

26 Of whom I have no certain thing to write unto my lord. Wherefore I have brought him forth before you, and specially before thee, O king Agrip'pa, that, after examination had, I might have somewhat to write.

27 For it seemeth to me unreasonable to send a prisoner, and not withal to signify the crimes laid against him.

Paul's Defense before Agrippa

26 Then Agrip'pa said unto Paul, Thou art permitted to speak for thyself. Then Paul stretched forth the hand, and answered for himself:

2 I think myself happy, king Agrip′pa, because I shall answer for myself this day before thee touching all the things whereof I am accused of the Jews:

3 Especially because I know thee to be expert in all customs and questions which are among the Jews: wherefore I beseech thee to hear me patiently.

4 My manner of life from my youth, which was at the first among mine own nation at Jerusalem, know all the Jews;

5 Which knew me from the beginning, if they would testify, that after the most straitest sect of our religion I lived a Pharisee.

6 And now I stand and am judged for the hope of the promise made of God unto our fathers:

7 Unto which promise our twelve tribes, instantly serving God day and night, hope to come. For which hope's sake, king Agrip′pa, I am accused of the Jews.

8 Why should it be thought a thing incredible with you, that God should raise the dead?

9 I verily thought with myself, that I ought to do many things contrary to the name of Jesus of Nazareth.

10 Which thing I also did in Jerusalem: and many of the saints did I shut up in prison, having received authority from the chief priests; and when they were put to death, I gave my voice against them.

11 And I punished them oft in every synagogue, and compelled them to blaspheme;

and being exceedingly mad against them, I
persecuted them even unto strange cities.

Paul Tells of His Conversion

12 Whereupon as I went to Damascus with
authority and commission from the chief
priests,

13 At midday, O king, I saw in the way a
light from heaven, above the brightness of the
sun, shining round about me and them which
journeyed with me.

14 And when we were all fallen to the
earth, I heard a voice speaking unto me, and
saying in the Hebrew tongue, Saul, Saul, why
persecutest thou me? it is hard for thee to
kick against the pricks.

15 And I said, Who art thou, Lord? And
he said, I am Jesus whom thou persecutest.

16 But rise, and stand upon thy feet: for I
have appeared unto thee for this purpose,
to make thee a minister and a witness both of
these things which thou hast seen, and of
those things in the which I will appear unto
thee;

17 Delivering thee from the people, and
from the Gentiles, unto whom now I send
thee,

18 To open their eyes, and to turn them
from darkness to light, and from the power
of Satan unto God, that they may receive
forgiveness of sins, and inheritance among
them which are sanctified by faith that is in
me.

Paul's Witness to Jews and Gentiles

19 Whereupon, O king Agrip′pa, I was not disobedient unto the heavenly vision:

20 But showed first unto them of Damascus, and at Jerusalem, and throughout all the coasts of Judea, and then to the Gentiles, that they should repent and turn to God, and do works meet for repentance.

21 For these causes the Jews caught me in the temple, and went about to kill me.

22 Having therefore obtained help of God, I continue unto this day, witnessing both to small and great, saying none other things than those which the prophets and Moses did say should come:

23 That Christ should suffer, and that he should be the first that should rise from the dead, and should show light unto the people, and to the Gentiles.

Paul Appeals to Agrippa to Believe

24 And as he thus spake for himself, Festus said with a loud voice, Paul, thou art beside thyself; much learning doth make thee mad.

25 But he said, I am not mad, most noble Festus; but speak forth the words of truth and soberness.

26 For the king knoweth of these things, before whom also I speak freely: for I am persuaded that none of these things are hidden from him; for this thing was not done in a corner.

27 King Agrip′pa, believest thou the prophets? I know that thou believest.

28 Then Agrip′pa said unto Paul, Almost thou persuadest me to be a Christian.

29 And Paul said, I would to God, that not only thou, but also all that hear me this day, were both almost, and altogether such as I am, except these bonds.

30 And when he had thus spoken, the king rose up, and the governor, and Bernice, and they that sat with them:

31 And when they were gone aside, they talked between themselves, saying, This man doeth nothing worthy of death or of bonds.

32 Then said Agrip′pa unto Festus, This man might have been set at liberty, if he had not appealed unto Caesar.

Paul Sails for Rome

27 And when it was determined that we should sail into Italy, they delivered Paul and certain other prisoners unto one named Julius, a centurion of Augustus' band.

2 And entering into a ship of Adramyt′-tium, we launched, meaning to sail by the coasts of Asia; one Aristar′chus, a Macedo′nian of Thessaloni′ca, being with us.

3 And the next day we touched at Sidon. And Julius courteously entreated Paul, and gave him liberty to go unto his friends to refresh himself.

4 And when we had launched from thence, we sailed under Cyprus, because the winds were contrary.

5 And when we had sailed over the sea of

Cili′cia and Pamphyl′i-a, we came to Myra, a city of Ly′ci-a.

6 And there the centurion found a ship of Alexandria sailing into Italy; and he put us therein.

7 And when we had sailed slowly many days, and scarce were come over against Cnidus, the wind not suffering us, we sailed under Crete, over against Salmo′ne;

8 And, hardly passing it, came unto a place which is called the Fair Havens; nigh whereunto was the city of Lase′a.

9 Now when much time was spent, and when sailing was now dangerous, because the fast was now already past, Paul admonished them,

10 And said unto them, Sirs, I perceive that this voyage will be with hurt and much damage, not only of the lading and ship, but also of our lives.

11 Nevertheless the centurion believed the master and the owner of the ship, more than those things which were spoken by Paul.

12 And because the haven was not commodious to winter in, the more part advised to depart thence also, if by any means they might attain to Phoinix, and there to winter; which is a haven of Crete, and lieth toward the southwest and northwest.

The Storm at Sea

13 And when the south wind blew softly, supposing that they had obtained their purpose, loosing thence, they sailed close by Crete.

14 But not long after there arose against it a tempestuous wind, called Euroc′lydon.

15 And when the ship was caught, and could not bear up into the wind, we let her drive.

16 And running under a certain island which is called Clauda, we had much work to come by the boat:

17 Which when they had taken up, they used helps, undergirding the ship; and, fearing lest they should fall into the quicksands, struck sail, and so were driven.

18 And we being exceedingly tossed with a tempest, the next day they lightened the ship;

19 And the third day we cast out with our own hands the tackling of the ship.

20 And when neither sun nor stars in many days appeared, and no small tempest lay on us, all hope that we should be saved was then taken away.

21 But after long abstinence, Paul stood forth in the midst of them, and said, Sirs, ye should have hearkened unto me, and not have loosed from Crete, and to have gained this harm and loss.

22 And now I exhort you to be of good cheer: for there shall be no loss of any man's life among you, but of the ship.

23 For there stood by me this night the angel of God, whose I am, and whom I serve,

24 Saying, Fear not, Paul; thou must be brought before Caesar: and, lo, God hath given thee all them that sail with thee.

25 Wherefore, sirs, be of good cheer: for I

believe God, that it shall be even as it was told me.

26 Howbeit we must be cast upon a certain island.

27 But when the fourteenth night was come, as we were driven up and down in A'dria, about midnight the shipmen deemed that they drew near to some country;

28 And sounded, and found it twenty fathoms: and when they had gone a little further, they sounded again, and found it fifteen fathoms.

29 Then fearing lest we should have fallen upon rocks, they cast four anchors out of the stern, and wished for the day.

30 And as the shipmen were about to flee out of the ship, when they had let down the boat into the sea, under color as though they would have cast anchors out of the foreship,

31 Paul said to the centurion and to the soldiers, Except these abide in the ship, ye cannot be saved.

32 Then the soldiers cut off the ropes of the boat, and let her fall off.

33 And while the day was coming on, Paul besought them all to take meat, saying, This day is the fourteenth day that ye have tarried and continued fasting, having taken nothing.

34 Wherefore I pray you to take some meat; for this is for your health: for there shall not a hair fall from the head of any of you.

35 And when he had thus spoken, he took bread, and gave thanks to God in presence of

them all; and when he had broken it, he
began to eat.

36 Then were they all of good cheer, and
they also took some meat.

37 And we were in all in the ship two
hundred threescore and sixteen souls.

38 And when they had eaten enough, they
lightened the ship, and cast out the wheat into
the sea.

The Shipwreck

39 And when it was day, they knew not the
land: but they discovered a certain creek with
a shore, into the which they were minded, if
it were possible, to thrust in the ship.

40 And when they had taken up the
anchors, they committed themselves unto the
sea, and loosed the rudder bands, and hoisted
up the mainsail to the wind, and made toward
shore.

41 And falling into a place where two seas
met, they ran the ship aground; and the fore-
part stuck fast, and remained unmovable, but
the hinder part was broken with the violence
of the waves.

42 And the soldiers' counsel was to kill the
prisoners, lest any of them should swim out,
and escape.

43 But the centurion, willing to save Paul,
kept them from their purpose; and commanded that they which could swim should
cast themselves first into the sea, and get to
land:

44 And the rest, some on boards, and some

on broken pieces of the ship. And so it came
to pass, that they escaped all safe to land.

Paul on the Island of Melita

28 And when they were escaped, then they
knew that the island was called Meli'ta.

2 And the barbarous people showed us no
little kindness: for they kindled a fire, and
received us every one, because of the present
rain, and because of the cold.

3 And when Paul had gathered a bundle of
sticks, and laid them on the fire, there came a
viper out of the heat, and fastened on his
hand.

4 And when the barbarians saw the venom-
ous beast hang on his hand, they said among
themselves, No doubt this man is a murderer,
whom, though he hath escaped the sea, yet
vengeance suffereth not to live.

5 And he shook off the beast into the fire,
and felt no harm.

6 Howbeit they looked when he should have
swollen, or fallen down dead suddenly: but
after they had looked a great while, and saw
no harm come to him, they changed their
minds, and said that he was a god.

7 In the same quarters were possessions of
the chief man of the island, whose name was
Pub'li-us; who received us, and lodged us
three days courteously.

8 And it came to pass, that the father of
Pub'li-us lay sick of a fever and of a bloody
flux: to whom Paul entered in, and prayed,
and laid his hands on him, and healed him.

9 So when this was done, others also, which
had diseases in the island, came, and were
healed:

10 Who also honored us with many honors;
and when we departed, they laded us with
such things as were necessary.

Paul Arrives at Rome

11 And after three months we departed in
a ship of Alexandria, which had wintered in
the isle, whose sign was Castor and Pollux.

12 And landing at Syracuse, we tarried there
three days.

13 And from thence we fetched a compass,
and came to Rhe´gi-um: and after one day the
south wind blew, and we came the next day
to Pute´oli:

14 Where we found brethren, and were desired to tarry with them seven days: and so
we went toward Rome.

15 And from thence, when the brethren
heard of us, they came to meet us as far as
Ap´pi-i Forum, and the Three Taverns; whom
when Paul saw, he thanked God, and took
courage.

16 And when we came to Rome, the centurion delivered the prisoners to the captain of
the guard: but Paul was suffered to dwell by
himself with a soldier that kept him.

Paul Preaches in Rome

17 And it came to pass, that after three
days Paul called the chief of the Jews together: and when they were come together,

he said unto them, Men and brethren, though I have committed nothing against the people, or customs of our fathers, yet was I delivered prisoner from Jerusalem into the hands of the Romans:

18 Who, when they had examined me, would have let me go, because there was no cause of death in me.

19 But when the Jews spake against it, I was constrained to appeal unto Caesar; not that I had aught to accuse my nation of.

20 For this cause therefore have I called for you, to see you, and to speak with you: because that for the hope of Israel I am bound with this chain.

21 And they said unto him, We neither received letters out of Judea concerning thee, neither any of the brethren that came showed or spake any harm of thee.

22 But we desire to hear of thee what thou thinkest: for as concerning this sect, we know that every where it is spoken against.

23 And when they had appointed him a day, there came many to him into his lodging; to whom he expounded and testified the kingdom of God, persuading them concerning Jesus, both out of the law of Moses, and out of the prophets, from morning till evening.

24 And some believed the things which were spoken, and some believed not.

25 And when they agreed not among themselves, they departed, after that Paul had spoken one word, Well spake the Holy Ghost by Isaiah the prophet unto our fathers,

26 Saying, Go unto this people, and say, Hearing ye shall hear, and shall not understand; and seeing ye shall see, and not perceive:

27 For the heart of this people is waxed gross, and their ears are dull of hearing, and their eyes have they closed; lest they should see with their eyes, and hear with their ears, and understand with their heart, and should be converted, and I should heal them.

28 Be it known therefore unto you, that the salvation of God is sent unto the Gentiles, and that they will hear it.

29 And when he had said these words, the Jews departed, and had great reasoning among themselves.

30 And Paul dwelt two whole years in his own hired house, and received all that came in unto him,

31 Preaching the kingdom of God, and teaching those things which concern the Lord Jesus Christ, with all confidence, no man forbidding him.

THE EPISTLE OF PAUL THE APOSTLE TO THE
ROMANS

Salutation

1 Paul, a servant of Jesus Christ, called to be an apostle, separated unto the gospel of God,

2 (Which he had promised afore by his prophets in the holy Scriptures,)

3 Concerning his Son Jesus Christ our Lord, which was made of the seed of David according to the flesh;

4 And declared to be the Son of God with power, according to the Spirit of holiness, by the resurrection from the dead:

5 By whom we have received grace and apostleship, for obedience to the faith among all nations, for his name:

6 Among whom are ye also the called of Jesus Christ:

7 To all that be in Rome, beloved of God, called to be saints: Grace to you, and peace, from God our Father and the Lord Jesus Christ.

Paul's Desire to Visit Rome

8 First, I thank my God through Jesus Christ for you all, that your faith is spoken of throughout the whole world.

9 For God is my witness, whom I serve with my spirit in the gospel of his Son, that without ceasing I make mention of you always in my prayers;

10 Making request, if by any means now at

length I might have a prosperous journey by the will of God to come unto you.

11 For I long to see you, that I may impart unto you some spiritual gift, to the end ye may be established;

12 That is, that I may be comforted together with you by the mutual faith both of you and me.

13 Now I would not have you ignorant, brethren, that oftentimes I purposed to come unto you, (but was let hitherto,) that I might have some fruit among you also, even as among other Gentiles.

14 I am debtor both to the Greeks, and to the Barbarians; both to the wise, and to the unwise.

15 So, as much as in me is, I am ready to preach the gospel to you that are at Rome also.

The Power of the Gospel

16 For I am not ashamed of the gospel of Christ: for it is the power of God unto salvation to every one that believeth; to the Jew first, and also to the Greek.

17 For therein is the righteousness of God revealed from faith to faith: as it is written, The just shall live by faith.

The Guilt of Mankind

18 For the wrath of God is revealed from heaven against all ungodliness and unrighteousness of men, who hold the truth in unrighteousness;

19 Because that which may be known of God is manifest in them; for God hath showed it unto them.

20 For the invisible things of him from the creation of the world are clearly seen, being understood by the things that are made, even his eternal power and Godhead; so that they are without excuse:

21 Because that, when they knew God, they glorified him not as God, neither were thankful; but became vain in their imaginations, and their foolish heart was darkened.

22 Professing themselves to be wise, they became fools,

23 And changed the glory of the uncorruptible God into an image made like to corruptible man, and to birds, and four-footed beasts, and creeping things.

24 Wherefore God also gave them up to uncleanness, through the lusts of their own hearts, to dishonor their own bodies between themselves:

25 Who changed the truth of God into a lie, and worshipped and served the creature more than the Creator, who is blessed for ever. Amen.

26 For this cause God gave them up unto vile affections: for even their women did change the natural use into that which is against nature:

27 And likewise also the men, leaving the natural use of the woman, burned in their lust one toward another; men with men working that which is unseemly, and receiving in

themselves that recompense of their error which was meet.

28 And even as they did not like to retain God in their knowledge, God gave them over to a reprobate mind, to do those things which are not convenient;

29 Being filled with all unrighteousness, fornication, wickedness, covetousness, maliciousness; full of envy, murder, debate, deceit, malignity; whisperers,

30 Backbiters, haters of God, despiteful, proud, boasters, inventors of evil things, disobedient to parents,

31 Without understanding, covenant-breakers, without natural affection, implacable, unmerciful:

32 Who, knowing the judgment of God, that they which commit such things are worthy of death, not only do the same, but have pleasure in them that do them.

The Righteous Judgment of God

2 Therefore thou art inexcusable, O man, whosoever thou art that judgest: for wherein thou judgest another, thou condemnest thyself; for thou that judgest doest the same things.

2 But we are sure that the judgment of God is according to truth against them which commit such things.

3 And thinkest thou this, O man, that judgest them which do such things, and doest the same, that thou shalt escape the judgment of God?

4 Or despisest thou the riches of his goodness and forbearance and long-suffering; not
knowing that the goodness of God leadeth
thee to repentance?

5 But, after thy hardness and impenitent
heart, treasurest up unto thyself wrath against
the day of wrath and revelation of the righteous judgment of God;

6 Who will render to every man according
to his deeds:

7 To them who by patient continuance in
well doing seek for glory and honor and immortality, eternal life:

8 But unto them that are contentious, and
do not obey the truth, but obey unrighteousness, indignation and wrath,

9 Tribulation and anguish, upon every soul
of man that doeth evil; of the Jew first, and
also of the Gentile;

10 But glory, honor, and peace, to every
man that worketh good; to the Jew first, and
also to the Gentile:

11 For there is no respect of persons with
God.

12 For as many as have sinned without law
shall also perish without law; and as many as
have sinned in the law shall be judged by the law;

13 (For not the hearers of the law are just
before God, but the doers of the law shall be
justified.

14 For when the Gentiles, which have not
the law, do by nature the things contained in
the law, these, having not the law, are a law
unto themselves:

15 Which show the work of the law written in their hearts, their conscience also bearing witness, and their thoughts the mean while accusing or else excusing one another;)

16 In the day when God shall judge the secrets of men by Jesus Christ according to my gospel.

The Jews and the Law

17 Behold, thou art called a Jew, and restest in the law, and makest thy boast of God,

18 And knowest his will, and approvest the things that are more excellent, being instructed out of the law;

19 And art confident that thou thyself art a guide of the blind, a light of them which are in darkness,

20 An instructor of the foolish, a teacher of babes, which hast the form of knowledge and of the truth in the law.

21 Thou therefore which teachest another, teachest thou not thyself? thou that preachest a man should not steal, dost thou steal?

22 Thou that sayest a man should not commit adultery, dost thou commit adultery? thou that abhorrest idols, dost thou commit sacrilege?

23 Thou that makest thy boast of the law, through breaking the law dishonorest thou God?

24 For the name of God is blasphemed among the Gentiles through you, as it is written.

25 For circumcision verily profiteth, if thou

keep the law: but if thou be a breaker of the
law, thy circumcision is made uncircumcision.

26 Therefore, if the uncircumcision keep the
righteousness of the law, shall not his uncircumcision be counted for circumcision?

27 And shall not uncircumcision which is by
nature, if it fulfil the law, judge thee, who by
the letter and circumcision dost transgress the
law?

28 For he is not a Jew, which is one outwardly; neither is that circumcision, which is
outward in the flesh:

29 But he is a Jew, which is one inwardly;
and circumcision is that of the heart, in the
spirit, and not in the letter; whose praise is
not of men, but of God.

3 What advantage then hath the Jew? or
what profit is there of circumcision?

2 Much every way: chiefly, because that
unto them were committed the oracles of
God.

3 For what if some did not believe? shall
their unbelief make the faith of God without
effect?

4 God forbid: yea, let God be true, but
every man a liar; as it is written, That thou
mightest be justified in thy sayings, and
mightest overcome when thou art judged.

5 But if our unrighteousness commend the
righteousness of God, what shall we say? Is
God unrighteous who taketh vengeance? (I
speak as a man)

6 God forbid: for then how shall God
judge the world?

7 For if the truth of God hath more abounded through my lie unto his glory; why yet am I also judged as a sinner?

8 And not rather, (as we be slanderously reported, and as some affirm that we say,) Let us do evil, that good may come? whose damnation is just.

There Is None Righteous

9 What then? are we better than they? No, in no wise: for we have before proved both Jews and Gentiles, that they are all under sin;

10 As it is written, There is none righteous, no, not one:

11 There is none that understandeth, there is none that seeketh after God.

12 They are all gone out of the way, they are together become unprofitable; there is none that doeth good, no, not one.

13 Their throat is an open sepulchre; with their tongues they have used deceit; the poison of asps is under their lips:

14 Whose mouth is full of cursing and bitterness:

15 Their feet are swift to shed blood:

16 Destruction and misery are in their ways:

17 And the way of peace have they not known:

18 There is no fear of God before their eyes.

19 Now we know that what things soever the law saith, it saith to them who are under the law: that every mouth may be stopped,

and all the world may become guilty before
God.

20 Therefore by the deeds of the law there
shall no flesh be justified in his sight: for by
the law is the knowledge of sin.

Righteousness through Faith

21 But now the righteousness of God without the law is manifested, being witnessed by
the law and the prophets;

22 Even the righteousness of God which is
by faith of Jesus Christ unto all and upon
all them that believe; for there is no difference:

23 For all have sinned, and come short of
the glory of God;

24 Being justified freely by his grace through
the redemption that is in Christ Jesus:

25 Whom God hath set forth to be a
propitiation through faith in his blood, to declare his righteousness for the remission of
sins that are past, through the forbearance of
God;

26 To declare, I say, at this time his
righteousness: that he might be just, and the
justifier of him which believeth in Jesus.

27 Where is boasting then? It is excluded.
By what law? of works? Nay; but by the
law of faith.

28 Therefore we conclude that a man is
justified by faith without the deeds of the law.

29 Is he the God of the Jews only? is he
not also of the Gentiles? Yes, of the Gentiles
also:

30 Seeing it is one God, which shall justify
1897 2316 1344
the circumcision by faith, and uncircumcision
4461 4102 203
through faith.

31 Do we then make void the law through
4102
faith? God forbid: yea, we establish the law.
2673 2673 3551
4102 1096 235 2476 3551

The Example of Abraham

4 What shall we say then that Abraham our
5101 2046 2046 11
father, as pertaining to the flesh, hath
3962 4561 2147
found?

2 For if Abraham were justified by works,
11 1344 2041
he hath whereof to glory; but not before God.
2745

3 For what saith the Scripture? Abraham
2316
believed God, and it was counted unto him
5101 1124 11
4100 2316 3049
for righteousness.

4 Now to him that worketh is the reward
1343
not reckoned of grace, but of debt.
2038 3049 3408
3049 5485 3783

5 But to him that worketh not, but be-
3049 2038 4100
lieveth on him that justifieth the ungodly, his
1344 765
faith is counted for righteousness.
4102 3049 1343

6 Even as David also describeth the blessed-
2509 1138 3108
ness of the man, unto whom God imputeth
444 2316 3049
righteousness without works,
1343 5565 2041

7 Saying, Blessed are they whose iniquities
3107 458
are forgiven, and whose sins are covered.
863 266 1943

8 Blessed is the man to whom the Lord
3107 2962
will not impute sin.
3049 3049 266

9 Cometh this blessedness then upon the
3108
circumcision only, or upon the uncircumcision
4061 203
also? for we say that faith was reckoned to
4102 3049
Abraham for righteousness.
11 1343

10 How was it then reckoned? when he was
3049 3049 5607 5607
in circumcision, or in uncircumcision? Not in
4061 203
circumcision, but in uncircumcision.
4061 203

11 And he received the sign of circumcision,
a seal of the righteousness of the faith which
he had yet being uncircumcised: that he
might be the father of all them that believe,
though they be not circumcised; that righteousness might be imputed unto them also:

12 And the father of circumcision to them
who are not of the circumcision only, but who
also walk in the steps of that faith of our
father Abraham, which he had being yet uncircumcised.

The Promise Realized through Faith

13 For the promise, that he should be the
heir of the world, was not to Abraham, or to
his seed, through the law, but through the
righteousness of faith.

14 For if they which are of the law be
heirs, faith is made void, and the promise
made of none effect:

15 Because the law worketh wrath: for
where no law is, there is no transgression.

16 Therefore it is of faith, that it might be
by grace; to the end the promise might be
sure to all the seed; not to that only which is
of the law, but to that also which is of the
faith of Abraham; who is the father of us all,

17 (As it is written, I have made thee a
father of many nations,) before him whom he
believed, even God, who quickeneth the dead,
and calleth those things which be not as
though they were:

18 Who against hope believed in hope, that
he might become the father of many nations,

according to that which was spoken, So shall thy seed be.

19 And being not weak in faith, he considered not his own body now dead, when he was about a hundred years old, neither yet the deadness of Sarah's womb:

20 He staggered not at the promise of God through unbelief; but was strong in faith, giving glory to God;

21 And being fully persuaded, that what he had promised, he was able also to perform.

22 And therefore it was imputed to him for righteousness.

23 Now it was not written for his sake alone, that it was imputed to him;

24 But for us also, to whom it shall be imputed, if we believe on him that raised up Jesus our Lord from the dead;

25 Who was delivered for our offenses, and was raised again for our justification.

Results of Justification

5 Therefore being justified by faith, we have peace with God through our Lord Jesus Christ:

2 By whom also we have access by faith into this grace wherein we stand, and rejoice in hope of the glory of God.

3 And not only so, but we glory in tribulations also; knowing that tribulation worketh patience;

4 And patience, experience; and experience, hope:

5 And hope maketh not ashamed; because

the love of God is shed abroad in our hearts by the Holy Ghost which is given unto us.

6 For when we were yet without strength, in due time Christ died for the ungodly.

7 For scarcely for a righteous man will one die: yet peradventure for a good man some would even dare to die.

8 But God commendeth his love toward us, in that, while we were yet sinners, Christ died for us.

9 Much more then, being now justified by his blood, we shall be saved from wrath through him.

10 For if, when we were enemies, we were reconciled to God by the death of his Son; much more, being reconciled, we shall be saved by his life.

11 And not only so, but we also joy in God through our Lord Jesus Christ, by whom we have now received the atonement.

Adam and Christ

12 Wherefore, as by one man sin entered into the world, and death by sin; and so death passed upon all men, for that all have sinned:

13 (For until the law sin was in the world: but sin is not imputed when there is no law.

14 Nevertheless death reigned from Adam to Moses, even over them that had not sinned after the similitude of Adam's transgression, who is the figure of him that was to come.

15 But not as the offense, so also is the free gift: for if through the offense of one

many be dead, much more the grace of God, and the gift by grace, which is by one man, Jesus Christ, hath abounded unto many.

16 And not as it was by one that sinned, so is the gift; for the judgment was by one to condemnation, but the free gift is of many offenses unto justification.

17 For if by one man's offense death reigned by one; much more they which receive abundance of grace and of the gift of righteousness shall reign in life by one, Jesus Christ.)

18 Therefore, as by the offense of one judgment came upon all men to condemnation; even so by the righteousness of one the free gift came upon all men unto justification of life.

19 For as by one man's disobedience many were made sinners, so by the obedience of one shall many be made righteous.

20 Moreover the law entered, that the offense might abound. But where sin abounded, grace did much more abound:

21 That as sin hath reigned unto death, even so might grace reign through righteousness unto eternal life by Jesus Christ our Lord.

Dead to Sin but Alive in Christ

6 What shall we say then? Shall we continue in sin, that grace may abound?

2 God forbid. How shall we, that are dead to sin, live any longer therein?

3 Know ye not, that so many of us as were

baptized into Jesus Christ were baptized into his death?

4 Therefore we are buried with him by baptism into death: that like as Christ was raised up from the dead by the glory of the Father, even so we also should walk in newness of life.

5 For if we have been planted together in the likeness of his death, we shall be also in the likeness of his resurrection:

6 Knowing this, that our old man is crucified with him, that the body of sin might be destroyed, that henceforth we should not serve sin.

7 For he that is dead is freed from sin.

8 Now if we be dead with Christ, we believe that we shall also live with him:

9 Knowing that Christ being raised from the dead dieth no more; death hath no more dominion over him.

10 For in that he died, he died unto sin once: but in that he liveth, he liveth unto God.

11 Likewise reckon ye also yourselves to be dead indeed unto sin, but alive unto God through Jesus Christ our Lord.

12 Let not sin therefore reign in your mortal body, that ye should obey it in the lusts thereof.

13 Neither yield ye your members as instruments of unrighteousness unto sin: but yield yourselves unto God, as those that are alive from the dead, and your members as instruments of righteousness unto God.

14 For sin shall not have dominion over you: for ye are not under the law, but under grace.

Servants of Righteousness

15 What then? shall we sin, because we are not under the law, but under grace? God forbid.

16 Know ye not, that to whom ye yield yourselves servants to obey, his servants ye are to whom ye obey; whether of sin unto death, or of obedience unto righteousness?

17 But God be thanked, that ye were the servants of sin, but ye have obeyed from the heart that form of doctrine which was delivered you.

18 Being then made free from sin, ye became the servants of righteousness.

19 I speak after the manner of men because of the infirmity of your flesh: for as ye have yielded your members servants to uncleanness and to iniquity unto iniquity; even so now yield your members servants to righteousness unto holiness.

20 For when ye were the servants of sin, ye were free from righteousness.

21 What fruit had ye then in those things whereof ye are now ashamed? for the end of those things is death.

22 But now being made free from sin, and become servants to God, ye have your fruit unto holiness, and the end everlasting life.

23 For the wages of sin is death; but the

gift of God is eternal life through Jesus Christ
5486 2316 166 2222 2424 5547
our Lord.
2962

An Analogy from Marriage

7 Know ye not, brethren, (for I speak to
50 50 80 2950
them that know the law,) how that the
1097 3551
law hath dominion over a man as long as he
3551 2961 444 3745
liveth?
2198

2 For the woman which hath a husband is
1135 5220 1210
bound by the law to her husband so long as
3551 435 2198
he liveth; but if the husband be dead, she is
2198 435 599 2673
loosed from the law of her husband.
3551 435

3 So then if, while her husband liveth, she
686 2198 435 2198
be married to another man, she shall be called
1096 2087 435 5537
an adulteress: but if her husband be dead, she
3428 435 599
is free from that law; so that she is no adul-
1658 3551
teress, though she be married to another man.
1096 1096 2087 435

4 Wherefore, my brethren, ye also are be-
80 2289
come dead to the law by the body of Christ;
3551 4983 5547
that ye should be married to another, even to
1096 2087
him who is raised from the dead, that we
1453 3498
should bring forth fruit unto God.
2592 2316

5 For when we were in the flesh, the mo-
4561 3804
tions of sins, which were by the law, did work
266 3551 1754
in our members to bring forth fruit unto
3196 2592
death.
2288

6 But now we are delivered from the law,
3570 2673 3551
that being dead wherein we were held; that
599 2722
we should serve in newness of spirit, and not
1398 2538 4151
in the oldness of the letter.
3821 1121

The Problem of Indwelling Sin

7 What shall we say then? Is the law sin?
5101 2046 2046 3551 266
God forbid. Nay, I had not known sin, but
1096 235 1097 1097 266 1508

by the law: for I had not known lust, except the law had said, Thou shalt not covet.

8 But sin, taking occasion by the commandment, wrought in me all manner of concupiscence. For without the law sin was dead.

9 For I was alive without the law once: but when the commandment came, sin revived, and I died.

10 And the commandment, which was ordained to life, I found to be unto death.

11 For sin, taking occasion by the commandment, deceived me, and by it slew me.

12 Wherefore the law is holy, and the commandment holy, and just, and good.

13 Was then that which is good made death unto me? God forbid. But sin, that it might appear sin, working death in me by that which is good; that sin by the commandment might become exceeding sinful.

14 For we know that the law is spiritual: but I am carnal, sold under sin.

15 For that which I do, I allow not: for what I would, that do I not; but what I hate, that do I.

16 If then I do that which I would not, I consent unto the law that it is good.

17 Now then it is no more I that do it, but sin that dwelleth in me.

18 For I know that in me (that is, in my flesh,) dwelleth no good thing: for to will is present with me; but how to perform that which is good I find not.

19 For the good that I would, I do not: but the evil which I would not, that I do.

20 Now if I do that I would not, it is no more I that do it, but sin that dwelleth in me.

21 I find then a law, that, when I would do good, evil is present with me.

22 For I delight in the law of God after the inward man:

23 But I see another law in my members, warring against the law of my mind, and bringing me into captivity to the law of sin which is in my members.

24 O wretched man that I am! who shall deliver me from the body of this death?

25 I thank God through Jesus Christ our Lord. So then with the mind I myself serve the law of God; but with the flesh the law of sin.

Life in the Spirit

8 There is therefore now no condemnation to them which are in Christ Jesus, who walk not after the flesh, but after the Spirit.

2 For the law of the Spirit of life in Christ Jesus hath made me free from the law of sin and death.

3 For what the law could not do, in that it was weak through the flesh, God sending his own Son in the likeness of sinful flesh, and for sin, condemned sin in the flesh:

4 That the righteousness of the law might be fulfilled in us, who walk not after the flesh, but after the Spirit.

5 For they that are after the flesh do mind the things of the flesh; but they that are after the Spirit, the things of the Spirit.

6 For to be carnally minded is death; but to be spiritually minded is life and peace.

7 Because the carnal mind is enmity against God: for it is not subject to the law of God, neither indeed can be.

8 So then they that are in the flesh cannot please God.

9 But ye are not in the flesh, but in the Spirit, if so be that the Spirit of God dwell in you. Now if any man have not the Spirit of Christ, he is none of his.

10 And if Christ be in you, the body is dead because of sin; but the Spirit is life because of righteousness.

11 But if the Spirit of him that raised up Jesus from the dead dwell in you, he that raised up Christ from the dead shall also quicken your mortal bodies by his Spirit that dwelleth in you.

12 Therefore, brethren, we are debtors, not to the flesh, to live after the flesh.

13 For if ye live after the flesh, ye shall die: but if ye through the Spirit do mortify the deeds of the body, ye shall live.

14 For as many as are led by the Spirit of God, they are the sons of God.

15 For ye have not received the spirit of bondage again to fear; but ye have received the Spirit of adoption, whereby we cry, Abba, Father.

16 The Spirit itself beareth witness with our spirit, that we are the children of God:

17 And if children, then heirs; heirs of God, and joint-heirs with Christ, if so be

that we suffer with him, that we may be also glorified together.

18 For I reckon that the sufferings of this present time are not worthy to be compared with the glory which shall be revealed in us.

19 For the earnest expectation of the creature waiteth for the manifestation of the sons of God.

20 For the creature was made subject to vanity, not willingly, but by reason of him who hath subjected the same in hope;

21 Because the creature itself also shall be delivered from the bondage of corruption into the glorious liberty of the children of God.

22 For we know that the whole creation groaneth and travaileth in pain together until now.

23 And not only they, but ourselves also, which have the firstfruits of the Spirit, even we ourselves groan within ourselves, waiting for the adoption, to wit, the redemption of our body.

24 For we are saved by hope: but hope that is seen is not hope: for what a man seeth, why doth he yet hope for?

25 But if we hope for that we see not, then do we with patience wait for it.

26 Likewise the Spirit also helpeth our infirmities: for we know not what we should pray for as we ought: but the Spirit itself maketh intercession for us with groanings which cannot be uttered.

27 And he that searcheth the hearts knoweth what is the mind of the Spirit, because he

maketh intercession for the saints according to the will of God.

More than Conquerors

28 And we know that all things work together for good to them that love God, to them who are the called according to his purpose.

29 For whom he did foreknow, he also did predestinate to be conformed to the image of his Son, that he might be the firstborn among many brethren.

30 Moreover, whom he did predestinate, them he also called: and whom he called, them he also justified: and whom he justified, them he also glorified.

31 What shall we then say to these things? If God be for us, who can be against us?

32 He that spared not his own Son, but delivered him up for us all, how shall he not with him also freely give us all things?

33 Who shall lay any thing to the charge of God's elect? It is God that justifieth.

34 Who is he that condemneth? It is Christ that died, yea rather, that is risen again, who is even at the right hand of God, who also maketh intercession for us.

35 Who shall separate us from the love of Christ? shall tribulation, or distress, or persecution, or famine, or nakedness, or peril, or sword?

36 As it is written, For thy sake we are killed all the day long; we are accounted as sheep for the slaughter.

37 Nay, in all these things we are more
than conquerors through him that loved us.

38 For I am persuaded, that neither death,
nor life, nor angels, nor principalities, nor
powers, nor things present, nor things to
come,

39 Nor height, nor depth, nor any other
creature, shall be able to separate us from the
love of God, which is in Christ Jesus our
Lord.

God's Election of Israel

9 I say the truth in Christ, I lie not, my
conscience also bearing me witness in the
Holy Ghost,

2 That I have great heaviness and continual
sorrow in my heart.

3 For I could wish that myself were accursed from Christ for my brethren, my kinsmen according to the flesh:

4 Who are Israelites; to whom pertaineth
the adoption, and the glory, and the covenants,
and the giving of the law, and the service of
God, and the promises;

5 Whose are the fathers, and of whom as
concerning the flesh Christ came, who is over
all, God blessed for ever. Amen.

6 Not as though the word of God hath
taken none effect. For they are not all Israel,
which are of Israel:

7 Neither, because they are the seed of
Abraham, are they all children: but, In Isaac
shall thy seed be called.

8 That is, They which are the children of

the flesh, these are not the children of God:
but the children of the promise are counted
for the seed.

9 For this is the word of promise, At this
time will I come, and Sarah shall have a son.
10 And not only this; but when Rebecca
also had conceived by one, even by our father
Isaac,

11 (For the children being not yet born,
neither having done any good or evil, that the
purpose of God according to election might
stand, not of works, but of him that calleth;)

12 It was said unto her, The elder shall
serve the younger.

13 As it is written, Jacob have I loved, but
Esau have I hated.

14 What shall we say then? Is there unrighteousness with God? God forbid.

15 For he saith to Moses, I will have mercy
on whom I will have mercy, and I will have
compassion on whom I will have compassion.

16 So then it is not of him that willeth, nor
of him that runneth, but of God that showeth
mercy.

17 For the Scripture saith unto Pharaoh,
Even for this same purpose have I raised thee
up, that I might show my power in thee, and
that my name might be declared throughout
all the earth.

18 Therefore hath he mercy on whom he
will have mercy, and whom he will he harden-
eth.

19 Thou wilt say then unto me, Why doth he
yet find fault? For who hath resisted his will?

20 Nay but, O man, who art thou that repliest against God? Shall the thing formed say to him that formed it, Why hast thou made me thus?

21 Hath not the potter power over the clay, of the same lump to make one vessel unto honor, and another unto dishonor?

22 What if God, willing to show his wrath, and to make his power known, endured with much long-suffering the vessels of wrath fitted to destruction:

23 And that he might make known the riches of his glory on the vessels of mercy, which he had afore prepared unto glory,

24 Even us, whom he hath called, not of the Jews only, but also of the Gentiles?

25 As he saith also in Hose′a, I will call them my people, which were not my people; and her beloved, which was not beloved.

26 And it shall come to pass, that in the place where it was said unto them, Ye are not my people; there shall they be called the children of the living God.

27 Isaiah also crieth concerning Israel, Though the number of the children of Israel be as the sand of the sea, a remnant shall be saved:

28 For he will finish the work, and cut it short in righteousness: because a short work will the Lord make upon the earth.

29 And as Isaiah said before, Except the Lord of Sab′a-oth had left us a seed, we had been as Sodom, and been made like unto Gomor′rah.

Righteousness Based on Faith

30 What shall we say then? That the Gentiles, which followed not after righteousness, have attained to righteousness, even the righteousness which is of faith.

31 But Israel, which followed after the law of righteousness, hath not attained to the law of righteousness.

32 Wherefore? Because they sought it not by faith, but as it were by the works of the law. For they stumbled at that stumblingstone;

33 As it is written, Behold, I lay in Zion a stumblingstone and rock of offense: and whosoever believeth on him shall not be ashamed.

10 Brethren, my heart's desire and prayer to God for Israel is, that they might be saved.

2 For I bear them record that they have a zeal of God, but not according to knowledge.

3 For they, being ignorant of God's righteousness, and going about to establish their own righteousness, have not submitted themselves unto the righteousness of God.

4 For Christ is the end of the law for righteousness to every one that believeth.

5 For Moses describeth the righteousness which is of the law, That the man which doeth those things shall live by them.

6 But the righteousness which is of faith speaketh on this wise, Say not in thine heart, Who shall ascend into heaven? (that is, to bring Christ down from above:)

7 Or, Who shall descend into the deep?
12

(that is, to bring up Christ again from the dead.)

8 But what saith it? The word is nigh thee, even in thy mouth, and in thy heart: that is, the word of faith, which we preach;

9 That if thou shalt confess with thy mouth the Lord Jesus, and shalt believe in thine heart that God hath raised him from the dead, thou shalt be saved.

10 For with the heart man believeth unto righteousness; and with the mouth confession is made unto salvation.

11 For the Scripture saith, Whosoever believeth on him shall not be ashamed.

12 For there is no difference between the Jew and the Greek: for the same Lord over all is rich unto all that call upon him.

13 For whosoever shall call upon the name of the Lord shall be saved.

14 How then shall they call on him in whom they have not believed? and how shall they believe in him of whom they have not heard? and how shall they hear without a preacher?

15 And how shall they preach, except they be sent? as it is written, How beautiful are the feet of them that preach the gospel of peace, and bring glad tidings of good things!

16 But they have not all obeyed the gospel. For Isaiah saith, Lord, who hath believed our report?

17 So then faith cometh by hearing, and hearing by the word of God.

18 But I say, Have they not heard? Yes...

verily, Their sound went into all the earth, and their words unto the ends of the world.

19 But I say, Did not Israel know? First Moses saith, I will provoke you to jealousy by them that are no people, and by a foolish nation I will anger you.

20 But Isaiah is very bold, and saith, I was found of them that sought me not; I was made manifest unto them that asked not after me.

21 But to Israel he saith, All day long I have stretched forth my hands unto a disobedient and gainsaying people.

The Remnant of Israel

11 I say then, Hath God cast away his people? God forbid. For I also am an Israelite, of the seed of Abraham, of the tribe of Benjamin.

2 God hath not cast away his people which he foreknew. Wot ye not what the Scripture saith of Eli′jah? how he maketh intercession to God against Israel, saying,

3 Lord, they have killed thy prophets, and digged down thine altars; and I am left alone, and they seek my life.

4 But what saith the answer of God unto him? I have reserved to myself seven thousand men, who have not bowed the knee to the image of Ba′al.

5 Even so then at this present time also there is a remnant according to the election of grace.

6 And if by grace, then is it no more of

works: otherwise grace is no more grace. But
if it be of works, then is it no more grace:
otherwise work is no more work.

7 What then? Israel hath not obtained that
which he seeketh for; but the election hath
obtained it, and the rest were blinded

8 (According as it is written, God hath
given them the spirit of slumber, eyes that
they should not see, and ears that they should
not hear;) unto this day.

9 And David saith, Let their table be made
a snare, and a trap, and a stumblingblock, and
a recompense unto them:

10 Let their eyes be darkened, that they
may not see, and bow down their back alway.

The Salvation of the Gentiles

11 I say then, Have they stumbled that they
should fall? God forbid: but rather through
their fall salvation is come unto the Gentiles,
for to provoke them to jealousy.

12 Now if the fall of them be the riches of
the world, and the diminishing of them the
riches of the Gentiles; how much more their
fulness?

13 For I speak to you Gentiles, inasmuch as
I am the apostle of the Gentiles, I magnify
mine office:

14 If by any means I may provoke to
emulation them which are my flesh, and might
save some of them.

15 For if the casting away of them be the
reconciling of the world, what shall the receiving of them be, but life from the dead?

16 For if the firstfruit be holy, the lump is also holy: and if the root be holy, so are the branches.

17 And if some of the branches be broken off, and thou, being a wild olive tree, wert graffed in among them, and with them partakest of the root and fatness of the olive tree;

18 Boast not against the branches. But if thou boast, thou bearest not the root, but the root thee.

19 Thou wilt say then, The branches were broken off, that I might be graffed in.

20 Well; because of unbelief they were broken off, and thou standest by faith. Be not high-minded, but fear:

21 For if God spared not the natural branches, take heed lest he also spare not thee.

22 Behold therefore the goodness and severity of God: on them which fell, severity; but toward thee, goodness, if thou continue in his goodness: otherwise thou also shalt be cut off.

23 And they also, if they abide not still in unbelief, shall be graffed in: for God is able to graff them in again.

24 For if thou wert cut out of the olive tree which is wild by nature, and wert graffed contrary to nature into a good olive tree; how much more shall these, which be the natural branches, be graffed into their own olive tree?

The Restoration of Israel

25 For I would not, brethren, that ye should be ignorant of this mystery, lest ye

should be wise in your own conceits, that blindness in part is happened to Israel, until the fulness of the Gentiles be come in.

26 And so all Israel shall be saved: as it is written, There shall come out of Zion the Deliverer, and shall turn away ungodliness from Jacob:

27 For this is my covenant unto them, when I shall take away their sins.

28 As concerning the gospel, they are enemies for your sakes: but as touching the election, they are beloved for the fathers' sakes.

29 For the gifts and calling of God are without repentance.

30 For as ye in times past have not believed God, yet have now obtained mercy through their unbelief:

31 Even so have these also now not believed, that through your mercy they also may obtain mercy.

32 For God hath concluded them all in unbelief, that he might have mercy upon all.

33 O the depth of the riches both of the wisdom and knowledge of God! how unsearchable are his judgments, and his ways past finding out!

34 For who hath known the mind of the Lord? or who hath been his counselor?

35 Or who hath first given to him, and it shall be recompensed unto him again?

36 For of him, and through him, and to him, are all things: to whom be glory for ever. Amen.

Exhortations for Christian Living

12 I beseech you therefore, brethren, by the mercies of God, that ye present your bodies a living sacrifice, holy, acceptable unto God, which is your reasonable service.

2 And be not conformed to this world: but be ye transformed by the renewing of your mind, that ye may prove what is that good, and acceptable, and perfect will of God.

3 For I say, through the grace given unto me, to every man that is among you, not to think of himself more highly than he ought to think; but to think soberly, according as God hath dealt to every man the measure of faith.

4 For as we have many members in one body, and all members have not the same office:

5 So we, being many, are one body in Christ, and every one members one of another.

6 Having then gifts differing according to the grace that is given to us, whether prophecy, let us prophesy according to the proportion of faith;

7 Or ministry, let us wait on our ministering; or he that teacheth, on teaching;

8 Or he that exhorteth, on exhortation: he that giveth, let him do it with simplicity; he that ruleth, with diligence; he that showeth mercy, with cheerfulness.

9 Let love be without dissimulation. Abhor that which is evil; cleave to that which is good.

10 Be kindly affectioned one to another with

brotherly love; in honor preferring one another;

11 Not slothful in business; fervent in
spirit; serving the Lord;

12 Rejoicing in hope; patient in tribulation;
continuing instant in prayer;

13 Distributing to the necessity of saints;
given to hospitality.

14 Bless them which persecute you: bless,
and curse not.

15 Rejoice with them that do rejoice, and
weep with them that weep.

16 Be of the same mind one toward another. Mind not high things, but condescend
to men of low estate. Be not wise in your own
conceits.

17 Recompense to no man evil for evil.
Provide things honest in the sight of all men.

18 If it be possible, as much as lieth in
you, live peaceably with all men.

19 Dearly beloved, avenge not yourselves,
but rather give place unto wrath: for it is
written, Vengeance is mine; I will repay,
saith the Lord.

20 Therefore if thine enemy hunger, feed
him; if he thirst, give him drink: for in so
doing thou shalt heap coals of fire on his
head.

21 Be not overcome of evil, but overcome
evil with good.

13 Let every soul be subject unto the higher
powers. For there is no power but of
God: the powers that be are ordained of God.

2 Whosoever therefore resisteth the power,

resisteth the ordinance of God: and they that resist shall receive to themselves damnation.

3 For rulers are not a terror to good works, but to the evil. Wilt thou then not be afraid of the power? do that which is good, and thou shalt have praise of the same:

4 For he is the minister of God to thee for good. But if thou do that which is evil, be afraid; for he beareth not the sword in vain: for he is the minister of God, a revenger to execute wrath upon him that doeth evil.

5 Wherefore ye must needs be subject, not only for wrath, but also for conscience' sake.

6 For, for this cause pay ye tribute also: for they are God's ministers, attending continually upon this very thing.

7 Render therefore to all their dues: tribute to whom tribute is due; custom to whom custom; fear to whom fear; honor to whom honor.

8 Owe no man any thing, but to love one another: for he that loveth another hath fulfilled the law.

9 For this, Thou shalt not commit adultery, Thou shalt not kill, Thou shalt not steal, Thou shalt not bear false witness, Thou shalt not covet; and if there be any other commandment, it is briefly comprehended in this saying, namely, Thou shalt love thy neighbor as thyself.

10 Love worketh no ill to his neighbor: therefore love is the fulfilling of the law.

11 And that, knowing the time, that now it is high time to awake out of sleep: for now is our salvation nearer than when we believed.

12 The night is far spent, the day is at hand: let us therefore cast off the works of darkness, and let us put on the armor of light.

13 Let us walk honestly, as in the day; not in rioting and drunkenness, not in chambering and wantonness, not in strife and envying:

14 But put ye on the Lord Jesus Christ, and make not provision for the flesh, to fulfil the lusts thereof.

Those Weak in Faith

14 Him that is weak in the faith receive ye, but not to doubtful disputations.

2 For one believeth that he may eat all things: another, who is weak, eateth herbs.

3 Let not him that eateth despise him that eateth not; and let not him which eateth not judge him that eateth: for God hath received him.

4 Who art thou that judgest another man's servant? to his own master he standeth or falleth. Yea, he shall be holden up: for God is able to make him stand.

5 One man esteemeth one day above another: another esteemeth every day alike. Let every man be fully persuaded in his own mind.

6 He that regardeth the day, regardeth it unto the Lord; and he that regardeth not the day, to the Lord he doth not regard it. He that eateth, eateth to the Lord, for he giveth God thanks; and he that eateth not, to the Lord he eateth not, and giveth God thanks.

7 For none of us liveth to himself, and no man dieth to himself.

8 For whether we live, we live unto the Lord; and whether we die, we die unto the Lord: whether we live therefore, or die, we are the Lord's.

9 For to this end Christ both died, and rose, and revived, that he might be Lord both of the dead and living.

10 But why dost thou judge thy brother? or why dost thou set at nought thy brother? for we shall all stand before the judgment seat of Christ.

11 For it is written, As I live, saith the Lord, every knee shall bow to me, and every tongue shall confess to God.

12 So then every one of us shall give account of himself to God.

13 Let us not therefore judge one another any more: but judge this rather, that no man put a stumblingblock or an occasion to fall in his brother's way.

14 I know, and am persuaded by the Lord Jesus, that there is nothing unclean of itself: but to him that esteemeth any thing to be unclean, to him it is unclean.

15 But if thy brother be grieved with thy meat, now walkest thou not charitably. Destroy not him with thy meat, for whom Christ died.

16 Let not then your good be evil spoken of:

17 For the kingdom of God is not meat and drink; but righteousness, and peace, and joy in the Holy Ghost.

18 For he that in these things serveth Christ is acceptable to God, and approved of men.

19 Let us therefore follow after the things which make for peace, and things wherewith one may edify another.

20 For meat destroy not the work of God. All things indeed are pure; but it is evil for that man who eateth with offense.

21 It is good neither to eat flesh, nor to drink wine, nor any thing whereby thy brother stumbleth, or is offended, or is made weak.

22 Hast thou faith? have it to thyself before God. Happy is he that condemneth not himself in that thing which he alloweth.

23 And he that doubteth is damned if he eat, because he eateth not of faith: for whatsoever is not of faith is sin.

15 We then that are strong ought to bear the infirmities of the weak, and not to please ourselves.

2 Let every one of us please his neighbor for his good to edification.

3 For even Christ pleased not himself; but, as it is written, The reproaches of them that reproached thee fell on me.

4 For whatsoever things were written aforetime were written for our learning, that we through patience and comfort of the Scriptures might have hope.

5 Now the God of patience and consolation grant you to be likeminded one toward another according to Christ Jesus:

6 That ye may with one mind and one

mouth glorify God, even the Father of our
Lord Jesus Christ.

The Gospel to the Gentiles

7 Wherefore receive ye one another, as
Christ also received us, to the glory of God.
8 Now I say that Jesus Christ was a
minister of the circumcision for the truth of
God, to confirm the promises made unto the
fathers:
9 And that the Gentiles might glorify God
for his mercy; as it is written, For this cause
I will confess to thee among the Gentiles, and
sing unto thy name.
10 And again he saith, Rejoice, ye Gentiles,
with his people.
11 And again, Praise the Lord, all ye Gentiles; and laud him, all ye people.
12 And again, Isaiah saith, There shall be a
root of Jesse, and he that shall rise to reign
over the Gentiles; in him shall the Gentiles
trust.
13 Now the God of hope fill you with all
joy and peace in believing, that ye may
abound in hope, through the power of the
Holy Ghost.
14 And I myself also am persuaded of
you, my brethren, that ye also are full of
goodness, filled with all knowledge, able also
to admonish one another.
15 Nevertheless, brethren, I have written
the more boldly unto you in some sort, as
putting you in mind, because of the grace that
is given to me of God,

16 That I should be the minister of Jesus Christ to the Gentiles, ministering the gospel of God, that the offering up of the Gentiles might be acceptable, being sanctified by the Holy Ghost.

17 I have therefore whereof I may glory through Jesus Christ in those things which pertain to God.

18 For I will not dare to speak of any of those things which Christ hath not wrought by me, to make the Gentiles obedient, by word and deed,

19 Through mighty signs and wonders, by the power of the Spirit of God; so that from Jerusalem, and round about unto Illyr'icum, I have fully preached the gospel of Christ.

20 Yea, so have I strived to preach the gospel, not where Christ was named, lest I should build upon another man's foundation:

21 But as it is written, To whom he was not spoken of, they shall see: and they that have not heard shall understand.

Paul Plans to Visit Rome

22 For which cause also I have been much hindered from coming to you.

23 But now having no more place in these parts, and having a great desire these many years to come unto you;

24 Whensoever I take my journey into Spain, I will come to you: for I trust to see you in my journey, and to be brought on my way thitherward by you, if first I be somewhat filled with your company.

25 But now I go unto Jerusalem to minister unto the saints.

26 For it hath pleased them of Macedonia and Achai'a to make a certain contribution for the poor saints which are at Jerusalem.

27 It hath pleased them verily; and their debtors they are. For if the Gentiles have been made partakers of their spiritual things, their duty is also to minister unto them in carnal things.

28 When therefore I have performed this, and have sealed to them this fruit, I will come by you into Spain.

29 And I am sure that, when I come unto you, I shall come in the fulness of the blessing of the gospel of Christ.

30 Now I beseech you, brethren, for the Lord Jesus Christ's sake, and for the love of the Spirit, that ye strive together with me in your prayers to God for me;

31 That I may be delivered from them that do not believe in Judea; and that my service which I have for Jerusalem may be accepted of the saints;

32 That I may come unto you with joy by the will of God, and may with you be refreshed.

33 Now the God of peace be with you all. Amen.

Personal Greetings

16 I commend unto you Phoebe our sister, which is a servant of the church which is at Cen'chre-ae:

2 That ye receive her in the Lord, as becometh saints, and that ye assist her in whatsoever business she hath need of you: for she hath been a succorer of many, and of myself also.

3 Greet Priscilla and Aquila, my helpers in Christ Jesus:

4 Who have for my life laid down their own necks: unto whom not only I give thanks, but also all the churches of the Gentiles.

5 Likewise greet the church that is in their house. Salute my well-beloved Epe'netus, who is the firstfruits of Achai'a unto Christ.

6 Greet Mary, who bestowed much labor on us.

7 Salute Andron'icus and Ju'ni-a, my kinsmen, and my fellow prisoners, who are of note among the apostles, who also were in Christ before me.

8 Greet Am'pli-as, my beloved in the Lord.

9 Salute Ur'bane, our helper in Christ, and Stachys my beloved.

10 Salute Apel'les approved in Christ. Salute them which are of Aristob'ulus' household.

11 Salute Hero'di-on my kinsman. Greet them that be of the household of Narcissus, which are in the Lord.

12 Salute Tryphae'na and Trypho'sa, who labor in the Lord. Salute the beloved Persis, which labored much in the Lord.

13 Salute Rufus chosen in the Lord, and his mother and mine.

14 Salute Asyn'critus, Phlegon, Hermas, Pat'robas, Hermes, and the brethren which are with them.

15 Salute Philol'ogus, and Julia, Ne'reus, and his sister, and Olym'pas, and all the saints which are with them.

16 Salute one another with a holy kiss. The churches of Christ salute you.

17 Now I beseech you, brethren, mark them which cause divisions and offenses contrary to the doctrine which ye have learned; and avoid them.

18 For they that are such serve not our Lord Jesus Christ, but their own belly; and by good words and fair speeches deceive the hearts of the simple.

19 For your obedience is come abroad unto all men. I am glad therefore on your behalf: but yet I would have you wise unto that which is good, and simple concerning evil.

20 And the God of peace shall bruise Satan under your feet shortly. The grace of our Lord Jesus Christ be with you. Amen.

21 Timothy my workfellow, and Lucius, and Jason, and Sosip'ater, my kinsmen, salute you.

22 I Tertius, who wrote this epistle, salute you in the Lord.

23 Gai'us mine host, and of the whole church, saluteth you. Eras'tus the chamberlain of the city saluteth you, and Quartus a brother.

24 The grace of our Lord Jesus Christ be with you all. Amen.

Concluding Doxology

25 Now to him that is of power to stablish you according to my gospel, and the preaching

of Jesus Christ, according to the revelation of
the mystery, which was kept secret since the
world began,

26 But now is made manifest, and by the
Scriptures of the prophets, according to the
commandment of the everlasting God, made
known to all nations for the obedience of
faith:

27 To God only wise, be glory through
Jesus Christ for ever. Amen.

THE FIRST EPISTLE
OF PAUL THE APOSTLE TO THE

CORINTHIANS

Salutation

1 Paul, called to be an apostle of Jesus Christ
through the will of God, and Sos'thenes our
brother,

2 Unto the church of God which is at
Corinth, to them that are sanctified in Christ
Jesus, called to be saints, with all that in
every place call upon the name of Jesus
Christ our Lord, both theirs and ours:

3 Grace be unto you, and peace, from God
our Father, and from the Lord Jesus Christ.

Thanksgiving for Spiritual Gifts

4 I thank my God always on your behalf,
for the grace of God which is given you by
Jesus Christ;

5 That in every thing ye are enriched by him, in all utterance, and in all knowledge;

6 Even as the testimony of Christ was confirmed in you:

7 So that ye come behind in no gift; waiting for the coming of our Lord Jesus Christ:

8 Who shall also confirm you unto the end, that ye may be blameless in the day of our Lord Jesus Christ.

9 God is faithful, by whom ye were called unto the fellowship of his Son Jesus Christ our Lord.

Divisions in the Church

10 Now I beseech you, brethren, by the name of our Lord Jesus Christ, that ye all speak the same thing, and that there be no divisions among you; but that ye be perfectly joined together in the same mind and in the same judgment.

11 For it hath been declared unto me of you, my brethren, by them which are of the house of Chlo′e, that there are contentions among you.

12 Now this I say, that every one of you saith, I am of Paul; and I of Apol′los; and I of Cephas; and I of Christ.

13 Is Christ divided? was Paul crucified for you? or were ye baptized in the name of Paul?

14 I thank God that I baptized none of you, but Crispus and Gai′us;

15 Lest any should say that I had baptized in mine own name.

16 And I baptized also the household of Steph′anas: besides,⁹⁰⁷ I know not³⁶²⁴ whether I baptized⁴⁷³⁴ any³⁰⁶³ other.²⁴³

17 For⁹⁰⁷ Christ¹⁵³⁶ sent²⁴³ me not to baptize, but⁵⁵⁴⁷ ⁶⁴⁹ to preach²⁰⁹⁷ the gospel: not with wisdom⁹⁰⁷ of words,³⁰⁵⁶ lest the cross⁴⁷¹⁶ of Christ⁵⁵⁴⁷ should⁴⁶⁷⁸ be²⁷⁵⁸ made²⁷⁵⁸ of none effect.

Christ the Power and Wisdom of God

18 For the preaching of the cross is to them that perish,³⁰⁵⁶ foolishness; but unto⁴⁷¹⁶ us which are saved,⁶²² it is the³⁴⁷² power of God.⁴⁹⁸²

19 For it is written,¹⁴¹¹ I will²³¹⁶ destroy the wisdom of the wise,¹¹²⁵ and will bring⁶²² to²⁶²² nothing the⁴⁶⁷⁸ understanding⁴⁶⁸⁰ of the prudent.¹¹⁴

20 Where⁴⁹⁰⁷ is the wise?⁴⁹⁰⁸ where is the scribe? where is the disputer⁴⁶⁸⁰ of this world? hath¹¹²² not God made foolish⁴⁸⁰⁴ the wisdom¹⁶⁵ of this world?²³¹⁶ ³⁴⁷¹

21 For after that in the⁴⁶⁷⁸ wisdom of God²⁸⁸⁹ the world by¹⁸⁹⁴ wisdom knew not⁴⁶⁷⁸God, it²³¹⁶ pleased God²⁸⁸⁹ by the⁴⁶⁷⁸ foolishness¹⁰⁹⁷ of preaching²³¹⁶ to²¹⁰⁶ save them²³¹⁶ that believe.³⁴⁷²

22 For⁴¹⁰⁰ the Jews require a sign, and the Greeks¹⁸⁹⁴ seek²⁴⁵³ after¹⁵⁴ wisdom:⁴⁵⁹²

23 But¹⁶⁷² we²²¹² preach⁴⁶⁷⁸ Christ crucified, unto the Jews²⁷⁸⁴ a stumblingblock,⁵⁵⁴⁷ and⁴⁷¹⁷ unto the Greeks foolishness;²⁴⁵³ ⁴⁶²⁵ ¹⁶⁷²

24 But³⁴⁷² unto them which are called, both Jews and Greeks, Christ the power²⁸²² of God, and²⁴⁵³ the wisdom¹⁶⁷² of God.⁵⁵⁴⁷ ¹⁴¹¹ ²³¹⁶

25 Because⁴⁶⁷⁸ the foolishness²³¹⁶ of God is wiser than men;³⁴⁷⁴ and the weakness²³¹⁶ of God is stronger⁴⁶⁸⁰ than men.⁴⁴⁴ ⁷⁷² ²³¹⁶ ²⁴⁷⁸

26 For⁴⁴⁴ ye see⁹⁹¹ your calling,²⁸²¹ brethren,⁸⁰ how

that not many wise men after the flesh, not many mighty, not many noble, are called:

27 But God hath chosen the foolish things of the world to confound the wise; and God hath chosen the weak things of the world to confound the things which are mighty;

28 And base things of the world, and things which are despised, hath God chosen, yea, and things which are not, to bring to nought things that are:

29 That no flesh should glory in his presence.

30 But of him are ye in Christ Jesus, who of God is made unto us wisdom, and righteousness, and sanctification, and redemption:

31 That, according as it is written, He that glorieth, let him glory in the Lord.

Proclaiming Christ Crucified

2 And I, brethren, when I came to you, came not with excellency of speech or of wisdom, declaring 'unto you the testimony of God.

2 For I determined not to know any thing among you, save Jesus Christ, and him crucified.

3 And I was with you in weakness, and in fear, and in much trembling.

4 And my speech and my preaching was not with enticing words of man's wisdom, but in demonstration of the Spirit and of power:

5 That your faith should not stand in the wisdom of men, but in the power of God.

The Revelation by God's Spirit

6 Howbeit we speak wisdom² among them
that are perfect: yet not the wisdom of this
world, nor of the princes of this world, that
come to nought:

7 But we speak the wisdom of God in a
mystery, even the hidden wisdom, which God
ordained before the world unto our glory;

8 Which none of the princes of this world
knew: for had they known it, they would
not have crucified the Lord of glory.

9 But as it is written, Eye hath not seen,
nor ear heard, neither have entered into the
heart of man, the things which God hath prepared for them that love him.

10 But God hath revealed them unto us by
his Spirit: for the Spirit searcheth all things,
yea, the deep things of God.

11 For what man knoweth the things of a
man, save the spirit of man which is in him?
even so the things of God knoweth no man,
but the Spirit of God.

12 Now we have received, not the spirit of
the world, but the Spirit which is of God;
that we might know the things that are freely
given to us of God.

13 Which things also we speak, not in the
words which man's wisdom teacheth, but
which the Holy Ghost teacheth; comparing
spiritual things with spiritual.

14 But the natural man receiveth not the
things of the Spirit of God: for they are
foolishness unto him: neither can he know
them, because they are spiritually discerned.

15 But he that is spiritual judgeth all things, yet he himself is judged of no man.

16 For who hath known the mind of the Lord, that he may instruct him? But we have the mind of Christ.

Laborers Together with God

3 And I, brethren, could not speak unto you as unto spiritual, but as unto carnal, even as unto babes in Christ.

2 I have fed you with milk, and not with meat: for hitherto ye were not able to bear it, neither yet now are ye able.

3 For ye are yet carnal: for whereas there is among you envying, and strife, and divisions, are ye not carnal, and walk as men?

4 For while one saith, I am of Paul; and another, I am of Apol'los; are ye not carnal?

5 Who then is Paul, and who is Apol'los, but ministers by whom ye believed, even as the Lord gave to every man?

6 I have planted, Apol'los watered; but God gave the increase.

7 So then neither is he that planteth any thing, neither he that watereth; but God that giveth the increase.

8 Now he that planteth and he that watereth are one: and every man shall receive his own reward according to his own labor.

9 For we are laborers together with God: ye are God's husbandry, ye are God's building.

10 According to the grace of God which is given unto me, as a wise masterbuilder, I have laid the foundation, and another buildeth there-

on. But let every man take heed how he buildeth thereupon.

11 For other foundation can no man lay than that is laid, which is Jesus Christ.

12 Now if any man build upon this foundation gold, silver, precious stones, wood, hay, stubble;

13 Every man's work shall be made manifest: for the day shall declare it, because it shall be revealed by fire; and the fire shall try every man's work of what sort it is.

14 If any man's work abide which he hath built thereupon, he shall receive a reward.

15 If any man's work shall be burned, he shall suffer loss: but he himself shall be saved; yet so as by fire.

16 Know ye not that ye are the temple of God, and that the Spirit of God dwelleth in you?

17 If any man defile the temple of God, him shall God destroy; for the temple of God is holy, which temple ye are.

18 Let no man deceive himself. If any man among you seemeth to be wise in this world, let him become a fool, that he may be wise.

19 For the wisdom of this world is foolishness with God: for it is written, He taketh the wise in their own craftiness.

20 And again, The Lord knoweth the thoughts of the wise, that they are vain.

21 Therefore let no man glory in men: for all things are yours;

22 Whether Paul, or Apol′los, or Cephas, or

the world, or life, or death, or things present, or things to come; all are yours;

23 And ye are Christ's; and Christ is God's.

The Ministry of the Apostles

4 Let a man so account of us, as of the ministers of Christ, and stewards of the mysteries of God.

2 Moreover it is required in stewards, that a man be found faithful.

3 But with me it is a very small thing that I should be judged of you, or of man's judgment: yea, I judge not mine own self.

4 For I know nothing by myself; yet am I not hereby justified: but he that judgeth me is the Lord.

5 Therefore judge nothing before the time, until the Lord come, who both will bring to light the hidden things of darkness, and will make manifest the counsels of the hearts: and then shall every man have praise of God.

6 And these things, brethren, I have in a figure transferred to myself and to Apol'los for your sakes; that ye might learn in us not to think of men above that which is written, that no one of you be puffed up for one against another.

7 For who maketh thee to differ from another? and what hast thou that thou didst not receive? now if thou didst receive it, why dost thou glory, as if thou hadst not received it?

8 Now ye are full, now ye are rich, ye have reigned as kings without us: and I would to

God ye did reign, that we also might reign with you.

9 For I think that God hath set forth us the apostles last, as it were appointed to death: for we are made a spectacle unto the world, and to angels, and to men.

10 We are fools for Christ's sake, but ye are wise in Christ; we are weak, but ye are strong; ye are honorable, but we are despised.

11 Even unto this present hour we both hunger, and thirst, and are naked, and are buffeted, and have no certain dwelling place;

12 And labor, working with our own hands: being reviled, we bless; being persecuted, we suffer it:

13 Being defamed, we entreat: we are made as the filth of the world, and are the off-scouring of all things unto this day.

14 I write not these things to shame you, but as my beloved sons I warn you.

15 For though ye have ten thousand instructors in Christ, yet have ye not many fathers: for in Christ Jesus I have begotten you through the gospel.

16 Wherefore I beseech you, be ye followers of me.

17 For this cause have I sent unto you Timothy, who is my beloved son, and faithful in the Lord, who shall bring you into remembrance of my ways which be in Christ, as I teach every where in every church.

18 Now some are puffed up, as though I would not come to you.

19 But I will come to you shortly, if the

Lord will, and will know, not the speech of them which are puffed up, but the power.

20 For the kingdom of God is not in word, but in power.

21 What will ye? shall I come unto you with a rod, or in love, and in the spirit of meekness?

Judgment of Immorality

5 It is reported commonly that there is fornication among you, and such fornication as is not so much as named among the Gentiles, that one should have his father's wife.

2 And ye are puffed up, and have not rather mourned, that he that hath done this deed might be taken away from among you.

3 For I verily, as absent in body, but present in spirit, have judged already, as though I were present, concerning him that hath so done this deed,

4 In the name of our Lord Jesus Christ, when ye are gathered together, and my spirit, with the power of our Lord Jesus Christ,

5 To deliver such a one unto Satan for the destruction of the flesh, that the spirit may be saved in the day of the Lord Jesus.

6 Your glorying is not good. Know ye not that a little leaven leaveneth the whole lump?

7 Purge out therefore the old leaven, that ye may be a new lump, as ye are unleavened. For even Christ our passover is sacrificed for us:

8 Therefore let us keep the feast, not with

old leaven, neither with the leaven of malice
and wickedness; but with the unleavened
bread of sincerity and truth.

9 I wrote unto you in an epistle not to
company with fornicators:

10 Yet not altogether with the fornicators of
this world, or with the covetous, or extortioners, or with idolaters; for then must ye
needs go out of the world.

11 But now I have written unto you not to
keep company, if any man that is called a
brother be a fornicator, or covetous, or an
idolater, or a railer, or a drunkard, or an
extortioner; with such a one, no, not to
eat.

12 For what have I to do to judge them
also that are without? do not ye judge them
that are within?

13 But them that are without God judgeth.
Therefore put away from among yourselves
that wicked person.

Going to Law before Unbelievers

6 Dare any of you, having a matter against
another, go to law before the unjust, and
not before the saints?

2 Do ye not know that the saints shall
judge the world? and if the world shall be
judged by you, are ye unworthy to judge the
smallest matters?

3 Know ye not that we shall judge angels?
how much more things that pertain to this
life?

4 If then ye have judgments of things per-

taining to this life, set them to judge who are least esteemed in the church.

5 I speak to your shame. Is it so, that there is not a wise man among you? no, not one that shall be able to judge between his brethren?

6 But brother goeth to law with brother, and that before the unbelievers.

7 Now therefore there is utterly a fault among you, because ye go to law one with another. Why do ye not rather take wrong? Why do ye not rather suffer yourselves to be defrauded?

8 Nay, ye do wrong, and defraud, and that your brethren.

9 Know ye not that the unrighteous shall not inherit the kingdom of God? Be not deceived: neither fornicators, nor idolaters, nor adulterers, nor effeminate, nor abusers of themselves with mankind,

10 Nor thieves, nor covetous, nor drunkards, nor revilers, nor extortioners, shall inherit the kingdom of God.

11 And such were some of you: but ye are washed, but ye are sanctified, but ye are justified in the name of the Lord Jesus, and by the Spirit of our God.

Glorify God in Your Body

12 All things are lawful unto me, but all things are not expedient: all things are lawful for me, but I will not be brought under the power of any.

13 Meats for the belly, and the belly for

meats: but God shall destroy both it and them. Now the body is not for fornication, but for the Lord; and the Lord for the body.

14 And God hath both raised up the Lord, and will also raise up us by his own power.

15 Know ye not that your bodies are the members of Christ? shall I then take the members of Christ, and make them the members of a harlot? God forbid.

16 What! know ye not that he which is joined to a harlot is one body? for two, saith he, shall be one flesh.

17 But he that is joined unto the Lord is one spirit.

18 Flee fornication. Every sin that a man doeth is without the body; but he that committeth fornication sinneth against his own body.

19 What! know ye not that your body is the temple of the Holy Ghost which is in you, which ye have of God, and ye are not your own?

20 For ye are bought with a price: therefore glorify God in your body, and in your spirit, which are God's.

Problems concerning Marriage

7 Now concerning the things whereof ye wrote unto me: It is good for a man not to touch a woman.

2 Nevertheless, to avoid fornication, let every man have his own wife, and let every woman have her own husband.

3 Let the husband render unto the wife due

benevolence: and likewise also the wife unto
the husband.

4 The wife hath not power of her own
body, but the husband: and likewise also the
husband hath not power of his own body, but
the wife.

5 Defraud ye not one the other, except it be
with consent for a time, that ye may give
yourselves to fasting and prayer; and come
together again, that Satan tempt you not for
your incontinency.

6 But I speak this by permission, and not
of commandment.

7 For I would that all men were even as I
myself. But every man hath his proper gift of
God, one after this manner, and another after
that.

8 I say therefore to the unmarried and
widows, It is good for them if they abide even
as I.

9 But if they cannot contain, let them
marry: for it is better to marry than to
burn.

10 And unto the married I command, yet
not I, but the Lord, Let not the wife depart
from her husband:

11 But and if she depart, let her remain unmarried, or be reconciled to her husband: and
let not the husband put away his wife.

12 But to the rest speak I, not the Lord: If
any brother hath a wife that believeth not, and
she be pleased to dwell with him, let him not
put her away.

13 And the woman which hath a husband

that believeth not, and if he be pleased to dwell with her, let her not leave him.

14 For the unbelieving husband is sanctified by the wife, and the unbelieving wife is sanctified by the husband: else were your children unclean; but now are they holy.

15 But if the unbelieving depart, let him depart. A brother or a sister is not under bondage in such cases: but God hath called us to peace.

16 For what knowest thou, O wife, whether thou shalt save thy husband? or how knowest thou, O man, whether thou shalt save thy wife?

17 But as God hath distributed to every man, as the Lord hath called every one, so let him walk. And so ordain I in all churches.

18 Is any man called being circumcised? let him not become uncircumcised. Is any called in uncircumcision? let him not be circumcised.

19 Circumcision is nothing, and uncircumcision is nothing, but the keeping of the commandments of God.

20 Let every man abide in the same calling wherein he was called.

21 Art thou called being a servant? care not for it: but if thou mayest be made free, use it rather.

22 For he that is called in the Lord, being a servant, is the Lord's freeman: likewise also he that is called, being free, is Christ's servant.

23 Ye are bought with a price; be not ye the servants of men.

24 Brethren, let every man, wherein he is called, therein abide with God.

25 Now concerning virgins I have no commandment of the Lord: yet I give my judgment, as one that hath obtained mercy of the Lord to be faithful.

26 I suppose therefore that this is good for the present distress, I say, that it is good for a man so to be.

27 Art thou bound unto a wife? seek not to be loosed. Art thou loosed from a wife? seek not a wife.

28 But and if thou marry, thou hast not sinned; and if a virgin marry, she hath not sinned. Nevertheless such shall have trouble in the flesh: but I spare you.

29 But this I say, brethren, the time is short: it remaineth, that both they that have wives be as though they had none;

30 And they that weep, as though they wept not; and they that rejoice, as though they rejoiced not; and they that buy, as though they possessed not;

31 And they that use this world, as not abusing it: for the fashion of this world passeth away.

32 But I would have you without carefulness. He that is unmarried careth for the things that belong to the Lord, how he may please the Lord:

33 But he that is married careth for the things that are of the world, how he may please his wife.

34 There is difference also between a wife

and a virgin. The unmarried woman careth for the things of the Lord, that she may be holy both in body and in spirit: but she that is married careth for the things of the world, how she may please her husband.

35 And this I speak for your own profit; not that I may cast a snare upon you, but for that which is comely, and that ye may attend upon the Lord without distraction.

36 But if any man think that he behaveth himself uncomely toward his virgin, if she pass the flower of her age, and need so require, let him do what he will, he sinneth not: let them marry.

37 Nevertheless he that standeth steadfast in his heart, having no necessity, but hath power over his own will, and hath so decreed in his heart that he will keep his virgin, doeth well.

38 So then he that giveth her in marriage doeth well; but he that giveth her not in marriage doeth better.

39 The wife is bound by the law as long as her husband liveth; but if her husband be dead, she is at liberty to be married to whom she will; only in the Lord.

40 But she is happier if she so abide, after my judgment: and I think also that I have the Spirit of God.

Food Offered to Idols

8 Now as touching things offered unto idols, we know that we all have knowledge. Knowledge puffeth up, but charity edifieth. 2 And if any man think that he knoweth

any thing, he knoweth nothing yet as he ought to know.

3 But if any man love God, the same is known of him.

4 As concerning therefore the eating of those things that are offered in sacrifice unto idols, we know that an idol is nothing in the world, and that there is none other God but one.

5 For though there be that are called gods, whether in heaven or in earth, (as there be gods many, and lords many,)

6 But to us there is but one God, the Father, of whom are all things, and we in him; and one Lord Jesus Christ, by whom are all things, and we by him.

7 Howbeit there is not in every man that knowledge: for some with conscience of the idol unto this hour eat it as a thing offered unto an idol; and their conscience being weak is defiled.

8 But meat commendeth us not to God: for neither, if we eat, are we the better; neither, if we eat not, are we the worse.

9 But take heed lest by any means this liberty of yours become a stumblingblock to them that are weak.

10 For if any man see thee which hast knowledge sit at meat in the idol's temple, shall not the conscience of him which is weak be emboldened to eat those things which are offered to idols;

11 And through thy knowledge shall the weak brother perish, for whom Christ died?

12 But when ye sin so against the brethren, and wound their weak conscience, ye sin against Christ.

13 Wherefore, if meat make my brother to offend, I will eat no flesh while the world standeth, lest I make my brother to offend.

The Rights of Those Who Preach the Gospel

9 Am I not an apostle? am I not free? have I not seen Jesus Christ our Lord? are not ye my work in the Lord?

2 If I be not an apostle unto others, yet doubtless I am to you: for the seal of mine apostleship are ye in the Lord.

3 Mine answer to them that do examine me is this:

4 Have we not power to eat and to drink?

5 Have we not power to lead about a sister, a wife, as well as other apostles, and as the brethren of the Lord, and Cephas?

6 Or I only and Barnabas, have not we power to forbear working?

7 Who goeth a warfare any time at his own charges? who planteth a vineyard, and eateth not of the fruit thereof? or who feedeth a flock, and eateth not of the milk of the flock?

8 Say I these things as a man? or saith not the law the same also?

9 For it is written in the law of Moses, Thou shalt not muzzle the mouth of the ox that treadeth out the corn. Doth God take care for oxen?

10 Or saith he it altogether for our sakes? For our sakes, no doubt, this is written: that

he that ploweth should plow in hope; and
that he that thresheth in hope should be partaker of his hope.

11 If we have sown unto you spiritual
things, is it a great thing if we shall reap
your carnal things?

12 If others be partakers of this power over
you, are not we rather? Nevertheless we have
not used this power; but suffer all things, lest
we should hinder the gospel of Christ.

13 Do ye not know that they which minister about holy things live of the things of
the temple? and they which wait at the altar
are partakers with the altar?

14 Even so hath the Lord ordained that
they which preach the gospel should live of
the gospel.

15 But I have used none of these things:
neither have I written these things, that it
should be so done unto me: for it were better
for me to die, than that any man should make
my glorying void.

16 For though I preach the gospel, I have
nothing to glory of: for necessity is laid upon
me; yea, woe is unto me, if I preach not the
gospel!

17 For if I do this thing willingly, I have a
reward: but if against my will, a dispensation
of the gospel is committed unto me.

18 What is my reward then? Verily that,
when I preach the gospel, I may make the
gospel of Christ without charge, that I abuse
not my power in the gospel.

19 For though I be free from all men, yet

have I made myself servant unto all, that I might gain the more.

20 And unto the Jews I became as a Jew, that I might gain the Jews; to them that are under the law, as under the law, that I might gain them that are under the law;

21 To them that are without law, as without law, (being not without law to God, but under the law to Christ,) that I might gain them that are without law.

22 To the weak became I as weak, that I might gain the weak: I am made all things to all men, that I might by all means save some.

23 And this I do for the gospel's sake, that I might be partaker thereof with you.

24 Know ye not that they which run in a race run all, but one receiveth the prize? So run, that ye may obtain.

25 And every man that striveth for the mastery is temperate in all things. Now they do it to obtain a corruptible crown; but we an incorruptible.

26 I therefore so run, not as uncertainly; so fight I, not as one that beateth the air:

27 But I keep under my body, and bring it into subjection: lest that by any means, when I have preached to others, I myself should be a castaway.

Warning against Idolatry

10 Moreover, brethren, I would not that ye should be ignorant, how that all our fathers were under the cloud, and all passed through the sea;

2 And were all baptized unto Moses in the
cloud and in the sea;

3 And did all eat the same spiritual meat;

4 And did all drink the same spiritual
drink; for they drank of that spiritual Rock
that followed them: and that Rock was Christ.

5 But with many of them God was not well
pleased: for they were overthrown in the
wilderness.

6 Now these things were our examples, to
the intent we should not lust after evil things,
as they also lusted.

7 Neither be ye idolaters, as were some of
them; as it is written, The people sat down to
eat and drink, and rose up to play.

8 Neither let us commit fornication, as some
of them committed, and fell in one day three
and twenty thousand.

9 Neither let us tempt Christ, as some of
them also tempted, and were destroyed of
serpents.

10 Neither murmur ye, as some of them
also murmured, and were destroyed of the
destroyer.

11 Now all these things happened unto
them for ensamples: and they are written for
our admonition, upon whom the ends of the
world are come.

12 Wherefore let him that thinketh he
standeth take heed lest he fall.

13 There hath no temptation taken you but
such as is common to man: but God is faithful, who will not suffer you to be tempted
above that ye are able; but will with the

temptation also make a way to escape, that ye may be able to bear it.

14 Wherefore, my dearly beloved, flee from idolatry.

15 I speak as to wise men; judge ye what I say.

16 The cup of blessing which we bless, is it not the communion of the blood of Christ? The bread which we break, is it not the communion of the body of Christ?

17 For we being many are one bread, and one body: for we are all partakers of that one bread.

18 Behold Israel after the flesh: are not they which eat of the sacrifices partakers of the altar?

19 What say I then? that the idol is any thing, or that which is offered in sacrifice to idols is any thing?

20 But I say, that the things which the Gentiles sacrifice, they sacrifice to devils, and not to God: and I would not that ye should have fellowship with devils.

21 Ye cannot drink the cup of the Lord, and the cup of devils: ye cannot be partakers of the Lord's table, and of the table of devils.

22 Do we provoke the Lord to jealousy? are we stronger than he?

Do All to the Glory of God

23 All things are lawful for me, but all things are not expedient: all things are lawful for me, but all things edify not.

24 Let no man seek his own, but every man another's wealth.

25 Whatsoever is sold in the shambles, that eat, asking no question for conscience' sake:

26 For the earth is the Lord's, and the fulness thereof.

27 If any of them that believe not bid you to a feast, and ye be disposed to go; whatsoever is set before you, eat, asking no question for conscience' sake.

28 But if any man say unto you, This is offered in sacrifice unto idols, eat not for his sake that showed it, and for conscience' sake: for the earth is the Lord's, and the fulness thereof:

29 Conscience, I say, not thine own, but of the other: for why is my liberty judged of another man's conscience?

30 For if I by grace be a partaker, why am I evil spoken of for that for which I give thanks?

31 Whether therefore ye eat, or drink, or whatsoever ye do, do all to the glory of God.

32 Give none offense, neither to the Jews, nor to the Gentiles, nor to the church of God:

33 Even as I please all men in all things, not seeking mine own profit, but the profit of many, that they may be saved.

11 Be ye followers of me, even as I also am of Christ.

The Covering of Women's Heads

2 Now I praise you, brethren, that ye remember me in all things, and keep the ordinances, as I delivered them to you.

3 But I would have you know, that the head of every man is Christ; and the head of the woman is the man; and the head of Christ is God.

4 Every man praying or prophesying, having his head covered, dishonoreth his head.

5 But every woman that prayeth or prophesieth with her head uncovered dishonoreth her head: for that is even all one as if she were shaven.

6 For if the woman be not covered, let her also be shorn: but if it be a shame for a woman to be shorn or shaven, let her be covered.

7 For a man indeed ought not to cover his head, forasmuch as he is the image and glory of God: but the woman is the glory of the man.

8 For the man is not of the woman; but the woman of the man.

9 Neither was the man created for the woman; but the woman for the man.

10 For this cause ought the woman to have power on her head because of the angels.

11 Nevertheless neither is the man without the woman, neither the woman without the man, in the Lord.

12 For as the woman is of the man, even so is the man also by the woman; but all things of God.

13 Judge in yourselves: is it comely that a woman pray unto God uncovered?

14 Doth not even nature itself teach you, that, if a man have long hair, it is a shame unto him?

15 But if a woman have long hair, it is a glory to her: for her hair is given her for a covering.

16 But if any man seem to be contentious, we have no such custom, neither the churches of God.

Disorder at the Lord's Supper

17 Now in this that I declare unto you I praise you not, that ye come together not for the better, but for the worse.

18 For first of all, when ye come together in the church, I hear that there be divisions among you; and I partly believe it.

19 For there must be also heresies among you, that they which are approved may be made manifest among you.

20 When ye come together therefore into one place, this is not to eat the Lord's supper.

21 For in eating every one taketh before other his own supper: and one is hungry, and another is drunken.

22 What! have ye not houses to eat and to drink in? or despise ye the church of God, and shame them that have not? What shall I say to you? shall I praise you in this? I praise you not.

The Institution of the Lord's Supper

23 For I have received of the Lord that which also I delivered unto you, That the Lord Jesus, the same night in which he was betrayed, took bread:

24 And when he had given thanks, he

brake it, and said, Take, eat; this is my body,
which is broken for you: this do in remembrance of me.

25 After the same manner also he took the
cup, when he had supped, saying, This cup
is the new testament in my blood: this do
ye, as oft as ye drink it, in remembrance of
me.

26 For as often as ye eat this bread, and
drink this cup, ye do show the Lord's death
till he come.

Partaking of the Supper Unworthily

27 Wherefore whosoever shall eat this
bread, and drink this cup of the Lord, unworthily, shall be guilty of the body and
blood of the Lord.

28 But let a man examine himself, and so
let him eat of that bread, and drink of that
cup.

29 For he that eateth and drinketh unworthily, eateth and drinketh damnation to
himself, not discerning the Lord's body.

30 For this cause many are weak and sickly
among you, and many sleep.

31 For if we would judge ourselves, we
should not be judged.

32 But when we are judged, we are chastened of the Lord, that we should not be
condemned with the world.

33 Wherefore, my brethren, when ye come
together to eat, tarry one for another.

34 And if any man hunger, let him eat at
home; that ye come not together unto con-

demnation. And the rest will I set in order when I come.

Spiritual Gifts

12 Now concerning spiritual gifts, brethren, I would not have you ignorant.

2 Ye know that ye were Gentiles, carried away unto these dumb idols, even as ye were led.

3 Wherefore I give you to understand, that no man speaking by the Spirit of God calleth Jesus accursed: and that no man can say that Jesus is the Lord, but by the Holy Ghost.

4 Now there are diversities of gifts, but the same Spirit.

5 And there are differences of administrations, but the same Lord.

6 And there are diversities of operations, but it is the same God which worketh all in all.

7 But the manifestation of the Spirit is given to every man to profit withal.

8 For to one is given by the Spirit the word of wisdom; to another the word of knowledge by the same Spirit;

9 To another faith by the same Spirit; to another the gifts of healing by the same Spirit;

10 To another the working of miracles; to another prophecy; to another discerning of spirits; to another divers kinds of tongues; to another the interpretation of tongues:

11 But all these worketh that one and the selfsame Spirit, dividing to every man severally as he will.

12 For as the body is one, and hath many members and all the members of that one body, being many, are one body: so also is Christ.

13 For by one Spirit are we all baptized into one body, whether we be Jews or Gentiles, whether we be bond or free; and have been all made to drink into one Spirit.

14 For the body is not one member, but many.

15 If the foot shall say, Because I am not the hand, I am not of the body; is it therefore not of the body?

16 And if the ear shall say, Because I am not the eye, I am not of the body; is it therefore not of the body?

17 If the whole body were an eye, where were the hearing? If the whole were hearing, where were the smelling?

18 But now hath God set the members every one of them in the body, as it hath pleased him.

19 And if they were all one member, where were the body?

20 But now are they many members, yet but one body.

21 And the eye cannot say unto the hand, I have no need of thee: nor again the head to the feet, I have no need of you.

22 Nay, much more those members of the body, which seem to be more feeble, are necessary:

23 And those members of the body, which we think to be less honorable, upon these we

bestow more abundant honor; and our uncomely parts have more abundant comeliness.

24 For our comely parts have no need: but God hath tempered the body together, having given more abundant honor to that part which lacked:

25 That there should be no schism in the body; but that the members should have the same care one for another.

26 And whether one member suffer, all the members suffer with it; or one member be honored, all the members rejoice with it.

27 Now ye are the body of Christ, and members in particular.

28 And God hath set some in the church, first apostles, secondarily prophets, thirdly teachers, after that miracles, then gifts of healings, helps, governments, diversities of tongues.

29 Are all apostles? are all prophets? are all teachers? are all workers of miracles?

30 Have all the gifts of healing? do all speak with tongues? do all interpret?

31 But covet earnestly the best gifts.

Love

And yet show I unto you a more excellent way.

13 Though I speak with the tongues of men and of angels, and have not charity, I am become as sounding brass, or a tinkling cymbal.

2 And though I have the gift of prophecy, and understand all mysteries, and all knowl-

edge; and though I have all faith, so that I could remove mountains, and have not charity, I am nothing.

3 And though I bestow all my goods to feed the poor, and though I give my body to be burned, and have not charity, it profiteth me nothing.

4 Charity suffereth long, and is kind; charity envieth not; charity vaunteth not itself, is not puffed up,

5 Doth not behave itself unseemly, seeketh not her own, is not easily provoked, thinketh no evil;

6 Rejoiceth not in iniquity, but rejoiceth in the truth;

7 Beareth all things, believeth all things, hopeth all things, endureth all things.

8 Charity never faileth: but whether there be prophecies, they shall fail; whether there be tongues, they shall cease; whether there be knowledge, it shall vanish away.

9 For we know in part, and we prophesy in part.

10 But when that which is perfect is come, then that which is in part shall be done away.

11 When I was a child, I spake as a child, I understood as a child, I thought as a child: but when I became a man, I put away childish things.

12 For now we see through a glass, darkly; but then face to face: now I know in part; but then shall I know even as also I am known.

13 And now abideth faith, hope, charity,

these three; but the greatest of these is
charity. 3187

26

Speaking in Tongues

14 Follow after charity, and desire spiritual
gifts, but rather that ye may prophesy.

2 For he that speaketh in an unknown
tongue speaketh not unto men, but unto God:
for no man understandeth him; howbeit in the
spirit he speaketh mysteries.

3 But he that prophesieth speaketh unto
men to edification, and exhortation, and comfort.

4 He that speaketh in an unknown tongue
edifieth himself; but he that prophesieth
edifieth the church.

5 I would that ye all spake with tongues,
but rather that ye prophesied: for greater is
he that prophesieth than he that speaketh with
tongues, except he interpret, that the church
may receive edifying.

6 Now, brethren, if I come unto you speaking with tongues, what shall I profit you, except I shall speak to you either by revelation,
or by knowledge, or by prophesying, or by
doctrine?

7 And even things without life giving sound,
whether pipe or harp, except they give a dis-
tinction in the sounds, how shall it be known
what is piped or harped?

8 For if the trumpet give an uncertain
sound, who shall prepare himself to the battle?

9 So likewise ye, except ye utter by the
tongue words easy to be understood, how

shall it be known what is spoken? for ye shall speak into the air.

10 There are, it may be, so many kinds of voices in the world, and none of them is without signification.

11 Therefore if I know not the meaning of the voice, I shall be unto him that speaketh a barbarian, and he that speaketh shall be a barbarian unto me.

12 Even so ye, forasmuch as ye are zealous of spiritual gifts, seek that ye may excel to the edifying of the church.

13 Wherefore let him that speaketh in an unknown tongue pray that he may interpret.

14 For if I pray in an unknown tongue, my spirit prayeth, but my understanding is unfruitful.

15 What is it then? I will pray with the spirit, and I will pray with the understanding also: I will sing with the spirit, and I will sing with the understanding also.

16 Else, when thou shalt bless with the spirit, how shall he that occupieth the room of the unlearned say Amen at thy giving of thanks, seeing he understandeth not what thou sayest?

17 For thou verily givest thanks well, but the other is not edified.

18 I thank my God, I speak with tongues more than ye all:

19 Yet in the church I had rather speak five words with my understanding, that by my voice I might teach others also, than ten thousand words in an unknown tongue.

20 Brethren, be not children in understanding: howbeit in malice be ye children, but in understanding be men.

21 In the law it is written, With men of other tongues and other lips will I speak unto this people; and yet for all that will they not hear me, saith the Lord.

22 Wherefore tongues are for a sign, not to them that believe, but to them that believe not: but prophesying serveth not for them that believe not, but for them which believe.

23 If therefore the whole church be come together into one place, and all speak with tongues, and there come in those that are unlearned, or unbelievers, will they not say that ye are mad?

24 But if all prophesy, and there come in one that believeth not, or one unlearned, he is convinced of all, he is judged of all:

25 And thus are the secrets of his heart made manifest; and so falling down on his face he will worship God, and report that God is in you of a truth.

26 How is it then, brethren? when ye come together, every one of you hath a psalm, hath a doctrine, hath a tongue, hath a revelation, hath an interpretation. Let all things be done unto edifying.

27 If any man speak in an unknown tongue, let it be by two, or at the most by three, and that by course; and let one interpret.

28 But if there be no interpreter, let him keep silence in the church; and let him speak to himself, and to God.

29 Let the prophets speak two or three, and
2980   4396   2980
let the other judge.
1252   243 1252

30 If any thing be revealed to another that
                601   243   2521
sitteth by, let the first hold his peace.
2521   4601   4413 4601   4601

31 For ye may all prophesy one by one,
        4601 1410   4395
that all may learn, and all may be comforted.
          3129   3870

32 And the spirits of the prophets are sub-
                4151   4396 5293
ject to the prophets.
5293   4396

33 For God is not the author of confusion,
        2316   181
but of peace, as in all churches of the saints.
1515   1577

34 Let your women keep silence in the
    4601   1135 4601   40
churches: for it is not permitted unto them to
1577   2010   2010   2980
speak; but they are commanded to be under
2980   5293
obedience, as also saith the law.
5293   2531   3551

35 And if they will learn any thing, let
            2309 3129 5100   1905
them ask their husbands at home: for it is a
1905 2398 435   3624
shame for women to speak in the church.
149   1135 2980   1577

36 What! came the word of God out from
        1831   3056   2316 1831
you? or came it unto you only?
2658   3441

37 If any man think himself to be a
1536   1380
prophet, or spiritual, let him acknowledge that
4396   4152 1921   1921
the things that I write unto you are the com-
                1125
mandments of the Lord.   1785
                2962

38 But if any man be ignorant, let him be
        5100   50   50   50
ignorant.
50

39 Wherefore, brethren, covet to prophesy,
        80   2206 4395
and forbid not to speak with tongues.
2967   2980   1100

40 Let all things be done decently and in order.
1096   1096   2156   5010

The Resurrection of the Dead

15 Moreover, brethren, I declare unto you
        80   1107
the gospel which I preached unto you,
2098   2097
which also ye have received, and wherein ye
3880
stand;
2476

2 By which also ye are saved, if ye keep in memory what I preached unto you, unless ye have believed in vain.

3 For I delivered unto you first of all that which I also received, how that Christ died for our sins according to the Scriptures;

4 And that he was buried, and that he rose again the third day according to the Scriptures:

5 And that he was seen of Cephas, then of the twelve:

6 After that, he was seen of above five hundred brethren at once; of whom the greater part remain unto this present, but some are fallen asleep.

7 After that, he was seen of James; then of all the apostles.

8 And last of all he was seen of me also, as of one born out of due time.

9 For I am the least of the apostles, that am not meet to be called an apostle, because I persecuted the church of God.

10 But by the grace of God I am what I am: and his grace which was bestowed upon me was not in vain; but I labored more abundantly than they all: yet not I, but the grace of God which was with me.

11 Therefore whether it were I or they, so we preach, and so ye believed.

12 Now if Christ be preached that he rose from the dead, how say some among you that there is no resurrection of the dead?

13 But if there be no resurrection of the dead, then is Christ not risen:

14 And if Christ be not risen, then is our preaching vain, and your faith is also vain.

15 Yea, and we are found false witnesses of God; because we have testified of God that he raised up Christ: whom he raised not up, if so be that the dead rise not.

16 For if the dead rise not, then is not Christ raised:

17 And if Christ be not raised, your faith is vain; ye are yet in your sins.

18 Then they also which are fallen asleep in Christ are perished.

19 If in this life only we have hope in Christ, we are of all men most miserable.

20 But now is Christ risen from the dead, and become the firstfruits of them that slept.

21 For since by man came death, by man came also the resurrection of the dead.

22 For as in Adam all die, even so in Christ shall all be made alive.

23 But every man in his own order: Christ the firstfruits; afterward they that are Christ's at his coming.

24 Then cometh the end, when he shall have delivered up the kingdom to God, even the Father; when he shall have put down all rule, and all authority and power.

25 For he must reign, till he hath put all enemies under his feet.

26 The last enemy that shall be destroyed is death.

27 For he hath put all things under his feet. But when he saith, All things are put

under him, it is manifest that he is excepted, which did put all things under him.

28 And when all things shall be subdued unto him, then shall the Son also himself be subject unto him that put all things under him, that God may be all in all.

29 Else what shall they do which are baptized for the dead, if the dead rise not at all? why are they then baptized for the dead?

30 And why stand we in jeopardy every hour?

31 I protest by your rejoicing which I have in Christ Jesus our Lord, I die daily.

32 If after the manner of men I have fought with beasts at Ephesus, what advantageth it me, if the dead rise not? let us eat and drink; for tomorrow we die.

33 Be not deceived: evil communications corrupt good manners.

34 Awake to righteousness, and sin not; for some have not the knowledge of God: I speak this to your shame.

35 But some man will say, How are the dead raised up? and with what body do they come?

36 Thou fool, that which thou sowest is not quickened, except it die:

37 And that which thou sowest, thou sowest not that body that shall be, but bare grain, it may chance of wheat, or of some other grain:

38 But God giveth it a body as it hath pleased him, and to every seed his own body.

39 All flesh is not the same flesh: but there

is one kind of flesh of men, another flesh of beasts, another of fishes, and another of birds.

40 There are also celestial bodies, and bodies terrestrial: but the glory of the celestial is one, and the glory of the terrestrial is another.

41 There is one glory of the sun, and another glory of the moon, and another glory of the stars; for one star differeth from another star in glory.

42 So also is the resurrection of the dead. It is sown in corruption, it is raised in incorruption:

43 It is sown in dishonor, it is raised in glory: it is sown in weakness, it is raised in power:

44 It is sown a natural body, it is raised a spiritual body. There is a natural body, and there is a spiritual body.

45 And so it is written, The first man Adam was made a living soul; the last Adam was made a quickening spirit.

46 Howbeit that was not first which is spiritual, but that which is natural; and afterward that which is spiritual.

47 The first man is of the earth, earthy: the second man is the Lord from heaven.

48 As is the earthy, such are they also that are earthy: and as is the heavenly, such are they also that are heavenly.

49 And as we have borne the image of the earthy, we shall also bear the image of the heavenly.

50 Now this I say, brethren, that flesh and

blood cannot inherit the kingdom of God; neither doth corruption inherit incorruption.

51 Behold, I show you a mystery; We shall not all sleep, but we shall all be changed,

52 In a moment, in the twinkling of an eye, at the last trump: for the trumpet shall sound, and the dead shall be raised incorruptible, and we shall be changed.

53 For this corruptible must put on incorruption, and this mortal must put on immortality.

54 So when this corruptible shall have put on incorruption, and this mortal shall have put on immortality, then shall be brought to pass the saying that is written, Death is swallowed up in victory.

55 O death, where is thy sting? O grave, where is thy victory?

56 The sting of death is sin; and the strength of sin is the law.

57 But thanks be to God, which giveth us the victory through our Lord Jesus Christ.

58 Therefore, my beloved brethren, be ye steadfast, unmovable, always abounding in the work of the Lord, forasmuch as ye know that your labor is not in vain in the Lord.

The Collection for the Saints

16 Now concerning the collection for the saints, as I have given order to the churches of Galatia, even so do ye.

2 Upon the first day of the week let every one of you lay by him in store, as God hath

prospered him, that there be no gatherings when I come.

3 And when I come, whomsoever ye shall approve by your letters, them will I send to bring your liberality unto Jerusalem.

4 And if it be meet that I go also, they shall go with me.

Plans for Travel

5 Now I will come unto you, when I shall pass through Macedonia: for I do pass through Macedonia.

6 And it may be that I will abide, yea, and winter with you, that ye may bring me on my journey whithersoever I go.

7 For I will not see you now by the way; but I trust to tarry a while with you, if the Lord permit.

8 But I will tarry at Ephesus until Pentecost.

9 For a great door and effectual is opened unto me, and there are many adversaries.

10 Now if Timothy come, see that he may be with you without fear: for he worketh the work of the Lord, as I also do.

11 Let no man therefore despise him: but conduct him forth in peace, that he may come unto me: for I look for him with the brethren.

12 As touching our brother Apol'los, I greatly desired him to come unto you with the brethren: but his will was not at all to come at this time; but he will come when he shall have convenient time.

Final Greetings

13 Watch ye, stand fast in the faith, quit you like men, be strong.

14 Let all your things be done with charity.

15 I beseech you, brethren, (ye know the house of Steph'anas, that it is the firstfruits of Achai'a, and that they have addicted themselves to the ministry of the saints,)

16 That ye submit yourselves unto such, and to every one that helpeth with us, and laboreth.

17 I am glad of the coming of Steph'anas and Fortuna'tus and Acha'icus: for that which was lacking on your part they have supplied.

18 For they have refreshed my spirit and yours: therefore acknowledge ye them that are such.

19 The churches of Asia salute you. Aquila and Priscilla salute you much in the Lord, with the church that is in their house.

20 All the brethren greet you. Greet ye one another with a holy kiss.

21 The salutation of me Paul with mine own hand.

22 If any man love not the Lord Jesus Christ, let him be Anath'ema, Maranath'a.

23 The grace of our Lord Jesus Christ be with you.

24 My love be with you all in Christ Jesus. Amen.

THE SECOND EPISTLE
OF PAUL THE APOSTLE TO THE
CORINTHIANS

Salutation

1 Paul, an apostle of Jesus Christ by the will of God, and Timothy our brother, unto the church of God which is at Corinth, with all the saints which are in all Achai´a:

2 Grace be to you, and peace, from God our Father, and from the Lord Jesus Christ.

Paul's Affliction

3 Blessed be God, even the Father of our Lord Jesus Christ, the Father of mercies, and the God of all comfort;

4 Who comforteth us in all our tribulation, that we may be able to comfort them which are in any trouble, by the comfort wherewith we ourselves are comforted of God.

5 For as the sufferings of Christ abound in us, so our consolation also aboundeth by Christ.

6 And whether we be afflicted, it is for your consolation and salvation, which is effectual in the enduring of the same sufferings which we also suffer: or whether we be comforted, it is for your consolation and salvation.

7 And our hope of you is stedfast, knowing, that as ye are partakers of the sufferings, so shall ye be also of the consolation.

8 For we would not, brethren, have you ignorant of our trouble which came to us in Asia, that we were pressed out of measure,

above strength, insomuch that we despaired
even of life:

9 But we had the sentence of death in ourselves, that we should not trust in ourselves,
but in God which raiseth the dead:

10 Who delivered us from so great a death,
and doth deliver: in whom we trust that he
will yet deliver us;

11 Ye also helping together by prayer for
us, that for the gift bestowed upon us by the
means of many persons thanks may be given
by many on our behalf.

The Postponement of Paul's Visit

12 For our rejoicing is this, the testimony
of our conscience, that in simplicity and godly
sincerity, not with fleshly wisdom, but by the
grace of God, we have had our conversation
in the world, and more abundantly to you-
ward.

13 For we write none other things unto
you, than what ye read or acknowledge; and
I trust ye shall acknowledge even to the
end;

14 As also ye have acknowledged us in part,
that we are your rejoicing, even as ye also are
ours in the day of the Lord Jesus.

15 And in this confidence I was minded to
come unto you before, that ye might have a
second benefit;

16 And to pass by you into Macedonia, and
to come again out of Macedonia unto you, and
of you to be brought on my way toward
Judea.

17 When I therefore was thus minded, did I use lightness? or the things that I purpose, do I purpose according to the flesh, that with me there should be yea, yea, and nay, nay?

18 But as God is true, our word toward you was not yea and nay.

19 For the Son of God, Jesus Christ, who was preached among you by us, even by me and Silva'nus and Timothy, was not yea and nay, but in him was yea.

20 For all the promises of God in him are yea, and in him Amen, unto the glory of God by us.

21 Now he which stablisheth us with you in Christ, and hath anointed us, is God;

22 Who hath also sealed us, and given the earnest of the Spirit in our hearts.

23 Moreover I call God for a record upon my soul, that to spare you I came not as yet unto Corinth.

24 Not for that we have dominion over your faith, but are helpers of your joy: for by faith ye stand.

2 But I determined this with myself, that I would not come again to you in heaviness.

2 For if I make you sorry, who is he then that maketh me glad, but the same which is made sorry by me?

3 And I wrote this same unto you, lest, when I came, I should have sorrow from them of whom I ought to rejoice; having confidence in you all, that my joy is the joy of you all.

4 For out of much affliction and anguish of

heart I wrote unto you with many tears; not that ye should be grieved, but that ye might know the love which I have more abundantly unto you.

Forgiveness for the Offender

5 But if any have caused grief, he hath not grieved me, but in part: that I may not overcharge you all.

6 Sufficient to such a man is this punishment, which was inflicted of many.

7 So that contrariwise ye ought rather to forgive him, and comfort him, lest perhaps such a one should be swallowed up with overmuch sorrow.

8 Wherefore I beseech you that ye would confirm your love toward him.

9 For to this end also did I write, that I might know the proof of you, whether ye be obedient in all things.

10 To whom ye forgive any thing, I forgive also: for if I forgave any thing, to whom I forgave it, for your sakes forgave I it in the person of Christ;

11 Lest Satan should get an advantage of us: for we are not ignorant of his devices.

Paul's Anxiety at Troas

12 Furthermore, when I came to Tro'as to preach Christ's gospel, and a door was opened unto me of the Lord,

13 I had no rest in my spirit, because I found not Titus my brother; but taking my leave of them, I went from thence into Macedonia.

Triumphant in Christ

14 Now thanks be unto God, which always causeth us to triumph in Christ, and maketh manifest the savor of his knowledge by us in every place.

15 For we are unto God a sweet savor of Christ, in them that are saved, and in them that perish:

16 To the one we are the savor of death unto death; and to the other the savor of life unto life. And who is sufficient for these things?

17 For we are not as many, which corrupt the word of God: but as of sincerity, but as of God, in the sight of God speak we in Christ.

Ministers of the New Covenant

3 Do we begin again to commend ourselves? or need we, as some others, epistles of commendation to you, or letters of commendation from you?

2 Ye are our epistle written in our hearts, known and read of all men:

3 Forasmuch as ye are manifestly declared to be the epistle of Christ ministered by us, written not with ink, but with the Spirit of the living God; not in tables of stone, but in fleshly tables of the heart.

4 And such trust have we through Christ to God-ward:

5 Not that we are sufficient of ourselves to think any thing as of ourselves; but our sufficiency is of God;

6 Who also hath made us able ministers of the new testament; not of the letter, but of the spirit: for the letter killeth, but the spirit giveth life.

7 But if the ministration of death, written and engraven in stones, was glorious, so that the children of Israel could not steadfastly behold the face of Moses for the glory of his countenance; which glory was to be done away;

8 How shall not the ministration of the spirit be rather glorious?

9 For if the ministration of condemnation be glory, much more doth the ministration of righteousness exceed in glory.

10 For even that which was made glorious had no glory in this respect, by reason of the glory that excelleth.

11 For if that which is done away was glorious, much more that which remaineth is glorious.

12 Seeing then that we have such hope, we use great plainness of speech:

13 And not as Moses, which put a veil over his face, that the children of Israel could not steadfastly look to the end of that which is abolished:

14 But their minds were blinded: for until this day remaineth the same veil untaken away in the reading of the old testament; which veil is done away in Christ.

15 But even unto this day, when Moses is read, the veil is upon their heart.

16 Nevertheless, when it shall turn to the Lord, the veil shall be taken away.

17 Now the Lord is that Spirit: and where the Spirit of the Lord is, there is liberty.

18 But we all, with open face beholding as in a glass the glory of the Lord, are changed into the same image from glory to glory, even as by the Spirit of the Lord.

4 Therefore, seeing we have this ministry, as we have received mercy, we faint not;

2 But have renounced the hidden things of dishonesty, not walking in craftiness, nor handling the word of God deceitfully; but, by manifestation of the truth, commending ourselves to every man's conscience in the sight of God.

3 But if our gospel be hid, it is hid to them that are lost:

4 In whom the god of this world hath blinded the minds of them which believe not, lest the light of the glorious gospel of Christ, who is the image of God, should shine unto them.

5 For we preach not ourselves, but Christ Jesus the Lord; and ourselves your servants for Jesus' sake.

6 For God, who commanded the light to shine out of darkness, hath shined in our hearts, to give the light of the knowledge of the glory of God in the face of Jesus Christ.

Living by Faith

7 But we have this treasure in earthen vessels, that the excellency of the power may be of God, and not of us.

8 We are troubled on every side, yet not

distressed; we are perplexed, but not in despair;

9 Persecuted, but not forsaken; cast down, but not destroyed;

10 Always bearing about in the body the dying of the Lord Jesus, that the life also of Jesus might be made manifest in our body.

11 For we which live are alway delivered unto death for Jesus' sake, that the life also of Jesus might be made manifest in our mortal flesh.

12 So then death worketh in us, but life in you.

13 We having the same spirit of faith, according as it is written, I believed, and therefore have I spoken; we also believe, and therefore speak;

14 Knowing that he which raised up the Lord Jesus shall raise up us also by Jesus, and shall present us with you.

15 For all things are for your sakes, that the abundant grace might through the thanksgiving of many redound to the glory of God.

16 For which cause we faint not; but though our outward man perish, yet the inward man is renewed day by day.

17 For our light affliction, which is but for a moment, worketh for us a far more exceeding and eternal weight of glory;

18 While we look not at the things which are seen, but at the things which are not seen: for the things which are seen are temporal; but the things which are not seen are eternal.

5 For we know that, if our earthly house of this tabernacle were dissolved, we have a building of God, a house not made with hands, eternal in the heavens.

2 For in this we groan, earnestly desiring to be clothed upon with our house which is from heaven:

3 If so be that being clothed we shall not be found naked.

4 For we that are in this tabernacle do groan, being burdened: not for that we would be unclothed, but clothed upon, that mortality might be swallowed up of life.

5 Now he that hath wrought us for the selfsame thing is God, who also hath given unto us the earnest of the Spirit.

6 Therefore we are always confident, knowing that, whilst we are at home in the body, we are absent from the Lord:

7 (For we walk by faith, not by sight:)

8 We are confident, I say, and willing rather to be absent from the body, and to be present with the Lord.

9 Wherefore we labor, that, whether present or absent, we may be accepted of him.

10 For we must all appear before the judgment seat of Christ; that every one may receive the things done in his body, according to that he hath done, whether it be good or bad.

The Ministry of Reconciliation

11 Knowing therefore the terror of the Lord, we persuade men; but we are made

manifest unto God; and I trust also are made manifest in your consciences.

12 For we commend not ourselves again unto you, but give you occasion to glory on our behalf, that ye may have somewhat to answer them which glory in appearance, and not in heart.

13 For whether we be beside ourselves, it is to God: or whether we be sober, it is for your cause.

14 For the love of Christ constraineth us; because we thus judge, that if one died for all, then were all dead:

15 And that he died for all, that they which live should not henceforth live unto themselves, but unto him which died for them, and rose again.

16 Wherefore henceforth know we no man after the flesh: yea, though we have known Christ after the flesh, yet now henceforth know we him no more.

17 Therefore if any man be in Christ, he is a new creature: old things are passed away; behold, all things are become new.

18 And all things are of God, who hath reconciled us to himself by Jesus Christ, and hath given to us the ministry of reconciliation;

19 To wit, that God was in Christ, reconciling the world unto himself, not imputing their trespasses unto them; and hath committed unto us the word of reconciliation.

20 Now then we are ambassadors for Christ, as though God did beseech you by us: we pray you in Christ's stead, be ye reconciled to God.

21 For he hath made him to be sin for us, who knew no sin; that we might be made the righteousness of God in him.

6 We then, as workers together with him, beseech you also that ye receive not the grace of God in vain.

2 (For he saith, I have heard thee in a time accepted, and in the day of salvation have I succored thee: Behold, now is the accepted time; behold, now is the day of salvation.)

3 Giving no offense in any thing, that the ministry be not blamed:

4 But in all things approving ourselves as the ministers of God, in much patience, in afflictions, in necessities, in distresses,

5 In stripes, in imprisonments, in tumults, in labors, in watchings, in fastings;

6 By pureness, by knowledge, by longsuffering, by kindness, by the Holy Ghost, by love unfeigned,

7 By the word of truth, by the power of God, by the armor of righteousness on the right hand and on the left,

8 By honor and dishonor, by evil report and good report: as deceivers, and yet true;

9 As unknown, and yet well known; as dying, and, behold, we live; as chastened, and not killed;

10 As sorrowful, yet alway rejoicing; as poor, yet making many rich; as having nothing, and yet possessing all things.

11 O ye Corinthians, our mouth is open unto you, our heart is enlarged.

12 Ye are not straitened in us, but ye are straitened in your own bowels.

13 Now for a recompense in the same, (I speak as unto my children,) be ye also enlarged.

Ye Are the Temple of the Living God

14 Be ye not unequally yoked together with unbelievers: for what fellowship hath righteousness with unrighteousness? and what communion hath light with darkness?

15 And what concord hath Christ with Be′li-al? or what part hath he that believeth with an infidel?

16 And what agreement hath the temple of God with idols? for ye are the temple of the living God; as God hath said, I will dwell in them, and walk in them; and I will be their God, and they shall be my people.

17 Wherefore come out from among them, and be ye separate, saith the Lord, and touch not the unclean thing; and I will receive you,

18 And will be a Father unto you, and ye shall be my sons and daughters, saith the Lord Almighty.

7 Having therefore these promises, dearly beloved, let us cleanse ourselves from all filthiness of the flesh and spirit, perfecting holiness in the fear of God.

Paul's Joy at the Church's Repentance

2 Receive us; we have wronged no man, we have corrupted no man, we have defrauded no man.

3 I speak not this to condemn you: for I have said before, that ye are in our hearts to die and live with you.

4 Great is my boldness of speech toward you, great is my glorying of you: I am filled with comfort, I am exceeding joyful in all our tribulation.

5 For, when we were come into Macedonia, our flesh had no rest, but we were troubled on every side; without were fightings, within were fears.

6 Nevertheless God, that comforteth those that are cast down, comforted us by the coming of Titus;

7 And not by his coming only, but by the consolation wherewith he was comforted in you, when he told us your earnest desire, your mourning, your fervent mind toward me; so that I rejoiced the more.

8 For though I made you sorry with a letter, I do not repent, though I did repent: for I perceive that the same epistle hath made you sorry, though it were but for a season.

9 Now I rejoice, not that ye were made sorry, but that ye sorrowed to repentance: for ye were made sorry after a godly manner, that ye might receive damage by us in nothing.

10 For godly sorrow worketh repentance to salvation not to be repented of: but the sorrow of the world worketh death.

11 For behold this selfsame thing, that ye sorrowed after a godly sort, what carefulness it wrought in you, yea, what clearing of your-

selves, yea, what indignation, yea, what fear, yea, what vehement desire, yea, what zeal, yea, what revenge! In all things ye have approved yourselves to be clear in this matter.

12 Wherefore, though I wrote unto you, I did it not for his cause that had done the wrong, nor for his cause that suffered wrong, but that our care for you in the sight of God might appear unto you.

13 Therefore we were comforted in your comfort: yea, and exceedingly the more joyed we for the joy of Titus, because his spirit was refreshed by you all.

14 For if I have boasted any thing to him of you, I am not ashamed; but as we spake all things to you in truth, even so our boasting, which I made before Titus, is found a truth.

15 And his inward affection is more abundant toward you, whilst he remembereth the obedience of you all, how with fear and trembling ye received him.

16 I rejoice therefore that I have confidence in you in all things.

The Offering for the Saints

8 Moreover, brethren, we do you to wit of the grace of God bestowed on the churches of Macedonia;

2 How that in a great trial of affliction, the abundance of their joy and their deep poverty abounded unto the riches of their liberality.

3 For to their power, I bear record, yea, and beyond their power they were willing of themselves;

4 Praying us with much entreaty that we would receive the gift, and take upon us the fellowship of the ministering to the saints.

5 And this they did, not as we hoped, but first gave their own selves to the Lord, and unto us by the will of God.

6 Insomuch that we desired Titus, that as he had begun, so he would also finish in you the same grace also.

7 Therefore, as ye abound in every thing, in faith, and utterance, and knowledge, and in all diligence, and in your love to us, see that ye abound in this grace also.

8 I speak not by commandment, but by occasion of the forwardness of others, and to prove the sincerity of your love.

9 For ye know the grace of our Lord Jesus Christ, that, though he was rich, yet for your sakes he became poor, that ye through his poverty might be rich.

10 And herein I give my advice: for this is expedient for you, who have begun before, not only to do, but also to be forward a year ago.

11 Now therefore perform the doing of it; that as there was a readiness to will, so there may be a performance also out of that which ye have.

12 For if there be first a willing mind, it is accepted according to that a man hath, and not according to that he hath not.

13 For I mean not that other men be eased, and ye burdened:

14 But by an equality, that now at this time your abundance may be a supply for their

want, that their abundance also may be a
supply for your want; that there may be
equality:

15 As it is written, He that had gathered
much had nothing over; and he that had
gathered little had no lack.

16 But thanks be to God, which put the
same earnest care into the heart of Titus for
you.

17 For indeed he accepted the exhortation;
but being more forward, of his own accord he
went unto you.

18 And we have sent with him the brother,
whose praise is in the gospel throughout all
the churches;

19 And not that only, but who was also
chosen of the churches to travel with us with
this grace, which is administered by us to the
glory of the same Lord, and declaration of
your ready mind:

20 Avoiding this, that no man should blame
us in this abundance which is administered
by us:

21 Providing for honest things, not only in
the sight of the Lord, but also in the sight
of men.

22 And we have sent with them our
brother, whom we have oftentimes proved
diligent in many things, but now much more
diligent, upon the great confidence which I
have in you.

23 Whether any do inquire of Titus, he is
my partner and fellow helper concerning you:
or our brethren be inquired of, they are the

messengers of the churches, and the glory of
Christ.
652 1577 1391
5547

24 Wherefore show ye to them, and before
the churches, the proof of your love, and of
our boasting on your behalf.
1731 4383
1577 1732 26

9 For as touching the ministering to the
saints, it is superfluous for me to write to
you:
2746 1248
40 4053·········· 1125·····

2 For I know the forwardness of your mind,
for which I boast of you to them of Macedonia, that Achaïa was ready a year ago; and
your zeal hath provoked very many.
1492 4288 4288
2744 3110
882 3903········· 4070
2205 2042 ·········4118–4119····

3 Yet have I sent the brethren, lest our
boasting of you should be in vain in this behalf; that, as I said, ye may be ready:
3992 3992 80
2745 2758············· 3313
2531 3903

4 Lest haply if they of Macedonia come
with me, and find you unprepared, we (that
we say not, ye) should be ashamed in this
same confident boasting.
3381 3381–4458 3110 2064
2147 532
2617·········

5 Therefore I thought it necessary to exhort
the brethren, that they would go before unto
you, and make up beforehand your bounty,
whereof ye had notice before, that the same
might be ready, as a matter of bounty, and
not as of covetousness.
5287 2746
2233 316 3870········
80 4281·········
4294·········
2129
4293·········
2092 2129

6 But this I say, He which soweth sparingly
shall reap also sparingly; and he which soweth
bountifully shall reap also bountifully.
4124
4687········· 5340
2325········· 5340 4687·········
2129 2325 2129

7 Every man according as he purposeth in
his heart, so let him give; not grudgingly,
or of necessity: for God loveth a cheerful
giver.
1538········· 2531······ 4255·
2588 3077
318 2316 25 2431

8 And God is able to make all grace abound
toward you; that ye, always having all suffi-
1395
2316 1415 4052······ 5485 4052
3842 841

ciency in all things, may abound to every good work:

9 (As it is written, He hath dispersed abroad; he hath given to the poor: his righteousness remaineth for ever.

10 Now he that ministereth seed to the sower both minister bread for your food, and multiply your seed sown, and increase the fruits of your righteousness:)

11 Being enriched in every thing to all bountifulness, which causeth through us thanksgiving to God.

12 For the administration of this service not only supplieth the want of the saints, but is abundant also by many thanksgivings unto God;

13 While by the experiment of this ministration they glorify God for your professed subjection unto the gospel of Christ, and for your liberal distribution unto them, and unto all men;

14 And by their prayer for you, which long after you for the exceeding grace of God in you.

15 Thanks be unto God for his unspeakable gift.

Paul's Defense of His Ministry

10 Now I Paul myself beseech you by the meekness and gentleness of Christ, who in presence am base among you, but being absent am bold toward you:

2 But I beseech you, that I may not be bold when I am present with that confidence,

wherewith I think to be bold against some, which think of us as if we walked according to the flesh.

3 For though we walk in the flesh, we do not war after the flesh:

4 (For the weapons of our warfare are not carnal, but mighty through God to the pulling down of strongholds;)

5 Casting down imaginations, and every high thing that exalteth itself against the knowledge of God, and bringing into captivity every thought to the obedience of Christ;

6 And having in a readiness to revenge all disobedience, when your obedience is fulfilled.

7 Do ye look on things after the outward appearance? If any man trust to himself that he is Christ's, let him of himself think this again, that, as he is Christ's, even so are we Christ's.

8 For though I should boast somewhat more of our authority, which the Lord hath given us for edification, and not for your destruction, I should not be ashamed:

9 That I may not seem as if I would terrify you by letters.

10 For his letters, say they, are weighty and powerful; but his bodily presence is weak, and his speech contemptible.

11 Let such a one think this, that, such as we are in word by letters when we are absent, such will we be also in deed when we are present.

12 For we dare not make ourselves of the number, or compare ourselves with some that

commend themselves: but they, measuring themselves by themselves, and comparing themselves among themselves, are not wise.

13 But we will not boast of things without our measure, but according to the measure of the rule which God hath distributed to us, a measure to reach even unto you.

14 For we stretch not ourselves beyond our measure, as though we reached not unto you; for we are come as far as to you also in preaching the gospel of Christ:

15 Not boasting of things without our measure, that is, of other men's labors; but having hope, when your faith is increased, that we shall be enlarged by you according to our rule abundantly,

16 To preach the gospel in the regions beyond you, and not to boast in another man's line of things made ready to our hand.

17 But he that glorieth, let him glory in the Lord.

18 For not he that commendeth himself is approved, but whom the Lord commendeth.

11 Would to God ye could bear with me a little in my folly: and indeed bear with me.

2 For I am jealous over you with godly jealousy: for I have espoused you to one husband, that I may present you as a chaste virgin to Christ.

3 But I fear, lest by any means, as the serpent beguiled Eve through his subtilty, so your minds should be corrupted from the simplicity that is in Christ.

4 For if he that cometh preacheth another Jesus, whom we have not preached, or if ye receive another spirit, which ye have not received, or another gospel, which ye have not accepted, ye might well bear with him.

5 For I suppose I was not a whit behind the very chiefest apostles.

6 But though I be rude in speech, yet not in knowledge; but we have been thoroughly made manifest among you in all things.

7 Have I committed an offense in abasing myself that ye might be exalted, because I have preached to you the gospel of God freely?

8 I robbed other churches, taking wages of them, to do you service.

9 And when I was present with you, and wanted, I was chargeable to no man: for that which was lacking to me the brethren which came from Macedonia supplied: and in all things I have kept myself from being burdensome unto you, and so will I keep myself.

10 As the truth of Christ is in me, no man shall stop me of this boasting in the regions of Achai'a.

11 Wherefore? because I love you not? God knoweth.

12 But what I do, that I will do, that I may cut off occasion from them which desire occasion; that wherein they glory, they may be found even as we.

13 For such are false apostles, deceitful workers, transforming themselves into the apostles of Christ.

14 And no marvel; for Satan himself is
transformed into an angel of light.

15 Therefore it is no great thing if his
ministers also be transformed as the ministers
of righteousness; whose end shall be according
to their works.

Paul's Sufferings as an Apostle

16 I say again, Let no man think me a
fool; if otherwise, yet as a fool receive me,
that I may boast myself a little.

17 That which I speak, I speak it not after
the Lord, but as it were foolishly, in this confidence of boasting.

18 Seeing that many glory after the flesh, I
will glory also.

19 For ye suffer fools gladly, seeing ye
yourselves are wise.

20 For ye suffer, if a man bring you into
bondage, if a man devour you, if a man take
of you, if a man exalt himself, if a man smite
you on the face.

21 I speak as concerning reproach, as though
we had been weak. Howbeit, whereinsoever any
is bold, (I speak foolishly,) I am bold also.

22 Are they Hebrews? so am I. Are they
Israelites? so am I. Are they the seed of
Abraham? so am I.

23 Are they ministers of Christ? (I speak
as a fool,) I am more; in labors more abundant, in stripes above measure, in prisons more
frequent, in deaths oft.

24 Of the Jews five times received I forty
stripes save one.

25 Thrice was I beaten with rods, once was I stoned, thrice I suffered shipwreck, a night and a day I have been in the deep;

26 In journeyings often, in perils of waters, in perils of robbers, in perils by mine own countrymen, in perils by the heathen, in perils in the city, in perils in the wilderness, in perils in the sea, in perils among false brethren;

27 In weariness and painfulness, in watchings often, in hunger and thirst, in fastings often, in cold and nakedness.

28 Beside those things that are without, that which cometh upon me daily, the care of all the churches.

29 Who is weak, and I am not weak? who is offended, and I burn not?

30 If I must needs glory, I will glory of the things which concern mine infirmities.

31 The God and Father of our Lord Jesus Christ, which is blessed for evermore, knoweth that I lie not.

32 In Damascus the governor under Ar′etas the king kept the city of the Dam′ascenes with a garrison, desirous to apprehend me:

33 And through a window in a basket was I let down by the wall, and escaped his hands.

Paul's Thorn in the Flesh

12 It is not expedient for me doubtless to glory. I will come to visions and revelations of the Lord.

2 I knew a man in Christ above fourteen years ago, (whether in the body, I cannot tell;

or whether out of the body, I cannot tell: God knoweth;) such a one caught up to the third heaven.

3 And I knew such a man, (whether in the body, or out of the body, I cannot tell: God knoweth;)

4 How that he was caught up into paradise, and heard unspeakable words, which it is not lawful for a man to utter.

5 Of such a one will I glory: yet of myself I will not glory, but in mine infirmities.

6 For though I would desire to glory, I shall not be a fool; for I will say the truth: but now I forbear, lest any man should think of me above that which he seeth me to be, or that he heareth of me.

7 And lest I should be exalted above meas-ure through the abundance of the revelations, there was given to me a thorn in the flesh, the messenger of Satan to buffet me, lest I should be exalted above measure.

8 For this thing I besought the Lord thrice, that it might depart from me.

9 And he said unto me, My grace is suffi-cient for thee: for my strength is made perfect in weakness. Most gladly therefore will I rather glory in my infirmities, that the power of Christ may rest upon me.

10 Therefore I take pleasure in infirmities, in reproaches, in necessities, in persecutions, in distresses for Christ's sake: for when I am weak, then am I strong.

11 I am become a fool in glorying; ye have compelled me: for I ought to have been com-

mended of you: for in nothing am I behind the very chiefest apostles, though I be nothing.

12 Truly the signs of an apostle were wrought among you in all patience, in signs, and wonders, and mighty deeds.

13 For what is it wherein ye were inferior to other churches, except it be that I myself was not burdensome to you? forgive me this wrong.

Paul Plans a Third Visit

14 Behold, the third time I am ready to come to you; and I will not be burdensome to you: for I seek not yours, but you: for the children ought not to lay up for the parents, but the parents for the children.

15 And I will very gladly spend and be spent for you; though the more abundantly I love you, the less I be loved.

16 But be it so, I did not burden you: nevertheless, being crafty, I caught you with guile.

17 Did I make a gain of you by any of them whom I sent unto you?

18 I desired Titus, and with him I sent a brother. Did Titus make a gain of you? walked we not in the same spirit? walked we not in the same steps?

19 Again, think ye that we excuse ourselves unto you? we speak before God in Christ: but we do all things, dearly beloved, for your edifying.

20 For I fear, lest, when I come, I shall not find you such as I would, and that I shall

be found unto you such as ye would not: lest there be debates, envyings, wraths, strifes, backbitings, whisperings, swellings, tumults:

21 And lest, when I come again, my God will humble me among you, and that I shall bewail many which have sinned already, and have not repented of the uncleanness and fornication and lasciviousness which they have committed.

13 This is the third time I am coming to you. In the mouth of two or three witnesses shall every word be established.

2 I told you before, and foretell you, as if I were present, the second time; and being absent now I write to them which heretofore have sinned, and to all other, that, if I come again, I will not spare:

3 Since ye seek a proof of Christ speaking in me, which to you-ward is not weak, but is mighty in you.

4 For though he was crucified through weakness, yet he liveth by the power of God. For we also are weak in him, but we shall live with him by the power of God toward you.

5 Examine yourselves, whether ye be in the faith; prove your own selves. Know ye not your own selves, how that Jesus Christ is in you, except ye be reprobates?

6 But I trust that ye shall know that we are not reprobates.

7 Now I pray to God that ye do no evil; not that we should appear approved, but that ye should do that which is honest, though we be as reprobates.

8 For we can do nothing against the truth, but for the truth.

9 For we are glad, when we are weak, and ye are strong: and this also we wish, even your perfection.

10 Therefore I write these things being absent, lest being present I should use sharpness, according to the power which the Lord hath given me to edification, and not to destruction.

Final Greetings

11 Finally, brethren, farewell. Be perfect, be of good comfort, be of one mind, live in peace; and the God of love and peace shall be with you.

12 Greet one another with a holy kiss.

13 All the saints salute you.

14 The grace of the Lord Jesus Christ, and the love of God, and the communion of the Holy Ghost, be with you all. Amen.

THE EPISTLE OF PAUL THE APOSTLE TO THE
GALATIANS

Salutation

1 Paul, an apostle, (not of men, neither by man, but by Jesus Christ, and God the Father, who raised him from the dead;)

2 And all the brethren which are with me, Unto the churches of Galatia:

3 Grace be to you, and peace, from God the Father, and from our Lord Jesus Christ,

4 Who gave himself for our sins, that he might deliver us from this present evil world, according to the will of God and our Father:

5 To whom be glory for ever and ever. Amen.

There Is No Other Gospel

6 I marvel that ye are so soon removed from him that called you into the grace of Christ unto another gospel:

7 Which is not another; but there be some that trouble you, and would pervert the gospel of Christ.

8 But though we, or an angel from heaven, preach any other gospel unto you than that which we have preached unto you, let him be accursed.

9 As we said before, so say I now again, If any man preach any other gospel unto you than that ye have received, let him be accursed.

10 For do I now persuade men, or God? or do I seek to please men? for if I yet

pleased men, I should not be the servant of
Christ.

Paul's Ministry of the True Gospel

11 But I certify you, brethren, that the
gospel which was preached of me is not after
man.

12 For I neither received it of man, neither
was I taught it, but by the revelation of Jesus
Christ.

13 For ye have heard of my conversation in
time past in the Jews' religion, how that beyond measure I persecuted the church of God,
and wasted it:

14 And profited in the Jews' religion above
many my equals in mine own nation, being
more exceedingly zealous of the traditions of
my fathers.

15 But when it pleased God, who separated
me from my mother's womb, and called me
by his grace,

16 To reveal his Son in me, that I might
preach him among the heathen; immediately I
conferred not with flesh and blood:

17 Neither went I up to Jerusalem to them
which were apostles before me; but I went into
Arabia, and returned again unto Damascus.

18 Then after three years I went up to
Jerusalem to see Peter, and abode with him
fifteen days.

19 But other of the apostles saw I none,
save James the Lord's brother.

20 Now the things which I write unto you,
behold, before God, I lie not.

21 Afterward I came into the regions of Syria and Cili′cia;

22 And was unknown by face unto the churches of Judea which were in Christ:

23 But they had heard only, That he which persecuted us in times past now preacheth the faith which once he destroyed.

24 And they glorified God in me.

2 Then fourteen years after I went up again to Jerusalem with Barnabas, and took Titus with me also.

2 And I went up by revelation, and communicated unto them that gospel which I preach among the Gentiles, but privately to them which were of reputation, lest by any means I should run, or had run, in vain.

3 But neither Titus, who was with me, being a Greek, was compelled to be circumcised:

4 And that because of false brethren unawares brought in, who came in privily to spy out our liberty which we have in Christ Jesus, that they might bring us into bondage:

5 To whom we gave place by subjection, no, not for an hour; that the truth of the gospel might continue with you.

6 But of those who seemed to be somewhat, (whatsoever they were, it maketh no matter to me: God accepteth no man's person:) for they who seemed to be somewhat in conference added nothing to me:

7 But contrariwise, when they saw that the gospel of the uncircumcision was committed unto me, as the gospel of the circumcision was unto Peter;

8 (For he that wrought effectually in Peter to the apostleship of the circumcision, the same was mighty in me toward the Gentiles;)

9 And when James, Cephas, and John, who seemed to be pillars, perceived the grace that was given unto me, they gave to me and Barnabas the right hands of fellowship; that we should go unto the heathen, and they unto the circumcision.

10 Only they would that we should remember the poor; the same which I also was forward to do.

Paul Rebukes Peter at Antioch

11 But when Peter was come to An'ti-och, I withstood him to the face, because he was to be blamed.

12 For before that certain came from James, he did eat with the Gentiles: but when they were come, he withdrew and separated himself, fearing them which were of the circumcision.

13 And the other Jews dissembled likewise with him; insomuch that Barnabas also was carried away with their dissimulation.

14 But when I saw that they walked not uprightly according to the truth of the gospel, I said unto Peter before them all, If thou, being a Jew, livest after the manner of Gentiles, and not as do the Jews, why compellest thou the Gentiles to live as do the Jews?

15 We who are Jews by nature, and not sinners of the Gentiles,

16 Knowing that a man is not justified by

the works of the law, but by the faith of Jesus Christ, even we have believed in Jesus Christ, that we might be justified by the faith of Christ, and not by the works of the law: for by the works of the law shall no flesh be justified.

17 But if, while we seek to be justified by Christ, we ourselves also are found sinners, is therefore Christ the minister of sin? God forbid.

18 For if I build again the things which I destroyed, I make myself a transgressor.

19 For I through the law am dead to the law, that I might live unto God.

20 I am crucified with Christ: nevertheless I live; yet not I, but Christ liveth in me: and the life which I now live in the flesh I live by the faith of the Son of God, who loved me, and gave himself for me.

21 I do not frustrate the grace of God: for if righteousness come by the law, then Christ is dead in vain.

The Spirit Received through Faith

3 O foolish Galatians, who hath bewitched you, that ye should not obey the truth, before whose eyes Jesus Christ hath been evidently set forth, crucified among you?

2 This only would I learn of you, Received ye the Spirit by the works of the law, or by the hearing of faith?

3 Are ye so foolish? having begun in the Spirit, are ye now made perfect by the flesh?

4 Have ye suffered so many things in vain?
if it be yet in vain.

5 He therefore that ministereth to you the
Spirit, and worketh miracles among you, doeth
he it by the works of the law, or by the
hearing of faith?

God's Covenant with Abraham

6 Even as Abraham believed God, and it
was accounted to him for righteousness.

7 Know ye therefore that they which are of
faith, the same are the children of Abraham.

8 And the Scripture, foreseeing that God
would justify the heathen through faith,
preached before the gospel unto Abraham,
saying, In thee shall all nations be blessed.

9 So then they which be of faith are blessed
with faithful Abraham.

10 For as many as are of the works of the
law are under the curse: for it is written,
Cursed is every one that continueth not in all
things which are written in the book of the
law to do them.

11 But that no man is justified by the law
in the sight of God, it is evident: for, The
just shall live by faith.

12 And the law is not of faith: but, The
man that doeth them shall live in them.

13 Christ hath redeemed us from the curse
of the law, being made a curse for us: for it
is written, Cursed is every one that hangeth on
a tree:

14 That the blessing of Abraham might
come on the Gentiles through Jesus Christ;

that we might receive the promise of the Spirit through faith.

15 Brethren, I speak after the manner of men; Though it be but a man's covenant, yet if it be confirmed, no man disannulleth, or addeth thereto.

16 Now to Abraham and his seed were the promises made. He saith not, And to seeds, as of many; but as of one, And to thy seed, which is Christ.

17 And this I say, that the covenant, that was confirmed before of God in Christ, the law, which was four hundred and thirty years after, cannot disannul, that it should make the promise of none effect.

18 For if the inheritance be of the law, it is no more of promise: but God gave it to Abraham by promise.

The Purpose of the Law

19 Wherefore then serveth the law? It was added because of transgressions, till the seed should come to whom the promise was made; and it was ordained by angels in the hand of a mediator.

20 Now a mediator is not a mediator of one, but God is one.

21 Is the law then against the promises of God? God forbid: for if there had been a law given which could have given life, verily righteousness should have been by the law.

22 But the Scripture hath concluded all under sin, that the promise by faith of Jesus Christ might be given to them that believe.

23 But before faith came, we were kept under the law, shut up unto the faith which should afterward be revealed.

24 Wherefore the law was our schoolmaster to bring us unto Christ, that we might be justified by faith.

25 But after that faith is come, we are no longer under a schoolmaster.

26 For ye are all the children of God by faith in Christ Jesus.

27 For as many of you as have been baptized into Christ have put on Christ.

28 There is neither Jew nor Greek, there is neither bond nor free, there is neither male nor female: for ye are all one in Christ Jesus.

29 And if ye be Christ's, then are ye Abraham's seed, and heirs according to the promise.

4 Now I say, That the heir, as long as he is a child, differeth nothing from a servant, though he be lord of all;

2 But is under tutors and governors until the time appointed of the father.

3 Even so we, when we were children, were in bondage under the elements of the world:

4 But when the fulness of the time was come, God sent forth his Son, made of a woman, made under the law,

5 To redeem them that were under the law, that we might receive the adoption of sons.

6 And because ye are sons, God hath sent forth the Spirit of his Son into your hearts, crying, Abba, Father.

7 Wherefore thou art no more a servant,

but a son; and if a son, then an heir of God
through Christ.

Warning against Returning to Bondage

8 Howbeit then, when ye knew not God,
ye did service unto them which by nature are
no gods.

9 But now, after that ye have known God,
or rather are known of God, how turn ye
again to the weak and beggarly elements,
whereunto ye desire again to be in bondage?

10 Ye observe days, and months, and times,
and years.

11 I am afraid of you, lest I have bestowed
upon you labor in vain.

12 Brethren, I beseech you, be as I am;
for I am as ye are: ye have not injured me
at all.

13 Ye know how through infirmity of the
flesh I preached the gospel unto you at the
first.

14 And my temptation which was in my
flesh ye despised not, nor rejected; but received me as an angel of God, even as Christ
Jesus.

15 Where is then the blessedness ye spake
of? for I bear you record, that, if it had been
possible, ye would have plucked out your own
eyes, and have given them to me.

16 Am I therefore become your enemy, because I tell you the truth?

17 They zealously affect you, but not well;
yea, they would exclude you, that ye might
affect them.

18 But it is good to be zealously affected always in a good thing, and not only when I am present with you.

19 My little children, of whom I travail in birth again until Christ be formed in you,

20 I desire to be present with you now, and to change my voice; for I stand in doubt of you.

The Allegory of Hagar and Sarah

21 Tell me, ye that desire to be under the law, do ye not hear the law?

22 For it is written, that Abraham had two sons, the one by a bondmaid, the other by a free woman.

23 But he who was of the bondwoman was born after the flesh; but he of the free woman was by promise.

24 Which things are an allegory: for these are the two covenants; the one from the mount Si'nai, which gendereth to bondage, which is Hagar.

25 For this Hagar is mount Si'nai in Arabia, and answereth to Jerusalem which now is, and is in bondage with her children.

26 But Jerusalem which is above is free, which is the mother of us all.

27 For it is written, Rejoice, thou barren that bearest not; break forth and cry, thou that travailest not: for the desolate hath many more children than she which hath a husband.

28 Now we, brethren, as Isaac was, are the children of promise.

29 But as then he that was born after the

flesh persecuted him that was born after the Spirit, even so it is now.

30 Nevertheless what saith the Scripture? Cast out the bondwoman and her son: for the son of the bondwoman shall not be heir with the son of the free woman.

31 So then, brethren, we are not children of the bondwoman, but of the free.

Stand Fast in Liberty

5 Stand fast therefore in the liberty wherewith Christ hath made us free, and be not entangled again with the yoke of bondage.

2 Behold, I Paul say unto you, that if ye be circumcised, Christ shall profit you nothing.

3 For I testify again to every man that is circumcised, that he is a debtor to do the whole law.

4 Christ is become of no effect unto you, whosoever of you are justified by the law; ye are fallen from grace.

5 For we through the Spirit wait for the hope of righteousness by faith.

6 For in Jesus Christ neither circumcision availeth any thing, nor uncircumcision; but faith which worketh by love.

7 Ye did run well; who did hinder you that ye should not obey the truth?

8 This persuasion cometh not of him that calleth you.

9 A little leaven leaveneth the whole lump.

10 I have confidence in you through the Lord, that ye will be none otherwise minded:

but he that troubleth you shall bear his judgment, whosoever he be.

11 And I, brethren, if I yet preach circumcision, why do I yet suffer persecution? then is the offense of the cross ceased.

12 I would they were even cut off which trouble you.

13 For, brethren, ye have been called unto liberty; only use not liberty for an occasion to the flesh, but by love serve one another.

14 For all the law is fulfilled in one word, even in this; Thou shalt love thy neighbor as thyself.

15 But if ye bite and devour one another, take heed that ye be not consumed one of another.

The Fruit of the Spirit and the Works of the Flesh

16 This I say then, Walk in the Spirit, and ye shall not fulfil the lust of the flesh.

17 For the flesh lusteth against the Spirit, and the Spirit against the flesh: and these are contrary the one to the other; so that ye cannot do the things that ye would.

18 But if ye be led of the Spirit, ye are not under the law.

19 Now the works of the flesh are manifest, which are these, adultery, fornication, uncleanness, lasciviousness,

20 Idolatry, witchcraft, hatred, variance, emulations, wrath, strife, seditions, heresies,

21 Envyings, murders, drunkenness, revelings, and such like: of the which I tell you

before, as I have also told you in time past,
that they which do such things shall not inherit the kingdom of God.

22 But the fruit of the Spirit is love, joy,
peace, long-suffering, gentleness, goodness,
faith,

23 Meekness, temperance: against such there
is no law.

24 And they that are Christ's have crucified
the flesh with the affections and lusts.

25 If we live in the Spirit, let us also walk
in the Spirit.

26 Let us not be desirous of vainglory,
provoking one another, envying one another.

6 Brethren, if a man be overtaken in a
fault, ye which are spiritual, restore such
a one in the spirit of meekness; considering
thyself, lest thou also be tempted.

2 Bear ye one another's burdens, and so
fulfil the law of Christ.

3 For if a man think himself to be something, when he is nothing, he deceiveth himself.

4 But let every man prove his own work,
and then shall he have rejoicing in himself
alone, and not in another.

5 For every man shall bear his own burden.

6 Let him that is taught in the word communicate unto him that teacheth in all good
things.

7 Be not deceived; God is not mocked:
for whatsoever a man soweth, that shall he
also reap.

8 For he that soweth to his flesh shall of

the flesh reap corruption; but he that soweth
to the Spirit shall of the Spirit reap life everlasting.

9 And let us not be weary in well doing:
for in due season we shall reap, if we faint
not.

10 As we have therefore opportunity, let
us do good unto all men, especially unto them
who are of the household of faith.

Paul Glories in the Cross

11 Ye see how large a letter I have written
unto you with mine own hand.

12 As many as desire to make a fair show
in the flesh, they constrain you to be circumcised; only lest they should suffer persecution
for the cross of Christ.

13 For neither they themselves who are
circumcised keep the law; but desire to have
you circumcised, that they may glory in your
flesh.

14 But God forbid that I should glory, save
in the cross of our Lord Jesus Christ, by
whom the world is crucified unto me, and I
unto the world.

15 For in Christ Jesus neither circumcision
availeth any thing, nor uncircumcision, but a
new creature.

16 And as many as walk according to this
rule, peace be on them, and mercy, and upon
the Israel of God.

17 From henceforth let no man trouble me:
for I bear in my body the marks of the Lord
Jesus.

Benediction

18 Brethren, the grace of our Lord Jesus Christ be with your spirit. Amen.

THE EPISTLE OF PAUL THE APOSTLE TO THE

EPHESIANS

Salutation

1 Paul, an apostle of Jesus Christ by the will of God, To the saints which are at Ephesus, and to the faithful in Christ Jesus:

2 Grace be to you, and peace, from God our Father, and from the Lord Jesus Christ.

Spiritual Blessings in Christ

3 Blessed be the God and Father of our Lord Jesus Christ, who hath blessed us with all spiritual blessings in heavenly places in Christ:

4 According as he hath chosen us in him before the foundation of the world, that we should be holy and without blame before him in love:

5 Having predestinated us unto the adoption of children by Jesus Christ to himself, according to the good pleasure of his will,

6 To the praise of the glory of his grace, wherein he hath made us accepted in the beloved:

7 In whom we have redemption through his

blood, the forgiveness of sins, according to the riches of his grace;

8 Wherein he hath abounded toward us in all wisdom and prudence;

9 Having made known unto us the mystery of his will, according to his good pleasure which he hath purposed in himself:

10 That in the dispensation of the fulness of times he might gather together in one all things in Christ, both which are in heaven, and which are on earth; even in him.

11 In whom also we have obtained an inheritance, being predestinated according to the purpose of him who worketh all things after the counsel of his own will:

12 That we should be to the praise of his glory, who first trusted in Christ.

13 In whom ye also trusted, after that ye heard the word of truth, the gospel of your salvation: in whom also, after that ye believed, ye were sealed with that Holy Spirit of promise,

14 Which is the earnest of our inheritance until the redemption of the purchased possession, unto the praise of his glory.

Prayer for Knowledge and Understanding

15 Wherefore I also, after I heard of your faith in the Lord Jesus, and love unto all the saints,

16 Cease not to give thanks for you, making mention of you in my prayers;

17 That the God of our Lord Jesus Christ, the Father of glory, may give unto you the

spirit of wisdom and revelation in the knowledge of him:

18 The eyes of your understanding being enlightened; that ye may know what is the hope of his calling, and what the riches of the glory of his inheritance in the saints,

19 And what is the exceeding greatness of his power to us-ward who believe, according to the working of his mighty power,

20 Which he wrought in Christ, when he raised him from the dead, and set him at his own right hand in the heavenly places,

21 Far above all principality, and power, and might, and dominion, and every name that is named, not only in this world, but also in that which is to come:

22 And hath put all things under his feet, and gave him to be the head over all things to the church,

23 Which is his body, the fulness of him that filleth all in all.

Saved by Grace

2 And you hath he quickened, who were dead in trespasses and sins;

2 Wherein in time past ye walked according to the course of this world, according to the prince of the power of the air, the spirit that now worketh in the children of disobedience:

3 Among whom also we all had our conversation in times past in the lusts of our flesh, fulfilling the desires of the flesh and of the mind; and were by nature the children of wrath, even as others.

4 But God, who is rich in mercy, for his great love wherewith he loved us,

5 Even when we were dead in sins, hath quickened us together with Christ, (by grace ye are saved;)

6 And hath raised us up together, and made us sit together in heavenly places in Christ Jesus:

7 That in the ages to come he might show the exceeding riches of his grace, in his kindness toward us, through Christ Jesus.

8 For by grace are ye saved through faith; and that not of yourselves: it is the gift of God:

9 Not of works, lest any man should boast.

10 For we are his workmanship, created in Christ Jesus unto good works, which God hath before ordained that we should walk in them.

One New Man in Christ

11 Wherefore remember, that ye being in time past Gentiles in the flesh, who are called Uncircumcision by that which is called the Circumcision in the flesh made by hands;

12 That at that time ye were without Christ, being aliens from the commonwealth of Israel, and strangers from the covenants of promise, having no hope, and without God in the world:

13 But now, in Christ Jesus, ye who sometime were far off are made nigh by the blood of Christ.

14 For he is our peace, who hath made

both one, and hath broken down the middle wall of partition between us;

15 Having abolished in his flesh the enmity, even the law of commandments contained in ordinances; for to make in himself of twain one new man, so making peace;

16 And that he might reconcile both unto God in one body by the cross, having slain the enmity thereby:

17 And came and preached peace to you which were afar off, and to them that were nigh.

18 For through him we both have access by one Spirit unto the Father.

19 Now therefore ye are no more strangers and foreigners, but fellow citizens with the saints, and of the household of God;

20 And are built upon the foundation of the apostles and prophets, Jesus Christ himself being the chief corner stone;

21 In whom all the building fitly framed together groweth unto a holy temple in the Lord:

22 In whom ye also are builded together for a habitation of God through the Spirit.

Paul's Ministry to the Gentiles

3 For this cause I Paul, the prisoner of Jesus Christ for you Gentiles,

2 If ye have heard of the dispensation of the grace of God which is given me to you-ward:

3 How that by revelation he made known unto me the mystery; (as I wrote afore in few words;

4 Whereby, when ye read, ye may understand my knowledge in the mystery of Christ,)

5 Which in other ages was not made known unto the sons of men, as it is now revealed unto his holy apostles and prophets by the Spirit;

6 That the Gentiles should be fellow heirs, and of the same body, and partakers of his promise in Christ by the gospel.

7 Whereof I was made a minister, according to the gift of the grace of God given unto me by the effectual working of his power.

8 Unto me, who am less than the least of all saints, is this grace given, that I should preach among the Gentiles the unsearchable riches of Christ;

9 And to make all men see what is the fellowship of the mystery, which from the beginning of the world hath been hid in God, who created all things by Jesus Christ:

10 To the intent that now unto the principalities and powers in heavenly places might be known by the church the manifold wisdom of God,

11 According to the eternal purpose which he purposed in Christ Jesus our Lord:

12 In whom we have boldness and access with confidence by the faith of him.

13 Wherefore I desire that ye faint not at my tribulations for you, which is your glory.

Prayer for Love Which Surpasses Knowledge

14 For this cause I bow my knees unto the Father of our Lord Jesus Christ,

15 Of whom the whole family in heaven and earth is named,

16 That he would grant you, according to the riches of his glory, to be strengthened with might by his Spirit in the inner man;

17 That Christ may dwell in your hearts by faith; that ye, being rooted and grounded in love,

18 May be able to comprehend with all saints what is the breadth, and length, and depth, and height;

19 And to know the love of Christ, which passeth knowledge, that ye might be filled with all the fulness of God.

20 Now unto him that is able to do exceeding abundantly above all that we ask or think, according to the power that worketh in us,

21 Unto him be glory in the church by Christ Jesus throughout all ages, world without end. Amen.

The Unity of the Spirit

4 I therefore, the prisoner of the Lord, beseech you that ye walk worthy of the vocation wherewith ye are called,

2 With all lowliness and meekness, with long-suffering, forbearing one another in love;

3 Endeavoring to keep the unity of the Spirit in the bond of peace.

4 There is one body, and one Spirit, even as ye are called in one hope of your calling;

5 One Lord, one faith, one baptism,

6 One God and Father of all, who is above all, and through all, and in you all.

7 But unto every one of us is given grace according to [1538] the [1325] measure of the gift of Christ. [5485] [3358] [1431] [5547]

8 Wherefore he saith, When he ascended up on high, [1352] he led captivity captive, [305] and gave gifts [531] unto men. [162] [161] [162] [1325]

9 (Now that [1390] he [444] ascended, what is it but that he also descended first into the [5101] lower [1508] parts of the earth? [2597] [2737] [3313]

10 He [1093] that descended is the same also that ascended up [2597] far above all heavens, that he [305] might fill all things.) [5231] [3772]

11 And [4137] he gave some, apostles; and some, prophets; and some, [1325] evangelists; [652] and some, pastors [4396] and teachers; [2099]

12 For the [4166] perfecting [1320] of the saints, for the work of the ministry, [2677] for the edifying [40] of the body of Christ: [2041] [1248] [3619]

13 Till [4983] we [5547] all come in the unity of the faith, [3360] and of the knowledge [2658] of the [1775] Son of God, [4102] unto a perfect [1922] man, unto the measure [5207] of the stature of the [5046] fulness of Christ: [2316] [3358]

14 That [2244] we henceforth be [4138] no more [5547] children, tossed to and fro, and carried about with [3516] every wind of doctrine, by the [4064] sleight of men, and [2831] cunning craftiness, whereby they lie in wait to [417] [1319] [2940] [444] deceive; [3834] [4106]

15 But speaking the truth in love, may grow [226] [26] up into him [226] in all things, which [26] is the [837] head, [837] even Christ: [2776]

16 From [5547] whom the whole body fitly joined together and compacted [3956] by that [4983] which every joint supplieth, [4883] according [4822] to the effectual working in the [2024] measure of every part, maketh in- [3358] [1538] [3313] [4160] [838]

crease of the body unto the edifying of itself
in love.

The New Life in Christ

17 This I say therefore, and testify in the
Lord, that ye henceforth walk not as other
Gentiles walk, in the vanity of their mind,
18 Having the understanding darkened, being alienated from the life of God through the
ignorance that is in them, because of the
blindness of their heart:

19 Who being past feeling have given themselves over unto lasciviousness, to work all uncleanness with greediness.

20 But ye have not so learned Christ;

21 If so be that ye have heard him, and
have been taught by him, as the truth is in
Jesus:

22 That ye put off concerning the former
conversation the old man, which is corrupt
according to the deceitful lusts;

23 And be renewed in the spirit of your
mind;

24 And that ye put on the new man, which
after God is created in righteousness and true
holiness.

25 Wherefore putting away lying, speak
every man truth with his neighbor: for we are
members one of another.

26 Be ye angry, and sin not: let not the sun
go down upon your wrath:

27 Neither give place to the devil.

28 Let him that stole steal no more: but
rather let him labor, working with his hands

the thing which is good, that he may have to
give to him that needeth.

29 Let no corrupt communication proceed
out of your mouth, but that which is good to
the use of edifying, that it may minister grace
unto the hearers.

30 And grieve not the Holy Spirit of God,
whereby ye are sealed unto the day of redemption.

31 Let all bitterness, and wrath, and anger,
and clamor, and evil speaking, be put away
from you, with all malice:

32 And be ye kind one to another, tender-
hearted, forgiving one another, even as God
for Christ's sake hath forgiven you.

Walk as Children of Light

5 Be ye therefore followers of God, as dear
children;

2 And walk in love, as Christ also hath
loved us, and hath given himself for us an
offering and a sacrifice to God for a sweet-
smelling savor.

3 But fornication, and all uncleanness, or
covetousness, let it not be once named among
you, as becometh saints;

4 Neither filthiness, nor foolish talking, nor
jesting, which are not convenient: but rather
giving of thanks.

5 For this ye know, that no whoremonger,
nor unclean person, nor covetous man, who is
an idolater, hath any inheritance in the kingdom of Christ and of God.

6 Let no man deceive you with vain words:

for because of these things cometh the wrath of God upon the children of disobedience.

7 Be not ye therefore partakers with them.

8 For ye were sometime darkness, but now are ye light in the Lord: walk as children of light;

9 (For the fruit of the Spirit is in all goodness and righteousness and truth;)

10 Proving what is acceptable unto the Lord.

11 And have no fellowship with the unfruitful works of darkness, but rather reprove them.

12 For it is a shame even to speak of those things which are done of them in secret.

13 But all things that are reproved are made manifest by the light: for whatsoever doth make manifest is light.

14 Wherefore he saith, Awake thou that sleepest, and arise from the dead, and Christ shall give thee light.

15 See then that ye walk circumspectly, not as fools, but as wise,

16 Redeeming the time, because the days are evil.

17 Wherefore be ye not unwise, but understanding what the will of the Lord is.

18 And be not drunk with wine, wherein is excess; but be filled with the Spirit;

19 Speaking to yourselves in psalms and hymns and spiritual songs, singing and making melody in your heart to the Lord;

20 Giving thanks always for all things unto God and the Father in the name of our Lord Jesus Christ;

21 Submitting yourselves one to another in
the fear of God.

Be Subject to One Another

22 Wives, submit yourselves unto your own
husbands, as unto the Lord.

23 For the husband is the head of the wife,
even as Christ is the head of the church: and
he is the saviour of the body.

24 Therefore as the church is subject unto
Christ, so let the wives be to their own husbands in every thing.

25 Husbands, love your wives, even as
Christ also loved the church, and gave himself
for it;

26 That he might sanctify and cleanse it
with the washing of water by the word,

27 That he might present it to himself a
glorious church, not having spot, or wrinkle,
or any such thing; but that it should be holy
and without blemish.

28 So ought men to love their wives as
their own bodies. He that loveth his wife
loveth himself.

29 For no man ever yet hated his own
flesh; but nourisheth and cherisheth it, even as
the Lord the church:

30 For we are members of his body, of his
flesh, and of his bones.

31 For this cause shall a man leave his
father and mother, and shall be joined unto
his wife, and they two shall be one flesh.

32 This is a great mystery: but I speak
concerning Christ and the church.

33 Nevertheless, let every one of you in particular so love his wife even as himself; and the wife see that she reverence her husband.

6 Children, obey your parents in the Lord: for this is right.

2 Honor thy father and mother; which is the first commandment with promise;

3 That it may be well with thee, and thou mayest live long on the earth.

4 And, ye fathers, provoke not your children to wrath: but bring them up in the nurture and admonition of the Lord.

5 Servants, be obedient to them that are your masters according to the flesh, with fear and trembling, in singleness of your heart, as unto Christ;

6 Not with eyeservice, as menpleasers; but as the servants of Christ, doing the will of God from the heart;

7 With good will doing service, as to the Lord, and not to men:

8 Knowing that whatsoever good thing any man doeth, the same shall he receive of the Lord, whether he be bond or free.

9 And, ye masters, do the same things unto them, forbearing threatening: knowing that your Master also is in heaven; neither is there respect of persons with him.

The Whole Armor of God

10 Finally, my brethren, be strong in the Lord, and in the power of his might.

11 Put on the whole armor of God, that ye

may be able to stand against the wiles of the
devil. 1410..... 2476...... 3180

1228

12 For we wrestle not against flesh and
blood, but against principalities, against powers, against the rulers of the darkness of this
world, against spiritual wickedness in high places.

13 Wherefore take unto you the whole
armor of God, that ye may be able to withstand in the evil day, and having done all, to
stand.

14 Stand therefore, having your loins girt
about with truth, and having on the breastplate of righteousness;

15 And your feet shod with the preparation
of the gospel of peace;

16 Above all, taking the shield of faith,
wherewith ye shall be able to quench all the
fiery darts of the wicked.

17 And take the helmet of salvation, and the
sword of the Spirit, which is the word of God:

18 Praying always with all prayer and supplication in the Spirit, and watching thereunto
with all perseverance and supplication for all
saints;

19 And for me, that utterance may be given
unto me, that I may open my mouth boldly,
to make known the mystery of the gospel,

20 For which I am an ambassador in bonds;
that therein I may speak boldly, as I ought to
speak.

Final Greetings

21 But that ye also may know my affairs,
and how I do, Tych′i·cus, a beloved brother

and faithful minister in the Lord, shall make
known to you all things:

22 Whom I have sent unto you for the
same purpose, that ye might know our affairs,
and that he might comfort your hearts.

23 Peace be to the brethren, and love with
faith, from God the Father and the Lord
Jesus Christ.

24 Grace be with all them that love our
Lord Jesus Christ in sincerity. Amen.

THE EPISTLE OF PAUL THE APOSTLE TO THE

PHILIPPIANS

Salutation

1 Paul and Timothy, the servants of Jesus
Christ, To all the saints in Christ Jesus
which are at Phil'ippi, with the bishops and
deacons:

2 Grace be unto you, and peace, from God
our Father and from the Lord Jesus Christ.

Paul's Prayer for the Philippian Christians

3 I thank my God upon every remembrance
of you,

4 Always in every prayer of mine for you
all making request with joy,

5 For your fellowship in the gospel from
the first day until now;

6 Being confident of this very thing, that he

which hath begun a good work in you will perform it until the day of Jesus Christ:

7 Even as it is meet for me to think this of you all, because I have you in my heart; inasmuch as both in my bonds, and in the defense and confirmation of the gospel, ye all are partakers of my grace.

8 For God is my record, how greatly I long after you all in the bowels of Jesus Christ.

9 And this I pray, that your love may abound yet more and more in knowledge and in all judgment;

10 That ye may approve things that are excellent; that ye may be sincere and without offense till the day of Christ;

11 Being filled with the fruits of righteousness, which are by Jesus Christ, unto the glory and praise of God.

To Me to Live Is Christ

12 But I would ye should understand, brethren, that the things which happened unto me have fallen out rather unto the furtherance of the gospel;

13 So that my bonds in Christ are manifest in all the palace, and in all other places;

14 And many of the brethren in the Lord, waxing confident by my bonds, are much more bold to speak the word without fear.

15 Some indeed preach Christ even of envy and strife; and some also of good will:

16 The one preach Christ of contention, not

sincerely, supposing to add affliction to my
bonds:

17 But the other of love, knowing that I
am set for the defense of the gospel.

18 What then? notwithstanding, every way,
whether in pretense, or in truth, Christ is
preached; and I therein do rejoice, yea, and
will rejoice.

19 For I know that this shall turn to my
salvation through your prayer, and the supply
of the Spirit of Jesus Christ,

20 According to my earnest expectation and
my hope, that in nothing I shall be ashamed,
but that with all boldness, as always, so now
also Christ shall be magnified in my body,
whether it be by life, or by death.

21 For to me to live is Christ, and to die
is gain.

22 But if I live in the flesh, this is the
fruit of my labor: yet what I shall choose I
wot not.

23 For I am in a strait betwixt two, having
a desire to depart, and to be with Christ;
which is far better:

24 Nevertheless to abide in the flesh is
more needful for you.

25 And having this confidence, I know that
I shall abide and continue with you all for
your furtherance and joy of faith;

26 That your rejoicing may be more abundant in Jesus Christ for me by my coming to
you again.

27 Only let your conversation be as it becometh the gospel of Christ: that whether I

come and see you, or else be absent, I may hear of your affairs, that ye stand fast in one spirit, with one mind striving together for the faith of the gospel;

28 And in nothing terrified by your adversaries: which is to them an evident token of perdition, but to you of salvation, and that of God.

29 For unto you it is given in the behalf of Christ, not only to believe on him, but also to suffer for his sake;

30 Having the same conflict which ye saw in me, and now hear to be in me.

Christ's Humiliation and Exaltation

2 If there be therefore any consolation in Christ, if any comfort of love, if any fellowship of the Spirit, if any bowels and mercies,

2 Fulfil ye my joy, that ye be likeminded, having the same love, being of one accord, of one mind.

3 Let nothing be done through strife or vainglory; but in lowliness of mind let each esteem other better than themselves.

4 Look not every man on his own things, but every man also on the things of others.

5 Let this mind be in you, which was also in Christ Jesus:

6 Who, being in the form of God, thought it not robbery to be equal with God:

7 But made himself of no reputation, and took upon him the form of a servant, and was made in the likeness of men:

8 And being found in fashion as a man, he humbled himself, and became obedient unto death, even the death of the cross.

9 Wherefore God also hath highly exalted him, and given him a name which is above every name:

10 That at the name of Jesus every knee should bow, of things in heaven, and things in earth, and things under the earth;

11 And that every tongue should confess that Jesus Christ is Lord, to the glory of God the Father.

Shining as Lights in the World

12 Wherefore, my beloved, as ye have always obeyed, not as in my presence only, but now much more in my absence, work out your own salvation with fear and trembling.

13 For it is God which worketh in you both to will and to do of his good pleasure.

14 Do all things without murmurings and disputings:

15 That ye may be blameless and harmless, the sons of God, without rebuke, in the midst of a crooked and perverse nation, among whom ye shine as lights in the world;

16 Holding forth the word of life; that I may rejoice in the day of Christ, that I have not run in vain, neither labored in vain.

17 Yea, and if I be offered upon the sacrifice and service of your faith, I joy, and rejoice with you all.

18 For the same cause also do ye joy, and rejoice with me.

19 But I trust in the Lord Jesus to send Timothy shortly unto you, that I also may be of good comfort, when I know your state.

20 For I have no man likeminded, who will naturally care for your state.

21 For all seek their own, not the things which are Jesus Christ's.

22 But ye know the proof of him, that, as a son with the father, he hath served with me in the gospel.

23 Him therefore I hope to send presently, so soon as I shall see how it will go with me.

24 But I trust in the Lord that I also myself shall come shortly.

25 Yet I supposed it necessary to send to you Epaphrodi'tus, my brother, and companion in labor, and fellow soldier, but your messenger, and he that ministered to my wants.

26 For he longed after you all, and was full of heaviness, because that ye had heard that he had been sick.

27 For indeed he was sick nigh unto death: but God had mercy on him; and not on him only, but on me also, lest I should have sorrow upon sorrow.

28 I sent him therefore the more carefully, that, when ye see him again, ye may rejoice, and that I may be the less sorrowful.

29 Receive him therefore in the Lord with all gladness; and hold such in reputation:

30 Because for the work of Christ he was

nigh unto death, not regarding his life, to
supply your lack of service toward me.

Pressing toward the Mark

3 Finally, my brethren, rejoice in the Lord.
To write the same things to you, to me
indeed is not grievous, but for you it is safe.

2 Beware of dogs, beware of evil workers,
beware of the concision.

3 For we are the circumcision, which worship God in the spirit, and rejoice in Christ
Jesus, and have no confidence in the flesh.

4 Though I might also have confidence in
the flesh. If any other man thinketh that he
hath whereof he might trust in the flesh, I
more:

5 Circumcised the eighth day, of the stock
of Israel, of the tribe of Benjamin, a Hebrew
of the Hebrews; as touching the law, a
Pharisee;

6 Concerning zeal, persecuting the church;
touching the righteousness which is in the
law, blameless.

7 But what things were gain to me, those I
counted loss for Christ.

8 Yea doubtless, and I count all things but
loss for the excellency of the knowledge of
Christ Jesus my Lord: for whom I have suffered the loss of all things, and do count them
but dung, that I may win Christ,

9 And be found in him, not having mine
own righteousness, which is of the law, but
that which is through the faith of Christ, the
righteousness which is of God by faith:

10 That I may know him, and the power of his resurrection, [1097] and the fellowship [1411] of his sufferings, [386] being made [2842] conformable unto his death; [3804] [4832]

11 [2288] If by any means I might attain unto the resurrection [1513] of the dead. [2658]

12 [1815] Not as though I had [3498] already attained, either were already perfect: [2983] [2235] but I follow [2983] after, if that I [5048] may [2235] apprehend [5048] that for which also [1377] I am apprehended [1499] of [2638] Christ Jesus. [2638]

13 [5547] Brethren, I count [2424] not myself to have apprehended: [80] but this [3049] one thing [1683] I do, [2638] for-getting those things which are behind, [1950] and reaching forth unto those things [3694] which are before, [1901] [1715]

14 I press toward the mark for the prize of the high [1377] calling of God [4649] in Christ Jesus. [1017]

15 Let [507] [2821] us therefore, [2316] as many [5547] as be [2424] perfect, be thus [5426] minded: [3767] and if [3745] in any thing ye be [5046] otherwise [5426] minded, [5426] God shall [5100] reveal even this [5426] unto you. [2088] [5426] [2316] [601]

16 Nevertheless, whereto we have already attained, [4133] let us walk [5348] by the same rule, let us mind the same [4748] thing. [2583]

17 [5426] Brethren, be followers together of me, [80] [1096] [4831] and mark them which walk so as ye have us [4648] [4043] [2531] for an ensample. [5179]

18 (For many walk, [4183] of whom [4043] I have told [3004] you often, and now tell you even weeping, that [4178] [3568] [3004] [2799] they are the enemies of the cross of Christ: [2190] [4716] [5547]

19 Whose end is destruction, whose God is their belly, [5056] and whose [684] glory is in their shame, [2316] who mind earthly things.) [2836] [1391] [152] [5426] [1919]

20 For our conversation is in heaven; from [4175] [5225] [3772]

whence also we look for the Saviour, the Lord
Jesus Christ:
21 Who shall change our vile body, that it
may be fashioned like unto his glorious body,
according to the working whereby he is able
even to subdue all things unto himself.

Rejoice in the Lord

4 Therefore, my brethren dearly beloved
and longed for, my joy and crown, so
stand fast in the Lord, my dearly beloved.
2 I beseech Eu-o′di-as, and beseech Syn′-
tyche, that they be of the same mind in the
Lord.
3 And I entreat thee also, true yokefellow,
help those women which labored with me in
the gospel, with Clement also, and with
other my fellow laborers, whose names are in
the book of life.
4 Rejoice in the Lord always: and again I
say, Rejoice.
5 Let your moderation be known unto all
men. The Lord is at hand.
6 Be careful for nothing; but in every thing
by prayer and supplication with thanksgiving
let your requests be made known unto God.
7 And the peace of God, which passeth all
understanding, shall keep your hearts and
minds through Christ Jesus.

Think on These Things

8 Finally, brethren, whatsoever things are
true, whatsoever things are honest, whatsoever
things are just, whatsoever things are pure,

53

whatsoever things are lovely, whatsoever
things are of good report; if there be any
virtue, and if there be any praise, think on
these things.

9 Those things, which ye have both learned,
and received, and heard, and seen in me, do:
and the God of peace shall be with you.

Acknowledgment of the Philippians' Gift

10 But I rejoiced in the Lord greatly, that
now at the last your care of me hath flourished
again; wherein ye were also careful, but ye
lacked opportunity.

11 Not that I speak in respect of want: for
I have learned, in whatsoever state I am,
therewith to be content.

12 I know both how to be abased, and I
know how to abound: every where and in all
things I am instructed both to be full and to
be hungry, both to abound and to suffer need.

13 I can do all things through Christ which
strengtheneth me.

14 Notwithstanding, ye have well done, that
ye did communicate with my affliction.

15 Now ye Philippians know also, that in
the beginning of the gospel, when I departed
from Macedonia, no church communicated
with me as concerning giving and receiving,
but ye only.

16 For even in Thessaloni′ca ye sent once
and again unto my necessity.

17 Not because I desire a gift: but I desire
fruit that may abound to your account.

18 But I have all, and abound: I am full,

having received of Epaphrodi′tus the things which were sent from you, an odor of a sweet smell, a sacrifice acceptable, well-pleasing to God. 19 But my God shall supply all your need according to his riches in glory by Christ Jesus.

20 Now unto God and our Father be glory for ever and ever. Amen.

Final Greetings

21 Salute every saint in Christ Jesus. The brethren which are with me greet you.

22 All the saints salute you, chiefly they that are of Caesar's household.

23 The grace of our Lord Jesus Christ be with you all. Amen.

THE EPISTLE OF PAUL THE APOSTLE TO THE

COLOSSIANS

Salutation

1 Paul, an apostle of Jesus Christ by the will of God, and Timothy our brother,

2 To the saints and faithful brethren in Christ which are at Colos′sae: Grace be unto you, and peace, from God our Father and the Lord Jesus Christ.

Prayer for Spiritual Wisdom

3 We give thanks to God and the Father of our Lord Jesus Christ, praying always for you,

4 Since we heard of your faith in Christ Jesus,

and of the love which ye have to all the saints,

5 For the hope which is laid up for you in heaven, whereof ye heard before in the word of the truth of the gospel;

6 Which is come unto you, as it is in all the world; and bringeth forth fruit, as it doth also in you, since the day ye heard of it, and knew the grace of God in truth:

7 As ye also learned of Ep'aphras our dear fellow servant, who is for you a faithful minister of Christ;

8 Who also declared unto us your love in the Spirit.

9 For this cause we also, since the day we heard it, do not cease to pray for you, and to desire that ye might be filled with the knowledge of his will in all wisdom and spiritual understanding;

10 That ye might walk worthy of the Lord unto all pleasing, being fruitful in every good work, and increasing in the knowledge of God;

11 Strengthened with all might, according to his glorious power, unto all patience and long-suffering with joyfulness;

12 Giving thanks unto the Father, which hath made us meet to be partakers of the inheritance of the saints in light:

13 Who hath delivered us from the power of darkness, and hath translated us into the kingdom of his dear Son.

Reconciliation through Christ's Death

14 In whom we have redemption through his blood, even the forgiveness of sins:

15 Who is the image[1504] of the invisible[517] God[2316], the firstborn of every creature:

16 For[4416] by him were all things[2937] created, that are in heaven, and that are in earth[2936], visible and invisible[3772], whether they be thrones[3707], or dominions[517], or principalities[2362], or powers[1849]: all things[2963] were created by him[746], and for him[2936]:

17 And[2936] he is before all things, and by him all things consist:

18 And he[4921] is the head of the body, the church: who is the beginning[2776], the[4983] firstborn from[1577] the dead; that in all[746] things he might[4416] have the preeminence[3498].[1096]

19 For it pleased[4409] the Father[3962] that in him should all fulness[2106] dwell;

20 And, having[4138] made[2730] peace through the blood of his[1517] cross, by him to reconcile[604] all things[129] unto himself[4716]; by him, I say, whether they be things in earth[1093], or things in heaven[3772].

Paul's Ministry to the Church

21 And you, that were sometime alienated[5607] and enemies[2190] in your mind[1271] by wicked[4190-4191] works[2041][526], yet now[2190] hath he reconciled

22 In the[3570] body[604] of his[604] flesh through death, to present[3936] you[4983] holy and[4561] unblamable[2288] and unreprovable[410] in his[40] sight[299][2714]:

23 If ye[2714] continue in the faith grounded[1489] and settled[1476], and be not[1961] moved away[4102] from[3334] the hope[2311] of the gospel[2098], which ye have heard[191], and which was preached to every creature[2784] which is under heaven[3772]; whereof I Paul[2937] am[3972] made[1096] a minister[1249];

24 Who now[466] rejoice[3568] in[5463] my sufferings[3804] for you, and fill up that[5303] which is behind of the

afflictions of Christ in my flesh for his body's sake, which is the church:

25 Whereof I am made a minister, according to the dispensation of God which is given to me for you, to fulfil the word of God;

26 Even the mystery which hath been hid from ages and from generations, but now is made manifest to his saints:

27 To whom God would make known what is the riches of the glory of this mystery among the Gentiles; which is Christ in you, the hope of glory:

28 Whom we preach, warning every man, and teaching every man in all wisdom; that we may present every man perfect in Christ Jesus:

29 Whereunto I also labor, striving according to his working, which worketh in me mightily.

2 For I would that ye knew what great conflict I have for you, and for them at Laodice'a, and for as many as have not seen my face in the flesh;

2 That their hearts might be comforted, being knit together in love, and unto all riches of the full assurance of understanding, to the acknowledgment of the mystery of God, and of the Father, and of Christ;

3 In whom are hid all the treasures of wisdom and knowledge.

4 And this I say, lest any man should beguile you with enticing words.

5 For though I be absent in the flesh, yet am I with you in the spirit, joying and be-

holding your order, and the steadfastness of
your faith in Christ.

6 As ye have therefore received Christ Jesus
the Lord, so walk ye in him:

7 Rooted and built up in him, and stab-
lished in the faith, as ye have been taught,
abounding therein with thanksgiving.

Dead but Risen with Christ

8 Beware lest any man spoil you through
philosophy and vain deceit, after the tradition
of men, after the rudiments of the world, and
not after Christ.

9 For in him dwelleth all the fulness of the
Godhead bodily.

10 And ye are complete in him, which is
the head of all principality and power:

11 In whom also ye are circumcised with
the circumcision made without hands, in putting off the body of the sins of the flesh by
the circumcision of Christ:

12 Buried with him in baptism, wherein
also ye are risen with him through the faith
of the operation of God, who hath raised him
from the dead.

13 And you, being dead in your sins and
the uncircumcision of your flesh, hath he
quickened together with him, having forgiven
you all trespasses;

14 Blotting out the handwriting of ordinances that was against us, which was contrary to us, and took it out of the way, nailing
it to his cross;

15 And having spoiled principalities and

powers, he made a show of them openly, triumphing over them in it.

16 Let no man therefore judge you in meat, or in drink, or in respect of a holyday, or of the new moon, or of the sabbath days:

17 Which are a shadow of things to come; but the body is of Christ.

18 Let no man beguile you of your reward in a voluntary humility and worshipping of angels, intruding into those things which he hath not seen, vainly puffed up by his fleshly mind,

19 And not holding the Head, from which all the body by joints and bands having nourishment ministered, and knit together, increaseth with the increase of God.

20 Wherefore if ye be dead with Christ from the rudiments of the world, why, as though living in the world, are ye subject to ordinances,

21 (Touch not; taste not; handle not;

22 Which all are to perish with the using;) after the commandments and doctrines of men?

23 Which things have indeed a show of wisdom in will-worship, and humility, and neglecting of the body; not in any honor to the satisfying of the flesh.

3 If ye then be risen with Christ, seek those things which are above, where Christ sitteth on the right hand of God.

2 Set your affection on things above, not on things on the earth.

3 For ye are dead, and your life is hid with Christ in God.

4 When Christ, who is our life, shall appear, then shall ye also appear with him in glory.

The Old Life and the New

5 Mortify therefore your members which are upon the earth; fornication, uncleanness, inordinate affection, evil concupiscence, and covetousness, which is idolatry:

6 For which things' sake the wrath of God cometh on the children of disobedience:

7 In the which ye also walked sometime, when ye lived in them.

8 But now ye also put off all these; anger, wrath, malice, blasphemy, filthy communication out of your mouth.

9 Lie not one to another, seeing that ye have put off the old man with his deeds;

10 And have put on the new man, which is renewed in knowledge after the image of him that created him:

11 Where there is neither Greek nor Jew, circumcision nor uncircumcision, Barbarian, Scyth′i-an, bond nor free: but Christ is all, and in all.

12 Put on therefore, as the elect of God, holy and beloved, bowels of mercies, kindness, humbleness of mind, meekness, long-suffering;

13 Forbearing one another, and forgiving one another, if any man have a quarrel against any: even as Christ forgave you, so also do ye.

14 And above all these things put on charity, which is the bond of perfectness.

15 And let the peace of God rule in your

hearts, to the which also ye are called in one body; and be ye thankful.

16 Let the word of Christ dwell in you richly in all wisdom; teaching and admonishing one another in psalms and hymns and spiritual songs, singing with grace in your hearts to the Lord.

17 And whatsoever ye do in word or deed, do all in the name of the Lord Jesus, giving thanks to God and the Father by him.

Social Duties of the New Life

18 Wives, submit yourselves unto your own husbands, as it is fit in the Lord.

19 Husbands, love your wives, and be not bitter against them.

20 Children, obey your parents in all things: for this is well-pleasing unto the Lord.

21 Fathers, provoke not your children to anger, lest they be discouraged.

22 Servants, obey in all things your masters according to the flesh; not with eyeservice, as menpleasers; but in singleness of heart, fearing God:

23 And whatsoever ye do, do it heartily, as to the Lord, and not unto men;

24 Knowing that of the Lord ye shall receive the reward of the inheritance: for ye serve the Lord Christ.

25 But he that doeth wrong shall receive for the wrong which he hath done: and there is no respect of persons.

4 Masters, give unto your servants that which is just and equal; knowing that ye also have a Master in heaven.

2 Continue in prayer, and watch in the same with thanksgiving;

3 Withal praying also for us, that God would open unto us a door of utterance, to speak the mystery of Christ, for which I am also in bonds:

4 That I may make it manifest, as I ought to speak.

5 Walk in wisdom toward them that are without, redeeming the time.

6 Let your speech be always with grace, seasoned with salt, that ye may know how ye ought to answer every man.

Final Greetings

7 All my state shall Tych'icus declare unto you, who is a beloved brother, and a faithful minister and fellow servant in the Lord:

8 Whom I have sent unto you for the same purpose, that he might know your estate, and comfort your hearts;

9 With Ones'imus, a faithful and beloved brother, who is one of you. They shall make known unto you all things which are done here.

10 Aristar'chus my fellow prisoner saluteth you, and Mark, sister's son to Barnabas, (touching whom ye received commandments: if he come unto you, receive him;)

11 And Jesus, which is called Justus, who are of the circumcision. These only are my fellow workers unto the kingdom of God, which have been a comfort unto me.

12 Ep'aphras, who is one of you, a servant

of Christ, saluteth you, always laboring fervently for you in prayers, that ye may stand perfect and complete in all the will of God.

13 For I bear him record, that he hath a great zeal for you, and them that are in La-odice′a, and them in Hi-erap′olis.

14 Luke, the beloved physician, and Demas, greet you.

15 Salute the brethren which are in La-odice′a, and Nymphas, and the church which is in his house.

16 And when this epistle is read among you, cause that it be read also in the church of the La-odice′ans; and that ye likewise read the epistle from La-odice′a.

17 And say to Archip′pus, Take heed to the ministry which thou hast received in the Lord, that thou fulfil it.

18 The salutation by the hand of me Paul. Remember my bonds. Grace be with you. Amen.

THE FIRST EPISTLE
OF PAUL THE APOSTLE TO THE
THESSALONIANS

Salutation

1 Paul, and Silva′nus, and Timothy, Unto the church of the Thessalo′ni-ans which is in God the Father, and in the Lord Jesus Christ: Grace be unto you, and peace, from God our Father, and the Lord Jesus Christ.

The Thessalonians' Faith and Example

2 We give thanks to God always for you all, making mention of you in our prayers;

3 Remembering without ceasing your work of faith, and labor of love, and patience of hope in our Lord Jesus Christ, in the sight of God and our Father;

4 Knowing, brethren beloved, your election of God.

5 For our gospel came not unto you in word only, but also in power, and in the Holy Ghost, and in much assurance; as ye know what manner of men we were among you for your sake.

6 And ye became followers of us, and of the Lord, having received the word in much affliction, with joy of the Holy Ghost:

7 So that ye were ensamples to all that believe in Macedonia and Achai′a.

8 For from you sounded out the word of the Lord not only in Macedonia and Achai′a, but also in every place your faith to God-ward is spread abroad; so that we need not to speak any thing.

9 For they themselves show of us what manner of entering in we had unto you, and how ye turned to God from idols to serve the living and true God;

10 And to wait for his Son from heaven, whom he raised from the dead, even Jesus, which delivered us from the wrath to come.

Paul's Ministry in Thessalonica

2 For yourselves, brethren, know our entrance in unto you, that it was not in vain:

2 But even after that we had suffered before, and were shamefully entreated, as ye know, at Phil′ippi, we were bold in our God to speak unto you the gospel of God with much contention.

3 For our exhortation was not of deceit, nor of uncleanness, nor in guile:

4 But as we were allowed of God to be put in trust with the gospel, even so we speak; not as pleasing men, but God, which trieth our hearts.

5 For neither at any time used we flattering words, as ye know, nor a cloak of covetousness; God is witness:

6 Nor of men sought we glory, neither of you, nor yet of others, when we might have been burdensome, as the apostles of Christ.

7 But we were gentle among you, even as a nurse cherisheth her children:

8 So being affectionately desirous of you, we were willing to have imparted unto you,

not the gospel of God only, but also our own souls, because[2098] ye were[2316] dear[3440] unto us.

[5590] 9 For[1360] ye remember,[1096] brethren,[27] our labor and travail: for laboring[3421] night[80] and day,[2873] because we would[3449] not be[2038] chargeable[3571] unto[2250] any of you, we preached unto[1912] you the gospel[5100] of God.

[2784] 10 Ye are witnesses, and[2098] God[2316] also, how holily and justly[3144] and unblamably[2316] we behaved[3743] ourselves among[1346] you that[274] believe:[1096]....

11 As ye know how[4100] we exhorted and comforted[2509] and charged[1492] every one of you, as a[3888-3870] father[3140] doth his[1538] children,

[3962] 12 That ye would[5043] walk worthy of God, who hath called you[4043] unto his[516] kingdom[2316] and[2564].... glory.

[1391] 13 For this cause also thank we God without ceasing, because, when[2168] ye received[2316] the[89] word of God which ye[3880] heard of us,[3880] ye received it not[3056] as[2316] the[189] word of men, but, as it[1209] is in truth, the word of[3056] God, which[444] effectually[2531] worketh also[230] in[3056] you that[2316] believe.[1754]....

14 For ye, brethren,[4100] became followers of the churches of God[80] which in[1096] Judea[3402] are in Christ Jesus:[1577] for ye[2316] also[5607] have suffered[2448 2449] like[5607] things of[5547] your[2424] own countrymen,[3958] even as[5023] they have of the[2398] Jews:[4853]

[2453] 15 Who both killed the Lord Jesus, and their[615] own prophets,[615] and have[2962] persecuted[2424] us; and[2398] they please[4396] not God,[1559] and are contrary to all[700] men:[700][2316][1727]

16 Forbidding[444] us to speak to the Gentiles that they[2967] might be saved,[2980] to fill up their[1484] sins always: for the[4982] wrath[378] is come upon them[266] to the[3842] uttermost.[3709][5348]....

Paul's Absence and Concern

17 But we, brethren, being taken from you for a short time in presence, not in heart, endeavored the more abundantly to see your face with great desire.

18 Wherefore we would have come unto you, even I Paul, once and again; but Satan hindered us.

19 For what is our hope, or joy, or crown of rejoicing? Are not even ye in the presence of our Lord Jesus Christ at his coming?

20 For ye are our glory and joy.

3 Wherefore when we could no longer forbear, we thought it good to be left at Athens alone;

2 And sent Timothy, our brother, and minister of God, and our fellow laborer in the gospel of Christ, to establish you, and to comfort you concerning your faith:

3 That no man should be moved by these afflictions: for yourselves know that we are appointed thereunto.

4 For verily, when we were with you, we told you before that we should suffer tribulation; even as it came to pass, and ye know.

5 For this cause, when I could no longer forbear, I sent to know your faith, lest by some means the tempter have tempted you, and our labor be in vain.

6 But now when Timothy came from you unto us, and brought us good tidings of your faith and charity, and that ye have good remembrance of us always, desiring greatly to see us, as we also to see you:

7 Therefore, brethren, we were comforted over you in all our affliction and distress by your faith:

8 For now we live, if ye stand fast in the Lord.

9 For what thanks can we render to God again for you, for all the joy wherewith we joy for your sakes before our God;

10 Night and day praying exceedingly that we might see your face, and might perfect that which is lacking in your faith?

11 Now God himself and our Father, and our Lord Jesus Christ, direct our way unto you.

12 And the Lord make you to increase and abound in love one toward another, and toward all men, even as we do toward you:

13 To the end he may stablish your hearts unblamable in holiness before God, even our Father, at the coming of our Lord Jesus Christ with all his saints.

A Life Pleasing to God

4 Furthermore then we beseech you, brethren, and exhort you by the Lord Jesus, that as ye have received of us how ye ought to walk and to please God, so ye would abound more and more.

2 For ye know what commandments we gave you by the Lord Jesus.

3 For this is the will of God, even your sanctification, that ye should abstain from fornication:

4 That every one of you should know how to

possess his vessel in sanctification and honor;
5 Not in the lust of concupiscence, even as
the Gentiles which know not God:

6 That no man go beyond and defraud his
brother in any matter: because that the Lord
is the avenger of all such, as we also have
forewarned you and testified.

7 For God hath not called us unto uncleanness, but unto holiness.

8 He therefore that despiseth, despiseth not
man, but God, who hath also given unto us
his Holy Spirit.

9 But as touching brotherly love ye need
not that I write unto you: for ye yourselves
are taught of God to love one another.

10 And indeed ye do it toward all the
brethren which are in all Macedonia: but we
beseech you, brethren, that ye increase more
and more;

11 And that ye study to be quiet, and to do
your own business, and to work with your
own hands, as we commanded you;

12 That ye may walk honestly toward them
that are without, and that ye may have lack of
nothing.

The Coming of the Lord

13 But I would not have you to be ignorant, brethren, concerning them which are
asleep, that ye sorrow not, even as others
which have no hope.

14 For if we believe that Jesus died and
rose again, even so them also which sleep in
Jesus will God bring with him.

15 For this we say unto you by the word of the Lord, that we which are alive and remain unto the coming of the Lord shall not prevent them which are asleep.

16 For the Lord himself shall descend from heaven with a shout, with the voice of the archangel, and with the trump of God: and the dead in Christ shall rise first:

17 Then we which are alive and remain shall be caught up together with them in the clouds, to meet the Lord in the air: and so shall we ever be with the Lord.

18 Wherefore comfort one another with these words.

5 But of the times and the seasons, brethren, ye have no need that I write unto you.

2 For yourselves know perfectly that the day of the Lord so cometh as a thief in the night.

3 For when they shall say, Peace and safety; then sudden destruction cometh upon them, as travail upon a woman with child; and they shall not escape.

4 But ye, brethren, are not in darkness, that that day should overtake you as a thief.

5 Ye are all the children of light, and the children of the day: we are not of the night, nor of darkness.

6 Therefore let us not sleep, as do others; but let us watch and be sober.

7 For they that sleep sleep in the night; and they that be drunken are drunken in the night.

8 But let us, who are of the day, be sober,

putting on the breastplate of faith and love; and for a helmet, the hope of salvation.

9 For God hath not appointed us to wrath, but to obtain salvation by our Lord Jesus Christ,

10 Who died for us, that, whether we wake or sleep, we should live together with him.

11 Wherefore comfort yourselves together, and edify one another, even as also ye do.

Paul Exhorts the Brethren

12 And we beseech you, brethren, to know them which labor among you, and are over you in the Lord, and admonish you;

13 And to esteem them very highly in love for their work's sake. And be at peace among yourselves.

14 Now we exhort you, brethren, warn them that are unruly, comfort the feeble-minded, support the weak, be patient toward all men.

15 See that none render evil for evil unto any man; but ever follow that which is good, both among yourselves, and to all men.

16 Rejoice evermore.

17 Pray without ceasing.

18 In every thing give thanks: for this is the will of God in Christ Jesus concerning you.

19 Quench not the Spirit.

20 Despise not prophesyings.

21 Prove all things; hold fast that which is good.

22 Abstain from all appearance of evil.

23 And the very God of peace sanctify you wholly; and I pray God your whole spirit and soul and body be preserved blameless unto the coming of our Lord Jesus Christ.

24 Faithful is he that calleth you, who also will do it.

Final Greetings and Benediction

25 Brethren, pray for us.

26 Greet all the brethren with a holy kiss.

27 I charge you by the Lord, that this epistle be read unto all the holy brethren.

28 The grace of our Lord Jesus Christ be with you. Amen.

THE SECOND EPISTLE
OF PAUL THE APOSTLE TO THE

THESSALONIANS

Salutation

1 Paul, and Silva'nus, and Timothy, Unto the church of the Thessalo'ni-ans in God our Father and the Lord Jesus Christ:

2 Grace unto you, and peace, from God our Father and the Lord Jesus Christ.

Judgment at Christ's Coming

3 We are bound to thank God always for you, brethren, as it is meet, because that your faith groweth exceedingly, and the charity of

every one of you all toward each other
aboundeth;

4 So that we ourselves glory in you in the
churches of God, for your patience and faith
in all your persecutions and tribulations that
ye endure:

5 Which is a manifest token of the righteous
judgment of God, that ye may be counted
worthy of the kingdom of God, for which ye
also suffer:

6 Seeing it is a righteous thing with God to
recompense tribulation to them that trouble
you;

7 And to you who are troubled rest with
us, when the Lord Jesus shall be revealed
from heaven with his mighty angels,

8 In flaming fire taking vengeance on them
that know not God, and that obey not the
gospel of our Lord Jesus Christ:

9 Who shall be punished with everlasting
destruction from the presence of the Lord,
and from the glory of his power;

10 When he shall come to be glorified in
his saints, and to be admired in all them that
believe (because our testimony among you was
believed) in that day.

11 Wherefore also we pray always for you,
that our God would count you worthy of this
calling, and fulfil all the good pleasure of his
goodness, and the work of faith with power:

12 That the name of our Lord Jesus Christ
may be glorified in you, and ye in him, according to the grace of our God and the
Lord Jesus Christ.

The Revealing of the Man of Sin

2 Now we beseech you, brethren, by the coming of our Lord Jesus Christ, and by our gathering together unto him,

2 That ye be not soon shaken in mind, or be troubled, neither by spirit, nor by word, nor by letter as from us, as that the day of Christ is at hand.

3 Let no man deceive you by any means: for that day shall not come, except there come a falling away first, and that man of sin be revealed, the son of perdition;

4 Who opposeth and exalteth himself above all that is called God, or that is worshipped; so that he as God sitteth in the temple of God, showing himself that he is God.

5 Remember ye not, that, when I was yet with you, I told you these things?

6 And now ye know what withholdeth that he might be revealed in his time.

7 For the mystery of iniquity doth already work: only he who now letteth will let, until he be taken out of the way.

8 And then shall that Wicked be revealed, whom the Lord shall consume with the spirit of his mouth, and shall destroy with the brightness of his coming:

9 Even him, whose coming is after the working of Satan with all power and signs and lying wonders,

10 And with all deceivableness of unrighteousness in them that perish; because they received not the love of the truth, that they might be saved.

11 And for this cause God shall send them strong delusion, that they should believe a lie:

12 That they all might be damned who believed not the truth, but had pleasure in unrighteousness.

Chosen to Salvation

13 But we are bound to give thanks always to God for you, brethren beloved of the Lord, because God hath from the beginning chosen you to salvation through sanctification of the Spirit and belief of the truth:

14 Whereunto he called you by our gospel, to the obtaining of the glory of our Lord Jesus Christ.

15 Therefore, brethren, stand fast, and hold the traditions which ye have been taught, whether by word, or our epistle.

16 Now our Lord Jesus Christ himself, and God, even our Father, which hath loved us, and hath given us everlasting consolation and good hope through grace,

17 Comfort your hearts, and stablish you in every good word and work.

Pray for Us

3 Finally, brethren, pray for us, that the word of the Lord may have free course, and be glorified, even as it is with you:

2 And that we may be delivered from unreasonable and wicked men: for all men have not faith.

3 But the Lord is faithful, who shall stablish you, and keep you from evil.

4 And we have confidence in the Lord[3982] touching you, that ye both do[4160] and will do[4160] the things which we command[2962] you.

5 And the Lord direct[3853] your hearts into the love of God,[26] [2316] and[2962] into[2720] the patient[2588] waiting[5281] for Christ.[5547]

The Obligation to Work

6 Now we command[3853] you, brethren, in the name of our Lord[3686] Jesus[2962] Christ,[2424] [5547] that ye with-[80] draw yourselves[4724] from every brother that walk-eth disorderly,[4724] and not after[80] the tradition[4043] which he received[814] of us.[3862]

7 For yourselves know[3880] how ye ought to[1163] follow us: for we behaved[1492] not ourselves dis-orderly[3401] [812] among you;[812]

8 Neither did we eat[812] any man's[5315] bread for[5100] nought; but wrought[5315] with labor and travail[740] [1432] night and day,[2038] that we might[2873] not be charge-[3449] able[3571] to any[2250] of you:[1912]

9 Not because[5100] we have not power,[1849] but to make ourselves an ensample[5179] unto you to follow[1325] us.

10 For[3401] even when we were with you, this we commanded[3853] you, that if any[1536] would not[2309] work, neither should he eat.[2038]

11 For we hear that there[2068] are some which walk among you[191] disorderly, working[5100] not at all,[4043] but are busybodies.[814] [2038]

12 Now them[4020] that are such we command and exhort[5108] by our Lord[3870] Jesus[2962] Christ,[2424] [3853] that with[5547] quietness[2271] they work,[2038] and eat[2068] their own bread.[740]

13 But ye,[80] brethren, be[1573] not weary[1573] in well[2569] doing.

14 And if any man obey not our word by
this epistle, note that man, and have no
company with him, that he may be ashamed.
15 Yet count him not as an enemy, but
admonish him as a brother.

Benediction

16 Now the Lord of peace himself give you
peace always by all means. The Lord be with
you all.

17 The salutation of Paul with mine own
hand, which is the token in every epistle: so
I write.

18 The grace of our Lord Jesus Christ be
with you all. Amen.

THE FIRST EPISTLE
OF PAUL THE APOSTLE TO

TIMOTHY

Salutation

1 Paul, an apostle of Jesus Christ by the
commandment of God our Saviour, and
Lord Jesus Christ, which is our hope;
2 Unto Timothy, my own son in the faith:
Grace, mercy, and peace, from God our
Father, and Jesus Christ our Lord.

Warning against False Doctrine

3 As I besought thee to abide still at
Ephesus, when I went into Macedonia, that

thou mightest charge some that they teach no other doctrine,

4 Neither give heed to fables and endless genealogies, which minister questions, rather than godly edifying which is in faith: so do.

5 Now the end of the commandment is charity out of a pure heart, and of a good conscience, and of faith unfeigned:

6 From which some having swerved have turned aside unto vain jangling;

7 Desiring to be teachers of the law; understanding neither what they say, nor whereof they affirm.

8 But we know that the law is good, if a man use it lawfully;

9 Knowing this, that the law is not made for a righteous man, but for the lawless and disobedient, for the ungodly and for sinners, for unholy and profane, for murderers of fathers and murderers of mothers, for manslayers,

10 For whoremongers, for them that defile themselves with mankind, for menstealers, for liars, for perjured persons, and if there be any other thing that is contrary to sound doctrine;

11 According to the glorious gospel of the blessed God, which was committed to my trust.

Paul's Thankfulness for Mercy

12 And I thank Christ Jesus our Lord, who hath enabled me, for that he counted me faithful, putting me into the ministry;

13 Who was before a blasphemer, and a

persecutor, and injurious: but I obtained mercy, because I did it ignorantly in unbelief.

14 And the grace of our Lord was exceeding abundant with faith and love which is in Christ Jesus.

15 This is a faithful saying, and worthy of all acceptation, that Christ Jesus came into the world to save sinners; of whom I am chief.

16 Howbeit for this cause I obtained mercy, that in me first Jesus Christ might show forth all long-suffering, for a pattern to them which should hereafter believe on him to life everlasting.

17 Now unto the King eternal, immortal, invisible, the only wise God, be honor and glory for ever and ever. Amen.

18 This charge I commit unto thee, son Timothy, according to the prophecies which went before on thee, that thou by them mightest war a good warfare;

19 Holding faith, and a good conscience; which some having put away, concerning faith have made shipwreck:

20 Of whom is Hymene′us and Alexander; whom I have delivered unto Satan, that they may learn not to blaspheme.

Instructions concerning Prayer

2 I exhort therefore, that, first of all, supplications, prayers, intercessions, and giving of thanks, be made for all men;

2 For kings, and for all that are in authority; that we may lead a quiet and peaceable life in all godliness and honesty.

3 For this is good [2570] and acceptable [587] in the sight of God our Saviour; [1799]....

4 Who [2316] will [4990] have all men to be saved, and [2309] [444] [4982] to come unto the knowledge of the truth. [2064] [1922] [225]

5 For there is one [1922] God, and one mediator [225] between God [2316] and men, [2316] the man [444] Christ [444] [5547] Jesus; [2316]

6 Who [2424] gave himself a ransom for all, to be [1325] [487] [3142]... testified in due time. [2398] [2540]

7 Whereunto I am ordained a preacher, and [5087] an apostle, (I speak the truth in Christ, and [652] [225] [5547] lie not,) a teacher of the Gentiles in faith and [5574] [1320] [1484] [4102] verity. [225]

8 I will therefore that men pray every [1014] [435] [4336] where, lifting up holy hands, without wrath [5117] [1869] [3741] [5495] [5565] [3709] and doubting. [1261]

9 In like manner also, that women adorn [5615] [1135] [2885] themselves in modest apparel, with shame- [2887] [2689] [127].. facedness and sobriety; not with braided hair; [4997] [4117]........... or gold, or pearls, or costly array; [5557] [3135] [4185] [2441]

10 But (which becometh women professing [4241] [1135] [1861] godliness) with good works. [2317]

11 Let the woman learn in silence with all [18] [2041] [3129] [1135] [3129] [2271] subjection. [5292]

12 But I suffer not a woman to teach, nor [2010] [1135] [1321]...... to usurp authority over the man, but to be [831].................. [435] in silence. [2271]

13 For Adam was first formed, then Eve. [76] [4111] [4111] [1534] [2096]

14 And Adam was not deceived, but the [76] [538] [538] woman being deceived was in the transgres- [1135] [538]............ [1096] [3847] sion.

15 Notwithstanding she shall be saved in [4982]............... childbearing, if they continue in faith and [5042] [3306] [4102] charity and holiness with sobriety. [26] [38] [4997]

Qualifications of Bishops

3 This is a true saying, If a man desire the office of a bishop, he desireth a good work.

2 A bishop then must be blameless, the husband of one wife, vigilant, sober, of good behavior, given to hospitality, apt to teach;

3 Not given to wine, no striker, not greedy of filthy lucre; but patient, not a brawler, not covetous;

4 One that ruleth well his own house, having his children in subjection with all gravity;

5 (For if a man know not how to rule his own house, how shall he take care of the church of God?)

6 Not a novice, lest being lifted up with pride he fall into the condemnation of the devil.

7 Moreover he must have a good report of them which are without; lest he fall into reproach and the snare of the devil.

Qualifications of Deacons

8 Likewise must the deacons be grave, not double-tongued, not given to much wine, not greedy of filthy lucre;

9 Holding the mystery of the faith in a pure conscience.

10 And let these also first be proved; then let them use the office of a deacon, being found blameless.

11 Even so must their wives be grave, not slanderers, sober, faithful in all things.

12 Let the deacons be the husbands of one

wife, ruling their children and their own
1135   4291   5043   2398........
houses well.
3624   2573
13 For they that have used the office of a
deacon well purchase to themselves a good
      1247............
degree, and great boldness in the faith which
2573   4046   3954   4102   2570
is in Christ Jesus.
898   4183
5547   2424

The Mystery of Our Religion

14 These things write I unto thee, hoping
to come unto thee shortly:
2064...   1125   16 79
15 But if I tarry long, that thou mayest
      5032   1492..
know how thou oughtest to behave thyself in
      1019   1163   390........
the house of God, which is the church of the liv-
3624   2316   1577   390
ing God, the pillar and ground of the truth.
2198   2316   4769   1477   225
16 And without controversy great is the
          3672....   3173
mystery of godliness: God was manifest in the
3466.   2150   2316. 5319........
flesh, justified in the Spirit, seen of angels,
4561   1344   4151   3700   32
preached unto the Gentiles, believed on in the
2784   1484   4100..........
world, received up into glory.
2889   353...........   1391

Prediction of Apostasy

4 Now the Spirit speaketh expressly, that in
      4151   4490
the latter times some shall depart from
5306.   2540   5100   868.........
the faith, giving heed to seducing spirits, and
4102   4337...   4108   4151
doctrines of devils;
1319   1140
2 Speaking lies in hypocrisy; having their
   5573........   5272   2398
conscience seared with a hot iron;
4893   2743........
3 Forbidding to marry, and commanding to
   2967   1060...   567..
abstain from meats, which God hath created
           1033   2316   2936.........
to be received with thanksgiving of them
         3336   2169
which believe and know the truth.
4103.   1921   225
4 For every creature of God is good, and
        2938   2316   2570
nothing to be refused, if it be received with
        2983   2983.........
thanksgiving:
579..........
2169

5 For it is sanctified by the word[3056] of God[2316] and prayer.[37] [1783]

A Good Minister of Jesus Christ

6 If thou put the brethren in remembrance of these[5294] things,[5294] thou shalt[80] be a good minister of Jesus Christ, nourished[5294] up in the words[2570][1249] of faith[2424][5547] and of good[1789] doctrine,[2570][1319] whereunto[3056] thou hast[4102] attained.

7 But[3877] refuse profane and old wives' fables, and exercise[3868] thyself[952] rather[1126] unto godliness.[3454]

8 For bodily[1128] exercise profiteth little:[2150] but godliness is[4984] profitable[1129] unto[5624] all[3641] things, having promise[2150] of the[5624] life that now is, and of that which[1860] is to[2222] come.[3568] [3195]

9 This[3195] is a faithful saying,[4103][3056] and worthy of all acceptation.[514]

10 For[594] therefore we both labor and suffer reproach, because we trust in the[2872] living[3679] God, who is the Saviour of[1679] all men,[444][2198] specially[2316] of those that believe.[4990][4103]

11 These things command and teach.

12 Let no man despise[3853] thy youth;[1321] but be thou an[2706] example of the[2706] believers,[3503] in word,[1096] in conversation,[5179] in charity,[4103] in[26] spirit, in[4151] faith,[3056] in[4102] purity.[391] [47]

13 Till I come, give attendance[4337] to reading,[2064] to exhortation,[320] to doctrine.

14 Neglect[3874] not the[1319] gift that is in thee, which was[272] given thee by[5486] prophecy, with the laying on[1325] of the hands of the[4394] presbytery.[1936]

15 Meditate upon[5495] these things;[4244] give thyself wholly[3191] to them; that thy profiting may appear[4297] to all.[5318]

16 Take heed[1907] unto thyself, and unto the doctrine; continue[1319] in them: for in doing this thou shalt[1961] both save[4982] thyself, and them[4160] that hear thee.[4982] [191] [191]

Responsibilities toward Others

5 Rebuke[1969] not an elder,[4245] but entreat[3870] him as a father;[3962] and the younger[3501] men as brethren;[80]

2 The elder[4245] women as mothers;[3384] the younger[3501] as sisters,[79] with all purity.[47]

3 Honor[5091] widows[5503] that are widows[5503] indeed.[3689]

4 But if any[5100] widow[5503] have children[5043] or nephews,[1549] let them learn[3129] first[3129] to show piety[2151] at home,[3624] and to requite[287] their parents:[2151] for that is good[2570] and acceptable[587] before[1799] God.[2316]

5 Now she that is a widow[5503] indeed,[3689] and desolate,[3443] trusteth[1679] in God,[2316] and continueth[4357] in supplications[1162] and prayers[4335] night[3571] and day.[2250]

6 But she that liveth[4684] in pleasure[3571] is dead[2348] while she liveth.[2198] [2198]

7 And these[3853] things give in charge, that they may be blameless.

8 But if any[423] provide[5100] not for[4306] his own,[4306] and[2398] specially for those[3122] of his own house,[3609] he hath denied[720] the faith,[4102] and is worse[5501] than an infidel.[571]

9 Let[4102] not a widow[5503] be taken into the number[2639] under[2639] threescore[5503] years[2094] old, having been[1096] the wife[1135] of one[1640] man,[1835] [435]

10 Well reported[3140] of for good[2570] works;[2041] if she have brought up[5044] children, if she have lodged[3580] strangers, if she have washed[3538] the saints'[40] feet,[4228] if she have relieved[1884] the afflicted,[2346] if she have[1872] diligently[1872] followed[18] every good[2041] work.

11 But the younger widows refuse: for when they have begun to wax wanton against Christ, they will marry;

12 Having damnation, because they have cast off their first faith.

13 And withal they learn to be idle, wandering about from house to house; and not only idle, but tattlers also and busybodies, speaking things which they ought not.

14 I will therefore that the younger women marry, bear children, guide the house, give none occasion to the adversary to speak reproachfully.

15 For some are already turned aside after Satan.

16 If any man or woman that believeth have widows, let them relieve them, and let not the church be charged; that it may relieve them that are widows indeed.

17 Let the elders that rule well be counted worthy of double honor, especially they who labor in the word and doctrine.

18 For the Scripture saith, Thou shalt not muzzle the ox that treadeth out the corn. And, The laborer is worthy of his reward.

19 Against an elder receive not an accusation, but before two or three witnesses.

20 Them that sin rebuke before all, that others also may fear.

21 I charge thee before God, and the Lord Jesus Christ, and the elect angels, that thou observe these things without preferring one before another, doing nothing by partiality.

22 Lay hands suddenly on no man, neither

be partaker of other men's sins: keep thyself pure.

23 Drink no longer water, but use a little wine for thy stomach's sake and thine often infirmities.

24 Some men's sins are open beforehand, going before to judgment; and some men they follow after.

25 Likewise also the good works of some are manifest beforehand; and they that are otherwise cannot be hid.

6 Let as many servants as are under the yoke count their own masters worthy of all honor, that the name of God and his doctrine be not blasphemed.

2 And they that have believing masters, let them not despise them, because they are brethren; but rather do them service, because they are faithful and beloved, partakers of the benefit.

Godliness with Contentment

These things teach and exhort.

3 If any man teach otherwise, and consent not to wholesome words, even the words of our Lord Jesus Christ, and to the doctrine which is according to godliness;

4 He is proud, knowing nothing, but doting about questions and strifes of words, whereof cometh envy, strife, railings, evil surmisings,

5 Perverse disputings of men of corrupt minds, and destitute of the truth, supposing that gain is godliness: from such withdraw thyself.

6 But godliness with contentment is great gain.

7 For we brought nothing into this world, and it is certain we can carry nothing out.

8 And having food and raiment, let us be therewith content.

9 But they that will be rich fall into temptation and a snare, and into many foolish and hurtful lusts, which drown men in destruction and perdition.

10 For the love of money is the root of all evil: which while some coveted after, they have erred from the faith, and pierced themselves through with many sorrows.

The Good Fight of Faith

11 But thou, O man of God, flee these things; and follow after righteousness, godliness, faith, love, patience, meekness.

12 Fight the good fight of faith, lay hold on eternal life, whereunto thou art also called, and hast professed a good profession before many witnesses.

13 I give thee charge in the sight of God, who quickeneth all things, and before Christ Jesus, who before Pontius Pilate witnessed a good confession;

14 That thou keep this commandment without spot, unrebukable, until the appearing of our Lord Jesus Christ:

15 Which in his times he shall show, who is the blessed and only Potentate, the King of kings, and Lord of lords;

16 Who only hath immortality, dwelling in

the light which no man can approach unto;
5457 676
whom no man hath seen, nor can see: to
444 1492 1410 1492
whom be honor and power everlasting. Amen.
5092 2904 166 281

17 Charge them that are rich in this world,
3853 4145 3568 165
that they be not high-minded, nor trust in un-
5309 5309 1679 83
certain riches, but in the living God, who
4149 2198 2316 3930
giveth us richly all things to enjoy;
4146 619

18 That they do good, that they be rich in
14 14 4147
good works, ready to distribute, willing to
2570 2041 2130 2843
communicate;

19 Laying up in store for themselves a good
597 2570
foundation against the time to come, that they
2310 3195
may lay hold on eternal life.
1949 166 2222

20 O Timothy, keep that which is com-
5599 5095 5442 3872
mitted to thy trust, avoiding profane and vain
1624 952 2757
babblings, and oppositions of science falsely
477 1108 5581
so called:

21 Which some professing have erred con-
5100 1861 795
cerning the faith. Grace be with thee. Amen.
4102 5485 281

THE SECOND EPISTLE
OF PAUL THE APOSTLE TO

TIMOTHY

Salutation

1 Paul, an apostle of Jesus Christ by the will of God, according to the promise of life which is in Christ Jesus,

2 To Timothy, my dearly beloved son: Grace, mercy, and peace, from God the Father and Christ Jesus our Lord.

Be Not Ashamed

3 I thank God, whom I serve from my forefathers with pure conscience, that without ceasing I have remembrance of thee in my prayers night and day;

4 Greatly desiring to see thee, being mindful of thy tears, that I may be filled with joy;

5 When I call to remembrance the unfeigned faith that is in thee, which dwelt first in thy grandmother Lois, and thy mother Eunice; and I am persuaded that in thee also.

6 Wherefore I put thee in remembrance, that thou stir up the gift of God, which is in thee by the putting on of my hands.

7 For God hath not given us the spirit of fear; but of power, and of love, and of a sound mind.

8 Be not thou therefore ashamed of the testimony of our Lord, nor of me his prisoner: but be thou partaker of the afflictions of the gospel according to the power of God;

9 Who hath saved us, and called us with a

holy calling, not according to our works, but according to his own purpose and grace, which was given us in Christ Jesus before the world began;

10 But is now made manifest by the appearing of our Saviour Jesus Christ, who hath abolished death, and hath brought life and immortality to light through the gospel:

11 Whereunto I am appointed a preacher, and an apostle, and a teacher of the Gentiles.

12 For the which cause I also suffer these things: nevertheless I am not ashamed; for I know whom I have believed, and am persuaded that he is able to keep that which I have committed unto him against that day.

13 Hold fast the form of sound words, which thou hast heard of me, in faith and love which is in Christ Jesus.

14 That good thing which was committed unto thee keep by the Holy Ghost which dwelleth in us.

15 This thou knowest, that all they which are in Asia be turned away from me; of whom are Phygel'lus and Hermog'enes.

16 The Lord give mercy unto the house of Onesiph'orus; for he oft refreshed me, and was not ashamed of my chain:

17 But, when he was in Rome, he sought me out very diligently, and found me.

18 The Lord grant unto him that he may find mercy of the Lord in that day: and in how many things he ministered unto me at Ephesus, thou knowest very well.

A Good Soldier of Jesus Christ

2 Thou therefore, my son, be strong in the grace that is in Christ Jesus.

2 And the things that thou hast heard of me among many witnesses, the same commit thou to faithful men, who shall be able to teach others also.

3 Thou therefore endure hardness, as a good soldier of Jesus Christ.

4 No man that warreth entangleth himself with the affairs of this life; that he may please him who hath chosen him to be a soldier.

5 And if a man also strive for masteries, yet is he not crowned, except he strive lawfully.

6 The husbandman that laboreth must be first partaker of the fruits.

7 Consider what I say; and the Lord give thee understanding in all things.

8 Remember that Jesus Christ of the seed of David was raised from the dead, according to my gospel:

9 Wherein I suffer trouble, as an evildoer, even unto bonds; but the word of God is not bound.

10 Therefore I endure all things for the elect's sake, that they may also obtain the salvation which is in Christ Jesus with eternal glory.

11 It is a faithful saying: For if we be dead with him, we shall also live with him:

12 If we suffer, we shall also reign with him: if we deny him, he also will deny us:

13 If we believe not, yet he abideth faithful: he cannot deny himself.

An Approved Workman

14 Of these things put them in remembrance, charging them before the Lord that they strive not about words to no profit, but to the subverting of the hearers.

15 Study to show thyself approved unto God, a workman that needeth not to be ashamed, rightly dividing the word of truth.

16 But shun profane and vain babblings: for they will increase unto more ungodliness.

17 And their word will eat as doth a canker: of whom is Hymene'us and Phile'tus;

18 Who concerning the truth have erred, saying that the resurrection is past already; and overthrow the faith of some.

19 Nevertheless the foundation of God standeth sure, having this seal, The Lord knoweth them that are his. And, Let every one that nameth the name of Christ depart from iniquity.

20 But in a great house there are not only vessels of gold and of silver, but also of wood and of earth; and some to honor, and some to dishonor.

21 If a man therefore purge himself from these, he shall be a vessel unto honor, sanctified, and meet for the master's use, and prepared unto every good work.

22 Flee also youthful lusts: but follow righteousness, faith, charity, peace, with them that call on the Lord out of a pure heart.

23 But foolish and unlearned questions avoid, knowing that they do gender strifes.

24 And the servant of the Lord must not

strive; but be gentle unto all men, apt to teach, patient;

25 In meekness instructing those that oppose themselves; if God peradventure will give them repentance to the acknowledging of the truth;

26 And that they may recover themselves out of the snare of the devil, who are taken captive by him at his will.

The Character of Men in the Last Days

3 This know also, that in the last days perilous times shall come.

2 For men shall be lovers of their own selves, covetous, boasters, proud, blasphemers, disobedient to parents, unthankful, unholy,

3 Without natural affection, trucebreakers, false accusers, incontinent, fierce, despisers of those that are good,

4 Traitors, heady, high-minded, lovers of pleasures more than lovers of God;

5 Having a form of godliness, but denying the power thereof: from such turn away.

6 For of this sort are they which creep into houses, and lead captive silly women laden with sins, led away with divers lusts,

7 Ever learning, and never able to come to the knowledge of the truth.

8 Now as Jannes and Jambres withstood Moses, so do these also resist the truth: men of corrupt minds, reprobate concerning the faith.

9 But they shall proceed no further: for their folly shall be manifest unto all men, as theirs also was.

Paul's Last Charge to Timothy

10 But thou hast fully known my doctrine,
manner of life, purpose, faith, longsuffering,
charity, patience,

11 Persecutions, afflictions, which came unto
me at An'ti-och, at Ico'ni-um, at Lystra; what
persecutions I endured: but out of them all
the Lord delivered me.

12 Yea, and all that will live godly in
Christ Jesus shall suffer persecution.

13 But evil men and seducers shall wax
worse and worse, deceiving, and being deceived.

14 But continue thou in the things which
thou hast learned and hast been assured of,
knowing of whom thou hast learned them;

15 And that from a child thou hast known
the holy Scriptures, which are able to make
thee wise unto salvation through faith which is
in Christ Jesus.

16 All Scripture is given by inspiration of
God, and is profitable for doctrine, for re-
proof, for correction, for instruction in righteousness:

17 That the man of God may be perfect,
thoroughly furnished unto all good works.

4 I charge thee therefore before God, and
the Lord Jesus Christ, who shall judge
the quick and the dead at his appearing and
his kingdom;

2 Preach the word; be instant in season, out
of season; reprove, rebuke, exhort with all
long-suffering and doctrine.

3 For the time will come when they will

not endure sound doctrine; but after their own lusts shall they heap to themselves teachers, having itching ears;

4 And they shall turn away their ears from the truth, and shall be turned unto fables.

5 But watch thou in all things, endure afflictions, do the work of an evangelist, make full proof of thy ministry.

6 For I am now ready to be offered, and the time of my departure is at hand.

7 I have fought a good fight, I have finished my course, I have kept the faith:

8 Henceforth there is laid up for me a crown of righteousness, which the Lord, the righteous judge, shall give me at that day: and not to me only, but unto all them also that love his appearing.

Personal Instructions

9 Do thy diligence to come shortly unto me:

10 For Demas hath forsaken me, having loved this present world, and is departed unto Thessaloni′ca; Crescens to Galatia, Titus unto Dalma′tia.

11 Only Luke is with me. Take Mark, and bring him with thee: for he is profitable to me for the ministry.

12 And Tych′icus have I sent to Ephesus.

13 The cloak that I left at Tro′as with Carpus, when thou comest, bring with thee, and the books, but especially the parchments.

14 Alexander the coppersmith did me much evil: the Lord reward him according to his works:

15 Of whom be thou ware also; for he hath greatly withstood 5442 our words. 5442

16 At my first answer no man stood with 3029 436 2251 3056 me, but all men forsook me: I pray God that 627 4836 it may not be laid to their charge. 1459

17 Notwithstanding the Lord stood with 3049 3049 3049 me, and strengthened me; that by me the 2962 3936 preaching might be fully known, and that all 1743 the Gentiles might hear: and I was delivered 2782 4135 out of the mouth of the lion. 4506 1484 191

18 And the Lord shall deliver me from 4750 3023 every evil work, and will preserve me unto his 2962 4506 heavenly kingdom: to whom be glory for ever 4190-4191 2041 4982 and ever. Amen. 2032 932 1391 165 165 281

Final Greetings

19 Salute Prisca and Aquila, and the house-782 4251 207 3624 hold of Onesiph'orus. 782

20 Eras'tus abode at Corinth: but Troph'-3683 imus have I left at Mile'tus sick. 2037 3306 2882 5161

21 Do thy diligence to come before winter. 620 620 3399 770 Eubu'lus greeteth thee, and Pudens, and 4704 4704 2064 5494 Linus, and Claudia, and all the brethren. 2103 782 4227 3044

22 The Lord Jesus Christ be with thy 2803 80 spirit. Grace be with you. Amen. 2962 2424 5547 4151 5485 281

THE EPISTLE OF PAUL TO

TITUS

Salutation

1 Paul, a servant of God, and an apostle of Jesus Christ, according to the faith of God's elect, and the acknowledging of the truth which is after godliness;

2 In hope of eternal life, which God, that cannot lie, promised before the world began;

3 But hath in due times manifested his word through preaching, which is committed unto me according to the commandment of God our Saviour;

4 To Titus, mine own son after the common faith: Grace, mercy, and peace, from God the Father and the Lord Jesus Christ our Saviour.

Qualifications of Elders and Bishops

5 For this cause left I thee in Crete, that thou shouldest set in order the things that are wanting, and ordain elders in every city, as I had appointed thee:

6 If any be blameless, the husband of one wife, having faithful children not accused of riot or unruly.

7 For a bishop must be blameless, as the steward of God; not self-willed, not soon angry, not given to wine, no striker, not given to filthy lucre;

8 But a lover of hospitality, a lover of good men, sober, just, holy, temperate;

9 Holding fast the faithful word as he hath

been taught, that he may be able by sound doctrine both to exhort and to convince the gainsayers.

10 For there are many unruly and vain talkers and deceivers, specially they of the circumcision:

11 Whose mouths must be stopped, who subvert whole houses, teaching things which they ought not, for filthy lucre's sake.

12 One of themselves, even a prophet of their own, said, The Cretians are always liars, evil beasts, slow bellies.

13 This witness is true. Wherefore rebuke them sharply, that they may be sound in the faith;

14 Not giving heed to Jewish fables, and commandments of men, that turn from the truth.

15 Unto the pure all things are pure: but unto them that are defiled and unbelieving is nothing pure; but even their mind and con-science is defiled.

16 They profess that they know God; but in works they deny him, being abominable, and disobedient, and unto every good work reprobate.

The Teaching of Sound Doctrine

2 But speak thou the things which become sound doctrine:

2 That the aged men be sober, grave, temperate, sound in faith, in charity, in patience.

3 The aged women likewise, that they be in

behavior as becometh holiness, not false accusers, not given to much wine, teachers of
good things;

4 That they may teach the young women to
be sober, to love their husbands, to love their
children,

5 To be discreet, chaste, keepers at home,
good, obedient to their own husbands, that
the word of God be not blasphemed.

6 Young men likewise exhort to be sober-
minded.

7 In all things showing thyself a pattern of
good works: in doctrine showing uncorrupt-
ness, gravity, sincerity,

8 Sound speech, that cannot be condemned;
that he that is of the contrary part may be
ashamed, having no evil thing to say of you.

9 Exhort servants to be obedient unto their
own masters, and to please them well in all
things; not answering again;

10 Not purloining, but showing all good
fidelity; that they may adorn the doctrine of
God our Saviour in all things.

11 For the grace of God that bringeth
salvation hath appeared to all men,

12 Teaching us that, denying ungodliness
and worldly lusts, we should live soberly,
righteously, and godly, in this present
world;

13 Looking for that blessed hope, and the
glorious appearing of the great God and our
Saviour Jesus Christ;

14 Who gave himself for us, that he might
redeem us from all iniquity, and purify unto

himself a peculiar people, zealous of good
works.

15 These things speak, and exhort, and
rebuke with all authority. Let no man despise
thee.

Be Careful to Maintain Good Works

3 Put them in mind to be subject to principalities and powers, to obey magistrates,
to be ready to every good work,

2 To speak evil of no man, to be no
brawlers, but gentle, showing all meekness
unto all men.

3 For we ourselves also were sometime
foolish, disobedient, deceived, serving divers
lusts and pleasures, living in malice and envy,
hateful, and hating one another.

4 But after that the kindness and love of
God our Saviour toward man appeared,

5 Not by works of righteousness which we
have done, but according to his mercy he
saved us, by the washing of regeneration, and
renewing of the Holy Ghost;

6 Which he shed on us abundantly through
Jesus Christ our Saviour;

7 That being justified by his grace, we
should be made heirs according to the hope
of eternal life.

8 This is a faithful saying, and these things
I will that thou affirm constantly, that they
which have believed in God might be careful
to maintain good works. These things are
good and profitable unto men.

9 But avoid foolish questions, and gene-

alogies, and contentions, and strivings about the law; for they are unprofitable and vain.

10 A man that is a heretic, after the first and second admonition, reject;

11 Knowing that he that is such is subverted, and sinneth, being condemned of himself.

Personal Instructions

12 When I shall send Ar'temas unto thee, or Tych'icus, be diligent to come unto me to Nicop'olis: for I have determined there to winter.

13 Bring Zenas the lawyer and Apol'los on their journey diligently, that nothing be wanting unto them.

14 And let ours also learn to maintain good works for necessary uses, that they be not unfruitful.

Benediction

15 All that are with me salute thee. Greet them that love us in the faith. Grace be with you all. Amen.

THE EPISTLE OF PAUL TO
PHILEMON

Salutation

PAUL, a prisoner of Jesus Christ, and Timothy our brother, Unto Phile'mon our dearly beloved, and fellow laborer,

2 And to our beloved Ap'phi-a, and Archip'pus our fellow soldier, and to the church in thy house:

3 Grace to you, and peace, from God our Father and the Lord Jesus Christ.

Philemon's Love and Faith

4 I thank my God, making mention of thee always in my prayers,

5 Hearing of thy love and faith, which thou hast toward the Lord Jesus, and toward all saints;

6 That the communication of thy faith may become effectual by the acknowledging of every good thing which is in you in Christ Jesus.

7 For we have great joy and consolation in thy love, because the bowels of the saints are refreshed by thee, brother.

Paul Pleads for Onesimus

8 Wherefore, though I might be much bold in Christ to enjoin thee that which is convenient,

9 Yet for love's sake I rather beseech thee, being such a one as Paul the aged, and now also a prisoner of Jesus Christ.

10 I beseech thee for my son Ones'imus, whom I have begotten in my bonds:

11 Which in time past was to thee unprofitable, but now profitable to thee and to me:

12 Whom I have sent again: thou therefore receive him, that is, mine own bowels:

13 Whom I would have retained with me, that in thy stead he might have ministered unto me in the bonds of the gospel:

14 But without thy mind would I do nothing; that thy benefit should not be as it were of necessity, but willingly.

15 For perhaps he therefore departed for a season, that thou shouldest receive him for ever;

16 Not now as a servant, but above a servant, a brother beloved, specially to me, but how much more unto thee, both in the flesh, and in the Lord?

17 If thou count me therefore a partner, receive him as myself.

18 If he hath wronged thee, or oweth thee aught, put that on mine account;

19 I Paul have written it with mine own hand, I will repay it: albeit I do not say to thee how thou owest unto me even thine own self besides.

20 Yea, brother, let me have joy of thee in the Lord: refresh my bowels in the Lord.

21 Having confidence in thy obedience I wrote unto thee, knowing that thou wilt also do more than I say.

22 But withal prepare me also a lodging:

for I trust that through your prayers I shall be given unto you.

Final Greetings

23 There salute thee Ep'aphras, my fellow prisoner in Christ Jesus;

24 Mark, Aristar'chus, Demas, Luke, my fellow laborers.

25 The grace of our Lord Jesus Christ be with your spirit. Amen.

THE EPISTLE OF PAUL THE APOSTLE TO THE

HEBREWS

God Has Spoken by His Son

1 God, who at sundry times and in divers manners spake in time past unto the fathers by the prophets,

2 Hath in these last days spoken unto us by his Son, whom he hath appointed heir of all things, by whom also he made the worlds;

3 Who being the brightness of his glory, and the express image of his person, and upholding all things by the word of his power, when he had by himself purged our sins, sat down on the right hand of the Majesty on high;

4 Being made so much better than the angels, as he hath by inheritance obtained a more excellent name than they.

The Son Superior to Angels

5 For unto which of the angels said he at any time, Thou art my Son, this day have I begotten thee? And again, I will be to him a Father, and he shall be to me a Son?

6 And again, when he bringeth in the first-begotten into the world, he saith, And let all the angels of God worship him.

7 And of the angels he saith, Who maketh his angels spirits, and his ministers a flame of fire.

8 But unto the Son he saith, Thy throne, O God, is for ever and ever: a sceptre of righteousness is the sceptre of thy kingdom.

9 Thou hast loved righteousness, and hated iniquity; therefore God, even thy God, hath anointed thee with the oil of gladness above thy fellows.

10 And, Thou, Lord, in the beginning hast laid the foundation of the earth; and the heavens are the works of thine hands.

11 They shall perish, but thou remainest: and they all shall wax old as doth a garment;

12 And as a vesture shalt thou fold them up, and they shall be changed: but thou art the same, and thy years shall not fail.

13 But to which of the angels said he at any time, Sit on my right hand, until I make thine enemies thy footstool?

14 Are they not all ministering spirits, sent forth to minister for them who shall be heirs of salvation?

So Great Salvation

2 Therefore we ought to give the more earnest heed to the things which we have heard, lest at any time we should let them slip.

2 For if the word spoken by angels was steadfast, and every transgression and disobedience received a just recompense of reward;

3 How shall we escape, if we neglect so great salvation; which at the first began to be spoken by the Lord, and was confirmed unto us by them that heard him;

4 God also bearing them witness, both with signs and wonders, and with divers miracles, and gifts of the Holy Ghost, according to his own will?

The Captain of Salvation Is Made Perfect through Suffering

5 For unto the angels hath he not put in subjection the world to come, whereof we speak.

6 But one in a certain place testified, saying, What is man, that thou art mindful of him? or the son of man, that thou visitest him?

7 Thou madest him a little lower than the angels; thou crownedst him with glory and honor, and didst set him over the works of thy hands:

8 Thou hast put all things in subjection under his feet. For in that he put all in subjection under him, he left nothing that is not

put under him. But now we see not yet all
things put under him.

9 But we see Jesus, who was made a little
lower than the angels for the suffering of
death, crowned with glory and honor; that he
by the grace of God should taste death for
every man.

10 For it became him, for whom are all
things, and by whom are all things, in bringing many sons unto glory, to make the captain
of their salvation perfect through sufferings.

11 For both he that sanctifieth and they
who are sanctified are all of one: for which
cause he is not ashamed to call them brethren,

12 Saying, I will declare thy name unto my
brethren, in the midst of the church will I
sing praise unto thee.

13 And again, I will put my trust in him.
And again, Behold I and the children which
God hath given me.

14 Forasmuch then as the children are partakers of flesh and blood, he also himself likewise took part of the same; that through death
he might destroy him that had the power of
death, that is, the devil;

15 And deliver them, who through fear of
death were all their lifetime subject to bondage.

16 For verily he took not on him the nature of angels; but he took on him the seed
of Abraham.

17 Wherefore in all things it behooved him
to be made like unto his brethren, that he
might be a merciful and faithful high priest in

things pertaining to God, to make reconciliation for the sins of the people.

18 For in that he himself hath suffered being tempted, he is able to succor them that are tempted.

Christy Superior to Moses

3 Wherefore, holy brethren, partakers of the heavenly calling, consider the Apostle and High Priest of our profession, Christ Jesus;

2 Who was faithful to him that appointed him, as also Moses was faithful in all his house.

3 For this man was counted worthy of more glory than Moses, inasmuch as he who hath builded the house hath more honor than the house.

4 For every house is builded by some man; but he that built all things is God.

5 And Moses verily was faithful in all his house as a servant, for a testimony of those things which were to be spoken after;

6 But Christ as a son over his own house; whose house are we, if we hold fast the confidence and the rejoicing of the hope firm unto the end.

A Rest for the People of God

7 Wherefore as the Holy Ghost saith, Today if ye will hear his voice,

8 Harden not your hearts, as in the provocation, in the day of temptation in the wilderness:

9 When your fathers tempted me, proved
me, and saw my works forty years.

10 Wherefore I was grieved with that
generation, and said, They do always err in
their heart; and they have not known my
ways.

11 So I sware in my wrath, They shall not
enter into my rest.

12 Take heed, brethren, lest there be in any
of you an evil heart of unbelief, in departing
from the living God.

13 But exhort one another daily, while it is
called To-day; lest any of you be hardened
through the deceitfulness of sin.

14 For we are made partakers of Christ, if
we hold the beginning of our confidence steadfast unto the end;

15 While it is said, To-day if ye will hear
his voice, harden not your hearts, as in the
provocation.

16 For some, when they had heard, did
provoke: howbeit not all that came out of
Egypt by Moses.

17 But with whom was he grieved forty
years? was it not with them that had sinned,
whose carcasses fell in the wilderness?

18 And to whom sware he that they should
not enter into his rest, but to them that believed not?

19 So we see that they could not enter in
because of unbelief.

4 Let us therefore fear, lest, a promise
being left us of entering into his rest,
any of you should seem to come short of it.

2 For unto us was the gospel preached, as well as unto them: but the word preached did not profit them, not being mixed with faith in them that heard it.

3 For we which have believed do enter into rest, as he said, As I have sworn in my wrath, if they shall enter into my rest: although the works were finished from the foundation of the world.

4 For he spake in a certain place of the seventh day on this wise, And God did rest the seventh day from all his works.

5 And in this place again, If they shall enter into my rest.

6 Seeing therefore it remaineth that some must enter therein, and they to whom it was first preached entered not in because of unbelief:

7 Again, he limiteth a certain day, saying in David, Today, after so long a time; as it is said, Today if ye will hear his voice, harden not your hearts.

8 For if Jesus had given them rest, then would he not afterward have spoken of another day.

9 There remaineth therefore a rest to the people of God.

10 For he that is entered into his rest, he also hath ceased from his own works, as God did from his.

11 Let us labor therefore to enter into that rest, lest any man fall after the same example of unbelief.

12 For the word of God is quick, and

powerful, and sharper than any two-edged sword, piercing even to the dividing asunder of soul and spirit, and of the joints and marrow, and is a discerner of the thoughts and intents of the heart.

13 Neither is there any creature that is not manifest in his sight: but all things are naked and opened unto the eyes of him with whom we have to do.

(3056)

Jesus the Great High Priest

14 Seeing then that we have a great high priest, that is passed into the heavens, Jesus the Son of God, let us hold fast our profession.

15 For we have not a high priest which cannot be touched with the feeling of our infirmities; but was in all points tempted like as we are, yet without sin.

16 Let us therefore come boldly unto the throne of grace, that we may obtain mercy, and find grace to help in time of need.

5 For every high priest taken from among men is ordained for men in things pertaining to God, that he may offer both gifts and sacrifices for sins:

2 Who can have compassion on the ignorant, and on them that are out of the way; for that he himself also is compassed with infirmity.

3 And by reason hereof he ought, as for the people, so also for himself, to offer for sins.

4 And no man taketh this honor unto himself, but he that is called of God, as was Aaron.

2

5 So also Christ glorified not himself to be made a high priest; but he that said unto him, Thou art my Son, today have I begotten thee.

6 As he saith also in another place, Thou art a priest for ever after the order of Melchiz′edek.

7 Who in the days of his flesh, when he had offered up prayers and supplications with strong crying and tears unto him that was able to save him from death, and was heard in that he feared;

8 Though he were a Son, yet learned he obedience by the things which he suffered;

9 And being made perfect, he became the author of eternal salvation unto all them that obey him;

10 Called of God a high priest after the order of Melchiz′edek.

The Danger of Slothfulness and Apostasy

11 Of whom we have many things to say, and hard to be uttered, seeing ye are dull of hearing.

12 For when for the time ye ought to be teachers, ye have need that one teach you again which be the first principles of the oracles of God; and are become such as have need of milk, and not of strong meat.

13 For every one that useth milk is unskilful in the word of righteousness: for he is a babe.

14 But strong meat belongeth to them that are of full age, even those who by reason of use have their senses exercised to discern both good and evil.

6 Therefore leaving the principles of the doctrine of Christ, let us go on unto perfection; not laying again the foundation of repentance from dead works, and of faith toward God,

2 Of the doctrine of baptisms, and of laying on of hands, and of resurrection of the dead, and of eternal judgment.

3 And this will we do, if God permit.

4 For it is impossible for those who were once enlightened, and have tasted of the heavenly gift, and were made partakers of the Holy Ghost,

5 And have tasted the good word of God, and the powers of the world to come,

6 If they shall fall away, to renew them again unto repentance; seeing they crucify to themselves the Son of God afresh, and put him to an open shame.

7 For the earth which drinketh in the rain that cometh oft upon it, and bringeth forth herbs meet for them by whom it is dressed, receiveth blessing from God:

8 But that which beareth thorns and briers is rejected, and is nigh unto cursing; whose end is to be burned.

9 But, beloved, we are persuaded better things of you, and things that accompany salvation, though we thus speak.

10 For God is not unrighteous to forget your work and labor of love, which ye have showed toward his name, in that ye have ministered to the saints, and do minister.

11 And we desire that every one of you do

show the same diligence to the full assurance of hope unto the end:

12 That ye be not slothful, but followers of them who through faith and patience inherit the promises.

13 For when God made promise to Abraham, because he could swear by no greater, he sware by himself,

14 Saying, Surely blessing I will bless thee, and multiplying I will multiply thee.

15 And so, after he had patiently endured, he obtained the promise.

16 For men verily swear by the greater: and an oath for confirmation is to them an end of all strife.

17 Wherein God, willing more abundantly to show unto the heirs of promise the immutability of his counsel, confirmed it by an oath:

18 That by two immutable things, in which it was impossible for God to lie, we might have a strong consolation, who have fled for refuge to lay hold upon the hope set before us:

19 Which hope we have as an anchor of the soul, both sure and steadfast, and which entereth into that within the veil;

20 Whither the forerunner is for us entered, even Jesus, made a high priest for ever after the order of Melchiz′edek.

The Priestly Order of Melchizedek

7 For this Melchiz′edek, king of Salem, priest of the most high God, who met

Abraham returning from the slaughter of the kings, and blessed him;

2 To whom also Abraham gave a tenth part of all; first being by interpretation King of righteousness, and after that also King of Salem, which is, King of peace;

3 Without father, without mother, without descent, having neither beginning of days, nor end of life; but made like unto the Son of God; abideth a priest continually.

4 Now consider how great this man was, unto whom even the patriarch Abraham gave the tenth of the spoils.

5 And verily they that are of the sons of Levi, who receive the office of the priesthood, have a commandment to take tithes of the people according to the law, that is, of their brethren, though they come out of the loins of Abraham:

6 But he whose descent is not counted from them received tithes of Abraham, and blessed him that had the promises.

7 And without all contradiction the less is blessed of the better.

8 And here men that die receive tithes; but there he receiveth them, of whom it is witnessed that he liveth.

9 And as I may so say, Levi also, who receiveth tithes, paid tithes in Abraham.

10 For he was yet in the loins of his father, when Melchiz'edek met him.

11 If therefore perfection were by the Levitical priesthood, (for under it the people received the law,) what further need was there

that another priest should rise after the order
of Melchiz'edek, and not be called after the
order of Aaron?

12 For the priesthood being changed, there
is made of necessity a change also of the law.

13 For he of whom these things are spoken
pertaineth to another tribe, of which no man
gave attendance at the altar.

14 For it is evident that our Lord sprang
out of Judah; of which tribe Moses spake
nothing concerning priesthood.

15 And it is yet far more evident: for that
after the similitude of Melchiz'edek there
ariseth another priest,

16 Who is made, not after the law of a
carnal commandment, but after the power of
an endless life.

17 For he testifieth, Thou art a priest for
ever after the order of Melchiz'edek.

18 For there is verily a disannulling of the
commandment going before for the weakness
and unprofitableness thereof.

19 For the law made nothing perfect, but
the bringing in of a better hope did; by the
which we draw nigh unto God.

20 And inasmuch as not without an oath he
was made priest:

21 (For those priests were made without an
oath; but this with an oath by him that said
unto him, The Lord sware and will not
repent, Thou art a priest for ever after the
order of Melchiz'edek:)

22 By so much was Jesus made a surety of
a better testament.

23 And they truly were many priests, because they were not suffered to continue by reason of death:

24 But this man, because he continueth ever, hath an unchangeable priesthood.

25 Wherefore he is able also to save them to the uttermost that come unto God by him, seeing he ever liveth to make intercession for them.

26 For such a high priest became us, who is holy, harmless, undefiled, separate from sinners, and made higher than the heavens;

27 Who needeth not daily, as those high priests, to offer up sacrifice, first for his own sins, and then for the people's: for this he did once, when he offered up himself.

28 For the law maketh men high priests which have infirmity; but the word of the oath, which was since the law, maketh the Son, who is consecrated for evermore.

The Mediator of a New Covenant

8 Now of the things which we have spoken this is the sum: We have such a high priest, who is set on the right hand of the throne of the Majesty in the heavens;

2 A minister of the sanctuary, and of the true tabernacle, which the Lord pitched, and not man.

3 For every high priest is ordained to offer gifts and sacrifices: wherefore it is of necessity that this man have somewhat also to offer.

4 For if he were on earth, he should not be a priest, seeing that there [1093] are priests that offer gifts [2409] according [5607] to the law: [2409] [4374]......

5 Who serve unto the [1435] example and shadow [3551] of heavenly [3000] things, as Moses [5262] was admonished [4639] of God [2032] when he was [2531] [3475] about [5537] to make the tabernacle: for, See, saith he, that [3195] thou make [2005] all things according [4633] to [3708] the [5346] pattern showed to thee in the mount. [5179] [1166] [4160]

6 But now hath [3735] he obtained a more excellent ministry, [3570] by [5177] how much also [5177] he [1313] is the mediator [3009] of a better [3745] covenant, which was established [3316] upon better [2909] promises. [1242] [3549]... [2909] [1860]

7 For if that first covenant had been faultless, [1242] then should no place [2] have been sought [273] for the second. [5117] [2212].................

8 For finding [1208] fault with them, he saith, Behold, the [3201] days come, saith the Lord, when I [2400] will make [2250] a new [2064] covenant with [2962] the house of Israel [4931] and with [2537] the house [1242] of Judah: [3624]

9 Not [2474] according to the [3624] covenant [2455] that I made with their fathers, in the [1242] day when I took [4160] them by the hand [3962] to lead them [2250] out [1949] of the [1949] land of Egypt; [1949] because [5495] they [1806] continued not [1806] in my [1093] covenant, [125] and I regarded them [1696] not, saith the Lord. [1242] [272] [272]

10 For this [2962] is the covenant that I will make with the house of Israel [1242] after those days, saith the Lord; [3624] I will put [2474] my laws into their mind, [2250] and write [2962] them in [1325] their hearts: [3551] and I will [1271] be to them [1924] a God, [1924] and they [2588] shall be to me a people: [2316]

11 And they shall not teach [2992] every man his neighbor, [3364] and [1321] every [1538] man his brother, saying, [4139] [1538]...... [80]

Know[1097] the Lord[2962]: for all shall[1492] know me, from the least[3398] to the greatest[3173].

12 For I will be merciful[2436] to their unrighteousness, and their sins[266] and their iniquities[93] will I remember[3415] no more.[458]

13 In[3415] that[3415] he[3364] saith,[2089] A new[2537] covenant, he hath[3822] made the first old. Now that which decayeth[3822] and waxeth[3822] old is ready[1451] to vanish[1095] away.

9 Then verily the first convenant had also ordinances of divine service,[2999] and a worldly[2886] sanctuary.[1345]

2 For[39] there was a tabernacle made;[4633] the first, wherein was the candlestick,[2680] and the table,[5132] and the showbread;[4286][740] which[3087] is called the sanctuary.

3 And[39] after the second veil,[1208] the tabernacle which is called the holiest[2665] of all;[4633]

4 Which had the golden[39] censer,[5552] and the ark[2369] of the covenant overlaid round about[2787] with gold,[5553] wherein[1242][24] was[4028] the golden[3840] pot[5552] that[4713] had manna,[3131] and Aaron's[2] rod[4464] that[985] budded, and the tables[4109] of the covenant;[1242]

5 And over[5231] it the cherubim[5502] of glory[1391] shadowing the mercy[2435] seat;[2683] of which we cannot now speak particularly.[3568]

6 Now[3313] when these things were thus[2680] ordained, the priests[2680] went always into[2680] the first tabernacle,[4633] accomplishing[2409][2005] the[1524] service[1275][2999] of God.[1524]

7 But into the second went the high[749] priest alone once every year,[1208] not without[3441] blood,[530][129] which he offered[1763] for himself,[5565] and for[129] the errors[4374] of the people;[1438]

8 The[51] Holy Ghost[2992] this signifying,[40] that the[1213]

way into the holiest of all was not yet made manifest, while as the first tabernacle was yet standing:

9 Which was a figure for the time then present, in which were offered both gifts and sacrifices, that could not make him that did the service perfect, as pertaining to the conscience;

10 Which stood only in meats and drinks, and divers washings, and carnal ordinances, imposed on them until the time of reformation.

11 But Christ being come a high priest of good things to come, by a greater and more perfect tabernacle, not made with hands, that is to say, not of this building;

12 Neither by the blood of goats and calves, but by his own blood he entered in once into the holy place, having obtained eternal redemption for us.

13 For if the blood of bulls and of goats, and the ashes of a heifer sprinkling the unclean, sanctifieth to the purifying of the flesh;

14 How much more shall the blood of Christ, who through the eternal Spirit offered himself without spot to God, purge your conscience from dead works to serve the living God?

15 And for this cause he is the mediator of the new testament, that by means of death, for the redemption of the transgressions that were under the first testament, they which are called might receive the promise of eternal inheritance.

16 For where a testament is, there must also of necessity be the death of the testator.

17 For a testament is of force after men are dead: otherwise it is of no strength at all while the testator liveth.

18 Whereupon neither the first testament was dedicated without blood.

19 For when Moses had spoken every precept to all the people according to the law, he took the blood of calves and of goats, with water, and scarlet wool, and hyssop, and sprinkled both the book and all the people,

20 Saying, This is the blood of the testament which God hath enjoined unto you.

21 Moreover he sprinkled likewise with blood both the tabernacle, and all the vessels of the ministry.

22 And almost all things are by the law purged with blood; and without shedding of blood is no remission.

Sin Put Away by Christ's Sacrifice

23 It was therefore necessary that the patterns of things in the heavens should be purified with these; but the heavenly things themselves with better sacrifices than these.

24 For Christ is not entered into the holy places made with hands, which are the figures of the true; but into heaven itself, now to appear in the presence of God for us:

25 Nor yet that he should offer himself often, as the high priest entereth into the holy place every year with blood of others;

26 For then must he often have suffered

since the foundation of the world: but now once in the end of the world hath he appeared to put away sin by the sacrifice of himself.

27 And as it is appointed unto men once to die, but after this the judgment:

28 So Christ was once offered to bear the sins of many; and unto them that look for him shall he appear the second time without sin unto salvation.

10 For the law having a shadow of good things to come, and not the very image of the things, can never with those sacrifices, which they offered year by year continually, make the comers thereunto perfect.

2 For then would they not have ceased to be offered? because that the worshippers once purged should have had no more conscience of sins.

3 But in those sacrifices there is a remembrance again made of sins every year.

4 For it is not possible that the blood of bulls and of goats should take away sins.

5 Wherefore, when he cometh into the world, he saith, Sacrifice and offering thou wouldest not, but a body hast thou prepared me:

6 In burnt offerings and sacrifices for sin thou hast had no pleasure.

7 Then said I, Lo, I come (in the volume of the book it is written of me) to do thy will, O God.

8 Above when he said, Sacrifice and offering and burnt offerings and offering for sin

thou wouldest not, neither hadst pleasure therein; which are offered by the law;

9 Then said he, Lo, I come to do thy will, O God. He taketh away the first, that he may establish the second.

10 By the which will we are sanctified through the offering of the body of Jesus Christ once for all.

11 And every priest standeth daily ministering and offering oftentimes the same sacrifices, which can never take away sins:

12 But this man, after he had offered one sacrifice for sins for ever, sat down on the right hand of God;

13 From henceforth expecting till his enemies be made his footstool.

14 For by one offering he hath perfected for ever them that are sanctified.

15 Whereof the Holy Ghost also is a witness to us: for after that he had said before,

16 This is the covenant that I will make with them after those days, saith the Lord; I will put my laws into their hearts, and in their minds will I write them;

17 And their sins and iniquities will I remember no more.

18 Now where remission of these is, there is no more offering for sin.

Let Us Draw Near and Hold Fast

19 Having therefore, brethren, boldness to enter into the holiest by the blood of Jesus,

20 By a new and living way, which he hath

consecrated for us, through the veil, that is to[2665][5123]........ say,[1457] his flesh;

[5123]21 And having[4561] a high priest over the house of God;[3173][2409] [3624]

[2316]22 Let us draw near with a true heart in full assurance of faith, having[228] our[2588] hearts[4136.] sprinkled from an[4102] evil conscience, and[2588] our bodies[4472] washed with pure[4190-4191] water.[4893]

[4983]23 Let[3068] us hold fast the[2513] profession[5204] of our faith[2722] without wavering;[2722]...... for he[3671] is faithful that[1680] promised;[186]............ [4103] [1861]

[1861]24 And let us consider one another to pro-[2657] [2657] [240]..........[3948]..... voke unto love[3948]. and to good works:[26] [2570][2041]

25 Not forsaking the assembling of ourselves together,[1459] as the manner of[1997] some is; but[1438] ex-horting[1997] one[2531] another:[1485] and so[5100] much the more,[3870] as ye see[5118]..... the day[3123]...... approaching.[3745][991] [2250] [1448]

26 For if we sin wilfully after that we have received the[264] knowledge[1596] of the truth, there re-[2983] maineth[2983] no[1922] more sacrifice[225] for sins,[620]

[620]27 But a certain fearful looking for of judg-[2089] [2378] ment and fiery indignation, which shall devour[5100]. [5398.] [1561] [2920] the[2920] adversaries.[4442] [2205] [3195] [2068]

[5227]28 He that despised Moses' law died with-[5100] out mercy under[114]........ two or three[3475] witnesses:[3551][599] [5565]

[5565][3628]29 Of how much sorer punishment, suppose[3144] ye, shall he be thought worthy, who hath[4214] [5501] [5098] [1380] trodden[515] under foot[.....515]the Son of God, and[2662]... hath[2662] counted the blood[5207] of the covenant,[2316] wherewith he was sanctified,[2233].........[129] an unholy[1242] thing, and hath done despite[37] unto the[2839] Spirit of grace?[1796]............................ [4151]

[5485]30 For we know him that hath said,[1492] Vengeance belongeth unto me, I will[2036]..... recom-[1557] [467]........

pense, saith the Lord. And again, The Lord shall judge his people.

31 It is a fearful thing to fall into the hands of the living God.

32 But call to remembrance the former days, in which, after ye were illuminated, ye endured a great fight of afflictions;

33 Partly, whilst ye were made a gazingstock both by reproaches and afflictions; and partly, whilst ye became companions of them that were so used.

34 For ye had compassion of me in my bonds, and took joyfully the spoiling of your goods, knowing in yourselves that ye have in heaven a better and an enduring substance.

35 Cast not away therefore your confidence, which hath great recompense of reward.

36 For ye have need of patience, that, after ye have done the will of God, ye might receive the promise.

37 For yet a little while, and he that shall come will come, and will not tarry.

38 Now the just shall live by faith: but if any man draw back, my soul shall have no pleasure in him.

39 But we are not of them who draw back unto perdition; but of them that believe to the saving of the soul.

Faith

11 Now faith is the substance of things hoped for, the evidence of things not seen.

2 For by it the elders obtained a good report.

3 Through faith we understand that the worlds were framed by the word of God, so that things which are seen were not made of things which do appear.

4 By faith Abel offered unto God a more excellent sacrifice than Cain, by which he obtained witness that he was righteous, God testifying of his gifts: and by it he being dead yet speaketh.

5 By faith Enoch was translated that he should not see death; and was not found, because God had translated him: for before his translation he had this testimony, that he pleased God.

6 But without faith it is impossible to please him: for he that cometh to God must believe that he is, and that he is a rewarder of them that diligently seek him.

7 By faith Noah, being warned of God of things not seen as yet, moved with fear, prepared an ark to the saving of his house; by the which he condemned the world, and became heir of the righteousness which is by faith.

8 By faith Abraham, when he was called to go out into a place which he should after receive for an inheritance, obeyed; and he went out, not knowing whither he went.

9 By faith he sojourned in the land of promise, as in a strange country, dwelling in tabernacles with Isaac and Jacob, the heirs with him of the same promise:

10 For he looked for a city which hath foundations, whose builder and maker is God.

11 Through faith also Sarah herself received strength to conceive seed, and was delivered of a child when she was past age, because she judged him faithful who had promised......

12 Therefore sprang there even of one, and him as good as dead, so many as the stars of the sky in multitude, and as the sand which is by the seashore innumerable.

13 These all died in faith, not having received the promises, but having seen them afar off, and were persuaded of them, and embraced them, and confessed that they were strangers and pilgrims on the earth.

14 For they that say such things declare plainly that they seek a country.

15 And truly, if they had been mindful of that country from whence they came out, they might have had opportunity to have returned.

16 But now they desire a better country, that is, a heavenly: wherefore God is not ashamed to be called their God: for he hath prepared for them a city.

17 By faith Abraham, when he was tried, offered up Isaac: and he that had received the promises offered up his only begotten son,

18 Of whom it was said, That in Isaac shall thy seed be called:

19 Accounting that God was able to raise him up, even from the dead; from whence also he received him in a figure.

20 By faith Isaac blessed Jacob and Esau concerning things to come.

21 By faith Jacob, when he was a dying,

blessed both the sons of Joseph; and worshipped, leaning upon the top of his staff.

22 By faith Joseph, when he died, made
mention of the departing of the children of
Israel; and gave commandment concerning his
bones.

23 By faith Moses, when he was born, was
hid three months of his parents, because they
saw he was a proper child; and they were not
afraid of the king's commandment.

24 By faith Moses, when he was come to
years, refused to be called the son of Pharaoh's
daughter;

25 Choosing rather to suffer affliction with
the people of God, than to enjoy the pleasures
of sin for a season;

26 Esteeming the reproach of Christ greater
riches than the treasures in Egypt: for he
had respect unto the recompense of the reward.

27 By faith he forsook Egypt, not fearing
the wrath of the king: for he endured, as seeing him who is invisible.

28 Through faith he kept the passover, and
the sprinkling of blood, lest he that destroyed
the firstborn should touch them.

29 By faith they passed through the Red
sea as by dry land: which the Egyptians
assaying to do were drowned.

30 By faith the walls of Jericho fell down,
after they were compassed about seven days.

31 By faith the harlot Rahab perished not
with them that believed not, when she had
received the spies with peace.

32 And what shall I more say? for the time would fail me to tell of Gideon, and of Barak, and of Samson, and of Jephthah; of David also, and Samuel, and of the prophets:

33 Who through faith subdued kingdoms, wrought righteousness, obtained promises, stopped the mouths of lions,

34 Quenched the violence of fire, escaped the edge of the sword, out of weakness were made strong, waxed valiant in fight, turned to flight the armies of the aliens.

35 Women received their dead raised to life again: and others were tortured, not accepting deliverance; that they might obtain a better resurrection:

36 And others had trials of cruel mockings and scourgings, yea, moreover of bonds and imprisonment:

37 They were stoned, they were sawn asunder, were tempted, were slain with the sword: they wandered about in sheepskins and goatskins; being destitute, afflicted, tormented;

38 Of whom the world was not worthy: they wandered in deserts, and in mountains, and in dens and caves of the earth.

39 And these all, having obtained a good report through faith, received not the promise:

40 God having provided some better thing for us, that they without us should not be made perfect.

The Chastening of the Lord

12 Wherefore, seeing we also are compassed about with so great a cloud of witnesses,

let us lay aside every weight, and the sin
which doth so easily beset us, and let us run
with patience the race that is set before us,

2 Looking unto Jesus the author and finisher
of our faith; who for the joy that was set before him endured the cross, despising the
shame, and is set down at the right hand of
the throne of God.

3 For consider him that endured such contradiction of sinners against himself, lest ye be
wearied and faint in your minds.

4 Ye have not yet resisted unto blood,
striving against sin.

5 And ye have forgotten the exhortation
which speaketh unto you as unto children,
My son, despise not thou the chastening of the
Lord, nor faint when thou art rebuked of him:

6 For whom the Lord loveth he chasteneth,
and scourgeth every son whom he receiveth.

7 If ye endure chastening, God dealeth with
you as with sons; for what son is he whom
the father chasteneth not?

8 But if ye be without chastisement, whereof
all are partakers, then are ye bastards, and
not sons.

9 Furthermore, we have had fathers of our
flesh which corrected us, and we gave them
reverence: shall we not much rather be in
subjection unto the Father of spirits, and live?

10 For they verily for a few days chastened
us after their own pleasure; but he for our
profit, that we might be partakers of his holiness.

11 Now no chastening for the present

seemeth to be joyous, but grievous: nevertheless, afterward it yieldeth the peaceable fruit of righteousness unto them which are exercised thereby. . . . .

Warning against Rejecting God's Grace

12 Wherefore lift up the hands which hang down, and the feeble knees; . . . .

13 And make straight paths for your feet, lest that which is lame be turned out of the way; but let it rather be healed. . . . .

14 Follow peace with all men, and holiness, without which no man shall see the Lord: . . . .

15 Looking diligently lest any man fail of the grace of God; lest any root of bitterness springing up trouble you, and thereby many be defiled;

16 Lest there be any fornicator, or profane person, as Esau, who for one morsel of meat sold his birthright.

17 For ye know how that afterward, when he would have inherited the blessing, he was rejected: for he found no place of repentance, though he sought it carefully with tears.

18 For ye are not come unto the mount that might be touched, and that burned with fire, ... nor unto blackness, and darkness, and tempest,

19 And the sound of a trumpet, and the voice of words; which voice they that heard entreated that the word should not be spoken to them any more: . . . .

20 (For they could not endure that which . . . .

was commanded, And if so much as a beast touch the mountain, it shall be stoned, or thrust through with a dart:

21 And so terrible was the sight, that Moses said, I exceedingly fear and quake:)

22 But ye are come unto mount Zion, and unto the city of the living God, the heavenly Jerusalem, and to an innumerable company of angels,

23 To the general assembly and church of the firstborn, which are written in heaven, and to God the Judge of all, and to the spirits of just men made perfect,

24 And to Jesus the mediator of the new covenant, and to the blood of sprinkling, that speaketh better things than that of Abel.

25 See that ye refuse not him that speaketh: for if they escaped not who refused him that spake on earth, much more shall not we escape, if we turn away from him that speaketh from heaven:

26 Whose voice then shook the earth: but now he hath promised, saying, Yet once more I shake not the earth only, but also heaven.

27 And this word, Yet once more, signifieth the removing of those things that are shaken, as of things that are made, that those things which cannot be shaken may remain.

28 Wherefore we receiving a kingdom which cannot be moved, let us have grace, whereby we may serve God acceptably with reverence and godly fear:

29 For our God is a consuming fire.

Service Well-pleasing to God

13 Let brotherly love [3306] continue. 2 Be [5360] not [3306] forgetful to entertain strangers: for thereby [1950] some [1950] have [5100] entertained [2990] [5381] angels [32] unawares. [3579]

3 Remember [2990] them that are in bonds, as bound [3403] with them; and them [1198] which suffer adversity, [4887] as being yourselves also [2558] in the body. [2558] [5607]

4 Marriage [4983] is honorable in all, and the bed undefiled: [1062] but whoremongers [5093] and adulterers [2845] God [283] will judge. [3432] [4205]

5 Let your [2316] conversation [2919] be without covetousness; and be content with such [5158] things as ye [866] have: for he hath said, [714] I will never [447] leave [3364] thee, [3918] nor [3918] forsake [2046] thee. [447]

6 So that [1459] we may boldly say, The Lord is my helper, and I will [2292] not [5399] fear what man [2962] shall do [998] unto me. [4160] [5399] [5101]

7 Remember them which have the rule over [3421] you, who have spoken [2233] unto you the word of God: whose faith [2980] follow, considering the end [3056] of their conversation. [2316] [4102] [3401] [333] [1545]

8 Jesus Christ [391] the same yesterday, and today, [2424] [5547] [5504] and for ever. [4594]

9 Be not carried about [165] with divers [4064] and strange doctrines: [4064] for it is a good thing [4164] that the heart be established [3581] [1322] with grace; [2570] not with meats, [2588] which have [950] not profited them [5485] that have been occupied [1033] therein. [5623] [5623] [4043]

10 We have an altar, [4043] whereof they have no right to eat which serve [2379] the tabernacle.

11 For the bodies of those beasts, [1849] [5315] [3000] [4633] whose blood is brought [4983] into the sanctuary [2226] by the [129] [39]

high priest for sin, are burned without the
camp.

12 Wherefore Jesus also, that he might
sanctify the people with his own blood, suffered without the gate.

13 Let us go forth therefore unto him without the camp, bearing his reproach.

14 For here have we no continuing city, but
we seek one to come.

15 By him therefore let us offer the sacrifice
of praise to God continually, that is, the fruit
of our lips, giving thanks to his name.

16 But to do good and to communicate
forget not: for with such sacrifices God is
well pleased.

17 Obey them that have the rule over you,
and submit yourselves: for they watch for your
souls, as they that must give account, that they
may do it with joy, and not with grief: for
that is unprofitable for you.

18 Pray for us: for we trust we have a good
conscience, in all things willing to live honestly.

19 But I beseech you the rather to do this,
that I may be restored to you the sooner.

Benediction and Final Greetings

20 Now the God of peace, that brought
again from the dead our Lord Jesus, that great
shepherd of the sheep, through the blood of
the everlasting covenant,

21 Make you perfect in every good work
to do his will, working in you that which
is well-pleasing in his sight, through Jesus

Christ; to whom be glory for ever and ever.
5547   1391   165   165
Amen.
281
22 And I beseech you, brethren, suffer the
word of exhortation: for I have written a
3056   3874   3870   80   430.
letter unto you in few words. 1989............
1989
23 Know ye that our brother Timothy is set
1097   1024
at liberty; with whom, if he come shortly, I
630   80   5095   630.
will see you.
3700
24 Salute all them that have the rule over
you, and all the saints. They of Italy salute
782   2233   2482   782
you.
40

25 Grace be with you all. Amen.
5485   281

JAMES

Salutation

1 James, a servant of God and of the Lord Jesus Christ, To the twelve tribes which are scattered abroad, Greeting.

Faith and Humility

2 My brethren, count it all joy when ye fall into divers temptations;

3 Knowing this, that the trying of your faith worketh patience.

4 But let patience have her perfect work, that ye may be perfect and entire, wanting nothing.

5 If any of you lack wisdom, let him ask of God, that giveth to all men liberally, and upbraideth not; and it shall be given him.

6 But let him ask in faith, nothing wavering: for he that wavereth is like a wave of the sea driven with the wind and tossed.

7 For let not that man think that he shall receive any thing of the Lord.

8 A double-minded man is unstable in all his ways.

9 Let the brother of low degree rejoice in that he is exalted:

10 But the rich, in that he is made low: because as the flower of the grass he shall pass away.

11 For the sun is no sooner risen with a burning heat, but it withereth the grass, and the flower thereof falleth, and the grace of the

fashion of it perisheth: so also shall the rich man fade away in his ways.

Trial and Temptation

12 Blessed is the man that endureth temptation: for when he is tried, he shall receive the crown of life, which the Lord hath promised to them that love him.

13 Let no man say when he is tempted, I am tempted of God: for God cannot be tempted with evil, neither tempteth he any man:

14 But every man is tempted, when he is drawn away of his own lust, and enticed.

15 Then when lust hath conceived, it bringeth forth sin; and sin, when it is finished, bringeth forth death.

16 Do not err, my beloved brethren.

17 Every good gift and every perfect gift is from above, and cometh down from the Father of lights, with whom is no variableness, neither shadow of turning.

18 Of his own will begat he us with the word of truth, that we should be a kind of firstfruits of his creatures.

Hearing and Doing the Word

19 Wherefore, my beloved brethren, let every man be swift to hear, slow to speak, slow to wrath:

20 For the wrath of man worketh not the righteousness of God.

21 Wherefore lay apart all filthiness and superfluity of naughtiness, and receive with

meekness the engrafted word, which is able to
4240 1721 3056 1410......... 4982
save your souls.
4982 5590

22 But be ye doers of the word, and not
1096 4163 3056
hearers only, deceiving your own selves.
202 3440 3884 1438.....

23 For if any be a hearer of the word, and
1536 202 3056
not a doer, he is like unto a man beholding
4163 1503.. 435 2657
his natural face in a glass:
1078 4383 2072

24 For he beholdeth himself, and goeth his
2657 1438 565
way, and straightway forgetteth what manner
565 2112 1950 3697......
of man he was.
3697

25 But whoso looketh into the perfect law
3879 5046 3551
of liberty, and continueth therein, he being
1657 3887 1096
not a forgetful hearer, but a doer of the work,
1953 202 4163 2041
this man shall be blessed in his deed.

26 If any man among you seem to be re-
1488 5100..... 3107 1722 4162 1380 2357
ligious, and bridleth not his tongue, but deceiv-
2357 5468 1100 538
eth his own heart, this man's religion is vain.
538 2588 2356 3152

27 Pure religion and undefiled before God
2513 2356 283 2316
and the Father is this, To visit the fatherless
3962 1980.... 3737
and widows in their affliction, and to keep
5503 2347 5083.....
himself unspotted from the world.
1438 784 575 2889

Warning against Partiality

2 My brethren, have not the faith of our
80 4102
Lord Jesus Christ, the Lord of glory, with
2962 2424 5547 1391
respect of persons.
4382

2 For if there come unto your assembly a
1525 4864
man with a gold ring, in goodly apparel, and
435 5554..... 5554.... 2986 2066
there come in also a poor man in vile raiment;
1525..... 4434 4508 2066

3 And ye have respect to him that weareth
1914.....
the gay clothing, and say unto him, Sit thou
2986 2066 2036 2521
here in a good place; and say to the poor,
5602 2573 2036 4434
Stand thou there, or sit here under my foot-
2476 1563 2521 5602 5286
stool:
5286

4 Are ye not then partial in yourselves, and are become judges of evil thoughts?

5 Hearken, my beloved brethren, Hath not God chosen the poor of this world rich in faith, and heirs of the kingdom which he hath promised to them that love him?

6 But ye have despised the poor. Do not rich men oppress you, and draw you before the judgment seats?

7 Do not they blaspheme that worthy name by the which ye are called?

8 If ye fulfil the royal law according to the Scripture, Thou shalt love thy neighbor as thyself, ye do well:

9 But if ye have respect to persons, ye commit sin, and are convinced of the law as transgressors.

10 For whosoever shall keep the whole law, and yet offend in one point, he is guilty of all.

11 For he that said, Do not commit adultery, said also, Do not kill. Now if thou commit no adultery, yet if thou kill, thou art become a transgressor of the law.

12 So speak ye, and so do, as they that shall be judged by the law of liberty.

13 For he shall have judgment without mercy, that hath showed no mercy; and mercy rejoiceth against judgment.

Faith without Works Is Dead

14 What doth it profit, my brethren, though a man say he hath faith, and have not works? can faith save him?

15 If a brother or sister be naked, and
destitute of daily[80] food, [79] [5225] [1131]
[3007]
16 And one[2184] of you[5160] say unto them, Depart
[5100] [2036] [5217]
in peace, be ye warmed and filled; notwith-
[1515] [2328] [2328] [5526]
standing ye give them not those things which
[1325] [2006]
are needful to the body; what doth it profit?
[2006] [4983] [5101] [3786]
17 Even so faith, if it hath not works, is
[4102] [2041]
dead, being alone.
[3498] [1438]
18 Yea, a man may say, Thou hast faith,
[235] [5100] [2046] [4102]
and I have works: show me thy faith without
[2041] [1166] [4102] [1537]
thy works, and I will show thee my faith by
[2041] [1166]....... [4102]
my works.
[2041]
19 Thou believest that there is one God;
[4100] [1520] [2316]
thou doest well: the devils also believe, and
[4160] [2573] [1140] [4100]
tremble.
[5425]
20 But wilt thou know, O vain man, that
[2309] [1097] [5599] [2756] [444]
faith without works is dead?
[4102] [5565] [2041] [3498]
21 Was not Abraham our father justified by
[1344] [11] [3962] [1344]
works, when he had offered Isaac his son upon
[2041] [399] [399]........ [2464] [5207] [1909]
the altar?
[2379]
22 Seest thou how faith wrought with his
[991] [4102] [4903]
works, and by works was faith made perfect?
[2041] [2041] [5048] [4102] [5048]
23 And the Scripture was fulfilled which
[1124] [4137]
saith, Abraham believed God, and it was im-
[3004] [11] [4100] [2316] [3049]
puted unto him for righteousness: and he was
[3049] [1343]
called the Friend of God. [2564]
[2564] [5384] [2316]
24 Ye see then how that by works a man
[3708] [5106] [2041]
is justified, and not by faith only.
[1344] [4102] [3440]
25 Likewise also was not Rahab the harlot
[3668] [1344] [4460] [4204]
justified by works, when she had received the
[1344] [2041] [5264] [5264]
messengers, and had sent them out another
[32] [1544]...... [1544] [2087]
way?
[3598]
26 For as the body without the spirit is
[4983] [5565]
dead, so faith without works is dead also.
[3498] [4102] [5565] [2041] [3498]

The Tongue

3 My brethren, be not many masters, knowing that we shall receive the greater condemnation.

2 For in many things we offend all. If any man offend not in word, the same is a perfect man, and able also to bridle the whole body.

3 Behold, we put bits in the horses' mouths, that they may obey us; and we turn about their whole body.

4 Behold also the ships, which though they be so great, and are driven of fierce winds, yet are they turned about with a very small helm, whithersoever the governor listeth.

5 Even so the tongue is a little member, and boasteth great things. Behold, how great a matter a little fire kindleth!

6 And the tongue is a fire, a world of iniquity: so is the tongue among our members, that it defileth the whole body, and setteth on fire the course of nature; and it is set on fire of hell.

7 For every kind of beasts, and of birds, and of serpents, and of things in the sea, is tamed, and hath been tamed of mankind:

8 But the tongue can no man tame; it is an unruly evil, full of deadly poison.

9 Therewith bless we God, even the Father; and therewith curse we men, which are made after the similitude of God.

10 Out of the same mouth proceedeth blessing and cursing. My brethren, these things ought not so to be.

11 Doth a fountain send forth at the same place sweet water and bitter?

12 Can the fig tree, my brethren, bear olive berries? either a vine, figs? so can no fountain both yield salt water and fresh.

The Wisdom from Above

13 Who is a wise man and endued with knowledge among you? let him show out of a good conversation his works with meekness of wisdom.

14 But if ye have bitter envying and strife in your hearts, glory not, and lie not against the truth.

15 This wisdom descendeth not from above, but is earthly, sensual, devilish.

16 For where envying and strife is, there is confusion and every evil work.

17 But the wisdom that is from above is first pure, then peaceable, gentle, and easy to be entreated, full of mercy and good fruits, without partiality, and without hypoc-risy.

18 And the fruit of righteousness is sown in peace of them that make peace.

Friendship with the World

4 From whence come wars and fightings among you? come they not hence, even of your lusts that war in your members?

2 Ye lust, and have not: ye kill, and desire to have, and cannot obtain: ye fight and war, yet ye have not, because ye ask not.

3 Ye ask, and receive not, because ye ask

amiss, that ye may consume it upon your lusts.

4 Ye adulterers and adulteresses, know ye not that the friendship of the world is enmity with God? whosoever therefore will be a friend of the world is the enemy of God.

5 Do ye think that the Scripture saith in vain, The spirit that dwelleth in us lusteth to envy?

6 But he giveth more grace. Wherefore he saith, God resisteth the proud, but giveth grace unto the humble.

7 Submit yourselves therefore to God. Resist the devil, and he will flee from you.

8 Draw nigh to God, and he will draw nigh to you. Cleanse your hands, ye sinners; and purify your hearts, ye double-minded.

9 Be afflicted, and mourn, and weep: let your laughter be turned to mourning, and your joy to heaviness.

10 Humble yourselves in the sight of the Lord, and he shall lift you up.

Judging a Brother

11 Speak not evil one of another, brethren. He that speaketh evil of his brother, and judgeth his brother, speaketh evil of the law, and judgeth the law: but if thou judge the law, thou art not a doer of the law, but a judge.

12 There is one lawgiver, who is able to save and to destroy: who art thou that judgest another?

Boast Not of Tomorrow

13 Go to now, ye that say, Today or to-morrow we will go into such a city, and continue there a year, and buy and sell, and get gain:

14 Whereas ye know not what shall be on the morrow. For what is your life? It is even a vapor, that appeareth for a little time, and then vanisheth away.

15 For that ye ought to say, If the Lord will, we shall live, and do this, or that.

16 But now ye rejoice in your boastings: all such rejoicing is evil.

17 Therefore to him that knoweth to do good, and doeth it not, to him it is sin.

Warning to the Rich

5 Go to now, ye rich men, weep and howl for your miseries that shall come upon you.

2 Your riches are corrupted, and your garments are moth-eaten.

3 Your gold and silver is cankered; and the rust of them shall be a witness against you, and shall eat your flesh as it were fire. Ye have heaped treasure together for the last days.

4 Behold, the hire of the laborers who have reaped down your fields, which is of you kept back by fraud, crieth: and the cries of them which have reaped are entered into the ears of the Lord of Sab'a-oth.

5 Ye have lived in pleasure on the earth, and been wanton; ye have nourished your hearts, as in a day of slaughter.

6 Ye have condemned and killed the just; and he doth not resist you.

Patience and Prayer

7 Be patient therefore, brethren, unto the coming of the Lord. Behold, the husbandman waiteth for the precious fruit of the earth, and hath long patience for it, until he receive the early and latter rain. 8 Be ye also patient; stablish your hearts: for the coming of the Lord draweth nigh. 9 Grudge not one against another, brethren, lest ye be condemned: behold, the judge standeth before the door. 10 Take, my brethren, the prophets, who have spoken in the name of the Lord, for an example of suffering affliction, and of patience. 11 Behold, we count them happy which endure. Ye have heard of the patience of Job, and have seen the end of the Lord; that the Lord is very pitiful, and of tender mercy.

12 But above all things, my brethren, swear not, neither by heaven, neither by the earth, neither by any other oath: but let your yea be yea; and your nay, nay; lest ye fall into condemnation.

13 Is any among you afflicted? let him pray. Is any merry? let him sing psalms. 14 Is any sick among you? let him call for the elders of the church; and let them pray over him, anointing him with oil in the name of the Lord: 15 And the prayer of faith shall save the sick, and the Lord shall raise him up; and if

he have committed sins, they shall be forgiven him.

16 Confess your faults one to another, and pray one for another, that ye may be healed. The effectual fervent prayer of a righteous man availeth much.

17 Eli′jah was a man subject to like passions as we are, and he prayed earnestly that it might not rain: and it rained not on the earth by the space of three years and six months.

18 And he prayed again, and the heaven gave rain, and the earth brought forth her fruit.

19 Brethren, if any of you do err from the truth, and one convert him;

20 Let him know, that he which converteth the sinner from the error of his way shall save a soul from death, and shall hide a multitude of sins.

THE FIRST EPISTLE GENERAL OF
PETER

Salutation

1 Peter, an apostle of Jesus Christ, To the strangers scattered throughout Pontus, Galatia, Cappado'cia, Asia, and Bithyn'i-a,

2 Elect according to the foreknowledge of God the Father, through sanctification of the Spirit, unto obedience and sprinkling of the blood of Jesus Christ: Grace unto you, and peace, be multiplied.

The Christian's Hope and Salvation

3 Blessed be the God and Father of our Lord Jesus Christ, which according to his abundant mercy hath begotten us again unto a lively hope by the resurrection of Jesus Christ from the dead,

4 To an inheritance incorruptible, and undefiled, and that fadeth not away, reserved in heaven for you,

5 Who are kept by the power of God through faith unto salvation ready to be revealed in the last time.

6 Wherein ye greatly rejoice, though now for a season, if need be, ye are in heaviness through manifold temptations:

7 That the trial of your faith, being much more precious than of gold that perisheth, though it be tried with fire, might be found unto praise and honor and glory at the appearing of Jesus Christ:

8 Whom having not seen, ye love; in whom,

25

though now ye see him not, yet believing, ye rejoice with joy unspeakable and full of glory:

9 Receiving the end of your faith, even the salvation of your souls.

10 Of which salvation the prophets have inquired and searched diligently, who prophesied of the grace that should come unto you:

11 Searching what, or what manner of time the Spirit of Christ which was in them did signify, when it testified beforehand the sufferings of Christ, and the glory that should follow.

12 Unto whom it was revealed, that not unto themselves, but unto us they did minister the things, which are now reported unto you by them that have preached the gospel unto you with the Holy Ghost sent down from heaven; which things the angels desire to look into.

A Call to Holy Living

13 Wherefore gird up the loins of your mind, be sober, and hope to the end for the grace that is to be brought unto you at the revelation of Jesus Christ;

14 As obedient children, not fashioning yourselves according to the former lusts in your ignorance:

15 But as he which hath called you is holy, so be ye holy in all manner of conversation;

16 Because it is written, Be ye holy; for I am holy.

17 And if ye call on the Father, who without respect of persons judgeth according to

every man's work, pass the time of your so-
1538 2041 390 5550 3940
journing here in fear:
5401

18 Forasmuch as ye know that ye were not
redeemed with corruptible things, as silver and
1492 1492 3084
gold, from your vain conversation received by
3084 5349 694
tradition from your fathers; 391
5553 3152 3970

19 But with the precious blood of Christ, as
3970
of a lamb without blemish and without
5093 129 5547
spot: 286 299 784

20 Who verily was foreordained before the
4267 4267
foundation of the world, but was manifest in
2602 2889
these last times for you, 5319
2078 5550

21 Who by him do believe in God, that
raised him up from the dead, and gave him
4100 4100 2316 1453
glory; that your faith and hope might be in
1453 3498 1325
God.
1341 4102 1680
2316

22 Seeing ye have purified your souls in
48 5590
obeying the truth through the Spirit unto
5218 225 4151
unfeigned love of the brethren, see that ye
505 5360
love one another with a pure heart fervently:
25 240
23 Being born again, not of corruptible
2513 2588 1619
seed, but of incorruptible, by the word of
313 5349
God, which liveth and abideth for ever.
4701 862 3056
2316 2198 3306 165
24 For all flesh is as grass, and all the glory
1360 4561 5528 1391
of man as the flower of grass. The grass
438 5528 5528
withereth, and the flower thereof falleth away:
3583 438 1601
25 But the word of the Lord endureth for
4487 2962 3306
ever. And this is the word which by the
165 4487 2097
gospel is preached unto you.

2 Wherefore laying aside all malice, and all
659 2549
guile, and hypocrisies, and envies, and all
1388 5272 5355
evil speakings,
2636
2 As newborn babes, desire the sincere milk
738 1025 1971 97 1051
of the word, that ye may grow thereby:
3050 3050 837

3 If so be ye have tasted that the Lord is gracious.

Christ the Living Stone

4 To whom coming, as unto a living stone, disallowed indeed of men, but chosen of God, and precious,

5 Ye also, as lively stones, are built up a spiritual house, a holy priesthood, to offer up spiritual sacrifices, acceptable to God by Jesus Christ.

6 Wherefore also it is contained in the Scripture, Behold, I lay in Zion a chief corner stone, elect, precious: and he that believeth on him shall not be confounded.

7 Unto you therefore which believe he is precious: but unto them which be disobedient, the stone which the builders disallowed, the same is made the head of the corner,

8 And a stone of stumbling, and a rock of offense, even to them which stumble at the word, being disobedient: whereunto also they were appointed.

God's Own People

9 But ye are a chosen generation, a royal priesthood, a holy nation, a peculiar people; that ye should show forth the praises of him who hath called you out of darkness into his marvelous light:

10 Which in time past were not a people, but are now the people of God: which had not obtained mercy, but now have obtained mercy.

Live as Servants of God

11 Dearly beloved, I beseech you as strangers and pilgrims, abstain from fleshly lusts, which war against the soul;

12 Having your conversation honest among the Gentiles: that, whereas they speak against you as evildoers, they may by your good works, which they shall behold, glorify God in the day of visitation.

13 Submit yourselves to every ordinance of man for the Lord's sake: whether it be to the king, as supreme;

14 Or unto governors, as unto them that are sent by him for the punishment of evildoers, and for the praise of them that do well.

15 For so is the will of God, that with well doing ye may put to silence the ignorance of foolish men:

16 As free, and not using your liberty for a cloak of maliciousness, but as the servants of God.

17 Honor all men. Love the brotherhood. Fear God. Honor the king.

The Example of Christ's Suffering

18 Servants, be subject to your masters with all fear; not only to the good and gentle, but also to the froward.

19 For this is thankworthy, if a man for conscience toward God endure grief, suffering wrongfully.

20 For what glory is it, if, when ye be buffeted for your faults, ye shall take it patiently? but if, when ye do well, and suffer

for it, ye take it patiently, this is acceptable with God.

21 For even hereunto were ye called: because Christ also suffered for us, leaving us an example, that ye should follow his steps:

22 Who did no sin, neither was guile found in his mouth:

23 Who, when he was reviled, reviled not again; when he suffered, he threatened not; but committed himself to him that judgeth righteously:

24 Who his own self bare our sins in his own body on the tree, that we, being dead to sins, should live unto righteousness: by whose stripes ye were healed.

25 For ye were as sheep going astray; but are now returned unto the Shepherd and Bishop of your souls.

The Behavior of Wives and Husbands

3 Likewise, ye wives, be in subjection to your own husbands; that, if any obey not the word, they also may without the word be won by the conversation of the wives;

2 While they behold your chaste conversation coupled with fear.

3 Whose adorning, let it not be that outward adorning of plaiting the hair, and of wearing of gold, or of putting on of apparel;

4 But let it be the hidden man of the heart, in that which is not corruptible, even the ornament of a meek and quiet spirit, which is in the sight of God of great price.

5 For after this manner in the old time the

holy women also, who trusted in God,
adorned themselves, being in subjection unto
their own husbands:
....

6 Even as Sarah obeyed Abraham, calling him
lord: whose daughters ye are, as long as ye do
well, and are not afraid with any amazement.

7 Likewise, ye husbands, dwell with them
according to knowledge, giving honor unto the
wife, as unto the weaker vessel, and as being
heirs together of the grace of life; that your
prayers be not hindered.

Suffer for Righteousness' Sake

8 Finally, be ye all of one mind, having
compassion one of another; love as brethren,
be pitiful, be courteous:

9 Not rendering evil for evil, or railing for
railing: but contrariwise blessing; knowing that
ye are thereunto called, that ye should inherit
a blessing.

10 For he that will love life, and see good
days, let him refrain his tongue from evil, and
his lips that they speak no guile:

11 Let him eschew evil, and do good; let
him seek peace, and ensue it.

12 For the eyes of the Lord are over the
righteous, and his ears are open unto their
prayers: but the face of the Lord is against
them that do evil.

13 And who is he that will harm you, if ye
be followers of that which is good?

14 But and if ye suffer for righteousness'
sake, happy are ye: and be not afraid of their
terror, neither be troubled;

15 But sanctify the Lord God in your hearts: and be ready always to give an answer to every man that asketh you a reason of the hope that is in you, with meekness and fear: 16 Having a good conscience; that, whereas they speak evil of you, as of evildoers, they may be ashamed that falsely accuse your good conversation in Christ. 17 For it is better, if the will of God be so, that ye suffer for well doing, than for evil-doing. 18 For Christ also hath once suffered for sins, the just for the unjust, that he might bring us to God, being put to death in the flesh, but quickened by the Spirit: 19 By which also he went and preached unto the spirits in prison; 20 Which sometime were disobedient, when once the long-suffering of God waited in the days of Noah, while the ark was a preparing, wherein few, that is, eight souls were saved by water. 21 The like figure whereunto even baptism doth also now save us, (not the putting away of the filth of the flesh, but the answer of a good conscience toward God,) by the resurrection of Jesus Christ: 22 Who is gone into heaven, and is on the right hand of God; angels and authorities and powers being made subject unto him.

Good Stewards of God's Grace

4 Forasmuch then as Christ hath suffered for us in the flesh, arm yourselves like-

wise with the same mind: for he that hath
suffered in the flesh hath ceased from sin;

2 That he no longer should live the rest of
his time in the flesh to the lusts of men, but
to the will of God.

3 For the time past of our life may suffice
us to have wrought the will of the Gentiles,
when we walked in lasciviousness, lusts, excess
of wine, revelings, banquetings, and abominable idolatries:

4 Wherein they think it strange that ye run
not with them to the same excess of riot,
speaking evil of you:

5 Who shall give account to him that is
ready to judge the quick and the dead.

6 For, for this cause was the gospel preached
also to them that are dead, that they might
be judged according to men in the flesh, but
live according to God in the spirit.

7 But the end of all things is at hand: be
ye therefore sober, and watch unto prayer.

8 And above all things have fervent charity
among yourselves: for charity shall cover the
multitude of sins.

9 Use hospitality one to another without
grudging.

10 As every man hath received the gift,
even so minister the same one to another, as
good stewards of the manifold grace of
God.

11 If any man speak, let him speak as the
oracles of God; if any man minister, let him
do it as of the ability which God giveth; that
God in all things may be glorified through

Jesus Christ: to whom be praise and dominion for ever and ever. Amen.

Suffering as a Christian

12 Beloved, think it not strange concerning the fiery trial which is to try you, as though some strange thing happened unto you:

13 But rejoice, inasmuch as ye are partakers of Christ's sufferings; that, when his glory shall be revealed, ye may be glad also with exceeding joy.

14 If ye be reproached for the name of Christ, happy are ye; for the Spirit of glory and of God resteth upon you: on their part he is evil spoken of, but on your part he is glorified.

15 But let none of you suffer as a murderer, or as a thief, or as an evildoer, or as a busybody in other men's matters.

16 Yet if any man suffer as a Christian, let him not be ashamed; but let him glorify God on this behalf.

17 For the time is come that judgment must begin at the house of God: and if it first begin at us, what shall the end be of them that obey not the gospel of God?

18 And if the righteous scarcely be saved, where shall the ungodly and the sinner appear?

19 Wherefore, let them that suffer according to the will of God commit the keeping of their souls to him in well doing, as unto a faithful Creator.

Tend the Flock of God

5 The elders which are among you I exhort, who am also an elder, and a witness of the sufferings of Christ, and also a partaker of the glory that shall be revealed:

2 Feed the flock of God which is among you, taking the oversight thereof, not by constraint, but willingly; not for filthy lucre, but of a ready mind;

3 Neither as being lords over God's heritage, but being ensamples to the flock.

4 And when the chief Shepherd shall appear, ye shall receive a crown of glory that fadeth not away.

5 Likewise, ye younger, submit yourselves unto the elder. Yea, all of you be subject one to another, and be clothed with humility: for God resisteth the proud, and giveth grace to the humble.

6 Humble yourselves therefore under the mighty hand of God, that he may exalt you in due time:

7 Casting all your care upon him; for he careth for you.

8 Be sober, be vigilant; because your adversary the devil, as a roaring lion, walketh about, seeking whom he may devour:

9 Whom resist steadfast in the faith, knowing that the same afflictions are accomplished in your brethren that are in the world.

10 But the God of all grace, who hath called us unto his eternal glory by Christ Jesus, after that ye have suffered a while, make you perfect; stablish, strengthen, settle you.

11 To him be glory and dominion for ever
and ever. Amen.
₁₃₉₁ ₂₉₀₄ ₁₆₅
₁₆₅ ₂₈₁

Final Greetings

12 By Silva'nus, a faithful brother unto you,
as I suppose, I have written briefly, exhorting,
₄₆₁₀ ₄₁₀₃ ₈₀
and testifying that this is the true grace of
₃₀₄₉ ₁₁₂₅ ₃₆₄₁ ₃₈₇₀
God wherein ye stand.
₁₉₅₇ ₂₂₇ ₅₄₈₅
₂₃₁₆ 13 The church that is at Babylon, elected
₂₄₇₆
together with you, saluteth you; and so doth
₈₉₇ ₄₈₉₉
Mark my son.
₇₈₂
₃₁₃₈ 14 Greet ye one another with a kiss of
₅₂₀₇
charity. Peace be with you all that are in
₇₈₂ ₂₄₀ ₅₃₇₀
Christ Jesus. Amen.
₂₆ ₁₅₁₅ ₂₈₁
₅₅₄₇ ₂₄₂₄

THE SECOND EPISTLE GENERAL OF

PETER

Salutation

1 Simon Peter, a servant and an apostle of
₄₈₂₆ ₄₀₇₄ ₁₄₀₁ ₆₅₂
Jesus Christ, To them that have obtained
₂₄₂₄ ₅₅₄₇ ₂₉₇₅
like precious faith with us through the right-
₂₄₇₂ ₄₁₀₂ ₁₃₄₃
eousness of God and our Saviour Jesus
₂₃₁₆ ₄₉₉₀ ₂₄₂₄
Christ:
₅₅₄₇
2 Grace and peace be multiplied unto you
₅₄₈₅ ₁₅₁₅ ₄₁₂₉
through the knowledge of God, and of Jesus
₁₉₂₂ ₂₃₁₆ ₂₄₂₄
our Lord.
₂₉₆₂

Make Your Calling and Election Sure

3 According as his divine power hath given
₂₃₀₄ ₁₄₁₁ ₁₄₃₃
unto us all things that pertain unto life and
₂₂₂₂

godliness, through the knowledge of him that
hath called us to glory and virtue:

4 Whereby are given unto us exceeding
great and precious promises; that by these ye
might be partakers of the divine nature, having
escaped the corruption that is in the world
through lust.

5 And besides this, giving all diligence, add
to your faith virtue; and to virtue, knowledge;

6 And to knowledge, temperance; and to
temperance, patience; and to patience, godliness;

7 And to godliness, brotherly kindness; and
to brotherly kindness, charity.

8 For if these things be in you, and abound,
they make you that ye shall neither be barren
nor unfruitful in the knowledge of our Lord
Jesus Christ.

9 But he that lacketh these things is blind,
and cannot see afar off, and hath forgotten
that he was purged from his old sins.

10 Wherefore the rather, brethren, give
diligence to make your calling and election
sure: for if ye do these things, ye shall never
fall:

11 For so an entrance shall be ministered
unto you abundantly into the everlasting
kingdom of our Lord and Saviour Jesus
Christ.

12 Wherefore I will not be negligent to put
you always in remembrance of these things;
though ye know them, and be established in
the present truth.

13 Yea, I think it meet, as long as I am in this tabernacle, to stir you up by putting you in remembrance;

14 Knowing that shortly I must put off this my tabernacle, even as our Lord Jesus Christ hath showed me.

15 Moreover I will endeavor that ye may be able after my decease to have these things always in remembrance.

Eyewitnesses of Christ's Glory

16 For we have not followed cunningly devised fables, when we made known unto you the power and coming of our Lord Jesus Christ, but were eyewitnesses of his majesty.

17 For he received from God the Father honor and glory, when there came such a voice to him from the excellent glory, This is my beloved Son, in whom I am well pleased.

18 And this voice which came from heaven we heard, when we were with him in the holy mount.

19 We have also a more sure word of prophecy; whereunto ye do well that ye take heed, as unto a light that shineth in a dark place, until the day dawn, and the day-star arise in your hearts:

20 Knowing this first, that no prophecy of the Scripture is of any private interpretation.

21 For the prophecy came not in old time by the will of man: but holy men of God spake as they were moved by the Holy Ghost.

False Prophets and Teachers

2 But there were false prophets also among
the people, even as there shall be false
teachers among you, who privily shall bring in
damnable heresies, even denying the Lord that
bought them, and bring upon themselves swift
destruction.

2 And many shall follow their pernicious
ways; by reason of whom the way of truth
shall be evil spoken of.

3 And through covetousness shall they with
feigned words make merchandise of you:
whose judgment now of a long time lingereth
not, and their damnation slumbereth not.

4 For if God spared not the angels that
sinned, but cast them down to hell, and delivered them into chains of darkness, to be
reserved unto judgment;

5 And spared not the old world, but saved
Noah the eighth person, a preacher of righteousness, bringing in the flood upon the
world of the ungodly;

6 And turning the cities of Sodom and
Gomor'rah into ashes condemned them with
an overthrow, making them an ensample unto
those that after should live ungodly;

7 And delivered just Lot, vexed with the
filthy conversation of the wicked:

8 (For that righteous man dwelling among
them, in seeing and hearing, vexed his righteous soul from day to day with their unlawful
deeds:)

9 The Lord knoweth how to deliver the
godly out of temptation, and to reserve the

unjust unto the day of judgment to be punished:

10 But chiefly them that walk after the flesh in the lust of uncleanness, and despise government. Presumptuous are they, self-willed, they are not afraid to speak evil of dignities.

11 Whereas angels, which are greater in power and might, bring not railing accusation against them before the Lord.

12 But these, as natural brute beasts made to be taken and destroyed, speak evil of the things that they understand not; and shall utterly perish in their own corruption;

13 And shall receive the reward of unrighteousness, as they that count it pleasure to riot in the daytime. Spots they are and blemishes, sporting themselves with their own deceivings while they feast with you;

14 Having eyes full of adultery, and that cannot cease from sin; beguiling unstable souls: a heart they have exercised with covetous practices; cursed children:

15 Which have forsaken the right way, and are gone astray, following the way of Ba'laam the son of Beor, who loved the wages of unrighteousness;

16 But was rebuked for his iniquity: the dumb ass speaking with man's voice forbade the madness of the prophet.

17 These are wells without water, clouds that are carried with a tempest; to whom the mist of darkness is reserved for ever.

18 For when they speak great swelling

words of vanity, they allure through the lusts of the flesh, through much wantonness, those that were clean escaped from them who live in error.

19 While they promise them liberty, they themselves are the servants of corruption: for of whom a man is overcome, of the same is he brought in bondage.

20 For if after they have escaped the pollutions of the world through the knowledge of the Lord and Saviour Jesus Christ, they are again entangled therein, and overcome, the latter end is worse with them than the beginning.

21 For it had been better for them not to have known the way of righteousness, than, after they have known it, to turn from the holy commandment delivered unto them.

22 But it is happened unto them according to the true proverb, The dog is turned to his own vomit again; and the sow that was washed to her wallowing in the mire.

The Promise of the Lord's Coming

3 This second epistle, beloved, I now write unto you; in both which I stir up your pure minds by way of remembrance:

2 That ye may be mindful of the words which were spoken before by the holy prophets, and of the commandment of us the apostles of the Lord and Saviour:

3 Knowing this first, that there shall come in the last days scoffers, walking after their own lusts,

4 And saying, Where is the promise of his coming? for since the fathers fell asleep, all things continue as they were from the beginning of the creation.

5 For this they willingly are ignorant of, that by the word of God the heavens were of old, and the earth standing out of the water and in the water:

6 Whereby the world that then was, being overflowed with water, perished:

7 But the heavens and the earth, which are now, by the same word are kept in store, reserved unto fire against the day of judgment and perdition of ungodly men.

8 But, beloved, be not ignorant of this one thing, that one day is with the Lord as a thousand years, and a thousand years as one day.

9 The Lord is not slack concerning his promise, as some men count slackness; but is long-suffering to us-ward, not willing that any should perish, but that all should come to repentance.

10 But the day of the Lord will come as a thief in the night; in the which the heavens shall pass away with a great noise, and the elements shall melt with fervent heat, the earth also and the works that are therein shall be burned up.

11 Seeing then that all these things shall be dissolved, what manner of persons ought ye to be in all holy conversation and godliness,

12 Looking for and hasting unto the coming of the day of God, wherein the heavens being

on fire shall be dissolved, and the elements
shall melt with fervent heat?

13 Nevertheless we, according to his promise, look for new heavens and a new earth,
wherein dwelleth righteousness.

14 Wherefore, beloved, seeing that ye look
for such things, be diligent that ye may be
found of him in peace, without spot, and
blameless.

15 And account that the long-suffering of
our Lord is salvation; even as our beloved
brother Paul also according to the wisdom
given unto him hath written unto you;

16 As also in all his epistles, speaking in
them of these things; in which are some
things hard to be understood, which they that
are unlearned and unstable wrest, as they do
also the other Scriptures, unto their own destruction.

17 Ye therefore, beloved, seeing ye know
these things before, beware lest ye also, being
led away with the error of the wicked, fall
from your own steadfastness.

18 But grow in grace, and in the knowledge
of our Lord and Saviour Jesus Christ. To him
be glory both now and for ever. Amen.

THE FIRST EPISTLE GENERAL OF

JOHN

The Word of Life

1 That which was from the beginning, which we have heard, which we have seen with our eyes, which we have looked upon, and our hands have handled, of the Word of life;

2 (For the life was manifested, and we have seen it, and bear witness, and show unto you that eternal life, which was with the Father, and was manifested unto us;)

3 That which we have seen and heard declare we unto you, that ye also may have fellowship with us: and truly our fellowship is with the Father, and with his Son Jesus Christ.

4 And these things write we unto you, that your joy may be full.

God Is Light

5 This then is the message which we have heard of him, and declare unto you, that God is light, and in him is no darkness at all.

6 If we say that we have fellowship with him, and walk in darkness, we lie, and do not the truth:

7 But if we walk in the light, as he is in the light, we have fellowship one with another, and the blood of Jesus Christ his Son cleanseth us from all sin.

Sin, Its Reality and Remedy

8 If we say that we have no sin, we deceive ourselves, and the truth is not in us.

9 If we confess our sins, he is faithful and just to forgive us our sins, and to cleanse us from all unrighteousness.

10 If we say that we have not sinned, we make him a liar, and his word is not in us.

2 My little children, these things write I unto you, that ye sin not. And if any man sin, we have an advocate with the Father, Jesus Christ the righteous:

2 And he is the propitiation for our sins: and not for ours only, but also for the sins of the whole world.

Tests of True Knowledge

3 And hereby we do know that we know him, if we keep his commandments.

4 He that saith, I know him, and keepeth not his commandments, is a liar, and the truth is not in him.

5 But whoso keepeth his word, in him verily is the love of God perfected: hereby know we that we are in him.

6 He that saith he abideth in him ought himself also so to walk, even as he walked.

7 Brethren, I write no new commandment unto you, but an old commandment which ye had from the beginning. The old commandment is the word which ye have heard from the beginning.

8 Again, a new commandment I write unto you, which thing is true in him and in you: because the darkness is past, and the true light now shineth.

9 He that saith he is in the light, and

hateth his brother, is in darkness even until now.

10 He that loveth his brother abideth in the light, and there is none occasion of stumbling in him.

11 But he that hateth his brother is in darkness, and walketh in darkness, and knoweth not whither he goeth, because that darkness hath blinded his eyes.

12 I write unto you, little children, because your sins are forgiven you for his name's sake.

13 I write unto you, fathers, because ye have known him that is from the beginning. I write unto you, young men, because ye have overcome the wicked one. I write unto you, little children, because ye have known the Father.

14 I have written unto you, fathers, because ye have known him that is from the beginning. I have written unto you, young men, because ye are strong, and the word of God abideth in you, and ye have overcome the wicked one.

15 Love not the world, neither the things that are in the world. If any man love the world, the love of the Father is not in him.

16 For all that is in the world, the lust of the flesh, and the lust of the eyes, and the pride of life, is not of the Father, but is of the world.

17 And the world passeth away, and the lust thereof: but he that doeth the will of God abideth for ever.

The Antichrist

18 Little children, it is the last time: and as ye have heard that antichrist shall come, even now are there many antichrists; whereby we know that it is the last time.

19 They went out from us, but they were not of us; for if they had been of us, they would no doubt have continued with us: but they went out, that they might be made manifest that they were not all of us.

20 But ye have an unction from the Holy One, and ye know all things.

21 I have not written unto you because ye know not the truth, but because ye know it, and that no lie is of the truth.

22 Who is a liar but he that denieth that Jesus is the Christ? He is antichrist, that denieth the Father and the Son.

23 Whosoever denieth the Son, the same hath not the Father: but he that acknowledgeth the Son hath the Father also.

24 Let that therefore abide in you, which ye have heard from the beginning. If that which ye have heard from the beginning shall remain in you, ye also shall continue in the Son, and in the Father.

25 And this is the promise that he hath promised us, even eternal life.

26 These things have I written unto you concerning them that seduce you.

27 But the anointing which ye have received of him abideth in you, and ye need not that any man teach you: but as the same anointing teacheth you of all things, and is truth, and is

no lie, and even as it hath taught you, ye shall abide in him.

The Children of God and Righteousness

28 And now, little children, abide in him; that, when he shall appear, we may have confidence, and not be ashamed before him at his coming.

29 If ye know that he is righteous, ye know that every one that doeth righteousness is born of him.

3 Behold, what manner of love the Father hath bestowed upon us, that we should be called the sons of God: therefore the world knoweth us not, because it knew him not.

2 Beloved, now are we the sons of God, and it doth not yet appear what we shall be: but we know that, when he shall appear, we shall be like him; for we shall see him as he is.

3 And every man that hath this hope in him purifieth himself, even as he is pure.

4 Whosoever committeth sin transgresseth also the law: for sin is the transgression of the law.

5 And ye know that he was manifested to take away our sins; and in him is no sin.

6 Whosoever abideth in him sinneth not: whosoever sinneth hath not seen him, neither known him.

7 Little children, let no man deceive you: he that doeth righteousness is righteous, even as he is righteous.

8 He that committeth sin is of the devil; for the devil sinneth from the beginning. For

this purpose the Son of God was manifested, that he might destroy the works of the devil.

9 Whosoever is born of God doth not commit sin; for his seed remaineth in him: and he cannot sin, because he is born of God.

10 In this the children of God are manifest, and the children of the devil: whosoever doeth not righteousness is not of God, neither he that loveth not his brother.

Love One Another

11 For this is the message that ye heard from the beginning, that we should love one another.

12 Not as Cain, who was of that wicked one, and slew his brother. And wherefore slew he him? Because his own works were evil, and his brother's righteous.

13 Marvel not, my brethren, if the world hate you.

14 We know that we have passed from death unto life, because we love the brethren. He that loveth not his brother abideth in death.

15 Whosoever hateth his brother is a murderer: and ye know that no murderer hath eternal life abiding in him.

16 Hereby perceive we the love of God, because he laid down his life for us: and we ought to lay down our lives for the brethren.

17 But whoso hath this world's good, and seeth his brother have need, and shutteth up

his bowels of compassion from him, how dwelleth[4698] the love of God in him?

[3306] 18 My little[26] children,[2316] let us not love in word,[3056] neither[5040] in tongue;[1100] but in deed[25] and in truth.[2041]

[225] 19 And hereby we know that we are of the truth,[225] and shall[3982] assure[1097] our hearts before him.

20 For if our[2588] heart condemn[2588] us,[1715] God is greater[3187] than our heart,[2588] and knoweth[2607] all[3956] things.[2316]

21 Beloved, if our[2588] heart condemn[1097] us not,[2607] then have[27] we confidence[2588] toward God.

22 And whatsoever[3954] we ask,[2316] we receive of him, because we keep his commandments,[154] [2983] and do those things that[5083] are pleasing[1785] in his sight.[4160]

23 And this is[701] his commandment,[1799] That we[1799] should believe on the name[1785] of his Son Jesus[5207] [2424] Christ,[4100] [5547] and love one another,[3686] as he gave[2531] us[1325] commandment.[25] [240]

[1785] 24 And he that keepeth his commandments dwelleth in him,[3306] and he[5083] in him.[1785] And hereby we know[1097] that he abideth[3306] in us, by the Spirit[4151] which he hath given[1325] us.

The Spirit of God and the Spirit of Antichrist

4 Beloved, believe not every spirit, but try the[27] spirits[4100] whether they are[3956] of[4151] God: be-[1381]cause many[4151] false prophets[4183] are[5578] gone[1831] out into[2316] the world.

2 Hereby[2889] know ye the Spirit of God: Every spirit that confesseth[1097] that Jesus Christ[2316] is come[4151] in the flesh[3670] is[2064] of[2424] God:[5547] [2064]

3 And every[4561] spirit[2316] that confesseth not that Jesus Christ[3956] is[4151] come in the flesh[3670] is not[2064] of God:[2424] [5547] and this[2064] is that spirit[4561] of antichrist,[2316] [500]

whereof ye have heard that it should come; and even now already[191] is it in the world.[2064]

4 Ye are[2075][3568] of God,[2316] little children,[2235] and have overcome[3528] them: because[5040] greater[3187] is he that is in you, than he that is in the world.[2889]

5 They are[1526] of the world:[2889] therefore speak they of the world,[2889] and the world[2889] heareth[191] them.[2980]

6 We are of God: he that knoweth God heareth[191] us; he that is not[2316] of God heareth not[1097][2316] us. Hereby know[1097] we the spirit[4151] of truth,[225] and the spirit[4151] of error.[4106][191]

God Is Love

7 Beloved,[27] let us love[25] one[240] another:[25] for love is of God;[2316] and every one that loveth[25] is born[1080] of God,[2316] and knoweth[1097] God.[3956]

8 He that loveth[25] not,[2316] knoweth[1097] not God;[2316] for God[2316] is love.[26]

9 In this was manifested[5319] the love[26] of God toward us, because that God sent[649] his only begotten Son[2316][5207] into the world,[2889] that we might[3439] live[2198] through him.

10 Herein is love,[26] not that we loved[25] God,[2316] but that he loved[26] us, and sent[649] his Son[5207] to be the propitiation[2434] for our sins.[266]

11 Beloved,[27] if God[2316] so loved[25] us, we ought[3784] also to love[25] one[240] another.

12 No man hath seen[2300] God[2316] at any time.[4455] If we love[25] one another,[240] God[2316] dwelleth[3306] in us, and his love[26] is perfected[5048] in us.

13 Hereby know[1097] we that we dwell[3306] in him, and he in us, because he hath given[1325] us of his Spirit.[4151]

14 And we have seen and do testify that the Father sent the Son to be the Saviour of the world.

15 Whosoever shall confess that Jesus is the Son of God, God dwelleth in him, and he in God.

16 And we have known and believed the love that God hath to us. God is love; and he that dwelleth in love dwelleth in God, and God in him.

17 Herein is our love made perfect, that we may have boldness in the day of judgment: because as he is, so are we in this world.

18 There is no fear in love; but perfect love casteth out fear: because fear hath torment. He that feareth is not made perfect in love.

19 We love him, because he first loved us.

20 If a man say, I love God, and hateth his brother, he is a liar: for he that loveth not his brother whom he hath seen, how can he love God whom he hath not seen?

21 And this commandment have we from him, That he who loveth God love his brother also.

Faith the Victory over the World

5 Whosoever believeth that Jesus is the Christ is born of God: and every one that loveth him that begat loveth him also that is begotten of him.

2 By this we know that we love the children of God, when we love God, and keep his commandments.

3 For this is the love of God, that we keep his commandments: and his commandments are not grievous.

4 For whatsoever is born of God overcometh the world: and this is the victory that overcometh the world, even our faith.

5 Who is he that overcometh the world, but he that believeth that Jesus is the Son of God?

The Witness concerning the Son

6 This is he that came by water and blood, even Jesus Christ; not by water only, but by water and blood. And it is the Spirit that beareth witness, because the Spirit is truth.

7 For there are three that bear record in heaven, the Father, the Word, and the Holy Ghost: and these three are one.

8 And there are three that bear witness in earth, the spirit, and the water, and the blood: and these three agree in one.

9 If we receive the witness of men, the witness of God is greater: for this is the witness of God which he hath testified of his Son.

10 He that believeth on the Son of God hath the witness in himself: he that believeth not God hath made him a liar; because he believeth not the record that God gave of his Son.

11 And this is the record, that God hath given to us eternal life, and this life is in his Son.

12 He that hath the Son hath life; and he that hath not the Son of God hath not life.

The Knowledge of Eternal Life

13 These things have I written unto you that believe on the name[1125] of the[1125] Son of God; that[4100] ye may know that[3686] ye have[5207] eternal[2316] life, and that[1492] ye may believe on the name[166] of the[2222] Son of God.[4100] [3686]

[5207][2316] 14 And this is the confidence that we have in him, that, if we ask any[3954] thing according to his will, he heareth[154] us:[5100]

[2307] 15 And if we[191] know that he hear us, whatsoever we ask, we[1492] know that[191] we have the petitions[154] that[1492] we desired of him.[155][154]

[155] 16 If any man see[154] his brother sin a sin which is not[5100] unto death[1492], he shall ask[80], and he[264][266] shall give him life for[2288] them that[154] sin not unto death.[1325] There is a[2222] sin unto death:[264] I do not say[2288][3004][3004] that[2288] he shall pray[266] for it.

[2065] 17 All unrighteousness[3956] is sin[93]: and there is a sin[266] not unto death.[266]

[266] 18 We know[2288] that whosoever is born of God sinneth not[1492]; but he that[3956] is begotten[1080] of God[2316] keepeth[264] himself[1438], and that[5083] wicked[1438] one[1080] toucheth[2316] him[5083] not.[4190-4191][680]

19 And we know that we are of God[1492], and[2316] the whole world lieth in wickedness.

20 And we[3650] know[2889][2749] that the[4190-4191] Son of God is come, and hath[1492] given us an[5207] understanding,[2316][2240] that we may[1325] know him that is true[1271]; and we are in him[1097] that is true, even in his[228] Son Jesus[5207][2424] Christ. This is the[228] true God, and eternal life.[228]

[5547] 21 Little children,[228] keep[2316] yourselves from[166] idols.[2222] Amen.[5040][5442][1438]
[1497]   [281]

JOHN

Salutation

THE elder unto the elect lady and her children, whom I love in the truth; and not I only, but also all they that have known the truth;

2 For the truth's sake, which dwelleth in us, and shall be with us for ever.

3 Grace be with you, mercy, and peace, from God the Father, and from the Lord Jesus Christ, the Son of the Father, in truth and love.

Abide in the Doctrine of Christ

4 I rejoiced greatly that I found of thy children walking in truth, as we have received a commandment from the Father.

5 And now I beseech thee, lady, not as though I wrote a new commandment unto thee, but that which we had from the beginning, that we love one another.

6 And this is love, that we walk after his commandments. This is the commandment, That, as ye have heard from the beginning, ye should walk in it.

7 For many deceivers are entered into the world, who confess not that Jesus Christ is come in the flesh. This is a deceiver and an antichrist.

8 Look to yourselves, that we lose not those things which we have wrought, but that we receive a full reward.

9 Whosoever transgresseth, and abideth not in the doctrine[3845] of Christ, hath not God[3306]. He that abideth[1322] in the doctrine[5547] of Christ, he[2316] hath both the[3306] Father and the[1322] Son.[5547]

10 If there[3962] come any unto[5207] you, and bring not this[1536] doctrine,[2064] receive[5100] him not into your[5342] house, neither[1322] bid him[2983] God-speed:

11 For[3614] he that[3004] biddeth him[5463] God-speed is partaker of his[3004] evil deeds.[5463] [2841]
[4190-4191 2041]

Final Greetings

12 Having many things to write unto you, I would not write[4183] with paper[1125] and ink: but I trust[1014] to come[1125] unto you,[5489] and speak[3188] face to face,[1679] that[2064] our joy[2980] may be full.[4750]
[4750]

13 The children of thy[5479] elect[4137] sister greet thee. Amen.[5043] [1588] [79] [782]
[281]

THE THIRD EPISTLE OF

JOHN

Salutation

THE elder unto the well-beloved Gai′us,[4245] whom I love[27] in the truth.[1050]

2 Beloved,[25] I wish above[225] all things that thou mayest prosper[27] and be in[2172] health,[3956] even as thy soul[5198] prospereth.[2137] [2531]
[5590] [2137]

3 For I rejoiced greatly, when the brethren came and testified[5463] of the[3029] truth[2064] that is in[80] thee, even[2064] as thou[3140] walkest in the[225] truth.
[2531] [4043] [225]

4 I have no greater joy than to hear that my children walk in truth.[3186] [5479] [191]
[5043] [4043] [225]

Gaius' Hospitality Commended

5 Beloved, thou doest faithfully whatsoever thou doest to the brethren, and to strangers;
6 Which have borne witness of thy charity before the church: whom if thou bring forward on their journey after a godly sort, thou shalt do well:
7 Because that for his name's sake they went forth, taking nothing of the Gentiles.
8 We therefore ought to receive such, that we might be fellow helpers to the truth.

The Opposition of Diotrephes

9 I wrote unto the church: but Diot're-phes, who loveth to have the preeminence among them, receiveth us not.
10 Wherefore, if I come, I will remember his deeds which he doeth, prating against us with malicious words: and not content therewith, neither doth he himself receive the brethren, and forbiddeth them that would, and casteth them out of the church.

The Good Report concerning Demetrius

11 Beloved, follow not that which is evil, but that which is good. He that doeth good is of God: but he that doeth evil hath not seen God.
12 Deme'tri-us hath good report of all men, and of the truth itself: yea, and we also bear record; and ye know that our record is true.

Final Greetings

13 I had many things to write, but I will not with ink and pen write unto thee:

14 But I trust I shall shortly see thee, and we shall speak face to face. Peace be to thee. Our friends salute thee. Greet the friends by name.

THE GENERAL EPISTLE OF
JUDE

Salutation

JUDE, the servant of Jesus Christ, and brother of James, To them that are sanctified by God the Father, and preserved in Jesus Christ, and called:

2 Mercy unto you, and peace, and love, be multiplied.

Judgment on False Teachers

3 Beloved, when I gave all diligence to write unto you of the common salvation, it was needful for me to write unto you, and exhort you that ye should earnestly contend for the faith which was once delivered unto the saints.

4 For there are certain men crept in unawares, who were before of old ordained to this condemnation, ungodly men, turning the grace of our God into lasciviousness, and denying the only Lord God, and our Lord Jesus Christ.

5 I will therefore put you in remembrance, though ye once knew this, how that the

Lord, having saved the people out of the land of Egypt, afterward destroyed them that believed not.

6 And the angels which kept not their first estate, but left their own habitation, he hath reserved in everlasting chains under darkness unto the judgment of the great day.

7 Even as Sodom and Gomor'rah, and the cities about them in like manner, giving themselves over to fornication, and going after strange flesh, are set forth for an example, suffering the vengeance of eternal fire.

8 Likewise also these filthy dreamers defile the flesh, despise dominion, and speak evil of dignities.

9 Yet Michael the archangel, when contending with the devil he disputed about the body of Moses, durst not bring against him a railing accusation, but said, The Lord rebuke thee.

10 But these speak evil of those things which they know not: but what they know naturally, as brute beasts, in those things they corrupt themselves.

11 Woe unto them! for they have gone in the way of Cain, and ran greedily after the error of Ba'laam for reward, and perished in the gainsaying of Korah.

12 These are spots in your feasts of charity, when they feast with you, feeding themselves without fear: clouds they are without water, carried about of winds; trees whose fruit withereth, without fruit, twice dead, plucked up by the roots;

13 Raging waves of the sea, foaming out their own shame; wandering stars, to whom is reserved the blackness of darkness for ever.

14 And Enoch also, the seventh from Adam, prophesied of these, saying, Behold, the Lord cometh with ten thousands of his saints,

15 To execute judgment upon all, and to convince all that are ungodly among them of all their ungodly deeds which they have ungodly committed, and of all their hard speeches which ungodly sinners have spoken against him.

16 These are murmurers, complainers, walking after their own lusts; and their mouth speaketh great swelling words, having men's persons in admiration because of advantage.

Warnings and Exhortations

17 But, beloved, remember ye the words which were spoken before of the apostles of our Lord Jesus Christ;

18 How that they told you there should be mockers in the last time, who should walk after their own ungodly lusts.

19 These be they who separate themselves, sensual, having not the Spirit.

20 But ye, beloved, building up yourselves on your most holy faith, praying in the Holy Ghost,

21 Keep yourselves in the love of God, looking for the mercy of our Lord Jesus Christ unto eternal life.

22 And of some have compassion, making a difference:

23 And others save with fear, pulling them
out of the fire; hating even the garment
4982   5401   726
spotted by the flesh.   5509
4442   3404
4696   4561

Concluding Doxology

24 Now unto him that is able to keep you
1410..........   5442....
from falling, and to present you faultless before the presence of his glory with exceeding
679 2476   299   2714
joy, 2714..........   1391   20.......

25 To the only wise God our Saviour, be
3441   4680. 2316   4990
glory and majesty, dominion and power, both
1391   3172   2904   1849
now and ever. Amen.
3568   165   281

THE REVELATION

OF ST. JOHN THE DIVINE

The Revelation of Jesus Christ

1 The Revelation of Jesus Christ, which God gave unto him, to show unto his servants things which must shortly come to pass; and he sent and signified it by his angel unto his servant John:

2 Who bare record of the word of God, and of the testimony of Jesus Christ, and of all things that he saw.

3 Blessed is he that readeth, and they that hear the words of this prophecy, and keep those things which are written therein: for the time is at hand.

Greetings to the Seven Churches

4 John to the seven churches which are in Asia: Grace be unto you, and peace, from him which is, and which was, and which is to come; and from the seven Spirits which are before his throne;

5 And from Jesus Christ, who is the faithful witness, and the first-begotten of the dead, and the prince of the kings of the earth. Unto him that loved us, and washed us from our sins in his own blood,

6 And hath made us kings and priests unto God and his Father; to him be glory and dominion for ever and ever. Amen.

7 Behold, he cometh with clouds; and every eye shall see him, and they also which pierced

him: and all kindreds of the earth shall wail because of him. Even so, Amen.

8 I am Alpha and Ome′ga, the beginning and the ending, saith the Lord, which is, and which was, and which is to come, the Almighty.

A Vision of the Son of Man

9 I John, who also am your brother, and companion in tribulation, and in the kingdom and patience of Jesus Christ, was in the isle that is called Patmos, for the word of God, and for the testimony of Jesus Christ.

10 I was in the Spirit on the Lord's day, and heard behind me a great voice, as of a trumpet,

11 Saying, I am Alpha and Ome′ga, the first and the last: and, What thou seest, write in a book, and send it unto the seven churches which are in Asia; unto Ephesus, and unto Smyrna, and unto Per′gamos, and unto Thyati′ra, and unto Sardis, and unto Philadelphia, and unto La-odice′a.

12 And I turned to see the voice that spake with me. And being turned, I saw seven golden candlesticks;

13 And in the midst of the seven candlesticks one like unto the Son of man, clothed with a garment down to the foot, and girt about the paps with a golden girdle.

14 His head and his hairs were white like wool, as white as snow; and his eyes were as a flame of fire;

15 And his feet like unto fine brass, as if

they burned in a furnace; and his voice as the sound of many waters.

16 And he had in his right hand seven stars: and out of his mouth went a sharp two-edged sword: and his countenance was as the sun shineth in his strength.

17 And when I saw him, I fell at his feet as dead. And he laid his right hand upon me, saying unto me, Fear not; I am the first and the last:

18 I am he that liveth, and was dead; and, behold, I am alive for evermore, Amen; and have the keys of hell and of death.

19 Write the things which thou hast seen, and the things which are, and the things which shall be hereafter;

20 The mystery of the seven stars which thou sawest in my right hand, and the seven golden candlesticks. The seven stars are the angels of the seven churches: and the seven candlesticks which thou sawest are the seven churches.

The Message to Ephesus

2 Unto the angel of the church of Ephesus write; These things saith he that holdeth the seven stars in his right hand, who walketh in the midst of the seven golden candlesticks.

2 I know thy works, and thy labor, and thy patience, and how thou canst not bear them which are evil: and thou hast tried them which say they are apostles, and are not, and hast found them liars:

3 And hast borne, and hast patience, and

for my name's sake hast labored, and hast not fainted.

4 Nevertheless I have somewhat against thee, because thou hast left thy first love.

5 Remember therefore from whence thou art fallen, and repent, and do the first works; or else I will come unto thee quickly, and will remove thy candlestick out of his place, except thou repent.

6 But this thou hast, that thou hatest the deeds of the Nicola′itans, which I also hate.

7 He that hath an ear, let him hear what the Spirit saith unto the churches; To him that overcometh will I give to eat of the tree of life, which is in the midst of the paradise of God.

The Message to Smyrna

8 And unto the angel of the church in Smyrna write; These things saith the first and the last, which was dead, and is alive;

9 I know thy works, and tribulation, and poverty, (but thou art rich) and I know the blasphemy of them which say they are Jews, and are not, but are the synagogue of Satan.

10 Fear none of those things which thou shalt suffer: behold, the devil shall cast some of you into prison, that ye may be tried; and ye shall have tribulation ten days: be thou faithful unto death, and I will give thee a crown of life.

11 He that hath an ear, let him hear what the Spirit saith unto the churches; He that overcometh shall not be hurt of the second death.

The Message to Pergamos

12 And to the angel of the church in Per'-gamos write; These things saith he which hath the sharp sword with two edges.

13 I know thy works, and where thou dwellest, even where Satan's seat is: and thou holdest fast my name, and hast not denied my faith, even in those days wherein An'tipas was my faithful martyr, who was slain among you, where Satan dwelleth.

14 But I have a few things against thee, because thou hast there them that hold the doctrine of Ba'laam, who taught Balak to cast a stumblingblock before the children of Israel, to eat things sacrificed unto idols, and to commit fornication.

15 So hast thou also them that hold the doctrine of the Nicola'itans, which thing I hate.

16 Repent; or else I will come unto thee quickly, and will fight against them with the sword of my mouth.

17 He that hath an ear, let him hear what the Spirit saith unto the churches; To him that overcometh will I give to eat of the hidden manna, and will give him a white stone, and in the stone a new name written, which no man knoweth saving he that receiveth it.

The Message to Thyatira

18 And unto the angel of the church in Thy-ati'ra write; These things saith the Son of God, who hath his eyes like unto a flame of fire, and his feet are like fine brass.

19 I know thy works, and charity, and service, and faith, and thy patience, and thy works; and the last to be more than the first. 20 Notwithstanding I have a few things against thee, because thou sufferest that woman Jez′ebel, which calleth herself a prophetess, to teach and to seduce my servants to commit fornication, and to eat things sacrificed unto idols.

21 And I gave her space to repent of her fornication; and she repented not. 22 Behold, I will cast her into a bed, and them that commit adultery with her into great tribulation, except they repent of their deeds. 23 And I will kill her children with death; and all the churches shall know that I am he which searcheth the reins and hearts: and I will give unto every one of you according to your works.

24 But unto you I say, and unto the rest in Thy-a-ti′ra, as many as have not this doctrine, and which have not known the depths of Satan, as they speak; I will put upon you none other burden.

25 But that which ye have already, hold fast till I come. 26 And he that overcometh, and keepeth my works unto the end, to him will I give power over the nations:

27 And he shall rule them with a rod of iron; as the vessels of a potter shall they be broken to shivers: even as I received of my Father.

28 And I will give him the morning star.

29 He that hath an ear, let him hear what the Spirit saith unto the churches.

The Message to Sardis

3 And unto the angel of the church in Sardis write; These things saith he that hath the seven Spirits of God, and the seven stars. I know thy works, that thou hast a name that thou livest, and art dead.

2 Be watchful, and strengthen the things which remain, that are ready to die: for I have not found thy works perfect before God.

3 Remember therefore how thou hast received and heard, and hold fast, and repent. If therefore thou shalt not watch, I will come on thee as a thief, and thou shalt not know what hour I will come upon thee.

4 Thou hast a few names even in Sardis which have not defiled their garments; and they shall walk with me in white: for they are worthy.

5 He that overcometh, the same shall be clothed in white raiment; and I will not blot out his name out of the book of life, but I will confess his name before my Father, and before his angels.

6 He that hath an ear, let him hear what the Spirit saith unto the churches.

The Message to Philadelphia

7 And to the angel of the church in Philadelphia write; These things saith he that is holy, he that is true, he that hath the key of

David, he that openeth, and no man shutteth;
and shutteth, and no man openeth.

8 I know thy works: behold, I have set before thee an open door, and no man can shut
it: for thou hast a little strength, and hast kept
my word, and hast not denied my name.

9 Behold, I will make them of the synagogue of Satan, which say they are Jews, and
are not, but do lie; behold, I will make them
to come and worship before thy feet and to
know that I have loved thee.

10 Because thou hast kept the word of my
patience, I also will keep thee from the hour
of temptation, which shall come upon all the
world, to try them that dwell upon the earth.

11 Behold, I come quickly: hold that fast
which thou hast, that no man take thy
crown.

12 Him that overcometh will I make a
pillar in the temple of my God, and he shall
go no more out: and I will write upon him
the name of my God, and the name of the
city of my God, which is new Jerusalem,
which cometh down out of heaven from my
God: and I will write upon him my new
name.

13 He that hath an ear, let him hear what
the Spirit saith unto the churches.

The Message to Laodicea

14 And unto the angel of the church of the
La-odice′ans write; These things saith the
Amen, the faithful and true witness, the be-
ginning of the creation of God.

15 I know thy works, that thou art neither cold nor hot: I would thou wert cold or hot. 16 So then because thou art lukewarm, and neither cold nor hot, I will spew thee out of my mouth. 17 Because thou sayest, I am rich, and increased with goods, and have need of nothing; and knowest not that thou art wretched, and miserable, and poor, and blind, and naked: 18 I counsel thee to buy of me gold tried in the fire, that thou mayest be rich; and white raiment, that thou mayest be clothed, and that the shame of thy nakedness do not appear; and anoint thine eyes with eyesalve, that thou mayest see. 19 As many as I love, I rebuke and chasten: be zealous therefore, and repent. 20 Behold, I stand at the door, and knock: if any man hear my voice, and open the door, I will come in to him, and will sup with him, and he with me. 21 To him that overcometh will I grant to sit with me in my throne, even as I also overcame, and am set down with my Father in his throne. 22 He that hath an ear, let him hear what the Spirit saith unto the churches.

The Heavenly Worship

4 After this I looked, and, behold, a door was opened in heaven: and the first voice which I heard was as it were of a trumpet talking with me; which said, Come up hither,

and I will show thee things which must be
hereafter.

2 And immediately I was in the Spirit: and,
behold, a throne was set in heaven, and one
sat on the throne.

3 And he that sat was to look upon like a
jasper and a sardine stone: and there was a
rainbow round about the throne, in sight like
unto an emerald.

4 And round about the throne were four
and twenty seats: and upon the seats I saw
four and twenty elders sitting, clothed in white
raiment; and they had on their heads crowns
of gold.

5 And out of the throne proceeded lightnings and thunderings and voices: and there
were seven lamps of fire burning before the
throne, which are the seven Spirits of God.

6 And before the throne there was a sea of
glass like unto crystal. And in the midst of the
throne, and round about the throne, were four
beasts full of eyes before and behind.

7 And the first beast was like a lion, and
the second beast like a calf, and the third
beast had a face as a man, and the fourth
beast was like a flying eagle.

8 And the four beasts had each of them six
wings about him; and they were full of eyes
within: and they rest not day and night, saying, Holy, holy, holy, Lord God Almighty,
which was, and is, and is to come.

9 And when those beasts give glory and
honor and thanks to him that sat on the
throne, who liveth for ever and ever,

10 The four and twenty elders fall down before him that sat on the throne, and worship him that liveth for ever and ever, and cast their crowns before the throne, saying,

11 Thou art worthy, O Lord, to receive glory and honor and power: for thou hast created all things, and for thy pleasure they are and were created.

The Unopened Book and the Lamb

5 And I saw in the right hand of him that sat on the throne a book written within and on the back side, sealed with seven seals.

2 And I saw a strong angel proclaiming with a loud voice, Who is worthy to open the book, and to loose the seals thereof?

3 And no man in heaven, nor in earth, neither under the earth, was able to open the book, neither to look thereon.

4 And I wept much, because no man was found worthy to open and to read the book, neither to look thereon.

5 And one of the elders saith unto me, Weep not: behold, the Lion of the tribe of Judah, the Root of David, hath prevailed to open the book, and to loose the seven seals thereof.

6 And I beheld, and, lo, in the midst of the throne and of the four beasts, and in the midst of the elders, stood a Lamb as it had been slain, having seven horns and seven eyes, which are the seven Spirits of God sent forth into all the earth.

7 And he came and took the book out of

the right hand of him that sat upon the throne. [1188] ..... [2521] ......

[2362] 8 And when he had taken the book, the four beasts and four [2983] and twenty [975] elders fell down [2226] before the Lamb, having [1501] every [4245] one [4098] of them [1799] harps, and [721] golden vials full of [1538] odors, which [2788] are the [5552] prayers of [5357] saints. [1073] [2368]

9 And they sung [4335] a new [40] song, saying, Thou art worthy [103] to take the book, [2537] [5603] and to [3004] open the seals thereof: [514] for [2983] thou [975] wast slain, and [455] hast redeemed [4973] us to God by thy [4969] blood out of every kindred, [59] and tongue, [2316] and people, [129] and nation; [3956]

[5443] 10 And hast [1100] made us unto [2992] our God kings [1484] and priests: and [4160] we shall reign on the [2316] [935] earth.

11 And [2409] I beheld, and [936] I heard the voice [1093] of many angels [1492] round about the [191] throne, and the [5456] beasts, [4183] [32] and the [2943] elders: and the [2362] number of them [2226] was ten thousand [4245] times ten thousand, and thousands of thousands;

12 Saying [5505] with a loud [5505] voice, Worthy is the [3004] Lamb that was slain [3173] to receive [5456] power, [514] and riches, [721] and [4969] wisdom, and strength, [2983] and honor, [1411] and glory, [4149] and [4678] blessing. [2479] [5092]

13 And [1391] every [2129] creature which is in heaven, and on the [3956] earth, and [2938] under the earth, [3772] and such as are in [1093] the sea, [5270] and all that [1093] are in them, heard I saying, [2281] Blessing, [3956] and honor, and glory, [191] and [3004] power, be [2129] unto him that [5092] sitteth upon the throne, [2904] and unto the Lamb for ever [2521] and ever. [2362] [721] [165]

14 And [165] the four beasts said, Amen. And the four and twenty [2226] elders [3004] fell down [281] and worshipped him [1501] that liveth [4245] for [4098] ever and ever. [4352] [2198] .... [165]

The Seals

6 And I saw when the Lamb opened one of the seals, and I heard, as it were the noise of thunder, one of the four beasts saying, Come and see.

2 And I saw, and behold a white horse: and he that sat on him had a bow; and a crown was given unto him: and he went forth conquering, and to conquer.

3 And when he had opened the second seal, I heard the second beast say, Come and see.

4 And there went out another horse that was red: and power was given to him that sat thereon to take peace from the earth, and that they should kill one another: and there was given unto him a great sword.

5 And when he had opened the third seal, I heard the third beast say, Come and see. And I beheld, and lo a black horse; and he that sat on him had a pair of balances in his hand.

6 And I heard a voice in the midst of the four beasts say, A measure of wheat for a penny, and three measures of barley for a penny; and see thou hurt not the oil and the wine.

7 And when he had opened the fourth seal, I heard the voice of the fourth beast say, Come and see.

8 And I looked, and behold a pale horse: and his name that sat on him was Death, and Hell followed with him. And power was given unto them over the fourth part of the earth, to

kill with sword, and with hunger, and with death, and with the beasts of the earth.

9 And when he had opened the fifth seal, I saw under the altar the souls of them that were slain for the word of God, and for the testimony which they held:

10 And they cried with a loud voice, saying, How long, O Lord, holy and true, dost thou not judge and avenge our blood on them that dwell on the earth?

11 And white robes were given unto every one of them; and it was said unto them, that they should rest yet for a little season, until their fellow servants also and their brethren, that should be killed as they were, should be fulfilled.

12 And I beheld when he had opened the sixth seal, and, lo, there was a great earthquake; and the sun became black as sackcloth of hair, and the moon became as blood;

13 And the stars of heaven fell unto the earth, even as a fig tree casteth her untimely figs, when she is shaken of a mighty wind.

14 And the heaven departed as a scroll when it is rolled together; and every mountain and island were moved out of their places.

15 And the kings of the earth, and the great men, and the rich men, and the chief captains, and the mighty men, and every bondman, and every free man, hid themselves in the dens and in the rocks of the mountains;

16 And said to the mountains and rocks,

Fall on us, and hide us from the face of him
that sitteth on the throne, and from the
wrath of the Lamb:

17 For the great day of his wrath is come;
and who shall be able to stand?

The 144,000 Which Are Sealed

7 And after these things I saw four angels
standing on the four corners of the earth,
holding the four winds of the earth, that the
wind should not blow on the earth, nor on the
sea, nor on any tree.

2 And I saw another angel ascending from
the east, having the seal of the living God:
and he cried with a loud voice to the four
angels, to whom it was given to hurt the earth
and the sea,

3 Saying, Hurt not the earth, neither the
sea, nor the trees, till we have sealed the
servants of our God in their foreheads.

4 And I heard the number of them which
were sealed: and there were sealed a hundred
and forty and four thousand of all the tribes
of the children of Israel.

5 Of the tribe of Judah were sealed twelve
thousand. Of the tribe of Reuben were sealed
twelve thousand. Of the tribe of Gad were
sealed twelve thousand.

6 Of the tribe of Asher were sealed twelve
thousand. Of the tribe of Naph'tali were sealed
twelve thousand. Of the tribe of Manas'seh
were sealed twelve thousand.

7 Of the tribe of Simeon were sealed twelve
thousand. Of the tribe of Levi were sealed

twelve thousand. Of the tribe of Is′sachar
were sealed twelve thousand.

8 Of the tribe of Zeb′ulun were sealed
twelve thousand. Of the tribe of Joseph were
sealed twelve thousand. Of the tribe of Benjamin were sealed twelve thousand.

The White-robed Multitude

9 After this I beheld, and, lo, a great
multitude, which no man could number, of all
nations, and kindreds, and people, and
tongues, stood before the throne, and before
the Lamb, clothed with white robes, and
palms in their hands;

10 And cried with a loud voice, saying,
Salvation to our God which sitteth upon the
throne, and unto the Lamb.

11 And all the angels stood round about
the throne, and about the elders and the four
beasts, and fell before the throne on their
faces, and worshipped God,

12 Saying, Amen: Blessing, and glory, and
wisdom, and thanksgiving, and honor, and
power, and might, be unto our God for ever
and ever. Amen.

13 And one of the elders answered, saying
unto me, What are these which are arrayed in
white robes? and whence came they?

14 And I said unto him, Sir, thou knowest.
And he said to me, These are they which
came out of great tribulation, and have washed
their robes, and made them white in the
blood of the Lamb.

15 Therefore are they before the throne of

God, and serve him day and night in his temple: and he that sitteth on the throne shall dwell among them.

16 They shall hunger no more, neither thirst any more; neither shall the sun light on them, nor any heat.

17 For the Lamb which is in the midst of the throne shall feed them, and shall lead them unto living fountains of waters: and God shall wipe away all tears from their eyes.

The Seventh Seal

8 And when he had opened the seventh seal, there was silence in heaven about the space of half an hour.

2 And I saw the seven angels which stood before God; and to them were given seven trumpets.

3 And another angel came and stood at the altar, having a golden censer; and there was given unto him much incense, that he should offer it with the prayers of all saints upon the golden altar which was before the throne.

4 And the smoke of the incense, which came with the prayers of the saints, ascended up before God out of the angel's hand.

5 And the angel took the censer, and filled it with fire of the altar, and cast it into the earth: and there were voices, and thunderings, and lightnings, and an earthquake.

The Trumpets

6 And the seven angels which had the seven trumpets prepared themselves to sound.

7 The first angel sounded, and there followed hail and fire mingled with blood, and they were cast upon the earth: and the third part of trees was burnt up, and all green grass was burnt up.

8 And the second angel sounded, and as it were a great mountain burning with fire was cast into the sea: and the third part of the sea became blood;

9 And the third part of the creatures which were in the sea, and had life, died; and the third part of the ships were destroyed.

10 And the third angel sounded, and there fell a great star from heaven, burning as it were a lamp, and it fell upon the third part of the rivers, and upon the fountains of waters;

11 And the name of the star is called Wormwood: and the third part of the waters became wormwood; and many men died of the waters, because they were made bitter.

12 And the fourth angel sounded, and the third part of the sun was smitten, and the third part of the moon, and the third part of the stars; so as the third part of them was darkened, and the day shone not for a third part of it, and the night likewise.

13 And I beheld, and heard an angel flying through the midst of heaven, saying with a loud voice, Woe, woe, woe, to the inhabiters of the earth by reason of the other voices of the trumpet of the three angels, which are yet to sound!

9 And the fifth angel sounded, and I saw a star fall from heaven unto the earth: and to him was given the key of the bottomless pit.

2 And he opened the bottomless pit; and there arose a smoke out of the pit, as the smoke of a great furnace; and the sun and the air were darkened by reason of the smoke of the pit.

3 And there came out of the smoke locusts upon the earth: and unto them was given power, as the scorpions of the earth have power.

4 And it was commanded them that they should not hurt the grass of the earth, neither any green thing, neither any tree; but only those men which have not the seal of God in their foreheads.

5 And to them it was given that they should not kill them, but that they should be tormented five months: and their torment was as the torment of a scorpion, when he striketh a man.

6 And in those days shall men seek death, and shall not find it; and shall desire to die, and death shall flee from them.

7 And the shapes of the locusts were like unto horses prepared unto battle; and on their heads were as it were crowns like gold, and their faces were as the faces of men.

8 And they had hair as the hair of women, and their teeth were as the teeth of lions.

9 And they had breastplates, as it were breastplates of iron; and the sound of their

wings was as the sound of chariots of many horses running to battle.

10 And they had tails like unto scorpions, and there were stings in their tails: and their power was to hurt men five months.

11 And they had a king over them, which is the angel of the bottomless pit, whose name in the Hebrew tongue is Abad'don, but in the Greek tongue hath his name Apol'ly-on.

12 One woe is past; and, behold, there come two woes more hereafter.

13 And the sixth angel sounded, and I heard a voice from the four horns of the golden altar which is before God,

14 Saying to the sixth angel which had the trumpet, Loose the four angels which are bound in the great river Euphra'tes.

15 And the four angels were loosed, which were prepared for an hour, and a day, and a month, and a year, for to slay the third part of men.

16 And the number of the army of the horsemen were two hundred thousand thousand: and I heard the number of them.

17 And thus I saw the horses in the vision, and them that sat on them, having breastplates of fire, and of jacinth, and brimstone: and the heads of the horses were as the heads of lions; and out of their mouths issued fire and smoke and brimstone.

18 By these three was the third part of men killed, by the fire, and by the smoke, and by the brimstone, which issued out of their mouths.

19 For their power is in their mouth, and in their tails: for their tails were like unto serpents, and had heads, and with them they do hurt.

20 And the rest of the men which were not killed by these plagues yet repented not of the works of their hands, that they should not worship devils, and idols of gold, and silver, and brass, and stone, and of wood; which neither can see, nor hear, nor walk:

21 Neither repented they of their murders, nor of their sorceries, nor of their fornication, nor of their thefts.

The Angel and the Little Book

10 And I saw another mighty angel come down from heaven, clothed with a cloud: and a rainbow was upon his head, and his face was as it were the sun, and his feet as pillars of fire:

2 And he had in his hand a little book open: and he set his right foot upon the sea, and his left foot on the earth,

3 And cried with a loud voice, as when a lion roareth: and when he had cried, seven thunders uttered their voices.

4 And when the seven thunders had uttered their voices, I was about to write: and I heard a voice from heaven saying unto me, Seal up those things which the seven thunders uttered, and write them not.

5 And the angel which I saw stand upon the sea and upon the earth lifted up his hand to heaven,

6 And sware by him that liveth for ever and ever, who created heaven, and the things that therein are, and the earth, and the things that therein are, and the sea, and the things which are therein, that there should be time no longer:

7 But in the days of the voice of the seventh angel, when he shall begin to sound, the mystery of God should be finished, as he hath declared to his servants the prophets.

8 And the voice which I heard from heaven spake unto me again, and said, Go and take the little book which is open in the hand of the angel which standeth upon the sea and upon the earth.

9 And I went unto the angel, and said unto him, Give me the little book. And he said unto me, Take it, and eat it up; and it shall make thy belly bitter, but it shall be in thy mouth sweet as honey.

10 And I took the little book out of the angel's hand, and ate it up; and it was in my mouth sweet as honey: and as soon as I had eaten it, my belly was bitter.

11 And he said unto me, Thou must prophesy again before many peoples, and nations, and tongues, and kings.

The Two Witnesses

11 And there was given me a reed like unto a rod: and the angel stood, saying, Rise, and measure the temple of God, and the altar, and them that worship therein.

2 But the court which is without the temple

leave out, and measure it not; for it is given
unto the Gentiles: and the holy city shall they
tread under foot forty and two months.

3 And I will give power unto my two witnesses, and they shall prophesy a thousand
two hundred and threescore days, clothed in
sackcloth.

4 These are the two olive trees, and the
two candlesticks standing before the God of
the earth.

5 And if any man will hurt them, fire proceedeth out of their mouth, and devoureth
their enemies: and if any man will hurt them,
he must in this manner be killed.

6 These have power to shut heaven, that it
rain not in the days of their prophecy: and
have power over waters to turn them to
blood, and to smite the earth with all plagues,
as often as they will.

7 And when they shall have finished their
testimony, the beast that ascendeth out of the
bottomless pit shall make war against them,
and shall overcome them, and kill them.

8 And their dead bodies shall lie in the
street of the great city, which spiritually is
called Sodom and Egypt, where also our Lord
was crucified.

9 And they of the people and kindreds and
tongues and nations shall see their dead bodies
three days and a half, and shall not suffer
their dead bodies to be put in graves.

10 And they that dwell upon the earth shall
rejoice over them, and make merry, and shall
send gifts one to another; because these two

prophets tormented them that dwelt on the earth.

11 And after three days and a half the Spirit of life from God entered into them, and they stood upon their feet; and great fear fell upon them which saw them.

12 And they heard a great voice from heaven saying unto them, Come up hither. And they ascended up to heaven in a cloud; and their enemies beheld them.

13 And the same hour was there a great earthquake, and the tenth part of the city fell, and in the earthquake were slain of men seven thousand: and the remnant were affrighted, and gave glory to the God of heaven.

14 The second woe is past; and, behold, the third woe cometh quickly.

The Seventh Trumpet

15 And the seventh angel sounded; and there were great voices in heaven, saying, The kingdoms of this world are become the kingdoms of our Lord, and of his Christ; and he shall reign for ever and ever.

16 And the four and twenty elders, which sat before God on their seats, fell upon their faces, and worshipped God,

17 Saying, We give thee thanks, O Lord God Almighty, which art, and wast, and art to come; because thou hast taken to thee thy great power, and hast reigned.

18 And the nations were angry, and thy wrath is come, and the time of the dead, that they should be judged, and that thou shouldest

give reward unto thy servants the prophets, and to the saints, and them that fear thy name, small and great; and shouldest destroy them which destroy the earth.

19 And the temple of God was opened in heaven, and there was seen in his temple the ark of his testament: and there were lightnings, and voices, and thunderings, and an earthquake, and great hail.

The Woman and the Dragon

12 And there appeared a great wonder in heaven; a woman clothed with the sun, and the moon under her feet, and upon her head a crown of twelve stars:

2 And she being with child cried, travailing in birth, and pained to be delivered.

3 And there appeared another wonder in heaven; and behold a great red dragon, having seven heads and ten horns, and seven crowns upon his heads.

4 And his tail drew the third part of the stars of heaven, and did cast them to the earth: and the dragon stood before the woman which was ready to be delivered, for to devour her child as soon as it was born.

5 And she brought forth a man child, who was to rule all nations with a rod of iron: and her child was caught up unto God, and to his throne.

6 And the woman fled into the wilderness, where she hath a place prepared of God, that they should feed her there a thousand two hundred and threescore days.

7 And there was war in heaven: Michael and his angels fought against the dragon; and the dragon fought and his angels,

8 And prevailed not; neither was their place found any more in heaven.

9 And the great dragon was cast out, that old serpent, called the Devil, and Satan, which deceiveth the whole world: he was cast out into the earth, and his angels were cast out with him.

10 And I heard a loud voice saying in heaven, Now is come salvation, and strength, and the kingdom of our God, and the power of his Christ: for the accuser of our brethren is cast down, which accused them before our God day and night.

11 And they overcame him by the blood of the Lamb, and by the word of their testimony; and they loved not their lives unto the death.

12 Therefore rejoice, ye heavens, and ye that dwell in them. Woe to the inhabiters of the earth and of the sea! for the devil is come down unto you, having great wrath, because he knoweth that he hath but a short time.

13 And when the dragon saw that he was cast unto the earth, he persecuted the woman which brought forth the man child.

14 And to the woman were given two wings of a great eagle, that she might fly into the wilderness, into her place, where she is nourished for a time, and times, and half a time, from the face of the serpent.

15 And the serpent cast out of his mouth

water as a flood after the woman, that he
might cause her to be carried away of the
flood.

16 And the earth helped the woman; and
the earth opened her mouth, and swallowed
up the flood which the dragon cast out of his
mouth.

17 And the dragon was wroth with the
woman, and went to make war with the
remnant of her seed, which keep the commandments of God, and have the testimony of
Jesus Christ.

The Two Beasts

13 And I stood upon the sand of the sea,
and saw a beast rise up out of the sea,
having seven heads and ten horns, and upon
his horns ten crowns, and upon his heads the
name of blasphemy.

2 And the beast which I saw was like unto
a leopard, and his feet were as the feet of a
bear, and his mouth as the mouth of a lion:
and the dragon gave him his power, and his
seat, and great authority.

3 And I saw one of his heads as it were
wounded to death; and his deadly wound was
healed: and all the world wondered after the
beast.

4 And they worshipped the dragon which
gave power unto the beast: and they worshipped the beast, saying, Who is like unto
the beast? who is able to make war with him?

5 And there was given unto him a mouth
speaking great things and blasphemies; and

power[1849] was[1325] given unto him to continue[4160] forty[5062] and two months.

6 And he[3376] opened his mouth in blasphemy against God, to[455] blaspheme his[4750] name,[988] and his tabernacle,[2316] and them[987] that dwell[3686] in heaven.

[4633] 7 And it was given[4637] unto him to make[3772] war with the saints,[1325] and to overcome[3528] them:[40] and[4171] power was[40] given him[3528] over all[4171] kindreds, and[1849] tongues,[1325] and nations.[5443]

[1100] 8 And all that[1484] dwell upon the earth shall worship him, whose[2730] names are not[1093] written[4352] in the book of life of the[3686] Lamb[1125] slain[1125] from the foundation[976] of[2222] the world.[721] [4969]

[2602] 9 If any man have[2889] an ear, let him hear.

[1536] 10 He that leadeth[5100] into captivity[3775] shall[191] go[191] into captivity:[1536] he that[4863] killeth with[161] the sword[5217] must be[161] killed[1536] with the[615] sword. Here is[3162] the patience[1163] and[615] the faith of the[3162] saints.[5602]

[5281] 11 And I beheld[4102] another beast coming up out of the earth;[1492] and he[243] had two[2342] horns[305] like[2768] [3664] a lamb, and he[1093] spake as a dragon.

[721] 12 And he exerciseth[2980] all the power[1404] of the first beast before[4160] him, and causeth[1849] the earth and them which[2342] dwell[1799] therein[2730] to worship[4160] the[1093] first beast,[2342] whose deadly[2730] wound[2288] was[4127] healed.[2323] [4352]

13 And he doeth[2342] great wonders,[2288] so that[4127] he[2323] maketh fire[4160] come[3173] down[4592] from heaven on the earth in the[4160] sight[4442] of men,[2597] [3772]

[1093] 14 And deceiveth[1799] them[444] that dwell on the earth by the means[4105] of those[2730] miracles which he had power[1093] to do in the sight[4592] of the beast; saying[1325] to them[4160] that dwell on the[1799] earth,[2342] that they should make[2730] an image to the beast,[1093] which had the wound[4160] by a[1504] sword, and did[2342] live.
[4127]   [3162]   [2198]

15 And he had power to give life unto the image of the beast, that the image of the beast should both speak, and cause that as many as would not worship the image of the beast should be killed.

16 And he causeth all, both small and great, rich and poor, free and bond, to receive a mark in their right hand, or in their foreheads:

17 And that no man might buy or sell, save he that had the mark, or the name of the beast, or the number of his name.

18 Here is wisdom. Let him that hath understanding count the number of the beast: for it is the number of a man; and his number is Six hundred threescore and six.

The Song of the 144,000

14 And I looked, and, lo, a Lamb stood on the mount Zion, and with him a hundred forty and four thousand, having his Father's name written in their foreheads.

2 And I heard a voice from heaven, as the voice of many waters, and as the voice of a great thunder: and I heard the voice of harpers harping with their harps:

3 And they sung as it were a new song before the throne, and before the four beasts, and the elders: and no man could learn that song but the hundred and forty and four thousand, which were redeemed from the earth.

4 These are they which were not defiled with women; for they are virgins. These are

they which follow the Lamb whithersoever he goeth. These were redeemed from among men, being the firstfruits unto God and to the Lamb.

5 And in their mouth was found no guile: for they are without fault before the throne of God.

The Messages of the Three Angels

6 And I saw another angel fly in the midst of heaven, having the everlasting gospel to preach unto them that dwell on the earth, and to every nation, and kindred, and tongue, and people,

7 Saying with a loud voice, Fear God, and give glory to him; for the hour of his judgment is come: and worship him that made heaven, and earth, and the sea, and the fountains of waters.

8 And there followed another angel, saying, Babylon is fallen, is fallen, that great city, because she made all nations drink of the the wine of the wrath of her fornication.

9 And the third angel followed them, saying with a loud voice, If any man worship the beast and his image, and receive his mark in his forehead, or in his hand,

10 The same shall drink of the wine of the wrath of God, which is poured out without mixture into the cup of his indignation; and he shall be tormented with fire and brimstone in the presence of the holy angels, and in the presence of the Lamb:

11 And the smoke of their torment as-

cendeth up for ever and ever: and they have no rest[305] day nor[165] night,[165] who worship the beast and his[372] image,[2250] and[3571] whosoever[4352] receiveth[2342] the mark[1504] of his[2983] name.[5480]

12 Here[3686] is the patience of the saints: here are they[5602] that keep the[5281] commandments[40] of God,[5602] and the faith[5983] of Jesus.[1785] [2316]

13 And I[4102] heard[2424] a voice from heaven saying unto me, Write,[191] Blessed[5456] are the dead[3772] which die in the Lord[1125] from[3107] henceforth:[3498] Yea,[599] saith the Spirit,[2962] that[534] they may rest[3483] from their labors;[4151] and their works[2041] do[190] follow[373] them.[2873]

The Harvest of the Earth

14 And I looked, and behold a white cloud, and upon the[1492] cloud one[2400] sat like unto the[3022] Son[3507] of man, having on[3507] his head[2521] a[3664] golden crown,[5207] and[444] in his hand a sharp[2776] sickle.[5552] [4735]

15 And another[5495] angel[3691] came[1407] out of the temple, crying[243] with[32] a loud[1831] voice to him that[3485] sat[2896] on the cloud,[3173] Thrust[5456] in thy sickle,[2521] and reap: for[3507] the time[3992] is come for thee[1407] to reap;[2325] for the harvest[5610] of[2064] the earth is ripe.[2325] [2326] [1093] [3583]

16 And he that sat on the cloud thrust in his sickle[2521] on the[1407] earth;[1093] and[3507] the earth[906] was reaped.[1093] [2325]

17 And another angel[243] came[32] out of the temple which[1831] is in heaven, he also having a sharp[3485] sickle.[3772]

18 And[3691] another[1407] angel came out from the altar,[243] which[32] had power[1831] over fire; and cried[2379] with a loud[1849] cry to[4442] him that had the[5455] sharp sickle,[3173] saying,[2906] Thrust in thy sharp sickle,[3691] and[1407] [3992] [3691] [1407]

gather the clusters of the vine of the earth; for her grapes are fully ripe.

19 And the angel thrust in his sickle into the earth, and gathered the vine of the earth, and cast it into the great winepress of the wrath of God.

20 And the winepress was trodden without the city, and blood came out of the winepress, even unto the horse bridles, by the space of a thousand and six hundred furlongs.

The Angels with the Last Plagues

15 And I saw another sign in heaven, great and marvelous, seven angels having the seven last plagues; for in them is filled up the wrath of God.

2 And I saw as it were a sea of glass mingled with fire: and them that had gotten the victory over the beast, and over his image, and over his mark, and over the number of his name, stand on the sea of glass, having the harps of God.

3 And they sing the song of Moses the servant of God, and the song of the Lamb, saying, Great and marvelous are thy works, Lord God Almighty; just and true are thy ways, thou King of saints.

4 Who shall not fear thee, O Lord, and glorify thy name? For thou only art holy: for all nations shall come and worship before thee; for thy judgments are made manifest.

5 And after that I looked, and, behold, the temple of the tabernacle of the testimony in heaven was opened:

6 And the seven angels came out of the temple, having the seven plagues, clothed in pure and white linen, and having their breasts girded with golden girdles.

7 And one of the four beasts gave unto the seven angels seven golden vials full of the wrath of God, who liveth for ever and ever.

8 And the temple was filled with smoke from the glory of God, and from his power; and no man was able to enter into the temple, till the seven plagues of the seven angels were fulfilled.

The Vials of Wrath

16 And I heard a great voice out of the temple saying to the seven angels, Go your ways, and pour out the vials of the wrath of God upon the earth.

2 And the first went, and poured out his vial upon the earth; and there fell a noisome and grievous sore upon the men which had the mark of the beast, and upon them which worshipped his image.

3 And the second angel poured out his vial upon the sea; and it became as the blood of a dead man: and every living soul died in the sea.

4 And the third angel poured out his vial upon the rivers and fountains of waters; and they became blood.

5 And I heard the angel of the waters say, Thou art righteous, O Lord, which art, and wast, and shalt be, because thou hast judged thus.

6 For they have shed the blood of saints
and prophets, and thou hast given them blood
to drink; for they are worthy.

7 And I heard another out of the altar say,
Even so, Lord God Almighty, true and
righteous are thy judgments.

8 And the fourth angel poured out his vial
upon the sun; and power was given unto him
to scorch men with fire.

9 And men were scorched with great heat,
and blasphemed the name of God, which hath
power over these plagues: and they repented
not to give him glory.

10 And the fifth angel poured out his vial
upon the seat of the beast; and his kingdom
was full of darkness; and they gnawed their
tongues for pain,

11 And blasphemed the God of heaven because of their pains and their sores, and repented not of their deeds.

12 And the sixth angel poured out his vial
upon the great river Euphrates; and the
water thereof was dried up, that the way of
the kings of the east might be prepared.

13 And I saw three unclean spirits like
frogs come out of the mouth of the dragon,
and out of the mouth of the beast, and out of
the mouth of the false prophet.

14 For they are the spirits of devils, working miracles, which go forth unto the kings of
the earth and of the whole world, to gather
them to the battle of that great day of God
Almighty.

15 Behold, I come as a thief. Blessed is he

that watcheth, and keepeth his garments, lest he walk naked, and they see his shame.

16 And he gathered them together into a place called in the Hebrew tongue Armaged´-don.

17 And the seventh angel poured out his vial into the air; and there came a great voice out of the temple of heaven, from the throne, saying, It is done.

18 And there were voices, and thunders, and lightnings; and there was a great earthquake, such as was not since men were upon the earth, so mighty an earthquake, and so great.

19 And the great city was divided into three parts, and the cities of the nations fell: and great Babylon came in remembrance before God, to give unto her the cup of the wine of the fierceness of his wrath.

20 And every island fled away, and the mountains were not found.

21 And there fell upon men a great hail out of heaven, every stone about the weight of a talent: and men blasphemed God because of the plague of the hail; for the plague thereof was exceeding great.

The Judgment of the Great Harlot

17 And there came one of the seven angels which had the seven vials, and talked with me, saying unto me, Come hither; I will show unto thee the judgment of the great whore that sitteth upon many waters;

2 With whom the kings of the earth have committed fornication, and the inhabitants of

the earth have been made drunk with the wine of her fornication.

3 So he carried me away in the spirit into the wilderness: and I saw a woman sit upon a scarlet-colored beast, full of names of blasphemy, having seven heads and ten horns.

4 And the woman was arrayed in purple and scarlet color, and decked with gold and precious stones and pearls, having a golden cup in her hand full of abominations and filthiness of her fornication:

5 And upon her forehead was a name written, MYSTERY, BABYLON THE GREAT, THE MOTHER OF HARLOTS AND ABOMINATIONS OF THE EARTH.

6 And I saw the woman drunken with the blood of the saints, and with the blood of the martyrs of Jesus. And when I saw her, I wondered with great admiration.

7 And the angel said unto me, Wherefore didst thou marvel? I will tell thee the mystery of the woman, and of the beast that carrieth her, which hath the seven heads and ten horns.

8 The beast that thou sawest was, and is not; and shall ascend out of the bottomless pit, and go into perdition: and they that dwell on the earth shall wonder, whose names were not written in the book of life from the foundation of the world, when they behold the beast that was, and is not, and yet is.

9 And here is the mind which hath wisdom. The seven heads are seven mountains, on which the woman sitteth.

10 And there are seven kings: five are
fallen, and one is, and the other is not yet
come; and when he cometh, he must continue
a short space.

11 And the beast that was, and is not, even
he is the eighth, and is of the seven, and
goeth into perdition.

12 And the ten horns which thou sawest are
ten kings, which have received no kingdom as
yet; but receive power as kings one hour with
the beast.

13 These have one mind, and shall give
their power and strength unto the beast.

14 These shall make war with the Lamb,
and the Lamb shall overcome them: for he is
Lord of lords, and King of kings: and they
that are with him are called, and chosen, and
faithful.

15 And he saith unto me, The waters which
thou sawest, where the whore sitteth, are
peoples, and multitudes, and nations, and
tongues.

16 And the ten horns which thou sawest
upon the beast, these shall hate the whore,
and shall make her desolate and naked,
and shall eat her flesh, and burn her with
fire.

17 For God hath put in their hearts to fulfil his will, and to agree, and give their kingdom unto the beast, until the words of God
shall be fulfilled.

18 And the woman which thou sawest is
that great city, which reigneth over the kings
of the earth.

The Fall of Babylon

18 And after these things I saw another angel come down from heaven, having great power; and the earth was lightened with his glory.

2 And he cried mightily with a strong voice, saying, Babylon the great is fallen, is fallen, and is become the habitation of devils, and the hold of every foul spirit, and a cage of every unclean and hateful bird.

3 For all nations have drunk of the wine of the wrath of her fornication, and the kings of the earth have committed fornication with her, and the merchants of the earth are waxed rich through the abundance of her delicacies.

4 And I heard another voice from heaven, saying, Come out of her, my people, that ye be not partakers of her sins, and that ye receive not of her plagues.

5 For her sins have reached unto heaven, and God hath remembered her iniquities.

6 Reward her even as she rewarded you, and double unto her double according to her works: in the cup which she hath filled, fill to her double.

7 How much she hath glorified herself, and lived deliciously, so much torment and sorrow give her: for she saith in her heart, I sit a queen, and am no widow, and shall see no sorrow.

8 Therefore shall her plagues come in one day, death, and mourning, and famine; and she shall be utterly burned with fire: for strong is the Lord God who judgeth her.

9 And the kings of the earth, who have committed[935] fornication and lived[1093] deliciously with her, shall bewail[4203] her, and lament[4763] for her, when they shall see[2799] the smoke of her[2875] burning,

10 Standing[991] afar off for[2586] the fear[5401] of her[4451] torment,[2476] saying,[3113] Alas, alas, that great city Babylon,[929] that mighty[3759] city! for in one[3173] hour[4172] is thy[897] judgment[2478] [4172] come.[5610] [2064]

11 And[2929] the[2064] merchants of the earth shall weep and mourn over[1713] her; for no man buyeth[1093] their[2799] merchandise[3996] any more:[59]

12 The merchandise[1117] of gold, and silver, and precious stones,[1117] and of pearls,[5557] and fine linen,[696] and purple,[5093] and silk,[3037] and scarlet,[3135] and all[1040] thyine wood,[4209] and all manner[4596] vessels of ivory,[2847] and all manner[2367] [3586] vessels of most precious[4632] wood,[1661] and of brass, and iron,[4632] and marble,[5093] [3586]

13 And cinnamon,[5475] and odors,[4604] and ointments,[3139] and frankincense,[2792] and wine,[2368] and oil,[3464] and fine flour,[3030] and wheat,[3631] and beasts,[1637] and sheep,[4585] and horses,[4621] and chariots,[2934] and slaves,[4263] and souls of men.[2462] [4480] [4983]

14 And the fruits[5590] [444] that thy soul lusted after[3703] are departed from thee, and all things which[5590] [1939] were dainty[565] and goodly are departed from thee, and thou shalt find[3045] them no more at all.[2986] [565]

15 The merchants[2147] of these things, which were made rich[1713] by her, shall stand afar off for[4147] the fear of her torment,[2476] weeping and wailing,[3113] [3996]

16 And saying,[5401] Alas,[929] alas, that great city,[2799] that was clothed in fine linen,[3759] and purple,[3173] and[4172] scarlet,[4016] and decked[1039] with gold, and precious[4210] stones,[2847] and pearls![5558] [5557] [5093]

17 For in one hour so great riches is come[3037] [3135] [5610] [5118] [4149] [2049]

to nought. And every shipmaster, and all the
company in ships, and sailors, and as many as
trade by sea, stood afar off,

18 And cried when they saw the smoke of
her burning, saying, What city is like unto this
great city!

19 And they cast dust on their heads, and
cried, weeping and wailing, saying, Alas, alas,
that great city, wherein were made rich all
that had ships in the sea by reason of her
costliness! for in one hour is she made
desolate.

20 Rejoice over her, thou heaven, and ye
holy apostles and prophets; for God hath
avenged you on her.

21 And a mighty angel took up a stone like
a great millstone, and cast it into the sea, saying, Thus with violence shall that great city
Babylon be thrown down, and shall be found
no more at all.

22 And the voice of harpers, and musicians,
and of pipers, and trumpeters, shall be heard
no more at all in thee; and no craftsman, of
whatsoever craft he be, shall be found
any more in thee; and the sound of a
millstone shall be heard no more at all in
thee;

23 And the light of a candle shall shine no
more at all in thee; and the voice of the
bridegroom and of the bride shall be heard
no more at all in thee: for thy merchants were
the great men of the earth; for by thy sorceries were all nations deceived.

24 And in her was found the blood of

prophets, and of saints, and of all that were slain upon the earth.

The Multitude in Heaven Praises God

19 And after these things I heard a great voice of much people in heaven, saying, Alleluia; Salvation, and glory, and honor, and power, unto the Lord our God:

2 For true and righteous are his judgments; for he hath judged the great whore, which did corrupt the earth with her fornication, and hath avenged the blood of his servants at her hand.

3 And again they said, Alleluia. And her smoke rose up for ever and ever.

4 And the four and twenty elders and the four beasts fell down and worshipped God that sat on the throne, saying, Amen; Alleluia.

5 And a voice came out of the throne, saying, Praise our God, all ye his servants, and ye that fear him, both small and great.

6 And I heard as it were the voice of a great multitude, and as the voice of many waters, and as the voice of mighty thunderings, saying, Alleluia: for the Lord God omnipotent reigneth.

7 Let us be glad and rejoice, and give honor to him: for the marriage of the Lamb is come, and his wife hath made herself ready.

8 And to her was granted that she should be arrayed in fine linen, clean and white: for the fine linen is the righteousness of saints.

The Marriage Supper of the Lamb

9 And he saith unto me, Write, Blessed are they which are called unto the marriage supper of the Lamb. And he saith unto me, These are the true sayings of God.

10 And I fell at his feet to worship him. And he said unto me, See thou do it not: I am thy fellow servant, and of thy brethren that have the testimony of Jesus: worship God: for the testimony of Jesus is the spirit of prophecy.

The Rider on the White Horse

11 And I saw heaven opened, and behold a white horse; and he that sat upon him was called Faithful and True, and in righteousness he doth judge and make war.

12 His eyes were as a flame of fire, and on his head were many crowns; and he had a name written, that no man knew, but he himself.

13 And he was clothed with a vesture dipped in blood: and his name is called The Word of God.

14 And the armies which were in heaven followed him upon white horses, clothed in fine linen, white and clean.

15 And out of his mouth goeth a sharp sword, that with it he should smite the nations; and he shall rule them with a rod of iron: and he treadeth the winepress of the fierceness and wrath of Almighty God.

16 And he hath on his vesture and on his thigh a name written, KING OF KINGS, AND LORD OF LORDS.

17 And I saw an angel standing in the sun; and he cried with a loud voice, saying to all the fowls that fly in the midst of heaven, Come and gather yourselves together unto the supper of the great God;

18 That ye may eat the flesh of kings, and the flesh of captains, and the flesh of mighty men, and the flesh of horses, and of them that sit on them, and the flesh of all men, both free and bond, both small and great.

19 And I saw the beast, and the kings of the earth, and their armies, gathered together to make war against him that sat on the horse, and against his army.

20 And the beast was taken, and with him the false prophet that wrought miracles before him, with which he deceived them that had received the mark of the beast, and them that worshipped his image. These both were cast alive into a lake of fire burning with brimstone.

21 And the remnant were slain with the sword of him that sat upon the horse, which sword proceeded out of his mouth: and all the fowls were filled with their flesh.

The Thousand Years

20 And I saw an angel come down from heaven, having the key of the bottomless pit and a great chain in his hand.

2 And he laid hold on the dragon, that old serpent, which is the Devil, and Satan, and bound him a thousand years,

3 And cast him into the bottomless pit, and

shut him up,[2808] and[2808] set a seal[4972] upon him, that he should deceive the[4105] nations[1883] no more,[2089] till[891] the thousand[4105] years should[1484] be fulfilled:[2089] and[891] after that he must[5507] be[2094] loosed[5055] a little season.

4 And I[1163] saw[3089] thrones,[3398] and they[5550] sat upon them, and[1492] judgment[2362] was given unto[2523] them: and I saw the souls[2917] of them[1325] that were beheaded[5590] for the witness of Jesus,[3990] and for the word of God, and[3141] which had[2424] not worshipped the[3056] beast,[2316] neither his image,[4352] neither[4352] had received[2342] his[3777] mark[1504] upon their foreheads,[2983] or in their[5480] hands; and they lived and[3359] reigned with Christ a[5495] thousand[2198] years.[936]

5 But[5547] the[5507] rest of[2094] the dead lived not again until the[3062] thousand years[3498] were[326] finished. This is[326] the first[5507] resurrection.[2094][5055]

6 Blessed and[306] holy is he that hath part in the first[3107] resurrection:[40] on such the second[3313] death hath no power,[386] but they shall be[1208] priests[2288] of God and[1849] of Christ, and shall reign[2409] with him a[2316] thousand[5547] years.[936]

7 And when[5507] the[2094] thousand years are expired, Satan shall be loosed[5507] out[2094] of his prison,[5055]

8 And[4567] shall[3089] go out to deceive the[5438] nations which are[1831] in the four quarters[4105] of the[1484] earth, Gog and Magog, to gather[1137] them together[1093] to battle:[1136] the[3098] number[4863] of whom is as the[4863] sand of[4171] the sea.[706][285]

9 And[2281] they went up on the breadth of the earth, and compassed[305] the camp[4114] of the saints about,[1093] and the beloved[3925] city: and fire[40] came down[2944] from God[25] out of[4172] heaven, and devoured[4442][2597] them.[2316][3772][2719]

10 And the devil that deceived them was[1228][4105][906]

cast into the lake of fire and brimstone, where the beast and the false prophet are, and shall be tormented day and night for ever and ever.

The Judgment at the Great White Throne

11 And I saw a great white throne, and him that sat on it, from whose face the earth and the heaven fled away; and there was found no place for them.

12 And I saw the dead, small and great, stand before God; and the books were opened: and another book was opened, which is the book of life: and the dead were judged out of those things which were written in the books, according to their works.

13 And the sea gave up the dead which were in it; and death and hell delivered up the dead which were in them: and they were judged every man according to their works.

14 And death and hell were cast into the lake of fire. This is the second death.

15 And whosoever was not found written in the book of life was cast into the lake of fire.

The New Heaven and the New Earth

21 And I saw a new heaven and a new earth: for the first heaven and the first earth were passed away; and there was no more sea.

2 And I John saw the holy city, new Jerusalem, coming down from God out of heaven, prepared as a bride adorned for her husband.

3 And I heard a great voice out of heaven saying, Behold, the tabernacle of God is with

men, and he will dwell with them, and they shall be his people, and God himself shall be with them, and be their God.

4 And God shall wipe away all tears from their eyes; and there shall be no more death, neither sorrow, nor crying, neither shall there be any more pain: for the former things are passed away.

5 And he that sat upon the throne said, Behold, I make all things new. And he said unto me, Write: for these words are true and faithful.

6 And he said unto me, It is done. I am Alpha and Ome'ga, the beginning and the end. I will give unto him that is athirst of the fountain of the water of life freely.

7 He that overcometh shall inherit all things; and I will be his God, and he shall be my son.

8 But the fearful, and unbelieving, and the abominable, and murderers, and whoremongers, and sorcerers, and idolaters, and all liars, shall have their part in the lake which burneth with fire and brimstone: which is the second death.

The New Jerusalem

9 And there came unto me one of the seven angels which had the seven vials full of the seven last plagues, and talked with me, saying, Come hither, I will show thee the bride, the Lamb's wife.

10 And he carried me away in the spirit to a great and high mountain, and showed me

that great city, the holy Jerusalem, descending out of heaven from God,

11 Having the glory of God: and her light was like unto a stone most precious, even like a jasper stone, clear as crystal;

12 And had a wall great and high, and had twelve gates, and at the gates twelve angels, and names written thereon, which are the names of the twelve tribes of the children of Israel:

13 On the east three gates; on the north three gates; on the south three gates; and on the west three gates.

14 And the wall of the city had twelve foundations, and in them the names of the twelve apostles of the Lamb.

15 And he that talked with me had a golden reed to measure the city, and the gates thereof, and the wall thereof.

16 And the city lieth foursquare, and the length is as large as the breadth: and he measured the city with the reed, twelve thousand furlongs. The length and the breadth and the height of it are equal.

17 And he measured the wall thereof, a hundred and forty and four cubits, according to the measure of a man, that is, of the angel.

18 And the building of the wall of it was of jasper: and the city was pure gold, like unto clear glass.

19 And the foundations of the wall of the city were garnished with all manner of precious stones. The first foundation was

jasper; the second, sapphire; the third, a
2393   1208   4552   5154
chalcedony; the fourth, an emerald;
5472   5067   4665

20 The fifth, sardonyx; the sixth, sardius;
         3991   4557   1622   4556
the seventh, chrysolite; the eighth, beryl; the
       1442   5555   3590   969
ninth, a topaz; the tenth, a chrysoprasus; the
1766   5116   1182   5556
eleventh, a jacinth; the twelfth, an amethyst.
1734   5192   1428   271

21 And the twelve gates were twelve pearls;
                        4440   3135
every several gate was of one pearl: and the
303-1538   4440   3135
street of the city was pure gold, as it were
4113   4172   2513 5553
transparent glass.
1307   5194

22 And I saw no temple therein: for the
Lord God Almighty and the Lamb are the
2962 2316 3485   721
temple of it.
3841

23 And the city had no need of the sun,
3485   2246
neither of the moon, to shine in it: for the
                4172   5532
glory of God did lighten it, and the Lamb
      1391 2316 4582 5316
is the light thereof.   721
       2316 5461

24 And the nations of them which are saved
        3088
shall walk in the light of it: and the kings of
              1484   4982
the earth do bring their glory and honor into
4043   5457   1391   935
it.
1093 5342   5092

25 And the gates of it shall not be shut at
              4440   2808   2808
all by day: for there shall be no night there.
2250   3571 1563

26 And they shall bring the glory and
        2250   1391
honor of the nations into it.
5092   1484

27 And there shall in no wise enter into it
                                          1525
any thing that defileth, neither whatsoever
            2840
worketh abomination, or maketh a lie: but
4160   946   5579 1508
they which are written in the Lamb's book of
      1125   721   975
life.
2222

22 And he showed me a pure river of
            1166   2513 4215
water of life, clear as crystal, proceeding
5204   2222 2986   2930   1607
out of the throne of God and of the Lamb.
5204   2222   2930   721

2 In the midst of the street of it, and on
        3319   4113   1782

either side of the river, was there the tree of life, which bare twelve manner of fruits, and yielded her fruit every month: and the leaves of the tree were for the healing of the nations.

3 And there shall be no more curse: but the throne of God and of the Lamb shall be in it; and his servants shall serve him:

4 And they shall see his face; and his name shall be in their foreheads.

5 And there shall be no night there; and they need no candle, neither light of the sun; for the Lord God giveth them light: and they shall reign for ever and ever.

Jesus to Come Soon

6 And he said unto me, These sayings are faithful and true: and the Lord God of the holy prophets sent his angel to show unto his servants the things which must shortly be done.

7 Behold, I come quickly. Blessed is he that keepeth the sayings of the prophecy of this book.

8 And I John saw these things, and heard them. And when I had heard and seen, I fell down to worship before the feet of the angel which showed me these things.

9 Then saith he unto me, See thou do it not: for I am thy fellow servant, and of thy brethren the prophets, and of them which keep the sayings of this book: worship God.

10 And he saith unto me, Seal not the sayings of the prophecy of this book: for the time is at hand.

11 He that is unjust, let him be unjust still: and he which[91] is filthy, let him be filthy[2089] still: and he that[4510] is righteous, let him be righteous[2089] still: and he that[1342] is holy, let[1344] him be[1344] holy still. [2089] 12 And, behold, I[40] come[37] quickly; and my[2089] reward is with[2400] me, to give[2064] every[5035] man according[3408] as his work shall be.[591] [1538]

13 I am[204] Alpha and Ome′ga, the beginning and the end, the[1] first and[5598] the last.[746]

14 Blessed[5056] are they that do his[2078] commandments, that[3107] they may have right[4160] to the tree[1785] of life, and may enter in through the gates[3586] into the[2222] city.[1525] [4440]

15 For[4172] without are dogs, and sorcerers, and whoremongers,[1854] and murderers,[2965] and idolaters,[5333] and whosoever[4205] loveth[5406] and maketh a lie.[1496]

16 I Jesus have[5368] sent mine[4160] angel to testify[5579] unto you[2424] these[3992] things in the churches.[32] I am[3140] the root and the offspring of David,[1577] and the bright[4491] and morning star.[1085] [1138]

[2986] 17 And the[3720] Spirit and the[792] bride say, Come. And let him that[4151] heareth say,[3565] Come. And[2064] let him that is athirst[191] come.[2036] And whosoever[2064] will,[2064] let him[1372] take the[2064] water of life freely.[2309]

[2983] 18 For I[2983] testify[5204] unto every[2222] man[1432] that heareth the words of the[4828] prophecy of this book,[191] If any man[3056] shall add[4394] unto these things, God[975] shall[5100] add unto him[2007] the plagues that are written in[2316] [2007] this book:[4127] [1125]

[975] 19 And if any man shall take away from the words of the book[5100] of this[851] prophecy, God shall[3056] take away his[976] part out of the book of[4394] life, and[2316] [851] out of the holy[3313] city, and from the[976] things[2222] which are written[40] in[4172] this book.
[1125] [975]

20 He which testifieth these things saith,
Surely I come quickly: Amen. Even so, come,
  3140   2064   5035   281   3483......   2064
Lord Jesus.
2962   2424
  21 The grace of our Lord Jesus Christ be
            5485   2962 2424   5547
with you all. Amen.
              281

Key Number Index to Standard Reference Works

The following index is designed to help the student locate any word quickly in either the Arndt & Gingrich <u>Lexicon</u> or the Moulton & Geden <u>Concordance</u> or Kittel's <u>Theological Dictionary</u> by using the numbering system of Strong and of the <u>Word Study Concordance</u>. First, determine the number of the word, using this <u>Word Study</u> <u>New</u> <u>Testament</u>). Then, locate that number in the adjoining column for Arndt & Gingrich, Moulton & Geden, or Kittel. For example, <u>hilasteerion</u> (propitiation), WSC #2435, will be found on page 376 in Arndt & Gingrich, on page 486 in Moulton & Geden, and on page 300, volume 3 of Kittel. The second column in each case below gives the number of occurrences (or the <u>frequency</u>) of that word. Starred numbers are found in the Proper Names Index in the Word Study Concordance.

WSC	F	A&G/M&G	K
1	4	1/46	1:1
2*	5	1/1	1:3
3*	1	1/1	1:4
4	1	1/1	
5	3	1/1	1:5
6*	4	1/1	1:6
7*	3	1/1	
8*	1	1/1	
9*	1	1/1	
10*	2	1/1	
11*	73	1/1	1:8
12	9	2/2	1:9
13*	2	2/2	
14	1	2/2	1:10
15	10	/2	1:10
16	1	2/2	1:10
17	1	2/2	1:10
18	102	2/2	1:10
19	4	3/4	1:10
20	5	3/4	1:19
21	11	3/4	1:19
22	4	4/4	
23	7	4/4	
24	1	4/4	
25	142	4/4	1:21
26	116	5/6	1.21
27	62	6/7	1:21
28*	2	6/8	1:55
29	3	6/8	
30	2	6/8	
31	1	7/8	1:56
32	186	7/8	1:74
33	2	8/10	
34	8	8/10	
35	1	8/10	1:662
36	1	8/10	
37	29	8/10	1:88
38	10	9/11	1:88
39	11	9/	
40	229	9/11	1:88
41	1	10/14	1:88
42	3	10/14	1:88
43	1	10/14	
44	1	10/14	
45	4	10/14	
46	2	10/14	
47	2	10/14	1:122
48	7	11/14	1:122
49	1	11/14	1:122
50	22	11/14	1:115
51	1	11/14	1:115
52	4	11/14	1:115
53	8	11/14	1:122
54	1	12/14	1:122
55	1	12/14	
56	2	12/14	1:115
57	1	12/14	1:115
58	11	12/15	
59	31	12/15	1:124
60	2	12/15	
61	1	13/15	
62	1	13/15	
63	1	13/15	
64	1	13/15	
65	2	13/15	
66	3	13/15	
67	12	13/15	
68	36	13/15	

WSC	F	A&G/M&G	K
69	4	13/16	2:333
70	2	14/16	
71	71	14/16	
72	1	14/17	1:128
73	6	14/17	1:134
74	1	15/17	1:134
75	7	15/17	1:134
76*	9	15/17	1:141
77	1	15/17	
78*	1	15/17	
79	24	15/17	1:144
80	346	15/17	1:144
81	2	16/21	1:144
82	1	16/21	
83	1	16/21	
84	1	16/21	
85	3	16/21	
86	11	16/21	1:146
87	1	16/21	3:921
88	2	17/21	
89	4	17/21	
90	1	17/	
91	27	17/21	1:149
92	3	17/22	1:149
93	25	17/22	1:149
94	12	17/22	1.149
95	1	18/22	
96	8	18/22	2:255
97	1	18/22	
98*	1	18/22	
99*	1	18/22	
100	1	18/22	
101	2	18/22	2:284
102	10	18/23	2:284
103	5	18/23	1:163
104	8	19/23	
105	4	19/23	
106	9	19/23	2:902
107*	2	19/23	
108*	1	19/23	
109	7	19/23	1:165
110	3	20/23	3:7
111	2	20/23	1:166
112	1	20/23	3:65
113	2	20/23	1:167
114	16	20/23	8:152
115	2	20/23	8:152
116*	4	20/24	
117*	2	20/24	
118	2	20/24	1:167
119	1	20/24	1:167
120	1	21/24	
121	2	21/24	
122	1	21/24	
123	6	21/24	
124*	5	21/24	
125*	24	21/24	
126	2	21/24	1:168
127	2	21/24	1:169
128*	2	21/24	
129	99	22/25	1:172
130	1	22/26	1:172
131	1	23/26	
132*	2	23/26	
133	1	23/26	
134	9	23/26	1:177
135	1	23/26	1:178
136	2	23/26	

WSC	F	A&G/M&G	K
137*	1	23/26	
138	3	23/26	1:180
139	9	23/26	1:180
140	1	23/26	1:180
141	1	23/26	1:180
142	102	23/	1:185
143	1	26/27	1:187
144	1	24/27	1:187
145	1	24/27	1:187
146	3	24/27	
147	1	24/27	
148	1	24/27	
149	3	24/27	
150	1	24/27	1:189
151	1	24/28	1:189
152	6	24/28	1:189
153	5	25/28	1:189
154	71	25/28	1:191
155	3	25/28	1:191
156	20	25/28	
157	1	26/28	
158	4	26/29	
159	1	26/29	
160	2	26/29	
161	3	26/29	1:195
162	2	26/29	1:195
163	3	26/29	1:195
164	1	26/29	1:195
165	128	26/29	1:197
166	71	27/30	1:197
167	10	28/31	3:413
168	1	28/	
169	30	28/31	3:413
170	2	28/32	3:455
171	1	28/32	3:455
172	2	28/32	3:469
173	14	28/32	
174	2	29/32	
175	7	29/32	3:614
176	1	29/32	1:689
177	2	29/32	
178	2	29/32	3:921
179	1	29/32	4:328
180	1	29/32	
181	5	29/32	3:444
182	1	29/32	3:444
183	1	29/32	
184*	1	29/135	
185	3	29/32	1:209
186	1	30/32	
187	1	30/33	
188	1	30/33	
189	24	30/33	1:216
190	92	30/33	1:210
191	437	31/34	1:216
192	2	32/38	2:339
193	1	32/38	2:339
194	1	32/38	
195	1	32/38	
196	1	32/38	
197	4	32/38	
198	1	32/38	
199	5	32/38	
200	4	32/39	
201	1	33/39	
202	4	33/39	
203	20	33/39	1:225
204	2	33/39	1:791

WSC	F	A&G/M&G	K
205	1	33/39	
206	6	33/39	
207*	6	33/39	
208	3	33/39	3:1098
209	1	33/39	
210	1	33/39	2:469
211	4	33/39	
212	2	34/39	1:226
213	2	34/39	1:226
214	2	34/39	1:227
215	1	34/39	
216	3	34/39	
217	8	34/40	1:228
218	9	34/40	1:229
219	1	34/40	
220	12	34/40	
221*	2	34/40	
222*	2	35/40	
223*	6	35/40	
224	2	35/40	
225	110	35/40	1:232
226	2	36/41	1:232
227	25	36/41	1:232
228	27	36/42	1:232
229	2	36/42	
230	21	36/42	
231	5	37/40	
232	1	37/42	
233	3	37/42	
234	1	37/42	
235	636	37/42	
236	6	38/43	1:251
237	1	38/43	
238	1	38/43	1:260
239	4	38/43	1:264
240	100	38/43	
241	1	39/44	1:264
242	3	39/44	
243	160	39/44	1:264
244	1	39/46	2:599
245	14	40/46	1:264
246	1	40/46	1:264
247	1	40/46	
248	3	40/46	
249	3	40/46	4:69
250	1	40/46	
251	1	40/46	
252	1	40/46	
253	1	40/46	4:313
254	11	40/46	
255	1	40/46	
256*	5	41/47	
257	2	41/47	
258	3	41/47	
259	1	41/47	
260	10	41/47	
261	1	41/47	
262	1	41/47	
263	1	41/47	
264	43	41/47	1:267
265	4	42/47	1:267
266	174	42/47	1:267
267	1	43/49	
268	47	43/50	1:317
269	2	44/50	4:527
270	1	44/50	
271	1	44/50	
272	5	44/50	

WSC	F	A&G/M&G	K
273	5	44/50	4:571
274	2	44/50	
275	2	44/50	4:589
267	2	44/50	
277	1	44/50	
278	2	44/51	4:626
279	1	45/51	4:948
280	2	45/51	4:632
281	152	45/51	1:335
282	1	45/52	
283	4	45/52	4:644
284 *	3	45/52	
285	5	45/52	
286	4	45/52	1:338
287	1	46/52	
288	8	46/52	1:342
289	1	46/52	
290	23	46/52	
291 *	1	46/53	
292	1	46/53	
293	2	46/53	
294	4	46/53	
295 *	1	46/53	
296	1	47/53	
297	14	47/53	
298	2	47/53	4:829
299	7	47/53	4:829
300 *	2	47/	
301 *	1	47/53	
302	191	47/53	
303	10	49/55	
303	5	49/55	
304	2	49/56	
305	81	49/56	1:518
306	6	50/57	
307	1	50/57	
308	26	50/57	
309	1	50/57	
310	3	50/57	
311	1	50/57	
312	18	50/57	1:56
313	2	51/57	1:665
314	33	51/57	1:343
315	9	51/58	1:344
316	8	51/58	1:344
317	1	52/58	
318	18	52/58	1:344
319	1	/58	
320	3	52/58	1:343
321	24	52/58	
322	2	53/59	2:25
323	1	53/59	2:25
324	2	53/59	
325	1	53/59	
326	5	53/59	2:832
327	2	53/59	
328	1	53/59	
329	1	53/59	
330	1	53/59	
331	6	53/59	1:353
332	4	54/59	
333	2	54/59	
334	1	54/59	1:353
335	1	54/59	
336	2	54/59	
337	23	54/59	
338	2	54/59	
339	2	55/59	
340	1	55/60	3:447
341	2	55/60	3:447
342	2	55/60	3:447
343	2	55/60	3:447
344	4	55/60	3:556
345	14	55/60	3:654
346	2	55/60	3:673
347	8	55/60	
348	1	55/	
349	5	55/60	3:898
350	16	55/60	3:921
351	1	56/60	3:921
352	4	56/60	
353	13	56/60	4:5
354	1	/61	4:5

WSC	F	A&G/M&G	K
355	3	56/61	
356	1	56/61	1:347
357	1	56/61	
358	1	57/61	
359	1	57/61	4:328
360	2	57/61	4:328
361	1	57/61	1:317
362	1	57/61	
363	6	57/61	
364	4	57/61	1:348
365	1	57/61	4:896
366	1	57/61	
367 *	11	58/61	
368	1	58/61	
369	1	58/61	
370	1	58/61	
371	2	58/61	
372	5	58/61	1:350
373	12	58/61	1:350
374	1	58/62	
375	4	58/62	
376	2	59/62	
377	11	59/62	
378	6	59/62	6:283
379	2	59/62	
380	1	59/62	
381	3	59/62	
382	1	59/62	
383	2	59/62	
384	1	59/62	
385	2	59/62	
386	42	59/62	1:368
387	3	60/63	
388	1	60/63	7:572
389	1	60/63	
390	11	60/63	7:714
391	13	60/63	7:714
392	1	61/63	8:27
393	9	61/63	1:351
394	2	61/63	1:353
395	10	64/64	1:351
396	2	62/64	
397	3	62/64	
398	2	62/64	
399	10	62/64	9:56
400	1	62/64	
401	1	62/64	
402	14	62/64	
403	1	63/64	9:608
404	1	63/64	9:608
405	1	63/64	
406 *	13	63/64	
407	1	63/64	1:360
408 *	1	63/64	
409	1	63/65	
410	5	63/65	1:356
411	11	63/65	
412	1	63/65	
413	1	63/65	
414	6	63/65	1:359
415	1	63/65	2:477
416	1	64/65	
417	31	64/65	
418	1	64/65	
419	1	64/65	1:357
420	1	64/65	3:469
421	2	64/65	1:358
422	1	64/65	
423	3	64/65	4:5
424	3	64/65	
425	5	64/66	1:367
426	2	64/66	
427	3	64/66	
428	1	65/66	
429	2	65/66	
430	15	65/66	1:359
431	1	65/66	
432	1	65/66	
433	3	65/66	1:360
434	1	65/66	
435	215	65/66	1:360
436	14	66/69	
437	1	66/69	5:199

WSC	F	A&G/M&G	K
438	4	66/69	
439	2	66/69	
440	1	66/69	
441	2	67/69	1:455
442	7	67/69	1:364
443	3	67/69	
444	559	67/69	1:364
445	1	68/75	
446	4	68/75	
447	4	69/75	1:367
448	1	69/65	
449	3	69/75	4:946
450	112	69/75	1:368
451 *	1	69/77	
452 *	4	69/77	
453	6	70/77	4:948
454	2	70/77	4:948
455	77	70/77	
456	2	70/78	
457	1	71/78	
458	15	71/78	4:1022
459	10	71/78	4:1022
460	2	71/78	
461	3	71/78	
462	2	71/78	5:489
463	2	72/78	1:359
464	1	72/78	1:134
465	2	72/78	1:251
466	1	72/78	6:283
467	7	72/78	2:166
468	2	72/78	2:166
469	1	72/78	2:166
470	2	72/79	3:921
471	2	72/79	
472	4	72/79	2:816
473	22	72/79	1:372
474	1	73/79	
475	1	73/79	
476	5	73/79	1:373
477	1	73/79	
478	1	73/79	
479	1	73/79	
480	8	73/79	
481	1	73/49	
482	3	73/79	1:375
483	10	74/79	
484	1	74/80	1:375
485	4	74/80	
486	1	74/80	4:293
487	1	74/80	4:328
488	2	74/80	
489	2	74/80	4:695
490 *	18	74/80	
491 *	1	75/80	
492	2	75/80	
493 *	1	75/80	
494 *	1	75/80	
495	1	75/80	
496	1	75/80	
497	1	75/80	
498	5	75/80	
499	2	75/80	8:246
500	5	75/80	9:493
500 *	5	75/	
501	4	75/80	
502	1	75/80	
503	1	75/80	
504	4	75/80	
505	6	76/81	8:559
506	4	76/81	8:27
507	9	76/81	1:376
508	2	76/57	
509	13	76/81	1:376
510	1	76/81	
511	2	76/81	1:376
512	2	76/81	
513	2	77/81	
514	41	77/81	1:379
515	7	77/82	1:379
516	6	78/82	
517	5	78/82	5:315
518	44	78/82	1:56
519	1	78/82	

WSC	F	A&G/M&G	K
520	16	78/82	
521	1	79/83	5:596
522	3	79/83	
523	3	79/83	1:191
524	1	79/83	
525	3	79/83	1:251
526	3	79/83	1:264
527	2	79/83	
528	7	79/83	
529	4	79/83	1:38
530	15	80/83	1:381
531	1	80/83	5:736
532	1	80/83	
533	13	80/83	
534	1	80/83	
535	1	80/83	
536	8	80/83	1:478
537	44	81/84	5:886
538	4	81/84	1:384
539	7	81/84	1:384
540	1	81/84	5:590
541	1	81/84	1:507
543	7	81/84	6:1
544	16	82/85	6:1
545	6	82/85	6:1
546	2	82/85	
547	4	82/85	
548	7	82/85	
549	1	82/85	
550	1	82/85	
551	1	82/85	6:23
552	1	82/85	
553	7	82/85	2:50
554	2	82/85	2:318
555	1	83/85	2:318
556	1	83/85	
557	1	83/85	
558	1	83/85	2:487
559 *	1	83/85	
560	1	83/85	2:517
561	6	83/85	
562	1	83/86	
563	1	83/86	
564	1	83/86	6:72
565	120	83/86	2:666
566	1	84/87	
567	6	84/87	
568	11	84/87	2:816
569	7	84/87	6:174
570	12	84/87	6:174
571	23	85/88	6:174
572	8	85/88	1:386
573	2	85/88	1:386
574	1	85/88	
575	656	85/88	
576	4	88/89	
577	2	88/89	
578	1	88/89	
579	1	88/89	
580	2	88/89	
581	1	88/89	
582	2	88/89	
583	4	89/89	
584	4	89/89	
585	1	89/89	
586	4	89/89	
587	2	89/89	2:50
588	6	89/89	2:50
589	6	89/89	
590	1	89/89	
591	48	89/89	2:166
592	1	90/90	5:452
593	9	90/90	2:255
594	2	90/90	2:50
595	2	90/90	
596	6	90/90	
597	1	90/90	
598	1	90/90	
599	111	90/90	3:7
600	8	91/91	1:387
601	26	91/92	3:556
602	18	91/92	3:556
603	2	92/92	1:393

WSC	F	A&G/M&G	K
604	3	92/92	1:251
605	1	92/92	1:387
606	4	92/92	3:654
607	4	92/92	
608	1	92/92	
609	6	92/92	3:830
610	1	92/92	3:921
611	249	92/93	3:921
612	4	93/95	3:921
613	6	93/95	3:957
614	3	93/95	3:957
615	75	93/95	
616	2	93/96	
617	4	93/96	
618	12	93/96	
619	2	94/96	
620	6	94/96	
621	1	94/369	
622	92	94/96	1:394
623*	1	95/97	1:394
624*	1	95/97	
625*	10	95/97	
626	16	95/97	
627	8	95/97	
628	2	95/97	4:295
629	10	95/97	4:328
630	69	95/98	
631	1	96/98	
632	1	96/98	
633	1	96/98	
634	1	96/98	
635	2	96/98	6:228
636	4	96/98	
637	1	96/819	
638	3	96/99	6:455
639	4	97/99	
640	1	97/99	
641	1	97/99	6:991
642	1	97/99	
643	1	97/370	
644	1	97/99	7:394
645	4	97/99	
646	2	97/99	1:512
647	3	97/99	
648	1	97/99	
649	133	98/99	1:398
650	6	98/101	
651	4	98/101	1:398
652	81	99/101	1:398
653	1	99/102	
654	10	99/102	7:714
655	1	100/102	
656	3	100/102	7:798
657	6	100/102	
658	1	100/102	
659	8	100/102	
660	2	100/102	
661	1	100/102	
662	1	100/102	8:181
663	2	101/102	8:106
664	2	101/102	8:106
665	1	101/102	
666	1	101/102	
667	5	101/102	
668	3	101/102	
669	3	101/102	1:447
670	1	101/103	
671	1	101/103	
672	3	101/103	
673	2	101/103	
674	1	101/103	
676	1	102/103	
677	3	102/103	6:745
678	1	102/103	6:768
679	1	102/103	
680	36	102/103	
681	4	102/103	
682*	1	102/103	
683	6	102/103	1:448
684	20	103/103	1:394
685	1	103/104	1:448
686	51	103/104	
687	3	103/104	
688*	2	103/104	
689*	3	103/104	
690*	1	104/104	
691	1	104/104	1:452
692	8	104/104	1:452
693	3	104/105	
694	20	104/105	
695	1	104/105	
696	5	104/105	
697*	2	104/105	
698*	1	104/105	
699	1	105/105	1:455
700	17	105/105	1:455
701	4	105/105	1:455
702*	1	105/105	
703	5	105/105	1:457
704	1	105/105	1:338
705	3	105/105	1:461
706	18	105/106	1:461
707*	4	106/106	
708*	5	106/106	
709	3	106/106	
710	3	106/106	
711*	1	106/106	
712	3	106/106	
713	3	106/106	
714	8	106/106	1:464
715	1	107/106	1:464
716	4	102/106	
717*	1	107/104,106	
718	1	107/106	
719	1	107/106	
720	31	107/107	1:469
721	30	107/107	1:338
722	3	108/107	
723	1	108/107	
724	3	108/107	
725	1	108/107	
726	13	108/107	1:472
727	5	108/108	
728	3	109/108	1:475
729	1	109/104	
730	3	109/108	
730	6	109/108	
731	1	109/108	
732	5	109/108	
733	2	109/108	
734*	1	109/108	
735*	5	109/108	
736	1	109/108	
737	36	109/108	
738	1	110/109	1:665
739	1	110/109	1:475
740	100	110/109	1:477
741	3	110/110	
742*	1	110/110	
743	2	110/110	1:74
744	12	110/110	1:478
745*	1	111/110	
746	58	111/110	1:478
747	4	112/111	1:478
748	1	112/111	
749	143	112/111	3:221
750	1	112/112	
751*	2	112/112	
752	2	112/112	7:798
753	1	112/112	
754	1	112/113	
755	3	112/113	
756	84	113/113	
757	2	113/113	1:478
758	37	113/113	1:478
759	4	113/114	
761	2	113/114	
762	4	114/114	
763	6	114/114	7:168
764	2	114/114	7:168
765	9	114/114	7:168
766	9	114/114	1:490
767	1	114/115	5:200
768*	2	114/115	
769	24	114/115	1:490
770	36	115/115	1:490
771	1	115/115	1:490
772	25	115/115	1:490
773*	19	115/116	
774*	1	115/116	
775*	1	115/116	
776	1	115/116	
777	1	115/116	
778	1	115/116	1:494
779	12	116/116	
780	2	116/116	
781	1	116/116	
782	60	116/116	1:496
783	10	116/117	1:496
784	4	116/117	1:502
785	1	116/117	
786	2	116/117	
787	1	117/117	
788	1	117/117	
789*	2	117/116	
790	1	117/117	1:503
791	2	117/117	
792	24	117/117	1:503
793	2	117/118	7:653
794	2	117/118	
795	3	117/118	
796	9	117/118	1:505
797	2	117/118	
798	4	117/118	1:503
799*	1	118/118	
800	4	118/118	
801	5	118/118	7:888
802	1	118/118	
803	3	118/118	1:506
804	3	118/118	1:506
805	3	118/118	1:506
806	3	118/118	1:506
807	2	118/118	
808	2	118/118	
809	1	119/118	
810	3	119/118	1:506
811	1	119/119	1:606
812	1	119/119	8:27
813	1	119/119	8:27
814	2	119/119	8:27
815	3	119/119	
816	14	119/119	
817	2	119/119	
818	6	119/119	
819	7	119/119	
820	4	119/119	
821	1	119/119	
822	2	120/119	
823	1	120/119	
824	3	120/119	
825*	1	120/119	
826	1	120/119	1:507
827	1	120/119	
828*	1	120/119	
829	2	120/119	1:508
830	2	120/119	
831	1	120/119	
832	3	120/119	
833	12	120/120	
834	2	121/120	
835	2	121/120	
836	1	121/120	
837	22	121/120	8:517
838	2	121/120	
839	15	121/120	
840	2	121/120	
841	2	121/120	1:464
842	1	122/120	1:464
843	1	122/120	3:921
844	2	122/120	
845	1	122/120	5:315
846	5117	122/120-130	
847	4	123/130	
848	659	122/122	
849	1	123/131	
850	1	123/131	
851	10	123/131	
852	1	124/131	
853	5	124/131	
854	1	124/131	
855	1	124/131	
856	2	124/131	
857	1	124/131	
858	1	124/131	
859	17	124/131	1:509
860	2	124/132	
861	8	124/132	9:93
862	7	125/131	9:93
863	146	125/131	1:509
864	1	126/133	
865	1	126/133	1:10
866	2	126/134	
867	1	126/134	
868	15	126/134	1:512
869	3	126/134	
870	4	126/134	
871	1	126/134	5:186
872	2	126/134	
873	10	126/134	5:452
874	7	127/134	5:467
875	2	127/134	
876	1	127/134	
877	4	127/134	9:220
878	11	127/134	9:220
879	1	127/134	8:545
880	4	127/134	
881*	2	127/135	
882*	11	127/135	
883*	1	127/135	
884	2	127/136	
884*	2	127/135	9:359
885*	1	127/135	
886	3	127/135	9:424
887	1	127/135	
888	2	128/135	
889	1	128/135	
890	1	128/135	
891	49	128/135	
892	2	128/136	
893	1	128/136	9:594
894	2	129/136	
895	1	129/136	
896*	1	129/136	
897*	12	129/136	1:514
898	1	129/136	
899	9	129/136	1:517
900	1	130/136	
901	3	130/136	
902	1	130/136	
903*	3	130/136	1:524
904*	1	130/136	
905	4	130/137	1:525
906	125	130/137	1:526
907	80	131/138	1:529
908	22	132/139	1:529
909	4	132/139	1:529
910*	14	132/139	1:529
911	3	132/139	
912*	11	132/139	
913*	1	132/140	
914*	4	132/140	
915	6	132/140	1:546
916	6	133/140	1:553
917	2	133/140	
918*	6	133/140	
919*	1	133/140	
920*	1	133/140	
921*	1	133/140	
922	6	133/140	1:553
923*	2	133/140	
924*	1	133/140	
925	1	133/140	
926	6	133/140	1:553
927	1	134/141	
928	12	134/141	1:561
929	6	134/141	1:561
930	1	134/141	1:561
931	3	134/141	1:561
932	162	134/141	1:564
933	1	135/143	
934	1	135/143	1:564
935	118	135/143	1:564

WSC	F	A&G/M&G	K
936	21	136/144	1:564
937	5	136/144	1:564
938	4	136/144	1:564
939	1	136/144	
940	1	136/145	1:594
941	27	136/145	1:596
942	1	137/145	
943	5	137/145	
944	1	137/145	
945	1	137/145	1:597
946	6	137/145	1:598
947	1	137/145	1:598
948	2	137/145	1:598
949	9	137/145	1:600
950	8	138/145	1:600
951	2	138/145	1:600
952	5	138/145	1:604
953	2	138/145	1:604
954*	7	138/146	1:605
955*	1	138/146	1:607
956	1	138/145	1:608
957	1	138/146	
958*	4	139/146	
959*	3	139/146	
960*	2	139/146	
961*	1	139/146	
962*	1	139/146	
963*	11	139/146	
964*	1	139/146	
965*	8	139/146	
966*	7	139/146	
967*	3	139/146	
968	12	139/147	
969	1	139/147	
970	4	140/147	
971	2	140/147	1:609
972	1	140/147	
973	1	140/147	1:609
974	4	140/147	
975	32	140/147	1:615
976	13	140/147	1:615
977	1	141/148	
978*	2	141/147	
979	11	141/148	
980	1	140/148	
981	1	141/148	
982	3	141/148	
983	1	141/148	
984	2	141/148	
985	4	141/148	
986*	1	142/148	
987	35	142/148	1:621
988	19	142/148	1:621
989	5	142/149	1:621
990	1	142/149	
991	135	142/149	5:315
992	2	143/150	
993*	1	143/	
994	11	143/150	1:625
995	1	144/150	
996	2	144/150	1:628
997	8	144/150	1:628
998	1	144/150	1:628
999	3	144/150	
1000	1	144/151	
1001	2	144/151	
1002	1	144/	
1003*	2	144/151	
1004	1	144/151	
1005*	2	144/151	
1006	9	144/151	
1007*	1	144/146,151	
1008	1	144/151	
1009	1	145/151	
1010	2	145/151	
1011	8	145/151	
1012	12	145/151	1:629
1013	2	145/151	1:629
1014	35	145/151	1:629
1015	2	146/152	
1016	8	146/152	
1017	2	146/152	1:637
1018	1	146/152	1:637

WSC	F	A&G/M&G	K
1019	2	146/152	
1020	1	146/152	
1021	3	146/152	
1022	1	146/152	
1023	3	146/152	1:639
1024	7	146/152	
1025	8	146/152	5:636
1026	7	147/152	
1027	12	147/152	1:640
1028	2	147/153	
1029	1	147/153	
1030	7	147/153	1:641
1031	1	147/153	1:641
1032	1	147/153	
1033	17	147/153	1:642
1034	1	147/153	
1035	11	147/153	1:642
1036	2	147/153	
1037	1	148/153	
1038	3	148/153	
1039	4	148/153	
1040	2	148/153	
1041	1	148/153	
1042*	1	148/153	
1043*	2	148/153	
1044	1	148/153	
1045*	1	148/153	
1046*	3	148/153,160	
1047	1	148/154	
1048*	1	148/154	
1049	5	148/154	
1050*	5	149/154	
1051	5	149/154	1:645
1052*	1	149/154	
1053*	4	149/154	
1054*	2	149/154	
1055	3	149/154	
1056*	63	149/154	
1057*	11	149/155	
1058*	3	149/155	
1059*	2	150/155	
1060	29	150/155	1:648
1061	1	150/155	
1062	16	150/155	1:648
1063	1069	151/156	
1064	9	151/157	
1065	11	152/157	
1066*	1	152/157	
1067	12	152/157	1:657
1068*	2	152/157	
1069	4	152/157	
1070	2	152/157	1:658
1071	1	152/157	1:658
1072	9	152/158	
1073	11	153/158	
1074	42	153/158	1:662
1075	1	153/158	1:662
1076	2	153/158	1:662
1077	2	153/158	
1078	3	154/158	1:681
1079	1	154/158	
1080	97	154/159	1:665
1081	9	155/159	1:665
1082*	3	155/160	
1083	2	155/158	
1084	2	155/160	1:665
1085	21	155/160	1:681
1086*	1	155/160	
1087	1	155/160	
1088	1	156/160	
1089	15	156/160	1:675
1090	1	156/160	
1091	1	156/160	
1092	19	156/161	
1093	252	156/161	1:677
1094	1	156/163	
1095		/163	
1096	677	157/164	1:681
1097	223	159/170	1:689
1098	1	161/172	
1099	4	161/172	
1100	50	161/172	1:719
1101	2	161/173	

WSC	F	A&G/M&G	K
1102	1	162/173	
1103	1	162/173	1:727
1104	1	162/173	
1105	1	162/173	
1106	9	162/173	1:689
1107	24	162/173	1:689
1108	29	162/173	1:689
1109	1	163/174	
1110	15	163/174	
1111	8	163/174	1:728
1112	4	163/174	1:728
1113	1	163/174	1:728
1114	1	163/174	1:737
1115*	3	164/174	
1116*	2	164/174	
1116*	3	164/174	
1117	3	164/174	
1118	19	164/174	
1119	12	164/175	1:738
1120	4	164/175	1:738
1121	15	164/175	1:742
1122	67	164/175	1:740
1123	1	165/176	
1124	51	165/176	1:742
1125	194	165/176	1:742
1126	1	166/179	
1127	23	166/179	2:333
1128	4	166/179	1:773
1129	1	166/179	1:773
1130	1	166/179	
1131	15	166/179	1:773
1132	3	167/179	1:773
1133	1	167/179	
1134	1	167/179	
1135	221	167/179	1:776
1136*	1	167/182	1:789
1137	9	167/182	1:791
1138*	59	168/184	
1139	13	168/182	2:1
1140	60	168/182	2:1
1141	1	168/183	2:1
1142	5	168/183	2:1
1143	1	168/183	
1144	11	168/183	
1145	1	169/183	
1146	1	169/183	
1147	8	169/183	2:20
1148*	1	169/183	
1149*	1	169/183	
1150	4	169/183	
1151	1	169/183	
1152*	1	169/183	
1153*	1	169/184	
1154*	15	169/184	
1155	4	169/184	
1156	1	169/184	
1157	1	169/184	
1158*	2	169/184	
1159	5	169/184	
1160	1	170/184	
1161	398	170/	
1162	19	170/185	2:40
1163	105	171/185	2:21
1164	1	171/186	
1165	1	171/186	2:25
1166	33	171/186	2:25
1167	1	172/186	
1168	1	172/186	
1169	3	172/186	
1170	1	172/187	
1171	2	172/187	
1172	4	172/187	2:34
1173	16	172/187	2:34
1174	1	172/187	
1175	1	172/187	2:1
1176	27	172/187	2:36
1177	2	173/	
1178	1	173/187	
1179*	3	173/187	
1180	5	173/187	
1181	4	173/187	
1182	3	173/188	
1183	2	173/188	

WSC	F	A&G/M&G	K
1184	5	173/188	2:50
1185	3	173/188	
1186	26	173/188	
1187	1	173/188	
1188	73	188/188	2:37
1189	22	174/189	2:40
1190*	1	174/189	
1191*	3	174/189	
1192	1	174/189	
1193	2	174/189	
1194	15	174/189	
1195	2	174/189	
1196	1	174/189	
1197	1	174/189	
1198	16	175/189	2:43
1199	20	175/189	2:43
1200	3	175/190	
1201	4	175/190	
1202	2	175/190	
1203	10	175/190	2:44
1204	1	175/190	
1205	13	175/190	
1206	1	175/190	
1207	1	176/191	
1208	43	176/191	
1209	59	176/191	2:50
1210	44	176/192	2:60
1211	6	177/192	
1212	4	177/192	
1213	7	177/192	2:61
1214*	3	177/192	
1215	1	177/192	
1216*	1	177/192	
1217	1	177/192	2:62
1218	4	178/193	2:63
1219	4	178/193	
1220	16	178/193	
1221	1	178/193	
1222	1	178/193	
1223	640	178/193	2:65
1224	3	180/200	
1225	1	180/200	2:71
1226	2	180/200	
1227	2	180/200	
1228	38	181/200	2:71
1229	3	181/201	1:56
1230	3	181/201	
1231	2	181/201	
1232	1	181/173	
1233	1	/201	
1234	2	/201	
1235	1	181/201	
1236	2	181/201	
1237	1	181/201	
1238	3	181/201	
1239	5	181/201	
1240	1	181/201	
1241	3	182/201	5:292
1242	33	182/201	2:104
1243	3	182/202	1:180
1244	2	182/202	1:180
1245	2	183/202	
1246	1	183/202	
1247	37	183/202	2:81
1248	34	183/202	2:81
1249	30	183/203	2:81
1250	8	184/203	
1251	1	184/203	
1252	19	184/203	3:921
1253	3	184/203	3:921
1254	1	184/203	
1255	2	184/203	
1256	13	184/203	2:93
1257	1	184/204	4:194
1258	6	184/204	
1259	1	185/204	1:251
1260	16	185/204	2:93
1261	14	185/204	2:93
1262	1	185/204	
1263	15	185/204	4:474
1264	1	185/204	
1265	5	185/205	
1266	12	185/205	

WSC	F	A&G/M&G	K
1267	1	186/205	
1268	1	186/205	
1269	1	186/205	
1270	1	186/205	4:948
1271	13	186/205	4:948
1272	8	186/205	
1273	1	186/205	
1274	1	186/205	
1275	7	186/193	
1276	6	186/205	
1277	1	186/205	
1278	2	186/205	
1279	5	186/205	
1280	5	186/206	
1281	1	186/206	6:632
1282	2	187/206	
1283	4	187/206	
1284	5	187/206	
1285	1	187/206	
1286	1	187/206	
1287	9	187/206	7:418
1288	2	187/206	
1289	3	187/206	
1290	3	187/206	2:98
1291	8	187/206	7:588
1292	1	187/206	
1293	3	188/206	7:588
1294	7	188/206	7:714
1295	8	188/207	
1296	2	188/207	8:27
1297	1	188/207	
1298	1	188/207	
1299	16	188/207	8:27
1300	1	188/207	
1301	2	188/207	8:140
1302	27	188/197	
1303	7	188/207	2:104
1304	10	189/207	
1305	1	189/207	
1306	1	189/207	
1307	1	109/207	
1308	13	189/207	9:56
1309	1	189/208	
1310	3	189/208	
1311	6	189/208	9:93
1312	6	189/208	9:93
1313	4	190/208	9:56
1314	1	190/208	
1315	2	190/208	
1316	1	190/208	
1317	2	190/208	2:135
1318	3	190/208	2:135
1319	21	190/208	2:135
1320	58	190/208	2:135
1321	97	191/209	2:135
1322	30	/210	2:135
1323	2	191/211	
1324*	3	191/211	
1325	413	191/211	2:166
1326	7	193/215	
1327	1	193/216	5:42
1328	1	193/216	2:661
1329	6	193/216	2:661
1330	42	193/216	2:666
1331	1	193/216	
1332	1	193/216	
1333	2	194/216	
1334	8	194/216	
1335	1	194/216	2:907
1336	4	194/216	
1337	1	194/216	
1338	3	194/216	
1339	3	194/217	
1340	2	194/217	
1341	1	194/217	2:174
1342	81	194/217	2:174
1343	92	195/218	2:174
1344	60	196/219	2:174
1345	10	197/219	2:174
1346	5	197/219	
1347	2	197/219	2:174
1348	3	197/219	
1349	4	197/219	2:174
1350	12	197/220	
1351	1	197/220	
1352	53	197/220	
1353	2	197/220	
1354*	1	198/220	
1355	3	198/220	
1356*	1	198/220	
1356	1	198/	
1357	1	198/220	5:449
1358	4	198/220	
1359*	1	198/220	
1360	22	198/221	
1361*	1	198/221	
1362	4	198/221	
1363	1	198/221	
1364	6	198/221	
1365	2	199/221	
1366	3	199/221	
1367	1	199/221	
1368	1	199/221	
1369	1	199/221	
1370	3	199/221	1:512
1371	2	199/221	2:225
1372	16	199/221	2:226
1373	1	199/221	2:226
1374	2	200/222	9:608
1375	10	200/222	
1376	1	200/222	2:229
1377	44	200/222	
1378	5	200/222	2:230
1379	1	200/222	2:230
1380	63	200/222	2:232
1381	23	201/223	2:255
1382	7	201/223	2:255
1383	2	202/223	2:255
1384	7	202/224	2:255
1385	6	202/224	
1386	1	202/224	
1387	1	202/224	
1388	12	202/224	
1389	1	202/224	
1390	4	202/224	
1391	168	202/224	2:232
1392	62	203/226	2:232
1393*	2	203/227	
1394	2	204/227	
1395	1	204/227	
1396	1	204/227	2:261
1397	5	204/227	2:261
1398	25	204/227	2:261
1399	3	204/227	2:261
1400	2	204/227	
1401	125	204/227	2:261
1402	8	205/229	2:261
1403	2	205/229	2:50
1404	13	205/229	2:281
1405	1	205/229	
1406	3	205/229	
1407	8	205/229	
1408	3	205/229	8:226
1409*	1	206/229	
1410	210	206/229	2:284
1411	120	206/231	2:284
1412	1	207/233	2:284
1413	3	207/233	2:284
1414	1	207/233	2:284
1415	35	207/233	2:284
1416	2	/233	
1417	135	208/233	2:318
1419	2	208/235	
1420	1	208/235	
1421	1	208/235	
1422	1	208/235	
1423	3	208/235	
1424	5	209/235	
1425	1	209/235	4:948
1426	1	209/235	
1427	72	209/235	2:321
1428	1	209/235	2:321
1429	1	209/236	2:321
1430	7	209/236	
1431	11	209/236	2:166
1432	9	209/236	2:166
1433	3	209/236	
1434	2	209/236	2:166
1435	19	210/237	2:166
1436	2	210/237	
1437	341	210/237,240	
1438	339	211/240	
1439	13	211/244	
1440	5	212/244	2:627
1441	1	212/244	2:627
1442	9	212/244	2:627
1443*	1	212/244	
1444*	1	212/	3:357
1445*	4	212/244	3:357
1446*	3	212/244	3:357
1447*	6	212/244	3:357
1448	43	212/245	2:330
1449	2	213/333	
1450	1	213/245	2:329
1451	30	213/245	2:330
1452	1	213/245	
1453	141	213/245	2:333
1454	1	214/247	2:333
1455	1	214/337	
1456	1	214/337	
1457	2	214/337	3:447
1458	7	214/247	3:487
1459	9	214/247	
1460	1	215/337	
1461	6	215/337	
1462	2	215/247	3:487
1463	1	215/247	2:339
1464	1	215/337	3:830
1465	5	215/337	3:830
1466	4	215/247	2:339
1467	2	215/247	2:339
1468	1	215/247	2:339
1469	1	215/337	3:921
1470	2	216/247	
1471	1	216/337	
1472	1	216/247	
1173	370	216/247	2:343
1474	1	216/255	
1475	1	216/255	
1476	3	217/255	2:362
1477	1	217/255	2:362
1478*	2	217/255	
1479	1	217/255	3:155
1480	1	217/256	
1481	1	217/256	
1482	2	217/256	2:364
1483	1	217/256	
1484	164	217/256	2:364
1485	12	217/258	2:372
1486	4	217/307	
1487	310	217/272	
1488	92	217/258	
1489	5	152/258	
1490	14	217/261	
1491	5	220/270	2:373
1492	663	219/263, 267	
			5:315
1493	1	220/270	2:375
1494	10	221/270	2:375
1495	4	220/270	2:375
1496	7	220/270	2:375
1497	11	220/270	2:375
1498	12	221/278	
1499	22	217/258	
1500	7	221/270	2:380
1501	12	221/270	
1502	1	221/270	
1503	2	221/349	
1504	23	221/270	2:381
1505	3	221/271	2:397
1506	2	221/271	2:397
1507	1	221/325	
1508	92	/261	
1509	3	217/261	
1510	141	221/271	2:398
1511	126	221/278	
1512	6	225/262	
1513	4	226/258	
1514	4	226/297	2:400
1515	92	226/297	2:400
1516	2	227/298	2:400
1517	1	227/298	2:400
1518	1	227/298	2:400
1519	1773	227/298	2:420,
			2:434
1520	271	229/299	
1521	10	231/303	
1522	5	231/303	1:216
1523	1	231/303	2:50
1524	4	231/303	
1525	198	231/303	2:666
1526	163	221/275	
1527	2	/299	
1528	1	231/306	3:487
1529	5	232/306	5:42
1530	1	232/306	
1531	17	232/306	6:566
1532	1	232/306	
1533	7	233/306	9:56
1534	16	233/306	
1535	65	233/306	
1536	79	/262	
1537	921	233/307	
1538	83	236/308	
1539	1	236/309	
1540	17	236/309	
1541	1	236/309	
1542	3	236/309	
1543	5	236/309	
1543	16	236/309	
1544	82	236/309	1:526
1545	2	237/310	
1546	1	237/310	
1547	5	237/155	
1548	2	237/155	
1549	1	237/310	
1550	1	237/310	
1551	8	237/311	
1552	1	237/311	
1553	3	237/311	2:63
1554	4	237/311	
1555	1	238/311	
1556	6	238/311	2:442
1557	9	238/311	2:442
1558	2	238/311	2:442
1559	2	238/311	
1560	1	238/311	
1561	1	238/311	2:50
1562	5	238/311	2:318
1563	98	238/311	
1564	27	238/312	
1565	251	238/313	
1566	2	239/315	
1567	7	239/315	2:892
1568	4	239/316	3:4
1569	1	239/316	3:4
1570	1	239/316	
1571	2	239/316	3:413
1572	1	240/316	
1573	6	240/337	
1574	2	240/316	2:446
1575	3	240/316	
1576	2	240/316	
1577	115	240/316	3:487
1578	3	241/317	
1579	1	241/317	
1580	1	241/317	
1581	11	241/318	3:830
1582	1	241/318	3:915
1583	1	241/318	
1584	1	241/318	4:16
1585	1	241/318	
1586	21	241/318	4:69
1587	3	242/318	
1588	23	243/318	4:69
1589	7	242/314	4:69
1590	6	242/319	
1591	5	242/319	
1592	2	242/319	4:796
1593	1	242/319	
1594	1	242/319	4:936
1595	1	242/319	2:469

WMC	F	A&G/M&G	K	WMC	F	A&G/M&G	K	WMC	F	A&G/M&G	K	WMC	F	A&G/M&G	F
1596	2	242/319		1676*	2	251/326	2:504	1757	2	265/336		1839	17	275/346	2:449
1597	2	242/319		1677	2	251/326	2:516	1758	3	265/336		1840	1	276/346	
1598	4	243/319	6:1	1678*	1	251/326		1759	8	265/336		1841	3	276/346	5:42
1599	2	243/319		1679	31	251/326	2:517	1760	3	265/336	3:167	1842	1	276/346	5:167
1600	1	242/319		1680	54	252/327	2:517	1761	4	265/336	3:167	1843	11	276/346	5:199
1601	13	243/319	6:161	1681*	1	253/327		1762	5	265/336		1844	1	277/346	5:457
1602	3	243/319		1682	2	253/327		1763	14	265/336		1845	1	277/347	5:457
1603	1	243/319	6:283	1683	37	253/327		1764	7	266/337	2:543	1846	2	277/347	
1604	1	243/319	6:283	1684	18	253/328		1765	2	266/337		1847	1	277/347	
1605	13	243/320		1685	1	253/328		1766	10	261/333		1848	11	277/347	
1606	3	243/320	6:332	1686	3	253/328		1767	1	266/337		1849	103	277/347	2:560
1607	34	243/320	6:566	1687	1	253/328	2:535	1768	4	264/335,337		1850	4	278/348	2:560
1608	1	244/320	6:579	1688	1	253/328		1769	1	266/335		1851	1	278/348	
1609	1	244/320	2:448	1689	12	253/328		1770	1	266/337		1852	1	278/348	8:545
1610	4	244/320		1690	5	254/328		1771	2	266/337	4:948	1853	1	278/348	8:545
1611	7	244/320	2:449	1691	88	216/252		1772	2	266/337	4:1022	1854	65	278/348	2:575
1612	1	244/320		1692	1	254/328		1773	1	266/337		1855	11	279/349	
1613	1	244/320		1693	1	254/328		1774	5	266/338		1856	2	279/349	
1614	16	244/320	2:460	1694*	1	254/328		1775	2	267/338		1857	3	279/349	
1615	2	244/321		1695*	1	254/328		1776	1	267/338		1858	1	279/349	
1616	1	245/321	2:460	1696	3	254/328	4:574	1777	10	267/338	2:816	1859	27	279/349	
1617	1	245/321		1697*	1	254/328		1778	3	267/338		1860	53	280/350	2:576
1618	2	245/321		1698	95	216/252		1779	2	267/338		1861	15	280/350	2:576
1619	1	245/321		1699	78	254/329		1780	2	267/338		1862	2	280/350	2:576
1620	4	245/321		1700	109	216/251		1781	17	267/338	2:544	1863	3	280/350	
1621	2	245/321		1701	1	255/329	5:625	1782	13	268/338		1864	1	281/350	1:134
1622	9	245/321		1702	13	255/329	5:625	1783	2	268/338	8:238	1865	1	281/351	
1623	14	245/321		1703	2	255/329	5:625	1784	5	268/338		1866*	1	281/351	
1624	5	245/321		1704	1	255/338	5:940	1785	71	268/339	2:544	1867	6	281/351	
1625	2	245/321		1705	1	255/330		1786	1	268/339		1868	11	281/351	2:586
1626	1	246/321	2:465	1705	4	255/330		1787	2	268/339		1869	19	281/351	1:185
1627	7	246/321		1706	7	255/330		1788	9	269/339		1870	11	281/351	
1628	7	246/322		1707	2	256/330		1789	1	269/339		1871	1	282/351	
1629	1	246/322		1708	1	256/330		1790	3	269/340		1872	4	282/351	1:210
1630	2	246/322		1709	1	256/338		1791	2	269/340		1873	1	282/351	1:216
1631	2	246/322		1710	2	256/330		1792	1	269/340		1874	1	282/351	
1632	18	246/322	2:467	1711	1	256/330		1793	5	269/340	8:238	1875	3	282/351	
1632	10	247/322	2:467	1712	1	256/330		1794	3	269/340		1876	1	282/351	
1633	1	247/322		1713	5	256/330		1795	1	269/340		1877	3	282/351	
1634	3	247/322		1714	1	255/330		1796	1	269/340	8:295	1878	1	282/351	
1635	2	247/322	2:469	1715	48	256/330		1797	2	270/340	8:545	1879	2	282/351	1:350
1636	15	247/322		1716	6	256/331		1798	1	270/340	8:545	1880	2	282/352	
1637	11	247/322	2:470	1717	2	257/331		1799	97	270/340		1881	2	282/352	
1638	1	247/323		1718	10	257/331	9:1	1800*	1	270/341		1882	1	282/352	5:449
1639*	1	247/323		1719	6	257/331		1801	1	270/341	5:543	1883	20	283/352	
1640	4	247/323	4:648	1720	1	257/331	2:536	1802*	3	270/341	2:556	1884	3	283/352	
1641	1	247/323		1721	1	252/331		1803	13	270/341		1885	2	283/352	
1642	3	247/323		1722	2781	257/331	2:537	1804	1	270/341	1:56	1886	1	283/352	
1643	5	248/323		1723	2	261/333		1805	4	271/341	1:124	1887	17	283/352	
1644	1	248/323		1724	1	261/333		1806	13	271/341		1888	1	123/131	
1645	2	248/323		1725	1	261/333		1807	8	271/342		1889*	3	283/352	
1646	13	248/323	4:648	1726	5	261/333		1808	2	271/342		1890	1	283/352	
1647	1	248/323		1727	8	261/333		1809	1	271/342	1:191	1891*	2	283/352	
1648*	2	248/323		1728	2	261/333		1810	5	271/342		1892	2	283/352	
1649	1	248/323	2:473	1729	1	261/337		1811	3	271/342	1:210	1893	27	283/352	
1650	2	248/323	2:473	1730	1	261/334		1812	2	271/342		1894	11	284/353	
1651	17	248/323	2:473	1731	11	262/334		1813	5	272/342		1895	1	284/353	
1652	2	249/324		1732	4	262/334		1814	1	272/342		1896	2	284/	
1653	31	249/324	2:477	1733	6	262/334		1815	1	272/342	1:368	1897	1	284/353	
1654	14	249/324	2:477	1734	3	262/334		1816	2	272/342		1898	1	284/353	
1655	2	249/324	2:477	1735	1	262/334		1817	3	272/342	1:368	1899	16	284/353	
1656	28	249/324	2:477	1736	3	262/334		1818	5	272/342	1:384	1900	1	284/353	
1657	11	259/324	2:487	1737	2	262/334		1819	1	272/342		1901	1	284/353	
1658	23	250/325	2:487	1738	2	262/334		1820	2	272/342		1902	2	284/353	2:318
1659	7	250/325	2:487	1739	1	262/335		1821	11	272/342	1:398	1903	1	284/353	
1660	1	250/325	2:666	1740	2	262/334	2:232	1822	2	273/343	1:475	1904	10	284/353	2:666
1661	1	250/325		1741	4	262/334	2:232	1823	1	273/343		1905	59	284/354	2:685
1662*	3	250/325		1742	8	263/334		1824	6	273/343		1906	1	285/354	2:685
1663*	1	250/325		1743	8	263/334	2:284	1825	2	273/343	2:333	1907	5	285/354	
1664*	2	250/325		1744	1	263/334		1826	4	273/343		1908	3	285/354	
1665*	9	250/324		1745	1	263/334		1827	1	273/323		1909	895	285/354	
1666*	1	250/325		1746	28	263/334	2:318	1828	1	273/343		1910	6	289/364	
1667	1	250/325		1747	1	263/335		1829	1	273/343		1911	18	289/364	1:526
1668	3	251/325		1748	2	264/335		1830	1	273/343	2:655	1912	3	290/364	
1669	1	251/325		1749	1	264/335		1831	222	273/343	2:666	1913	3	290/365	
1670	6	251/325		1750	1	264/335		1832	32	274/345	2:560	1914	3	290/365	
1670	2	251/325	2:503	1751	1	264/335		1833	3	275/346		1915	4	290/365	
1671*	1	251/326	2:504	1752	25	264/335		1834	6	275/346	2:907	1916	1	290/150	
1672*	27	251/326	2:504	1753	8	264/335	2:635	1835	9	275/346		1917	4	290/365	
1673*	2	251/326	2:504	1754	21	264/336	2:635	1836	5	275/346		1918	1	290/365	
1674*	2	251/326	2:504	1755	2	265/336	2:635	1837	1	275/346		1919	7	290/365	1:677
1675*	3	251/326	2:504	1756	3	265/336	2:635	1838	1	275/346		1920	1	290/365	

WSC	F	A&G/M&G	K	WSC	F	A&G/M&G	K	WSC	F	A&G/M&G	K	WSC	F	A&G/M&G	K
1921	42	290/365	1:689	2003	7	302/372	8:27	2083	4	314/392	2:699	2162	1	327/405	
1922	20	291/366	1:689	2004	10	302/372		2084	1	314/392	1:719	2163	1	327/405	
1923	5	291/366	1:742	2005	11	302/372	8:49	2085	2	314/392	2:135	2164	1	327/405	
1924	5	291/366	1:742	2006	1	302/372		2086	1	315/392	2:896	2165	14	327/405	2:772
1925	9	291/366		2007	42	302/372	8:152	2087	99	315/392	2:702	2166*	2	328/405	
1926	2	292/366		2008	29	303/373	2:623	2088	1	315/393		2167	2	328/405	2:772
1927	2	292/366		2009	1	303/373	2:623	2089	119	315/393		2168	39	328/405	9:359
1928	1	292/366		2010	19	303/373		2090	40	316/394	2:704	2169	15	328/405	9:359
1929	11	292/366		2011	1	303/373		2091	1	316/395	2:704	2170	1	329/406	9:359
1930	1	292/366		2012	3	303/374		2092	17	316/395	2:704	2171	3	329/406	2:775
1931	1	292/366		2013	5	303/374		2093	3	316/395		2172	7	329/406	2:775
1932	2	292/366	2:588	2014	4	304/374	9:1	2094	49	317/395		2173	3	329/406	
1933	5	292/366	2:588	2015	6	304/374	9:1	2095	6	317/396		2174	1	330/406	
1934	14	292/367	2:892	2016	1	304/374	9:1	2096*	2	317/396		2175	3	330/406	2:808
1935	1	292/367		2017	1	304/374	9:310	2097	55	317/396	2:707	2176	10	330/406	
1936	4	292/367	8:152	2018	5	304/374		2098	77	318/397	2:707	2177	1	330/406	
1937	16	293/367	3:167	2019	3	304/374		2099	3	318/397	2:707	2178	5	330/406	1:381
1938	1	293/367	3:167	2020	2	304/374	9:310	2100	3	318/398	1:455	2179*	1	/406	
1939	38	293/367	3:167	2021	3	304/374		2101	3	319/398	1:455	2180*	5	330/406	
1940	1	293/367		2022	1	304/374		2102	1	319/398		2181*	15	330/406	
1941	32	293/367	3:487	2023	5	305/374		2103*	1	319/398		2182	1	330/407	
1942	1	294/368		2024	2	305/374		2104	3	319/398		2183	2	330/407	
1943	1	294/368		2025	2	305/374		2105	1	319/398		2184	1	330/407	
1944	3	294/368	1:448	2026	8	305/374	5:119	2106	21	319/398	2:738	2185	2	330/407	
1945	7	294/368	3:654	2027	1	305/368		2107	9	319/399	2:738	2186	21	330/407	
1946*	1	296/368		2028	1	305/374	5:242	2108	2	320/399	2:635	2187*	1	331/406	
1947	1	294/368		2029	2	305/374	5:315	2109	1	320/399	2:635	2188	1	331/407	
1948	1	294/368		2030	1	305/374	5:315	2110	1	320/399	2:635	2189	6	331/407	2:811
1949	19	295/368	4:5	2031	1	305/374		2111	3	320/399		2190	32	331/407	2:811
1950	8	295/368		2032	20	305/375	5:497	2112	80	320/399		2191	5	332/408	2:815
1951	2	295/369		2033	87	306/375	2:627	2113	2	321/399		2192	709	332/408	2:816, 6:1091
1952	1	295/369		2034	4	306/376	2:627	2114	3	321/399					
1953	1	295/369		2035	1	305/376	2:627	2115	1	321/399		2193	148	334/415	
1954	1	295/369		2036	976	225/288		2115	1	/399		2194*	3	336/416	
1955	1	295/369	4:328	2037*	3	306/376		2116	2	321/399		2195*	3	336/416	
1956	2	295/369	4:328	2038	39	306/376	2:635	2117	8	321/399		2196*	1	336/416	
1957	1	295/369	4:474	2039	6	307/376	2:635	2117	8	321/400		2197*	11	336/417	
1958	1	295/369		2040	16	307/377	2:635	2118	1	321/400		2198	142	336/417	2:832
1959	3	296/369		2041	176	307/377	2:635	2119	3	321/400	3:455	2199*	12	337/418	
1960	1	296/369		2042	2	308/379		2120	2	321/400	3:455	2200	3	337/419	2:875
1961	18	296/369		2043	1	308/379		2121	2	321/400	3:455	2201	2	337/419	
1962	1	296/369		2044	1	308/379		2122	2	321/400		2202	1	337/419	
1963	1	296/369		2045	6	308/376	2:655	2123	7	322/400		2203*	2	338/419	
1964	1	296/369	5:457	2046	71	/387		2124	2	322/400		2204	2	338/419	2:875
1965	1	296/369	5:457	2047	4	308/379	2:657	2125	2	322/401	2:751	2205	17	338/419	2:877
1966	5	296/353		2048	35	308/379	2:657	2126	3	322/401	2:751	2206	12	338/419	2:877
1967	2	296/369	2:590	2048	15	308/379		2127	44	322/401	2:754	2207	5	338/419	2:877
1968	13	297/369		2049	5	309/380	2:657	2128	8	323/401		2208*	2	338/419	
1969	1	297/370		2050	5	309/380	2:657	2129	16	323/401	2:754	2209	4	338/419	2:888
1970	1	/99		2051	1	309/380		2130	1	323/401		2210	6	339/419	2:888
1971	9	297/370		2052	7	309/380	2:660	2131*	1	323/401		2211*	1	339/419	
1972	2	297/370		2053	2	309/380		2132	1	323/401	4:948	2212	119	339/419	2:892
1973	1	298/370		2054	9	309/380		2133	2	323/401	4:948	2213	5	339/421	
1974	1	298/370		2055	1	309/380		2134	2	323/402		2214	6	339/421	2:892
1975	1	298/370		2056	2	309/380		2135	8	323/402	2:765	2215	8	340/421	
1976	1	298/370		2057*	1	309/380		2136*	1	324/402		2216*	3	340/421	
1977	2	298/370	6:991	2058	2	309/380	2:661	2137	4	324/402		2217	4	340/421	
1978	2	298/370	7:200	2059	4	309/380	2:661	2138	1	324/402		2218	6	340/421	2:896
1979	1	298/370		2060*	2	310/389		2139	1	324/402		2219	13	340/421	2:902
1980	11	298/370	2:599	2061*	1	310/380		2140	1	324/402		2220	4	340/421	2:902
1981	1	298/370	7:368	2062	4	310/380		2141	1	324/402		2221	2	340/421	
1982	5	298/370	7:394	2063*	2	310/380		2142	1	324/402		2222	134	340/422	2:832
1983	2	298/370	2:599	2064	642	310/381	2:666	2143	1	324/402		2223	8	341/423	5:292
1984	4	299/370	2:599	2065	58	311/388	2:685	2144	5	324/402	2:50	2224	2	342/423	5:292
1985	5	299/270	2:599	2066	7	312/389		2145	1	324/402		2225	2	342/423	2:832
1986	1	299/371		2067	1	312/389		2146	1	324/402	6:768	2226	23	342/423	2:832
1987	14	300/371		2068	65	312/389	2:689	2147	178	325/402	2:769	2227	12	342/424	2:832
1988	7	300/371	2:622	2069*	1	313/391		2148*	1	326/402		2228	357	342/424	
1989	3	300/371	7:588	2070	53	221/274		2149	1	326/404		2229	1	334/	
1990	1	300/371		2071	193	221/285		2150	15	326/404	7:168	2230	1	149/424	
1991	4	300/371	7:653	2071	1	/288		2151	2	326/404	7:168	2231	1	343/425	
1992	24	300/371	7:588	2072	2	313/391	2:696	2152	4	326/404	7:168	2232	22	344/425	
1993	1	301/371		2073	3	313/391		2153	2	326/404		2233	28	344/425	2:907
1994	39	301/372	7:714	2074*	3	313/391		2154	1	326/404	2:770, 7:200	2234,2236	5	344/425	
1995	1	301/372	7:714	2075	92	221/274						2235	59	344/425	
1996	7	301/372		2076	906	221/273	2:21	2155	2	326/404	7:548	2237	5	344/426	2:909
1997	2	301/372	7:798	2077	16	221/278		2156	3	327/404		2238	2	345/426	
1998	1	301/372		2078	58	313/391	2:697	2157	1	327/404		2239	1	345/426	
1999	2	301/371		2079	1	314/392		2158	5	327/405	2:770	2240	27	345/426	2:926
2000	1	301/372		2080	8	314/392	2:698	2159	2	327/405		2241	2	345/426	
2001	1	302/372		2081	14	314/392		2160	1	327/405		2242*	1	345/423	
2002	1	302/372	7:1094	2082	2	314/392		2161*	1	327/405					

WSC	F	A&G/M&G	K
2243*	30	345/423	2:928
2244	8	345/427	2:941
2245	2	346/427	
2246	32	346/427	
2247	2	346/427	
2248	178	216/255	
2249	127	346/253	
2250	389	346/427	2:943
2251	9	348/432	
2252	16	348/281	
2253	1	348/432	
2254	177	216/255	
2255	5	348/	
2256	1	348/432	
2257	410	216/254	
2258	454	221/281	
2259	2	348/432	
2260	1	349/	
2261	2	349/432	
2262*	1	349/432	
2263	1	349/432	
2264*	44	349/432	
2265*	3	349/433	
2266*	6	349/433	
2267*	1	349/433	
2268*	21	349/433	
2269*	3	349/433	2:953
2270	5	349/434	
2271	4	350/434	
2272	2	350/434	
2273	1	350/424,434	
2274	3	350/434	
2275	2	350/434	
2276	2	350/433	
2277	2	221/278	
2278	2	350/434	2:954
2279	3	350/434	
2280*	2	350/434	
2281	92	350/434	
2282	2	351/435	
2283*	1	351/435	3:1
2284	4	351/435	3:4
2285	3	351/435	3:4
2286	1	351/435	
2287	1	351/435	
2288	119	351/435	3:7
2289	11	352/437	3:7
2290	11	352/437	
2291*	1	352/437	
2292	6	352/437	3:25
2293	8	352/437	3:25
2294	1	352/437	
2295	1	352/437	3:27
2296	46	352/437	3:27
2297	1	353/438	3:27
2298	7	357/438	3/27
2299	3	353/438	
2300	24	353/438	5:315
2301	1	354/438	3:42
2302	3	354/438	3:42
2303	7	354/438	
2304	3	354/439	3:65
2305	1	354/439	
2306	1	354/439	
2307	64	354/439	3:44
2308	1	355/439	3:44
2309	209	355/439	3:44
2310	16	356/442	3:63
2311	6	356/442	3:63
2312	1	356/442	3:65
2313	1	357/	4:527
2314	1	357/442	4:527
2315	1	357/442	6:332
2316	1343	357/442	3:65
2317	1	358/457	3:123
2318	1	357/457	3:123
2319	1	359/457	
2320	1	359/457	3:65
2321*	2	359/457	
2322	4	359/457	3:128
2323	44	359/457	3:128
2324	1	359/457	3:128
2325	21	359/457	3:132
2326	13	360/458	3:132
2327	2	360/458	
2328	6	360/458	
2329	1	360/458	
2330	3	360/458	
2331*	4	360/458	
2332*	5	360/458	
2333*	1	360/458	
2334	57	360/458	5:315
2335	1	360/459	
2336	1	361/459	
2337	1	361/459	
2338	3	361/459	
2339	1	361/459	
2340	1	361/459	
2341	1	361/459	
2342	46	361/459	3:133
2343	8	362/460	3:136
2344	18	362/460	3:136
2345	3	362/460	
2346	10	362/460	3:139
2347	45	362/460	3:139
2348	13	363/461	3:7
2349	6	363/461	3:7
2350	4	363/461	
2351	7	363/461	
2352	4	363/461	
2353	1	363/461	
2354	4	363/461	3:148
2355	1	363/685	3:148
2356	4	364/461	3:155
2357	1	364/461	3:155
2358	2	364/462	3:159
2359	15	364/462	
2360	3	364/462	
2361	1	364/462	
2362	61	364/462	3:160
2363*	4	365/463	
2364	29	365/463	
2365	2	365/463	
2366	1	356/463	
2367	1	365/463	
2368	6	365/463	
2369	1	365/463	
2370	1	365/463	
2371	1	365/463	
2372	18	365/463	3:167
2373	1	366/463	
2374	39	366/464	3:173
2375	1	366/464	5:292
2376	2	366/464	
2377	4	366/464	
2378	29	366/464	3:180
2379	23	367/465	3:180
2380	14	367/465	3:180
2381*	12	367/465	
2382	5	368/465	5:292
2383*	2	368/465	
2384*	27	368/465	
2385*	42	368/466	
2386	3	368/466	3:194
2387*	1	368/466	
2388*	1	368/466	
2389*	1	368/466	
2390	28	368/466	3:194
2391*	1	369/467	
2392	3	369/467	3:194
2393	4	369/467	
2394*	5	369/467	
2395	7	369/467	3:194
2396	27	269/467	
2397	1	370/263	
2398	113	370/467	2:373
2399	5	371/469	3:215
2400	213	371/469	
2401*	1	372/471	
2402	1	372/471	
2403*	1	372/471	3:217
2404*	1	372/471	
2405	2	372/471	3:221
2406	2	372/471	3:221
2407	1	372/471	3:221
2408*	3	372/471	3:218
2409	32	372/471	3:221
2410*	7	372/471	
2411	71	373/472	3:221
2412	1	373/472	3:221
2413	2	373/473	3:221
2414*	59	373/473	7:292
2415*	2	374/473	7:292
2416	1	374/473	3:221
2417	1	374/473	3:221
2418	1	374/474	3:221
2419*	83	374/474	5:292
2420	4	374/475	3:221
2421*	5	374/475	
2422*	1	374/475	
2423*	2	374/475	
2424*	975	374/475	3:284
2424*	2	/485	
2424*	1	/485	
2425	41	374/485	3:293
2426	1	375/486	3:293
2427	2	375/486	3:293
2428	1	375/486	3:296
2429	1	375/486	
2430*	2	376/486	
2431	1	376/486	3:297
2432	1	376/486	3:297
2433	2	376/486	3:300
2434	2	376/486	3:300
2435	2	376/486	3:300
2436	2	376/486	3:300
2437*	1	376/486	
2438	4	376/486	
2439	2	376/486	
2440	61	376/486	
2441	6	377/487	
2442	1	377/693	
2443	665	377/487	3:323
2444	6	379/495	
2445*	10	379/495	
2446*	15	379/495	6:595
2447	3	379/496	3:334
2448,2449*	45	379/496	3:357
2450	1	380/496	3:357
2451*	1	380/496	3:357
2452*	1	380/496	
2453*	198	380/496	
2454	2	380/498	3:357
2455*	45	380/499	
2456*	1	381/499	
2457*	2	381/499	
2458*	1	381/499	
2459*	3	381/499	
2460	2	381/499	
2461	1	381/499	
2462	16	381/499	3:336
2463	20	381/500	3:339
2464*	20	381/500	
2465	1	381/500	1:74
2466*	1	/501	
2467	2	/267	
2468	5	381/278	
2469*	11	/500	
2470	8	381/500	3:343
2471	3	382/500	3:343
2472	1	382/500	3:343
2473	1	382/500	
2474*	70	/500	3:357
2475*	9	/501	3:357
2476	155	382/501	7:636
2477	1	383/503	3:391
2478	27	383/503	3:397
2479	11	384/503	3:397
2480	29	384/504	3:397
2481	1	384/504	
2482*	4	/504	
2483*	1	384/504	
2484*	1	/504	
2485	2	385/504	
2486	20	385/504	
2487	3	385/504	3:402
2488*	2	/504	
2489*	2	385/504	
2490*	1	385/505	
2491*	133	385/506	
2491*	92	/505	
2491*	1	/506	
2491*	4	/506	
2492*	1	/506	
2493*	1	/506	
2494*	1	386/506	
2495*	9	/506	3:406
2495*	4	/506	
2496*	2	/506	
2497*	1	386/506	
2498*	2	/507	
2499,2500*	7	386/507	
2501*	6	/507	
2501*	1	/507	
2501*	9	/507	
2501*	1	/507	
2501*	1	/507	
2501*	16	/507	
2501*	1	/507	
2502*	2	/507	
2503	1	386/507	
2504	72	386/507	
2505	1	387/508	
2506	3	387/508	3:411
2507	9	387/508	3:411
2508	2	387/508	3:413
2509	13	387/508	
2510	1	387/509	
2511	30	388/509	3:413
2512	7	388/509	3:413
2513	28	388/509	3:413
2514	1	389/509	3:413
2515	3	389/509	
2516	6	389/509	3:440
2517	5	389/510	
2518	22	389/510	3:431
2519	3	389/510	
2520	2	389/510	3:437
2521	89	390/510	3:440
2522	1	390/511	
2523	48	390/511	3:440
2524	4	391/512	
2525	22	391/512	3:444
2526	4	391/512	
2527	1	391/512	
2528	1	391/512	
2529	1	391/512	5:315
2530	5	392/512	
2531	182	392/512	
2532	766	392/	
2533*	3	/514	
2535*	3	/514	1:6
2536*	2	/514	
2537	44	394/514	3:447
2538	2	395/515	3:447
2539	6	395/515	
2540	86	395/515	3:455
2541*	30	/516	
2542*	2	/516	
2542*	17	396/516	
2543,2544	4	396/516	
2545	12	397/516	3:464
2546	11	397/516	
2547	9	397/516	
2548	23	397/517	
2549	11	397/517	3:469
2550	1	398/517	3:469
2551	4	398/517	3:468
2552	1	398/517	5:904
2553	4	398/517	5:904
2554	1	398/517	3:469
2555	5	398/517	3:469
2556	51	398/517	3:469
2557	4	399/518	3:469
2558	2	399/518	

WSC	F	A&G/M&G	K
2559	6	399/518	3:469
2560	16	399/518	4:1091
2561	1	399/518	
2562	1	399/518	
2563	12	399/518	
2564	106	399/518	3:487
2565	1	400/520	
2566	1	401/	
2567	1	401/520	2:135
2568*	1	401/	
2569	1	401/520	
2570	102	401/520	3:536
2571	4	401/521	3:556
2572	8	401/521	3:556
2573	37	402/521	
2574	6	402/522	3:592
2575	4	402/522	
2576	2	407/522	
2577	3	403/522	
2578	4	403/522	3:594
2579	13	403/522	
2580*	4	/522	
2581*	2	/522	
2582*	1	/522	
2583	5	403/522	3:596
2584*	16	/543	
2585	1	404/523	3:603
2586	13	404/523	
2587*	2	/523	
2588	160	404/523	3:605
2589	89	405/525	3:605
2590	66	405/525	3:614
2591*	1	405/525	
2592	8	406/525	3:614
2593	1	406/526	
2594	1	406/526	3:617
2595	6	406/526	
2596	481	406/526	
2597	80	409/531	1:518
2598	3	409/532	
2599	1	409/532	
2600	1	410/532	
2601	2	410/532	
2602	11	410/532	3:620
2603	1	410/532	
2604	1	410/532	1:56
2605	17	410/532	1:56
2606	3	410/532	1:658
2607	3	410/532	1:689
2608	4	410/533	
2609	10	411/533	
2610	1	411/533	1:134
2611	1	411/533	
2612	1	411/533	
2613	5	411/533	3:621
2614	1	411/533	
2615	2	411/533	2:261
2616	2	411/533	
2617	13	411/533	1:189
2618	12	411/533	
2619	3	412/533	3:556
2620	4	412/533	3:645
2621	11	412/534	3:654
2622	2	412/534	
2623	2	412/534	
2624	1	412/534	
2625	3	412/534	
2626	2	412/534	
2627	4	412/534	
2628	2	412/534	
2629	1	412/534	
2630	1	413/534	
2631	3	413/534	3:921
2632	19	413/534	3:921
2633	2	413/534	3:921
2634	4	413/534	3:1039
2635	5	413/534	4:3
2636	2	413/534	4:3
2637	1	413/535	4:3
2638	15	413/535	4:5
2639	1	414/535	

WSC	F	A&G/M&G	K
2640	1	414/979	4:194
2641	25	414/535	4:194
2642	1	415/535	4:267
2643	4	415/535	1:251
2644	6	415/535	1:251
2645	1	415/535	
2646	3	415/535	4:328
2647	17	415/535	4:328
2648	1	415/536	4:390
2649	4	415/536	4:474
2650	1	415/536	
2651	2	415/526	
2652	2	415/533	
2653	1	415/533	
2654	1	415/536	
2655	3	415/536	
2656	1	416/536	
2657	15	416/536	4:948
2658	13	416/536	3:623
2659	1	416/536	3:626
2660	1	416/536	3:626
2661	4	416/536	1:379
2662	5	416/536	5:940
2663	9	416/536	3:627
2664	4	416/536	3:627
2665	6	417/537	3:628
2666	7	417/537	6:135
2667	2	417/537	6:161
2668	1	417/537	
2669	2	417/537	
2670	2	417/537	
2671	6	418/537	1:448
2672	6	418/537	1:448
2673	27	418/537	1:452
2674	1	418/537	
2675	13	418/537	1:475
2676	1	419/538	1:475
2677	1	419/538	1:475
2678	4	419/538	
2679	2	419/538	
2680	11	419/538	
2681	4	419/538	7:368
2682	2	419/538	
2683	1	419/538	
2684	1	419/538	7:413
2685	1	419/538	7:413
2686	1	419/538	
2687	2	420/538	7:588
2688	1	420/538	
2689	1	420/538	7:588
2690	2	420/538	7:714
2691	1	420/538	3:631
2692	2	420/538	7:714
2693	1	420/538	
2694	1	420/538	
2695	1	420/538	
2696	1	420/538	7:939
2697	1	420/538	
2698	3	420/538	
2699	1	420/538	8:106
2700	1	420/	
2701	1	420/538	
2701.5	9	/540	
2702	3	420/539	
2703	2	421/539	
2704	2	421/539	9:93
2705	6	421/539	9:113
2706	9	421/539	3:631
2707	1	421/539	3:631
2708	2	421/539	
2709	1	421/539	3:633
2710	2	421/539	
2711	1	422/539	
2712	1	422/539	2:375
2713	5	422/539	
2714	5	422/539	2:560
2715	2	422/539	2:560
2716	24	422/539	3:634
2717	2	423/540	
2718	13	423/540	
2719	6	423/530	
2720	3	423/540	

WSC	F	A&G/M&G	K
2721	1	423/540	
2722	19	423/540	2:816
2723	22	424/540	3:636
2724	4	424/541	3:636
2725	7	424/541	3:636
2726	1	424/541	
2727	8	424/541	3:638
2728	1	425/541	3:334
2729	2	425/541	3:397
2730	47	425/541	5:199
2731	1	425/541	
2732	2	425/541	5:119
2733	1	425/542	
2734	1	425/542	2:696
2735	1	426/220	
2736	11	426/542	3:640
2737	1	426/542	3:640
2738	2	426/542	3:642
2739	4	426/542	3:642
2740	1	426/542	3:643
2741	2	426/542	
2742	3	426/542	3:643
2743	1	426/542	3:643
2744	38	426/542	3:645
2745	11	427/542	3:645
2746	12	427/543	3:645
2747*	2	/544	
2748*	1	/543	
2749	26	427/543	3:654
2750	1	428/543	
2751	4	428/543	
2752	1	428/543	3:656
2753	27	428/543	
2754	1	428/544	3:659
2755	1	428/544	3:659
2756	18	428/544	3:659
2757	2	429/544	
2758	5	429/544	3:659
2759	5	429/544	3:663
2760	3	429/544	
2761	1	429/544	
2762	2	429/544	
2763	3	430/544	
2764	1	430/544	
2765	2	430/544	
2766	1	430/544	
2767	3	430/544	
2768	11	430/544	3:669
2769	1	430/545	
2770	16	430/545	3:672
2771	3	430/545	3:672
2772	1	430/545	
2773	1	430/545	
2774	2	431/545	
2775	1	431/546	
2776	76	431/545	3:673
			1:791
2777	1	431/545	
2778	4	431/546	
2779	5	431/546	
2780	1	431/546	
2781	1	431/546	
2782	8	432/546	3:683
2783	3	432/546	3:683
2784	61	432/546	3:683
2785	1	432/547	
2786*	6	/547	6:100
2787	6	433/547	
2788	4	433/547	
2789	2	433/547	
2790	2	433/547	
2791*	8	/547	
2792	1	433/548	
2793	4	433/548	
2794	9	433/548	
2795	8	433/548	3:718
2796	1	433/548	
2797*	1	/543	
2798	11	434/548	3:720
2799	40	434/548	3:722
2800	2	434/548	3:726

WSC	F	A&G/M&G	K
2801	9	434/548	3:726
2802*	1	/549	
2803*	1	/549	
2804*	3	/549	
2805	9	434/548	3:722
2806	15	434/	3:726
2707	6	434/549	3:744
2808	16	435/549	
2809	1	435/549	
2810*	1	435/549	
2811	1	435/549	
2812	16	435/549	3:754
2813	12	435/549	3:754
2814	4	435/550	3:757
2815*	1	/550	
2816	18	435/550	3:758
2817	14	436/550	3:758
2818	15	436/550	3:758
2819	13	436/550	3:758
2820	1	436/550	3:758
2821	11	436/550	3:487
2822	11	437/551	3:487
2823	2	437/551	
2824	3	437/551	
2825	10	437/551	
2826	2	437/551	
2827	7	437/551	
2828	1	437/551	
2829	2	437/551	
2830	2	437/551	
2831	1	437/551	
2832*	1	/551	
2833	1	438/551	
2834*	1	/551	
2835	2	438/551	
2836	23	438/551	3:786
2837	18	438/552	
2838	1	438/552	
2839	12	438/552	3:789
2840	15	439/552	3:789
2841	8	439/552	3:789
2842	20	439/552	3:789
2843	1	440/553	3:789
2844	10	440/553	3:789
2845	4	440/553	
2846	1	441/553	
2847	6	441/553	3:810
2848	2	441/553	3:810
2849	2	441/553	3:814
2850	1	441/553	3:817
2851	2	441/553	3:814
2852	5	441/553	3:818
2853	10	442/553	3:822
2854	1	442/553	
2855	3	442/553	
2856	4	442/553	3:823
2857*	1	/553	
2859	6	443/553	3:824
2860	1	443/554	
2861	5	443/554	
2862	1	443/554	
2863	2	443/554	
2864	1	443/554	
2865	11	443/554	
2866	1	443/554	
2867	2	444/554	3:827
2868	5	444/554	
2869	3	444/554	
2870	1	444/554	3:830
2871	1	444/554	
2872	23	444/554	3:827
2873	19	444/554	3:827
2874	2	444/555	
2875	8	444/555	3:830
2876	1	445/555	
2877	8	445/555	
2878	2	445/555	3:860
2879*	1	/555	
2880	2	445/555	
2881*	2	445/555	
2882*	6	/555	

WSC	F	A&G/M&G	K
2883*	10	/555	
2884	1	445/555	
2885	10	445/555	3:867
2886	2	446/555	3:867
2887	2	446/555	3:867
2888	1	446/555	3:905
2889	187	446/556	3:867
2890*	1	/557	
2891	1	448/557	
2892	3	448/557	
2893	1	448/557	
2894	6	448/557	
2895	12	448/558	
2896	59	448/558	3:898
2897	1	449/558	
2898	4	449/558	
2899	5	449/559	3:904
2900	1	449/559	3:905
2901	4	449/558	3:905
2902	47	449/559	3:905
2903	4	450/559	
2904	12	450/559	3:905
2905	7	450/559	3:898
2906	6	450/559	3:898
2907	2	450/559	
2908	1	450/560	
2909	19	450/560	
2910	7	451/560	3:915
2911	3	451/560	
2912*	2	451/560	
2913*	1	/560	
2914*	5	/560	
2915	2	451/560	
2916	2	451/560	
2917	28	451/560	3:921
2918	2	452/560	
2919	114	452/560	3:921
2920	48	453/562	3:921
2921*	2	/562	
2922	3	454/562	3:921
2923	17	454/562	3:921
2924	1	454/563	3:921
2925	9	454/563	3:954
2926-7	20	455/563	3:957
2928	16	455/563	3:957
2929	1	455/563	
2930	2	455/563	
2931	1	455/563	3:957
2932	7	456/563	
2933	4	456/563	
2934	4	456/563	
2935	1	456/563	
2936	14	456/564	3:1000
2937	19	456/564	3:1000
2938	4	457/564	3:1000
2939	1	457/564	3:1000
2940	1	457/564	
2941	1	457/564	3:1035
2942	2	457/564	
2943	4	457/564	
2944	5	457/564	
2945	7	458/564	
2946	1	458/564	
2947	1	458/564	
2948	4	458/564	
2949	5	458/564	
2950	1	458/565	3:1037
2951	1	458/565	
2952	4	458/565	3:1101
2953*	3	458/565	
2954*	5	/565	
2955	3	458/565	
2956*	6	459/565	
2957*	1	/565	
2958*	1	/565	
2959	2	459/565	3:1039
2960	2	459/565	3:1039
2961	7	459/565	3:1039
2962	749	459/565	3:1039
2963	4	461/575	3:1039
2964	2	461/574	3:1098
2965	5	462/574	3:1101
2966	1	462/574	
2967	23	462/574	
2968	28	462/574	
2969	1	462/575	
2970	3	462/575	
2971	1	463/575	
2972*	1	/575	
2973*	1	/575	
2974	14	463/575	
2975	4	463/575	4:1
2976*	15	/575	
2977	4	463/575	
2978	3	463/575	
2979	2	462/575	4:3
2980	295	464/575	4:3, 4:69
2981	4	465/578	
2982	2	465/578	
2983	263	465/578	4:5
2984*	1	/581	
2985	9	466/581	4:16
2986	9	467/581	4:16
2987	1	467/581	
2988	1	467/581	
2989	7	467/581	4:16
2990	6	467/582	
2991	1	467/582	
2992	143	467/582	4:29
2993*	5	467/582	
2994*	2	467/582	
2995	1	468/584	4:57
2996*	1	/584	
2997	1	468/584	
2998	2	468/584	
2999	5	468/584	4:58
3000	21	468/584	4:58
3001	4	468/584	4:65
3002*	1	/584	
3003	4	469/584	4:68
3004	1343	469/584	4:69
3005	1	471/597	4:194
3006	1	471/597	4:193
3007	6	471/597	
3008	3	471/597	4:215
3009	6	472/597	4:215
3010	1	472/597	4:215
3011	5	472/597	4:215
3012	2	472/597	
3013	1	472/597	4:232
3014	7	473/597	4:233
3015	9	473/597	4:233
3016	3	473/598	
3017*	5	473/598	4:234
3018*		/598	4:234
3018*		/598	4:234
3018*	3	473/598	4:234
3019*	3	473/598	4:239
3020*	1	473/598	
3021	2	473/598	4:241
3022	25	473/598	4:241
3023	9	473/598	4:251
3024	1	474/598	
3025	5	474/598	4:254
3026	1	474/598	
3027	15	474/599	4:257
3028	1	474/598	
3029	14	474/599	
3030	2	474/599	4:263
3031	2	474/599	4:263
3032	1	/599	4:265
3033	1	474/599	
3034	8	475/599	4:267
3035	3	475/599	4:268
3036	9	475/599	4:267
3037	60	475/599	4:268
3038	1	475/600	
3039	2	475/600	4:280
3040	3	476/600	
3041	10	476/600	
3042	12	476/600	
3043	2	476/600	
3044*	1	476/600	
3045	1	478/601	
3046	2	476/601	
3047	1	476/601	
3048	2	476/601	4:282
3049	41	476/601	4:284
3050	2	477/601	4:69
3051	4	477/601	4:69
3052	1	477/601	4:69
3053	2	477/601	4:284
3054	1	478/601	4:69
3055	1	478/601	4:69
3056	330	478/601	4:69
3057	1	480/605	
3058	4	480/605	4:293
3059	3	480/605	4:293
3060	2	480/605	4:293
3061	3	480/605	
3062	41	481/605	
3063	14	481/605	
3064	1	481/605	
3065*	3	/606	
3066*	2	/606	
3067	2	481/606	4:295
3068	6	481/606	4:295
3069*	3	/606	
3070*	2	/606	
3071*	1	/606	
3072*	1	482/606	
3073*	1	482/606	
3074	6	482/606	4:308
3075	1	482/606	4:312
3076	26	482/606	4:313
3077	16	483/606	4:313
3078	1	483/607	
3079	3	483/607	
3080	1	483/607	
3081	1	483/607	
3082	3	/607	
3082	3	/607	
3083	2	483/607	4:328
3084	3	483/607	4:328
3085	3	484/607	4:328
3086	1	484/607	4:328
3087	12	484/607	4:324
3088	14	484/607	4:324
3089	43	484/607	4:328
3090	1	/608	
3091	4	/608	
3092	1	/608	
3093	1	/608	
3094	12	485/608	
3095	1	485/608	4:356
3096	1	485/608	4:356
3097	6	486/608	4:356
3098*	1	/608	
3099*	1	/608	
3100	4	486/608	
3101	268	486/608	4:390
3102	1	487/611	4:390
3103*	1	/611	
3104*	1	/628	
3105	5	487/611	4:360
3106	2	487/611	4:362
3107	58	487/612	4:362
3108	3	488/612	4:362
3109*	22	488/612	
3110*	5	/612	
3111	1	488/612	4:370
3112	10	488/612	4:372
3113	14	489/613	4:374
3114	10	489/613	4:374
3115	14	489/613	4:374
3116	1	489/613	
3117	5	489/613	
3118	1	489/613	
3119	3	489/613	4:1091
3120	4	489/613	
3121*	1	/613	
3122	12	490/613	
3123	85	490/614	
3124*	1	/614	
3125	1	491/614	
3126*	4	491/614	4:388
3126	4	/614	4:388
3127*	1	/615	
3128*	3	/615	
3129	25	491/615	4:390
3130	1	49*/615	
3131	5	491/615	4:462
3132	1	492/615	
3133	1	492/615	
3134	1	492/615	4:466
3135	9	492/615	4:472
3136*	3	/615	
3137*	54	/615	
3138*	8	/616	
3139	1	493/616	
3140	79	493/616	4:474
3141	37	494/617	4:474
3142	20	494/617	4:474
3143	3	495/618	
3144	34	495/618	4:474
3145	1	496/618	4:514
3146	7	496/618	4:515
3147	1	496/618	4:515
3148	6	496/618	4:515
3149	3	496/618	
3150	1	496/619	4:519
3151	1	496/619	4:519
3152	6	496/619	4:519
3153	3	496/619	4:519
3154	1	496/619	4:519
3155	2	497/619	4:519
3156*	5	497/611	
3157*	1	/611	
3158*	2	497/611	
3159*	2	497/611	
3160*	1	497/619	
3161*	2	497/619	
3162	29	497/619	4:524
3163	4	497/619	4:527
3164	4	497/619	4:527
3165	301	216/252	
3166	1	497/131	
3167	2	497/619	4:529
3168	3	498/619	4:529
3169	1	498/619	4:529
3170	8	498/619	4:529
3171	1	498/620	
3172	3	498/620	4:529
3173	195	498/620	4:529
3174	1	499/622	4:529
3175	3	499/622	
3176	1	499/622	
3177	7	499/622	
3178	3	500/622	4:545
3179	5	500/622	
3180	2	500/622	5:42
3181	1	500/704	
3182	3	500/622	4:545
3183	2	500/622	4:545
3184	7	500/622	4:545
3185	1	500/622	
3186	1	500/622	
8187	45	500/622	
3188	3	500/623	
3189	3	501/623	4:549
3190*	1	/623	
3191	3	501/623	
3192	4	501/623	4:552
3193	1	501/623	
3194*	1	/623	
3195	110	501/623	
3196	34	502/625	4:555
3197*	2	/625	
3198*	9	/625	4:568

WSC	F	A&G/M&G	K
3199	10	501/623	
3200	1	503/625	
3201	3	503/625	4:571
3202	1	503/625	4:571
3303	195	503/625	
3304	4	504/628	
3305	8	504/628	
3306	120	504/628	4:589
3307	14	505/629	
3308	6	506/629	4:589
3309	19	506/629	4:589
3310	10	506/629	
3311	2	506/629	
3312	1	506/630	
3313	43	506/630	4:594
3314	2	507/630	
3315	1	507/630	4:598
3316	6	507/630	4:598
3317	4	508/630	
3318*	2	508/630	
3319	61	508/630	
3320	1	509/631	4:625
3321	3	509/631	
3322	1	509/631	
3323*	2	/631	
3324	8	509/631	
3325	1	509/631	
3326	473	509/631	7:766
3327	12	511/636	1:518
3328	1	512/636	
3329	2	512/636	
3330	5	512/636	
3331	3	512/636	8:152
3332	2	512/636	
3333	4	512/636	3:487
3334	1	512/636	3:718
3335	6	512/636	4:5
3336	1	512/637	4:5
3337	2	512/637	1:251
3338	6	512/637	4:626
3339	4	513/637	4:742
3340	34	513/637	4:948
3341	24	513/637	4:948
3342	9	514/637	
3343	8	514/638	
3344	3	514/638	7:714
3345	5	514/638	7:954
3346	6	5.5/638	8:152
3347	1	515/638	
3348	8	515/638	2:816
3349	1	515/638	4:630
3350	4	515/638	
3351	2	515/638	
3352	1	515/638	
3353	6	516/638	2:816
3354	10	516/638	4:632
3355	1	516/638	
3356	1	516/639	5:904
3357	1	516/639	
3358	13	516/639	4:632
3359	8	516/639	4:635
3360	17	517/639	
3361	675	517/639	
3362	60	210/240	
3363	97	/494	
3364	5	194/646	
3364	94	/646	
3365	2	519/647	
3366	57	519/647	
3367	92	519/648	
3368	1	520/648	
3369	1	520/648	
3370*	1	/649	
3371	21	520/649	
3372	3	520/649	
3373	1	520/649	
3374	1	520/649	4:637
3376	18	520/649	4:638
3377	7	520/649	
3378	5	521/719	

WSC	F	A&G/M&G	K
3379	25	521/649	
3380	2	521/650	
3381	12	521/639	
3382	1	521/650	
3383	37	527/650	
3384	85	521/650	4:642
3385	15	522/651	
3386	1	522/651	
3387	4	/639	
3388	2	522/651	
3389	1	522/651	
3391	80	229/299	
3392	5	522/651	4:644
3393	1	522/651	4:644
3394	1	522/651	4:644
3395	1	523/651,325	
3396	4	523/651	
3397	16	523/651	
3398	30	523/652	4:648
3399*	3	/652	
3400	1	523/652	
3401	4	523/652	4:659
3402	7	524/652	4:659
3403	2	524/652	4:675
3404	42	524/652	4:683
3405	3	525/653	4:695
3406	1	525/653	4:695
3407	2	525/653	4:695
3408	29	525/653	4:695
3409	2	525/653	4:695
3410	1	525/653	
3411	4	525/653	4:695
3412*	1	/653	
3413*	2	/653	
3414	9	526/653	
3415	21	526/652	
3416*	1	/654	
3417	7	526/654	4:675
3418	7	526/654	4:675
3419	42	526/654	4:675
3420	1	526/654	4:675
3421	21	526/654	4:675
3422	3	527/655	
3423	3	527/655	
3424	1	527/655	
3425	1	527/655	4:735
3426	3	527/655	
3427	241	216/252	
3428	7	527/655	4:729
3429	6	528/655	4:729
3430	4	528/655	4:729
3431	14	528/655	4:729
3432	4	528/655	4:729
3433	6	528/655	4:735
3434*	1	/655	
3435	3	528/655	4:736
3436	1	528/656	4:736
3437	1	528/656	4:571
3438	2	529/656	4:574
3439	9	529/656	4:737
3440	66	529/656	
3441	47	529/657	
3442	2	530/657	
3443	1	530/657	
3444	3	530/657	4:742
3445	1	530/657	4:742
3446	2	530/657	4:742
3447	1	530/657	
3448	6	530/657	4:760
3449	3	530/657	
3450	586	216/251	
3451	1	530/657	
3452	1	530/658	
3453	1	530/658	4:802
3454	5	530/658	4:762
3455	1	531/658	
3456	1	531/658	4:796
3457	1	531/658	
3458	4	531/658	
3459	1	531/658	

WSC	F	A&G/M&G	K
3460*	1	/658	
3461	9	531/658	
3462	1	531/658	4:800
3463	3	531/658	
3464	14	531/658	4:800
3465*	2	/658	
3466	27	531/658	4:802
3467	1	532/659	
3468	1	532/659	4:829
3469	2	532/659	
3470	1	533/659	4:829
3471	4	533/659	4:832
3472	5	533/659	4:832
3473	1	533/659	4:832
3474	13	533/659	4:832
3475*	24	/659	
3475*	49	/659	
3475*	4	/659	
3475*	3	/659	4:848
3476*	3	/660	
3477*	1	/660	
3478*	12	/660	
3479*	4	/661	4:874
3480*	15	534/660	4:874
3481*	1	/661	
3482*	6	/661	
3483	34	534/661	
3484*	1	/661	
3485	46	535/661	4:880
3486*	1	/662	
3487	2	535/662	
3488*	1	/662	
3489	2	536/662	4:891
3490	1	536/662	
3491	1	536/662	
3492	3	536/662	
3493*	1	/662	
3494	5	536/662	
3495	10	536/662	
3496*	1	536/	
3497*	1	/661	
3498	132	536/662	4:892
3499	3	537/663	4:892
3500	2	537/663	4:892
3501	24	537/664	4:896
3502	1	538/669	
3503	5	538/664	
3504	1	538/664	
3506	2	538/664	
3507	26	538/664	4:902
3508*	3	/664	
3509	1	538/664	4:902
3510	1	539/664	4:911
3511	1	539/664	
3512	1	539/664	
3513	1	539/664	
3514	2	539/664	
3515	1	539/664	4:912
3516	14	539/664	4:912
3517*	1	539/665	
3518*	1	/665	
3519	1	540/665	
3520	9	540/665	
3521	8	540/665	4:924
3522	21	540/665	4:924
3523	2	540/665	
3524	3	540/665	4:936
3525	6	540/665	4:936
3526*	1	/665	
3527*	1	541/665	
3528	28	541/665	4:942
3529	1	541/666	4:942
3530*	5	541/666	
3531*	2	541/666	
3532*	1	542/666	
3533*	1	541/666	
3534	4	541/666	4:942
3535*	1	/666	
3536*	2	542/666	
3537	1	542/666	

WSC	F	A&G/M&G	K
3538	17	542/666	4:946
3539	14	542/666	4:948
3540	6	542/666	4:948
3541	1	543/666	
3542	2	543/667	
3543	15	543/667	
3544	9	543/667	4:1022
3545	2	543/667	4:1022
3546	1	543/667	
3547	3	543/667	2:135
3548	1	543/667	4:1022
3549	2	544/667	4:1022
3550	1	544/667	4:1022
3551	197	544/667	4:1022
3552	1	545/669	4:1091
3553	1	545/669	4:1091
3554	12	545/669	4:1091
3555	1	545/669	
3556	1	545/669	
3557	3	545/669	
3558	7	546/669	
3559	3	546/669	4:948
3560	8	546/669	4:948
3561	1	546/670	
3562	1	546/670	
3563	24	546/670	4:948
3564*	1	547/670	
3565	8	547/670	4:1099
3566	16	547/670	4:1099
3567	3	547/670	
3568	139	547/670	4:1106
3569	520	/670	
3570	20	548/672	
3571	65	548/672	4:1123
3572	2	549/673	
3573	2	549/673	
3574	1	549/673	
3575*	8	/673	
3576	2	549/673	4:1126
3577	1	549/673	
3578	2	549/673	5:1
3579	10	550/673	5:1
3580	1	550/673	5:1
3581	14	550/673	5:1
3582	2	550/673	
3583	16	550/673	
3584	7	550/674	
3585	2	551/674	
3586	19	551/674	5:37
3587	3	551/674	
3588	543	551/674	
3589	2	555/683	
3590	5	555/683	
3591	1	555/683	5:41
3592	12	555/683	
3593	1	555/683	
3594	5	555/683	5:42
3595	5	555/684	5:42
3596	1	556/684	
3597	2	555/684	
3598	102	556/684	5:42
3599	12	557/685	
3600	4	557/685	5:115
3601	2	557/685	5:115
3602	2	557/685	5:116
3603	11		
3604*	1	/685	
3605	1	557/685	
3606	15	557/685	
3607	2	558/685	
3608	5	558/685	
3609	3	559/686	5:119
3610	4	559/686	
3611	9	559/686	5:119
3612	1	559/686	
3613	2	559/686	5:119
3614	95	559/686	5:119
3615	2	560/687	
3616	1	560/687	2:44
3617	12	560/687	2:44

WSC	F	A&G/M&G	K	WMC	F	A&G/M&G	K	WSC	F	A&G/M&G	K	WSC	F	A&G/M&G	K
3618	39	560/687	5:119	3698	1	579/700		3776	2	600/731		3853	30	618/753	5:761
3619	18	561/688	5:119	3699	82	579/700		3777	94	600/731		3854	37	618/753	
3621	1	562/688		3700	1	580/701	5:315	3778	192	600/731		3855	10	619/754	1:128
3622	7	562/688	5:119	3700	58	580/702		3778	80	600/736		3856	2	619/754	2:25
3623	10	562/688	5:119	3701	4	580/701	5:315	3778	81	600/733		3857	3	619/754	5:765
3624	114	562/688	5:119	3702	1	580/701		3778	3	600/736		3858	5	619/754	
3625	16	563/689	5:119	3703	1	580/701		3779	213	602/737		3859	1	619/205	
3626	1	564/690		3704	56	580/701		3780	56	602/740		3860	121	619/754	2:166
3627	2	564/690	5:159	3705	12	580/701	5:315	3781	7	603/740	5:559	3861	1	621/756	2:232
3628	5	564/690	5:159	3706	4	581/702	5:315	3782	2	603/740	5:559	3862	13	621/756	2:166
3629	3	564/690	5:159	3707	1	581/702	5:315	3783	2	603/740	5:559	3863	4	621/756	2:877
3630	2	564/690		3708	59	581/702	5:315	3784	36	603/740	5:559	3864	1	621/756	
3631	33	564/690	5:162	3709	36	582/703	5:382	3785	4	603/741		3865	1	621/756	
3632	1	565/690		3710	8	583/703	5:382	3786	3	604/741		3866	1	621/756	8:152
3633	1	565/690		3711	1	583/703	5:382	3787	2	604/741	2:261	3867	2	621/756	
3633	2	565/690		3712	2	583/703		3788	102	604/741	5:315	3868	11	621/756	1:191
3634	15	565/690		3713	3	583/703	5:447	3789	14	604/742	5:566	3869	1	622/756	
3635	1	565/691		3714	2	583/704		3790	1	605/742		3870	108	622/756	5:773
3636	3	565/691	5:166	3715	1	583/704	5:447	3791	2	605/		3871	1	623/757	
3637	1	565/691		3716	1	583/704	5:449	3792	1	605/742		3872	2	623/756	8:152
3638	9	565/691		3717	2	583/704	5:449	3793	175	605/742	5:582	3873	2	623/757	3:654
3639	4	566/591	5:167	3718	1	584/704	8:106	3794	1	606/744	5:590	3874	29	623/758	5:773
3640	5	566/691	6:174	3719	1	584/704		3795	5	606/744		3875	5	623/758	5:800
3641	43	566/691	5:171	3720	1	584/704		3796	3	606/744		3876	3	624/758	1:216
3642	1	567/691	9:608	3721	1	584/704		3797	1	606/745		3877	4	624/758	1:210
3643	1	567/691		3722	3	584/704		3798	15	606/744		3878	2	624/758	1:216
3644	1	567/691	5:167	3723	4	584/704		3799	3	606/745		3879	5	624/758	5:814
3645	1	567/691	5:167	3724	8	584/704	5:452	3800	4	606/745	5:591	3880	50	624/758	4:5
3646	3	567/692		3725	11	584/704		3801	15	/281		3881	2	625/759	
3647	1	567/692	3:758	3726	3	584/704,338		3802	1	607/745	5:593	3882	1	625/759	
3648	2	567/692	3:758				5:457	3803	5	607/745	5:593	3883	1	625/759	
3649	1	567/692	5:173	3727	10	584/704	5:457	3804	16	607/745	5:904	3884	2	625/759	
3650	112	567/692	5:174	3728	4	584/704	5:457	3805	1	607/745	5:904	3885	10	625/759	
3651	1	567/693	5:174	3729	5	585/704	5:467	3806	3	607/745	5:904	3886	5	625/759	
3652*	1	/693		3730	2	585/704	5:467	3807	3	608/745	5:596	3887	3	625/759	4:574
3653	1	568/693	7:751	3731	1	585/704	5:467	3808	2	608/745	5:626	3888	4	626/759	5:816
3654	4	568/693		3732	3	585/704		3809	6	608/745	5:596	3889	1	626/759	5:816
3655	1	568/693		3733	2	585/705		3810	2	608/745	5:596	3890	1	626/759	5:816
3656	4	568/693		3734	1	585/705		3811	13	608/745	5:596	3891	1	626/759	4:1022
3657	1	568/693		3735	65	585/705	5:475	3812	1	609/746		3892	1	626/759	4:1022
3658	1	568/		3736	3	586/705		3813	51	609/746	5:636	3893	1	626/759	6:122
3659	1	568/693		3737	2	586/705	5:487	3814	13	609/746		3894	2	626/759	6:122
3660	27	568/693	5:176	3738	1	587/706		3815	1	609/747	5:625	3895	1	626/759	6:161
3661	12	569/698	5:185	3739	1393	587/706		3816	24	609/747	5:636,	3896	1	626/760	
3662	1	569/694		3740	3	589/712					5:654	3897	1	626/760	
3663	2	569/693	4:904	3741	8	589/712	5:489	3817	5	610/747		3898	1	627/760	
3664	47	569/694	5:186	3741	8	589/712	5:489	3819	6	610/747	5:717	3899	5	627/760	
3665	2	570/694	5:186	3742	2	589/712	5:489	3820	19	610/747	5:717	3900	23	627/760	6:161
3666	15	570/694	5:186	3743	1	589/712	5:489	3821	1	610/747	5:717	3901	1	627/760	
3667	6	570/694	5:186	3744	6	590/712	5:493	3822	4	610/747	5:717	3902	1	627/760	
3668	30	570/695		3745	115	590/712		3823	1	610/747	5:721	3903	4	627/760	
3669	1	571/695	5:186	3747	5	590/713		3824	2	611/749	1:681	3904	6	627/760	7:1
3670	23	571/695	5:199	3748	153	590/713		3825	142	611/747		3905	1	627/760	
3671	6	571/695	5:199	3749	2	591/715		3826	1	612/749		3906	6	627/760	8:140
3672	1	572/695	5:199	3750	1	591/715		3827	1	612/835		3907	1	628/760	8:140
3673	1	562/695		3751	8	591/715	5:496	3828*	5	612/749		3908	19	628/760	8:152
3674	3	572/695		3752	122	592/715		3829	1	612/749		3909	1	628/761	
3675	1	572/695		3753	105	592/717		3830	1	612/749		3910	1	628/761	
3676	3	572/695		3754	1293	592/718		3831	1	612/749	5:722	3911	2	628/761	
3677	6	572/696	5:220	3755	6	594/713		3832	1	612/749		3912	1	628/761	
3678	1	573/696	5:283	3756	1453	594/719		3833	3	612/749	5:292	3913	1	628/761	
3679	10	573/696	5:238	3757	27	594/719		3834	5	612/749	5:722	3914	4	629/761	
3680	5	573/696	5:238	3758	1	595/720		3835	1	613/749	5:722	3915	1	629/761	
3681	1	573/696	5:238	3759	47	595/721		3836	1	613/749		3916	19	629/761	
3682*	2	573/696		3760	1	595/721		3837	7	613/749		3917	1	629/761	
3683*	2	573/696		3761	137	595/721		3838	2	613/749	8:49	3918	23	629/761	5:858
3684	2	573/696		3762	235	596/723		3839	1	613/749		3919	1	630/761	5:824
3685	1	573/696		3763	16	596/725		3840	3	613/749		3920	1	630/761	5:824
3686	230	573/696	5:242	3764	5	596/725		3841	10	613/749	3:905	3921	1	630/761	
3687	10	577/699	5:242	3765	48	596/725		3842	42	614/750		3922	2	630/761	2:666
3688	6	577/699	5:283	3766	1	597/726		3843	9	614/750		3923	1	630/762	
3689	10	577/699		3767	526	597/726		3844	200	614/750	5:727	3924	3	630/762	
3690	7	577/699		3768	23	597/726		3845	4	616/752	5:736	3925	10	630/762	
3691	8	578/699	5:288	3769	5	598/726		3846	2	616/752		3926	1	631/762	
3692	2	578/699		3770	8	596/727	5:497	3847	7	617/752	5:736	3927	3	631/762	2:63
3693	7	578/699	5:289	3771	2	598/727	5:497	3848	5	617/752	5:736	3928	31	631/762	2:666
3694	36	578/699	5:289	3772	284	598/727	5:497	3849	2	617/752		3929	1	631/762	1:509
3695	1	578/700	5:292	3773*	1	/730		3850	50	617/752	5:744	3930	16	631/762	
3696	5	579/700	5:292	3774*	1	/730		3851	1	618/752		3931	1	632/762	
3697	5	579/700		3775	37	600/730	5:543	3852	5	618/753	5:761	3932	1	632/762	

WSC	F	A&G/M&G	K	WSC	F	A&G/M&G	K	WSC	F	A&G/M&G	K	WSC	F	A&G/M&G	K
3933	14	632/762	5:826	4011*	3	650/741		4091*	55	/786		4171	18	691/832	6:502
3934*	1	/763		4012	331	650/791	6:53	4092	1	664/803		4172	164	691/832	6:516
3935	1	636/763		4013	6	651/795		4093	1	664/803		4173	2	692/834	
3936	2	633/763	5:837	4014	4	651/795		4094	5	664/803		4174	2	692/834	6:516
3936	39	633/763	5:837	4015	2	651/795		4095	75	664/803	6:135	4175	1	692/834	6:516
3937*	1	633/763		4016	24	651/795		4096	1	664/804		4176	2	693/834	6:516
3938	1	634/763		4017	7	652/795		4097	9	664/804	6:160	4177	3	693/834	6:516
3939	2	634/763	5:841	4018	2	652/795		4098	90	664/804	6:161	4178	18	693/834	
3940	2	634/763	5:841	4019	1	652/795		4099*	2	/805		4179	1	693/834	
3941	4	634/763	5:841	4020	1	652/795		4100	248	665/805	6:174	4180	1	693/834	6:545
3942	5	634/764	5:854	4021	2	652/795		4101	2	668/808		4181	1	693/834	
3943	2	634/764		4022	4	652/795	2:666	4102	244	668/808	6:174	4182	1	694/834	6:484
3944	1	634/764		4023	3	652/795		4103	66	670/811	6:174	4183	365	694/834	
3945	1	634/764	5:186	4024	7	652/795	5:292	4104	1	671/811	6:174	4184	1	696/838	7:548
3946	2	634/764	5:186	4025	1	653/795		4105	39	671/812	6:228	4185	3	696/838	
3947	2	634/764		4026	4	653/795		4106	10	671/812	6:228	4186	2	696/838	
3948	2	634/764	5:857	4027	1	653/796	3:413	4107	1	672/812	6:228	4187	1	696/838	
3949	2	635/764	5:382	4028	3	653/796		4108	5	672/812	6:228	4188	2	696/838	6:135
3950	1	635/764	5:382	4029	5	653/796	3:654	4109	3	672/812		4189	7	697/838	6:546
3951	1	635/764	5:857	4030	2	653/796	5:292	4110	1	672/812	6:254	4190-1	78	697/839	6:546
3952	24	635/764	5:858	4031	1	654/796		4111	2	672/812	6:254	4192	3	698/839	
3953	2	635/764		4032	1	654/796		4112	1	672/812	6:254	4193*	1	698/840	
3954	51	635/764	5:871	4033	1	654/796		4113	9	672/812		4194*	4	698/840	
3955	9	636/765	5:871	4034	2	654/796	4:16	4114	4	672/813		4195*	2	698/840	
3956	1243	636/765	5:886	4035	2	645/796	4:194	4115	3	672/813		4196*	2	698/840	
3957	29	638/788	5:896	4036	5	654/796	4:313	4116	1	673/813		4197	2	698/840	
3958	42	637/778	5:904	4037	1	654/796	4:574	4117	1	673/813		4198	154	698/840	6:566
3959*	1	640/778		4038	1	654/796		4118-9	59	673/813		4199	3	699/841	
3960	10	640/778	5:939	4039	1	654/796		4120	3	673/813		4200	2	699/841	
3961	5	640/779	5:940	4040	1	654/796		4121	9	673/814	6:263	4201*	1	699/842	
3962	418	640/779	5:945	4041	1	654/796	6:57	4122	5	673/814	6:266	4202	26	699/842	6:579
3963*	1	642/783		4042	1	654/796		4123	4	673/814	6:266	4203	8	700/842	6:579
3964	1	642/784		4043	96	654/796	5:490	4124	10	673/814	6:266	4204	12	700/842	6:579
3965	3	643/783	5:945	4044	1	655/797		4125	5	673/814		4205	10	700/842	6:579
3966	4	642/783		4045	3	655/797	6:161	4126	5	673/814		4206,4208			
3967	1	642/783	5:945	4046	2	655/797		4127	21	674/814			4	700/842	
3968	8	642/783		4047	5	655/797		4128	32	674/814	6:274	4207	2	700/842	
3969*	1	642/784		4048	1	655/797		4129	12	674/815	6:274	4209	5	700/842	
3970	1	642/784		4049	1	656/797		4130	24	663/815		4210	3	700/842	
3971	3	642/784	5:945	4050	4	565/798	6:51	4131	2	675/815		4211	1	700/842	
3972*	1	642/784		4051	5	656/798	6:58	4132	1	675/815		4212	3	701/842	
3972*	163	642/784		4052	39	656/798	6:58	4133	31	675/815		4213	3	701/843	
3973	15	643/785		4053	22	657/798		4134	17	675/815	6:283	4214	27	701/843	6:135
3974*	2	643/785		4054	4	657/798		4135	5	676/816	6:283	4215	16	701/843	6:595
3975	2	644/786	5:1022	4055-6	13	657/799		4136	4	676/816	6:283	4216	1	701/843	6:595
3976	3	644/786		4057	3	657/799		4137	90	676/816	6:283	4217	7	701/843	
3977	1	644/786		4058	10	657/799	6:63	4138	17	678/817	6:283	4218	32	701/843	
3978	1	644/786		4059	18	658/799	6:72	4139	1	678/817		4219	19	701/843	
3979	2	644/786		4060	8	658/799		4139	17	678/817	6:311	4220	1	702/844	
3980	4	644/786	6:1	4061	36	658/799	6:72	4140	1	678/817	6:128	4221	33	702/844	6:135
3981	1	644/786	6:1	4062	1	658/800		4141	1	679/817		4222	15	702/844	6:135
3982	55	644/686	6:1	4063	1	659/800		4142	6	679/817		4223*	1	/844	
3983	23	645/787	6:12	4064	5	659/800		4143	67	679/817		4224	1	702/844	
3984	2	645/787	6:23	4065	1	659/800	3:631	4144	3	679/818		4225	3	703/844	
3985	39	646/787	6:23	4066	10	659/800		4145	28	679/818	6:318	4226	47	702/844	
3986	21	646/788	6:23	4067	1	659/800	6:84	4146	4	679/818		4227*	1	703/845	
3987	2	646/788	6:23	4068	1	659/800	6:93	4147	12	679/818	6:318	4228	93	703/845	6:624
3988	1	647/788	6:1	4069*	1	659/		4148	3	686/819	6:318	4229	11	703/845	6:632
3989	2	647/788		4070	2	659/800		4149	1	680/819	6:318	4230	1	704/846	6:632
3990	1	647/788		4071	14	659/800		4150	1	680/819		4231	1	704/846	6:632
3991	4	647/788		4072	4	659/800		4151	385	680/819	6:332	4232	8	704/846	
3992	81	647/788	1:398	4072	1	660/800		4152	26	685/824	6:332	4233	2	704/846	6:632
3993	1	648/789	6:37	4073	16	660/800	6:95	4153	2	685/824		4234	6	704/846	6:632
3994	6	648/789		4074*	1	660/800		4154	7	685/824	6:332	4235	1	705/847	
3995	1	648/789		4075	4	661/802		4155	2	686/824	6:455	4236	9	705/847	
3996	10	648/789	6:40	4076	1	661/802		4156	3	686/824	6:455	4237	1	705/846	
3997	5	648/789	6:40	4077	12	661/802	6:112	4157	2	686/824		4238	38	705/847	6:632
3998	1	648/789	6:37	4078	1	661/802		4158	1	686/824		4239	3	705/847	6:645
3999	1	648/789		4079	2	661/802		4159	28	686/824		4240	3	705/847	6:645
4000	6	648/789		4080	2	662/802		4160	576	687/824	6:458	4241	7	706/847	
4001	2	648/790		4081	6	662/802	6:118	4161	2	689/831	6:458	4242	2	706/847	
4002	38	648/790		4082	6	662/802	6:119	4162	1	689/831	6:458	4243	2	706/847	6:651
4003	1	648/790		4083	4	662/802		4163	6	689/831	6:458	4244	3	706/847	6:651
4004	7	648/790		4084	12	662/803		4164	10	690/831	6:484	4245	67	706/847	6:651
4005	3	648/790	6:44	4085	1	662/803		4165	11	690/831	6:485	4246	3	707/848	6:651
4006	6	649/790	6:1	4086	1	663/803		4166	18	691/831	6:485	4247	1	707/848	
4007	4	649/		4087	4	663/803	6:122	4167	5	691/831	6:485	4248	1	707/848	
4008	23	649/790		4088	4	663/803	6:122	4168	5	691/831	6:485	4249	1	707/848	
4009	4	649/791		4089	2	663/803	6:122	4169	34	691/831		4250	14	707/849	
4010*	2	649/791		4090	2	663/803		4170	7	691/832	6:502	4251*	1	/849	

WSC	F	A&G/M&G	K	WSC	F	A&G/M&G	K	WSC	F	A&G/M&G	K	WSC	F	A&G/M&G	K
4252*	5	/849		4330	1	719/861		4410	4	732/873	6:865	4490	1	743/882	
4253	49	708/849	6:683	4331	1	719/861	2:330	4411	5	732/873	6:865	4491	17	743/882	6:985
4254	18	708/849	1:128	4332	1	719/761		4412	60	732/873	6:865	4492	2	743/882	
4255	1	709/850		4333	1	720/861		4413	100	732/874	6:865	4493	1	743/882	
4256	1	709/850		4334	86	720/861	2:666	4414	1	734/875		4494	1	743/882	
4257	1	709/850		4335	37	720/863	2:775	4415	1	734/875	6:865	4495-6	8	743/882	6:991
4258	2	709/850		4336	87	720/863	2:775	4416	9	734/875	6:865	4497*	2	744/882	
4259	1	709/850		4337	24	721/864		4417	5	734/875	6:883	4498*	1	744/882	
4260	5	709/850		4338	1	722/864		4418	1	734/875		4499*	1	744/882	
4261	2	709/850		4339	4	722/864	6:727	4419	2	734/875		4500	1	744/882	
4262	1	709/850		4340	4	722/864		4420	5	734/875		4501	7	744/882	6:998
4263	41	709/850	6:689	4341	30	722/864	3:487	4421	1	734/875		4502*	1	744/883	
4264	2	710/850		4342	10	722/865	3:617	4422	2	734/875		4503*	1	744/883	3:1
4265	1	710/850		4343	1	723/865	3:617	4423	1	735/875		4504*	2	744/883	
4266	1	710/850		4344	1	723/865		4424*	1	/875		4505	4	744/883	
4267	5	710/851	1:689	4345	1	723/865	3:758	4425	2	735/875		4506	18	744/883	6:998
4268	2	710/851	1:689	4346	1	723/865		4426	1	735/875		4507	1	745/883	
4269	2	710/851		4347	4	723/865		4427	1	735/875		4508	1	745/883	
4270	5	710/851	1:742	4348	6	723/865	6:745	4428	1	735/875		4509	1	745/883	
4271	3	711/851		4349	1	723/865	6:745	4429	3	735/875		4510	2	745/883	
4272	1	711/851		4350	8	723/865	6:745	4430	5	735/875	6:161	4511	3	745/883	
4273	3	711/851		4351	2	723/865		4431	2	735/875	6:161	4512	1	745/883	
4274	1	711/851	8:226	4352	60	623/865	6:758	4432	3	735/876	6:885	4513*	1	745/	
4275	2	711/851	5:315	4353	1	724/866	6:758	4433	1	735/876	6:885	4514*	12	745/883	
4276	1	711/851	2:517	4354	2	724/866		4434	34	735/876	6:885	4515*	1	745/883	
4277	3	711/851		4355	14	724/866	4:5	4435	1	736/876	6:915	4516*	8	745/883	
4278	2	712/851		4356	1	724/866	4:5	4436*	1	736/876	6:917	4517	2	745/883	
4279	1	712/851	2:576	4357	6	724/866	4:574	4437	3	736/876		4518	2	746/884	
4280	(4277)			4358	1	724/866		4438	1	736/876	6:915	4519	2	746/884	
	9	711/851		4359	1	725/866		4439	10	736/876	6:921	4520	1	746/884	7:1
4281	9	712/851		4360	2	725/867		4440	18	736/876	6:921	4521	68	746/884	7:1
4282	2	712/851	2:704	4361	1	725/867		4441	12	737/876		4522	1	746/885	
4283	1	712/851	2:707	4362	1	725/867		4442	74	737/876	6:928	4523*	14	747/885	7:45
4284	1	712/851	6:692	4363	8	725/867		4443	2	738/877		4524*	2	747/885	
4285	1	712/851	2:907	4364	1	725/867		4444	4	738/878	6:953	4525	1	747/885	7:54
4286	12	713/851	8:152	4365	1	725/867		4445	2	738/878	6:956	4526	4	747/885	7:56
4287	1	713/852	6:694	4366	2	725/867		4446	6	738/878	6:956	4527*	2	747/885	
4288	5	713/852		4367	7	725/867	8:27	4447	1	738/878	6:928	4528*	3	747/885	
4289	3	713/852	6:694	4368	1	726/867		4448	6	738/878	6:928	4529*	1	747/885	
4290	1	713/852	6:700	4369	18	726/867	8:152	4449	2	738/878		4530*	1	748/885	
4291	8	713/852		4370	3	726/867		4450	2	738/878	6:928	4531	15	747/885	7:65
4292	1	714/852	3:487	4371	1	726/867		4451	3	738/878	6:928	4532*	2	748/885	
4293	4	714/852	1:56	4372	1	726/867	6:766	4453	22	738/878		4533*	3	748/885	
4294	1	714/852		4373	1	726/867	6:766	4454	12	739/878	6:959	4534*	1	748/885	
4295	1	712/851	2:907	4374	48	726/867	9:56	4455	6	739/878		4535	1	748/885	7:65
4295	5	714/852	3:654	4375	1	727/868		4456	5	739/878	5:1022	4536	11	748/885	7:71
4296	2	714/852	3:683	4376	9	727/868	9:56	4457	3	739/878	5:1022	4537	12	748/885	7:71
4297	3	714/852	6:703	4377	7	727/868		4458	16	740/258		4538	1	748/885	7:71
4298	6	714/852	6:703	4378	1	727/868		4459	103	739/879		4539*	2	748/886	
4299	1	715/852	3:921	4379	1	727/868		4460*	2	740/880		4540*	11	748/886	7:88
4300	1	715/852		4380	1	728/868	6:768	4461	17	740/880	6:961	4541*	9	748/886	7:88
4301	3	715/852	4:5	4381	1	728/868	6:768	4462	2	740/880	6:961	4542*	2	749/886	7:88
4302	3	715/852		4382	4	728/868	6:768	4463	2	740/880	6:966	4543*	1	749/886	
4303	1	715/852	4:474	4383	78	728/868	6:768	4464	12	740/880	6:966	4544*	1	749/886	
4304	1	715/852		4384	1	729/867		4465	2	740/880	6:966	4545*	3	749/886	
4305	1	715/853	4:589	4385	1	729/869		4466*	1	740/880		4546*	1	749/886	
4306	3	715/853	4:948	4386	10	729/870		4467	1	741/880	6:972	4547	2	749/886	5:292
4307	2	715/853	4:948	4387	1	729/870		4468	1	741/880	6:972	4548	1	749/886	
4308	2	716/853	5:315	4388	3	729/870		4469	1	741/880	6:973	4549*	9	749/886	
4309	6	716/853	5:452	4389	1	729/870		4470	2	741/880		4550	8	749/886	7:94
4310	1	716/853	5:904	4390	2	729/870		4471*	1	741/880		4551*	1	749/886	
4311	9	716/853		4391	2	729/870		4472	4	741/880	6:976	4552	1	749/886	
4312	1	716/853		4392	7	729/870		4473	2	741/880	6:976	4553	1	749/886	
4313	2	716/853		4393	2	730/870		4474	5	741/881		4554*	3	749/886	
4314	711	716/853	6:720	4394	19	730/870	6:781	4475	3	741/881		4555	1	750/886	
4315	1	718/860		4395	28	730/870	6:781	4476	3	742/881		4556	1	750/886	
4316	1	718/860		4396	149	730/871	6:781	4477*	1	742/881	3:1	4557	1	750/886	
4317	4	718/860	1:128	4397	2	731/872	6:781	4478*	1	742/881		4558	1	750/886	
4318	3	718/860	1:128	4398	2	731/872	6:781	4479*	1	742/881		4559	11	750/886	7:98
4319	3	718/861		4399	1	731/872	9:88	4480	1	742/881		4560	1	750/887	7:98
4320	1	718/861		4400	2	731/872	6:862	4481*	1	742/881		4561	151	750/887	7:98
4321	1	718/861		4401	1	732/872		4482	1	742/881		4562*	1	752/890	
4322	2	718/861		4402*	1	732/873		4483	(2036)			4563	3	752/888	
4323	2	718/861	1:353	4403	3	732/873			26	742/881		4564*	4	752/888	
4324	1	718/861		4404	10	732/873		4484*	1	742/881		4565*	1	752/888	
4325	1	719/861		4405	4	732/873		4485	1	742/881		4566*	1	752/888	7:151
4326	1	719/861	2:40	4406	10	732/852		4486	7	742/881		4567*	36	752/888	7:151
4327	14	719/861	2:50	4407	1	732/873		4487	70	742/881	4:69	4568	2	752/889	
4328	16	719/861	6:725	4408	2	732/873		4488*	1	743/882		4569*	17	752/889	
4329	2	719/861	6:725	4409	1	732/873	6:865	4489	1	743/882		4570	8	752/889	7:165

WSC	F	A&G/M&G	K
4571	196	779/910	
4572	40	753/889	
4573	1	753/889	7:168
4574	2	753/889	7:168
4575*	3	753/889	
4576	10	753/890	7:168
4577	1	753/890	
4578	14	753/890	7:196
4579	5	753/890	7:196
4580*	1	754/890	
4581*	1	754/890	
4582	9	754/890	
4583	2	754/890	
4584*	1	754/890	
4585	1	754/890	
4586	4	754/890	7:168
4587	3	754/890	7:168
4588*	1	754/890	
4589*	1	755/890	
4590*	1	755/890	
4591	6	755/890	7:200
4592	77	755/890	7:200
4593	1	756/891	7:200
4594	41	756/891	7:269
4595	1	756/892	7:94
4596	1	756/894	
4597	3	756/892	7:275
4598	1	758/892	7:275
4599	1	756/892	
4600	2	756/892	
4601	9	757/892	
4602	2	757/892	
4603	5	757/892	
4604	1	757/892	
4605*	11	757/892	
4606*	1	757/002	
4607	1	757/892	7:278
4608	1	757/892	
4609*	13	758/892	
4610*	4	758/893	
4611	13	758/893	
4612	1	758/893	
4613*	76	758/893	
4614*	4	759/893	7:282
4615	5	759/893	7:287
4616	6	759/894	
4617	1	759/894	7:291
4618	3	759/894	
4619	1	759/894	
4620	1	759/894	
4621	14	759/894	
4622*	7	759/894	7:292
4623	11	760/894	
4624	30	760/894	7:339
4625	15	760/894	7:339
4626	3	760/895	
4627	3	761/895	
4628	3	761/895	
4629	1	761/895	
4630*	1	761/895	
4631	1	761/895	
4632	23	761/895	7:358
4633	20	762/895	7:368
4634	1	762/895	7:368
4635	1	762/895	7:368
4636	2	762/895	7:368
4637	5	762/896	
4638	3	763/896	7:368
4639	7	763/896	7:394
4640	3	763/896	7:401
4641	3	763/896	3:605
4642	6	763/896	5:1022
4643	1	763/896	5:1022
4644	1	763/896	5:1022
4645	6	763/896	5:1022
4646	4	763/896	7:403
4647	1	763/896	7:409
4648	6	764/896	7:413
4649	1	764/896	7:413
4650	5	764/896	7:418
4651	5	764/896	
4652	3	764/896	7:423
4653	16	765/896	7:423
4654	8	764/896	7:423
4655	32	764/897	7:423
4656	1	765/897	7:423
4657	1	765/897	7:445
4658*	1	765/897	7:447
4659	2	765/897	7:450
4660	3	765/897	
4661	1	765/897	
4662	1	765/897	
4663	3	765/897	7:452
4664	1	765/897	
4665	1	765/897	
4666	2	765/897	7:457
4667*	1	766/897	
4668*	1	766/897	
4669	1	766/897	7:457
4670*	10	766/897	
4671	221	779/910	
4672*	12	766/898	7:459
4673	1	766/898	
4674	27	766/898	
4675	498	779/909	
4676	4	766/898	
4677*	1	766/898	
4678	51	766/898	7:465
4679	2	767/899	7:465
4680	22	767/899	7:465
4681*	2	768/899	
4682	4	768/899	
4683	2	768/899	
4684	2	768/899	
4685	2	768/899	
4686	7	768/899	
4687	53	768/899	7:536
4688	1	769/900	
4689	2	769/900	7:528
4690	44	769/900	7:536
4691	1	769/901	
4692	6	769/901	
4693	6	769/901	
4694	1	770/901	
4695	2	770/901	
4696	2	770/901	
4697	12	770/901	7:548
4698	11	770/901	7:548
4699	3	770/901	
4700	3	770/901	
4701	1	770/901	7:536
4702	3	770/901	7:536
4703	5	770/901	7:536
4704	11	771/901	7:559
4705,4707	3	771/902	7:559
4706	1	771/902	
4708,4709	3	771/902	7:559
4710	12	771/902	
4711	5	771/902	
4712	6	771/902	
4713	1	771/902	
4714	9	771/902	7:568
4715	1	772/902	
4716	28	772/902	7:572
4717	46	772/902	7:572
4718	3	773/903	
4719	5	773/903	
4720*	1	773/903	
4721	3	773/903	
4722	4	773/903	7:585
4723	4	773/903	
4724	2	773/903	7:588
4725	1	773/903	
4726	2	773/903	7:600
4727	6	773/903	7:600
4728	3	773/903	7:604
4729	3	774/904	7:604
4730	4	774/904	7:604
4731	4	774/904	7:609
4732	3	774/904	7:609
4733	1	774/904	7:609
4734*	3	774/904	
4735	8	774/904	7:615
4736*	7	774/904	
4737	3	775/904	7:615
4738	5	775/904	
4739	8	775/904	7:636
4740	1	775/904	7:653
4741	13	775/904	7:653
4742	1	776/905	7:567
4743	1	776/905	
4744	1	776/905	7:665
4745	4	776/905	
4746	1	776/905	
4747	7	776/905	7:666
4748	5	777/905	7:666
4749	9	777/905	7:687
4750	78	777/905	7:692
4751	1	777/906	
4752	2	777/906	7:701
4753	8	778/906	7:701
4754	7	778/906	7:701
4755	10	778/906	7:701
4756	2	778/906	7:701
4757	26	778/906	7:701
4758	1	778/907	7:701
4759	1	778/907	
4760	1	778/907	7:701
4761	1	778/907	
4762	18	778/907	7:714
4763	2	779/907	
4764	1	779/907	
4765	4	779/907	7:730
4766	7	779/907	
4767	1	779/907	
4768	2	779/907	
4769	4	779/907	7:732
4770*	1	779/908	
4771	178	779/908	
4772	3	780/914	7:736
4773	12	780/914	7:736
4774	1	780/915	1:689
4775	2	780/923	
4776	2	780/923	7:766
4777	1	780/923	5:904
4778	1	780/923	
4779	8	780/923	3:487
4780	1	781/923	7:743
4781	1	781/923	
4782	1	781/923	
4783	1	781/923	
4784	1	781/923	
4785	1	781/923	9:604
4786	2	781/923	
4787	1	781/923	
4788	4	781/923	7:744
4789	4	781/923	3:758, 7:766
4790	3	781/924	3:789
4791	4	782/924	3:789
4792	1	782/924	
4793	3	782/924	3:921
4794	1	782/924	
4795	1	782/915	
4796	7	782/926	9:359
4797	1	782/926	
4797	4	783/926	
2798	1	783/926	
4799	1	783/915	
4800	3	783/922	7:766
4801	2	783/922	
4802	10	783/922	7:747
4803	3	783/922	7:747
4804	1	783/922	7:747
4805	1	783/922	7:748
4806	2	783/922	7:766
4807	1	783/915	7:751
4808	16	783/915	7:751
4809	1	784/915	7:751
4810	4	784/915	7:751
4811	2	784/915	7:751
4812	1	784/915	
4813	1	784/915	
4814	6	784/915	
4815	16	784/915	7:759
4816	8	784/915	
4817	1	784/915	
4818	1	784/924	4:313
4819	8	784/915	
4820	6	785/919	
4821	2	785/919	1:564, 7:766
4822	6	785/919	7:763
4823	5	785/916	
4824	8	785/916	
4825	1	785/916	
4826*	7	785/916	
4827	1	786/924	4:390
4828	4	786/924	4:474
4829	1	786/924	
4830	2	786/924	
4831	1	786/924	4:659
4832	2	786/916	4:766
4833	1	786/916	7:766
4834	2	786/924	5:904
4835	1	786/916	5:905
4836	2	786/924	
4837	1	786/924	
4838	4	786/924	
4839	1	786/759	
4840	1	786/924	
4841	2	786/924	5:904, 7:766
4842	2	787/924	
4843	1	787/925	
4844	1	787/925	
4845	3	787/925	6:283
4846	5	787/925	6:455
4847	1	787/925	
4848	4	787/925	
4849	1	787/916	
4850	1	787/925	6:651
4851	17	787/916	9:56
4852	1	788/926	
4853	1	788/916	
4854	1	788/916	7:766
4855	1	788/926	
4856	6	788/916	
4857	1	788/916	9:278
4858	1	788/916	9:278
4859	1	788/916	9:278
4860	1	789/916	9:604
4861	1	789/916	
4862	125	789/916	7:766
4863	62	789/917	
4864	57	790/917	7:798
4865	1	791/918	
4866	2	791/918	1:167
4867	3	791/918	
4868	3	791/918	
4869	3	791/918	1:195
4870	2	791/918	1:210
4871	1	791/918	
4872	2	791/918	
4873	9	792/918	3:654
4874	3	792/918	7:852
4875	1	792/919	
4876	6	792/919	
4877	1	792/972	
4878	2	792/919	1:375
4879	3	792/919	
4880	3	792/919	3:766
4881	1	792/919	
4882	1	792/919	

WSC	F	A&G/M&G	K
4883	2	792/919	7:855
4884	4	792/919	
4885	1	793/919	7:856
4886	4	793/919	7:856
4887	1	793/919	
4888	1	793/919	2:232
			7:766
4889	10	793/919	2:261
4890	1	793/920	
4891	1	793/920	7:766
4892	22	793/920	7:860
4893	32	794/920	7:899
4894	4	/920	7:899
4895	2	794/920	
4896	1	794/920	
4897	2	794/920	
4898	2	794/920	
4899	1	794/920	
4900	1	794/918	
4901	1	795/920	4:474
4902	1	795/921	
4903	5	795/921	7:871
4904	13	795/921	7:871
4905	32	795/921	2:666
4906	5	796/921	
4907	7	796/921	7:888
4908	4	796/921	7:888
4909	6	796/921	
4910	2	796/921	
4911	1	796/922	
4912	12	796/922	7:877
4913	1	797/922	
4914	2	797/922	
4915	1	797/922	
4916	2	797/922	7:766
4917	2	797/922	
4918	2	797/922	
4919	1	797/922	
4920	26	797/922	7:888
4921	3	798/923	7:896
4921	13	798/923	7:896
4922	1	798/924	
4923	1	798/924	
4924	1	799/924	
4925	1	799/924	5:119
4926	1	799/924	
4927	1	799/924	
4928	2	799/924	7:877
4929	2	799/925	
4930	6	799/925	8:49
4931	7	799/925	8:49
4932	2	800/925	
4933	4	800/925	8:140
4934	4	800/925	
4935	1	800/925	
4936	3	800/926	
4937	8	801/926	7:919
4938	1	801/926	7:919
4939	1	801/926	
4940	1	801/926	
4941*	1	801/926	
4942	1	801/926	8:559
4943	1	801/926	
4944	1	801/926	
4945	1	801/926	
4946*	1	801/926	
4947*	8	801/926	
4948*	1	801/926	
4949*	1	/926	
4950	1	802/926	
4951	5	802/926	
4952	1	802/926	
4953	1	802/927	7:200
4954	1	802/925	7:1024
4955	1	802/902	
4956	2	802/927	
4957	5	802/925	7:766
4958	2	802/925	7:588
4959	1	802/925	7:600
4960	1	803/925	7:666
4961	2	803/925	7:701
4962	1	803/927	

WSC	K	A&G/M&G	K
4963	2	803/927	
4964	2	803/925	
4965*	1	803/927	
4966*	2	803/927	
4967	3	803/927	7:925
4968	1	803/927	
4969	10	803/927	7:925
4970	11	803/927	
4971	1	803/927	
4972	26	803/927	7:939
4973	16	804/927	7:939
4974	1	804/927	
4975	3	804/928	
4976	2	804/928	7:954
4977	10	805/928	7:959
4978	8	805/928	7:959
4979	1	805/928	
4980	2	805/928	
4981	2	805/928	
4982	111	805/928	
4983	146	806/929	7:1024
4984	2	807/931	7:1024
4985	1	807/931	
4986*	1	807/931	
4987	2	808/931	7:1094
4988*	2	808/931	
4989	1	808/931	
4990	24	808/931	7:965
4991	45	808/931	7:965
4992	4	809/932	
4992	1	809/932	7:965
4993	6	809/932	7:1097
4994	1	809/932	7:1097
4995	1	809/932	7:1097
4996	1	809/932	
4997	3	809/932	7:1097
4998	4	810/932	7:1097
4999*	1	810/	
5000*	2	810/932	
5001	1	810/932	8:27
5002	1	810/932	
5003	1	810/932	
5004	2	810/932	
5005	2	811/932	
5006	1	811/932	
5007	15	811/932	
5008	1	811/933	
5009	4	811/933	
5010	10	811/933	
5011	8	811/933	8:1
5012	7	812/933	8:1
5013	14	812/933	8:1
5014	4	812/933	8:1
5015	17	812/933	
5016	2	813/934	
5017	2	813/934	
5018*	2	813/934	
5019*	3	813/934	
5020	1	813/934	
5021	8	813/934	8:27
5022	4	813/934	
5023	4	813/	
5024	247	600/737	
5025	12	600/737	
5025	9	600/737	
5026	31	600/735	
5026	57	600/736	
5026	34	600/735	
5027	1	813/934	
5028	7	814/934	
5029	2	814/934	
5030	10	814/934	
5031	2	814/934	
5032	5	814/934	
5033	1	814/934	
5034	1	814/934	
5035	13	814/935	
5036	1	814/935	
5037	204	815/935	
5038	9	815/935	
5039	1	815/935	
5040*	9	815/935	5:636

WSC	F	A&G/M&G	K
5041	1	815/935	
5042	1	815/935	
5043	99	815/935	5:636
5044	1	816/936	
5045	2	816/936	
5046	19	816/936	8:49
5047	2	817/936	8:49
5048	24	817/936	8:49
5049	1	818/937	
5050	2	818/937	8:49
5051	1	818/937	8:49
5052	1	818/937	
5053	12	818/937	
5054	1	818/937	
5055	26	818/937	8:49
5056	42	818/937	8:49
5057	22	820/938	8:88
5058	3	820/938	
5059	16	820/938	8:113
5060*	1	820/938	
5061*	2	820/938	
5062	22	820/939	8:127
5063	2	820/939	8:127
5064	42	820/938	8:127
5065	2	821/939	
5066	1	821/939	8:27
5067	10	821/939	8:127
5068	1	821/939	
5069	1	821/940	
5070	5	821/940	
5071	4	821/940	
5072	1	821/940	
5073	1	821/940	
5074	3	821/940	
5075	3	821/939	
5076	4	821/939	
5077	1	821/940	
5078	3	821/940	
5079	4	821/940	
5080	1	822/940	
5081	1	822/940	
5082	4	822/940	
5083	75	822/940	8:140
5084	2	823/941	8:140
5085*	3	823/941	
5086*	1	823/941	
5087	96	823/941	8:152
5088	19	824/942	
5089	3	824/942	
5090*	1	824/942	
5091	21	824/942	8:169
5092	43	825/943	8:169
5093	14	825/943	
5094	1	825/943	
5095*	24	826/943	
5096*	1	826/944	
5097	2	826/944	
5098	1	826/944	
5099	1	826/944	
5100	452	827/949	
5101	538	828/954	
5102	2	828/954	
5103*	13	828/954	
5104	1	828/628	
5105	2	828/954	
5106	4	828/954	
5107	1	828/954	
5108	61	828/954	
5109	1	829/955	
5110	2	829/955	
5111	16	829/955	8:181
5112	1	829/955	8:181
5113	1	829/955	8:181
5114	1	829/955	
5115	1	829/955	
5116	1	829/955	
5117	92	830/955	8:187
5118	21	831/956	
5119	159	831/957	
5120	1		
5121	3	831/958	
5122	1	831/958	

WSC	F	A&G/M&G	K
5123	17	831/735	
5124	320	/734	
5125	19	/737	
5126	64	/735	
5127	77	/735	
5128	27	/737	
5129	89	/735	
5130	69	/737	
5131	4	831/958	
5132	15	832/958	8:209
5133	1	832/958	
5134	1	832/959	
5135	2	832/959	
5136	1	832/959	
5137	7	832/959	
5138	2	832/959	
5139*	1	832/959	
5140*	68	833/959	8:216
5141	4	833/960	
5142	8	833/960	
5143	20	833/960	8:226
5144	11	833/960	
5145	2	833/960	
5146	2	833/960	
5147	4	834/960	
5148	1	834/960	
5149	1	834/960	
5150	1	834/960	
5151	12	834/960	8:216
5152	1	834/960	
5153	1	834/961	
5154	57	834/961	8:216
5155	1	834/961	
5156	5	834/961	
5157	1	834/961	
5158	13	835/961	
5159	1	835/961	
5160	16	835/961	
5161*	3	835/962	
5162	1	835/962	
5163	1	835/962	
5164	1	835/962	
5165	2	836/962	
5166	3	836/962	
5167	1	836/962	6:63
5168	2	836/962	
5169	1	836/962	
5170*	1	836/962	
5171	1	836/962	
5172	2	836/962	
5173*	1	836/962	
5174*	6	836/962	
5175*	1	836/962	
5176	6	836/962	8:236
5177	13	837/962	8:238
5178	1	837/962	
5179	16	837/963	8:246
5180	14	838/963	8:260
5181*	1	838/963	
5182	1	838/461	
5183*	1	838/963	
5184*	11	838/963	
5185	53	838/963	8:270
5186	3	838/964	8:270
5187	3	838/964	
5188	1	839/964	
5189	1	839/964	
5190*	5	839/964	
5191	1	839/964	
5192	1	839/964	
5193	3	839/964	
5194	2	839/964	
5195	5	839/964	8:295
5196	3	839/964	8:295
5197	2	839/964	8:295
5198	12	839/964	8:308
5199	14	840/964	8:308
5200	1	840/964	
5201	3	840/965	
5202	1	840/965	
5203	1	840/965	
5204	79	840/965	8:314

WSC	F	A&G/M&G	K	WSC	F	A&G/M&G	K	WSC	F	A&G/M&G	K	WSC	F	A&G/M&G	K
5205	6	841/965		5287	5	854/980	8:572	5368	25	866/990	9:113	5449	14	877/997	9:251
5206	5	841/966	8:334	5288	4	855/980	7:588	5369*	1	867/990	2:909	5450	1	877/997	
5207	381	841/966	8:334	5289	1	855/981	7:588	5370	7	867/990	9:113	5451	1	878/997	
5208	1	843/970		5290	35	855/981		5371*	1	867/990		5452	11	878/997	
5209	437	/914		5291	1	855/981		5372*	1	867/990		5453	3	878/997	
5210	243	843/910		5292	4	855/981	8:27	5373	1	867/990	9:113	5454	2	878/997	
5211*	2	843/970		5293	40	855/981	8:27	5374*	1	867/990		5455	42	878/997	9:278
5212	10	843/970		5294	2	856/982		5375*	4	867/990		5456	141	878/998	9:278
5213	621	/913		5295	1	856/982		5376*	38	867/990		5457	70	879/999	9:310
5214	4	844/970	8:489	5296	2	856/982	8:246	5377	1	868/991		5458	2	880/1000	9:310
5215	2	844/970	8:489	5297	3	856/982		5378*	1	868/991		5459	1	880/1000	9:310
5216	583	/913		5298	2	856/982		5379	1	868/991		5460	5	880/1000	9:310
5217	81	844/970	8:504	5299	2	856/982	8:590	5380	1	868/991		5461	11	880/1000	9:310
5218	15	844/971	1:216	5300	1	856/982		5381	2	868/991	5:1	5462	2	880/1000	9:310
5219	21	845/971	1:216	5301	2	856/982		5382	3	868/991	5:1	5463	74	881/1000	9:359
5220	1	845/971		5302	16	856/982	8:592	5383	1	868/991		5464	4	882/1001	
5221	5	845/972	3:623	5303	9	857/982	8:592	5384	29	868/991	9:113	5465	7	882/1001	
5222	1	845/972	3:623	5304	2	857/982	8:592	5385	1	869/991	9:172	5466*	1	882/1001	
5223	2	845/972		5305	12	857/982	8:592	5386	1	869/991	9:172	5467	2	882/1001	
5224	14	845/972		5306	1	857/982	8:592	5387	1	869/991		5468	2	882/1001	
5225	48	845/972		5307	1	857/982		5388	1	869/991		5469	2	882/1001	
5226	1	846/972		5308	11	857/982		5389	3	869/991		5470	1	883/1001	
5227	2	846/972		5309	2	857/983		5390	1	869/991		5471	1	882/1001	
5228	160	846/972	8:507	5310	13	857/983	8:602	5391	1	869/989		5472	1	882/1001	
5229	3	847/974		5311	6	858/983	8:602	5392	8	869/991		5473	1	883/1001	
5230	1	847/974		5312	20	858/983	8:602	5393*	1	869/991		5474	2	883/1001	
5231	3	847/974		5313	2	858/983	8:602	5394	2	869/991		5475	5	883/1001	
5232	1	847/974	8:517	5314	2	859/983		5395	7	870/991		5476	2	883/1001	
5233	1	848/974	5:736	5315	97	312/		5396	1	870/992		5477*	2	883/1002	
5234	1	848/974	8:520	5316	31	859/983	9:1	5397	1	870/992		5478*	1	883/1001	
5235	5	848/974	8:520	5317*	1	860/984		5398	3	870/993		5479	59	803/1002	9:359
5236	8	848/975	8:520	5318	21	860/984	9:1	5399	93	870/992	9:189	5480	9	884/1002	9:416
5237	1	848/975		5319	49	860/984	9:1	5400	1	871/992		5481	1	884/1002	9:418
5238	1	848/975	2:460	5320	3	860/984		5401	47	871/993	9:189	5482	1	884/1002	
5239	1	848/975		5321	2	861/984	9:1	5402*	1	872/993		5483	23	884/1002	9:359
5240	1	848/975		5322	1	861/984		5403*	3	872/993		5484	9	885/1003	
5241	1	848/975	8:238	5323*	1	861/984		5404	2	872/993		5485	156	885/1003	9:359
5242	5	848/975	8:523	5324	1	861/984	9:1	5405*	1	872/993		5486	17	885/1005	9:359
5243	1	849/975	8:525	5325	1	861/985		5406	7	872/993		5407	2	007/1005	9:359
5244	5	849/975	8:525	5326	2	861/985	9:1	5407	12	872/994		5488*	2	887/1005	
5245	1	849/975	4:942	5327	1	861/985		5408	10	872/994		5489	1	887/1005	
5246	2	849/975		5328*	5	861/985		3409	6	872/994	9:56	5490	1	887/1005	
5247	2	849/975	8:528	5329*	3	861/985		5410*	1	872/994		5491	7	887/1005	
5248	2	849/975	6:58	5330*	100	861/985	9:11	5411	5	872/994	9:56	5492	1	887/1005	
5249	1	849/975		5331	3	861/986		5412	2	872/994	9:56	5493	1	887/1005	
5250	1	849/975	6:263	5332	1	861/986		5413	5	873/994	9:56	5494	6	888/1005	
5251	1	849/975	8:602	5333	1	862/986		5414	1	873/994		5495	779	888/1005	9:424
5252	1	850/975		5334	1	862/986		5415*	1	873/994		5496	2	889/1007	9:424
5253	4	850/975		5335	4	862/986		5416	1	873/994		5497	1	889/1007	9:424
5254	1	850/975		5336	4	862/986	9:49	5417	2	873/994		5498	1	889/1007	9:424
5255	3	850/975	1:216	5337	4	862/986		5418	4	873/994		5499	6	889/1007	9:424
5256	3	850/975	8:530	5338	3	862/986		5419	4	873/994		5500	2	889/1007	9:424
5257	20	850/976	8:530	5339	10	862/986		5420	2	873/994		5501	11	889/1007	
5258	6	850/976	8:545	5340	2	862/986		5421	7	873/994		5502*	1	889/1007	9:438
5259	230	850/978,976		5341	1	862/986		5422	1	873/994		5503	26	889/1008	9:440
5260	1	851/978		5342	64	862/986	9:56	5423	1	873/994		5504	3	890/407	
5261	1	851/978	1:742	5343	31	863/987		5424	2	873/994	9:220	5505	23	890/1008	
5262	6	851/978	2:25	5344*	9	863/988		5425	1	873/995		5506	22	890/1008	
5263	6	851/978		5345	2	864/988		5426	29	874/995	9:220	5507	11	890/1008	9:466
5264	4	852/978		5346	58	864/988		5427	4	875/995	9:220	5508*	1	890/1008	
5265	3	852/978	5:292	5347*	13	864/988		5428	2	874/995	9:220	5509	11	890/1008	
5266	10	852/978	5:292	5348	7	864/988	9:88	5429	14	874/995	9:220	5510	3	890/1009	
5267	1	852/978	8:557	5349	6	864/989	9:93	5430	1	874/995		5511	2	890/1009	
5268	2	852/979		5350	3	864/989		5431	1	874/995		5512	2	890/1009	
5269	1	852/979		5351	8	865/989	9:93	5432	4	875/995		5513	1	890/1009	
5270	9	852/979		5352	1	865/989		5433	1	875/995		5514*	1	890/1009	
5271	1	852/979	8:559	5353	2	865/989		5434	1	875/995		5515	4	890/1009	
5272	7	852/979	8:559	5354	1	865/989		5435*	3	875/995		5516	1	891/	
5273	20	853/979	8:559	5355	9	865/989		5436*	1	875/995		5517	4	891/1009	9:472
5274	4	853/979	4:5	5356	9	965/989	9:93	5437	2	875/995		5518	2	891/1009	
5275	1	853/979		5357	12	866/989		5438	47	875/995	9:236	5519	14	891/1009	
5276	1	853/979	4:254	5358	1	866/989	1:10	5439	1	876/996		5520	1	891/1009	
5277	1	853/979		5359	2	866/989		5440	1	876/996		5521	2	891/1009	
5279	7	853/980		5360	6	866/989	1:144	5441	3	876/996		5522	2	891/1010	
5280	3	854/980	1:348	5361	1	866/989	1:144	5442	30	876/996	9:236	5523*	2	891/1009	
5281	32	854/980	4:574	5362	1	866/989		5443	31	876/996	9:236	5524	1	892/1009	
5282	3	854/980	4:948	5363	2	866/990	9:107	5444	6	877/997		5525	1	892/1009	
5283	1	854/980	4:948	5364	1	866/990	9:107	5445	5	877/997		5526	15	892/1009	
5284	2	854/980		5365	1	866/990		5446	3	877/997	9:251	5527	1	892/1009	
5285	1	854/980		5366	2	866/990		5447	1	877/997	9:251	5528	15	892/1009	
5286	9	854/980		5367	1	866/990		5448	7	877/997		5529	1	892/1010	

WSC	F	A&G/M&G	K	WSC	F	A&G/M&G	K	WSC	F	A&G/M&G	K	WSC	F	A&G/M&G	K
5530	11	892/1010		5557	13	897/1019		5584	4	900/1022		5611*	4	905/1026	
5531	1	893/1010		5558	2	897/1019		5585	2	900/1022	9:604	5612*	1	905/1026	
5532	49	893/1010		5559	1	897/1019		5586	3	901/1022	9:604	5613*	492	905/1026,1030	
5533	2	893/1010		5560	15	897/1019		5587	1	901/1022		5614*	6	907/1031	9:682
5534	1	893/1010		5561	27	897/1019		5588	1	901/1022		5615*	17	907/1031	
5535	5	893/1010		5562	10	897/1020		5589	3	901/1022		5616*	34	907/1031	
5536	7	893/1010	9:480	5563	13	898/1020		5590	105	901/1022	9:608	5617*	1	908/1032	
5537	9	893/1011	9:480	5564	10	898/1020		5591	6	902/1023	9:608	5618*	42	908/1032	
5538	1	894/1011	9:480	5565	39	898/1020		5592	3	902/1023		5619*	1	908/1032	
5539	1	894/1011		5566	1	899/1020		5593	4	902/1023		5620*	83	908/1032	
5540	2	894/1011		5567	5	899/1021	8:489	5594	1	903/1023		5621*	5	908/1033	
5541	1	894/1011	9:483	5568	7	899/1021	8:489	5595	2	903/1023		5622*	2	908/1033	
5542	1	894/1011	9:483	5569	2	899/1021	1:144	5596	4	903/1024		5623*	15	908/1033	
5543	7	894/1011	9:483	5570	1	899/1021	1:398	5597	1	903/1024		5624*	4	909/1033	
5544	10	894/1011	9:483	5571	3	899/1021	9:594	5598	4	903/1024					
5545	3	894/1011	9:493	5572	1	899/1021		5599	16	903/1024					
5546*	3	895/1011	9:493	5573	1	899/1021		5600	66	221/277					
5547*	569	895/1011	9:493	5574	12	899/1021	9:594	5601*	3	903/502,1024					
5548	5	895/1018	9:493	5575	3	900/1021	4:474	5602	60	903/1024					
5549	5	896/1018		5576	6	900/1021	4:474	5603	7	903/1024	1:163				
5550	53	896/1018	9:581	5577	2	900/1021	4:474	5604	4	904/1025	9:667				
5551	1	896/1018		5578	11	900/1021	6:781	5605	3	905/1025	9:667				
5552	18	896/1018		5579	9	900/1021	9:594	5606	2	904/1025					
5553	9	896/1019		5580	2	900/1021		5607	154	221/279					
5554	1	896/1019		5581	1	900/1022	5:242	5608*	1	904/1025					
5555	1	896/1019		5582	1	900/1022	9:594	5609*	1	904/1025					
5556	1	897/1019		5583	10	900/1022	9:594	5610*	108	904/1025	9:675				